INTRO-
DUCTION
TO
CHILDREN'S
LITERATURE

McGRAW-HILL
BOOK COMPANY

New York St. Louis San Francisco Auckland Bogotá Düsseldorf
Johannesburg London Madrid Mexico Montreal New Delhi
Panama Paris São Paulo Singapore Sydney Tokyo Toronto

INTRODUCTION TO CHILDREN'S LITERATURE

Joan I. Glazer
Rhode Island College

Gurney Williams III

This book was set in Trump by Black Dot, Inc.
The editors were Alison Meersschaert and James R. Belser;
the designer was Jo Jones;
the production supervisor was Charles Hess.
Ornamental drawings were done by Joseph Gillians.
Von Hoffmann Press, Inc., was printer and binder.

See Acknowledgments on pages 707–710. Copyrights included on this page by reference.

Cover illustration by Reynold Ruffins
Cover characters adapted from illustrations by Kate Greenaway, in *Under the Window*, F. Warne & Co., 1910; Ernest H. Shephard, in A. A. Milne, *Winnie-The-Pooh*, E. P. Dutton, 1926; Maurice Sendak, in *Where the Wild Things Are*, Harper & Row, 1963; Beatrix Potter, in *The Tale of Peter Rabbit*, F. Warne & Co., 1902; and John Tenniel, in Lewis Carroll, *Alice's Adventures in Wonderland*, Macmillan and Co., 1865.

INTRODUCTION TO CHILDREN'S LITERATURE

Library of Congress Cataloging in Publication Data

Glazer, Joan I
    Introduction to children's literature.

    Bibliography: p.
    Includes index.
    1. Books and reading for children.
2. *Children's literature. I. Williams, Gurney,*
date   joint author. II. Title.
Z1037.A1G57   028.5   78-12202
ISBN 0-07-023380-2

CONTENTS

PART II LITERATURE AND CHILDREN TOGETHER

goals • Coordinating literature with other subjects • Chart
of goals in literature and other courses • Case studies
illustrating how literature can be combined with science,
mathematics, and social studies

FOREWORD

A study of children's literature properly begins with reading the books. But how does one begin, when there are so many? Each year, hundreds of new titles are added to the thousands already in print. It is a bewildering array, and students new to the subject will welcome an introductory text that guides and orders their study. Here they will find help in selecting books to read, assistance in classifying them for study, criteria for their evaluation, and more.

For students who intend to share literature with children, knowing how to select, classify, and evaluate books is only the beginning of study. Learning ways to present literature to youngsters is the next important consideration. In *Introduction to Children's Literature,* students will discover an unusually rich source of methods, fully developed through illustrations and examples.

A successful text for children's literature is one that both informs about the books and inspires the reading of them. Among books for children are some of the best of all books; experiencing them is to be delighted, inspired, enlightened. The authors of *Introduction to Children's Literature* know this, and, along with quantities of useful information, they are able to convey a sense of the potential for pleasure to be found in children's literature by students of all ages.

Glenna Davis Sloan
Professor of Education
Queens College of the
City University of New York

PREFACE

Exploring children's books, discovering literature, and presenting it to young readers—these are fascinating tasks for adults today.

We began writing this book with the assumption that an introduction to these tasks should be as fresh and intriguing as children's books themselves. It should reflect the vitality of the literature and the joy that is generated when children first meet books they will never forget. It should avoid presenting page after page of titles with sketchy descriptions that mean little to students who are not already familiar with the field.

We have tailored this book for students—in English, education, or library science courses—who may never have studied the subject. This book does not attempt to catalogue children's literature. Nor does it name every important book. Rather, as an introduction, it presents a balanced selection of books with enough explanation for each example to interest students in literature they may not yet have read. We think these books are exciting, for adults as well as children, and we have tried to convey their power and artistry in a way that will send many of our readers on a hunt for the actual books, or others like them (listed in end-of-chapter bibliographies).

Introduction to Children's Literature comprises two major sections. Part One is a survey of genres: picture books, Mother Goose and concept books, poetry, traditional literature, fantasy, contemporary realism, historical fiction, biography, and informational books. These chapters contain criteria for evaluating books in each genre. Often, the text provides recommendations for matching books to children at different ages; but the age designations are merely rough guidelines, for children frequently read books published for older or younger readers. The first section closes with a chapter on trends in literature—and trends in adult thinking about children—since the seventeenth century.

Part Two suggests practical strategies for bringing books and children together. Case studies help to illustrate how to choose and present books, understand and enhance children's responses, organize books into units, and organize units into year-long programs of literature. The chapters show how to plan numerous activities step by step, and how to avoid missteps. But the goal in Part Two is not to present students with a set of specific activities based on certain books. The chapters have been written to suggest general techniques or processes of working with books so that students can plan their own activities around literature available to them. The final chapter is a report on how social and economic factors shape what is published now and what will appear in the years ahead.

Several special features in this book have been designed to draw readers closer to the literature. In "Issue" boxes scattered throughout the text, readers encounter contrasting viewpoints about children and books from experts in the field. These "mini-debates"—each presenting two opinions on one subject—call on students to draw their own conclusions and defend them. Anecdotes about authors and artists at work sharpen understanding about how books are created. Most of the chapters in Part One begin with such anecdotes, each illustrating a central point about the genre being discussed.

Another particularly useful feature is the color section in Chapter 2. Pictures here specifically illustrate discussions in the text about differences in media and style. In one set of color pictures, the subject is the same, showing contrasts in media. In another set, the medium is held constant, illustrating contrasting styles. The color section does more than display some good art. It also helps convey general concepts students can apply to many different illustrations.

Back-of-the-book features include lists of prizewinning books, a list of children's book publishers with data on what they publish, and a full subject-title-author index. Material quoted in the text appears with the original year of publication, as well as the page number, in parentheses, so that students can determine how old the writing is without turning to references. (When no page number appears, the book is unpaginated.) The full citations are arranged alphabetically by the author's name at the end of each chapter.

We hope all these features will be useful. But most of all, we hope that *Introduction to Children's Literature* conveys some of the vitality that we have found in children's books. You probably already know something of that vitality. All of us, even those who have never studied children's literature, can call up fantastic realms from our imaginations. Talking toads and glass slippers endure in our memories. Tom Sawyer or other active characters from realistic fiction mirrored us as children. Their personalities linger. We remember children's books as lively, colorful, and engrossing. We hope this book shows that they still are.

Acknowledgments

A large number of remarkably supportive and thoughtful people helped us as we wrote this book. We are deeply grateful to the following reviewers who made valuable suggestions after reading part or all the various drafts of the manuscript: Dr. Mercedes Ballou, Northern Kentucky University; Dr. Donald J. Bissett, Wayne State University; Professor Ruth Kearney Carlson, California State University at Hayward; Dr. Patricia Cianciolo, Michigan State University; Professor Gertrude Corcoran, School of Education, San Jose State University; Professor Glenna Davis Sloan, Queens College; Professor Patricia Grasty, West Chester State College; Dr. Ruth K. MacDonald, Northeastern University; Professor DayAnn McClenathan, State University of New York at Buffalo; Professor Diane Monson, University of Washington; Dr. Gordon Pruett, Northeastern University; and Dr. John W. Stewig, University of Wisconsin.

We also appreciate valuable and professional help from librarians Nancy Brown, Bronxville, N. Y., Public Library; Alice Forsstrom, Warwick, R. I., Public Library; and Jackie Smith, Providence Public Library.

Finally, we are especially grateful to our editor, Alison Meersschaert, for her intelligence, humor, and patience over the past two years.

We bow in thanks to all who helped with this book, but we accept any deficiencies in it as ours alone.

Joan I. Glazer

Gurney Williams III

PART ONE

How do you find literature among the more than 39,000 children's books in print? What do we know about children to help us match good books with young readers? Part One explores both questions. It surveys each of the major categories – or genres – of children's books and offers criteria adults can use to evaluate and choose books for young readers. And it presents useful theories about who children are, what they need, and how they grow.

EX-
PLORING
THE
REALM
OF LITERA-
TURE

CHAPTER
1

CHILDREN AND LITERATURE

MEET THE CHILD, JUDGE THE BOOK

Some adult readers accused British writer Jill Paton Walsh of encouraging children to play with deadly serpents. The charge was based on a scene in her book *Goldengrove* (1972) in which a boy finds a snake on a cliff path, grabs it behind the head, and hurls it off the cliff. Critics asked: Was this good fare for children?

To find out how dangerous the situation really was, she called a museum and requested the department dealing with snakes. "Reptiles speaking," said an official in the department when he picked up the phone. He was not any friendlier than Walsh's critics, but he had a different complaint, Walsh reported. "He thought it was very irresponsible of me to encourage children to go throwing innocent snakes off cliffs.

"If we were to try to foresee every possible reaction of that kind, we would not write about anything," she added (1973, p. 31).

Children's literature arouses adult passions. Society pushes and tugs at Walsh and other writers of children's books, and at teachers and librarians who work with young readers. Some adults object to anything that might scare children. Some expect children's books to teach lessons, although men and women in different eras have disagreed about what is to be taught. Seventeenth-century Puritans, for instance, thought books for the young should preach piety, so children could be saved from temptation and hell. On the other hand, a twentieth-century Russian running the 1977 International Book Fair in Moscow expressed a different idea about what children's books should teach. "Peace and progress," Director Yuri V. Torsuyev told a reporter for *The New York Times* (Sept. 4, 1977). And Walsh's museum critic apparently wanted a book on the benevolence of snakes.

Sometimes authors today are urged for the good of the child to write by a rule. Here is one rule, for instance: *Ease the slow reader along by repeating words and phrases frequently.* One critic, Margery Fisher, tells how the strategy worked in her family.

> I was picking out books for my eldest grandaughter who is a late reader of nearly eight. I was thinking in theoretical terms. I thought, "Ah yes, reluctant reader, repetition to help her along." And I found an easy book with a repetitive pattern. When she came to the fourth repetition of words and situations she heaved a great sigh and said "Not again." So I left her by the bookshelf. (1970, p. 17)

(Chapter-opening illustration from *Did You Carry the Flag Today, Charlie?* by Rebecca Caudill, Illustrated by Nancy Grossman. Illustration copyright © 1966 by Nancy Grossman. Reproduced by permission of Holt, Rinehart and Winston, Publishers.)

Listening to a parent read is a valuable introduction to the world of books. (Illustration by Emily McCully from *Black Is Brown Is Tan* by Arnold Adoff. Illustrations copyright © 1973 by Emily Arnold McCully. By permission of Harper & Row, Publishers, Inc.)

Many writers such as Walsh, and many young readers, are stubborn. They resist rules and generalizations. Walsh argues that her first responsibility is to her book. Literature stands on its own, she argues, apart from usefulness or popularity. And the child, left free by the bookshelf, chooses unpredictably, mulling through catalogs and comic books as often as good literature.

Perhaps you stand somewhere in the middle, treasuring excellent writing while respecting the child (and mulling through catalogs yourself, sometimes). There, between good books and young readers, you face some hard questions.

One question arises from the health of children's book publishing today. American publishing houses produce some 2,200 hardbound books for children every year, an average of approximately eight books each weekday, not counting paperbacks. *Children's Books in Print* (1977), a useful index of children's books, lists 39,250 titles in print that are available for purchase. How do you select from this vast field? What books stand on their own as literature? A later section of this chapter (Evaluating the Elements of Literature) will offer general guidelines.

Another question lurks behind all debates on literature and education: Who is the child? You answer the question for yourself every time you give a book to a young reader. You might suggest Dorothy Kunhardt's *Pat the Bunny* (1940) for a 3-year-old, for instance, because you know the child will like to touch the piece of flannel surrounded in the book by the outline of a rabbit, or the patch of roughness on a picture of a father's unshaven face. You might offer Judy Blume's *Are You There God? It's Me, Margaret* to an 11-year-old girl because you know she can identify with Margaret's impatience at her body's lazy drift into womanhood.

"Are you there God? It's me, Margaret," Margaret prays.

"I just did an exercise to help me grow. Have you thought about it God? About my growing, I mean. I've got a bra now. It would be nice if I had something to put in it." (1970)

Both selections depend on assumptions about who the children are.

Some adults in every age have been quite certain about their answers. Educators in other generations identified offspring as sinful, as sensible, as lovable scamps, and as miniature versions of parents. All these idealized children of the adult imagination survive. You can recognize them in conversations at PTA meetings, in teacher conferences, even in comic strips and TV shows about children. Chapter 10 traces the roots of some common ideas about who children are.

Most adults think they already know. But research over the past century has undermined easy generalizations. It has become clear that there is no simple answer, and that childhood itself is immensely complicated.

WHO IS THE CHILD?

The little girl in Lewis Carroll's fantasy, *Alice in Wonderland* (1865), has just eaten some cake which makes her grow like an opening telescope. "Goodbye, feet!" she calls. Her head bumps the roof of the hall. Naturally, she worries about herself.

"I wonder if I've changed in the night? Let me think: *was* I the same when I got up this morning? I almost think I can remember feeling a little different. But if I'm not the same, the next question is 'Who in the world am I?' Ah, *that's* the great puzzle!" And she began thinking over all the children she knew that were the same age as herself, to see if she could have been changed for any of them. (1965 edition, p. 17)

Children sometimes seem to grow like Alice. One morning, the shirt that fit last week becomes too small. The jungle gym bar that was too high before spring vacation comes within reach on the first day back at school.

Changes in thinking and feeling can be even more surprising. A 5-year-old suddenly acts like a 2-year-old when a new brother comes home from the hospital. One 7-year-old reads the sports stories in a daily newspaper; another 7-year-old wants to hear the same fairy tale read aloud each bedtime, day after day.

The "great puzzle" is fitting together pieces of odd data like these to make a clear picture of the rapidly changing child.

Several researchers in this century have tried to solve the puzzle. Sometimes they begin by gathering a group of children the same age and searching for similarities in how they are growing. Sometimes researchers contrast children of different ages. Whatever the process, there is no easy solution.

Research has shown, however, that children go through recognizable stages of growth. And these stages can be related roughly to the child's age, although individuals differ widely in when they arrive at a stage of growth, and when they move on.

It is essential in working with children, and introducing them to books, to know something of the stages. How do children think and learn? How do they answer questions of right and wrong? How do they gain skill in language? The answers to each of these questions can help identify an individual child, and may indicate which books are beyond—or beneath—a young reader.

There is research on all these questions.

HOW DO CHILDREN GROW AND LEARN?
In the 1920s and 1930s, two groups of psychologists battled over the question of learning. One group, centered in America and England, contended that learning came from experience with the environment—the world of people and things around the child. The second group, centered in Europe, thought that heredity was the key to learning. Learning depended, they thought, on a set of inherited characteristics, a "given" nature.

Social scientists staked territory on one side or the other. Reputations rose and fell apart over the question. The *nature versus nurture* debate raged as World War II began.

Piaget's Theory of Cognitive Development

Switzerland was neutral in the war. And one Swiss researcher, *Jean Piaget* (1896-   ), refused to take sides in the controversy.

Piaget didn't begin his career as a psychologist. As a 10-year-old, he published a short article on a sparrow he had seen in a public park. And when he was still a schoolboy, he began writing scholarly articles on mollusks—clams, snails, and many other species. Later he became interested in psychology, and his early investigations in the quiet lakes of Switzerland led him to believe that both environment and heredity shaped living organisms. As he moved from mollusks to young people,

> He discovered that children harbored notions concerning nature and the physical world that they had neither inherited nor learned in the classic sense. He found, for example, that young children believed the moon followed them when they went for a walk at night, that dreams came in through the window while they were asleep, and that anything that moved, including waves and windblown curtains, was alive. (Evans, 1973, p. vii)

Such ideas, Piaget suggested, arose when children organized experience in their minds with limited ability. The ability to organize grew as the child grew, in regular stages. Learning and understanding came both from the experience with the world—nurture—and from the innate ability in the brain to make sense of the experience—nature.

Piaget suggested that there are four stages in the growth of natural ability, and they always follow the same order.

Sensorimotor Just after birth, the child moves mostly at random, hitting the side of a crib, listening, sucking, crying. The child in this stage is exploring the world constantly, using all five senses.

A portrait of a boy in this stage appears in Joan Lexau's children's book, *Emily and the Klunky Baby and the Next-Door Dog* (1972). Emily has been assigned to watch her brother while her divorced mother fills out tax returns. The little girl pulls out some crayons to pass the time.

> "Here's a green crayon," she whispered to the baby. "But you can only draw on the paper." The baby bit off the pointy part of the crayon.

"It's not candy!" Emily said. She had to fish the crayon out of the baby's mouth.

The baby dumped the crayon box on the rug and ran to the kitchen. Just in time Emily took the pots away from him. "You can't bang pots now," she whispered. "We have to be quiet for Mama."

The baby howled.

"Shut up," Emily yelled. The baby did not shut up.

Newborn children cannot distinguish themselves from things around them. But in the course of the first two years of life or so, before language begins, the child's understanding changes. Children learn through banging pots, chewing crayons, and other actions that they are different from objects. They begin to understand relationships, for instance, that if a toy they want is out of reach on a blanket, they can pull the blanket toward them. The world becomes more comprehensible through the child's senses and through growing *motor ability*—skill at moving. By the end of the sensorimotor period, a revolution has taken place: the child has become aware of an "outside" world of permanent objects, and an "inside" world of self.

Preoperational Somewhere around the age of 2 and continuing to about 6 or 7, the child begins to understand symbols. Language is one set of symbols. Children in this stage also start drawing pictures from memory, experiencing mental images of objects that they cannot see and enjoying fantasies and dreams. But they have not yet gained what Piaget calls *operational* status: they are not yet able to manipulate their mental images in a systematic way.

In one experiment, for instance, Piaget found that children looking at a collection of objects such as pyramids on a table were unable to describe what the objects would look like if they were sitting on the other side of the table. Emily, the little girl with the "klunky" brother, runs into a similar preoperational problem when she walks around the block and comes upon her house from the other side. She cannot understand why she arrives at home when she has walked so far.

"Mama," Emily said. "If you go for a walk and you keep going and going, then do you come back here?"

"Go around the world, you mean?" Mama said. "Well, it's too far to walk, and there are oceans in the way."

"You'd have to cross streets too," Emily said.

"Yes," her mother said. "If you didn't cross any streets, you'd go around the block and come right back here."

"Oh," Emily said. "Oh!"

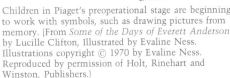
Children in Piaget's preoperational stage are beginning to work with symbols, such as drawing pictures from memory. (From *Some of the Days of Everett Anderson* by Lucille Clifton, Illustrated by Evaline Ness. Illustrations copyright © 1970 by Evaline Ness. Reproduced by permission of Holt, Rinehart and Winston, Publishers.)

In another set of experiments, Piaget asked 4-year-olds to walk on all fours and then to explain verbally how they had done it. The descriptions were often all wrong.

"I'm moving everything at the same time," one 4-year-old explained, inaccurately (Piaget, 1976, p. 2).

Operational By the time a child is about 7, Piaget found improving accuracy of description. By about 9, children know exactly what they are doing as they scramble across the floor. Children in this stage are able to perform many other mental operations as well. One is called *conservation*. A child in the operational stage realizes for the first time that a change in appearance of a quantity of something need not change its quantity—that quantity is conserved. For example, in one Piagetian experiment, an equal amount of liquid is poured into two identical beakers. The children agree there is the same amount of liquid in each beaker. Then one beaker is emptied into a shorter, wider beaker. A child in the preoperational stage will conclude that there is less liquid in the short beaker than in the tall one, because the height has dropped. The operational child, however, recognizes that only the appearance is different.

Formal operational Finally, from about 11 or 12 on, children begin to develop more advanced kinds of mental operations. The period gets its name from Piaget's observation that children in this stage can understand the form or stucture or thought, apart from its content. They can juggle several conflicting hypotheses at once—tentative assumptions subject to verification—and systematically decide which hypothesis is true.

An example of such newly emerged reasoning power appears in James Harvey's *Beyond the Gorge of Shadows* (1965). A 16-year-old boy named Gahyaz challenges the belief of his prehistoric tribe that there are no other people on earth. Gahyaz's companion, Maitsoh, thinks he is crazy or lying to suggest such heretical theories. But then the two boys hike to a distant cave where Maitsoh finds pieces of charcoal and splintered animal bones. Above the bones, the wall is charred as if from a fire. The exploration also turns up a stone scraper and a spear point. From the evidence, Maitsoh decides that his assumptions about Gahyaz were wrong.

"There was no doubt in his mind, none at all, that other men had once lived here. There was no question they had hunted and killed their meat, cooked it over fires and cracked the bones for marrow like the people of his own band. Maitsoh's senses reeled" (p.68). They reeled not because he had *seen* the other people but because his maturing mind had been able to hypothesize that they existed.

A later section in this chapter will show how Piaget's discoveries about children—and other research—can help bring books and young readers together. Piaget himself has warned, however, that the age ranges in the four stages are just approximations. They are useful as guideposts in the search for the child, but they can be misleading. When an American psychologist, Richard I. Evans, pressed him on the point in an interview, Piaget said that children vary widely in how they grow. And some never pass completely through all the stages.

Evans: *Looking at this entire developmental process, from the sensory-motor all the way through to the higher operational levels, I'm sure that you do not believe that these are fixed. In other words, there is quite a bit of flexibility and individual differences within this developmental model, is there not?*

Piaget: *Oh yes, of course, there can be fixations at certain stages; there can be delays and accelerations. But I would even go further. Within the formal operational level, it is entirely possible that some people, for instance those in manual professions, specialized laborers of various sorts, may reach the formal operational level in their particular professional domain, but not right across the board. (Evans, 1973, p. 27)*

Other Theories About Thinking and Learning

Piaget continues to be widely respected and quoted, but not all educators agree that his principles of development are useful in the classroom. And despite his statement that there can be delays and accelerations in a child's movement from one stage to another, some psychologists today think that his theories are too rigid.

You can find vestiges of the nature-nurture controversy in their discussions about thinking and learning.

One theorist, *Jerome Bruner* of Harvard, agrees with Piaget that there are distinct stages of mental growth. Bruner's stages are similar to Piaget's. In the first, children view the world in terms of action toward objects. To Emily's little brother, a crayon is to eat. Children in the second stage are able to think in pictures or images; they need not touch or move objects to learn. In the third stage, children gain the ability to reason abstractly and to make hypotheses, using language to represent the world.

But Bruner does not agree that the sequence of stages is unalterable. He argues that mental growth depends "in very considerable measure" (1966, p. 21) on mastering techniques taught by the culture in which the child lives—on nurturing by parents, teachers, or others. In other words, adults could help Emily understand the mystery behind her adventurous walk around the block. Mental development can be accelerated, Bruner argues, especially with teaching materials that encourage children to explore the world for themselves. Is Emily's brother too young to be exposed to writing with the crayons he likes to chew? Bruner would argue that he is not—that the "klunky" child will learn faster if consistently exposed to symbols like pictures and written words, as well as concrete objects.

Robert Gagné, another contemporary psychologist, goes a step further than Bruner in breaking with Piaget. Gagné does not believe that a child's mind grows in a fixed sequence of stages. Growth, Gagné asserts, results from learning alone, not from some internal process of maturation.

But in Gagné's view, learning does not mean merely swallowing a tumbler of facts, dates, road maps, or sense impressions. Children also learn to *process* knowledge—as Maitsoh used evidence in the cave to reason out the existence of other people. Children develop mental *capabilities*—Gagné's word to describe skill in processing or performing mental tasks. These capabilities, he asserts, are learned in orderly, step-by-step fashion. Maitsoh attained his inductive reasoning power by mastering simpler skills, one by one, in what Gagné calls a *learning hierarchy*—a ladder of many small steps, each supporting higher and higher levels of learning. Teachers can help children up the ladder, according to Gagné's theory (1970, 1974).

Piaget, Bruner, and Gagné agree on one central point: Each child is unique. And no one can know a child's learning ability or mental maturity simply from knowing how old the child is.

How Do Children Judge Right and Wrong?

Similarly, no one can tell how a child will judge right and wrong just by knowing the child's age. But there are general patterns of change. *Lawrence Kohlberg*, a researcher at Harvard University, has reported that everyone passes through the same sequence of moral stages. At each of six stages, people have a different view of law, civil liberties, authority, and other areas where questions of right and wrong are debated.

Kohlberg verified the stages through an 18-year study of fifty American males. Researchers interviewed them every three years from ages 10 to 28. In every interview, subjects were asked questions like this:

> Before the civil war, we had laws that allowed slavery. According to the law if a slave escaped, he had to be returned to his owner like a runaway horse. Some people who didn't believe in slavery disobeyed the law and hid the runaway slaves and helped them to escape. Were they doing right or wrong? (Kohlberg, 1973, p. 372)

A 10-year-old named Johnny answered like this:

> They were doing wrong because the slave ran away himself; they're being just like slaves themselves trying to keep em away. (p. 373)

That response, Kohlberg says, is an example of moral thinking in the first stage.

Preconventional morality Children in the first stage bow to authority or superior power. Does the law allow slavery? Then the slaves were wrong to try to escape, and the people who helped share the

guilt. Answers from other subjects show that the threat of punishment is reason enough to behave.

Three years later, Johnny's answer had changed. At 13, he argued:

> If a person is against slavery and maybe likes the slaves or maybe dislikes the owner, it's okay for him to break the law if he likes, provided he doesn't get caught. (p. 373)

The rule in the second stage: Do what is rewarding. Live as you like, but avoid getting caught breaking the law.

Conventional morality In the next two stages, people come to recognize structure in society. At stage three, Johnny wants to please. He is aware of what "good boys" are supposed to do, and that becomes reason enough to behave well. At stage four, he respects the law as a way to maintain society the way most people want it to be. Still, at this stage, he begins to recognize that some laws are unpopular.

"Laws are made by the people," Johnny says at age 19. "But you might [break the law and help the slaves] because you feel it's wrong. If fifty thousand people break the law, can you put them all in jail? Can fifty thousand people be wrong? (p. 373).

When the subject Kohlberg called Johnny was last interviewed at 24, he had not yet gone beyond conventional morality. According to Kohlberg, most Americans function at stage four, although some people do move to another stage in their late twenty's.

Beyond conventional morality In the last of Kohlberg's stages, the individual is guided by self-developed moral principles and not by concern with authority. The individual in stage five decides that some laws are bad in themselves—apart from their popularity— because they are unjust. A person in Kohlberg's stage six, with a strong awareness of justice and reliance on conscience, will sometimes argue that bad laws *must* be broken.

There are several other discoveries in Kohlberg's work. One is that there is nothing uniquely American about the stages. When researchers studied residents of a Turkish village, they found the

Piaget, Bruner, and Gagné agree on one central point: Each child is unique. (Reprinted with the permission of Charles Scribner's Sons from *Amelia Mixed the Mustard and Other Poems* by Evaline Ness, copyright © 1975 by Evaline Ness.)

same stages, in the same order. A second discovery was that people generally have trouble understanding moral reasoning more than one stage above their own. A child who settles questions of right and wrong on the basis of punishment (stage one), for instance, would have trouble understanding an appeal like "Nice boys and girls don't do that" (stage three).

Again, age designations mean little by themselves. You cannot know children's value systems by asking how old they are. Children often switch back and forth between the stages. Sometimes they think at one stage and act another.

Several critics of Kohlberg have argued that in fact the theory does not apply to everyone. One critic, E. L. Simpson, asserts that people would have to have a high degree of literacy just to talk about the principles in stages five and six—beyond conventional morality. So Kohlberg's theories probably do not apply in societies where the educational system is weak, Simpson writes (1974). He also argues that moral development is related to sex. Because of cultural influences, women are pushed into stage three—wanting to please, like "good girls"—sooner than men. And they stay in stage three longer. Kohlberg's research fails to reveal this cultural pressure, Simpson argues, because most of Kohlberg's subjects were male.

Still, Kohlberg's work does uncover patterns of difference in the way children decide moral issues, and many children—male and female—do progress through stages he identified. His theories can help explain children's reactions to books.

Here is one example. At the end of one version of "Snow White and the Seven Dwarfs," the wicked stepmother has to put on red-hot shoes and dances until she drops dead. Adults may find this a cruel and unusual punishment, even for a purveyor of poisoned apples. Not young children. One 6-year-old was satisfied to see her die.

"She was hurting Snow White," explained the normal first-grader, whose sense of right and wrong demanded punishment for wrongdoing.

How Do Children Acquire Language?

No matter where they live or who their parents are, healthy children cry when they are hungry or in pain. They add babbling to this repertoire of sound in their first year; this doubletalk usually peaks when the child is about 8 to 9 months old. And studies of children in Russia, Germany, and America show that physically normal babies in their babbling produce sounds from other languages as well as from their native tongues.

The similarities in vocal sounds seem to support a theory that language is innate—as ingrained in normal children as the instinct to seek a mother's breast for food.

But many psychologists are dissatisfied with this theory. Researcher E. Brooks Smith and his associates (1970), for example, argue that instinct or innate ability alone cannot adequately explain certain curious traits of language. If language is as immutable as the sucking instinct, why do some words age and drop out of use? Why do normal people make what others consider mistakes in speaking and writing? Language seems far removed in these cases from the realm of natural reflex.

The theories of Smith and others today suggest once again that nature and nurture combine to shape the child.

Like Piaget, Smith writes that children go through several stages as they acquire ability in expressing themselves and understanding others. And like Piaget, Smith qualifies his theory. Stages overlap. And cultural influences intervene during a natural progression from the crying of a newborn to the creative slang of a teenager.

Piaget's child moves at a regular pace from stage to stage, sometimes remaining at one stage of overall mental development for years. The child in Smith's theory of language development seems to race from random crying and babbling, to talking in words of one syllable, to copying adult speech, to intuitively grasping rules of language—all before the first day of kindergarten. At each stage, adults supply essential information to the child. Children in early stages appropriate words and word order, all in one piece. Within the first four years they seize upon unspoken rules from their culture and try to apply the rules, often with a logic that seems beyond their years.

Rule: *Adding "-ed" to a verb puts it into the past tense.*

Logical application: *A 4-year-old child says, "Mommy taked me to the doctor."*

Throughout early school years, a child gradually brings grammar into line with prevailing standards. "The need for effectiveness is so strong that he is constantly pushed and shoved in the direction of the language of his community," Smith writes. "Like a plastic mask, his language develops within the language mold of his community, eventually taking on the same structure and dimension" (p.25).

As they grow, children learn words and structures peculiar to their society. Children in one Eskimo tribe, for example, pick up more than 100 different words for snow. Snow atop ice, for instance is *tuva*. Wet spring snow is *masa*. Wind-driven snow is *tiqsiq* (Thomson, 1975, pp. 140-141).

Listening to and discussing stories can aid children's
language development. (Reprinted with permission of
Macmillan Publishing Co., Inc. From *Will I Have a
Friend?* by Miriam Cohen. Illustrated by Lillian
Hoban. Illustration copyright © 1967 by Lillian
Hoban.)

The amount of snow, the casual conversations of parents, changing conventions of grammar—these and other elements of a child's
world shape the growth of language.

Several other studies show that literature, too, can nurture language development.

In one study by educator Dorothy H. Cohen, published in 1968,
7-year-olds were tested for reading ability in October of their
second-grade year. Then, 155 of the children in an experimental
group entered a program enriched with literature read to them aloud
every day of the school year. Their teachers chose from fifty books
with realistic stories. After hearing these stories, children participated in follow-up activities such as acting out the story, discussing
words, and traveling on a field trip.

A second group of 130 children heard stories only occasionally if
at all. Otherwise, the two groups followed the same curriculum.
Both groups were tested again in June.

The children in the experimental group showed an improvement
in vocabulary, word knowledge, and reading comprehension sig-

nificantly greater than improvement in the group that heard no stories. Simply hearing stories and becoming involved in books—without reading the books themselves—gave children a boost in reading ability.

The studies by Cohen, Piaget, Kohlberg, Smith and others are not the last word on who the child is. These experts cannot tell you how one boy or girl thinks. Your own curiosity and sensitivity may be more useful than studies in exploring the mystery of a child you want to know.

But research can sharpen common sense, and give some ideas on where to start in answering questions about young readers.

Common sense alone is often wrong. Here are three propositions about children and books that *sound* somewhat commonsensical. *Each, however, is false as a general statement.*

Children do not really need books about nature because, with fresh minds and unjaded senses, they understand the world and how it works—often better than adults.
There ought to be more stories for youngest readers about heroes who act for the good of society, not just to win a princess or pot of gold. Children, as natural idealists, would respond more to such heroes than to the flat, somewhat selfish knights of fairy tales.
Storytelling sessions are amusing and entertaining for the preschool child, but once formal training in reading begins, *listening* to stories does not significantly increase the child's ability with language.

What do studies show to be true? Piaget's work indicates that children have trouble understanding the workings of the physical world until they are 6 or 7. Kohlberg's research shows that young children behave to avoid punishment or, at a higher stage, for personal reward. And Cohen's report indicates that second-graders who listen to stories from books do significantly better on reading tests than other second-graders who are given just the usual curriculum. The point is, adult intuitions about children cannot always be trusted.

WHAT CHILDREN'S LITERATURE IS—AND IS NOT

Children cannot be easily defined. Nor can their literature. Authors of children's books are free to write on almost any subject, to use bold and imaginative language, to please the reader. Well-wrought, ingenious stories are the basic stock of all literature.

There are a handful of obvious differences that set children's books apart. They tend to be shorter than adult novels. Illustrations are far more important than in books for older readers. Plots are simpler. There may be more emphasis on the actions than on the musings of main characters. And the main characters themselves tend to be children.

Children's literature today does *not* have to teach lessons or morals. The best of it does not condescend. Stories of sweetly starched children and their encounters with cute elves or wonderful woodland creatures make modern readers gag. Such saccharine tales might have made it into print a century ago, but today good editors strain them quickly out of mail from would-be writers.

"There are hundreds, literally, of stories about adopted birds, squirrels, chipmunks, skunks, rabbits and even foxes and gophers," writes children's book editor Jean Karl, describing the menagerie that arrives in her morning mail. "They are almost all alike. They tell how the poor orphaned baby was found, how it was fed with a medicine dropper or a doll's bottle, how it grew and became a pet, both beloved and mischievous, and finally how it was sent back to the wilds for its own good" (Karl, 1970, p. 28). She sends such animals back to the writers.

Today's author can go far beyond cute and cliché-infested rabbits. *Watership Down,* by Richard Adams (1974), is about power struggles, survival, destruction of the earth's resources, the dangers of dictatorship, and death, among other things. It is also a children's book, and its chief characters are rabbits. But they are creatures in real literature. (There is more on the book in Chapter 6.) Other children's books today cover sensitive areas once reserved for adults only. There are books about physical and mental handicaps, alcoholism, divorce, racial discrimination, and the difficulties of aging. (Chapter 7 explores the apparently unlimited field of modern realistic fiction for children.)

Some writers report that there is even more freedom in the domain of children's books than in adult literature. "In the publishing field today I see more restrictions on what I can do in adult books than in so-called juveniles," writes American author Sylvia Louise Engdahl (1972, p. 250). In *The Far Side of Evil* (1971), a science fiction story centering on a planet with the power to blow itself up, Engdahl deals with "some of the grimmest topics that could be chosen: brain-washing, imminent nuclear war, and the sacrifice of innocent lives. At first, I feared it might be entirely too grim for a junior novel [a novel for teenagers], but nobody seems to have been bothered on that score" (1972, p. 252).

More than that, she contends that the hopeful tone of the book would have disqualified it for serious attention from critics of adult

Some children's books today cover sensitive areas
once reserved for adults only. (Illustration by Charles
Robinson from *A Taste of Blackberries* by Doris
Buchanan Smith. Illustrations copyright © 1973 by
Thomas Y. Crowell Company, Inc. By permission of
Thomas Y. Crowell Company, Inc.)

21

literature. Writers for children are freer than authors for adults to be optimistic, an attitude that grownups today are often supposed to tuck away with other childish things. Happy, visionary endings are still possible in children's books, and the main characters, like real children, can still dream, and expect the best of life.

The freedom to be hopeful, however, is not a license for cuteness. Engdahl warns:

> Let me emphasize that by optimism, I am referring not to the outmoded, sugar-sweet happy ending, but to the portrayal of whatever ordeals a story's characters have undergone, whatever griefs they are left with, as being in some way purposeful—as leading somewhere. (p. 251)

The endangered planet in *The Far Side of Evil* may not survive. The threat of holocaust still hangs over its people, and there is no rosy sunset as the book ends. But the main character, a girl named Elana sent to the planet to observe it, never loses her idealistic hope that someday people will not want to kill each other.

Of course, authors writing for children are also free to explore realms of nonsense, or the foibles of family life, or countless other situations where problems are no more grim than dropping the top of a toothpaste tube down the drain. But whether the problems presented in books are global, or merely niggling, the best of the literature offers a fresh look often lacking in adult books.

The freshness, of course, comes from the author. And in the author it begins with an understanding of who the child is. A British writer, Peter Abbs, suggests:

> In writing for children an author must return to the child in himself. He must reexperience the world as if anew, with all the vulnerable freshness of a child, all the simplicity and uncertainty of a child and with an openness to the unconscious. . . . (1975, p. 123)

EVALUATING THE ELEMENTS OF LITERATURE

The literature begins with the child, but good books are written by authors who go on to use strong material with adult sophistication. The elements are basic to all literature—*plot, setting, characterization, theme,* and *style.* There is no formula for combining these elements. The chemistry is different for each book.

Here is how one book is put together. The children's novel *The Door in the Wall,* by Marguerite de Angeli, published in 1949, is a classic. It won the Newbery Award as the best children's book of that year, and for decades readers have ratified the honor by continuing to read it.

Why does it succeed? Look at the elements.

Plot

"It's about this boy who gets sick and can't walk," begins a young reader's desciption of *Door in the Wall*.

Children often identify a book by its plot, by what happens. When they love a book, they pass on the plot like a gift to friends or parents in a breathless synopsis: "And then the boy went to a monastery and then he learned how to whittle and made a cross and . . ."

Here is a full synopsis of de Angeli's book.

Robin de Bureford is the 10-year-old son of Sir John de Bureford, who has gone off to the Scottish Wars. Robin's mother also leaves home to serve the queen, and the boy himself is to go to the castle of Sir Peter Lindsay as a page, following the custom in fourteenth-century England. But before he can leave, he becomes ill, not with the plague then killing many Londoners, but with an unexplained sickness that cripples his legs. A monk, Brother Luke, carries him to a monastery where he learns to whittle and read and swim. He also learns to walk with crutches he has made himself.

A letter from his father tells him that he and Brother Luke can go on to the castle of Sir Peter. There, he begins training as a page, building confidence despite his disability and overcoming bitterness and anger. One evening Welsh soldiers advance on the castle under cover of fog. They surround it. Robin disguises himself as a poor shepherd. With his crutches tied to his back, he swims an icy river near the castle, passes through the Welsh lines, and carries the message for help. Allies of Sir Peter arrive and break the siege. The Scottish wars end. Robin's father and mother arrive at Sir Peter's castle. The king himself honors Robin for his bravery, and the boy learns that he and his parents will go back, reunited, to their home in London.

The plot of *Door in the Wall* is sometimes called *progressive*, because it progresses toward a climax, or peak event: Robin overcomes his disability and saves the castle. Other books are built on *parallel* plots, with two sets of action occurring simultaneously. Usually, the parallel lines of plot come together at the end of the book. Some novels have a major plot and one or more *subplots*, lesser story lines that support the main action. Another large group of books for children have *episodic* stories: each chapter tells a different tale, each with its own climax, complete in itself.

An example of a book with an episodic plot is Arnold Lobel's *Frog and Toad Together* (1972), a runner-up for the Newbery Award in 1973. Each of the five chapters in this easy-to-read fantasy is a whole story. In one, "Dragons and Giants," a book of fairy tales about the battles of brave people makes Frog wonder whether he and Toad are brave. The pale green frog and his light brown friend set off on a quest to find out, and begin to climb a mountain. As in many classic tales, the two face three trials. The first is an encounter with a huge snake who looms at Frog and Toad out of a dark cave and says, "Hello lunch."

"I am not afraid," Toad cries (p. 45). They climb higher, and survive an avalanche of boulders and then a close brush with a hawk. "We are not afraid!" scream Frog and Toad (p. 48), and they run all the way home where Toad stays in bed and Frog stays in the closet, "for a long time, just feeling very brave together" (p. 51).

The same vulnerable characters appear in each of the tales, and in each, the plot carries them quickly into a problem. In each, their friendship and cooperation help them through.

Events in this book spawn other events. The animals' reading leads directly to climbing a hill, which leads to the subsequent action and danger. In books with progressive plots, what happens in Chapter 1 is frequently the cause of adventures in Chapter 2, all the way to the end of the book.

Novelist E. M. Forster once developed a simple test for plots. If a book says, "The king died and then the queen died," that is merely a report of two unconnected events. If a book says, "The king died and then the queen died of grief," that is a plot (Forster, 1954, p. 130).

The Door in the Wall is built on a good plot. Events interlock. The disease that cripples Robin in the first chapter affords him a good disguise in the book's climactic scenes when he must pass through enemy lines. Swinging on his crutches, soaked after his swim in the river, Robin presents no threat to the Welsh guard who stops him. "Art tha' but a shepherd boy, then?" the guard asks. "And hast fallen into the river? Come, then, lad, and warm tha' self by the fire. Be not frighted. We'll not hurt thee" (p. 94).

Robin passes on. It is no coincidence, either, that Robin can swim the icy river. His skill can be traced to the teaching of Brother Luke, who cared for Robin because his father had to go to war, which we have learned in Chapter 1.

Setting

In some books, setting is specific. *Door in the Wall*, for instance, is set in medieval England amid drafty stone rooms, great halls, and

Frog and Toad decide that they *look* brave, and so
begin their adventures. (Illustration from *Frog and
Toad Together*, written and illustrated by Arnold
Lobel. Copyright © 1971, 1972 by Arnold Lobel. By
permission of Harper & Row, Publishers, Inc.)

The illustrations for *The Door in the Wall* help to
establish the medieval setting. (Illustration from *The
Door in the Wall* by Marguerite de Angeli. Copyright
© 1949 by Marguerite de Angeli. Reproduced by
permission of Doubleday & Company, Inc.)

walled cities. In other books, authors underline the universality of
their stories by deliberately leaving place and time vague.

When the setting is specific, it must be true to the author's perception of time and place. For novels set in the past, this means
painstaking research. (There is more on the ups and downs of such
research in Chapter 8.) The work of historians often provides a
backdrop for such stories, a panorama from which authors pick important detail.

After such research, authors may be tempted to drop in more of
the setting than the reader wants to know. But successful settings
never intrude. Place and time enter gently, often with references to
what is seen, heard, tasted, touched, or smelled by characters in the
story.

The setting of *Door in the Wall*, for example, comes to the reader through Robin's senses. On the opening page, Robin pulls a coverlet over his head and shuts his eyes to try to keep out the deafening sound of church bells: "It seemed to Robin they were all inside his head screaming to be let out" (p. 7).

Other details of setting come through sight and touch.

> Robin thought of his father and how he had looked on that last day when he rode off to the Scottish wars at the head of the column. Now, remembering, Robin could almost feel the weight of his father's mailed glove on his shoulder as he said good-by. Then he had been straight and strong, standing there in the courtyard as the men rode forth. (p. 7)

But time and place are more than a backdrop. They also set off the opening events of *Door in the Wall*, even before Robin and other characters begin to act on their own. The London plague claims the maid who takes care of Robin in his mother's absence, driving the boy into the care of the monks.

Details of medieval England also make the plot more believable. Lame Robin's growing strength, for instance, is not merely reported; it is proved in the way he masters the place where he lives:

> He was able to go about easily from keep to tower, from hall to chapel, from turret to dungeon. Even the twisting stairs held no terror for him, because he had learned to place the crutches carefully and swiftly where they would hold and balance him. (p. 78)

Characterization

The setting gives Robin a chance to show himself, and his character is drawn in several other ways. He appears in straight narration, for instance. The second paragraph of the book reports, like a calling card, that he is the son of a noble family. But his character comes out in other, subtler ways that tell much more. Readers learn who Robin is through techniques of character delineation—portrayal—used in all literature.

Robin is revealed in his actions Is Robin bitter and angry at the beginning of the book? De Angeli does not say so. Instead, she shows his anger, and several other allied emotions at the same time, in sharp action, when Ellen the cook brings him porridge in bed:

> Robin gathered all his strength and flung his arm toward the bowl of porridge, sending it flying out of Ellen's hands and spreading its contents all over her. He was ashamed as soon as he had done it, but Ellen did look funny with the mess hanging from her chin. (p.10)

In his thoughts Readers enter his mind and feel the longing there. If only his mother were here, he dreams. "The damp, sweaty feeling would leave his head, his legs would obey him and take him where he wanted to go, racing up and down alleyways or along the high street" (p. 10).

In his speech "Forthright," "bold," "articulate"—rather than attaching these labels to Robin, de Angeli lets him introduce himself by what he says, for instance to Brother Luke in their first meeting. "But I cannot walk," Robin explains. "See you, my two legs are as useless as if they were logs of wood" (p. 15). And, when he meets his father for the first time since becoming a cripple, he asks an agonizing question: "Sir, mind you not that I must go thus, bent over, and with these crutches to help me walk?" (p. 120).

In the way others see him His father answers, and in deft strokes draws a much-changed Robin for readers. "The courage you have shown," Sir John replies, "the craftsmanship proven by the harp, and the spirit in your singing all make so bright a light that I cannot see whether or no your legs are misshapen" (p. 120).

The portrait that emerges is not static. From a self-pitying dreamer confined to his bed, Robin becomes a brave and active youth near the end of the book, with manual skills to make up for his bent legs, and songs to offer to the king. De Angeli does more than delineate the character; she also develops him.

Robin grows naturally. Brother Luke cannot transform him just by carting him to a monastery. Robin's early try at whittling there, for instance, ends in failure when he chisels right through the cross of walnut wood he is trying to make. Robin is ready to give up. It takes two years and a life-threatening mission outside the castle to bring about the changes. His growth is so believable that children sometimes ask what happened to him after the end of the book.

Robin provides a good standard for judging main characters in other books. How does the author tell you about them? Do they emerge naturally from what they do, think, and say? Do they show weaknesses as well as strengths? If they change in the course of the book, is the pace of change believable? At the end of the book, do you know them enough to imagine what might happen if the book continued? Do you care about them?

Theme

"It's about a boy. . . . It's a book about England in the Middle Ages. . . . It's about how a cripple saves a castle. . . ." Different readers

ISSUE

WHAT LANGUAGE SHOULD CHARACTERS USE?

As a writer I am interested in language and in people and in how the two things go together, for they do bear considerably upon each other. I have been particularly concerned with the language of children and of people less glib and articulate than I am. . . . When I am using for my protagonist a semiliterate ten- or twelve-year-old, I do not think that he should reveal the world in my voice and in my terms, or that he should speak fluently in my vocabulary. I think he should have to struggle with language and find himself ill at ease with it and occasionally get it wrong. I think sometimes even familiar things should be outside his powers of exact description, as I know him to be blessed occasionally with a word or a phrase of piercing insight. But I think the battle to make himself understood to others as well as to himself is very much an innate part of what I am attempting to get across in many of my books. When my characters speak, I hope they speak naturally and in words that come naturally to them. (p. 252)

> Steele, Mary Q. "'As Far as You Can Bear to See': Excellence in Children's Literature," *The Horn Book*, June 1975, pp. 250–255.

Most of the junior novels sound exactly alike, and many are written in the first person. . . . It is as if the writers felt that only a banal, flat-footed, unevocative way of writing—utterly lacking in the overtones and elliptical expressions the accomplished writer takes pleasure in—would be tolerated by his audience. But surely there can be no more unrewarding prose than is found in these books, written as if by the teenagers themselves. Scarcely ever do their writers educate the ear, give it a chance to become fine-tuned, expand its experience of word play, or provide the reader any opportunity to reach into subtle comprehensions or to grow aesthetically. On the contrary, they offer only those word arrangements teenagers themselves use every day of their lives, which are most often extremely limited modes of expression. (p. 80)

> Cameron, Eleanor. "McLuhan, Youth, and Literature", part III, *The Horn Book*, February 1973, pp. 79–85.

What is the basic difference in the viewpoints of these two children's authors? What concerns do they share? How might each respond to the comments of the other?

may focus on character, setting, or plot to describe *Door in the Wall*. But underlying all three elements, there is a theme; the book is about a fundamental truth.

De Angeli's theme appears in a Bible citation on the page before the first chapter:

> I know thy works: Behold I have set before thee an open door and no man shall shut it: for thou hast a little strength and hast not denied my name. (Rev. 3:8)

There are walls around us all, the book says—personal disabilities as well as restrictions imposed by custom. But none of us needs to be a prisoner. The thread of that idea passes through the book and knits all the elements together. De Angeli brings readers back again and again to the truth she has found in the Bible citation, while studiously avoiding climbing to a pulpit to preach. Just as plot, setting, and character develop naturally, the theme emerges easily, without being labeled as truth or moral. Reading, Brother Luke says, is one door in the wall.

"Yes," Robin says. "I see now what you mean by the door in the wall" (p. 29), and the story moves on without harping on the message. Sir Peter, proprietor of the castle, expands a little on the theme later when he meets Robin: "Each of us has his place in the world. . . . If we cannot serve in one way, there is always another. If we do what we are able, a door always opens to something else" (p. 71). And at the end of the story, after Robin awakes from a nap at a holiday feast and wonders where he is, Brother Luke raises the theme again like the last notes of a recurring chorus.

> "Thou'rt here, Sir Robin," said the friar.
> "Safe with all thy loved ones. 'Tis the feast of Christmas, and thou has found the door in thy wall." (p. 121)

The theme never overwhelms the plot.

Over centuries, books for children have often turned into tracts. Themes have often popped out like messages in a fortune cookie, surrounded by hollow characterization and a dry plot.

The famous rags-to-riches stories by Horatio Alger in the last century, dragged out sermonlike themes about the importance of honesty and hard work. In one passage of *Ragged Dick* (1868), Alger manages to combine preachment with some clumsy characterization. Ragged Dick is not without faults, Alger begins.

ISSUE

WHAT MAKES A STEREOTYPE?

The problem of this investigation consisted of an analysis of characterizations of minority group Americans as presented in contemporary children's literature. . . . (p. 13)

None of the Indians, Chinese, Japanese or Negroes was identified as Roman Catholic while virtually all of the Spanish-American characters were. . . . (p. 15)

Spanish-Americans [were shown] as having brown skin and black hair and favoring traditional costumes only in the case of the Mexican subgroup [persons of Mexican descent living in the Southwest]. . . . (p. 16)

Spanish-Americans were shown as poor people of the lower-class having no college aspirations and holding a variety of non-professional jobs. . . . (p. 16)

The first hypothesis of the study, that stereotypes of the respective minority groups would not be identified in the literature analyzed, has to be rejected. Stereotypes were identified. (p. 17)

> Gast, David K. "Minority Americans in Children's Literature,"
> *Elementary English*, Vol. 44, January 1967, pp. 12–23.

While this writer found Mr. Gast's information correct, the characters were never found lacking in individuality and human dignity. Hidalgo in *Hidalgo and the Gringo Train*, for instance, is identified as a dark, little boy living in the country and as a Catholic. As the same time, he is pictured as an intensely curious boy, eager to learn to read a book which has captured his imagination. While Miguel in *And Now Miguel* also fits Mr. Gast's pattern, the boy reveals special qualities entirely his own, a certain wonder about himself, an eagerness to grow into responsibility. It seems, then, that Mr. Gast confuses stereotype and accurate cultural information. (p. 449)

> Blatt, Gloria T. "The Mexican-American in Children's Literature,"
> *Elementary English*, April 1968, pp. 446–451.

How would you describe the difference between a stereotype and a character portrayal based on accurate cultural information? What would you need to know in order to decide if a particular character were stereotyped or not? If a writer were to describe you in stereotypical terms, what might you expect to read about yourself?

But there were some good points about him nevertheless. He was above doing anything mean or dishonorable. He would not steal, or cheat, or impose upon younger boys, but was frank and straight-forward, manly and self-reliant. His nature was a noble one, and had saved him from all mean faults. I hope my young readers will like him as I do. . . . Perhaps although he was only a bootblack, they may find something in him to imitate. (p. 18)

By contrast, Robin is no paragon of noble qualities. And the truth he approaches cannot be expressed by slogans. Good books are based on complex and important themes, presented with subtlety through plot, characterization, and setting.

Style

The presentation itself—the choice of words and the way they are put together—can draw readers into the book, or drive them away. Look at these two passages describing old houses.

> Tommy took Stephanie's hand and they walked up to the big old front door of Halfway House. It looked like it hadn't been opened in about seventy-seven years. And it was covered with musty, dusty spider webs.
> "It's probably locked. Let's go home!" said Tommy.
> But just then—ccrreeeeaaakkk—the door opened—all by. . . . itself!!!!

> They set out again, and made good speed, reaching the village of Heath-cot by dusk. There they found an inn at the edge of town, its thatch pulled down over its eyes of windows wherein could be seen a smoky light from the fire.
> A creaking sign showed the picture of the White Hart.
> "An innocent name," said the friar. "But this place hath a fearsome look."

The first passage is straightforward, but heavy-handed. The rollicking rhyme of "musty, dusty" seems out of place in what is supposed to be an ominous setting. And the Morse code of dashes and dots in the last sentence does not make the setting any more spooky. Finally, readers are bound to be frustrated trying to put four shrieking exclamation marks into the word "itself." (There is another problem with the passage, unrelated to its style: the door in the picture under the text is not covered with musty, dusty spider webs or even spider webs. A similar problem arises a few pages later when the story says Tommy's eyes were "as big as saucers" and Stephanie was white as a—guess what—sheet. In the picture, Tommy's eyes are their usual teaspoon size, and Stephanie is as pink-cheeked as she was on the first page of the book.) The first passage is from *A Visit to The Haunted House* by Dean Walley.

By contrast, the second version calls up a vivid picture of a menacing road house. The phrase "thatch pulled down over its eyes of windows" is fresh. The scene does not need labels or exclamation marks because the style itself conveys mystery and awe. The second passage is on page 55 of *The Door in the Wall*.

Authors face basic questions about style as they begin a book. They can choose, for instance, to write in the third person, as de Angeli does, telling the story as a narrator watching the action from outside. Or, like many authors of modern fiction, they can write in the first person, taking the role of a main character. First-person narratives create a sense of comradeship with the teller. But third-person books allow authors to present several perspectives on the action.

Writers can also choose the pace of their story—the speed of the trip from London to the castle in the country, for instance. They can make events in the plot whisk by like markers on a highway. Or they can slow the pace to take a close look at one scene, or to listen to one character's anger at what is happening.

Style permeates every sentence. It sets mood. De Angeli's style, for instance, evokes a sense of the traditional tale. Her stately language rings like the words of a saga told in the glow of the fire after a medieval feast.

Her style meets several criteria. The language itself sings. She chooses active verbs. She thrusts readers into scenes by letting them in on the sounds of bells, street smells, tastes, and textures ("geese roasted with feathers on," p. 121), as well as sights. She varies sentence length, and frees characters to speak conversationally, with room to take a breath. And best of all, her style is never more noticeable than the story. It is a clear window on Robin's world.

The Door in the Wall is good literature. Do children like it? That is another question.

BRINGING BOOKS TO CHILDREN

Lloyd Alexander, an American children's book writer, tells a story about a boy who hated kreplach, a small package of dough containing meat filling. The boy's mother asked a psychologist how to change his taste. The psychologist suggested showing the boy each step in the process of making kreplach. So the mother called her son into the kitchen the next day as she rolled out dough, cut it into squares, and began to fold the corners over the filling. The boy was fascinated until she had tucked the last corner under the ground meat. Then he was horrified. "It's kreplach!" he shouted.

It is the same with books, Alexander writes. "What if a book meets all these criteria and the reader still doesn't like it?" (in Painter, 1970, p. 25).

Alice in Wonderland, for instance, bores many children. The language in *The Door in the Wall* may strike some children as stuffy. Yet both of these books are good literature. Both are built of strong materials—good plots, rich settings, well-developed characters, important themes, and artistic styles—and in both, the materials meld well.

The likes and dislikes of children do not determine the quality of literature. Obviously, if one child likes *Alice,* the book does not become twice as good because *two* people like it; popularity is a literary criterion only in Wonderland logic. Books must be judged as literature on their own merits. And children should be given excellent literature.

Still, in the presence of something good, some of them shout, "It's kreplach!"

No one can say with certainty what a child will like. "I don't know the answer," Alexander writes (ibid.). Another children's book author, Esther Hautzig, agrees that bringing books to children is never simple.

> Books are like people, like friends, and one's chemical reactions to them cannot be really duplicated by anyone else's—much like fingerprints. A book may be universally liked but liked by a thousand people for a thousand different reasons and understood, or read, on a thousand different levels. (1970, p. 467)

There is a spectrum of solutions to the problem of bringing books and children together. At one extreme, children may be put into strict categories based on research about age or stage. Then everyone in a class or category gets the same book. Under this system, books appear in a child's life in progression from simple toward difficult. Children tend to look down on last year's book ("That's baby stuff; it's a second-grade book") and up to next year's ("I can't read that; it's a fourth-grade book"). This convenient and authoritarian approach to matching children and books is yielding today to the realization that within a third-grade class, for instance, there are some children who need and want books that once would have been reserved for fourth- or second-graders.

At another extreme, children do all their own choosing without

34

ISSUE

HOW VALUABLE IS THE NEWBERY AWARD?

The times have changed, but not so children's librarians. Who cares what children are asking for and demanding, we have our high standards of literature to maintain. We have our Newbery winners which stand for "the most distinguished contribution to American literature" for the year they are published. . . . I do not deny that the award winners these past 50 years are not the best a particular year had to offer, I just think that the award should admit that it reflects the judgment of adults with little regard for what children are reading. If this would be pointed out, maybe parents, teachers, and librarians would not force the title on an unwitting child. (p. 15)

> Kalkhoff, Ann. "Innocent Children or Innocent Librarians,"
> in *Issues in Children's Book Selection* (New York: Bowker, 1973), pp. 11-19.

Much has been written about the Newbery Awards; more will be written. Discussion and controversy only prove the prestige and success of the awards. . . . I have never served on a Newbery-Caldecott Committee, but I have been impressed with the expertise, enthusiasm, or at least with the honesty and sincerity of people whom I have known on the committee. Any of them would, I think, agree with me that one value of the awards has been the provision of opportunity at this national level for discussion of books, not in terms of expense, social relevance, or relation to the curriculum, but for that quality the Newbery Awards have assisted us in recognizing: excellence. (p. 34)

> Sullivan, Peggy. "Victim of Success? A Closer Look at the Newbery Award,"
> in *Issues in Children's Book Selection* (New York: Bowker, 1973), pp. 31-34.

What do you see as values in the giving of children's book awards such as the Newbery Award? What are possible criticisms of such practices? If you were asked to decide whether the Newbery Award should be continued, what would be the critical factors in your decision?

Children, like adults, select books that are meaningful
to them. (Illustrations copyright © 1978 by Ray Cruz.
From *Alexander Who Used to Be Rich Last Sunday*
by Judith Viorst. Used by permission of Atheneum
Publishers.)

guidance. Margery Fisher, a critic and mother of six children, tells
how she would match books and readers.

> If I was in the ideal school with all the power in the world I should simply
> have a large room with books all over the floor or all over the tables and
> leave children there. (1970, p. 21)

Certainly there are times when children should be left alone in a
library and—as a fundamental principle—they should not be forced
to read books that are meaningless to them, no matter how good the
books are. But at many other times, children naturally look to adults
to help them find good books.

Parents, teachers, librarians—all become brokers sometimes between literature and children. The most realistic approach today lies
somewhere between the extremes.

Adults need to arm themselves with a strong sense of what is
good literature. They also need to recognize individual tastes, differences in how children grow and what they like. It does little good,
warns critic Northrop Frye, to tell a young boy that the book he has
just plucked off the shelf is no good.

ISSUE

IS THERE EVER JUSTIFICATION FOR GIVING MEDIOCRE BOOKS TO CHILDREN?

In addition to the Feminists on Children's Media there are two groups currently writing and publishing their own titles. Granted the publications by the Feminists Press and Lollipop Power Inc. are second or even third rate, but they fill a need. At their low price and paperback format, we can purchase them as ephemeral and replace them as soon as superior works come along. (p. 16)

Kalkhoff, Ann. "Innocent Children or Innocent Librarians,"
in *Issues in Children's Book Selection* (New York: Bowker, 1973), pp. 11-19.

Child readers bring certain expectations to a book including a desire to find enjoyment and meaning in it, and I argue that if the author does not meet those demands, the work will leave the reader feeling empty and cheated. Because readers can rarely identify the reasons for the feelings of dissatisfaction they sometimes have after completing a mediocre book, the danger exists that the child may attach an impression of shallowness and superficiality to the topics or characters in the book instead of to the author. As a result, in promoting a mediocre book simply because it deals with a rarely-discussed issue or because it portrays a woman or minority character in a favorable manner, we may be promoting the very attitudes we hope to erase. (pp. 139-140)

Richardson, Carmen C. "Rediscovering the Center in Children's Literature,"
Language Arts, February 1978, pp. 138-145.

According to Richardson, what might be the result of children's reading of publications by a company such as Lollipop Power, publications which might be "second or even third rate," but which "fill a need"? How could Kalkhoff defend her position? What assumptions underlie Kalkhoff's position? Richardson's?

He has to feel values for himself, and should follow his individual rhythm in doing so. In the meantime, he can read almost anything in any order, just as he can eat mixtures of food that would have his elders reaching for the baking soda. A sensible teacher or librarian can soon learn how to give guidance to a youth's reading that allows for undeveloped taste and still doesn't turn him into a gourmet or dyspeptic before his time. (1964, p. 116)

There are a couple of steps to good literary guidance: judging books to find good literature, and then meeting the child's particular interests. Before you know the child well, you can begin with what you know generally of children of different ages.

Succeeding chapters recommend books for young readers in four age groups, comprising children from age 3 to their mid-teens. But the age designations used in this book are not written in stone. They are merely a starting point for people who want to bring books and children together. Here is what the designations mean. And here, at the same time, is a thumbnail summary of research about who children are, and the kinds of books they tend to like.

Preschool

Newborn children do not distinguish themselves from objects and people around them. By the preschool period—the years from 3 to 5—they recognize the outside world. They can choose books themselves, turn pages, although sometimes with difficulty, react to pictures, and toss away books that bore them.

They tend to enjoy slapstick humor—watching a cook on TV's *Sesame Street* dropping an armload of cakes, for instance. They like rhymes, and they toy with the sounds of words. Some begin reading toward the end of the period, a few even sooner.

But preschool children have trouble in some areas that will seem familiar to them in just a few years. They have little concept of time or distance, for instance. What adults consider common sense is garbled. One 4-year-old girl who watched her father leave for work on a train every day assumed he worked full time on a train.

Moral decisions for preschool children often rest on the threat of punishment; intention does not count.

Books for preschool children tend to be short, with plenty of pictures, and no subplots, parallel plots, or flashbacks. Mother Goose rhymes (Chapter 3) are popular. Folktales (Chapter 5) with repetition, such as "The Three Billy Goats Gruff," help bridge short attention spans. Stories about evil and good make sense to preschool

The humor in the books about Curious George has
given them lasting appeal for preschool and primary
children. (From *Curious George Takes a Job* by H. A.
Rey, illustrated by the author. Copyright © renewed
1975 by H. A. Rey. Reprinted by permission of
Houghton Mifflin Company.)

children, particularly when evil—the bad giant, the troll, the
witch—is routed in the end.

"Witches should be sour, like good lemons, and as tart and zest-
ful," writes children's book author Philippa Pearce. "The only good
witch is a really bad one. That's the acid test" (in Field, 1969, p. 58).

Primary

The child from 6 to 8, in the early school years, rapidly gains in
reading ability. With this growth in verbal skill comes growing appreciation of puns, jokes, and riddles, although slapstick humor remains popular. Children in the first few grades also come closer to
comprehending the world around them. They can identify a bird, for
instance, even when it appears at an odd angle in a picture. Most
moral choices still rest on the threat of punishment, but a child may
also make decisions on how to act on the basis of possible rewards.
Concepts of time and distance are still vague.

Books for primary school children can present several points of
view—the child can juggle them successfully—but stories still tend

39

to be short. Young readers can now hold a favorite character in mind, following with keen interest the adventures of a monkey or elephant, for instance, through a series of books read at different times. Children as young as 6 are able to spot inconsistencies in plot or character.

Intermediate

Pressure grows on children 9 to 11 years old to join a pack, to become a member of a group, gang or team. Parents often feel the first pangs of separation as their sons and daughters begin to move—at least in spirit—away from family. But children in the middle grades are not as independent as they sometimes seem. In their encounters with literature they may need constant help from adults because books that interest them often surpass their reading level.

Books for intermediate-grade children can begin to focus on problems of growing up and getting along with other people. Boys and girls may choose differently. For both sexes, sense of humor becomes more subtle, sometimes based on aggression or hostility. Children in this period can readily understand characters in books who make moral choices on the basis of expected reward, but they can also begin to appreciate acting properly to please others. It is not too late to read aloud to children in fourth, fifth, or sixth grades; many enjoy hearing stories they are not yet skilled enough to read to themselves.

Early Adolescence

Most children 12 to 14 can reason with abstract concepts, understand time and distance accurately and sustain concentration on a single task for long periods. But there are major differences in ability and interest between individual adolescents, variations which become gradually apparent and more pronounced in each successive grade.

Books for early adolescents vary as much as their readers. Some seventh-graders like adult books; some eighth-graders stop reading altogether under growing pressures of puberty. Most students in these years have developed enough insight to understand involved books like Barbara Picard's *One is One* (1965). It follows Stephen de Beauville from age 7 to 27, from declared coward to knight to artist in a monastery. Set in the Middle Ages, the story has familiar resonance for early teenagers trying to find out who they are.

Young teenagers are also old enough to become critics of books, to

Adolescent readers can understand complex stories
such as *One Is One*. (Illustration by Victor
Ambrus from *One is One* by Barbara Leonie Picard,
published by Oxford University Press 1965.)

analyze form as well as content and to make up their own minds
about what is good literature, apart from what teachers tell them.
Critic Northrop Frye describes such independence.

> I recently went past two teen-age girls looking at the display in front of a
> movie which told them that inside was the thrill of a lifetime, on no
> account to be missed, and I heard one of them say: "Do you suppose it's
> any good?" (1964, p. 138)

Adults, of course, should ask that question about books for children of any age. Popular tastes are subject to fad and sometimes
change as often as the marquees of movie theaters. So, of course, do

41

the tastes of individual children as they grow through ages and stages. But there are enough good books for children today for an astute adult to select exciting fare for any individual child.

Judge the book, and meet the child. Good literature, well chosen for a reader, is here today and here tomorrow, remembered and still read even after the reader has grown up.

SUMMARY

1 Matching books to children requires knowing who the child is, as well as selecting good literature from the 39,250 children's books in print.

2 Who is the child? Research over the past century has undermined easy generalizations about how children grow and learn. One persistent controversy—the nature-nurture debate—focuses on whether children inherit their ability to learn or whether they mature through experience with the world around them.

3 Psychologist Jean Piaget believes that both environment and heredity shape living organisms. He suggests that all children go through four stages of development. At first they understand the world through their senses alone; mental operations come into play in later stages, and eventually, at some time after age 11 or 12, children are able to deal with abstractions.

4 Piaget's theories are not universally accepted. Psychologist Jerome Bruner, for instance, agrees with Piaget that there are distinct stages. But Bruner does not agree that their sequence is unalterable, and he suggests that development can be accelerated by use of proper teaching materials.

5 In a study of fifty American males, Lawrence Kohlberg reports finding six stages of development in the way people judge right from wrong. He suggests that children have trouble understanding principles of morality more than one stage above their own. Again, age alone does not determine stage.

6 Psychologist E. Brooks Smith and his colleagues suggest that language acquisition also proceeds in stages and that children pass through many of these stages before they reach kindergarten. Contesting the theory that language is simply innate, Smith argues that many influences outside the child nurture growth of speaking, reading, and writing ability. A study by Dorothy Cohen indicates that exposure to literature can be one such influence.

7 What is good children's literature? Like children, literature is not easily defined, but the elements of *plot, setting, characterization, theme,* and *style* are basic to all literature. Using some basic criteria, each of these elements can be analyzed for excellence.

8 The quality of literature alone, however, does not ensure acceptance by a particular child. As the research shows, the audience for children's literature is diverse. Preschool children generally enjoy short stories with plenty of pictures, and no subplots or flashbacks, but reading interests diverge widely as children grow.

BIBLIOGRAPHY

Adult References

Abbs, Peter. "Penelope Lively, Children's Fiction and the Failure of Adult Culture," *Children's Literature in Education,* vol. 18, Fall 1975, pp. 118–124.

Blatt, Gloria T. "The Mexican-American in Children's Literature," *Elementary English,* April 1968, pp. 446–451.

Bruner, Jerome S. *Toward a Theory of Instruction* (New York: Norton, 1966).

Cameron, Eleanor. "McLuhan, Youth, and Literature,"part III, *The Horn Book,* February 1973, pp. 79–85.

Children's Books in Print 1977-1978 (New York: Bowker, 1977).

Cohen, Dorothy H. "The Effect of Literature on Vocabulary and Reading Achievement," *Elementary English,* February 1968, pp. 209–213.

Engdahl, Sylvia Louise. "Why Write for Today's Teenagers?" *The Horn Book,* June 1972, pp. 249–254.

Evans, Richard Isadore. *Jean Piaget: The Man and His Ideas,* trans. Eleanor Duckworth (New York: Dutton, 1973).

Field, Elinor Whitney (comp.). *Horn Book Reflections* (Boston: The Horn Book, 1969).

Fisher, Margery. "Is Fiction Educational?" *Children's Literature in Education,* vol. 1, March 1970, pp. 11–21.

Forster, E. M. *Aspects of the Novel* (New York: Harcourt, 1954).

Frye, Northrop. *The Educated Imagination* (Bloomington: Indiana University Press, 1964).

Gagné, Robert M. *The Conditions of Learning,* 2d ed. (New York: Holt, 1970).

———*Essentials of Learning for Instruction* (Hinsdale, Ill.: Dryden, 1974).

Gast, David K. "Minority Americans in Children's Literature," *Elementary English,* vol. 44, January 1967, pp. 12–23.

Hautzig, Esther. *"The Endless Steppe*—For Children Only?" *The Horn Book,* October 1970, pp. 461–468.

Kalkhoff, Ann. "Innocent Children or Innocent Librarians," in *Is-*

sues in Children's Book Selection (New York: Bowker, 1973, pp. 11-19).

Karl, Jean. *From Childhood To Childhood* (New York: John Day, 1970).

Kohlberg, Lawrence. "Moral Development and the New Social Studies," *Social Education,* May 1973, pp. 369-375.

Painter, Helen W. (ed.). *Reaching Children and Young People through Literature* (Newark, Del.: International Reading Association, 1970).

Piaget, Jean. *The Grasp of Consciousness: Action and Concept in the Young Child,* trans. Susan Wedgwood (Cambridge: Harvard University Press, 1976).

Richardson, Carmen C. "Rediscovering the Center in Children's Literature," *Language Arts,* February 1973, pp. 138-145.

Simpson, E. L. "Moral Development Research: A Case Study of Scientific Cultural Bias," *Human Development,* vol. 17, 1974, pp. 81-106.

Smith, E. Brooks, Kenneth S. Goodman, and Robert Meredith. *Language and Thinking in School,* 2d ed. (New York: Holt, 1976).

Steele, Mary Q. "'As Far as You Can Bear to See': Excellence in Children's Literature," *The Horn Book,* June 1975, pp. 250-255.

Sullivan, Peggy. "Victim of Success? A Closer Look at the Newbery Award," in *Issues in Children's Book Selection* (New York: Bowker, 1973, pp. 31-34).

Thomson, David S., and the editors of Time-Life Books. *Language* (New York: Time-Life Books, 1975).

Walsh, Jill Paton. "The Writer's Responsibility," *Children's Literature in Education,* vol. 10, March 1973, pp. 30-36.

Children's Book References

Adams, Richard. *Watership Down* (New York: Macmillan, 1974).

Alger, Horatio Jr. *Ragged Dick* (Boston: Loring, 1868). In Haviland, Virginia, and Margaret N. Coughlin, *Yankee Doodle's Literary Sampler of Prose, Poetry and Pictures* (New York: Crowell, 1974, pp. 263–271).

Blume, Judy. *Are You There God? It's Me, Margaret* (New York: Dell, 1970).

Carroll, Lewis. *Alice in Wonderland,* illus. John Tenniel (New York: Random House, 1965). (1865)

De Angeli, Marguerite. *The Door in the Wall* (Garden City, N.Y.: Doubleday, 1949).

Engdahl, Sylvia Louise. *The Far Side of Evil,* illus. Richard Cuffari (New York: Atheneum, 1971).

Harvey, James. *Beyond the Gorge of Shadows* (New York: Lothrop, Lee and Shepard, 1965).

Kunhardt, Dorothy. *Pat the Bunny* (Racine, Wis.: Golden, 1968). (1940)

Lexau, Joan. *Emily and the Klunky Baby and the Next-Door Dog,* illus. Martha Alexander (New York: Dial, 1972).

Lobel, Arnold. *Frog and Toad Together* (New York: Harper, 1972).

Picard, Barbara. *One Is One,* illus. Victor Ambrus (London: Oxford University Press, 1965).

Walley, Dean. *A Visit to the Haunted House,* illus. Arlene Noel (Kansas: Hallmark Cards Inc.).

Walsh, Jill Paton. *Goldengrove* (New York: Farrar, 1972).

CHAPTER 2

PICTURE BOOKS

A FIRST LOOK AT CHILDREN'S LITERATURE

Robert McCloskey bought four ducks at the Washington Market in New York City, took them to his apartment, and turned them loose. Then, for weeks, as they waddled and quacked from room to room, McCloskey crawled behind with Kleenex and sketch pad, making hundreds of drawings.

McCloskey, an accomplished artist, collected stacks of pictures of full-grown mallards. Then he brought home half a dozen live ducklings. Again, he followed them around like a bird dog. The stack of drawings grew. Earlier, he had studied stuffed ducks at the Museum of Natural History in New York and interviewed an expert in birds at Cornell University. He had learned how ducks molt, and how they mate. He had discovered how to tell which ducks were pure mallard and which were part puddle duck.

The result of his exhaustive research: *Make Way for Ducklings* (1941), a children's picture storybook.

The plot is simple. Mr. and Mrs. Mallard want to establish a home for their eight ducklings in Boston. After the eggs hatch on a quiet island in the Charles River, Mrs. Mallard leads a march of ducklings to live in a pond at the Public Gardens. The line of ducks wends through Boston streets. In McCloskey's realistic pictures, many of them drawn from a duck's perspective, giant cars threaten the brood. A towering policeman stops traffic so the Mallard family can enter a gate of the garden where they take up residence, fed by tourists' peanuts.

Children as young as 2 or 3 can follow the story with the help of the pictures. But the research, techniques, and training that made it possible for McCloskey to tell the story in words and picture were sophisticated. The book may have started with a childlike imagination—McCloskey got the idea for *Ducklings* by watching real ducks in Boston and by dreaming like a child about what might happen to them. But he used painstaking study, and skills acquired from years as an art student, to create a classic children's book.

A glance at a children's classic like McCloskey's may not reveal the serious work and skill between its covers. People who produce these books are accustomed to misunderstanding. One artist, Roger Duvoisin, says he is sometimes introduced at parties as "Roger Duvoisin, author of *Petunia, the Silly Goose.*" The introduction is sure to bring a wink and a smile, he says (in Haviland, 1973, p. 179).

But Duvoisin and McCloskey, and many others who write and illustrate children's books, served long apprenticeships creating art for adults before they turned to children's literature. Their subjects

(Chapter-opening illustration reprinted with permission of Macmillan Publishing Co., Inc. from *Rosie's Walk* by Pat Hutchins. Copyright © 1968 by Patricia Hutchins.)

today may be silly ducks, geese, hippos, or bugs—wink!—but the artists often approach their subjects with the seriousness of a master painter climbing toward a chapel ceiling.

A later section in this chapter will offer suggestions on how to select picture books to match children's needs and tastes. Selection is easier, however, after you have become aware of the dimensions in picture books. For instance, you cannot define them as "first" books, as the next section will show. Many are too advanced for young readers. Later sections will illustrate how the making of picture books calls on the most advanced skills of modern artists. And the results of their labor appear in every type or category *(genre)* of children's literature.

In other words, these are not just nursery books. Give them a second look, because picture books can give you a view of the whole field of children's literature.

MORE THAN A PRETTY PHASE: THE VARIETY OF MODERN PICTURE BOOKS

Children usually see books with pictures long before they can read words. Even before they can talk well, they weigh the books on their laps. They open them at random and point at colors, bending fingers as they press down on the page. Often, adults guide the exploration. Parents bounce children on their knees to the cantering rhythms of nursery rhymes, for instance. (The next chapter deals with these and other specialized kinds of picture books.) Often, adults are not needed. Selma Lanes, a writer and editor, says some books are so extravagantly illustrated that children do not even notice the words.

> More than once I have brought new picture books of old favorites of mine home fom the library only to have my five-year-old son tell me when I finally sat down to read one: " . . . I already looked at that myself. I don't want to listen to it." (Lanes, 1971, p. 56)

But children's interest in pictures is not a passing phase; it does not wane after they are taught to read words. The surprising fact is that as children learn to read they usually learn to find more in pictures as well. Some books rich in pictures, in fact, are too advanced for 5-year-olds or first-graders. And teachers and librarians cannot always gauge their difficulty by counting the number of words.

Wordless picture books, (sometimes called *textless picture books* or *books without words*), are often cataloged erroneously at the bottom of a bookcase marked for youngest children. The books tell a

49

McCloskey made hundreds of
sketches of ducks as he planned
Make Way for Ducklings. (From
Make Way for Ducklings by
Robert McCloskey. Copyright ©
1941, 1969 by Robert
McCloskey. Reprinted by
permission of The Viking Press.)

story without words, and many, like Brinton Turkle's *Deep in the Forest* (1976), *are* simple enough for preschool children. The action in Turkle's book begins on the title page as a bear cub wanders away from its mother and two other cubs. The lone cub arrives at a small log cabin, finds a table with three chairs, three bowls, and three

Frog's eventful trip to a restaurant is told through illustrations alone. (Excerpted from the book *Frog Goes to Dinner* by Mercer Mayer. Copyright © 1974 by Mercer Mayer. Used by permission of The Dial Press.)

beds. The sizes of the chairs, bowls, and beds seem to fit another story: large, medium, and just right. A golden-haired girl returns with her family to find the cub in her bed and her things in shambles. The cub flees for home to rub noses with its mother. Even 4- or 5-year-olds find the plot as good as Goldilocks.

There is universal appeal as well in artist Diane de Groat's wordless *Alligator's Toothache* (1977). A timid alligator with a toothache refuses to open his mouth for a dentist. The alligator's friends trick him by delivering the dentist on a silver platter with a cover. His jaws unlock and the dentist whisks·away the bad tooth.

Another artist, Mercer Mayer, has produced several wordless books popular with 6-, 7-, and 8-year-olds. Pictures in *A Boy, A Dog and A Frog* (1967) follow a boy and his dog on the trail of a frog. The frog escapes and then, lonely, tracks the boy all the way home to his bathtub. The action is easy to understand.

Not all wordless books are as simple. Martha Alexander's book, *Bobo's Dream* (1970), for instance, is complicated by a kind of subplot; it is more appropriate for children 7 to 9. Bobo is a pet dachshund who gnaws a bone while his young master reads a picture book. Falling orange leaves and the boy's football helmet set the season. A shaggy mongrel steals the bone. Bobo's master recovers it and then reads on while Bobo takes a nap. In the dog's dream, presented in a series of balloons, some big children steal his master's football. Bobo, a giant of a dachshund in his dream, is called to the rescue. He glares at the bullies and their puny mongrel, and intimidates them into returning the ball. When Bobo wakes up, the dream has given him courage. He yaps at the mongrel to protect his bone, and walks proudly home.

Other wordless picture books are too complicated even for children in the early grades. *The Silver Pony* (1973) by Lynd Ward, for instance, is the story of a boy and his dream of a flying young horse. In eighty pictures, the boy takes fantastic trips on the pony's back, performing heroic deeds—he saves a lamb from a lion, for instance. Lynd marks the passage of time by increasing the number of stars in the sky with each new night. Finally the boy dreams that he and his pony are shot down by rockets. At the same time his family actually finds him deathly ill outside their farmhouse. He recovers and his parents present him with a real pony, wingless but silver. The book calls for sustained attention; first graders are likely to get lost, but intermediate-grade children can usually understand the pictures without a word of explanation.

Books of one sentence or so tell most of the story with pictures, using just a few words. Again, age designation can be misleading. A

Some wordless books, such as *The Silver Pony*, are too
complicated for children in the early grades. (From
The Silver Pony by Lynd Ward, illustrated by the
author. Copyright © 1973 by Lynd Ward. Reprinted by
permission of Houghton Mifflin Company.)

book like *Rosie's Walk* (1968), by Pat Hutchins, for instance, might
appeal in different ways to children from preschool to fourth or fifth
grade. Here is the text in its entirety.

> Rosie the hen went for a walk across the yard around the pond over the
> haystack past the mill through the fence under the beehives and got back
> in time for dinner.

The words, printed up to half an inch high, do not reveal the main plot: a fox stalks Rosie every step of her barnyard tour. The red-masked fox leaps at her, missing repeatedly, and finally races away pursued by a yellow horde of bees. Young children do not need the words to follow Rosie's incautious walk. Bright oranges and yellows enliven pages decorated with wildflowers and graceful bugs as the fox suffers one mishap after another. Older children can read the laconic text a few words at a time.

Jose Aruego needs few words to tell a funny story about two water buffalo. "Look what I can do!" says one, dancing a jig. "I can do it too!" says the other, and soon both buffalo gambol like overweight ballet dancers through a jungle. In *Look What I Can Do* (1971), the exuberant animals get carried away;—they fall off a cliff, nearly drown in a river, and drag themselves up on a beach. Another buffalo finds them and begins dancing. "Look what I can do!" the stranger boasts. The first two buffalo sit on him.

Aruego introduces the cartoon-style carabao (water buffalo) in the first few pages against a white backdrop, then follows them into a jungle of orange and yellow flowers and wide-eyed animals scurrying to keep out of their way. A 5-year-old can tell what is happening with little coaching. But there is enough action—will the buffaloes survive the fall off the cliff into rocky rapids?—to keep children in the first few grades interested.

Words and pictures weigh equally in other books, such as *Make Way for Ducklings*. Although all the books mentioned so far in this sampling tell stories, the term *picture storybook* is often reserved specifically for narratives told by a roughly equal partnership of artwork and words. Picture storybooks are usually only thirty-two or forty-eight pages long, but still attempt to introduce at least one character well, and sometimes to show how the character changes in the course of the story.

Ludwig Bemelmans's *Madeline*, published in 1939, tells a wisp of a story about a little girl who dares to be different from eleven other little girls living with a nun, Miss Clavel, in Paris. The other girls under Miss Clavel's wing stay together in a conforming clump, but Madeline strikes out on her own, unafraid of mice or tigers at the zoo, and proud of her distinctive scar after an emergency appendectomy. The bigger girls look up to her;—they want an operation too. In colorful paintings and bouncing verse, artist Bemelmans vividly characterized Madeline, Paris, and Miss Clavel, who leans forward so much as she rushes about that she often looks as though she is about to fall down.

Writer and artist Marie Hall Ets tells a more substantial tale in a picture storybook about a Mexican-American family, *Bad Boy,*

Madeline's antics make her stand out from Miss
Clavel's other charges and endear her to young
readers. (From *Madeline's Rescue* by Ludwig
Bemelmans. Copyright © 1951, 1953 by Lugwig
Bemelmans. Reprinted by permission of The Viking
Press.)

Good Boy (1967). Roberto, who appears in drawings to be about 5
years old, is the middle child in a family with five children. He takes
the brunt of a family argument when his father orders his mother
out of the house; days after the quarrel, she refuses to come home.
The two youngest children are taken to Mexico to live with a relative, and the two older children are already in school. But Roberto is
forced to go to a day-care center where at first he cannot understand
the English spoken by his teacher. Eventually he learns enough English to write a letter asking his mother to return to the family.
When she does, young Roberto wins new respect from his father.

ISSUE

CAN PICTURES BE LITERARY?

Picture books also appeal to little children through the eye. But it is not, as with the adult, the appeal of aesthetic pleasure in the artist's line, color harmony, composition and style. A little child's approach to pictures is first of all a literary one. He expects them to tell him the story he cannot read for himself. Pictures are his first introduction to books and through them his interest is caught. (p. 116)

Smith, Lillian H. *The Unreluctant Years*
(Chicago: American Library Association, 1953).

The picture book today has become a showcase for the artist. He has taken over the picture book to such an extent that in many cases it no longer offers the child even the hint of a *potential* literary experience. . . . To the degree that it dilutes the opportunities for a child to respond to a word story, the modern picture book becomes a nonliterary commodity. It can limit a child's interest in real books and even impart a neutral or negative attitude toward words. (p. 28)

Groff, Patrick. "The Picture Book Paradox,"
PTA Magazine, March 1973, pp. 26-29.

What does Smith mean by "literary"? How does Groff use the term? If the two agreed on the meaning of "literary," would they still have a difference of opinion? Why or why not?

What influence do you think picture books have on a child's later reading? On what do you base your opinion?

Most picture storybooks are meant to be read aloud to children from preschool to grades two or three; the average third-grader can handle their vocabulary.

Sometimes, however, understanding the vocabulary does not ensure understanding of what is being read. For instance, *Through the Window* (1970), by artist Charles Keeping, is the story in words and pictures of a young boy named Jacob and what he sees outside from his vantage at home. Jacob spots familiar people on the streets of London, but suddenly the scene through the lacy border of the window becomes grim. Runaway horses dash by. Then an old lady appears, carrying the limp body of her dog, which has been trampled. Younger readers often miss the connection between the horses and the dog. They cannot easily understand why the curtains border every page. They fail to connect the death of the lady's pet with the frequent appearance of reflections from a cross on a church across the way. The illustrations are too sophisticated for most children below the fourth or fifth grade.

Pictures carry every one of these books. The text makes no mention of the villain in *Rosie's Walk*. The talking Mallard family in *Make Way for Ducklings* does not know the name of the "horrid thing" that nearly runs over Mr. Mallard on the streets of Boston; it takes a picture to tell the reader it is a two-wheeler bike. The dependence on pictures separates these books from *illustrated books*. In illustrated books the text alone is sufficient to tell the story, and these books are generally aimed at children with advanced reading skills.

But is should be clear by now that no one ought to put picture books somewhere near the floor of the library, for nonreading toddlers and preschoolers only. Many picture books are sophisticated enough to capture adults' interest at the same time they speak to the child.

One mother began interpreting every page of a wordless picture book to her 6-year-old daughter. "Shh," the little girl said. "Read it like grownups read." So mother and daughter turned the pages quietly, smiling as if they were enjoying the same funny novel.

THE MAKING OF MODERN PICTURE BOOKS
Some Background

The sophistication evident in today's children's literature came slowly to picture books. For centuries after the invention of the printing press in the mid-1400s, most book illustrators had to cut their designs into wood. They would gouge the surface of a flat board, leaving raised areas where they wanted lines or blocks of print. The projection of wood surface above the hollows is called a *relief*. Then artists would apply ink to the wood and press the wet, carved block against paper. Pictures showed white space above the indentations in the block, and black lines where the inky relief met the paper. There are sharp contrasts in these early woodcuts, as if scenes were lit by a harsh spotlight which burned away color.

Printing from flat metal plates offered an alternative to woodcuts as early as the late fifteenth century. Artists etched pictures into copper, brass, or zinc, covered the plate with ink, and wiped the surface clean. Enough ink remained in the hollows cut into the metal to flow onto paper placed under pressure against the plate. The method, the opposite of relief printing, is called *intaglio* printing. (*Intaglio* comes from latin words meaning "to cut in.")

Until the beginning of the last century, children's books printed by either method were black-and-white, unless artists or readers added hues by hand to the printed page. The content of pictures was somewhat gray as well, offering static, idealized people frozen in statuelike poses. Printers had experimented for several hundred years with techniques of adding colors—using two woodcuts inked separately and then fitted together, for instance. But results were often blotchy.

Then in the 1800s new techniques of printing took hold. One major advance was *lithography*, a method that was neither relief nor intaglio. Artists drew designs with greasy ink on the surface of a smooth, flat stone. Then they brushed the whole surface of the stone with ordinary ink and washed it with water. The rinsing carried away the ink except where it was held in the water-repellent grease. They pressed paper against the stone, and inky areas transfered the drawing. Other advances permitted more use of color.

Content became more colorful, too, as several artists in the 1800s began turning out imaginative books, some of which are still in circulation today.

George Cruikshank (1792-1878) was one of these pioneering artists. Son of a political cartoonist, George himself began roasting politicians—Tories, Whigs, and Radicals alike—when he was still a teenager. He illustrated his first book in 1820 with spirited and funny drawings in a version of fairy tales collected by two German brothers, Jakob and Wilhelm Grimm. Cruikshank favored wild costumes for his characters, and sometimes drew enlarged heads, a style developed by seventeenth-century artists and still used by cartoonists.

Walter Crane (1845-1915), son of a portrait painter, learned his trade as apprentice to a wood engraver, and studied Italian master painters and Japanese color prints. In the mid-1860s, he turned to children's books. Working with a famous printer named Edmund Evans, he published a series of nursery rhyme books including *Baby's Opera*. It presented words and music to popular children's verse, as well as dignified but upbeat drawings. His illustration for "King Cole" shows fiddlers three in formal pose and uniform. But each member of the trio—one with long curly hair, one with short straight hair, and one bald—is curiously individual, scratching out the music in his own way as a parrot perched on the king's throne conducts.

Two other illustrators, both born in 1846, set standards followed by children's book artists ever since.

Kate Greenaway (1846-1901) was shy of public recognition, but her pink-cheeked children with placid faces were so well dressed they influenced styles in children's clothes wherever her books appeared.

As a child, *Randolph Caldecott* (1846-1886) liked to cut wood into the shapes of animals. But his father, an accountant, apparently thought art was not a proper field for his son, and young Caldecott became a banker. One of his banks was located in the farmlands of Shropshire. Here in the country, he lived with a farmer who helped introduce Caldecott to prancing pigs and horses, cows and dogs, which later romped through his book illustrations. He switched from banking to books in the 1870's, moving to London but continuing his studies of animals, sometimes dissecting them to study their structure. In his art, his subjects were usually mobile and lively—though Caledcott himself in later years suffered rheumatic fever and had trouble climbing two flights of stairs.

One of his illustrations for *The Diverting History of John Gilpin: Showing How He Went Farther Than He Intended, and Came Home Safe Again,* by William Cowper, shows Gilpin clinging to a runaway horse as it gallops through a village, disrupting geese and astounding staid country folk. In 1938, the American Library Association began giving an annual award named after Caldecott for the most distinguished illustrations in an American picture book. The design of the medal struck for the award is adapted from the picture of grim Mr. Gilpin on his wild horse ride. (There is more on Caldecott and Greenaway in the Mother Goose section of the next chapter. And Chapter 10 presents a broader picture of changes in children's literature over the past few centuries.)

Like many twentieth-century artists, including Robert McCloskey and Roger Duvoisin, Caldecott did not begin his career as a children's book illustrator. His first major job, in 1875 was illustrating a book for adults—Washington Irving's *Sketch-Book*. Like all other trend-setting artists in the nineteenth century, and the best of those who followed them, Caldecott was a mature craftsman, careful of detail even when he was most whimsical.

The Labor behind Modern Picture Book Literature

How much detail can there be in a simple children's book? Look at *Spectacles* (1968), a little (7 inches wide, 6 inches high) picture book of about forty pages illustrated with bright colors by Ellen Raskin, a New York writer and artist. The premise: A little girl named Iris

The design of the Caldecott Award medal was adapted from this illustration by Randolph Caldecott. (Illustration from *R. Caldecott's Picture Book #1* by Randolph Caldecott. Used by permission of the publishers, Frederick Warne & Co., Inc.)

Fogel has gone too long without glasses, and one day a fire-breathing dragon knocks at her door. The dragon turns out to be Great-aunt Fanny standing against a background of trees and a distant house that suggests a dragon's form. Iris's friend Chester, seen without spectacles, looks just like a "giant pygmy nuthatch on our front lawn". . . . A "chestnut mare in the parlor" is a babysitter standing next to a couch. Finally, a blue elephant—an eye doctor to those who can see him—prescribes glasses.

The appearance of the book is deceiving. The blocks of color appear to have been brushed evenly within black outlines, the kind of coloring children do more or less accurately in the first grade. In reality, adding color to *Spectacles* was back-straining work for Raskin.

Black-and-white books are much easier to produce. They need pass through the presses only once, to pick up black ink on white paper. If a publisher wants to add red decorations, it becomes slightly more complicated. The book will have to go through twice, once to receive the black ink and once to pick up the impressions from a new set of plates coated with red ink. Putting yellow and blue into the picture means two additional trips for the book through the presses.

Spectacles has four colors, counting black, and that means four trips and four sets of plates.

How are these plates made? One method, developed over the last century or so, involves photographing a color picture several times through different filters, each allowing certain colors to pass through and blocking others. The printer can then make up plates from the photographs, each plate for a different color. That is one method of *color separation*, but the process is expensive and tricky. (The process was used on color pages in this book.) Ellen Raskin chose a different—and, for the artist, more difficult—method of making her book.

The first step in making *Spectacles* was getting the idea for the story. "That was easy," Raskin writes. "I'm terribly nearsighted." Her publisher was interested.

Next she made a model of her book, called a *dummy* or a *comprehensive layout* (*comp*, for short), including pictures and text. She revised it many times, finally sending words for the story to a typesetter who sent back a printed text to be pasted down on the final version.

Then she turned to the pictures, and the harder work. For the illustration of Great-aunt Fanny, for instance, she began by making a final drawing of the black lines and areas. Then she taped a sheet of transparent acetate—like heavy cellophane—over the drawing. Next she laid down a sheet of darker transparent paper with an adhesive backing; it clung to the acetate.

Slowly and carefully she cut the darker paper with a razor blade to fit exactly over each area where yellow, or green, would appear. This included the smoke coming out of the chimney in the background, Aunt Fanny's face and ankles, and a couple of trees. The sheet of acetate was sent to the printer to make a place for the shade of yellow she chose. By the same method she prepared other sheets of acetate for the blue and red patches in the pictures. (The blue would cover the same areas of the trees as the yellow, to make green boughs.)

This page, a comparatively simple one to make, required her to prepare one illustration board and four separate sheets of acetate. After careful checking, the printer lined up the separate components so the colors would fit within the lines.

Raskin repeated the process for every color page in the book. To make one short story, she had to lean over the drawing board and create—by drawing and cutting—eighty-eight detailed pieces of art (Raskin, 1969).

For this picture of Great-aunt Fanny, which looks comparatively simple, artist Ellen Raskin prepared one illustration board and an acetate sheet for each of the four colors used in printing it. (Copyright © 1968 by Ellen Raskin. All rights reserved. From *Spectacles* by Ellen Raskin. Used by permission of Atheneum Publishers.)

That is one example of the kind of work that goes into a modern picture book. Of course there are many different materials for making a picture, coupled with a whole constellation of styles. It is easier to appreciate the labor, and evaluate what you see, if you understand *media*—the paints, brushes, and other tools, and the surfaces used—and *style*, the artist's use of color, line, and space.

Media

You will find a mouse or a rat in several of the pictures in the color section. But each of the rodents has been created with different artistic materials, or media. And each helps support the spirit of the particular story it illustrates.

63

Marcia Brown's *woodcuts*, for instance, match the magical, primitive tone of *Once a Mouse* (1961), a retelling of an ancient Indian tale. The mouse is little more than a blot with whiskers. But the crow chasing it is powerful, thrusting its wings to the sky, stretching its spidery talons and threatening with a gaping mouth as sharp as crossed cutlasses. Even the ground seems ready to gobble the mouse. The grain of the wood adds ridges to the earth, giving it a hard and hostile texture. Using magic to turn the little animal into a cat, a wise man saves the mouse from the dangers of a world cut sharply into wood.

The rat in Brian Wildsmith's version of another traditional tale, *The Lion and the Rat* (1963), also lives in a challenging jungle. But here the mystery and power of a lush animal kingdom is supported by *opaque paint*—paint heavy enough to prohibit light from passing through it. Wildsmith's rat seems to have an inner light of his own shining out through a turquoise face and orange-brown body the color of fire. Unlike the hapless little animal in *Once a Mouse*, this rat has powerful resources: when a trap snares a lion in the jungle, only the rat—of all the animals—can free it by gnawing through strands of the giant net.

There are several kinds of opaque paint. *Acrylics* are quick-drying paints made from plastics; they appear vivid and shining on the page. *Tempera*, made by mixing coloring powder into a sticky substance such as egg yolk and thinning with water, gives a comparatively flat look. (Artist Maurice Sendak uses tempera for his paintings in *Where the Wild Things Are* (1963); see example in the color section.) *Oils*, made with coloring powder and linseed oil, can be used to give a bright, bumpy effect that calls out to be touched.

Watercolor paint, unlike opaque media, usually allows light to pass through. Sometimes watercolor is called *wash*. These paints, specially treated powders thinned with water, often convey delicacy and softness. For instance, gentle watercolors invite readers into the domestic scene in Beatrix Potter's *The Tale of Two Bad Mice*. Watercolors capture the faded pastels of some flowered wallpaper in a dollhouse invaded by two adventurous mice. And the medium adds fluffiness to the animals' fur.

But watercolors can be used quite differently, as you can see by comparing the watercolor paintings in the color section. The man-and-wife artist team of Leo and Diane Dillon, for instance, use broad-brush watercolors combined with *pastels* in *Why Mosquitoes Buzz in People's Ears* (Aardema, 1975), a modern version of an African folktale. (Pastel is a dried paste made of ground chalk and other materials.) The colors here look like bold makeup painted stroke by stroke on a mask.

In contrast, the soft, green clouds of pollution hanging over a city in Sheila Heins's watercolors for *The Last Free Bird* (Stone, 1967) intermingle above the boxlike buildings. There is no border to the murky clouds, no clear limit to the danger lurking in the sky. Heins's mysterious paintings forbode extinction for a declining race of birds.

Turning to another mouse in another medium, look at Feodor Rojankovsky's Miss Mousey in *Frog Went A-Courtin'* (Langstaff, 1955). Rojankovsky's color comes from *crayons.* The medium gives a slightly grainy aura to the pictures, as if a child had helped make them. The crayon, supplemented with pen and ink, pleasantly matches a child's simple song, about a frog who marries a mouse.

Simpler still are the field mice in Leo Lionni's *Frederick*, a modern (1967) folktale about a mouse who gathers sun, colors, and words while his relatives collect food for the winter. Lionni's pictures are *collages*, made by cutting or tearing pieces of paper and gluing them on a background. The technique reduces mice to a few simple components; ears and bodies, tails and limbs, and bright eyes. Used with great skill, the technique allows Lionni to reveal differences in character between the mice. Frederick is the one with half-lidded or fully closed eyes in the first few pages of the story. Later, in the depth of winter, his eyes open wide as he stands on his hind legs and recalls the rays of sun he has stored in his memory. His eyes stay bright as he leads the other mice, with their eyes closed, to envision the colors of summer and harvest seasons.

The story is about fundamental needs—the mice need rich memories and poetry as much as they need nourishing food—and the collages provide a back-to-basics quality to the pictures. Readers can almost feel the rough edges of torn paper used to make the mice.

There are more media for color pictures than there are basic colors in the rainbow. There are also variations in black-and-white techniques used in modern children's books. Artist Arnold Lobel uses *crosshatching*, crisscross patterns of lines, to add shading to line drawings throughout *The Quarreling Book* (Zolotow, 1963). A bad day in the James household begins when a grumpy Mr. James marches off to work in the rain without kissing Mrs. James goodbye. She passes his grouchiness on to Jonathon James, who turns against Sally James, and the anger passes from person to person like an ugly rumor until a little dog helps make everyone happy again.

Crosshatching darkens Mr. James's face, makes the rain appear to come down in waves, and scatters dark shadows through the house of children trapped inside on a wet day. Later the rain turns to a few benign dotted lines; Mr. James's face clears as he looks up to see the last patch of crosshatched cloud move away from the sun.

65

Arnold Lobel used crosshatching to add shading to
this illustration. (Illustrations by Arnold Lobel from
The Quarreling Book by Charlotte Zolotow. Pictures
copyright © 1963 by Arnold Lobel. By permission of
Harper & Row, Publishers, Inc.)

Another variation in black-and-white technique is *scratchboard*.
Artist Barbara Cooney used the process frequently for her pictures in
Chanticleer and the Fox (1958), adapted from the fourteenth-
century *Canterbury Tales* told by English poet Geoffrey Chaucer.
Scratchboard in this book adds a silvery sheen to black surfaces,
making animal fur look thick, adding sparkle to the tops of trees in a
dark forest, and rich grain to a wooden table. Cooney got these
bright effects by covering portions of a white board with black ink,
and then scratching away at the blackness to reveal some of the
white beneath. She further brightened the book—about a proud
rooster stolen away by a fox—by adding bright reds, blues, greens,
and yellows over the basic black-and-white.

Black-and-white *photography* is the medium used by Tana Hoban
in *Look Again!* (1971). There are no words on these pages, but the
layout provides a tacit challenge to identify objects in the pictures.
A square hole on the first page offers a glimpse of something on the
following page. Cobwebs? Bugs with long antennae? It turns out to
be a close-up of a dandelion. The following page shows a child blow-

ing its seeds away. The next box reveals a few shaggy lines like fur-covered jail bars. It is the forehead of a zebra. The book calls for careful observation.

Photography, woodcuts, paints—opaque and watercolor—and pen and ink are among the most popular materials artists use to make picture books. Other media used less frequently today include chalk, pastel, and stone lithography. Artists explore new media all the time. A New York editor talking with a small group of cartoonists one day came up with what he thought was a put-down for one of the artists. "When are you going to stop drawing with half-melted Hershey bars?" he asked. No one laughed much. It sounded too much like an idea that ought to be tried.

Style

It becomes obvious from exploring the differences between the watercolors in the color section that different artists use the same medium in different ways. Differences in the use of blank space, line, solids, and color define *style*. Artistic style, the particular way an artist uses media, can be as an individual as a signature or a smile.

No one could confuse the worldly rabbit painted by Maurice Sendak in Charlotte Zolotow's *Mr. Rabbit and the Lovely Present* (1962) with the young *Peter Rabbit* by Beatrix Potter; it is easy to identify each artist by the rabbit.

Style has a second meaning. Each of the watercolors fits a general category of style depending on how realistic the picture is. Donald Carrick's paintings for *The Accident* (by Carol Carrick, 1976) reveal scenes almost as they would look through a camera's viewfinder. Christopher and his father look like real people as they face the death of Christopher's dog, Bodger: Carrick paints in a *realistic* or *representational* style. Sendak's rabbit, on the other hand, is painted in an *impressionistic* style, and a sense of the way light reflects and sparkles is imparted through hundreds of small brush strokes. Real rabbits do not look like points or strokes of light. Impressionism, developed in the 1870s in France, calls on the viewer to supply the reality suggested in the painting.

Farther still from the camera's eye is the *cartoon* style of *Little Toot* (Gramatky, 1939). The little tugboat on its first voyage on the open sea, where it rescues an ocean liner, has several exaggerated human features: wide eyes, red cheeks, and cavernous mouth. Like many cartoon characters, Toot is a thing come to life. Its hull appears as soft as a duck's body. It waves its masthead like the tail of a puppy.

Finally, some styles bear only distant similarities to reality. The

Dillons' paintings for *Why Mosquitoes Buzz* are reminiscent of African folk art. They draw a mosquito with more concern for evoking a traditional style than for recreating a bug. Heins's city in *The Last Free Bird* reduces all the millions of shapes and colors of a crowded skyline to a few rough lines, an example of *abstract* style.

Some artists work well in several of these stylistic categories, while others are best known in one style. Potter, for instance, painted realistic animals and settings based on the actual countryside of England's Lake District. The style is compatible with the homey, sensible stories she told.

No matter whether the pictures are realistic or abstract, in all the best picture books, the style—like the medium—is wedded to the story.

The Barn (1968), by John Schoenherr, is about a skunk on a hunting expedition when it becomes hunted itself. Schoenherr's animals do not act or talk like people. They behave just like animals trying to survive predators' attacks. What style is appropriate? Realism.

In an entirely different kind of story, Don Freeman tells a tale about a talking animal, a shaggy-haired lion invited to a party (*Dandelion*, 1964). Dandelion orders his mane curled, buys a checkered sports jacket and flowers, and appears at the home of Jennifer Giraffe, who fails to recognize him as any lion she knows. Realism would not work here. Realistic pictures of a lion getting its hair done would be entirely inappropriate to the fantasy theme. The cartoon style Freeman uses is natural. (There are several more benchmark pictures in the color insert showing how artists use media, style, and color to match different subjects.)

Every artist begins with a blank canvas as challenging as the sheer, snowy face of a mountain. Some of the tools used in meeting the challenge of the canvas have been in use a long time: the different media, the freedom to use different styles, and the high plateau of lively wit attained by a few artists in the last century, for example. Each artist adds particular talents to these tools, covering new ground. The results of their various approaches accompany every piece of literary territory explored in Part One of this book.

A BROAD VIEW OF LITERATURE THROUGH PICTURE BOOKS

The distinctions between different genres are usually fairly clear, although occasionally there are subtleties that make classification difficult at the borders of the categories.

Fiction is invented. Lions do not get their hair done, except in fiction; the James family in *The Quarreling Book* is imaginary. But if you look closely at these two books, you will see that there is a

ISSUE

HOW IMPORTANT IS "GOOD ART" IN PICTURE BOOKS?

A child can develop an appreciation of beauty through his handling of well-illustrated books. One need not settle for the lifeless illustrations that crowd the pages of many children's books, when quantities of beautiful and vital ones are available at libraries and book stores merely for the asking. It is not expecting too much that the books published for children of all ages should include drawings that are made by the greatest artists. It is never too early to give a young child books that are illustrated with the best and most substantial pictures so that his inborn tendencies to be imaginative and curious do not dwindle into dormancy or that his creative spirit become stunted by lack of nourishment. (p. 10)

> Cianciolo, Patricia. *Illustrations in Children's Books*
> (Dubuque, Iowa: Wm. C. Brown, 1970).

The function of the art in such a book [a picture story book] should be primarily to tell a story. The story is the thing. It only matters in a secondary sense how well drawn or how colorful the pictures are. Indeed, it does not matter that not one picture from the book is suitable for framing. Each picture should best function in concert with all other pictures in the book. Therein lies the art of a picture book: how well it tells the story, how well it interacts picture to picture, and how well it supports and extends the text. (p. 146)

> Lorraine, Walter. "The Art of the Picture Book,"
> *Wilson Library Bulletin*, October 1977, pp. 144–147.

What is the function of the art in picture books according to each of these writers? What picture books do you know which have illustrations which would meet the criteria of both writers? How important do you think it is that books for children "include drawings that are made by the greatest artists"?

border *within* the general category of fiction. Lions will *never* get their hair done, so far as we can guess now. That is *fantasy*, one whole realm of fiction. Fantasies contain elements that could not be, in actuality—sometimes an odd character, sometimes a curious occurrence. (Much of traditional literature, covered in Chapter 5, is fantasy; Chapter 6 introduces modern fantasy.)

But the James family? Their tiff may be exaggerated, but it is not unreal. Somewhere as you read this, rain is making someone grouchy. The story could happen. It is *realistic* fiction. But there is more. We are approaching another border. Their story could happen now. It is *contemporary realism* (Chapter 7). If their quarrel were about which side to sign up with in the American Revolution, it could not be happening now. Realistic fiction set in the past is called historical realism, or usually, *historical fiction* (Chapter 8).

Those are the major categories of fiction. Now, a warning: crossing the line into nonfiction does not carry you from the rarefied atmosphere of a dream world into the air of actuality. Writers and artists create fiction from real experience. The eye of the owl tracking the skunk in Schoenherr's story of survival, *The Barn*, is frightening partly because it recalls images of a real owl's eyes. The humor in *Dandelion* comes partly because the story is resonant of real people and places. A sign in Lou Kangaroo's barber shop where the lion gets his hair done, for instance, advertises: "Try Lou's Shampoo, The Best in Kalamazoozoo." The fantasy is just a small step from reality. Similarly *poetry,* usually located in the realm of fiction, appeals powerfully to real senses and emotions; many poems extract the core of what happened to the poet and convey it more clearly than any nonfiction account could.

Crossing the wispy line into nonfiction, we find two further sections. One is *biography*, life stories of real people. The other is *informational books*, presenting hard facts on subjects such as science or nature. (Biography and informational books are discussed in Chapter 9.) But there is plenty of room in nonfiction for invention. Look at some examples in picture books.

Nonfiction

David Macaulay's *Cathedral* (1973) is one of the best-known factually based books of the 1970s. In dozens of realistic pen-and-ink drawings, he shows how a French cathedral grows from the dreams of some thirteenth-century clergymen.

Macaulay's detailed drawings show the construction of a cathedral and provide perspective on the size and intricacy of the project. (From *Cathedral* by David Macauley, illustrated by the author. Copyright © 1973 by David Macauley. Reprinted by permission of Houghton Mifflin Company.)

Early pictures introduce the workmen in 1252, some just back from the crusades, clearing a forest to get wood, cutting chunks of stone from a quarry, and burning some of the thatched-roof houses to clear space for the cathedral site. Construction takes eighty-six years, and as it proceeds, the surrounding walled city of Chutreaux changes. The houses, for instance, convert from thatched to slate roofs. This kind of detail in pictures gives readers a treasure of facts about life in medieval France.

But there is some fiction behind the facts. The cathedral, as a preface points out, is imaginary. While the techniques correspond accurately to ancient construction methods, Macaulay invented some specifics. Fiction: in 1306 work stops, the text tells us, because the local clergy run temporarily out of funds. Fiction: master builder Robert of Cormont dies in 1329 after a fall from some high scaffolding.

Other fictional details appear in the pictures. One of the houses to the right of the growing cathedral, for instance, develops a hole in its slate roof around 1306. The hole is still there three decades later, in another picture dated 1338. Is there a story behind that old gap? We called up Macaulay, a teacher at the Rhode Island School of Design, to find out.

He laughed. "You'll have to make up your own story about the hole," he said. Macaulay explained that to save the work of redrawing the whole city for each new page, he photographed a drawing of the background, and then added only the new detail on the cathedral to make several pages. He used the same background photograph for three of the last pictures in the book, he said, and just forgot to fix the hole.

Macaulay said he had added fictional touches to make the hard facts about cathedral construction palatable. "It's the way I like to learn," he said.

Another book with pictures by the Dillons, *Ashanti to Zulu* (Musgrove, 1976), introduces customs among twenty-six different African peoples. Wagenia men, members of one of the tribes, fish from wooden catwalks erected over the dangerous rapids of the Congo River, the book tells readers. Handwoven bamboo traps, some of them 10 feet wide at the mouth, snare the catch. That is hard fact, researched by author Margaret Musgrove in Ghana, at the University of Massachusetts and at Yale University. The Dillons's pictures, done in pastels, watercolors, and acrylics, are based on their own research. But the book is enriched by their interpretation. Fishermen balance precariously on the catwalk over the frothy water. A baby sleeps in a sling on its mother's back. A flattened, white sun looks hot as molten steel. In the foreground, the most prominent feature in the picture is a long-beaked bird decorated with soft reds, greens, and yellows. While the Wagenia family looks out over the river, the bird looks straight at the reader as if posing for a portrait. Sociological fact comes alive in a dreamlike setting.

You can find nonfiction at every station between wordless picture books and illustrated books. Erich Fuchs' *Journey to the Moon* (1969), is a wordless story about the Apollo 11 moon shot. Helen Jordan tells *How a Seed Grows* (1960), integrating a simple text, accessible to second- or third-graders, and sketchlike pen-and-ink drawings enlivened with broad strokes of green, orange, and brown. *The Blacksmiths*, by Leonard Everett Fisher (1976), is an illustrated book—text predominates over the scratchboard pictures—about the forging and fitting of horseshoes. Each of these books presents facts with drama and flair. Even Jordan's book, about the relatively quiet growth of a seed, builds gentle suspense in text and drawings about what happens to a bean seed planted in an eggshell. At first, the seed just soaks up water, as a black-and-white cross section of the shell shows. Now it gets fat and pregnant: the same cross section is set against a bright green background. And now the hair roots push down into the egg, and a sprout breaks up toward the sun.

Stories about real people can be retold dramatically as well, without being unfaithful to historical fact. Aliki's *Diogenes, the Story of the Greek Philosopher* (1968), introduces a complex personality in a series of simple anecdotes highlighting his life. His father is accused of coining false money, and Diogenes is banished. In Athens, he learns from watching a starving mouse to give up comfort and accept a simple life. In broad daylight, he carries a lantern, looking for an honest man. . . .

Even young children, with no clear sense of historical time, can understand these episodes. The illustrations are reminiscent of art on ancient Greek vases.

The choice of facts, the artistry used in presenting them, the arrangement of facts to build interest as a book progresses—these elements can make nonfiction as lively as any fictional story.

Fiction: Fantasy

The main character in Roger Duvoisin's *Petunia* (1950) is a silly goose who seems vaguely familiar. Finding a red book in her meadow is all she needs to believe that she has become omniscient. The fact that she cannot read the book does not crimp her growing conceit: "Her neck stretched out several notches." Friends notice

Fisher made this scratchboard illustration by covering
white board with black ink, then scratching some of
the black away to reveal the white underneath. (From
The Blacksmiths, written and illustrated by Leonard
Everett Fisher. Copyright © 1976 by Leonard Everett
Fisher. Used by permission of the publisher.)

the change. They begin to believe she really is wise, and take their
problems to her. Straw, a horse, has a toothache. Without hesitation,
Petunia diagnoses the problem: *teeth*.

74

"Look at me. [Petunia tells the horse.] Do I have teeth? Of course not. So I have no toothache. I am going to stop that pain right now. I am going to pull ALL those teeth out."

The overweening goose goes too far when she tries to read the label on a strange box the other animals have found at the side of a road. "CANDIES," she tells them. "That's what it says on that box." The animals plunge into the firecrackers in the box, and the firecrackers blow up, exploding Petunia's pride at the same time.

Obviously none of this could really happen. Geese cannot talk or cart books around, except in fantasy. But the story appeals in part because Petunia displays real human weakness. Her neck stretched with pride—in one picture her head has disappeared at the top of the page—looks remarkably like the neck of the nasty little kid who knew all the answers in the third grade.

A large collection of classic picture books present animals with human foibles readily familiar to children. In many of these books of fantasy, cartoon-style drawings exaggerate the traits that make monkeys, elephants, and lions act like people.

Curious George (1941), by H. A. Rey, is a monkey with a face like a little boy. In this story and each of its sequels, George's curiosity leads him into slapstick mishaps. When he plays with a telephone, he accidentally calls the fire department; responding to his false alarm, the firemen find him and throw him in jail, where he escapes on some telephone wires, grabs the string attached to some balloons, floats off over the city, and,. . . .

Decades after George made his debut, children still want more of the indestructible monkey. Perhaps one reason is that again and again George gets into intriguing mishief without ever paying the cost—spankings, dressings down—that real children would pay. No matter what he does, the "man in the yellow hat," a cowboylike figure who originally found George in the jungle, takes him back.

A lion created by Roger Duvoisin and his wife, Louise Fatio, makes mischief too, again without the threat of real danger. The idea for *The Happy Lion* (1954) came to Louise Fatio in France one day when a lion escaped from a circus and wandered peacefully through a small French town. In the book, the door of the cage is left open, and the lion decides to leave the zoo to visit friends in town. The friends, however, are not as happy to see him as he had expected. They tend to faint or scream. Before firemen can capture him, the lion's friend François wishes him "Bonjour" and suggests they walk back to the zoo together. The lion decides that from now on he will let people visit him because when they come to the zoo, they are more polite and sensible.

Another jungle-animal-made-good is Babar, an elephant who appears in a series of books by Jean DeBrunhoff beginning with *The Story of Babar* in 1933. Babar is born in a great forest, and runs away when his mother is shot by a hunter. He arrives in a city where an old lady "who has always been fond of little elephants" gives him clothes and money, supporting him until his cousins arrive. On his return to the forest, he is crowned king. The death of Babar's mother is a stark scene: she collapses and seems to wither after the hunter shoots her. But the story is just far enough removed from reality— remember, it is an *elephant's* mother—that children can tolerate the killing.

Another perennial picture book elephant is the kind-hearted Horton, the creation of artist and writer Dr. Seuss, a pseudonym for Theodor Geisel. Geisel was doodling one day when a cartoon sketch of an elephant on transparent paper happened to fall on a sketch of a tree. "After a short while," Geisel told an interviewer, "it was obvious to me that Horton was sitting in the tree hatching an egg" (in Hopkins, 1969, p. 256). The result of this discovery was *Horton Hatches the Egg* (1940). Mayzie, a lazy bird, wants to flee her nest for a Florida vacation. So Horton agrees to be her sitter for a short time, and climbs cautiously up into her little tree. But Mayzie likes Palm Beach too much to be a proper mother and Horton is stuck on his perch, through rain, blizzards, and the ridicule of other animals, reciting a poem to himself:

> I meant what I said
> And I said what I meant . . .
> An elephant's faithful
> One hundred per cent!

What finally hatches is about 50 percent elephant: it has ears, tail, and trunk just like Horton, and wings like a bird.

The richness of detail of the cartoon drawings helps readers accept the fantasy. Do you have trouble believing that an elephant could climb a tree? What if he propped it up first? Horton does, placing forked sticks beneath the spindly branch he wants to climb. The climb itself is just a few short steps beyond the realistic preparations. Horton's bulky props prevent a strain on credibility.

In 1957, Dr. Seuss produced a benchmark book, *The Cat in the Hat,* with the same kind of cartoon characters and jingling verse that enliven *Horton*. But there is a major difference. Children as young as 6 can read this book, which is built on a basic vocabulary list of just 220 words, without help.

Cat in the Hat was one of the first of what are often called *easy-to-read* books, sometimes built on a specifically selected group of words familiar to beginning readers. It is a fantasy, told in doggerel, about how a zany cat invades a house inhabited by two bored children and their pet fish on a rainy day. Since *Cat* appeared, easy-to-read books have proliferated in fantasy, realistic fiction, and nonfiction.

The simplicity demanded for such books can constrict writers, although some books have won wide recognition as literature. In 1971, *Frog and Toad Are Friends* (1970), by artist and writer Arnold Lobel, was a Caldecott Honor Book. And several years later, Lobel's *Frog and Toad Together* (1972) became a Newbery Honor Book in the annual competition for the best writing in a children's book by an American author. In both books, three-color pictures, separated by Lobel himself, show a lush, swampy land as backdrop for the adventures of a kindly frog and toad. Lobel, incidentally, did not work from a standard word list on these fantasies. He wrote what he wanted to say, keeping characters per line and lines per page to a minimum, and trusting ear and intuition to make the books simple.

A similar nonformula system was used by a first-grade teacher named Else Holmelund Minarik when she began writing about a quiet young bear. Minarik's first book, published in 1957 at about the same time Dr. Seuss' cat made his slapstick debut, was called *Little Bear*. It comprised four gentle, easy-to-read stories. Artist Maurice Sendak provided pictures with the flavor of a human family album: Mother Bear wears long flowing brown, black, and gray dresses characteristic of the 1890s.

In one episode, the childlike bear puts on a space helmet made of an old box and two springs, and announces that he is going to fly to the moon. He climbs to the top of a hill, jumps off a little tree with his eyes closed, pretends he has landed on the moon, and wanders home. "Here is a house that looks just like my house," he says at his threshold (p. 44). And inside the lunar house, lunch and his mother's huge lap await him.

Minarik once told an interviewer that her stories had arisen out of a recurring dream. "I was being pursued by a big bear," she recalled. "I would run and run but always awoke before the bear caught up with me. One night I got tired of running. I stopped. The bear stopped. And we began talking with each other. Ever since we've

ISSUE

IN THE NIGHT KITCHEN: "HEAVY, SELF-CONSCIOUS, POINTLESS," OR "A WORK OF ART"?

As in *Where the Wild Things Are*, the author-illustrator tells a simple story of a young child running the gamut of a psychological fantasy, until he returns to everyday reality. Disturbed by "a racket in the night," Mickey "fell through the dark, out of his clothes . . . into the Night Kitchen." Unresisting, he was mixed into the batter of a cake by three monstrous, yet comical cooks dressed in white and only came to himself when the cake was about to be put into the oven. From then on, Mickey decided that he was not a mere ingredient, and escaping in an airplane of dough, which he had hastily constructed, "he flew up . . . over the top of the Milky Way in the Night Kitchen" and diving into a gigantic white bottle full of milk, he was able to supply the bakers with the ingredient—the milk—which they needed. Joyful and triumphant, Mickey returned to his bed. . . .

Only adults will recognize the advertisements and hardware contemporary with the artist's childhood, although some children may recognize the genesis of the Night Kitchen from the commercial slogan "Baked while you sleep." And psychologists—and others—will discover where subconscious elements may appear to impinge on storytelling and picturization. It will not, however, be the first time in the history of mankind that a work of art will have had a disturbing effect. (pp. 44, 45)

Heins, Paul. Review in *The Horn Book*, February 1971, pp. 44-45.

It just may be that America's children have been waiting with bated breath for this opportunity to vicariously wallow nude in cake dough and skinny-dip in milk—not to mention the thrill of kneading, punching, pounding, and pulling. Somehow, I doubt it.

Perhaps, at the sub-conscious level, our children need liberation from the Puritan convention that, while children should be seen and not heard, only selected parts of the anatomy should be seen in public. If that is the case, then Mr. Sendak has struck a literary blow for the Kid Lib movement. It can never again be said that the penis has not been displayed in children's books—Mickey's dangles conspiciously throughout most of his adventures. (Sendak has already given his readers a ground-level view of the vagina in his illustrations for George MacDonald's *The Light Princess*.) As to Freudian sex symbols, there are so many that it is a romp to identify and discuss them.

As Little Orphan Annie was wont to say, "Gloryosky, Sandy!"

It seems that Mr. Sendak has used one of the most weary of all literary devices—that of a dream—to get into his story which proves in its execution, in both text and illustration, to be heavy, self-conscious, pointless, and —worst of all—dull. (pp. 262-263)

Root, Shelton L. Review in *Elementary English*, February 1971, pp. 262-263.

In the Night Kitchen created somewhat of an uproar when it was published. As can be seen from these two reviews, opinions varied. How would you describe and assess the illustrations? Read the entire book. Do you feel that there are subconscious elements which "impinge on storytelling and picturization"? What for you, if anything, would constitute too much or inappropriate symbolism in a book for young children?

been good friends" (in Hopkins, 1969, p. 188). The stories may have arisen from dreams, but the world of the bear—and the realms of animals in all good fantasy—seem familiar to children.

Talking animals populate many picture books. Some fantasies, however, have different kinds of curious elements. One story in Lore Segal's funny *Tell Me a Trudy* (1977) is about Martians hiding in the bathroom around bedtime. A little girl named Trudy thinks somebody bad lurks behind the bathroom door, or maybe the shower curtain or under a terrycloth robe. She writes to Superman for help. When he arrives, Trudy introduces him to the rest of the family: "This is Superman. He's come about the bathroom." Trudy's mother offers cookies. After dark, Superman checks out the bathroom and beats up four Martians behind the robe, turns down an invitation for supper, and flies out the window. His visit is every child's dream. "Was that really Superman?" Trudy's brother asks. "Well," Trudy answers, "the bad guys in the bathroom are all gone."

Poetry in Picture Book Form

Is poetry fantasy? What about this poem, *Spring Is* (1976), a book by Janina Domanska?

Spring is showery, flowery, bowery.
Summer is hoppy, poppy, floppy.
Autumn is wheezy, sneezy, freezy.
Winter is slippy, drippy, nippy.

In Domanska's illustrations, a dachshund gambols about, and rabbits climb hills using walking sticks and slide around on ice as if

79

skating: all fantasy. Yet the text carries a realistic sense of the seasons.

Another book of poetry in picture book format, George Mendoza's *And I Must Hurry for the Sea Is Coming In* (1969), is also tinged with dreamlike images. Lavish color photographs show a boy taking to the sea alone in a large sailboat, as the lines of poetry add a touch of mystery:

> the sea is coming in
> though wind and sea are set against me
> I will take my boat
> And I will go into the dawn wind. . . .

At the end of the book, the pictures tell the story. The boy appears lying on a sidewalk in a city. A hydrant spills water into the street, and he plucks his toy sailboat out of the water.

Poems in both these books could be read on their own. The pictures, however, carry the texts deeper into imaginary realms, challenging the reader to question what is dream and what is real.

Fiction: Realism

Realism, remember, is fiction that could be fact. Realistic stories are made of material from real life, past or present. That excludes talking bears, juggling cats, and elephants hatching eggs. It does not exclude exaggeration and caricature, fantasylike dreams, and mysterious emotions. Some of the best realism, in fact, explores feelings as powerful as giant talking mother bears in fantasy.

It could happen now A boy named Robert finds out one day that a "little friend" is coming to live with him each day while the friend's mother works. The intruder, in a book called *Stevie* by John Steptoe (1969), turns out to be a crybaby who wants everything he sees. He breaks toys and leaves footprints on Robert's bed. He keeps falling down and hurting himself. "I used to have a lot of fun before old stupid came to live with us," Robert says. Then Stevie moves out. The next morning, Robert forgets he is gone and pours two bowls of cornflakes. Then he remembers some of the good times: pretending there is a boogie man under the covers, finding dead rats in the park,

Robert sits thinking about Stevie in this book of realistic fiction. (Illustration from *Stevie* by John Steptoe. Copyright © 1969 by John L. Steptoe. By permission of Harper & Row, Publishers, Inc.)

and playing cowboys and Indians on the stoop. "Aw, no! I let my cornflakes get soggy thinkin' about him," Robert says.

Steptoe's paintings, using several media and completed when he was 18 years old, portray real city life distilled through imagination into glowing colors and rich black shadows.

It could have happened then   A young English boy named George finds himself marching to Concord with soldiers to put down some upstart colonists. In Nathaniel Benchley's easy-to-read *George the Drummer Boy* (1977), the lad in the service of the crown recognizes that the march is a bad idea. Don Bolognese's illustrations reveal detail of costume and setting around Boston during the revolution. The place and time may be unfamiliar, but children today easily recognize the fear on the boy's face as he walks to war.

Many picture books like these reveal emotions children are likely to recognize. *My Grandson Lew*, by Charlotte Zolotow (1974), is about a boy's sudden loneliness for his grandfather who has been dead for four years. Zolotow's writing is lean and poetic, accompanied by soft, realistic watercolors by artist William Pène du Bois. The boy, Lewis, calls up old sights and sounds as he talks with his mother in the middle of the night.

> Blue eyes
> said Lewis.
> I remember how his beard scratched
> but I remember his eyes more.
> He gave me eye-hugs
> nights like this
> when I woke up
> and called. (p. 8)

And remembering helps her remember, too. Lewis concludes:

> I miss him.

> So do I, Lew's mother said.
> But now
> we will remember him together
> and neither of us
> will be so lonely
> as we would be
> if we had to remember him
> alone. (p. 32)

Writer Judith Viorst captures the nightmare of a day gone wrong in *Alexander and the Terrible, Horrible, No Good, Very Bad Day*

a

b

Artists may conceive of the same story in different ways.
(a) From *London Bridge Is Falling Down!* illustrated by Peter Spier. Copyright © 1967 by Peter Spier. Reproduced by permission of Doubleday & Company, Inc. (b) From *London Bridge Is Falling Down: The Song and Game* illustrated by Ed Emberley, by permission of Little, Brown and Co. Copyright © 1976 by Edward R. Emberley.

"A pretty little dandyman," says she,
"Who swears he wants to marry me."

"Frederick, why don't you work?" they asked.
"I *do* work," said Frederick.
"I gather sun rays for the cold dark winter days."

e

f

The medium used by the artist gives character to the subject.
(a) Woodcut. From *Once a Mouse* by Marcia Brown, copyright ©
1961 Marcia Brown, used with the permission of Charles Scribner's
Sons. (b) Opaque paint. From *The Lion and the Rat* by Brian
Wildsmith, 1963, by permission of Oxford University Press.
(c) Crayon, soft pencil. From *Frog Went A-Courtin'*, copyright 1955
by John M. Langstaff and Feodor Rojankovsky. Reproduced by
permission of Harcourt Brace Jovanovich, Inc. (d) Watercolor.
Illustration from *The Tale of Two Bad Mice* used by permission of
the publishers, Frederick Warne & Company, Inc. (e) Collage. From
Frederick by Leo Lionni. Copyright © 1967 by Leo Lionni.
Reproduced by permission of Pantheon Books. (f) Pen and ink with
three-color overlays. Reprinted with permission of Macmillan
Publishing Co., Inc. from *The Surprise Party* by Pat Hutchins.
Copyright © 1969.

c

d

e

These artists have all used watercolor, but their styles vary greatly.

(a) Abstract. From the book *The Last Free Bird* by Stone and Heins. Copyright © 1967 by A. Harris Stone and Sheila Heins. Published by Prentice-Hall, Inc., Englewood Cliffs, New Jersey. (b) Stylized. Excerpted from the book *Why Mosquitoes Buzz in People's Ears* with text by Verna Aerdema. Illustrations by Leo and Diane Dillon. Illustrations copyright © 1975 by Leo and Diane Dillon. Used by permission of The Dial Press, Inc. (c) Cartoon. By permission of G. P. Putnam's Sons from *Little Toot* by Hardie Gramatky. Copyright © 1939 by Hardie Gramatky; renewed 1967 by Hardie Gramatky. (d) Impressionistic. Illustration from *Mr. Rabbit and the Lovely Present* with text by Charlotte Zolotow. Illustrations by Maurice Sendak. Illustrations copyright © 1970 by Maurice Sendak. Reprinted by permission of Harper & Row, Publishers, Inc. (e) Representational. From *The Accident* with text by Carol Carrick. Illustrations by Donald Carrick. Copyright © 1967. Used with permission of The Seabury Press, Inc.

The final effect rests on the artist's use of style, color, and medium, as well as skill and imagination.
Illustration from *Where the Wild Things Are* by Maurice Sendak. Copyright © 1963 by Maurice Sendak. Reprinted by permission of Harper & Row, Publishers, Inc.

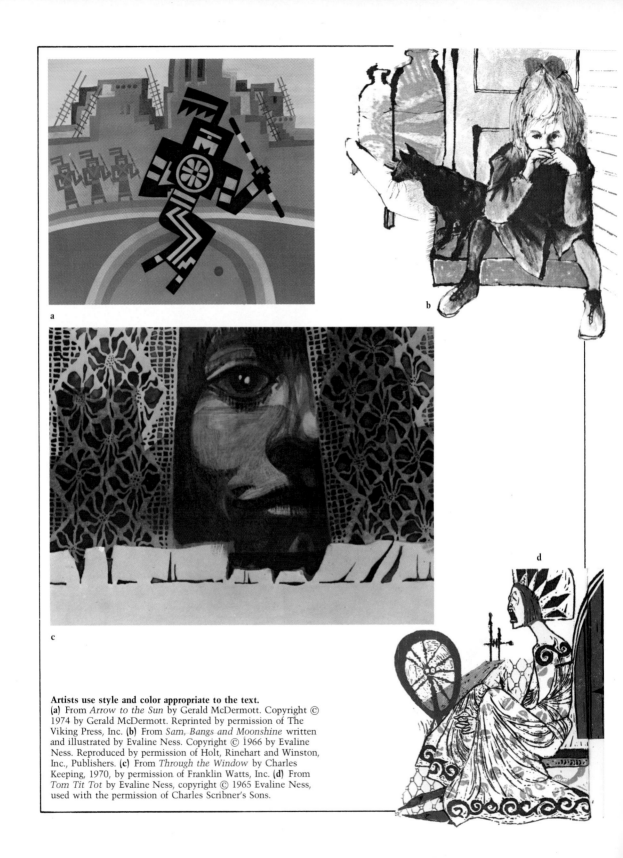

Artists use style and color appropriate to the text.
(a) From *Arrow to the Sun* by Gerald McDermott. Copyright ©
1974 by Gerald McDermott. Reprinted by permission of The
Viking Press, Inc. (b) From *Sam, Bangs and Moonshine* written
and illustrated by Evaline Ness. Copyright © 1966 by Evaline
Ness. Reproduced by permission of Holt, Rinehart and Winston,
Inc., Publishers. (c) From *Through the Window* by Charles
Keeping, 1970, by permission of Franklin Watts, Inc. (d) From
Tom Tit Tot by Evaline Ness, copyright © 1965 Evaline Ness,
used with the permission of Charles Scribner's Sons.

I went to sleep with gum in my mouth and now there's gum in my hair and when I got out of bed this morning I tripped on the skateboard and by mistake I dropped my sweater in the sink while the water was running and I could tell it was going to be a terrible, horrible, no good, very bad day.

The humor of Alexander's terrible, no good, very bad day is captured in Ray Cruz's illustrations. (Picture copyright © 1972 by Ray Cruz. From *Alexander and the Terrible, Horrible, No Good, Very Bad Day* by Judith Viorst. Used by permission of Atheneum Publishers.)

(1972). It begins in Alexander's bedroom, as unkempt as Alexander's hair in Ray Cruz's line drawings, just after the boy has woken up.

I went to sleep with gum in my mouth and now there's gum in my hair and when I got out of bed this morning I tripped on the skateboard and by mistake I dropped my sweater in the sink while the water was running and I could tell it was going to be a terrible, horrible, no good, very bad day.

He finds no car kit or code ring in his breakfast cereal box, and there is not enough room in the car on the way to school. At counting time, Alexander forgets sixteen, and at lunch time he discovers that his mother forgot to put dessert in his bag. Relief never comes, not even at bedtime, when the Mickey Mouse night-light burns out.

The book is comforting for a child—or adult—whose day has been merely terrible.

There is emotional support as well in British writer and artist Pat Hutchins's book *Titch* (1971) about a jot of a boy, the youngest in his family. Four-color, cartoonlike pictures with a minimum of props and background match the simple style of the story. Titch cannot ride his trike nearly fast enough to keep up with the two-wheelers ridden by his older brother and sister. His tiny pinwheel cannot compete with their kites, nor his wooden whistle with their drum and trumpet band. But Titch has something they do not have: a tiny seed. And, triumphantly, it grows into a plant bigger than them all.

Books such as *Titch* can help young readers to understand what seem to be foreign emotions. Other picture books of realistic fiction can help introduce readers to what may be strange settings or customs.

Ianthe Thomas's *Lordy Aunt Hattie* (1973), for instance, is about a little black girl named Jeppa Lee living with her aunt in the rural south. As Aunt Hattie puts it, "It's a day so hot that the cotton snakes done slithered down under the cotton-bulb shade." Huckleberry bushes bow under the weight of purple berries, and clouds of red dust trail a wagon on its way to market. Thomas di Grazia's pictures, using several media, radiate the warmth of a hazy sky hanging over snowy white cotton, bald patches of red earth, and deep green grass. The book may be eye-opening to children in the city.

Roger Duvoisin introduces another kind of country in his watercolors for *Hide and Seek Fog,* written by Alvin Tresselt and published in 1965. Fog mutes the colors of a seaside village, drives people from the beach in ghostly droves, and clings to the rigging of lobster boats trapped in the harbor. Tresselt's text is close to poetry.

But out of doors the fog
twisted about the cottages like slow-motion smoke.
It dulled the rusty scraping of the beach grass.
If muffled the chattery talk of the low tide waves.
And it hung, wet and dripping,
from the bathing suits and towels on the clothesline.

By comparison, illustrator Peter Parnall conveys the open, dry atmosphere of the desert in his pen-and-ink drawings for Byrd Baylor's *Hawk, I'm Your Brother* (1976). A young boy, Rudy Soto, wants to be able to soar over canyons like a hawk. He steals a redtail hawk from its nest before it can fly, hoping to capture enough magic from the bird to let him take off. At the end of a summer, Rudy

Peter Parnall uses clean line drawings and ample
blank areas to show the open space of Rudy Soto's
desert home. (Reprinted with the permission of
Charles Scribner's Sons from *Hawk, I'm Your Brother*
by Byrd Baylor, illustrated by Peter Parnall, copyright
© 1976 by Peter Parnall.)

realizes that the struggling bird is not content. *One* of them should
fly, he thinks. He frees the bird, then shares vicariously in its cir-
cling flight over the desert expanse.

Rudy is at home in the desert. Another adventurous character
from picture book realism is at home in the city. Peter is a black boy
who appears in several books by New York artist and writer Ezra
Jack Keats. In *The Snowy Day* (1962), Peter makes tracks and snow
angels in freshly fallen snow, then tries to keep a snowball in his
pocket when he goes inside. In *Whistle for Willie* (1964), he learns to
whistle, bringing his dog Willie to him on the run. And in *Goggles!*
(1969), Peter and his friend Archie outwit older boys who try to take
away some yellow motorcycle goggle frames Peter finds in an empty
lot. Keats, who grew up in Brooklyn, turns the lot full of junk into an
exciting playground: an old pipe big enough to be a tunnel for Willie
leads to a secret hideout made out of a door, a board with a hole in it,
and part of an old bed. Laundry flutters over TV antennas on the

85

rooftops of nearby apartments. In oils and collage, *Goggles!* gives a close-up view of city life.

Artist and writer Taro Yashima gives another perspective on the city in *Umbrella* (1958). A 3-year-old girl named Momo hopes for rain as she looks out her apartment window with a view of the skyline, presented here in muted colors. Momo wants to try her new red boots and umbrella. Eventually, the waters come and she descends to the noisy street where raindrops make a "ponpolo ponpolo" sound on her big black umbrella. The illustrations introduce a clean but crowded city, without the intriguing junk in *Goggles!*

Of course any city may be foreign land to rural readers, but Momo's face as she tries to walk like a "grown-up lady" (p. 18) under her umbrella looks familiar, like the face of 3-year-olds anywhere who have set out on adventure. Children in *Hide and Seek Fog* are the only people who enjoy the mist; they play hide-and-seek "in and out among the gray-wrapped rocks." Archie and Peter are the only people who find fun in the deserted city lot and its assorted refuse. These books help establish common ground between children with different backgrounds.

The fiction and the nonfiction in this section are a kind of preview of the field of children's literature. There is, of course, much more to be seen, many more books to choose from. Some picture books are flashier than these. Some have covers in three dimensions. Other gimmicky publications pop with gaudy colors at supermarket check-out counters, and explode up at readers with tricky paper constructions when opened at home.

On the other hand, there is also real literature to choose from. How *do* you choose? What kinds of pictures do children like? When does a picture book become literature?

SELECTING PICTURE BOOKS

Children do not choose picture books by genre, style, or media. They are not woodcut fans versus wash fans; they do not ask where the impressionist shelf is. They like stories.

Knowledge of how picture books are made can help teachers and librarians see more in a book; but technical knowledge can also trap adults into missing the story in concern over brushstrokes. Artist Marcia Brown warns:

> One wonders how much it helps to know if a picture was done in crayon or wash, woodcut or acrylic, if one does not see that the artist woefully missed the point and mood of the story . . . if hands that are meant to hold, can't; if images crowd the page and distort the focus and meaning of the story and suffocate its message. (in Kingman, 1968, p. 15)

Each stroke of a brush or choice of a word in a picture book is important, but just as important is how all the parts fit together to appeal to children. Look at one example.

Where the Wild Things Are, with words and pictures by Maurice Sendak (1963), is the story of a boy's fantasy the night he is sent to bed without supper. Max is mischievous. He cracks a wall by driving in a nail with a huge claw hammer, and he scares his terrier by brandishing a fork and chasing the dog downstairs. "Wild Thing!" his mother calls him. She sends him to his room. There, the fantasy begins. The bed, windows, and door begin to fade, and a forest takes root "until his ceiling hung with vines and the walls became the world all around." Max sails away on a little pink boat called MAX, and after a long voyage lands where the Wild Things live.

They are among the best monsters in fiction. Their yellow eyes bulge with menace as they gnash their spiky teeth. One has a head like a lion's, and scaly legs. Another looks like giant rooster, and another like a monstrous bull with human feet.

They are angry, but they are vulnerable. One wears a shirt with red and yellow stripes, like a child's. And one, with wavy red hair, has softer, maybe sympathetic, eyes. The Wild Things are easily conquered. "Be still!" Max commands, and then tames them by staring into their yellow eyes, "and they were frightened and called him the most wild thing of all." Max is king.

"Let the wild rumpus start!" the king commands. His mollified subjects become light-footed. In a dance often compared to a ballet, they swing from trees. They carry Max triumphant in a procession. Then they tire. And Max, lonely, smells good things to eat. He sails away from the Wild Things, back to his room where he finds his supper waiting for him, still hot.

The artistic technique in *Wild Things* is sophisticated. Yet Sendak himself once said the book "is an example of how I felt as a child. It is a child's level of seeing things" (in Hopkins, 1969, p. 252).

The combination of mature artistry and childlike imagination makes *Wild Things* good literature. It meets several standards, criteria you can apply to any picture book.

Text and Illustrations Must Work Together

Style, medium, and colors must match the text It would be difficult to illustrate a story about fog with sharp-edged woodcuts. Bright yellow and orange acrylics would be inappropriate in a story about a haunted house. The tempera used in *Wild Things* is rich but not overpowering, and the cross-hatching serves to subdue the colors as well as to provide shading and detail. Deep blues and greens establish the mood of a primeval forest, a perfect place for children to meet hulking monsters.

Illustrations must conform to the text Sendak the writer says that Max was wearing his wolf suit; Sendak the artist was compelled to draw the suit. It is an uncommon wolf suit, embellished with a bushy tail. Artists are free to add such decoration, but every added touch must be consistent with the written story, or children begin to turn off. "Incongruities of text and picture are unforgivable to the child," writes artist Bettina Ehrlich, "and considered to be as absurd as it would seem to an adult to read, 'His green hat was red'" (Ehrlich, 1952, pp. 305-306).

A picture should be near the text it illustrates When text tells us that Max's mother sends him to bed without supper, the picture on the page opposite shows the boy standing in his bedroom. Children find it confusing if words describe an action that appears in pictures earlier or later in the book. For instance, imprecise placement of text in one well-known Mother Goose book may lead some readers to confuse Solomon Grundy, a man in a nursery rhyme, with a pig. (See the discussion of Format in "Evaluating Mother Goose Books" in Chapter 3.)

Text and pictures should combine to build the story Early pages of *Wild Things* develop anticipation for later action. In the second picture of the book, a picture tacked on a wall shows the head of one of the Wild Things. The drawing is signed "by Max." The pictures and words build like a crescendo as Max goes to his room and begins to dream. At first, Sendak's pictures cover part of a page. Then they completely fill one page, and then spill onto the next page, until the borders of the book are barely able to contain all the frolicsome monsters. After the climactic "rumpus" scene—Sendak painted it to music—the paintings begin to get smaller and finally disappear. The last page holds just a line of text about Max's dinner: "and it was still hot."

Writing Should Approximate Poetry

"There is still among laymen a lack of comprehension of the discipline needed to pare a text to a basic line that looks simple," writes Marcia Brown. "A picture book is as concise as poetry. Text and pictures combine to form an essence that expands in the child's mind" (in Kingman, 1968, p. 24).

ISSUE

HOW MUCH DETAIL IS TOO MUCH?

Children under six or seven tend to see 'wholes', so figures in pictures need to be strong and clear in outline, otherwise they may appear just as a lot of unrelated detail. Nor must the value of the spoken work be forgotten in relation to children's looking. The tendency nowadays to attach importance to visual aids in education, showing young children pictures, diagrams, etc., needs to be considered in relation to the way in which they see and remember things. (p. 7)

Cass, Joan E. *Literature and the Young child*
(London: Longmans, 1967).

However, when it comes to illustrations in a book, the contents of the picture, its "readability," and a certain quality which I should like to call "intimacy" or "lovability" are more important. The picture should offer a lot to read; it should, above all, go into detail. A picture which offers few facts and which one has finished "reading" in a second is unsatisfying for the small child however great its artistic merits in design, composition and color may be.

It cannot be emphasized enough that the picture is not taken in as a whole any more than the type face of a page is taken in as a whole by the reading adult. The picture is *dissected* into its details, and the more meaning it conveys the better. (pp. 306–307)

Erlich, Bettina. "Story and Picture in Children's Books,"
The Horn Book, October, 1952, pp. 301–308.

Select two picture books whose content is appropriate for a young child. Select one with pictures which are "strong and clear in outline," and another with pictures which "offer a lot to read . . . go into detail." Read each of them to the same four- or five-year-old child. When you have finished, ask the child to tell you what was in several pictures in each of the books.

Which of the above statements does your experience with this one child seem to support? Compare your results with those of other students in your class.

Sendak's writing sometimes has the power of a primitive tribal chant. The Wild Things "roared their terrible roars and gnashed their terrible teeth and rolled their terrible eyes and showed their terrible claws." Time passes in a dream cadence that recalls the way children understand days, weeks, and years. Max sails "off through night and day and in and out of weeks and almost over a year to where the Wild Things are."

Words in some picture books can easily become engraved on children's memories, particularly when lines are light and rhythmical. A refrain from Wanda Gág's *Millions of Cats*, for instance, is hard to forget; it is part of a story of an old couple who wanted a cat and wound up with

> Cats here, cats there
> Cats and kittens everywhere,
> Hundreds of cats,
> Thousands of cats,
> Millions and billions and trillions of cats.

The lines were first published in 1928; their poetry has helped them survive.

This kind of apparently simple, childlike expression is not easy to write. A British author and illustrator, Edward Ardizzone, described the challenge:

> Writing the text for a picture book . . . has its particular difficulties, the main one being that the tale has to be told in so few words, yet must read aloud easily and sound well when read. Another difficulty is that at the turn of each page, and one rarely has more than one hundred-twenty words between the turns, the text must end with a natural break, a note of interrogation or suspense. With rare exceptions, the professional writer who is no artist finds this extremely difficult, if not impossible, to do. (1959, pp. 41–42)

Pictures Must Stand Alone as Art

Are children old enough for good art? Yes. Sendak's book, for one, is painted with the care of a master. The two-page procession of the Wild Things carrying Max depicts five huge, prancing monsters without a hint of overcrowding. Wild Things at the head and tail of the procession curve their clawed hands into the air, providing a graceful beginning and end to the parade. The menace remaining in the monster's eyes prevents the story from turning syrupy after Max's conquest; even though Max is king, there is still a chance he could be gobbled up.

Crosshatching helps establish the texture of the monsters' hides, but there are not so many lines that they distract readers from the whole picture. The art of *Wild Things* was good enough to win the Caldecott Award in 1964, and to set off rumpuslike dances in kindergartens all across the country.

Are children equally at home with *all* styles of art? One study published in 1976 suggests not. The study by British educator Gerald Smerdon summarized the reactions of 381 English students, from infants to teenagers, to a series of pictures. All twelve black-and-white drawings showed a castle, rendered by the same artist from the same perspective. But there were major differences among the castles. They covered a spectrum from realism to abstraction, from an almost photographic view at one extreme to a jumble of lines at the other. Smerdon flashed the pictures in pairs on a screen and asked children to choose which they liked. He was trying not only to uncover children's taste in artistic style, but also to see whether age or sex made any difference. His conclusion: Age and sex didn't matter, with minor exceptions. Children clearly preferred realism.

Results of the study may be useful to teachers or librarians trying to wean young children away from the literal images flickering on a TV screen to picture books. Children do seem to demand that pictures verify text. When Petunia, the silly goose created by Roger Duvoisin, miscounts chicks in her barnyard, children's fingers naturally poke at the page to check her count.

But there are some caveats about the conclusions. The research used black-and-white art only; color might have attracted many children to the abstract castle. Many more might have liked the nonrealistic style if the castle had been in the context of a story like Sheila Heins's abstract city in *Last Free Bird.*

And even if children do begin as literalists, teachers can broaden their appreciation by introducing other styles. They can start by presenting a realistic mouse like artist Brian Wildsmith's in *The Lion and the Rat,* and then present the more abstract mouse in Marcia Brown's woodcuts from *Once a Mouse.* In both books, the artwork by itself is powerful.

Judging Format

Good art requires the right settings, or frame; in books, the "frame" is the format.

The book's size, the appearance of its type, the design of its dust jacket and title page, the spacing of text and pictures—all these elements of format support or detract from the picture book. And

Don't stroke that dog, Shirley,
you don't know where he's been

the quality of binding and paper determine durability. In *Wild Things*, the dust jacket and front cover show a sleeping Wild Thing with Max's boat in the background; the picture propels the reader into the book. The binding is sewn so that in the middle of the rumpus, the book opens wide to show a two-page spread of rumpus-ing monsters.

Is the Book Appropriate?

Any children sentenced to a stretch in a lonely room can empathize with Max. They have dreamt valiant dreams, in shame, of showing the world, and they have plummeted from their bravado when they realized how hungry they could get without love and supper. So the story itself is appropriate. As Sendak says, it is a child's level of seeing things.

But appropriateness involves more than that.

Does the book avoid perpetuating stereotypes? One picture book from not so long ago, *A Visit to the Dentist* (1959) by Bernard Garn, concludes with a little girl's dream that someday she will be a dental assistant, mixing cement and getting instruments ready for the doctor. The message is clearly sexist.

By contrast, Harlow Rockwell's *My Doctor* (1973) tells a simple story about a boy's visit to a doctor, who happens to be a woman. The book helps to counteract the stereotype that all doctors are male, but it is not an anti-sexist tract. Readers are likely to be more interested in pieces of office equipment shown in the book—scales, stethoscope, tongue depressors, and needles—than in the gender of the person using them.

Is the story within the child's range of comprehension? Here is a beautiful passage from a picture book called *Wildfire:*

> Daylight revealed charred ruins of the valley sunk beneath a haze of sour smoke. A slow snow of ash drifted down among the high black

The design of this book helps tell the story. On the top is the "real" day at the beach; on the bottom, Shirley's imaginings as she gazes out at the ocean. (Illustrations from *Come Away from the Water, Shirley* by John Burningham. Copyright © 1977 by John Burningham. By permission of Thomas Y. Crowell Company, Inc. and Jonathan Cape, Ltd.)

tombstones that marked the death of firs and cedars. Ribbons of white smoke curled upward from the black and ugly earth. Huge cones still dangled from the skeleton of the lone sugar pine. The shadow of a vulture floated on the smoke beneath a dull red sun. (Valens, 1963)

The passage is good writing, but first graders are not likely to understand it; fourth or fifth graders, on the other hand, probably would. Remember that different picture books appeal to different ages.

Does the Art Avoid Condescension?

The best of the books in this chapter are the work of skilled artists who know their craft. Robert McCloskey may have crawled around at child height for a few weeks while studying mallards, but the ducks he drew in *Make Way for Ducklings* were sophisticated. Sendak may have lived at the child's level in dreaming of *Wild Things*, but he worked at the drawing board as an adult. Attempts to duplicate childish drawings, writes artist Bettina Ehrlich, are always doomed.

> The adult artist has neither the naïveté nor the imagination to produce the picture writing of the child, and to attempt it is as objectionable as it would be for an adult writer to express himself in baby language or to spell as a child does. (1952, p. 308)

Over the last century or so, picture books for children have come of age. And today you can judge them by stringent artistic standards. Today it is appropriate to ask of each book: Is the art mature enough for the child?

SUMMARY

1. Children often begin their acquaintance with literature by encountering stories told largely through pictures, but there are many picture books for older children as well. Even some *wordless picture books* are too complicated for children in early grades. *Books of one sentence* or so might appeal in different ways to children from preschool to fourth or fifth grades. The term *picture storybook* is often reserved for narratives told by a roughly equal partnership of artwork and words, while in *illustrated books* the text alone is sufficient to tell the story. There is, in other words, a wide variety in the way pictures are used in children's books, and often there is a high level of sophistication.

2. Several artists in the last century contributed to the variety of styles and the sophisticated use of media in today's picture books. *George Cruikshank, Walter Crane, Kate Greenaway,* and *Raldolph Caldecott* were among the most famous of the nineteenth-century artists whose books were produced with pioneering colorprinting processes.

3. Printing techniques have advanced far enough today that artists can render illustrations in many different ways. Some are adept at using *color separation,* a photographic process that allows each drawing in their books to be reproduced in the colors of the original. Ellen Raskin is one artist who has developed her own method of color separation, a complicated, exacting process which required 88 separate pieces of art for one short story.

4. The color section in this chapter illustrates the use of different media, including *woodcuts, opaque paint, watercolor* or *wash, crayon,* and *collage.* The media convey the artist's *style*—the way the individual craftsperson uses blank space, line, solids, and color. The insert also contains a spectrum of styles. *Realistic* or *representational* pictures show scenes almost as they would look through a camera's viewfinder. *Impressionistic* style gives a sense of the subject through hundreds of small brushstrokes that seem to catch the way light reflects and sparkles. *Cartoon* styles are further removed from a camera's-eye view than impressionistic styles, and *abstract* art bears only distant similarities to concrete reality. In the best picture books, media and style match the story.

5. The stories in picture books fall into every genre of literature, and examples in this chapter represent each category covered in Part One. *Fiction* is divided basically into two realms: *realism,* stories which could happen or could have happened, and *fantasy,* stories containing elements that could not exist in the real world. *Nonfiction* includes *biography* and *informational books,* although there is plenty of room in nonfiction for imagination and invention.

6. Certain general standards can be applied in selecting the best literature from a wide variety of books with pictures. These are among the most important criteria: Text and illustrations must work together; writing should approximate poetry; the pictures must stand alone as art; the format—or frame—of the book should provide a good setting for the artwork; the book should fall within the child's range of comprehension without condescension and without perpetuating stereotypes.

BIBLIOGRAPHY

Adult References

Ardizzone, Edward. "Creation of a Picture Book," *Top of the News*, December 1959, pp. 40–46.

Cass, Joan E. *Literature and the Young Child* (London: Longmans, 1967).

Cianciolo, Patricia. *Illustrations in Children's Books* (Dubuque, Iowa: Wm. C. Brown, 1970).

Ehrlich, Bettina. "Story and Picture in Children's Books," *The Horn Book*, October 1952, pp. 301–308.

Groff, Patrick. "The Picture Book Paradox," *PTA Magazine*, March 1973, pp. 26-29.

Haviland, Virginia. *Children and Literature, Views and Reviews* (Glenview, Ill.: Scott, Foresman, 1973).

Heins, Paul. Review of *In the Night Kitchen, The Horn Book*, February 1971, pp. 44–45.

Hopkins, Lee Bennett. *Books Are by People* (New York: Citation Press, 1969).

Kingman, Lee, Joanna Forster, and Ruth Giles Lontoft. *Illustrators of Children's Books: 1957-1966* (Boston: The Horn Book, 1968).

Lanes, Selma. *Down the Rabbit Hole* (New York: Atheneum, 1971).

Lorraine, Walter. "The Art of the Picture Book," *Wilson Library Bulletin*, October 1977, pp. 144–147.

Raskin, Ellen. *Author-Illustrator, Color-Separator* (publisher's brochure) (New York: Atheneum, 1969).

Root, Shelton L. Review of *In the Night Kitchen, Elementary Education*, February 1971, pp. 262–263.

Smerdon, Gerald. "Children's Preferences in Illustration" *Children's Literature in Education*, vol. 20, Spring 1976, pp. 17–31.

Smith, Lillian H. *The Unreluctant Years* (Chicago: American Library Association, 1953).

Children's Book References

Aardema, Verna. *Why Mosquitoes Buzz in People's Ears*, illus. Leo and Diane Dillon (New York: Dial, 1975).

Alexander, Martha. *Bobo's Dream* (New York: Dial, 1970).

Aliki. *Diogenes, the Story of the Greek Philosopher* (Englewood Cliffs, N. J.: Prentice Hall, 1968).

Aruego, Jose. *Look What I Can Do.* (New York: Scribner's, 1971).

Baylor, Byrd. *Hawk, I'm Your Brother,* illus. Peter Parnall (New York: Scribner's 1976).

Bemelmans, Ludwig. *Madeline* (New York: Viking, 1951). (1939)

Benchley, Nathaniel. *George the Drummer Boy,* illus. Don Bolognese (New York: Harper, 1977).

Brown, Marcia. *Once a Mouse* (New York: Scribner's, 1961).

Carrick, Carol. *The Accident,* illus. Donald Carrick (New York: Seabury, 1976).

Cooney, Barbara. *Chanticleer and the Fox* (New York: Crowell, 1958).

Cowper, William. *The Diverting History of John Gilpin,* illus. Randolph Caldecott (London: Warne).

DeBrunhoff, Jean. *The Story of Babar* (New York: Random House, 1960). (1933)

De Groat, Diane. *Alligator's Toothache* (New York: Crown, 1977).

Domanska, Janina. *Spring Is* (New York: Greenwillow Books, 1976).

Duvoisin, Roger. *Petunia* (New York: Knopf, 1950).

Ets, Marie Hall. *Bad Boy; Good Boy* (New York: Crowell, 1967).

Fatio, Louise. *The Happy Lion,* illus. Roger Duvoisin (New York: McGraw- Hill, 1954).

Fisher, Leonard Everett. *The Blacksmiths* (New York: Watts, 1976).

Freeman, Don. *Dandelion* (New York: Viking, 1964).

Fuchs, Erich. *Journey to the Moon* (New York: Delacorte, 1969).

Gág, Wanda. *Millions of Cats* (New York: Coward-McCann, 1928).

Garn, Bernard J. *A Visit to the Dentist,* illus. Arthur Krusz (New York: Grosset, 1959).

Geisel, Theodor. *Horton Hatches the Egg* (New York: Random House, 1940).

————. *The Cat in the Hat* (New York: Random House, 1957).

Gramatky, Hardie. *Little Toot* (New York: Putnam's, 1939).

Hoban, Tana. *Look Again!* (New York: Macmillan, 1971).

Hutchins, Pat. *Rosie's Walk* (New York: Macmillan, 1968).

————. *Titch* (New York: Macmillan, 1971).

Jordan, Helen. *How a Seed Grows,* illus. Joseph Low (New York: Crowell, 1960).

Keats, Ezra Jack. *The Snowy Day* (New York: Viking, 1962).

————. *Whistle for Willie* (New York: Viking, 1964).

————. *Goggles!* (New York: Macmillan, 1969).

Keeping, Charles. *Through the Window* (New York: Watts, 1970).

Langstaff, John. *Frog Went A-Courtin',* illus. Feodor Rojankovsky (New York: Harcourt, 1955).

Lionni, Leo. *Fredrick* (New York: Pantheon, 1967).

Lobel, Arnold. *Frog and Toad are Friends* (New York: Harper, 1970).
———. *Frog and Toad Together* (New York: Harper, 1972).
Macaulay, David. *Cathedral* (Boston: Houghton Mifflin, 1973).
Mayer, Mercer. *A Boy, A Dog, and A Frog* (New York: Dial, 1967).
McCloskey, Robert. *Make Way for Ducklings* (New York: Viking, 1941).
Mendoza, George. *And I Must Hurry for the Sea Is Coming In*, illus. DeWayne Dalrymple (Englewood Cliffs, N.J.: Prentice Hall, 1969).
Minarik, Else Holmelund. *Little Bear*, illus. Maurice Sendak (New York: Harper, 1957).
Musgrove, Margaret. *Ashanti to Zulu*, illus. Leo and Diane Dillon (New York: Dial, 1976).
Potter, Beatrix. *The Tale of Peter Rabbit*, (London, Warne)
———. *The Tale of Two Bad Mice*, (London, Warne).
Raskin, Ellen. *Spectacles* (New York: Atheneum, 1968).
Rey, H. A. *Curious George* (Boston: Houghton Mifflin, 1941).
Rockwell, Harlow. *My Doctor* (New York: Macmillan, 1973).
Schoenherr, John. *The Barn*, (Boston: Little, Brown, 1968).
Segal, Lore. *Tell Me a Trudy*, illus. Rosemary Wells (New York: Farrar, 1977).
Sendak, Maurice. *Where the Wild Things Are* (New York: Harper, 1963).
Steptoe, John. *Stevie* (New York: Harper, 1969).
Stone, A. Harris. *The Last Free Bird*, illus. Sheila Heins (Englewood Cliffs, N. J.: Prentice-Hall, 1967).
Thomas, Ianthe. *Lordy Aunt Hattie*, illus. Thomas di Grazia (New York: Harper, 1973).
Tresselt, Alvin. *Hide and Seek Fog*, illus. Roger Duvoisin (New York: Lothrop, Lee and Shepard, 1965).
Turkle, Brinton. *Deep in the Forest* (New York: Dutton, 1976).
Valens, Evans G. *Wildfire*, illus. Clement Hurd (New York: World, 1963).
Viorst, Judith. *Alexander and the Terrible, Horrible, No Good, Very Bad Day*, illus. Ray Cruz (New York: Atheneum, 1972).
Ward, Lynd. *The Silver Pony* (Boston: Houghton Mifflin, 1973).
Wildsmith, Brian. *The Lion and the Rat* (New York: Watts, 1963).
Yashima, Taro. *Umbrella* (New York: Viking, 1958).
Zolotow, Charlotte. *Mr. Rabbit and the Lovely Present*, illus. Maurice Sendak (New York: Harper, 1962).
———. *The Quarreling Book*, illus. Arnold Lobel (New York: Harper, 1963).
———. *My Grandson Lew*, illus. William Pène du Bois (New York: Harper, 1974).

RECOMMENDED PICTURE BOOKS

Anno, Mitsumasa. *Anno's Journey* (Cleveland: Collins/World, 1978).
This textless book pictures the changes as a rural area goes to village, then town, then city.

Ardizzone, Edward. *Little Tim and the Brave Sea Captain* (New York: Walck, 1955).
Tim's adventures at sea are portrayed in watercolor and line drawings.

Brown, Margaret Wise. *The Runaway Bunny,* illus. Clement Hurd (New York: Harper, 1972). (1942)
A little bunny is comforted by his mother who tells him that no matter where he is, she will be able to find him and care for him.

Burningham, John. *Mr. Gumpy's Outing* (New York: Holt, 1971).
Mr. Gumpy invites each of the animals aboard his boat on the condition that they behave. They don't, the boat overturns, and all go home for tea and drying off.

Burton, Virginia Lee. *The Little House* (Boston: Houghton Mifflin, 1942).
The little house, unhappy when the city grows up around it, finally is moved back to the country.

Carrick, Carol. *The Foundling,* illus. Donald Carrick (New York: Seabury, 1977).
Christopher resists his parents' efforts to give him a puppy to replace his dog which has been killed, but then the boy finds a stray puppy himself.

Clifton, Lucille. *Amifika,* illus. Thomas DiGrazia (New York: Dutton, 1977).
Amifika overhears his mother say they will get rid of something his daddy does not remember, and begins to fear that he just may be that something.

Cohen, Miriam. *When Will I Read?* illus. Lillian Hoban (New York: Greenwillow, 1977).
Jim wants desparately to read, and finds that he can when he sees that part of the sign on a hamster cage has been torn off, and he knows what the remainder says.

Emberley, Barbara. *Drummer Hoff,* illus. Ed Emberley (Englewood Cliffs, N.J.: Prentice-Hall, 1967).
In this cumulative rhyme, Drummer Hoff fires a cannon.

Fisher, Aileen. *Listen Rabbit,* illus. Symeon Shimin (New York: Crowell, 1964).
This poem tells a realistic story about a boy who wants a wild rabbit for a pet.

Gackenbach, Dick. *Do You Love Me?* (New York: Seabury, 1975).

Six-year-old Walter is distraught when he accidentally kills a hummingbird he is trying to catch, but his older sister helps him understand, and brings him a puppy he can cuddle.

Freschet, Berniece. *The Web in the Grass,* illus. Roger Duvoisin (New York: Scribner's, 1972).

Duvoisin's beautiful yet accurate illustrations help explicate the "life story" of a spider.

Hoban, Russell. *A Birthday for Frances,* illus. Lillian Hoban (New York: Harper, 1968).

Frances suffers pangs of jealousy when the family celebrates her sister's birthday.

Isadora, Rachel. *Max* (New York: Macmillan, 1976).

On his way to play baseball, Max stops at his sister's dancing class and finds himself intrigued with ballet steps.

Kahl, Virginia. *The Duchess Bakes a Cake* (New York: Scribner's, 1955).

The cake rises to unbelievable proportions in this exaggerated tale of too much yeast.

Lexau, Joan. *I'll Tell on You,* illus. Gail Owens (New York: Dutton, 1976).

Rose must decide whether to tell on her friend Mark when he does not admit that it was his dog which bit a younger child.

Lindgren, Astrid. *The Tomten,* adapted from a poem by Victor Rydberg, illus. Harald Wiberg (New York: Coward-McCann, 1961).

The Tomten, a gentle troll-like creature which only animals and children can understand, strolls quietly around the farm at night.

Lionni, Leo. *Swimmy* (New York: Pantheon, 1963).

Swimmy teaches all the little fish to swim together to give themselves protection from the larger fish.

Marshall, James. *George and Martha Rise and Shine* (Boston: Houghton Mifflin, 1976).

This book has five short stories about two hippopotamus friends; each tale has a humorous twist.

Miles, Miska. *Wharf Rat,* illus. John Schoenherr (Boston: Little Brown, 1972).

This realistic animal story describes the life of a rat as he searches for food along the wharf, and as he experiences the effects of an oil spill.

Oxenbury, Helen. *Pig Tale* (New York: Morrow, 1973).
  After a fling at city life and material goods, two pigs, Bertha and
  Briggs, decide to return to the freedom of country living.
Ryan, Cheli Duran. *Hildilid's Night,* illus. Arnold Lobel (New York:
  Macmillan, 1971).
  Hildilid expends so much energy trying to get rid of the night that
  she is too exhausted to enjoy the day.
Shulevitz, Uri. *Dawn* (New York: Farrar, 1974).
  A boy and his grandfather camp overnight by a lake, rise before
  dawn to have breakfast, and row out onto the lake as the sun rises.
Sonneborn, Ruth. *Friday Night is Papa Night,* illus. Emily McCully
  (New York: Viking, 1970).
  When Papa is late getting home, Pedro hears him and welcomes
  him home by having the light on for him.
Steig, William. *Caleb and Kate* (New York: Farrar, 1977).
  Kate does not realize that the dog at her heels is actually her hus-
  band Caleb who has been transformed by a witch.
Uchida, Yoshiko. *The Rooster Who Understood Japanese,* illus.
  Charles Robinson (New York: Scribner's, 1976).
  Miyo tries to help Mrs. Kitamura find a way to keep her rooster
  after a new neighbor threatens to call the police because of its
  crowing.

Udry, Janice May. *What Mary Jo Shared,* illus. Eleanor Mill
  (Chicago: Whitman, 1966).
  Mary Jo solves the problem of what to take to school for show-
  and-tell time by taking her father.
Waber, Bernard. *Mice on My Mind* (Boston: Houghton Mifflin,
  1977).
  The cat in this story has an obsession with mice, and neither cold
  showers nor psychiatrists are able to help.
Ward, Lynd. *The Biggest Bear* (Boston: Houghton Mifflin, 1952).
  Johnny's bear cub grows too large to keep as a pet, and poses a
  problem for both Johnny and his family.
Yashima, Taro. *Crow Boy* (New York: Viking, 1955).
  A young Japanese boy is not appreciated by his classmates until a
  sixth-grade teacher helps them see his talents.

CHAPTER 3

MOTHER GOOSE AND CONCEPT BOOKS

MISS MUFFET TO ABC TO 1 2 3

One British critic in 1952 enumerated the "unsavoury elements" he had discovered in a selection of writings for children. There were eight general references to murder, he said. There were two cases of choking to death, one case of death by devouring, one case of cutting a person in half, one case of death by shriveling, one case of "the desire to have a limb severed," and 185 other "cases" and "allusions," all unsuitable for children.

The long and grisly list reads like an indictment of horror films. But the critic, Geoffrey Handley-Taylor, was aiming at a more venerable target: Mother Goose rhymes (in Baring-Gould, 1962, pp. 20-21).

There have been other assaults, some dating back centuries. Too violent, several critics have said. Not educational, others have argued. In what some critics consider a subtler kind of assault, the old rhymes have been translated into modern idiom: in *Walt Disney's Mother Goose* (1976), Miss Muffet is Minnie Mouse.

But Mother Goose rhymes have survived all of this. Many of the poems are now hundreds of years old, passed along in the lilting voices of parents who call up magical words and images for their children again and again. The rhythms are sometimes bumpy and irregular, some of the words archaic. Some poems are ominous: young children and animals are often buffeted about, in a cruel world, with little hope of living happily ever after. Still, the rhymes have crept into the nursery at bedtime, and there they have remained. Where did they come from? How do they survive?

The British call them nursery rhymes; in the United States they are called Mother Goose rhymes, but the old poems for children are the same by either name. Along with alphabet, counting, and concept books—which are discussed later in the chapter—Mother Goose is an introduction to more advanced kinds of children's literature. Unlike alphabet books, though, most of Mother Goose was not originally meant for children.

Origins

Most of the Mother Goose rhymes collected and illustrated today for children were made up in their original wording by adults for adults. British writers Iona and Peter Opie point out in their introduction to

Humpty Dumpty sat on a wall,
Humpty Dumpty had a great fall;

All the King's horses
and all the King's men

Cannot put Humpty Dumpty
together again.

Political satire continues to be found in Mother Goose rhymes and illustrations, as shown here in a Humpty Dumpty who resembles Adolf Hitler. (Illustration from *The Tall Book of Mother Goose* by Feodor Rojankovsky. Copyright © 1942 by Western Publishing Company, Inc. By permission of Western Publishing Company, Inc.)

the *Oxford Dictionary of Nursery Rhymes* (1973, pp. 3–4) that some of the poetry is taken from ballads or folk songs such as "One Misty Moisty Morning." Other poems are converted drinking songs ("Nose, Nose, Jolly Red Nose"), or songs of battle ("At the Siege of Belleisle"). And some are clearly political commentary ("William and Mary, George and Ann").

A few come from popular songs of this century, but most of the poems are much older. The Opies found that close to 10 percent of rhymes they studied were in existence a century before the American Revolution (p. 7). Tradition holds that some counting rhymes (such as "eeny, meeny, mony, my," used to select a child to be "it" in games) are older than that—as old as rites used by Druids, ancient priests in Gaul and Britain. There is no proof, but legend holds that these priests used such rhymes to choose human sacrifices (p. 12).

The Opies conclude "almost without hesitation" (p. 4) that the only rhymes written especially for children before 1800 were rhyming alphabets, lullabies, and verses accompanying children's games. All the others now in the family of Mother Goose were made up for mature audiences.

One reason they infiltrated the nursery was the attitude parents had toward their offspring two centuries ago when the poems were first published for children. The Opies point out that in the seventeenth and eighteenth centuries, children were treated as "grown-ups in miniature."

> In paintings we see them wearing clothes which were replicas of those worn by their elders . . . Many parents saw nothing unusual in their children hearing strong language or savouring strong drink. (p. 5)

Another reason was that faced with a damp or squalling child, parents called with little thought on songs they like themselves.

Was There a Real Mother Goose?

There is confusion about who the stouthearted lady was. And there is no clear explanation of why she became associated with early collections of children's poems, although it is reasonably certain that her association in English dates from the eighteenth century. One persistent legend is that she was an American, Elizabeth Goose of Boston, stepmother of ten and mother to six of her own children.

The story is that one of her sons-in-law, a printer named Thomas Fleet, heard Mrs. Goose telling old tales to one after another of his children. He had half a dozen children. And sometime during their upbringing, he tired of listening to the reruns. As revenge for his boredom, he collected his mother-in-law's stories in a book he called *Songs for the Nursery or Mother Goose's Melodies for Children.* Supposedly, the book was published in 1719. The title page displayed a gooselike animal with a long neck, apparently honking. So the legend goes.

No scholar takes the story seriously today. There is no trace of Fleet's book and the strongest advocate of its existence is suspect: a man named John Fleet Eliot, great grandson of Thomas Fleet, who did not claim to have seen the book himself.

The more reliable trail leads to France. The phrase *conte de la Mère Oye* (Mother Goose story) has been tracked there to writings from the middle of the seventeenth century. And a French author named Perrault printed a book with the frontispiece "Contes de ma Mère L'Oye" in 1696–97. It included such classic stories as "Sleeping Beauty" and "Little Red Riding Hood," and was translated into English in 1729, the first known appearance of the famous mother in our language (Opie and Opie, 1973, p. 39). Later in the eighteenth century, Mother Goose became associated exclusively with children's rhymes.

Adult scholars since then have made extraordinary efforts to analyze Mother Goose poetry. Margaret Chisholm, dean of the School of Library and Information Services at the University of Maryland, made a kind of odessey to Ireland, Scotland, Wales, and England to track down roots of the rhymes. She reports (1972) that "Mary, Mary Quite Contrary" refers to Mary Queen of Scots; Jack and Jill were originally figures in Norse mythology, and the poem about them refers to the ebb and flow of the tide; and "Baa Baa Black Sheep" is about weaving wool in thirteenth-century England. The Opies point out (1973, p. 27) that "Sing a Song of Sixpense" has at different times, by different scholars, been earnestly exposed as a reference to the choirs of monasteries, the printing of the English Bible, the evils of clergymen, and the workings of the solar system.

THE APPEAL TO CHILDREN

Curious as all this may be, it is of no import to children. It does not even matter that some of the words are strange. "What does 'curds and whey' mean?" we asked one 5-year-old girl named Kim. "It's something to eat," she said. "Do you like the poem about Miss Muffet?" we asked. Kim said yes and added that she had heard on TV's *Sesame Street* that Miss Muffet was not afraid of spiders any more. "But *I* am," she said. And she recited the poem, without coaching, as if it belonged to her.

It does. Mother Goose has survived not because it teaches moral or historical lessons. The rhymes live on because of their elementary strength: generations of editing by parents and children have winnowed down the words until they are most appealing, most magical, to children. Mother Goose succeeds as literature in several ways.

Rhythm of the Language

Read this out loud:

> This is the way the gentlemen ride,
>> Gallop-a-trot,
>> Gallop-a-trot!
> This is the way the gentlemen ride,
>> Gallop-a-gallop-a-trot!

The content of the verse makes little difference. Its message in prose is something like "gentlemen ride their horses at a gallop." But just try saying *that* out loud gracefully. The child does not need to know what "gallop" means; in the poem it is fun to say. And it is fun to hear, particularly if a parent is bouncing the child precariously in time with the rhythm.

Listening to these sounds, the child begins to realize the power of words. Words set off the rollicking ride; some sounds seem to thump into the chest as well as the ears, and the sensation is pleasant.

Content

Snappy punchlines, sudden twists of plot, broad-brush stories, and vignettes of characters happy and lamentable—the poems are filled with enough vitality to hold the interest of sleepy children.

There is a short and funny story, for instance, in the poem about "Three Wise Men of Gotham":

> Three wise man of Gotham
> Went to sea in a bowl;
> If the bowl had been stronger
> My song had been longer.

Children and adults find satisfaction in the amusing and calculated insult of "Dr. Fell":

> I do not like thee, Doctor Fell;
> The reason why I cannot tell;
> But this I know and know full well,
> I do not like thee, Doctor Fell!

But many of the brief stories end unhappily. Humpty Dumpty is shattered. Jack and Jill fall down the hill. In "The Little Moppet," a girl with a doll meets a villain, a "proud beggar," and tells her woeful story in six lines:

I had a little moppet,
I put it in my pocket,
And fed it with corn and hay.
There came a proud beggar,
And swore he should have her;
and stole my little moppet away.

Happy or sad, Mother Goose offers action. Something happens every few words, as in the story, titled "A Melancholy Song," of a little girl who meets some young men while running an errand:

... Yet didn't you see, yet didn't you see,
What naughty tricks they put upon me?
They broke my pitcher
And spilt the water
And huffed my mother
And chid her daughter,
And kissed my sister instead of me.

Participation

"This little pig went to market" is an excuse for a tickling assault on the child's toes; parents can play the game by tugging at a little toe with each line of the poem. Preschool children enjoy the anticipation. Other rhymes provide the force for group games. Preschoolers who haven't ever considered cooperating with each other drop to the floor with remarkable teamwork when cued by the last line of "Ring around the Rosie": "We all fall down."

Associations

The child probably first hears Mother Goose rhymes in the nursery, from a loving parent. No author could ask for a better introduction to a body of writing. When the words of the poems are repeated at home, and later in school, they resonate with feelings from early childhood; they carry some of the warmth of the parents who first spoke them.

Cradles may plunge out of trees, and spiders big enough to sit down may brush Miss Muffet's dress—but even these potentially terrifying poems hold the fascination of recalled dreams.

109

USES AND VALUE

The appeal of the poetry in Mother Goose rhymes makes them useful for preschool and first-grade teachers. Anyone reading the poems will find an interested audience: they have probably heard the words before, in a pleasant setting, and the repetition helps combat the foreignness of the classroom.

One way for the teacher to begin is to read several of the poems aloud until the class shows its preferences. It is not hard to gauge response to these poems; the best of them trigger wiggles of recognition in a group. Even if the children do not know all the words, they mumble through in time with the rhythm until they encounter a run of words they remember.

A teacher can choose the poem drawing the most response and then repeat it several times until the whole class is able to chant the verses. The value: Children calling out the sing-song words are taking the first step toward poetry appreciation.

There is a variety of good poetry to savor. The English writer and critic G. K. Chesterton once said that the Mother Goose line "Over the hills and far away" was one of the best in all English poetry. But even less beautiful phrases help children learn to enjoy language. Lines such as "trip upon trenchers/And dance upon dishes," from "A Melancholy Song," develop a feeling for alliteration—repetition of the same consonant sound. Simple rhyming patterns, such as "A swarm of bees in May/Is worth a load of hay," make it easy to remember the verses and establish a sense of how slight changes in sound make a large difference in meaning.

Simple questions put to children about meaning—such as "What happened first in the poem?"—help set the poem in the listeners' minds. And questions about how the children *feel* about what happened can spark lively discussion.

Even Handley-Taylor's "unsavoury elements" can help a child to grow emotionally. Discussions of content need not avoid mysterious or violent sides of the poetry. Child psychologist Bruno Bettelheim points out that some fairy tales—and, we can add, some Mother Goose rhymes—are a kind of antidote to beliefs that children's literature must be unflaggingly sweet.

"Many parents believe that only conscious reality or pleasant and

Many Mother Goose rhymes, such as the one about the Queen of Hearts, tell appealing short stories. (Illustration by Blanche Fisher Wright from *The Real Mother Goose.* Copyright 1916, 1944 Rand McNally & Company.)

111

Goosey, goosey, gander,
Whither shall I wander?
Upstairs and downstairs,
And in my lady's chamber.

There I met an old man
That wouldn't say his prayers;
I took him by the left leg,
And threw him down the stairs.

Adults often disagree about the possible effects on
children of the violence in some nursery rhymes.
(From *Brian Wildsmith's Mother Goose* by Brian
Wildsmith. Copyright © 1964 by Brian Wildsmith.
Used by permission of Franklin Watts, Inc.)

wish-fulfilling images should be presented to the child—that he
could be exposed only to the sunny side of things," Bettelheim
writes (1976). "But such one-sided fare nourishes the mind only in a
one-sided way, and real life is not all sunny" (p. 7).

The young child, in fact, finds in the first few years of life that imagination and dreams sometimes run to witches, spiders, and bad giants as well as to fantasies about birthdays and sugar plums. It is obvious, at least to children, that children sometimes feel like kicking something.

"Children will always have ideas about throwing old men downstairs, hurting pussy cats or stealing things," writes Nicholas Tucker, a psychologist who frequently writes on children's literature, "whether they read nursery rhymes or not, and it may do them much more good to exorcise such feelings in print than to brood over them in private" (in Haviland, 1973, p. 262).

Tucker says that the rhyme, meter, and song of Mother Goose rhyme help put its content, even when violent, into an "acceptable, stylized context, where violence is resolved rather than magnified" (ibid.).

EVALUATING MOTHER GOOSE BOOKS

The poems themselves do not change much with age. Some of them were rewritten in the late 1700s to sanitize the bawdiness of the original adult songs. Writers in this century have occasionally tried to contribute new and wholesome verse to the wealth of Mother Goose: "Every perfect person owns/Just two hundred and six bones," is one such couplet, written by a Mrs. Winifred Sacville Stoner Jr. in 1925, and quickly forgotten (in Baring-Gould, 1962, p. 19).

But most of the words remain the same. There are, however, major differences in the way they are presented in the dozens of Mother Goose collections available today. The quality of the setting—particularly the work of the illustrator—is the major criterion for judging the collections.

Illustrations

In one Mother Goose poem, Hector Protector is a passive lad, wrapped and sent back and forth like a mute package:

> Hector Protector was dressed all in green.
> Hector Protector was sent to the queen.
> The queen did not like him;
> No more did the king.
> So Hector Protector was sent back again.

But when drawn by artist Maurice Sendak, Hector comes alive. The verse becomes half of a book, *Hector Protector and As I Went*

113

over the Water (1965). The boy's problems begin, as Sendak tells the story in pictures, with his mother. She dresses him in prissy green clothes with a feathered hat and ruffled collar. "I hate green!" he yells. She gives him a cake to take to the queen, but he drop-kicks it just outside the door of his house, at the edge of a dark wood where a gigantic lion, with somewhat human eyes, says "Grr-r." Hector subdues the lion with the broad side of a toy sword, then rides the animal into the forest. Here he tames a wild snake, enters the Queen's room on the lion with the docile snake wrapped around his sword. The startled royal court quickly casts him out of the palace. The words of the poem run out.

But Sendak continues the story for six more pages as Hector says goodbye to his doleful animals, meets his angry mother, gets sent to bed, and tries to cajole a bird outside his window to bring him some of the smashed cake. In the last picture, the bird itself has eaten the whole cake; it looks mildly ill, and says "Oh!"

Sendak's approach follows one tradition for illustrating Mother Goose: the artist embellishes the story, adding wordless subplots to complement the poetry. Sendak's model for this approach is Randolph Caldecott, a nineteenth-century illustrator who set standards that today's artists are still trying to meet.

Watch how Caldecott extends the action of the poem "Three Jovial Huntsmen," for example, in his *Picture Book No. 2* (published around 1880 and still available today). The poem is about three red-coated, horn-tooting horsemen galloping breakneck through rolling English hills, looking for foxes. They find only a scarecrow, a grinding stone, farm animals, children, and lovers in the course of a "rattlin' day."

But there is a lot going on in Caldecott's detailed drawings which never appears in the words. At one point, one of the riders falls off his horse, who prances away up a hill without him. The man's two boisterous friends, holding their hats, are so caught up in the hunt that they never notice the empty saddle behind them. The lone rider picks up his hunting horn and blows a blast. But the other mounts are now over the first hill and climbing a second, far away. In desparation, the lost rider climbs a tree and blows again, and now one of his friends waves reassurance while the other reins in the riderless horse.

All of this is told in just three pictures on two pages (24 and 25). The words of the poem never refer to the adventure.

A second approach to illustration is more literal: the artist faithfully captures the scene in the poem without augmenting its meaning or extending its story. Kate Greenaway's delicate drawings for *Mother Goose of the Old Nursery Rhymes* (also published in the

Jack Sprat could eat no fat,
His wife could eat no lean;
And so betwixt them both, you see,
They licked the platter clean.

Wallace Tripp added humor to his illustrations of
Mother Goose Rhymes. (From *Granfa' Grig Had a Pig
and Other Rhymes without Reason from Mother
Goose* by Wallace Tripp, by permission of Little,
Brown and Company. Illustrations Copyright © 1976
by Wallace Tripp.

1880s and still available) are static by comparison with Caldecott's.
She puts warm detail in the settings: Jack Horner's corner is in an
old-fashioned kitchen with a brick oven and a few cooking utensils.
But the figure of Jack looking at a plum appears pensive and still.
(There is more on Caldecott and Greenaway in Chapter 2.)

A more modern collection, *Brian Wildsmith's Mother Goose*
(1964) has large, eye-catching figures in bold colors. There are imaginative touches: the pig on the way to market carries a basket-
strapped to its back. Poems are placed logically: "Baa Baa Black
Sheep" is opposite "Mary Had a Little Lamb." The drawings do not
depart much from the poetry. Wildsmith's and Greenaway's figures
often appear to be posing to represent a moment in the brief narrative of the poem.

Which approach works? There are values in each. Sendak says the
literal approach is "respectful, honest, often beautiful and, I imagine, for the literal-minded child, the best possible accompaniment to
the rhymes" (in Haviland, 1973, p. 190). But Sendak's sympathy is
clearly with Caldecott and other interpretative artists. "This is the

115

real Mother Goose—marvelously imagined improvisations that playfully and rhythmically bounce off and around the verses without ever incongruously straying" (p. 191).

The child, of course, is the ultimate judge of which Mother Goose is "real." Teachers aware of the differences will offer several different collections, in several illustrative styles, to match individual tastes.

Format

The Greenaway drawings are only 4½ inches long and just 2¼ inches wide overall; most of the figures in the drawings are about as big as Tom Thumb. That may be a cozy size for individual readers, but groups of children sitting some distance from a teacher holding the book will come to think that all Mother Goose characters look alike. Wildsmith's collection is more appropriate for group reading. So are Caldecott's books.

In *The Real Mother Goose,* (1965) a famous collection that has gone through more than sixty printings since it first appeared in 1916, many of the drawings are large enough for group use. But in this classic collection, another problem arises: so many poems are printed per page that it sometimes becomes difficult for a child to tell which of Blanche Fisher Wright's cheerful illustrations go with which poem.

Below "Burnie Bee," for instance, a verse whose last line is "Take your wings and fly away," there is a picture of the three wise men of Gotham afloat in their bowl looking at birds in flight over the sea. On another page, the poem about the life and death of Solomon Grundy is next to a picture of a barber shaving a pig. The layout may not be a problem for children hearing the poems read to them; but a young student trying to read the poems and counting on pictures to help with difficult words may find the format confusing.

Coverage and Appropriateness

The Real Mother Goose is useful in a classroom library because it includes more than 160 rhymes—it can fill almost any request from the floor. Smaller collections should be judged in part by what rhymes are presented. Are there a few unusual, lively additions? Sendak, for one, favors including lesser-known but "witty, rambunctious" verses such as "I had a little husband, no bigger than my thumb,/I put him in a pint pot, and there I bid him drum . . . " in favor of "saccharine and pallid" chestnuts such as "Mary Had a Little Lamb."

Some witty collections, of course, are inappropriate for children. In *Charles Addams's Mother Goose* (1967) Jack Sprat and his wife are shown with the platter before them, empty except for the remains of their dinner—a pocket watch, collar, and pair of glasses. Eve Merriam, in *The Inner City Mother Goose*, (1969) rewrites verses to focus on urban problems, particularly in black ghettoes. One verse:

There was a crooked man
And he did very well. (p. 11)

The message is clear, clever, and vital—but not for 3-year-olds.

CONCEPT BOOKS

A nimble rabbit leaps over a snail. A carrier pigeon floats above some telephone wires. A four-engined jet flies over a wagon drawn by eight oxen. An old oak stands next to a straggly pea vine with unruly tendrils. To a child first looking at two adjoining pages of a book called *Fast-Slow-High-Low*, (1972) the pictures appear haphazard and puzzling.

But try climbing a few intellectual steps with a young reader. Step one: Many of the objects—the plane, rabbit, and telephone lines—are familiar. What are they doing here together on these two pages? Even preschool children who cannot read the only two words on the pages, "fast-slow", can begin to climb the next step. The rabbit is more fleet than the snail. The plane beats the ox cart. It may take some explaining for preschool children, but it soon becomes clear that the telephone does its job faster than the carrier pigeon, and the pea grows more rapidly than the oak. Part of the initial puzzle has been solved. These are drawings of fast versus slow.

Other pages in the book, by artist and writer Peter Spier, illustrate full versus empty, light versus dark, and other contrasting characteristics. And now the child can climb the next step: This is a book about *opposites*.

Spier's *Fast-Slow* is an example of what is sometimes called a concept book. A jumble of data falls into patterns under the force of a general concept or idea. The concept creates order out of the clutter, makes pieces fit. Unlike Mother Goose, which is colored with mystery and dreamlike images, concept books bring the everyday world into sharp focus for young children. These are books about relationships: rabbits call out to be compared with snails, circles bump into triangles, and stray noises are connected with the animals or machines that produce them.

117

This page gives many examples to illustrate the meanings of "smooth" and "rough" as part of an entire book exploring the concept of opposites. (Illustration from *Fast-Slow, High-Low* by Peter Spier. Copyright © 1972 by Peter Spier. Reproduced by permission of Doubleday & Company, Inc.)

Specific examples give weight to general ideas. A picture of a shy hippopotamus looking back at its bulk spread over two pages is solid evidence of weight in *Heavy Is a Hippopotamus* (1954) (a book by writer Miriam Schlein). Photographer Tana Hoban's *Over, Under and Through* (1973) introduces each block of black-and-white photographs with words representing the general concept, followed by several pages of examples. The word "over," is followed a few pages later by a picture of a boy leapfrogging over a fire hydrant.

One child's strategy in reading such a book is *inductive*: jumping from picture to picture, perhaps pointing, until the specific examples suggest the concept. Another child's strategy is *deductive*: recognizing the concept first, then finding examples and labeling each picture "over . . . over . . . over. . . ."

Some concept books appear to favor one strategy over another. Most ABC books first present an abstract symbol, then show how it is used in particular instances. But many concept books, including ABC and counting books, are flexible enough to match the child's reading whims. You can start with the examples and move to the symbol. Jump back and forth between general and specific. Skip pages. Many of these books can be adapted on the spot to meet individual curiosities.

Uses and Value

There is a picture of a child riding one of the oxen in Spier's fast-slow pages. How did the rider get there? Is it frightening to ride up there? The picture arouses curiosity; the child can imagine the experience of riding bareback. Another Spier book, *Crash! Bang! Boom!* (1972), offers dozens of pictures of things and their related noises. A police siren goes "you—you—you . . . ." The sharpening of a straight razor on a strop sounds like "fit-fit-fit." Some of the pictures are familiar; in one, a hand flips through a book ("fluf fluf fluf-a-luff"). Others, like the drawing of the straight razor, may be foreign to children. But even for children who cannot read the text, Spier's books have the appeal of a first visit to a large and noisy toy store.

But while entertaining, most concept books also make intellectual demands on readers. *The Indoor Noisy Book* (1939), by Margaret Wise Brown, tells a story about a dog named Muffin who has to stay in bed because of a cold. The dog hears all the noises in the house and has to try to make sense of the sounds. Some are easy, at least for Muffin. "Bbbbbbbbbbbbbbbb" is the noise the cook makes beating eggs in the kitchen.

But another sound is harder to identify: what do the "tiny footsteps" on the stairs mean? "Was it a little bug coming to see Muffin?" There is a picture of a huge ladybug climbing stairs. Most young readers instantly become detectives and reject the bug theory.

"Was it an elephant coming to see Muffin?" The picture shows an elephant wearing a hat, climbing the stairs. Children shake their heads. It cannot be an elephant. "Was it a clown with a firecracker?" Wrong again. The easy-going challenge of the book is to associate the sound with its likely source: "It was the cat, of course."

Other concept books encourage young readers to see the relationships between squares and rectangles, circles and ovals, light and dark. In *The Sesame Street Book of Shapes* (1970) a pointy-headed puppet named Bert tells the Cookie Monster that some cookies are shaped like circles. This painless introduction of the circle concept is followed by a page of splashy circles in different sizes and colors.

119

ISSUE

HOW EFFECTIVE ARE JOAN WALSH ANGLUND'S DRAWINGS?

A multitude of books greatly enjoyed by children are not stories. What is their appeal to children? Do the criteria that make story books interesting to children also make the non-story books appealing? What draws children to Ruth Krauss's *A Hole Is to Dig,* to Margaret Wise Brown's *The Golden Egg Book,* and to Joan Walsh Anglund's *Spring Is a New Beginning.*

Basically these books are popular because they are good writing even though there is no plot. . . .

Spring Is a New Beginning causes the adult to experience waves of beauty, sadness, and joyousness almost at the same time. To children this book brings together a multitude of concepts they have had about spring, in a new and beautiful way. The simplicity of the presentations, the concentration on one thought, and the appeal to the emotions of the reader make these books rightfully take their place among the sophisticated children's literature of our time. (p. 92)

Smith, James A., and Dorothy M. Park. *Word Music and Word Magic: Children's Literature Methods.* (Boston: Allyn and Bacon, 1977).

Mrs. Anglund's fabricated children, their faces no more expressive than Parker House rolls, sit or stand like display dummies in their made-to-order environments. Certainly Mrs. Anglund's tableaux have an immediate and insinuating charm. They are cute, occasionally even droll, and it is tempting to remember our pasts in such cozy clichés. Yet, by consciously manipulating her child characters to fulfill the requirements of preconceived tableaux of childhood, Mrs. Anglund stiffens and falsifies children. . . .

It would be hard to expect much semblance of reality when Mrs. Anglund's children must serve to illustrate such imprecise and adult sentiments as :

It (spring) is a gentle farewell
to yesterday
and the birth of new hope.

or:

It (love) is the happy way we feel
when we save a
bird that has been hurt . . .
or calm a frightened colt.

It perhaps says something of Mrs. Anglund's all-pervasive, sugar-coated sentimentality that even picket fences in her world seem always to have rounded points. (pp. 37, 39)

Lanes, Selma G. *Down the Rabbit Hole* (New York: Atheneum, 1971).

The illustration above is from *Spring Is a New Beginning.* How would you characterize Anglund's drawings? Why might they have appeal for some adults? Do you think they have equal appeal for some children? Why or why not? Perhaps you will want to read the entire book and see if you agree with Smith and Park that the writing is good and that the book is sophisticated.

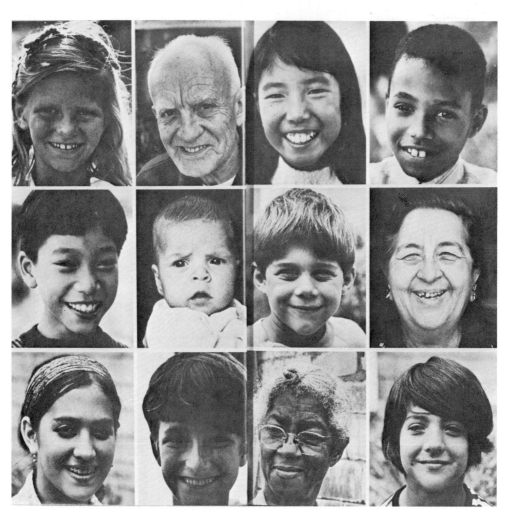

Children can begin to make generalizations based on
specific examples as they look at concept books.
(From *Faces* by Barbara Brenner, and illustrated by
George Ancona. Copyright © 1970 by Barbara
Brenner, illustrations © 1970 by George Ancona.
Reprinted by permission of the publishers, E. P.
Dutton.)

Then comes the challenge. The book asks the reader to find examples of circles in photographs of bicycles and telephones. Other TV
characters introduce squares, rectangles, and triangles. Finally, the
child is asked to spot each of the different shapes in several pages of
photographs and drawings. Deducing from general concepts, the

reader plays a valuable game: "That's a circle...there's a square...that's a triangle...."

Experience with these books is practice for dealing the sometimes threatening data of everyday life. What *is* that noise on the stair? I'm bigger than my brother, right? Which way is left? Different concept books can help answer all these practical preschool questions.

In addition, almost all concept books help develop language skills. Some teach tools such as the names of shapes. Others are so gracefully written they help foster delight in poetic language. The season of fall, for instance, is presented with active verbs and poetic language by Marjorie Auerbach in *A Day of Autumn* (1967):

> Run among leaves.
> Throw them in armfuls,
> Push them in piles.
> Scatter the scratchy leaves,
> Kick into piles of leaves,
> Lie high on banks of leaves,
> Crackly and soft.

Two specific kinds of concept books help children to understand relationships between common abstract symbols and their use in everyday expression. Many *alphabet* and *counting* books follow the same formula: a left-hand page introduces the symbol, and pictures and text on the right-hand page put the symbol to work, or show what it represents.

ABC BOOKS

"A" doesn't always stand for "apple" anymore. Today, it is just as likely to stand for "aardvark," "always," or even, in writer Eric Carle's *All About Arthur* (1974), for "an absolutely absurd accordian playing ape."

Some modern ABC books are not even designed, primarily, to introduce the alphabet. Muriel Feelings's *Jambo Means Hello* (1974), for instance, introduces another culture. There is one Swahili word for each letter in the book (except Q and X which represent sounds not used in the African language). "C" is for "chakula," the word for food, and the reader learns that villagers farm together and divide the harvest. Tom Feelings's softly shaded paintings of proud Africans help to introduce another culture. But the alphabet is incidental. The content and vocabulary are more appropriate to a third-grader than to a preschool child.

123

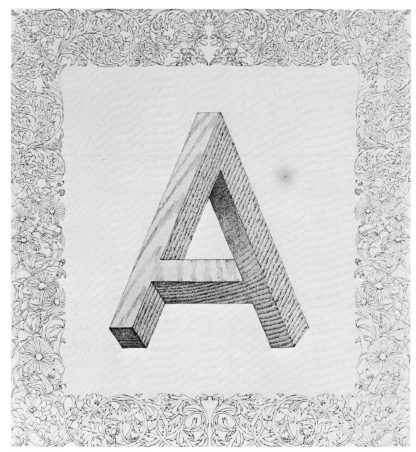

Some of the letters in this alphabet book present
optical illusions. (Illustration from *Anno's Alphabet:
An Adventure in Imagination* by Mitsumasa Anno.
Copyright © 1974 by Fukuinkan-Shoten. By
permission of Thomas Y. Crowell, Publishers, Inc.)

Other ABC books include lessons in science, short stories, or
word and picture tours through the inner city. Some are matched to
adult as well as children's interests. *Anno's Alphabet* (1975), by
Japanese artist Mitsumasa Anno, is designed around paintings of
wooden letters realistic down to their splinters. Several of the letters
are optical illusions, and many show elaborate engineering. Anno's
"P," for instance, converts to "R" by unlatching part of the "P,"
sliding it out of the groove, and allowing it to drop down. The appeal
of this wizardry spans generations.

Anno's book is appropriate for all ages. Most ABC books are not. The choice—from a wide and expanding shelf—depends on the role the book is expected to play. Several roles are possible.

A Book of Pictures

Like other works in this chapter, some ABC books offer a rich, unpredictable assortment of illustrations. Preschool children need not focus on letters or text. Instead, the teacher can point to pictures and ask a group of children to identify objects. Questions stimulate discussion. "Have you ever seen this before?" "Where?" "How do you know what it is?"

The major criterion for selection is clarity in the illustrations. And most of the pictures should depict objects familiar to the children. Three-year-olds are more likely to respond to a drawing of a dog than a doubloon.

A Book of Letters

In a venerable tradition, the reader first encounters the letter, then associates it with a word representing a picture. A simple variation on this "A is for apple" approach reverses the order: the child first sees the letter in use, and then—moving from specific to the general, inductively—recognizes the letter by itself.

A first-grade teacher opens an ABC book at random, covers the letter, and then shows the picture to readers. "What's the first letter of the word for this?" the teacher asks. The children can say the answer, or write it. Then the letter is uncovered.

Which books work best? Again, the most successful provide clear and familiar illustrations, several for each letter. Look at a couple of examples.

Agatha's Alphabet (1975), by Lucy Floyd and Kathryn Lasky and illustrated by Dora Leder, presents upper- and lowercase letters. And there are several pictures with each letter. "P" for instance is associated with a prisoner guarded by a policeman. Penguins, a penny, a pig, and a princess approach the prison on a path.

A Is for Always (1968), by Joan Walsh Anglund, also offers upper and lower case letters. The alphabet is related to abstract ideas. "C" is for "courteous" and "E" for "efficient." The illustrations show children demonstrating the concepts. "Efficient" is the caption for a picture of a child dusting furniture.

Which book would you choose to foster letter recognition?

125

A Book That Tells a Story

All About Arthur (1974), is a tale of a lonely ape who travels around the country—and through the alphabet—looking for friends. He finds his share. For example: "In Kansas City he met a kind kangaroo named Kenneth who had just knocked over a kettle while kissing his kooky wife Kate."

Another storybook, *Apricot ABC* (1969) by Miska Miles, is a narrative about what happens when a golden apricot falls out of a tree. A bee finds it; from then on, the reader hardly notices the flow of other letters as a *c*hicken eats some of the apricot, scaring away a *f*rog, *g*rasshopper, and *h*ummingbird. By the end of the alphabet, the cycle is about to begin again. The fallen apricot is growing into a seedling.

How naturally does the story fit into the alphabetic structure? Are there sudden breaks in the continuity because of the difficulty of using all the letters in order? Is it a good story? Those are criteria for selection.

A Book That Develops a Theme

Several alphabet books for older children—age 7 to 10—explore a theme, using the alphabet as a simple organizing structure. *ABC Science Experiments* (1970), for instance, suggests an easy project for each letter.

"Try to write on waxed paper with a pencil," the book by Harry Milgrom suggests at the letter "P" for "pencil." "What happens?" Nothing. An explanation—"waxed paper is too smooth"—appears at the end of the book.

Adam's ABC (1971), written by Dale Fife and illustrated by Don Robertson, is a collection of a boy's adventures in a city. The youngster's joy over everyday life—his appreciation of an elephant carved from ebony, and his sister's afro haircut—lets a theme emerge naturally: there is a lot to celebrate about being black.

To older children and adults, the use of alphabetical structure is often a kind of signal. It means the book is trying to touch on many different facets of its subject. The alphabet helps Fife to say that there are dozens of different and sparkling facets to Adam's life; his experience of urban life runs from A to Z.

For other authors, the alphabet can be an albatross. The letters sometimes get in the way of the theme, or create hurdles to smooth reading. Anne Alexander's *ABC of Cars and Trucks* (1956) hits a pothole on the letter "Y", which stands, the author says, for "your car."

Counting books for beginners should have objects which are clearly delineated. (From *Numbers of Things* by Helen Oxenbury. Copyright © 1968 by Franklin Watts, Inc.)

COUNTING BOOKS

Counting books, too, can develop themes, tell stories, introduce numerals—the written symbols for numbers—or provide pictures for young children to discuss. The concepts conveyed by these books are not always as simple as 1, 2, 3.

Muriel Feelings's contribution to the field, *Moja Means One, Swahili Counting Book* (1971), teaches readers to count to ten in the African language. Supported by Tom Feelings's illustrations, it, like the Feelings's alphabet book, presents detailed African village scenes. Maurice Sendak's *One Was Johnny* (1962) tells the story of a boy who lives by himself. As he counts, he is joined by offensive

127

visitors including a rat, cat, dog, and robber. The crowd becomes burdensome. After ten, Johnny counts backward until he is once again alone, and pleased about his solitude. Young Johnny's control over his menagerie is satisfying to children just learning to control their lives; numbers are a natural backdrop for the story.

Counting books follow the format of ABC books, introducing the symbol and then showing with pictures and words what it refers to. But children may already know number concepts when they open these books. Children ordinarily begin exploring numbers by manipulating and counting real objects, such as by blowing out two birthday candles, or watching as a parent measures out four scratchy scoops of coffee.

Evaluating Counting Books

Even if children have some number concept, counting books can be confusing.

Compare *Count and See* (1972), by photographer Tana Hoban, with *Brian Wildsmiths's 1, 2, 3's* (1965) and with Eric Carle's *The Very Hungry Caterpillar* (1969). Hoban's book of photographs clearly shows the number of objects—birthday candles, eggs in a carton—and the background never intrudes. In artist Wildsmith's book, vividly colored geometric shapes combine to form a design for a picture somehow related to the number. At nine, for instance, an abstract owl is made of nine geometric shapes on a gray background. But a child without a strong sense of "nineness" will have trouble interpreting the owl. Its chest, one of the nine shapes, comprises dozens of little triangles. The unwritten and confusing rule: These chest triangles do not count.

In Carle's book, the caterpillar begins eating its way through one apple, then two pears, three plums, and so on. Holes in the pages through each fruit leave a kind of caterpillar trail. But young readers may lose the count, because the holes reveal yesterday's meal, and today's, and part of several upcoming feasts, all showing at once.

So Wildsmith's and Carle's books would be better used with children who have a good grasp of number concepts from one to twenty. The clarity of Hoban's book makes it useful for preschool readers.

Some clearly designed counting books are admirably complex as well; an example is Marc Brown's *One Two Three, An Animal Counting Book* (1976). Groups of animals clearly represent each number, but members of each group are extravagantly different. At seven, for instance, each of seven cats has a different coat, some with rows of fur like thatched roofs, some with whorls of fur like fingerprints. Some expressions are demented, some homely, some embarrassed. Numeral 7s flash in the eyes of several of the cats; one prissy feline has a collar with seven studs. Later in the book, seventeen snakes squirm across two pages. Twenty turtles on another page appear caught in a traffic jam. Numerals are repeated frequently on the animals' bodies, each time in a different spot.

Like all good concept books, Brown's intricate *One Two Three* challenges and then supports the reader. A whole zoo of mostly strange animals become as familiar as housecats, tamed and domesticated by concepts useful for a lifetime.

SUMMARY

Several specialized kinds of picture books were introduced in this chapter, including Mother Goose rhymes and alphabet, counting, and concept books.

1. *Mother Goose* verses were for the most part originally written for adults, with the exception of rhyming alphabets, lullabies, and verses accompanying children's games. Legend holds that the figure of Mother Goose was patterned after an American, Elizabeth Goose of Boston, but no scholar today takes the legend seriously. More probably the name Mother Goose comes from a translation of a seventeenth-century French book called *Contes de ma Mère L'Oye* (*Mother Goose Stories*), by Perrault; in the eighteenth century, Mother Goose became associated exclusively with children's rhymes.
2. Mother Goose rhymes have survived for several reasons. Their language is powerful and rhythmic. They are self-contained stories filled with action. Many can be used as the basis for games and group activities. Mother Goose rhymes remain interesting to older children, perhaps because the verses bring back pleasant memories of the times they were first heard at home.
3. These happy associations make the rhymes particularly valuable to teachers of young children. Mother Goose fits naturally into the curricula of preschool or first-grade teachers who want to lay a groundwork of appreciation for good language. And the content of the rhymes matches young children's interests, even when it strikes adults as violent.
4. While the poems themselves remain popular, not all collections are alike: the setting for the rhymes varies from book to book. There are several criteria to help evaluate collections. *Illustrations* should complement and enrich the text, whether they convey the literal meaning of the verse or extend and embellish it. *Format* is a critical concern in presenting Mother Goose to groups; many collections are

129

too small to be read aloud to more than a few children at a time. And adults should analyze *coverage and appropriateness* to ensure that the collections contain a fresh variety, possibly including some little known verses such as "I had a little husband . . . . "

5. Mother Goose rhymes are filled with dreamlike stories and mysterious images. By contrast, *concept books* explain the everyday world to children. In pictures and simple text, they suggest a general concept—such as the difference between "fast" and "slow"—and give specific examples—a rabbit leaps over a snail. Concept books call on children to see relationships: a hippopotamus is related to the concept of heaviness, for example. Understanding the relations can help children better understand their world. Many of the best concept books also help develop language skills. Two specific kinds of concept books, alphabet books and counting books, present the relationships between common symbols and their use in everyday expression.

6. *Alphabet books* introduce letters and show them in use. But many modern alphabet books do more, conveying the flavor of another culture, for example, or teaching some basic facts of science. Teachers can use such books to familiarize students with letters, but many titles also serve as storybooks, or as a source for a colorful variety of pictures. Several alphabet books for older children use the alphabet to develop a theme.

7. *Counting books* introduce children to numerals; they can also develop themes, tell stories, and provide pictures for discussion. Like alphabet books, some counting books are too complex to use with preschool children. Adults selecting titles for children should pay particular attention to how clearly pictures illustrate numbers.

RECOMMENDED MOTHER GOOSE BOOKS

Alderson, Brian. *Cakes and Custard,* illus. Helen Oxenbury (New York: Morrow, 1975).
   This book has both traditional and modern verses, and some versions slightly different from the standards. The illustrations are humorous, almost cartoons.

Briggs, Raymond. *The Mother Goose Treasury* (New York: Coward-McCann, 1966).
   This book includes more than 400 rhymes, each illustrated with one picture and some with several pictures.

Brooke, Leslie. *Ring O'Roses* (London: Warne, 1923).
   The illustrations depict the humor in many of the verses and impart an "English" flavor to this collection.

Chorao, Kay. *The Baby's Lap Book* (New York: Dutton, 1977).
The rhymes are cleverly placed in this collection, with one illustration showing both the three blind mice, and the mouse which had run up the clock. Jack Horner with his plum sits opposite Little Miss Muffet with her curds and whey.

Cooney, Barbara. *Mother Goose in French*, trans. Hugh Latham (New York: Crowell, 1964).
The rhymes are in French, with phrases translated into English at the back of the book. The illustrations reflect the charm of a small French town Cooney visited.

De Angeli, Marguerite. *The Book of Nursery and Mother Goose Rhymes* (Garden City, N.Y.: Doubleday, 1953).
A comprehensive collection of rhymes, this book is noteworthy for the full-page watercolor illustrations of some of the verses.

De Kay, Ormonde Jr. *Rimes de la Mère Oie*, illus. Push Pin Studios (Boston: Little, Brown, 1971).
These Mother Goose rhymes translated into French preserve the original rhyme scheme and meter. The illustrations vary from small silhouettes to double-page color pictures.

Galdone, Paul. *The History of Simple Simon* (New York: McGraw-Hill, 1966).
This is one of several Mother Goose rhymes illustrated in single editions by Galdone. His illustrations are clear and colorful, making the rhymes easy for young children to follow.

Jeffers, Susan. *Three Jovial Huntsmen, A Mother Goose Rhyme* Scarsdale, N.Y.: Bradbury, 1973).
The illustrations have many hidden animals, which children enjoy finding, as the huntsmen search unsuccessfully for their quarry.

Petersham, Maud and Miska Petersham. *The Rooster Crows* (New York: Macmillian, 1945).
Subtitled *A Book of American Rhymes and Jingles*, this book has many favorites of American children. The illustrations earned the Caldecott Award.

Reed, Phillip. *Mother Goose and Nursery Rhymes* (New York: Atheneum, 1963).
The rhymes have been illustrated with wood engravings, printed in six colors. Exceptional use of space makes the format outstanding. Some unfamiliar rhymes are included.

Rojankovsky, Feodor. *The Tall Book of Mother Goose* (New York: Harper, 1942).
A basic collection of Mother Goose rhymes, this book is enhanced by action-filled illustrations. The setting is rural America.

Tripp, Wallace. *Granfa' Grig Had a Pig and Other Rhymes Without Reason from Mother Goose* (Boston: Little, Brown, 1976).

Tripp's illustrations have a zany humor which will appeal to older children and adults. Many of the pictures tell a story in themselves, with characters speaking as if in a cartoon.

Watson, Clyde. *Father Fox's Pennyrhymes,* illus. Wendy Watson (New York: Crowell, 1971).

This collection of rhymes has a homespun charm with its Early American setting. A family of foxes, dressed as humans, illustrates each of the verses.

Wyndham, Robert. *Chinese Mother Goose Rhymes,* illus. Ed Young (Cleveland: World, 1968).

These are authentic Chinese rhymes and riddles, in Chinese and in English, selected by the author. The book is read vertically with Chinese calligraphy running lengthwise on the page.

RECOMMENDED ALPHABET BOOKS

Baskin, Leonard. *Hosie's Alphabet* (New York: Viking, 1972).

A single object is named for each letter. The adjectives used in the descriptions (a *primordial* protozoa) are too advanced for young readers in terms of meaning, but the sounds have appeal. Caldecott Honor Book for the illustrations.

Brown, Marcia. *All Butterflies* (New York: Scribner's, 1974).

Each page illustrates two letters in a simple picture or story, such as "all butterflies," or "cat dance." The woodcut illustrations give a feeling of motion.

Burningham, John. *John Burningham's ABC* (New York: Bobbs-Merrill, 1967). (1964)

The left page gives upper-and lower-case letters, and one word—D for dogs, K for king—and the right page illustrates the word. Letters and illustrations are extremely clear, making this a useful book for the very young child.

Deasy, Michael. *City ABC's,* photographs by Robert Perron (New York: Walker and Co., 1974).

This book is illustrated with photographs of a city. The text is necessary to know what is being depicted—the *manhole,* or the *rooftop,* or the *overpass,*—when all are shown in a single illustration.

Delaunay, Sonia. *Alphabet* (New York: Crowell, 1972).

The text is short poems and rhymes "chosen from classic and traditional literature of childhood." The rhymes are organized so that each begins with the appropriate letter; the illustrations show the letter in a design.

Eastman, P.D. *The Alphabet Book* (New York: Random House, 1974).

Two objectives are shown for each letter—"Lion with lamb," and "Penguins in parachutes," for instance. Simple, direct, and humorous illustrations, and consistency of letter sounds, make this a useful book for letter or sound recognition.

Eichenberg, Fritz. *Ape in a Cape: An Alphabet of Odd Animals* (New York: Harcourt, 1952).

A short rhyme illustrates each letter: a "bear in despair" trying to escape a swarm of bees, or a "vulture with culture" reading by candlelight. Caldecott Honor Book for the illustrations.

Emberley, Ed. *Ed Emberley's ABC* (Boston: Little, Brown, 1978).

In a series of four panels for each letter, Emberley shows how the letters are formed. In one set, a tiger and a turtle build a "T" out of tinker toys; in another, two dogs use a bulldozer to dig a huge "D" in the lawn. A few of the letters appear in the middle or at the end of the word rather than at the beginning.

Falls, C.B. *ABC Book* (Garden City, N.Y.: Doubleday, 1923).

A single object is shown for each letter. The woodcuts are clear and colorful.

Farber, Norma. *This Is the Ambulance Leaving the Zoo,* illus. Tomie de Paola (New York: Dutton, 1975).

This is an alphabetically told story, in which the *a*mbulance leaves the zoo, a *b*us stops to let it pass, *c*ars pile up, and so on until the patient, a *y*ak, leaves the *v*eterinarian's, which is just beyond the *u*nderpass.

Isaac, Joanne. *Tom Thumb's Alphabet* (New York: Putnam, 1970).

This book contains old English rhymes, some changed slightly from their original forms. The letters are clear; the verses are carefully illustrated with etchings.

Mendoza, George. *Norman Rockwell's Americana ABC* (New York: Harry N. Abrams, Inc., 1975).

The book begins with the statement, "Who am I? I am America, as deep and warm, great and tall, as Norman Rockwell painted me . . ." Each letter is then accompanied by a statement beginning "I am" and illustrated with a full-page reproduction of one of Rockwell's paintings.

Munari, Bruno. *Bruno Munari's ABC* (Cleveland: World, 1960). Two or three examples are given for each letter, each a common object and easily recognizable by young children.

Oxenbury, Helen. *ABC of Things* (New York: Watts, 1971).

The book gives each letter and two or three words which begin with it. Many of the illustrations are humorous, such as an eagle

133

sitting on an elephant's trunk, angrily saying something to his bewidlered host.

Peter Piper's Alphabet, illus. Marcia Brown (New York: Scribner's 1959).

Each letter is illustrated with a tongue-twister, following the pattern of "Peter Piper picked a peck of pickled peppers." This text was first published in London in 1813.

RECOMMENDED CONCEPT BOOKS

Anacona, George. *I Feel* (New York: Dutton, 1977).

Photographs show children expressing a variety of emotions. Readers could use the full-page black-and-white pictures to make up their own stories about why the subjects feel the way they do.

Binzen, William. *Year After Year* (New York: Coward, 1976).

Color photography of seasonal changes, and two scenes shot in each season, make this a useful book for discussing the concept with young children. The poetry adds dimension to the book and gives it appeal for older children as well.

Bunting, Eve. *Winter's Coming,* illus. Howard Knotts (New York: Harcourt, 1977).

This book shows the preparations for winter made by each member of the family.

Carle, Eric. *The Grouchy Ladybug* (New York: Crowell, 1977).

This book presents size comparisons, and time sequence as the grouchy ladybug challenges animal after animal to a fight, but demures when each accepts with the excuse that none is large enough.

Corey, Dorothy. *You Go Away* (Chicago: Albert Whitman & Co., 1976).

This book for the very youngest gives a series of examples of people in the family "going away" and "coming back," from going away to do the laundry to going on a trip.

Emberley, Ed. *The Wing on a Flea: A Book About Shapes* (Boston: Little,Brown, 1961).

The reader is encouraged to look for circles, triangles, and rectangles in everyday objects.

Green, Mary McBurney. *Is It Hard?* illus. Lucienne Bloch (Reading, Young Scott, 1960).

Four children discover that what is easy for one of them is hard for another.

Hoban, Tana. *Big Ones Little Ones* (New York: Greenwillow, 1976). Photographs show adult and young animals.

Pairs of animals present the concepts of young and old, adult and child, and big and small. Wordless.

Klein, Leonore. *How Old Is Old?* (New York: Harvey House, 1967). Animals are "old" at different ages; whether a person is "old" depends upon who is making the judgment.

Lapp, Eleanor J. *The Mice Came In Early This Year*, illus. by David Cunningham (New York: Whitman, 1976).
Text describes seasonal changes as winter nears. Watercolor illustrations.

Lasker, Joe. *Lentil Soup* (Chicago: Albert Whitman & Co., 1977).
Days of the week are presented, as well as ordinal numbers, as Meg tries each day to cook lentil soup for Matt so that it will be as good as his mother's was. Success comes only when she leaves the kitchen in anger and the soup overcooks.

Reiss, John J. *Shapes* (Scarsdale, N.Y.: Bradbury, 1974).
Basic shapes appear in two and three dimensions. The book closes with examples of more complex shapes such as octagons and hexagons.

Schlein, Miriam. *Fast Is Not a Lady Bug*, illus. Leonard Kessler (New York: W.R. Scott, 1953).
This book presents the idea that speed is relative.

Ruben, Patricia. *True or False?* (Philadelphia: Lippincott, 1978).
For each photograph in the book there is a true/false question. Some relate to concepts of size, number, or shape. Others require some use of logic.

Tresselt, Alvin. *How Far is Far?* illus. Ward Brackett (New York: Parents Magazine Press, 1964).
Descriptive language is used to give responses to questions such as "how high is up?" and "how deep is down?"

RECOMMENDED COUNTING BOOKS

Anno, Mitsumasa. *Anno's Counting Book* (New York: Crowell, 1977).
This counting book begins with zero, shown by an empty landscape. Each number is then illustrated by the appropriate amount of houses, trees, children, adults, birds, and other objects filling the landscape.

Baum, Arline, and Joseph Baum. *One Bright Monday Morning* (New York: Random House, 1962).
The story tells what was seen each morning "while on my way to school," each time increasing the number of blades of grass and so on, until the realization that "It's SPRING."

Carle, Eric. *My Very First Book of Numbers* (New York: Crowell, 1974).

The pages in this book are cut in half, like Dutch doors. The reader tries to match the numeral displayed in the top half with the appropriate number of objects displayed in the bottom half.

Gretz, Susanna. *Teddy Bears 1 to 10* (Chicago: Follett, 1969).

The numbers one through ten are shown by teddy bears engaged in various activities. The illustrations are clear, appropriate for three- or four-year-olds.

Hoban, Russel. *Ten What? A Mystery Counting Book,* illus. Sylvie Selig (New York: Scribner's, 1974).

Beginning with "one urgent message," two secret agents start the search. Finally "ten were delivered," lollipops, that is. Each illustration shows a variety of objects, always the number for that page.

Holl, Adelaide. *Let's Count,* illus. Lucinda McQueen (Reading, Mass.: Addison-Wesley, 1976).

The text, in verse, describes from one to ten animals and then reverses the order, going from ten to one. The animals are all doing something, from sliding in the snow to drinking lemonade.

Krüss, James. *Three by Three,* illus. Johanna Rubin (New York: Macmillan, 1972). (Copyright 1963 by Annette Betz Verlag, Munchen)

When three roosters crow, the three hunters begin the hunt. At the end of the day, the three hunters go home with their three dogs, but without the three foxes.

Mack, Stan. *10 Bears in My Bed* (New York: Pantheon, 1974).

A little boy enters his bedroom to find ten bears in his bed. Each time he commands "roll over," one bear leaves, riding a toy. When the bed is empty, he climbs in, taking his teddy bear with him, and still dreaming of bears riding his toys.

Maestro, Betsy, and Giulio Maestro. *Harriet Goes to the Circus* (New York: Crown, 1977).

This book presents ordinal numbers as an elephant named Harriet gets up early to be first in line for the circus. As other animals line up behind her, they are labeled second, third, and so on, until a door to the right of the last in line is opened, and the order is reversed.

Maestro, Giulio. *One More and One Less* (New York: Crown, 1974).

"This is One," the opening page reports, over a prominent numeral "1" across from a picture of a single chicken. "One and one more is Two. 1+1=2," the book continues, and one more is added for each page. The group grows to ten and then, one by one, leaves.

Mendoza, George. *The Marcel Marceau Counting Book,* photographs by Milton H. Greene (Garden City, N.Y.: Doubleday, 1971).

Marceau is photographed pantomiming an occupation connected with a particular hat he is wearing. As he finishes with each hat, it is added to the collection, illustrating numbers one through twenty.

Oxenbury, Helen. *Numbers of Things* (New York: Watts, 1968).
The numeral, the word, and the name of the object are given on the left page, with an illustration on the right page. The number of objects is clear. Variety in design adds interest.

Peppe, Rodney. *Circus Numbers* (New York: Delacorte Press, 1969).
Upon entering the big top, one sees one ringmaster, two horses, and circus illustrations for the numbers up to ten. The book concludes with "How many people?" showing a page of faces.

Sugita, Yutaka. *One to Eleven* (London: Evans Brothers Ltd., 1971).
The wordless book shows only the numeral and the objects illustrating it. One character appears in all the illustrations. Clear and bright.

Wahl, John and Stacey. *I Can Count the Petals of a Flower* (Reston, Va.: National Council of Teachers of Mathematics, 1976).
Close-up color photographs illustrate each number by showing a flower with that number of petals. The last page, titled "Count carefully for a surprise," shows pairs of the same species with differing numbers of petals.

BIBLIOGRAPHY

Adult References

Baring-Gould, William S., and Ceil Baring-Gould, *The Annotated Mother Goose* (New York: Bramhall House, 1962).

Bettelheim, Bruno. *The Uses of Enchantment* (New York: Knopf, 1976).

Bodger, Joan. "Mother Goose. Is the Old Girl Relevant?" *Wilson Library Bulletin*, December 1969, pp. 402–408.

Chisholm, Margaret. "Mother Goose—Elucidated." *Elementary English*, December 1972, pp. 1141–1144.

Hall, Mary Anne, and Jane Matango. "Children's Literature: A Source for Concept Enrichment," *Elementary English*, April 1975, pp. 487–494.

Haviland, Virginia. *Children and Literature, Views and Reviews* (Glenview, Ill.:Scott Foresman, 1973).

Lanes, Selma G. *Down the Rabbit Hole* (New York: Atheneum, 1971).

Nadasan, Ardell. "Mother Goose Sexist?" *Elementary English*, March 1974, pp. 375–378.

Opie, Iona, and Peter Opie, *The Oxford Dictionary of Nursery Rhymes* (Oxford: Clarendon Press, 1973).

Smith, James A., and Dorothy M. Park. *Word Music and Word Magic: Children's Literature Methods* (Boston: Allyn and Bacon, 1977).

Thomas, Della. "Count Down on the 1-2-3's," *School Library Journal*, Mar. 15, 1971, pp. 95–102.

Children's Book References

Mother Goose Books

Addams, Charles. *The Charles Addams Mother Goose* (New York: Windmill Books, 1967).

Caldecott, Randolph. *Picture Book No. 2* (London: Warne).

Disney, Walt. *Walt Disney's Mother Goose,* illus. Walt Disney Studio (Racine, Wis.: Western, 1976). (14th printing)

Greenaway, Kate. *Mother Goose or the Old Nursery Rhymes* (London: Warne).

Merriam, Eve. *The Inner City Mother Goose,* illus. Lawrence Rutzkin (New York: Simon and Schuster, 1969).

Sendak, Maurice. *Hector Protector and As I Went over the Water* (New York: Harper, 1965).

Wildsmith, Brian. *Brian Wildsmith's Mother Goose* (New York: Watts, 1964).

Wright, Blanche Fisher. *The Real Mother Goose* (Chicago: Rand McNally, 1965). (1916)

Concept Books

Auerbach, Majorie. *A Day of Autumn* (New York: Knopf, 1967).

Brown, Margaret Wise. *The Indoor Noisy Book,* illus. Leonard Weisgard (New York: Harper, 1939).

Hoban, Tana. *Over, Under and Through* (New York: Macmillan, 1973).

Schlein, Miriam. *Heavy Is a Hippopotamus,* illus. Leonard Kessler (New York: W. R. Scott, 1954).

Sesame Street Book of Shapes (Boston: Little, Brown, 1970).

Spier, Peter. *Crash! Bang! Boom!* (Garden City, N.Y.: Doubleday, 1972).

————. *Fast-Slow, High-Low: A Book of Opposites* (Garden City, N.Y.: Doubleday, 1972).

ABC Books

Alexander, Anne. *ABC of Cars and Trucks,* illus. Ninon (Garden City, N.Y.: Doubleday, 1956). (Copyright 1954, Child Life.)

Anglund, Joan Walsh. *A Is for Always* (New York: Harcourt, 1968).

Anno, Mitsumasa. *Anno's Alphabet* (New York: Crowell, 1975).

Carle, Eric. *All about Arthur* (New York: Watts, 1974).

Feelings, Muriel. *Jambo Means Hello. Swahili Alphabet Book,* illus. Tom Feelings (New York: Dial, 1974).

Fife, Dale. *Adam's ABC,* illus. Don Robertson (New York: Coward-McCann, 1971).

Floyd, Lucy, and Kathryn Lasky. *Agatha's Alphabet,* illus. Dora Leder (Chicago: Rand McNally, 1975).

Miles, Miska. *Apricot ABC,* illus. Peter Parnall (Boston: Little, Brown, 1969).

Milgram, Harry. *ABC Science Experiments,* illus. Donald Crews (New York: Crowell, 1970).

Counting Books

Brown, Marc. *One Two Three, An Animal Counting Book* (Boston: Little, Brown, 1976).

Carle, Eric. *The Very Hungry Caterpillar* (New York: World, 1969).

Feelings, Muriel. *Moja Means One, Swahili Counting Book,* illus. Tom Feelings (New York: Dial, 1971).

Hoban, Tana. *Count and See* (New York: Macmillan, 1972).

Sendak, Maurice. *One Was Johnny, A Counting Book* (New York: Harper, 1962).

Wildsmith, Brian. *Brian Wildsmith's 1, 2, 3's* (New York: Watts, 1965).

CHAPTER
4

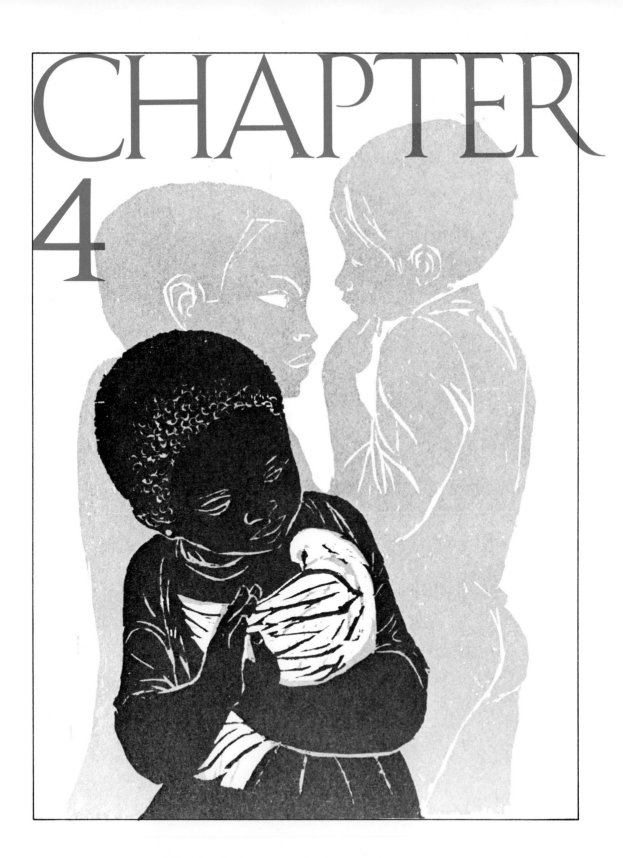

POETRY

BRINGING POEMS FOR CHILDREN TO LIFE

Poet William Jay Smith was writing in the living room of his Greenwich Village apartment when his 4-year-old son interrupted like a one-man marching band.

Young David Smith strode up and down the room in time to the dumpity-dum rhythm of something he had just composed: "A Jack in the box/Fell in the coffee/And Hurt himself."

That night, tossing in a four-poster bed "that made me feel like a child again myself," Smith augmented his son's idea into a full poem:

A Jack-in-the-box
On the pantry shelf
Fell in the coffee
and hurt himself.
Nobody looked
To see what had happened:
There by the steaming
Hot urn he lay;
So they picked him up
With the silverware,
And carried him off
On the breakfast tray.

David loved the complete poem when his father read it to him the next day. And Smith immediately set off on a quest to draw more poetry out of his son.

"For the next few weeks I listened to my son and watched his every movement," he wrote later. "There was no line, no bone structure, no shadow that I did not wish to explore. I wanted to give him the delight that he had given me, and in such a way that he would not realize he was being given anything." In a few weeks, Smith had finished a whole collection of poems. Filled with hope, he read them out loud to a friend who was an art critic.

The reading was a disaster. "He listened and gazed at me as if I had gone stark raving mad," Smith wrote. "The leaps and connections that seemed perfectly natural to a four-year-old were ones that he had forgotten ever having been made; the relationships and situations which struck the four-year-old as funny he found either embarrassing or strange." Children, on the other hand, enjoyed the poems published under the title *Laughing Time* (1955). Many wrote the author to say that David's poems, shaped by his father, had made them laugh out loud (in Haviland and Smith, 1969, pp. vi–vii).

Poetry is a natural language for young children. Some of the first words babies respond to are impromtu, poemlike phrases, soft parental sounds made in steady rhythm, precursors of Mother Goose verses (see Chapter 3). Poetry remains a natural language when children start speaking. Ask a 2-year-old boy named Jamie to say a poem and he will dictate:

Poem poem poem poem
Poemy poem . . .

In the early years of grade school, children can produce creditable poetic images without effort. One little girl in an elevator asked Flora Arnstein, a poetry teacher, "What shelf do we get off at?" And her grandson once told her he could not look long at the sun because it made his "eyes all out of breath" (1970, p. 16).

But then something happens. Children begin to lose their delight in poetry. By the time they are adults, many people—perhaps Smith's critic friend was one—recall only the pain of having to memorize dull poetry. Poems, often merely sermons in rhyme or overly precious stories of irrelevant elves, remain crammed in their minds like furniture in an attic.

"How natural and harmonious it all is at the beginning," Smith writes. "And yet what happens along the way later to make poetry to many children the dullest and the least enjoyable of literary expressions? It is usually along about the fifth grade in our schools that children decide poetry is not for them" (1969, p. v).

The problem is not a lack of good poetry. In the small children's library in the village of Bronxville, New York, for instance, there are roughly 200 volumes of poetry, many of them new. But they are dusty. "Occasionally a parent takes out a book for a child," the children's librarian reports. "Most of the books are shelf sitters." In a survey of children's poetry preferences, Ann Terry, a children's literature specialist at the University of Houston, writes that nationally there is an "abundance" of poetry for children.

"Never before in the history of literature have such a quantity and variety of poems been published especially for children's enjoyment," she reports (1974, p. 1). But children do not get a taste of the new abundance. A doctoral study by Chow Loy Tom (1969) showed that teachers presented "Paul Revere's Ride" to their students more often than any other poem. "Paul Revere's Ride," a bouncy story about the American patriot, was written in 1861. And most of the forty-one poems most frequently read to students by teachers were written prior to 1928.

One conclusion of the Terry study: teachers trying to foster children's interest in poetry may actually be driving them away.

Poetry is made of lively materials. Young children find poetry exhilarating. But older children often find it deadly. Why? This chapter explores the reasons, and suggests ways to keep poetry alive all through the school years.

THE LIVELY MATERIALS OF POETRY

Here is a poem by an inventive and popular children's poet, Eve Merriam. Try reading it aloud.

Cheers

The frogs and the serpents each had a football team,
And I heard their cheer leaders in my dream:
"Bilgewater, bilgewater," called the frog,
"Bilgewater, bilgewater,
Sis, boom, bog!
Roll 'em off the log,
Slog 'em in the sog,
Swamp 'em, swamp 'em,
Muck mire quash!"

"Sisyphus, Sisyphus," hissed the snake,
"Sibilant, syllabub,
Syllable-loo-ba-lay.
Scylla and Charybdis,
Sumac, asphodel,
How do you spell Success?
With an S-S-S!" (1966)

If you said it in prose, "Cheers" would come out something like this: "There were two football teams in a dream, one of frogs and one of snakes. They each had cheers for their teams, one based on Greek mythology (for example, referring to Sisyphus, the cruel king of Corinth condemned for eternity to roll a stone up a hill in Hades only to have it roll down again when he neared the top) and the other based on swamps."

The poem makes much more sense. Part of the reason for its

Body movement enhances the sound and rhythm of language. (Arthur Sirdofsky/Editorial Photocolor Archives.)

power is Merriam's use of several strong poetic materials: *hard-working words, powerful sounds,* and *compelling rhythms.*

Hard-Working Words

Words in good poetry often juggle meanings and feelings several at a time. What does "Bilgewater" say to you, for instance? It *denotes*—identifies, labels—water in the bottom of a boat. But it means much more than that. For instance, it *connotes*—suggests or implies—"Nonsense!" and also "Phooey!" The several messages in the word make it an extraordinarily good cheer for a frog.

Poets plumb words for extra meaning and emotions, for what poet John Ciardi calls *personality.* "Billingsgate, riparian, pismire, omnium-gatherum, rasp, bang, bodacious, lazy-susan, crepuscular —every word releases its own aura of feeling," Ciardi writes (1959, p. 764).

Such hard-working words, carefully chosen, give poetry a powerful density of expression. There is no fat or bone; as Eve Merriam says in "How to Eat a Poem" (1966), there is nothing to throw away.

145

Powerful Sounds

Merriam's "Cheers" begins with a *couplet*, two successive lines ending in rhyming words; the rhyme scheme then varies throughout the poem. Rhymes help bind the poem together and make it pleasant to say.

There are other powerful sounds. A series of *b*'s breaks up the first few lines of the frog chant, like little croaks. This repetition of a consonant is called *alliteration*. Merriam also repeats a vowel sound, the short *i* in "Sisyphus," in the first four lines of the snake cheer; this vowel repetition is called *assonance*. Some of the words carry extra power because they sound like what they mean. "Slog," for instance, means "to strike with a heavy blow." Use of the word is an example of *onomatopoeia* (pronounced "on-aw-mat-ah-PEE-ah"); words such as "buzz," "cuckoo," "crack," and "plink" are also onomatopoeic.

Compelling Rhythms

After the first slightly irregular couplet, the cheering animals come on with locomotive rhythms, driven home by alliteration. In other poems, rhythms can suggest the light steps of dancing, the slow cadence of a funeral march, or the irregular start-and-stop antics of a baseball player caught between bases during an attempted steal. In "Cheers," the rhythm is foot-stomping and heavy, like the steady waves of noise from a crowd of football fans.

Poets often call on two other lively materials, *imagery* and *figurative language*.

Imagery

In a collection of children's poems called *Hailstones and Halibut Bones* (1961), Mary O'Neill translates colors into sensory experiences, desribing how they look, feel, smell, sound, and taste. Here is "What is Brown?"

> Brown is the color of a country road
> Back of a turtle
> Back of a toad.
> Brown is cinnamon
> And morning toast
> And the good smell of
> The Sunday roast.
> Brown is the color of work

146

And the sound of a river,
Brown is bronze and a bow
And a quiver.
Brown is the house
On the edge of town
Where wind is tearing
The shingles down.
Brown is a freckle
Brown is a mole
Brown is the earth
When you dig a hole.
Brown is the hair
On many a head
Brown is chocolate
And gingerbread.
Brown is a feeling
You get inside
When wondering makes
Your mind grow wide.
Brown is a leather shoe
And a good glove—
Brown is as comfortable
As love.

Readers can see brown, smell it, feel it fitting on their hands; these sensory descriptions are called *imagery*.

Figurative Language: Unexpected Comparisons

Here is how poet Gerald Raftery sees city residences, in "Apartment House":

A filing-cabinet of human lives
Where people swarm like bees in tunneled hives,
Each to his own cell in the towered comb,
Identical and cramped—we call it home. (in Larrick, 1968)

Home is a filing cabinet of lives: that surprising, direct comparison is called a *metaphor*. People swarm to it *like* bees: that indirect comparison, bridged by the word "like," is called a *simile*. Both kinds of comparisons are called *figurative language*.

Poetry may take many different forms, some strangely shaped, some curt, some disciplined, some relaxed. But the materials available to the poet remain the same no matter what the form: hard-working words, powerful sounds, compelling rhythms, imagery, and

147

figurative language. A writer begins with these materials and then works, as James Stephens writes in his poem "I am Writer," to "make it sing,/And make it new . . ." (1938).

WHAT IS POETRY?

What does the poet make? Competent poets themselves cannot agree. They compliment poetry, or talk about what it is not, and sometimes make poems about it, but offer widely differing definitions of it.

Myra Cohn Livingston, an outstanding children's poet, once wrote that poetry "is not a something to be rationalized or explained; it is not an abstract principle; it is not part of an All-About book which arms with facts; it is not a piece of logic with which to startle others or to alter the course of scientific knowledge" (1964, p. 355). Those are some of the things poetry is not, to her.

Patrick J. Groff, an educator, says in similar style that poetry "is not the kind of writing that appears in newspapers and popular media or the kind of writing that is found in classroom textbooks" (1966, p. 458). Robert Frost, the great American poet, also defined poetry, playfully, in negative terms. Poetry, said Frost, is what got lost in the translation.

But what *is* poetry? Myra Livingston says, romantically, that it is "not the rose with a name, a color. . . . It is the scent" (1964, p. 360). (She echoes another romantic definition first published in 1926 by poet Eleanor Farjeon: "What is poetry? Who knows?/Not a rose, but the scent of the rose. . . .") Groff tries to arrive at a nuts-and-bolts definition: "Poetry for children is writing that (in addition to using, in most cases, the mechanics of poetry) transcends the literal meaning of expository writing" (1966, p. 458). Flora J. Arnstein writes that all poetry is "the presentation in words of experience either actual or imagined." She adds: "Of course it goes without saying that poetry is something more than that as well . . ." (1970, p. 2).

If any of these definitions seem foggy to you, you are in the company of poets and poetry critics. Groff himself, before gamely offering up his own definition, notes ironically that writers on children's literature keep on publishing new definitions of poetry all the time,

The use of sensory descriptions is central to the concept of poetry. Mary O'Neill explores the sights, smells, and moods associated with various colors. (From *Hailstones and Halibut Bones* by Mary O'Neill, illustrated by Leonard Weisgard. Illustrations Copyright © 1961 by Leonard Weisgard. Reproduced by permission of Doubleday & Company, Inc.)

149

OYSTERS

Oysters
are creatures
without
any features.

Humorous verse is popular with children and provides
a starting point for the sharing of poetry. (Reprinted
with permission of Macmillan Publishing Co., Inc.
from *Zoo Doings and Other Poems* by Jack
Prelutsky, illustrated by José Aruego. Illustrations
copyright © 1970 by Macmillan Publishing Co., Inc.)

"and often each new response appears more grand and splendiferous
than the last" (1966, p. 456).

Carl Sandburg (1878-1967), the respected American poet and
biographer, offered good perspective on the struggle to say what

poetry is. In *Early Moon* (1930), in a section called "Short Talk on Poetry," Sandburg wrote:

> When Walt Whitman says, "The poet is the answerer," we are interested. If we could know just what he means by "the answerer" we would know what he means by "the poet." One poet says poetry must be "cold, lonely and distant," not knowing that some readers of poetry are glad to have books which are warm, friendly and so near that they almost breathe with life.
>
> Another poet has said poetry is "emotion remembered in tranquility." What does that mean? It is anybody's guess what that means. To know exactly what it means we would have to know exactly what is emotion, what is tranquility, and what we do when we remember. Otherwise it is an escape from words into words, "passing the buck," or winding like a weasel through language that ends about where it begins. "He came out of the same hole he went in at." (1958 ed., p. 17)

Dancing around the holes, we can at least try to extract a common element from these descriptions of poetry: Poetry is dense and powerful language, made with care from lively materials. But this is not a definition (because it also applies to good prose).

Poetry takes many forms. A young reader's perception may be that all lines of poetry are smooth on the left and bumpy on the right. But many kinds of poetry do not follow that form; and some lines that *do* are not poetry, such as "Roses are red" greeting card rhymes and hair-spray jingles.

The best of such poemlike writing is sometimes called *verse*, rhymes with steady rhythm but lacking the power of real poetry. Some verse does have enough force to delight both young children and adults with a taste for whimsy. Such verse is often called *nonsense* verse, and many nonsense verses appear in a collection illustrated by Wallace Tripp, called *A Great Big Ugly Man Came Up and Tied His Horse to Me* (1973). Here is the title verse, author unkown:

A I was standing in the street,
As quiet as could be,
A great big ugly man came up
And tied his horse to me.

In Tripp's cover drawing, the horse appears concerned about being tied up to a badger. And the badger, wearing a red coat with gold buttons, looks alarmed but stoical. The situation is carried to a logical conclusion inside the book when the horse walks away, with dignity, carrying the badger in a bundle under his chin.

151

Tripp's spirited animals complement the rhymes. A raccoon in a stocking cap stops a doctor in a snow-covered field and announces:

I do not love thee, Doctor Fell,
The reason why I cannot tell;
But this alone I know full well,
I do not love thee, Doctor Fell.

Perhaps the reason is that the doctor is wearing a coon-skin cap.

Some of Tripp's humor has nothing to do with verses or children; a bottle of wine in one scene is labeled "Chateau de Former Self." A painting in a dining room scene titled "Pride Goeth Before a Fall" shows a pride of lions walking past a waterfall. Young children will not understand puns like these; adults may groan. The verses may not be poetry, but a first-grader's reaction at the end of the book is likely to be "Again."

One of the most difficult forms of nonsense verse to compose is the limerick, five lines of carefully organized silliness. The name comes from a line of old verse that goes "Will you come up to Limerick?" which, oddly, would not fit into the rhythm of a genuine limerick. In classical form, the first, second, and fifth lines of a limerick rhyme; the third and fourth have a separate rhyme and rhythm of their own. The acknowledged master of the form was Edward Lear (1812-1888), a writer who often embellished his verse with funny drawings. A typical piece of nonsense from Lear:

There was an Old Man with a beard,
Who said, "It is just as I feared!–
Two owls and a Hen,
Four larks and a Wren,
Have all built their nests in my beard."

Most forms of serious poetry fall into one of two categories: *narrative* or *lyric*.

Narrative poetry tells a story, like this one by Eloise Greenfield.

Harriet Tubman

Harriet Tubman didn't take no stuff
Wasn't scared of nothing neither
Didn't come in this world to be no slave
And wasn't going to stay one either

"Farewell!" she sang to her friends one night
She was mighty sad to leave 'em

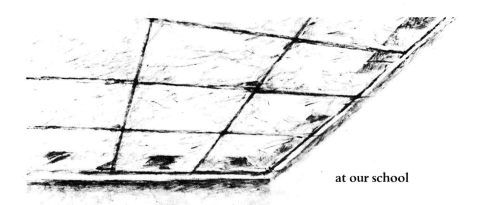

at our school

the skylights have big holes
through their glass panes
there is glass all over
all the floors

it is a day for wearing shoes
even on the mats

Adoff describes his family's experiences in living
through a tornado in this narrative poem. (Illustration
excerpted from the book *Tornado!* illustrated by
Ronald Himler. Copyright © 1977 by Ronald Himler.
Reprinted by permission of Delacorte Press)

But she ran away that dark, hot night
Ran looking for her freedom

She ran to the woods and she ran through the woods
With the slave catchers right behind her
And she kept on going till she got to the North
Where those mean men couldn't find her

Nineteen times she went back South
To get three hundred others

153

She ran for her freedom nineteen times
To save Black sisters and brothers
Harriet Tubman didn't take no stuff
Wasn't scared of nothing neither
Didn't come in this world to be no slave
And didn't stay one either

   And didn't stay one either (1978)

Lyric poetry describes something—an object, scene, personal feeling—in lines with a singing quality; you can imagine them set to music. The word "lyric" comes from the Greek word, *lura*, a stringed instument: the ancient Greeks often strummed a lyre as a poet read, mingling voice with music. Here is a famous children's lyrical poem, called "The Swing," by the Scottish poet Robert Louis Stevenson (1850-1894).

   How do you like to go up in a swing,
   Up in the air so blue?
   Oh, I do think it the pleasantest thing
   Ever a child can do!

   Up in the air and over the wall,
   Till I can see so wide,
   Rivers and trees and cattle and all
   Over the countryside.

   Till I look down on the garden green,
   Down on the roof so brown—
   Up in the air I go flying again,
   Up in the air and down!

Most of the forms of poetry which follow are narrative or lyric.

Ballad
A long narrative poem, a ballad usually relates a single incident, spinning out the story at a leisurely pace, sometimes with dialogue

This narrative poem, "Who Look at Me?", by June Jordan is illustrated with paintings by various artists. (Charles H. Alston. *Family*. (1955). Oil on canvas. 48¼ × 35¾ inches. Collection of Whitney Museum of American Art. Artists and Student Assistance. Fund.)

between characters. Repeated refrains or choruses sometimes stretch out the action. Usually the narrative advances in four-line stanzas, blocks of poetry, such as this one, the beginning of the traditional English ballad "Robin Hood and Allan-a-Dale":

Come listen to me, you gallants so free,
All you that love mirth for to hear,
And I will tell of a bold outlaw
That lived in Nottinghamshire.

In twenty-seven stanzas, Robin Hood rescues Allan-a-Dale's true love, who has been kidnapped by a king. The lovers are married by Little John,

And thus having ended this merry wedding,
The bride lookt as fresh as a queen,
And so they return'd to the merry green-wood,
Amongst the leaves so green.

No one knows who wrote this poem or others like it. The author of a *literary ballad*, on the other hand, is known. *The Ballad of the Burglar of Babylon* (1968), for example, is a poem by Elizabeth Bishop about a contemporary man who chooses to die rather than spend his life in jail. Here are the opening stanzas:

Micuçú was a burglar and killer,
    An enemy of society.
He had escaped three times
    From the worst penitentiary.

They don't know how many he murdered
    (Though they say he never raped),
And he wounded two policemen
    This last time he escaped.

They said, "He'll go to his auntie,
    Who raised him like a son.
She has a little drink shop
    On the hill of Babylon."

He did go straight to his auntie,
    And he drank a final beer.
He told her, "The soldiers are coming,
    And I've got to disappear.

There are now many collections of modern Haiku available. (From *Come Along!* by Rebecca Caudill. Illustrated by Ellen Raskin. Copyright © 1969 by Rebecca Caudill. Copyright © 1969 by Ellen Raskin. Reproduced by permission of Holt, Rinehart and Winston, Publishers.)

"Ninety years they gave me.
   Who wants to live that long?
I'll settle for ninety hours,
   On the hill of Babylon.

"Don't tell anyone you saw me.
   I'll run as long as I can.
You were good to me, and I love you,
   But I'm a doomed man."

Haiku

It is pronounced "HIGH-coo"; the Japanese name for the poem comes from ancient Chinese words meaning, literally, "amusement sentence." Haiku are unrhymed lyric poems with three lines and a total of seventeen syllables: five in the first line, seven in the second, and five in the third. They usually refer to a moment in nature

157

or a sudden insight; often they connect two things in nature, in this example the grasshopper and the dew:

> Grasshopper,
> Do not trample to pieces
> The pearls of bright dew.

These lines were written by Issa, well-known haiku poet who was born in central Japan in 1762. (The syllable count is off because of the problem of translation.) Americans have written haiku, too; here is one by Rebecca Caudill:

> Forsythia blooms,
> And little winds of springtime
> Ring the golden bells. (1969)

Free Verse

In contrast to Haiku, free verse has no formal governing rules, no required rhythm, no rhyme, no prescribed length of line. The form is not new.

"We have heard much in our time about free verse being modern," Carl Sandburg wrote, "as though it is a new-found style for men to use in speaking and writing, rising out of the machine age, skyscrapers, high speed and jazz" (1958, p. 24). But, as Sandburg points out, free verse is older than alphabets. Much of the Bible and many of the poems of American Indians are free verse.

Venerable as it is, it can adapt to tell a contemporary story, like this children's poem by Nikki Giovanni:

parents never understand

well i can't 'cause
yesterday when mommy had
this important visitor she said
run along joey and let mommy talk
and i ran along upstairs to see
bobby and eddie and we were playing
and i forgot and i had to come down
stairs and get dry clothes and mommy said how
could an eight year old boy wet his pants
and i looked at the visitor and smiled a really nice
smile and said i guess in america anything

can happen
so mommy said i have to
stay in today (1971)

Concrete Poetry

Concrete poetry uses the shapes of words or lines to make a poem, so that the work illustrates itself. Some concrete poetry is built out of more conventional forms, like John Updike's "Mirror":

When you look	kool uoy nehW
into a mirror	rorrim a otni
it is not	ton si ti
yourself you see,	,ees uoy flesruoy
but a kind	dnik a tub
of apish error	rorre hsipa fo
posed in fearful	lufraef ni desop
symmetry.	.yrtemmys (1957)

Sometimes a concrete poem is made of a few key words, like Froman's "On the Beach" (reproduced on the next page).

And sometimes the poem is simply a collection of letters or other symbols.

Other Forms

Other forms are as disciplined as the steps of formal ballet, with names that sound as fluid and spicy as poetry: villanelle, tercet and quatrain, clerihew and cinquain. Tercet is three rhymed lines; quatrains have four lines. A villanelle has nineteen lines comprising five tercets and a final quatrain governed by rules about what lines are repeated. Clerihews are humorous quatrains, usually about a person identified in the first line. And a cinquain (pronounced sing-CANE) is a five-line stanza like this one, written to teach what the form is, from David McCord:

This is
The form of the
Cinquain. The five lines have
2,4,6,8,2 syllables
As here. (1970)

Those are just a few of poetry's forms.

WAVE
WAVE WAVE
WAVE WAVE WAVE

FOAM FOAM FOAM

SAND SAND SAND SAND SAND SAND SAND SAND SAND SAND SA
SAND SAND SAND SAND SAND SANDS NDSAND SAND SAND SAND SAND SAND SANDSAND
SAND SAND SAND SAND SANDSANDS NDSAND SAND S AND SANDSANDSAND
SAND SAND SAND SAND SAND SAND SANDS SAND SAND SAND SANDSANDSAND
SAND SAND SAND SANDS NS AND SAND SAND SANDSANDSANDS
SAND SANDSA NS SAND SAND SAND DSANDSAND SANDS AND SANDSANDS
SAND SANDSA CLAM NDSANDSAND SAND SANDSAND SAND SAND SAND SANDS AND SANDSANDSA
NDSAND SAN SHELL SANDSANDSAND SAND SAN D SAND SANDS AND SANDSANDSA
SANDSAND SANDSANDSAND NDSA PEBBLES SAND SAND SANDSANDS
NDSAND SAND SANDSANDSANDS NDSA S NDSANDSAND SANDSAND SAN
NDSANDSANDSANDSAND STARFISH NDSAND SAND SAND SANDSANDSAND SANDSAND SAND
DSANDSANDSANDSA STAR FISH SANDS AND SANDSANDSAND SANDSANDSAND SAND
ANDSANDSANDSAND SANDSAND SANDSANDSANDSANDSANDSAND SANDSAND SANDSANDS
DSANDSANDSAND SANDS ANDSANDSANDSANDSANDSAND SANDSANDSANDSAN
ND AND N SANDSANDSANDSSANDANDSANDSANDSANDSANDS N
NO AND N N S D N N A N D
D D N D S D D D

HARD
GREY
ROCK

CLAM
SHELL

POETRY AS A NATURAL LANGUAGE

Young children do not need to know the forms before they appropriate poemlike speech as a natural language. Kornei Chukovsky, a leading Russian children's poet and linguistic scholar, wrote that children as young as 3 begin to pair off words, learning the meaning of one and then trying to match it with another: "Yesterday it was raw outside," someone says. A child asks: "And today—is it cooked?" (1925; 1971 edition, p. 61).

· As part of the pairing of words, children take delight in discovering rhymes. A mother asks where the broom is and her son answers: "Over there, on the stair," and then begins to chant: "Over there, on the stair; over there, on the stair . . ." (p. 62). The rhyming is fun; it also makes it easier to speak. A 2-year-old may stumble with "Good night," but have no trouble with "night night." "Mother" is hard to say; "Mama" is easy.

"In the beginning of our childhood we are all 'versifiers,'" Chukovsky writes. "It is only later that we begin to learn to speak in prose" (p. 64).

Almost all preschool children create words and rhymes to match movements in skipping, jumping, or repetitious work. In the first few grades, Chukovsky says, children's self-made poetry becomes slightly more literary. A 6-year-old named Ania wrote these lines after watching a woman spank a little boy:

My mama is clever
She spanks me never.
Hey, mommie, mommie,

Always love, love me—
I now love you double,
And will give you no trouble. (pp. 69–70)

No one told Ania to write two tercets, but that is very nearly what she did to convey some powerful feelings, including unspoken fear.

WHY CHILDREN GET BORED WITH POETRY

Poetry filled Ania's need to say something. Older children do not lose the need. During the early years of elementary school, children are hungry to read good poetry, expressing what they are not yet able to say themselves. So why do children lose interest in poetry?

The problem is not unique to the United States. Chukovsky complains that many Russian school children are taught "hackneyed lines, absurd rhythms, cheap rhymes." Poetic talent withers in classrooms where "corrections" made in students' verses are "almost invariably worse than the original version" (p. 73).

Overly dissected poetry dies in the classroom. Poorly chosen poetry never has a chance to live. The two major reasons children lose interest are teachers who analyze too ambitiously and teachers who choose too lazily.

Overanalysis

Children in grade school are sometimes in the position of the little brown bat in Randall Jarrell's *The Bat Poet* (1963). In the story by the late American poet, the bat awakens during the day to hear the song of the mockingbird. The song impresses him, and he decides to write some poems of his own.

But none of the other bats appreciates the poetry. Finally the mockingbird consents to listen and the bat recites:

> A shadow is floating through the moonlight.
> Its wings don't make a sound.
> Its claws are long, its beak is bright.
> Its eyes try all the corners of the night.
>
> It calls and calls: all the air swells and heaves
> And washes up and down like water.
> The ear that listens to the owl believes
> In death. The bat beneath the eaves,
>
> The mouse beside the stone are still as death—
> The owl's air washes them like water.
> The owl goes back and forth inside the night,
> And the night holds its breath. (p. 12)

What does the mockingbird think?

> "Why, I like it," said the mockingbird. "Technically it's quite accomplished. The way you change the rhyme-scheme's particularly effective."
>
> The bat said: "It is?"
>
> "Oh yes," said the mockingbird. "And it was clever of you to have that last line two feet short."
>
> The bat said blankly: "Two feet short?"
>
> "It's two feet short," said the mockingbird a little impatiently. "The next-to-the-last line's iambic pentameter, and the last line's iambic trimeter."

ISSUE

ARE CHILD POETS
TOO YOUNG TO PUBLISH?

The poems in this anthology were selected with the help of dozens of persons across the country. Their faith in young people is evidenced by cartons of literary magazines and unpublished manuscripts which they gathered from young poets and urged them to submit on their own. . . . The youngest contributor was in the fourth grade when he wrote his poem for this book; the oldest was eighteen and still in high school.

   Many of these poems first appeared in school newspapers and literary magazines—a few of them slick publications with full-color illustrations, others crudely dittoed in bleary lavender ink. Some of the most striking poems have come from out-of-school writers' workshops and the underground student press where innovation and protest flourish. (pp. viii-x)

Larrick, Nancy. *I Heard a Scream in the Street* (New York: Dell, 1970).

Among my files are hundreds of mimeographed booklets from schools and libraries, newsletters, vanity press pamphlets, magazines, and trade books containing the so-called poetry of children. Most of it is shoddy, presented with pride by conscientious teachers, librarians, parents, anthologists or editors who, unfortunately, know little of the tools, the voice, or the craft of poetry. We do our children a striking disservice when we accept for publication this work in the name of poetry. I am far from suggesting that we should not encourage young people to write, to learn, to develop, or to discover something of the feelings and thoughts which lie at the heart of the creative experience. But many years of teaching have convinced me that making this learning process an end in itself does ultimate harm to the child's growth. At an age when children should be striving to improve by profiting from error, their work is accepted as complete, finished, perfect. (p. 571)

Livingston, Myra Cohn. "But Is It Poetry?"
The Horn Book, December 1975, pp. 571-580.

What reasons can you give which would support the publication of poems by children? Which ones would militate against it? In the 1960s and 1970s, there has been an increase in the publication of children's work. Why do you suppose this is so?

The bat looked so bewildered that the mockingbird said in a kind voice: "An iambic foot has one weak syllable and one strong syllable; the weak one comes first. That last line of yours has six syllables and the one before it has ten: when you shorten the last line like that it gets the effect of the night holding its breath."

"I didn't know that," the bat said. "I just made it like holding your breath."

"To be sure, to be sure!" said the mockingbird. "I enjoyed your poem very much. When you've made up some more do come round and say me another."

The bat said that he would, and fluttered home to his rafter. Partly he felt very good—the mockingbird had liked his poem—and partly he felt just terrible. He thought: "Why, I might as well have said it to the bats. What do I care how many feet it has? The owl nearly kills me, and he says he likes the rhyme-scheme!" (pp. 14–15)

Teachers can easily become classroom mockingbirds. Even praise can cripple a child's poem if it is coupled with condescending analysis.

The drive to dissect is built on a misconception: that the bat began with a prose message about the danger of owls and decided to give it a high-tone setting, or that Ania wanted to be as cute as a greeting card in telling her mother she would be a good girl. Under this misconception, poetry is dressing: add layers of rhyme and rhythm to make a poem, cap with alliteration, and make sure there are enough syllables to button down the message. The poet does not mean to show too much of the body of meaning under the poem. The challenge under this misconception is to find out what the poem really means at some deeper level, to penetrate the cloak.

But the bat wanted only to sing, and Ania chose the best language she knew to communicate how she felt. Paraphrasing the poems, or parsing lines apart, discourages the bat and will bore the child.

Similarly, aggressive analysis can cut the life from a poem. The classroom questions that weaken a child's interest in poetry are often well meaning. "What is the bat really trying to say?" (Acceptable answer: "It's a story about how owls hunt animals and the animals are scared.") "Can you name two animals the owl is trying to catch?" (Acceptable answer: "Bat and mouse.") "What's the shadow, really?" ("It's really the owl.") In a few awful minutes, the child is equipped to cross out the poem and replace it with right answers.

But what if the child does not understand the poem? Perhaps a few brief definitions of unfamiliar words will help, but if not, there may be another major reason for reader boredom: poor selection.

Poor Selection

In the opinion of Agnes Repplier, a nineteenth-century writer, selection of poetry for children is simple. In an Atlantic magazine article in 1892, she asserted that children love mysterious "shadowy" lines such as

When the long dun wolds are ribb'd with snow,
And loud the Norland Whirlwinds blow,
  Oriana,
 Alone I wander to and fro,
  Oriana.

She wonders "who shall forget" such lines "that rang through our little hearts like the shrill sobbing of winter storms, of that strange tragedy that oppressed us more with fear than pity!"

Lots of grade-school children today would find those lines easily forgotten. And they would just as soon forget many of the newer poems presented to them for study and, sometimes, memorization.

But some adult "experts" won't let them forget. Agnes Repplier's deadly certainty about children's preferences is not unusual. Adults in every generation have been certain about children's taste in poetry. Seventeenth-century Puritan primers taught neat moral lessons in rhyme ("In Adam's fall/We sinned all"). Modern teachers, librarians, and specialists in children's literature choose poems for children with absolute assurance that they know children's needs and interests.

Much of the time, the adults have been wrong. At least half a dozen surveys within the past half century have compared children's real poetry interests with those of teachers and others who claimed to know what children liked. In every survey, the poetry tastes of teachers differed widely from those of children. One of these studies, by Ann Terry at the University of Houston, concludes that today's elementary school teachers seldom read or share poetry with their students, but, when they do, the poems "are frequently inappropriate selections for stimulating lasting interest. Teachers' choices rarely reflect students' prior experience with poetry or their current level of enjoyment" (1974, p. 58).

Poems whose language is too old or obscure for children remain unpopular with young readers from age to age. ("When the long dun wolds are ribb'd with snow" would appear to be a likely reject.) Poems that preach small sermons appear on "least liked" lists; yet children over the years have been subjected to uplifting—and condescending—verses.

Take It Easy

Pushing is for shopping carts.
Pushing is for swings,
Baby buggies, mowers, doors,
And many other things.

Pushing in the line at school
And in the busline, too,
Or in the cafeteria
Is NOT the thing to do.

So be polite and DO NOT PUSH,
Or prod or poke or squeeze,
Or use your bony shoulders
Or your knobby little knees.

Every generation seems to produce some "poetry"
designed to teach a lesson. (From *School Is Not a
Missle Range* by Norah Smardige. Illustrated by Ron
Martin. Copyright © 1977 by Abingdon. Used by
permission.)

Here is modern example, from a children's book with good intentions, *Free to Be You and Me* (Ms. Foundation, 1974). The poem is
called "Housework," by Sheldon Harnick, and it exhorts children to
disregard TV commercials in which housewives look gloriously

happy while scrubbing or mopping the floor. The final verse commands:

> Children,
> when you have a house of your own
> make sure, when there's housework to do,
> that you don't have to do it alone.
> Little boys, little girls,
> when you're big husbands and wives,
> if you want all the days of your lives
> to seem sunny as summer weather
> make sure, when there's housework to do,
> that you do it together.

The last four lines sound suspiciously like a TV commercial.

Children themselves may be the last to complain about poorly chosen writing. Poet William Jay Smith remembers dutifully copying out boring verse line by line in a notebook when he was in the fifth grade. Years later, after digging up the book, he realized what a chore the poetry had been for him as a boy. At certain points in one doggedly sentimental verse, "my pen seemed to falter, scratch and blur; the banality of the language was clearly too much for me" (1969, p. vi).

Edwin Muir (1887-1959), a famous Scottish poet and critic, said he recognized moral lessons and comforting endings as false when he was a boy, "and though professing an outward respect, was inwardly bored. I suppose I felt, without knowing it, that childhood was regarded by grown-ups as an artificial state for which this artificial verse had to be fabricated. The magic which had delighted me in the old songs and ballads sung in our house was not to be found in these improving poems" (in Hamilton, 1973, p. 270).

Children can learn to explore many forms of poetry, but teachers leading the expedition have to begin with a small step: listen to the poems and verses the child feels at home with, and savor the magic there before moving on.

WHERE TO BEGIN: CHILDREN'S PREFERENCES

The Ann Terry study focuses on the critical intermediate years—the fourth, fifth, and sixth grades—years when poetry interest often declines. During the survey, teachers presented tapes of 113 selected poems read by a radio announcer. The teachers asked children to evaluate each poem, using a five-point grading system ranging from "great" to "hated." Snoopy, the dog from Charles Schulz's "Peanuts" comic strip, illustrated the children's report form: dancing for joy (to represent "It's great!"), and slumped in dejection (for "I hate it!").

Children listened to ten to twelve poems a day for two weeks, hearing each poem twice; at the end of each session, they wrote comments on the last poem. Terry also surveyed teachers' preferences and asked about poetry use in the classroom.

Terry analyzed the returns to find the twenty-five most popular poems and the twenty-five most unpopular. She also investigated content, other poetic elements, poetic form, and age to try to discover whether there were general characteristics children liked or disliked. Here is some of what she found.

Most Popular, Least Popular

Of the 113 poems and verses, "Mummy Slept Late and Daddy Fixed Breakfast," by poet and critic John Ciardi, was most popular. When you read it, see if you can guess why it went over with young readers.

Mummy Slept Late and Daddy Fixed Breakfast

Daddy fixed the breakfast.
He made us each a waffle.
It looked like gravel pudding.
It tasted something awful.

"Ha, ha," he said, "I'll try again.
This time I'll get it right."
But what I got was in between
Bituminous and anthracite.

"A little too well done? Oh well,
I'll have to start all over."
That time what landed on my plate
Looked like a manhole cover.

I tried to cut it with a fork:
The fork gave off a spark.
I tried a knife and twisted it
Into a question mark.

I tried it with a hack-saw.
I tried it with a torch.
It didn't even make a dent.
It didn't even scorch.

The next time Dad gets breakfast
When Mommy's sleeping late,
I think I'll skip the waffles.
I'd sooner eat the plate! (1962)

Least popular was William Carlos Williams's "The Red Wheel-barrow" (often cited by critics as a successful adult poem).

so much depends
upon

a red wheel
barrow

glazed with rain
water

beside the white
chickens (1938)

What factors might explain why children disliked this poem?

How Do Children Choose?

Terry investigated whether a poem's content, age, poetic elements, and form had any bearing on children's preferences. She found that they all did.

Content Terry divided the poetry in the study into nine categories of content, including humor, familiar experience, people, animals, nature, fantasy, historical events, adventure, and social commentary.

Students showed a strong preference for humorous poetry and verse; limericks were high on the list, and so was Karla Kuskin's "Hughbert and the Glue."

Hughbert had a jar of glue.
From Hugh the glue could not be parted,
At least could not be parted far,
For Hugh was glued to Hughbert's jar.
But that is where it all had started.
The glue upon the shoe of Hugh
Attached him to the floor.
The glue on Hughbert's gluey hand
Was fastened to the door.

169

Cried a man on the Salisbury Plain,
"Don't disturb me—I'm counting the rain;
   Should you cause me to stop
   I might miss half-a-drop
And would have to start over again."

Limericks were high on the list of poetry preferences
of intermediate grade children in a study by Ann
Terry. (Illustrations copyright © 1978 by Joseph Low.
From *A Lollygag of Limericks* by Myra Cohn
Livingston. Used by permission of Atheneum
Publishers.)

While two of Hughbert's relatives
Were glued against each other.
His mother, I believe, was one.
The other was his brother.
The dog and cat stood quite nearby.
They could not move from there.
The bird was glued securely
Into Hughbert's mother's hair.

Hughbert's father hurried home
And loudly said to Hugh:
"From now on I would rather
That you did not play with glue." (1964)

Likes and dislikes were also influenced by familiar experience. Sometimes young listeners disliked a poem because they felt uncomfortable with its subject. One girl, for instance, did not enjoy a poem about basketball because, she said, "I can't make a basket when I play" (p. 25). And a boy disliked a poem about daffodils because he was allergic to flowers.

Some poems based on familiar experiences, however, seemed to be universal favorites, such as "Questions" by Marci Ridlon.

> What did you do?
> Where did you go?
> Why weren't you back
> An hour ago?
> How come your shirt's
> Ripped on the sleeve?
> Why are you wet?
> When did you leave?
>
> What scratched your face?
> When did you eat?
> Where are your socks?
> Look at your feet!
>
> How did you get
> Paint in your hair?
> Where have you been?
> Don't kick the chair!
>
> Say something now,
> I'll give you til ten.
> . . . .
> "See if I ever
> Come home again." (1969)

Students also seemed to like poems about animals, for instance, Irene Rutherford McLeod's "Lone Dog."

> I'm a lean dog, a keen dog, a wild dog, and lone;
> I'm a rough dog, a tough dog, hunting on my own;
> I'm a bad dog, a mad dog, teasing silly sheep;
> I love to sit and bay the moon, to keep fat souls from sleep.
>
> I'll never be a lap dog, licking dirty feet,
> A sleek dog, a meek dog, cringing for my meat,
> Not for me the fireside, the well-filled plate,
> But shut door, and sharp stone, and cuff, and kick, and hate.

171

Not for me the other dogs, running by my side,
Some have run a short while, but none of them would bide.
O mine is still the lone trail, the hard trail, the best,
Wide wind, and wild stars, and hunger of the quest! (1915)

Age Contemporary poems—written within the last fifteen or
twenty years—seemed to be favored over older classics. Children in
all three grades, but especially in grade six, seemed to like the contemporary quality of Paul Dehn's "Little Miss Muffet."

    Little Miss Muffet
    Crouched on a tuffet,
Collecting her shell shocked wits.
    There dropped (from a glider)
    An H-bomb beside her
Which frightened Miss Muffet to bits. (1958)

Another favorite was "We Real Cool" by Gwendolyn Brooks.

        The Pool Players
    Seven at the Golden Shovel
    We real cool. We
    Left school. We

    Lurk late. We
    Strike straight. We

    Sing sin. We
    Thin gin. We

    Jazz June. We
    Die soon. (1971)

Poetic Elements Terry's analysis indicates that young readers especially liked rhythm and rhyme. Rhyme was the major attraction of
"We Real Cool" for one fourth grader who said, "I like it because it
rhymes and it's real cool" (p. 20). Many other students liked the
rhythm in David McCord's "The Pickety Fence."

The pickety fence
The pickety fence
Give it a lick it's
The pickety fence
Give it a lick it's

Poet David McCord shares some of his poetry with an interested audience. (Photograph by Charles Carey. From *The Boston Globe,* November 29, 1977.)

A clickety fence
Give it a lick it's
A lickety fence
Give it a lick
Give it a lick
Give it a lick
With a rickety stick
Pickety
Pickety
Pickety
Pick (1925)

Powerful sounds combined with humorous content contributed to students' enjoyment of Laura E. Richards' "Eletelephony."

Once there was an elephant,
Who tried to use the telephant—
No! No! I mean an elephone
Who tried to use the telephone—
(Dear me! I am not certain quite
That even now I've got it right.)

173

Howe'er it was, he got his trunk
Entangled in the telephunk;
The more he tried to get it free,
The louder buzzed the telephee—
(I fear I'd better drop the song
Of elephop and telephong!) (1955)

Poems relying on figurative language and imagery—Williams'
"The Red Wheelbarrow," for instance—were unpopular. Its use of
sight imagery fell flat with children and, as a second strike, it did not
rhyme. Terry theorized that the poem was too sophisticated for
elementary school students.

Form The third and lethal strike against "Wheelbarrow" was probably its form; intermediate-grade children tended not to enjoy free
verse. Students also generally panned haiku. One target was a poem
by Buson.

What happiness
Crossing this summer river,
Sandals in hand! (in Lewis, 1964)

Why the dislike? "I hate it because its too short," one fifth grader
wrote. Sixth graders commented: "It did not have any poem in
it. . . . I like the words but the way they sound is awful. . . . It doesn't
make any sense at all. . . . Too short and I don't understand it. . . . I
liked this last one because it was about summer, but I still hate
haiku" (p. 19).

Is There Poetry in the Classroom?

One stunning discovery in the Terry data was that most teachers
seldom read poetry in their classes. Only one teacher in forty-two
who responded read poems every day; thirty-four out of the forty-
two presented poems approximately once a month or less. This
means the vast majority of children participated in classroom poetry
sessions less than nine times a year.

The preferences Terry discovered grew out of sparse exposure to
poetry, at least in the classroom. On the basis of meager experience,
fourth-, fifth-, and sixth-graders liked amusing, contemporary narratives with strong rhythm and rhyme.

The Terry findings may be a starting point for teachers trying to
keep poetry alive in the years when students tend to turn away. But
where do teachers go from there? How can they broaden children's

interests in poetry, and nurture the interest all through the school years?

HOW TO CONTINUE:
FOSTERING A TASTE FOR OTHER FLAVORS

It cannot be done in nine sessions a year. A once-a-month visit to a dark corner in the curriculum, where the old poems lie crumbling, puts poetry in the same category as housecleaning.

A child's interest grows when appropriate poetry becomes a delightful part of day-to-day life of the classroom. There are several practical ways to encourage enjoyment of poetry. Teachers can begin by enjoying it themselves.

Build a Private Poetry Collection

Poetry will never fit naturally in the classroom unless teachers feel comfortable with poems. That probably requires a little pleasant work: browsing through anthologies such as *Time for Poetry* [May Hill Arbuthnot and Sheldon Root, (eds), 1968], keeping a notebook of stray poems, and exploring several different poets' collections.

The best introduction for a poem is a good reading by a teacher who likes it. Teachers are better equipped to maintain the rhythm of a poem than a child whose reading falters at unfamiliar words. Avoid overly dramatic readings which can befog the meaning. At first it may be helpful to tape readings after school. Then listen from behind a student's desk. (Chapter 11 contains other suggestions for presenting poetry.)

Make Appropriate Selections

A teacher's favorite poems, however, may not be adequate fare for students. It depends in part on their experience.

Poems do not come coded for age levels; it is up to the teacher to judge where and when a poem fits. "To say that there are 'first-grade' or 'fifth-grade' poems is unfair to children and poetry," writes Leland B. Jacobs, a widely respected authority on children's literature. "Rather, the teacher selects poetry, whether it is primarily written for children or adults, which meets the children's minds and spirits . . ." (in Cohen, 1972, p. 33).

Selection, as the Terry study shows, can be tricky.

Is the audience at home with threshers and balers and life in a barnyard? Then Judith Thurman's "Zebra" may seem foreign:

white sun
black
fire escape,

morning
grazing like a zebra
outside my window. (1976)

Match Poems to What Is Happening

Some childhood experiences are as common in Red Oaks, Iowa, as in New York City. And there are poems to match each experience— sudden loneliness, fright at the first clap of thunder, even dismay at a runny nose. Teachers may want to memorize some of this topical poetry so it comes up naturally in the classroom.

A startling thunderstorm could provide the cue to give second-graders a page from Aileen Fisher's "I Like Weather" (1963):

Weather is full
of the nicest sounds:
it sings
and rustles
and pings
and pounds
and hums
and tinkles
and strums
and twangs
and whishes
and sprinkles
and splishes
and bangs
and mumbles
and grumbles
and rumbles
and flashes
and CRASHES.

A gentler rain might provide the occasion to try Lilian Moore's "Rain Rivers":

It's raining.
Street streams and rain rivers
are flowing,
and little twig boats
are towing
leaf barges. (1967)

Spring is showery,

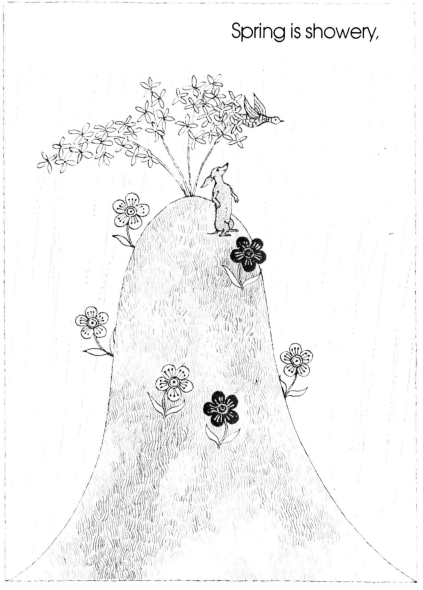

This poem, appropriate for preschool and primary
children, is fully illustrated in picture book format.
("Spring is Showery" from *Spring Is.* Copyright ©
1976 by Janine Domanska. By permission of
Greenwillow Books, a division of William Morrow &
Company Inc.)

177

More certain than downpours outside are runny noses inside. Dorothy Aldis's verse, "My Nose," is a concise complaint.

My Nose
It doesn't breathe,
It doesn't smell,
It doesn't feel
So very well.

I am discouraged
With my nose.
The only thing it
Does is blows. (1928)

Other poems express sadness at change: a friend moves away or becomes a stranger, a favorite teacher is transferred, a sister grows up. Poems are no panacea for a child's bewilderment at such change. They are not "useful words to live by." They can express feelings powerfully at times when a child may find it hard to talk or listen. Here, for instance, is Langston Hughes's deceptively simple "Poem":

I loved my friend
He went away from me
There's nothing more to say.
The poem ends,
Soft as it began—
I loved my friend. (1932)

And Richard J. Margolis knew how a lot of children feel when he wrote in "Only the Moon and Me":

When I am crying
I don't want to be tickled. (1969)

Of course, many poems celebrate change, such as this one, called "A Year Later," by Mary Ann Hoberman:

Last summer I couldn't swim at all
I couldn't even float!
I had to use a rubber tube
Or hang on to a boat;
I had to sit on shore
While everybody swam.
But now it's this summer
And I can! (1959)

178

ISSUE

CAN AN ESKIMO PICTURE ILLUSTRATE A NAVAHO SONG?

While each poem has an accompanying attribution, no mention is made of the pictured objects, their tribal or geographic source, except in the awkwardly arranged credits at the back of the book . . . an Eskimo picture illustrates a Navaho song, a Mojave doll from Arizona illustrates an Eskimo song. . . . There is no need to misspell Leonard W. Doob as Doop, or Ruth Stephan as Stephen. . . . Poets should not assume a license to be careless. This does a disservice to the scientists who bothered to learn languages and listen to chants.

Behn, Harry, In *The New York Times*, writing of the book *Out of the Earth I Sing: Poetry and Songs of Primitive Peoples of the World*, Richard Lewis (ed.) (New York: Norton, 1968).

The appearance on the same page of a poem and photograph not representing the same culture can hardly be considered a fault, since they harmonize so beautifully in subject matter and text. (p. 188)

Marx, Marion. *The Horn Book*,
April 1968, pp. 187–188.

Look at the book in question, *Out of the Earth I Sing*. What is the effect of combining art and poetry in this book? Should both be from the same culture? Why or why not? What is the editor's responsibility for giving accurate credits?

Introduce Families of Poems

After frequent exposure to poetry, children will begin to find patterns. They can see, for instance, how Eve Merriam, in writing "Toaster Time," used some of the same basic materials as Patricia Hubbell in writing "Our Washing Machine."

Our Washing Machine

Our washing machine went whisity whirr
Whisity whisity whisity whirr
One day at noon it went whisity click
Whisity whisity whisity click
Click grr click grr click grr click
   Call the repairman
   Fix it . . . Quick! (1963)

Toaster Time

Tick tick tick tick tick tick tick
Toast up a sandwich quick quick
   quick
Hamwich
Or jamwich
Lick lick lick

Tick tick tick tick tick tick—
   Stop!
POP! (1966)

These two poems are part of the same family, built on aural imagery, heavy with alliteration. Teachers can introduce many other kinds of families: two poems with the same subject, or two limericks on different subjects. What is alike about the poems? What is different? How did one poet feel about the subject compared with the other? What other noises should Merriam and Hubbell write poems about? Questions like those about several poems at once can bring children closer to lively poetry in many different forms, and help them develop poetic discrimination.

Let Children Choose

The teacher may introduce new poetry, but students should have access as well to a shelf of poetry books so they can seek out poems on their own or reread poems already presented. One way to encourage use of a "poetry corner" is to read aloud from illustrated poetry collections without showing listeners the illustrations. Let the audience form its own images. But make the book available so that later, in private exploration of the same book, children can discover how someone else's imagination played on the same poem.

Encourage a Response

Whenever possible, the response should be physical: swaying, clapping, dancing, or calling out a chorus such as this one from the book *Four Fur Feet* (1961), by Margaret Wise Brown:

> Oh, he walked around the world
> on his four fur feet
> his four fur feet
> his four fur feet
> And he walked around the world
> on his four fur feet
> and never made a sound—O.

It takes little encouragement for young children to join the refrain, even years before they can read it. Older children scouting collections of poetry may want to pass on what they have found to others. One way is to let students scrawl poems they like in letters big or small on newsprint covering a bulletin board. Older students may also enjoy writing their own poetry or memorizing poems they like. But neither activity should be forced, or interest will flag.

One Farmington, Michigan, high school girl named Mary Long, for instance, apparently found it chilling to have to produce "Poetry under Pressure":

> Six poems due tomorrow—
> Three written.
> A poem
> written on demand
> is difficult to do
> and can hardly
> be aesthetically satisfying.
> After all—
> when three ounces of pop
> fill a six-ounce glass
> you know it's mostly ice. (1974)

There is no good reason to require children to memorize poems once a teacher has brought good poetry out of its cultural closet and set it free in the classroom. Students in such a classroom still have to *learn* poems, as John Ciardi says:

> Poetry has only a remote place in the gross of our culture. As has, for example, the opera. Therefore, Americans generally need to be taught in school how to experience both poetry and the opera. In Milan, on the

Children can participate in the reading of a poem by
joining in on the refrain, as is possible in this book.
(From *Four Fur Feet* by Margaret Wise Brown,
illustrated by Remy Charlip. Illustrations Copyright ©
1961 by Remy Charlip. Reproduced by permission of
Young Scott Books, a Division of Addison-Wesley
Publishing Co.)

other hand, no one need go to school in order to learn how to experience an opera: the Milanese do not study opera, they *inhale* it. And in Chile, people on the streets of Santiago take poetry in the same way, as an essential part of the world they move in. A Milanese and a Chilean would have to go to school to learn, for example, how to watch a football game in an experienceable way. Certainly few people in the United States need to go to that school: in Green Bay it is football that is inhaled as a living thing, and opera and poetry that have to be learned. (1975, p. 2)

But learning poems is not the same thing as memorizing poems. Ciardi continues about what the ideal response to poetry should be:

If the reader cared enough for poetry, he would have no need to study it. He would live into it. As the Milanese citizen becomes an encyclopedia of opera information, as the Chilean knows his country's poets, as even retarded boys in the United States are capable of reciting endlessly detailed football stories, so those who are passionate for any given thing become alive to it by natural process. (Ibid.)

Does anyone tell baseball fans they have to remember batting averages? No, the numbers just refuse to go away. They haunt like the notes of a persistent melody. So it is with a well-made, well-chosen poem: it is hard to forget.

SUMMARY

1 Children have a natural affinity for poetry when they are young—delighting in Mother Goose, for instance—but frequently they lose interest after the first few years of school.

2 The problem is not a lack of good poems for children. *Eve Merriam's* poem, "Cheers," is one of many that successfully combine several elements traditionally found in poetry.

Hardworking words Words in poetry *denote*—identify or label—subjects, but they also *connote*—suggest or imply—many different meanings.

Powerful sounds "Cheers" gains power from the use of *alliteration*, the repetition of the same consonant sound; *assonance*, the repetition of the same vowel sound; and *onomatopoeia*, the use of words that sound like what they mean.

Compelling rhythms The rhythm of "Cheers" matches the subject; in certain lines it sounds like the foot-stomping rhythm of a stadium crowd.

Other poems make use of *imagery*—vivid descriptions based on sense impressions—and *figurative language*—interesting and sometimes surprising comparisons.

3 Poetry for children ranges from amusing *verse* and *limericks* to more substantial forms, including *narratives*—which tell a story—and *lyric* poems—which describe something in lines with a singing quality. There are *ballads*, long narratives usually about a single incident, and *haiku*, three-line lyrics with a total of seventeen syllables. And there are as many other different kinds of poetry as there are steps in ballet.

4 Despite the variety of poems, and the powerful language in the best poems, children often lose interest. In many instances, teachers choose poems without considering children's needs or interests, and frequently adults analyze poetry too ambitiously, knocking the life out of the writing.

5 What can be done to maintain interest in poetry? To begin with, teachers can study children's preferences in poetry, and present material children are likely to enjoy. One study by children's literature specialist *Ann Terry* indicates that children like amusing, contemporary narrative poems with strong rhythm and rhyme. They generally dislike haiku, and poems relying heavily on figurative language and imagery.

6 Having built a program based on popular poems, teachers can go on to broaden children's interests. Students are most likely to be caught up in new material if the teacher enjoys poetry and if the subject is appropriate to the children's interests and experiences. Enjoyment is also enhanced when teachers encourage a response. Clapping, swaying, dancing, calling out a chorus—these activities heighten interest in younger children. Older children may enjoy writing poetry on their own. But writing poems under the pressure of a classroom assignment, or memorizing poetry, can discourage children from delighting in good poetry all through their school years.

BIBLIOGRAPHY

Recommended Poetry Books

Adams, Adrienne (comp. and illustrator). *Poetry of Earth* (New York: Scribner's, 1972).
   This is a collection of thirty-three poems, each about the earth and/or its creatures, complemented by illustrations in tan, umber, blue-gray, and pale russet.

Adoff, Arnold. *My Black Me; A Beginning Book on Black Poetry* (New York: Dutton, 1974).
   This anthology of poems by black poets includes poems of protest and poems of pride.

Baron, Virginia Olsen. *The Seasons of Time,* illus. Yasuhide Kobashi (New York: Dial, 1968).
This collection of ancient Japanese Tanka poetry, illustrated with brush-and-ink drawings, is divided into sections for Spring, Summer, Autumn, Winter, and This World.

Behn, Harry. *Cricket Songs,* illus. pictures "from Sesshu and other Japanese masters." (New York: Harcourt, 1964).
Introduces a variety of poets who write haiku.

Belting, Natalia Maree. *Whirlwind Is a Ghost Dancing,* illus. Leo Dillon and Diane Dillon (New York: Dutton, 1974).
These poems of North American Indians are primarily related to myths of creation and explanations of nature, and are rich in figurative language and imagery. Illustrations combine Indian motifs with the artists' own interpretations.

Bierhorst, John (ed.). *In the Trail of the Wind* (New York: Farrar, 1971).
Poems and ritual orations of Indians of North and South America are grouped under headings such as "The Beginning," and "The Words of War." Notes about each of the selections are supplied.

Clifton, Lucille. *Everett Anderson's Year,* illus. Ann Grifalconi (New York: Holt, 1974).
One of several books about Everett Anderson, this offers a poem for each month, recounting special events in 7-year-old Everett's life, and his reactions to them.

De Gastold, Carmen Bernos, trans. Rumer Godden. *Prayers From the Ark,* illus. Jean Primrose (London: Macmillan, 1967). (1963, in English)
Each animal on the ark offers its special prayer to God. There is a gentle humor in the characterizations of the animals' thoughts and wishes.

Doob, Leonard W. (ed.). *A Crocodile Has Me by the Leg,* illus. Solomon Irein Wangboje (New York: Walker and Co., 1966).
Woodcut illustrations by a Nigerian artist, in black and red, give added flavor to this collection of traditional poetry from Africa.

Dunning, Steven, Edward Lueders, and Hugh Smith (eds.). *Reflections on a Gift of Watermelon Pickle . . .* (New York: Lothrop, Lee & Shepard, 1967).
The modern poems in this collection range from the serious to the lighthearted, and present a variety of forms.

————. *Some Haystacks Don't Even Have Any Needle* (Glenview, Ill.: Scott, Foresman, 1969).
This collection of poetry by modern American poets emphasizes modern times and language. It is illustrated with reproductions of works of modern art.

Farber, Norma. *Six Impossible Things Before Breakfast*, illus. Tomie De Paola, Charles Mikolaycak, Friso Henstra, Trina Schart Hyman, Lydia Dabcovich, and Hilary Knight (Reading, Mass.: Addison-Wesley, 1977).

Each of the six poems or stories is illustrated by a different artist. The poems are fairly long narratives.

Hoberman, Mary Ann. *Bugs*, illus. Victoria Chess (New York: Viking, 1976).

The book opens with a poem with two narrators, one who likes bugs and one who does not. There follows a series of poems, about different insects, in a variety of poetic forms.

Hopkins, Lee Bennett (ed.). *To Look at Any Thing*, illus. John Earl (New York: Harcourt, 1978).

Hopkins and Earl worked together matching poetry with photographs which capture the "faces" in natural objects—flowers, rocks, wood.

———. *Sing Hey for Christmas Day*, illus. Laura Jean Allen (New York: Harcourt, 1975).

This is one of several collections of poems around a holiday theme which Hopkins has edited. They capture the mood of the season, and most are appropriate for young children.

. . . *I Never Saw Another Butterfly* . . . Children's Drawings and Poems from Terezin Concentration Camp 1942–1944 (New York: McGraw-Hill, 1964).

These poems and drawings express the joys and the grim understandings of these children who knew they were soon to die. The material was chosen from documents housed in the State Jewish Museum in Prague.

Jacobs, Leland B. (ed.). *Poetry for Chuckles and Grins*, illus. Tomie De Paola (Champaign, Ill.: Garrard, 1968).

Cartoon-style illustrations reflect the mood of this humorous poetry for young children.

Jarrell, Randall. *A Bat is Born* (from *The Bat Poet*), illus. John Schoenherr (Garden City, N.Y.: Doubleday, 1978).

The grace and movement of Jarrell's poem about a newborn bat clinging to its mother as she flies through the night is repeated in Schoenherr's illustrations, which accentuate the feeling of movement by the curve and flow of the blue/black background.

Livingston, Myra Cohn. *4-Way Stop and Other Poems*, illus. James J. Spanfeller (New York: Atheneum, 1976).

The poems cover a range of moods and experiences, but all are within the grasp of elementary-school children. Several concrete and shape poems are included.

McCord, David. *One At a Time,* illus. Henry B. Kane (Boston: Little, Brown, 1977).
This collection of McCord's previously published poems includes many of the best known.

Ness, Evaline (comp. and illustrator). *Amelia Mixed the Mustard and Other Poems* (New York: Scribner's, 1975).
These twenty poems, all about women, are illustrated with lively woodcuts which embellish the character of each lady.

Neville, Mary. *Woody and Me,* illus. Ronni Solbert (New York, 1966).
The narrator of these twenty-nine poems tells about the activities and feelings of his older brother Woody and himself. Children will recognize many of the situations.

Plotz, Helen (comp.). *As I Walked Out One Evening; A Book of Ballads* (New York: Greenwillow, 1976).
Cowboy songs, songs about tall-tale heroes, and many other songs are included along with traditional ballads. The forms and origins of the ballad are discussed in the introduction.

Prelutsky, Jack. *Nightmares; Poems to Trouble Your Sleep,* illus. Arnold Lobel (New York: Greenwillow, 1976).
Poems about vampires, ghouls, ogres and the like will indeed make the reader shudder. Marvelously macabre.

Read, Herbert (comp.). *This Way, Delight,* illus. Juliet Kepes (New York: Pantheon, 1956).
A wide selection of works by adult poets, from Shakespeare to T.S. Eliot, is organized to lead "gradually from the simpler poems to the more difficult."

Silverstein, Shel. *Where the Sidewalk Ends;* The Poems and Drawings of Shel Silverstein (New York: Harper, 1974).
This is a representative sampling of Silverstein's zany wit, in poetry and illustration.

Snyder, Zilpha K. *Today is Saturday,* photographs by John Arms (New York: Atheneum, 1969).
Poems about the everyday experiences of children are well-illustrated with photographs. Many rhyme schemes are represented in this collection.

Starbird, Kaye. *A Snail's a Failure Socially and Other Poems, Mostly About People,* illus. Kit Dalton (Philadelphia: Lippincott, 1966).
These poems about people and animals show insight into human foibles, and a gentle appreciation of how people and animals cope.

Swenson, May. *Poems to Solve* (New York: Scribner's 1966).
The first thirteen of these poems are sophisticated riddles.

All are for fairly mature readers.

Tippett, James S. *Crickety Cricket!* The Best-Loved Poems of James S. Tippett, illus. Mary Chalmers (New York: Harper, 1973).

The poems for young children selected for this collection are organized into four sections: one about city life, one about transportation, one about animals and insects, and one about autumn and winter.

Adult References

Arnstein, Flora J. *Poetry and the Child* (New York: Dover 1970). (1962)

Chukovsky, Kornei. *From Two to Five,* trans. and ed. Miriam Morton (Berkeley: University of California Press, 1971). (1925)

Ciardi, John. *How Does a Poem Mean?* (Boston: Houghton Mifflin, 1975). (1959)

Cohen, Monroe D. (ed.). *Literature with Children* (Washington, D.C.: Association for Childhood Education International, 1972).

Groff, Patrick J. "Where Are We Going with Poetry for Children?" *The Horn Book,* August 1966, pp. 456–463.

Hamilton, Virginia (ed.). *Children and Literature, Views and Reviews* (Glenview, Ill.: Scott, Foresman, 1973).

Haviland, Virginia, and William Jay Smith. *Children and Poetry* (Washington: U.S. Government Printing Office, 1969).

Larrick, Nancy. *I Heard a Scream in the Street* (New York: Dell, 1970).

Livingston, Myra Cohn. "Not the Rose . . . ," *The Horn Book,* August 1964, pp. 355–360.

———. But Is It Poetry? *The Horn Book,* December 1975, pp. 571–580.

Marx, Marion. Review of *Out of the Earth I Sing: Poetry and Songs of Primitive Peoples of the World,* Richard Lewis (ed.). *The Horn Book,* April 1968, pp. 187–188.

McCord. David. "Excerpts from 'Write Me Another Verse,' " *The Horn Book,* August 1970, pp. 364–369.

Sandburg, Carl. *Early Moon* (New York: Harcourt, 1958). (1930)

Stephens, James. *Kings and the Moon* (New York: The Macmillan Company, 1938).

Terry, Ann. *Children's Poetry Preferences* (Urbana, Ill.: National Council of Teachers of English, 1974).

Tom, Chow Loy. *What Teachers Read to Pupils in the Middle Grades,* unpublished doctoral dissertation, Ohio State University, 1969.

Poetry References

Aldis, Dorothy. *Here, There and Everywhere,* illus. Majorie Flack (New York: Minton, 1928).

Arbuthnot, May Hill, and Sheldon L. Root, Jr. (eds.). *Time for Poetry,* 3d ed., illus. Arthur Paul (Glenview, Ill.: Scott, Foresman, 1968). (1952)

Bishop, Elizabeth. *The Ballad of the Burglar of Babylon,* illus. Ann Grifalconi (New York: Farrar, 1968).

Brooks, Gwendolyn. *The World of Gwendolyn Brooks* (New York: Harper, 1971).

Brown, Margaret Wise. *Four Fur Feet,* illus. Remy Charlip (New York: William R. Scott, 1961).

Caudill, Rebecca. *Come Along,* illus. Ellen Raskin (New York: Holt, 1969).

Ciardi, John. *You Read to Me, I'll Read to You,* illus. Edward Gorey (Philadelphia: Lippincott, 1962).

Dehn, Paul. *Punch*, Feb. 5, 1958.

Farjeon, Eleanor. *Poems for Children* (Philadelphia: Lippincott, 1951). (1926)

Fisher, Aileen. *I Like Weather*, illus. Janina Domanska (New York: Crowell, 1963).

Froman, Robert. *Seeing Things* (New York: Crowell, 1974).

Giovanni, Nikki. *Spin a Soft Black Song*, illus. Charles Bible (New York: Hill and Wang, 1971).

Greenfield, Eloise. *Honey, I Love and Other Love Poems,* illus. Diane Dillon and Leo Dillon (New York: Crowell, 1978).

Hoberman, Mary Ann. *Hello and Good-by,* illus. Norman Hoberman (Boston: Little, Brown, 1959).

Hubbell, Patricia. *The Apple Vendor's Fair*, illus. Julie Maas (New York: Atheneum, 1963).

Hughes, Langston. *The Dream Keeper, and other Poems,* illus. Helen Sewell (New York: Knopf, 1932).

Jarrell, Randall. *The Bat Poet,* illus. Maurice Sendak (New York: Macmillan, 1964). (1963)

Kuskin, Karla. *The Rose on My Cake* (New York: Harper, 1964).

Larrick, Nancy. *On City Streets,* illus. David Sagarin (New York: M. Evans, 1968).

———. *I Heard a Scream in the Street* (New York: Dell, 1970).

Lewis, Richard (ed.). *The Moment of Wonder* (New York: Dial, 1964).

———. *Out of the Earth I Sing—Poetry and Songs of Primitive Peoples of the World* (New York: Norton, 1968).

Long, Mary, in M. Joe Eaton and Malcolm Glass (eds.). *Grab Me a Bus* (New York: Scholastic Book Services, 1974).

Margolis, Richard J. *Only the Moon and Me,* illus. Marcia Kay Keegan. (New York: Lippincott, 1969).

McCord, David. *Every Time I Climb a Tree*, illus. Marc Simont (Boston: Little, Brown, 1967). (1925)

McLeod, Irene Rutherford. *Songs to Save a Soul* (London: Chatto & Windus, 1915).

Merriam, Eve. *There Is No Rhyme for Silver,* illus. Joseph Schindelman (New York: Atheneum, 1966). ("Toaster Time")

———. *It Doesn't Always Have to Rhyme,* illus. Malcolm Spooner (New York: Atheneum, 1966). ("Cheers," "How to Eat a Poem.")

Moore, Lilian. *I Feel the Same Way,* illus. Robert Quackenbush (New York: Atheneum, 1967).

Ms. Foundation. *Free To Be . . . You and Me* (New York: McGraw-Hill, 1974).

O'Neill, Mary. *Hailstones and Halibut Bones,* illus. Leonard Weisgard (Garden City, N.Y.: Doubleday, 1961).

Richards, Laura E. *Tirra Lirra; Rhymes Old and New,* illus. Marguerite Davis (Boston: Little, Brown, 1955).

Ridlon, Marci. *That Was Summer,* illus. Mia Carpenter (Chicago: Follett, 1969).

Smith, William Jay. *Laughing Time* (Boston: Little, Brown, 1955).

Thurman, Judith. *Flashlight and Other Poems,* illus. Reina Rubel (New York: Atheneum, 1976).

Tripp, Wallace. *A Great Big Ugly Man Came Up and Tied His Horse to Me* (Boston: Little, Brown, 1973).

Updike, John. *The Carpentered Hen and Other Tame Creatures* (New York: Harper, 1958).

Williams, William Carlos. *Collected Earlier Poems* (New York: New Directions, 1938).

TRA-DITIONAL LITERA-TURE

FAMILIAR TALES, DIFFERENT VOICES

In one classic German story, a girl named Ashputtel cannot go to a ball because her stepmother orders her to pick lentils out of cinders. Magically, she gets a pair of slippers and silver robe, goes to several balls, loses a slipper, and gains a prince.

In an old Filipino story, a stepdaughter named Maria is kept from going to a ball because she has to wash clothes in a river. A crab claiming to be her reincarnated mother arranges for some beautiful clothes and slippers. In a venerable Greek story, a young girl is running from the prince when her slipper falls into a horse trough. The prince finds it and goes looking for her, and —surprise!—they are married.

The girl is familiar. We know her as Cinderella, but people in other countries know the same character by different names, in different costumes. The Chinese call her Beauty; the Japanese call her Banizara; the Danes have named her Mette Wooden-hood. There are at least 500 versions of her story in Europe alone. Time after time in country after country—even where there are no princes— the slipper fits. The story wears well.

Cinderella is old. Forms of her story have been traced back more than a thousand years. In a *Saturday Review* cartoon (April 22, 1969, p. 36), she appears as an aging frizzy-haired queen next to a sagging king. "Remember the night we met and I lost my glass slipper?" she asks. She is also young, adopted in different forms by today's children all over the world.

Cinderella is a character of traditional literature. In some ways her story is typical of all the stories in this chapter. The author or authors is unknown. No one knows for sure where the story began. It was carried from country to country in the voices of thousands of tellers who changed it as they spoke it. Listeners, mainly adults, heard the tale for centuries before anyone wrote it down.

"Cinderella" is a fairy tale, a fast-moving story of magic, part of a large body of short stories called *folktales.* There are several other lively categories of traditional literature, that were centuries old before the printing press was invented in the middle of the fifteenth century. *Fables* are stories, usually about animals, that teach a lesson, often summarized in a one-line moral at the end of the tale. *Myths* are longer stories of gods, ancient heroes, ancestors, and natural phenomena. *Epics* are narratives of mortal heroes whose lives are closely watched and often directed by the heavens.

Some of this traditional literature is closely related to poetry (see

---

(Chapter-opening illustration from *The Sleeping Beauty* retold and illustrated by Trina Schart Hyman, by permission of Little, Brown and Company. Copyright © 1977 by Trina Schart Hyman.)

previous chapter). Classic epics were long poems following strict rules of style. Folktales often use repetitive phrases (for instance, "Little pig, little pig, let me come in./Not by the hair of my chinny-chin chin") which sound something like the choruses of ballads. Sometimes the tales end with short verses. Content, too, is often poetic. Writers of modern fantasy, by contrast, usually start at the real world and then take just a small step away from plausibility (see Chapter 6). Readers can map the imaginary kingdoms of modern fantasy. But the kingdoms in traditional stories, like the emotions in a good poem, cannot always be charted. It is easy to get lost, for instance, galloping through the green forest land of King Arthur, the legendary British hero who commanded his knights on romantic quests. In King Arthur's countryside, "any road or stream may meet any other road or stream," writes Elizabeth Cook, a British educator at Cambridge University. "Islands do not stay in the same place, and fountains, lakes, hermitages and castles may spring into view in any clearing between the trees. Either in the saddle or at the feast, the knight is likely to be surprised by running hounds, or deer, or ladies pursued by churls. Everything is in movement. This is the world of dreaming . . . " (1969, p. 30).

And like poetry, much of the literature is meant to be spoken.

LITERATURE WITH MANY VOICES

The great halls of kings in the Middle Ages (about A.D. 500 to A.D. 1450) were smokey and dismal. The tables of the king and his court bordered a fire in the middle of the room, and the only chimney was a hole in the slanted roof. Narrow slits in the walls squinted out at the countryside, onto battlegrounds where feudal lords fought continually.

No wonder storytellers were welcome in the hall. With their stock of serious tales of heroic crusaders, and bawdy poems accompanied by lutes and other stringed instruments, they raised the king's spirits and helped his court feel secure, at least for the night.

There must have been thousands of them. Just for one occasion, the wedding of Margaret of England in 1290, a king employed 426 minstrels to entertain with song and story. Many in the bands of bards that wandered from castle to castle were poor; they made their tales and prayed for a chance to perform by the fire. But others became part of the courts they entertained, and lived in princely fashion. In Wales, the leaders of storytellers were called *pinkerdd*, and sat a mere ten chairs from the sovereign. Kings agreed on the pinkerdd's value: if a storyteller should be captured it would take 126 cows to ransom him. (These and other colorful details about the

Medieval minstrels often carried their tales from
castle to castle, part of the oral tradition of literature.
(From *Merry Ever After* by Joe Lasker. Copyright ©
1976 by Joe Lasker. Reprinted by permission of The
Viking Press.)

traditions of storytelling come from Colwell, 1968, and Sawyer,
1942.)

It was a small price to pay because there was more to the storyteller's art than mere entertainment. There were no books, and
storytellers were often chroniclers, recreating past events in their

tales. Some accompanied kings into battle and later wrote songs, poems, and stories to exaggerate victories for the king's court, or to soften defeat. Some stories that echoed in the stone halls dealt with natural phenomona—how the world began, what caused the changing of seasons, the rumbling of thunder, and the flashing of lightning. Others dealt with equally universal human themes—rivalry between sisters and brothers, the son's jealousy of the father, sin, guilt, and retribution. The storytellers drew their material not only from what they saw, but also from what they heard through other tellers, and from what they felt as humans no different from us.

Storytelling, the art behind all traditional literature, did not begin in the Middle Ages. No one knows exactly when the *oral tradition*, passing on stories by telling them out loud, originated. Ancient Egyptian records show that the sons of Cheops, the pharaoh who built the pyramids 4,000 years before Christ, took turns entertaining their father with odd tales, each trying to top the other. In ancient India people came to believe that just listening to stories could cure sickness, overcome depression, and wash away sin. Around 150 years before Christ, Romans conquered Greece, and Greek myths and other stories were carried by traveling Latin storytellers to all the territories in the Roman empire.

Modern scholars have tried to explore how the stories began and how they migrated. Why, investigators have wondered, does Cinderella/Ashputtel appear in different clothing in different countries? One explanation, called *monogenesis*, is that originally just one society (in this case, a middle eastern society) knew the story; its tellers passed it on to other societies while traveling. The listeners then changed the story to suit their own tastes before passing it on. Another explanation of why so many tales are alike is called *polygenesis*: similar stories grew spontaneously in separate countries because societies, though different, shared the same needs and emotions.

Whatever their origin, folk literature did travel in different voices and dialects. Storytellers slung musical instruments on their backs, crossing cultural lines and mixing and blending heritages from many lands as they collected and spread stories all over the world. Joseph Jacobs, a pioneer in publishing folktales for children, once said that he had discovered "an English version of an Italian adaptation of a Spanish translation of a Latin version of a Hebrew translation of an Arabic translation of an Indian original" (in Colwell, 1968, p. 178).

The heavy international traffic in spoken stories continued all through the Middle Ages. Then technology began to catch up with itinerant tellers. About A.D. 1450, Johann Gutenberg of Germany invented movable type and printer's ink. Books from the newly developed printing press were wildly popular among the educated classes of Europe; within a couple of decades of Gutenberg's experiments, 40,000 books were in print. For several centuries storytellers continued to draw tales from uneducated people, and to pass them on while evening fires flickered. But the tradition began to decline. Whale oil, kerosene, and gas began burning in the 1800s, extending the day and encroaching on the time once reserved for storytelling. Inventor Thomas Edison lit up the streets of Menlo Park, New Jersey, with electric light bulbs in 1879, and his invention made it easy to enjoy books at night. Storytelling suffered.

But the art of spoken literature has not died. In Japan today, tellers use wooden clappers to call children together to hear stories. Storytellers enliven the marketplace of Morocco. In the United States, librarians offer story hours for small groups. Television allows storytellers to reach millions of children, although TV tellers miss the listener response which helps change and shape tales as they are told. Some black people in this country still remember the rhythms of a singing drum played by a folk hero named High John de Conquer. Westerners still sing songs of legendary cowboys.

You will add a dimension to many of the excerpts in this chapter if you read them aloud, and imagine the way they sounded when audiences first encountered them centuries ago.

FOLKTALES

As you read this Norwegian tale listen to the sound effects, the alliteration (repetition of the same consonant sound), and the rhythm, particularly near the climatic confrontation between the troll and the biggest Gruff.

Once on a time there were three billy-goats who were to go up to the hillside to make themselves fat, and the name of all three was "Gruff."

On the way up was a bridge over a burn they had to cross; and under the bridge lived a great ugly Troll, with eyes as big as saucers and a nose as long as a poker.

So first of all came the youngest billy-goat Gruff to cross the bridge.

"Trip, trap; trip, trap!" went the bridge.

"Who's that tripping over my bridge?" roared the Troll.

"Oh, it is only I, the tiniest billy-goat Gruff; and I'm going up to the hillside to make myself fat," said the billy-goat, with such a small voice.

"Now, I'm coming to gobble you up," said the Troll.

"Oh no, pray don't take me. I'm too little, that I am," said the billy-goat; "wait a bit till the second billy-goat Gruff comes, he's much bigger."

Marcia Brown is one of many illustrators who have chosen to illustrate a single edition of a folk tale. (Illustration reproduced from *The Three Billy Goats Gruff* by P. C. Asbjørnsen and J. E. Moe. Illustrations by Marcia Brown. Illustrations copyright © 1957 by Marcia Brown. By permission of Harcourt Brace Jovanovich, Inc.)

"Well, be off with you," said the Troll.

A little while after came the second billy-goat Gruff to cross the bridge.

"TRIP, TRAP! TRIP, TRAP! TRIP, TRAP!" went the bridge.

"WHO'S THAT tripping over my bridge?" roared the Troll.

"Oh, it's the second billy-goat Gruff, and I'm going up to the hillside to make myself fat," said the billy-goat, who hadn't such a small voice.

"Now, I'm coming to gobble you up," said the Troll.

"Oh no, don't take me; wait a little till the big billy-goat Gruff comes, he's much bigger."

"Very well, be off with you," said the Troll.

But just then came the big billy-goat Gruff.

"TRIP, TRAP! TRIP, TRAP! TRIP, TRAP!" went the bridge, for the billy-goat was so heavy that the bridge creaked and groaned under him. "WHO'S THAT tramping over my bridge?" roared the Troll.

"IT'S I! THE BIG BILLY-GOAT GRUFF," said the billy-goat, who had an ugly hoarse voice of his own.

"Now, I'm coming to gobble you up," roared the Troll.

"Well, come along! I've got two spears,

And I'll poke your eyeballs out at your ears;
I've got besides two curling-stones,
And I'll crush you to bits, body and bones."

That was what the big billy-goat said; and so he flew at the Troll and poked his eyes out with his horns, and crushed him to bits, body and bones, and tossed him out into the burn, and after that he went up to the hillside. There the billy-goats got so fat they were scarce able to walk home again; and if the fat hasn't fallen off them, why, they're still fat; and so—

Snip, snap, snout,
This tale's told out. (in Thompson, 1974, pp. 1-2)

"The Three Billy-Goats Gruff" is an example of a folktale. Like all traditional literature, its author is unkown, although it was popularized in the early 1840s by Norwegian story collectors, notably Peter Christian Asbjornsen and Jorgen E. Moe. In 1859, a Britisher, Sir George Dasent, translated it into English.

Many of the hundreds of folktales available to us today are associated with their collectors. The Mother Goose stories probably take their name from Charles Perrault's *Contes de ma Mère L'Oye*, which comprised eight folktales (not nursery rhymes) for adult readers (see "Was There a Real Mother Goose," in Chapter 3). The collection included "Puss in Boots" and "Sleeping Beauty." Late in the 1800s, Joseph Jacobs became one of the first collectors to present stories specifically for children; he is responsible for introducing such stories as "The Three Bears," "The Three Little Pigs," and "Henny Penny."

The Brothers Grimm

The most famous of all the early collectors of folktales are two German brothers, Jakob and Wilhelm Grimm. There are several misunderstandings about the Grimm fairy tales, published in three editions dated 1812, 1816, and 1856. To begin with, the brothers did not create the stories. Like other collectors, they searched them out from living storytellers and from other collections, including Perrault's.

Secondly, they did not track down the stories to entertain young readers. "The book of folktales was not at all written for children," wrote Jakob Grimm, "but they like it very much and I am glad they do" (in Kamenetsky, 1974, p. 379).

The Grimms' passion was language. They believed that by listening to the stories of uneducated people, they could learn more about

ISSUE

ARE THE GRIMM TALES DULL?

In their effort to integrate the various folktales in their *Kinder und Hausmärchen*, the Brothers Grimm actually had to "translate" them from more than twenty dialects into high German. In this process alone they were bound to take certain liberties, if only for the sake of clarity and smoothness in style. They weeded out needless repetitions, simplified the plot structure, substituted for indirect speech some lively conversations, added some action where the description became too involved, and even modified the titles of the tales. Wilhelm especially rewrote and changed the tales at various times, without, however, sacrificing his respect for the oral tradition. With the poet's sensitivity he developed a feeling for the oral style and used his skills as a storyteller to enhance the natural flow of speech. (p. 380)

> Christa Kamenetsky, in *Elementary Education*,
> March 1974, pp. 379-383.

They [the Grimms] wrote as scholars, not as storytellers, and were obviously more concerned to preserve evidence for future anthropologists than to put their stories into words that would hold the attention of children. They wrote down events and details as they heard them, making alterations only if they sounded incoherent. After reading the lively French fairy tales it is dull to read their narrative; but their sequences of magical adventures, objects, persons, and places are in themselves significant and beautiful. It is only the language that is dull. (p. 41)

> Elizabeth Cook, *The Ordinary and the Fabulous*
> (Cambridge: Cambridge University Press, 1969).

What reasons might explain why two authors have opposing opinions of the Grimms's writing? Which do you agree with? As you read a tale told by the Grimms, imagine that you want to retell it to a group of children. What would you edit out, if anything? Why? Which seems most important in keeping stories alive, content or form? Message or medium?

early Europeans and their migrations. Eventually the brothers' explorations of language led them to write a German dictionary and book of grammar—for adults.

Critics today differ on whether their storytelling style is graceful or heavy. Some German critics in 1812 gave bad reviews to the first edition of the brothers' work. But their stories, including "Snow White," "Rapunzel," "Hansel and Gretel," and "The Frog Prince," were popular with readers. In their lifetimes, the Grimms saw their stories flourish in translation in more than a dozen countries.

Why the popularity? One major reason is that the stories collected by the Grimms and others follow a familiar and simple formula.

THE FOLKTALE FORMULA

Stories begin quickly. Characters are uncomplicated. Plots move swiftly along well-trod paths, and all questions are answered before the story ends. But there is also plenty of room for flexibility, from beginning to happy ending.

The Many Versions of Once upon a Time

"Once upon a time . . ." tells the reader or listener that the story happened in the past, but the opening is vague about when, and the words do not give away any of the plot. Young children cannot say exactly what "once upon a time" means, nor do they care. The phrase is like theme music, rhythmically signaling to listeners that if they are not quiet, they will miss something.

There are many versions. "Once there was and twice there wasn't . . ." is the opening of "Just Say Hic." "The Frog King" begins: "In the olden times, when wishing was some good . . . ." An African tale called "How the Spider Got a Thin Waist" starts with the words "Many dry seasons ago, before the oldest man in our village can remember, before the dry and the rain and the dry and the rain that any one of us can talk about to his children . . . ."

The phrase, whatever it is, ends. The plot begins immediately. Within the first few sentences the audience knows who the characters are, often by name, and what their problem is. The confrontation is set up in the first two sentences: goats versus a great ugly troll. Another story, "Cap o' Rushes," begins: "Well, there was once a very rich gentleman, who had three daughters, and he thought he'd see how fond they were of him." "Molly Whuppie" opens with "Once upon a time, there was an old woodcutter who had too many children. Work as hard as he might, he couldn't feed them all." In

Beauty demonstrates her love for her father and saves his life by going to live at the palace of the Beast. (From *Beauty and the Beast* (a retelling) by Phillippa Pearce, illustrations by Alan Barrett. Illustrations copyright © 1972 by Alan Barrett. Reproduced by permission of Longman Publishers)

each story, there is a problem or a challenge faced by a small number of stock characters.

Uncomplicated Characters

A 6-year-old listening to the story of the three goats Gruff interrupted with a question after the first sentence. Gruff was a frightening name, she said. "Are the goats good or bad?"

She had learned that characters in folktales are uncomplicated. They tend to be either good or bad. They are not believable by ordinary standards. For instance, meet Beauty, the paragon in *Beauty and the Beast* (retold by Philippa Pearce):

The third and youngest daughter was quite different from the other two. She was beautiful—so beautiful that she was known as Beauty. She was also good and kind. Everyone loved Beauty, except for her sisters, who were jealous of her. (1972)

Many other characters are not merely good; they tower over normal mortals, like the girl in "The Frog Prince" who was so lovely "that even the sun, that looked on many things, could not but marvel when he shone upon her face."

Not all daughters can match this. In "King Grisly-Beard," there's a bad princess:

A great king had a daughter who was very beautiful, but so proud and haughty and conceited that none of the princes who came to ask her in marriage were good enough for her, and she only made sport of them.

(Grimm, trans. Taylor, 1973)

Frequently several characters are introduced at once to set off contrasts between them. Here is the opening of *The Fool of the World and the Flying Ship* (retold by Arthur Ransome):

There were once upon a time an old peasant and his wife and they had three sons. Two of them were clever young men who could borrow money without being cheated, but the third was the Fool of the World. He was as simple as a child, simpler than some children, and he never did anyone a harm in his life. (1968)

Unlike characters in a novel or some modern fantasy, evil daughters never repent. Bad witches refuse to recant cruel spells. Fools never grow in wisdom. When a poor boy becomes a prince, or the tattered girl by the fire wins the heart of the prince, it is only because their true nature emerges. They have not changed.

A Variety of Fools, and Other Motifs

Some characters and other elements in folktales appear regularly in story after story. The youngest and smallest of siblings is successful after others in the family fail. Wishes are granted. Magic objects such as rings, beans, or tablecloths are standard props in many tales. These elements are called *motifs*. They recur so frequently that a well-known folklorist, Stith Thompson, was able to index them. He found, for instance, that fools appeared in more than a thousand stories. He counted and categorized the variety of fools and "other unwise persons" in his *Motif-Index of Folk Literature*.

Fools (and other unwise persons)

Fools (general)
Absurd misunderstandings
Absurd Disregard of facts . . .
Gullible fools
Talkative fools
Inquisitive fools
Foolish imitation
Literal fools
Foolish extremes
Thankful fools
Cowardly fools
Bungling fools . . . (1955, p. 8)

The longer and more involved the tale, the more motifs. In "Billy Goats Gruff," for instance, there are four motifs. Animals talk. There is a monster (the troll). The goats use trickery. And the number three is significant.

Why three? No one is sure, but no one questions its appeal. Repeatedly, folktale heroes face three tasks. Families have three children. Spirits grant three wishes or give three gifts. Even phrases come in waves of three—the three goats have similar lines for the troll and the bridge makes the same noises three times. "It could be four, or two," writes Michael Hornyansky, "but three is easier to remember. It is a magic number, with the feeling of a reliable sample" (1965, p. 20).

Curiously, three is not the magic number in all folktales. In Native American folktales, for instance, four is a magic number. But three goats Gruff are enough for a story to grow in action and suspense without going on too long.

The Quick Pace of Plot

A life-and-death confrontation between the poker-nosed troll and the first goat develops within the first 200 words of the billy-goats Gruff story. Within 500 words, three goats have risked their lives and the troll has been horribly dispatched. If you read the story silently, episodes flip by with the speed of jerky scenes from an old-time silent movie. Even read out loud the story develops quickly, arouses suspense, and builds to a climax: ". . . crushed him to bits, body and bones." It ends a few words later with a little verse.

Does "this tale's told out" seem out of place? Not if you remember that the story was meant to be spoken. Storytellers, as performers, had no curtains or blackouts to cut them off from their audiences at the end of a tale. Instead they used familiar devices— short verses, sayings, asides to the reader, or phrases built on "happily ever after"—to let listeners know they were done.

The Inevitable Fate of Villains

The troll is crushed. The wicked queen in "Snow White," the story goes, "had to put on the red-hot slippers and dance till she dropped down dead." The teller does not linger over the punishment, nor does the story give so much detail about the fate of the villain that the punishment becomes the focus of the story. The characters are so abstract, and unreal, that audiences recognize there is nothing personal in the punishment. Critic Lillian Smith writes, "Both the child's attitude and the characteristic narrative method of the folktale have an impersonal quality important to remember. In the telling it is a matter of emphasis and intention; in the listener, the child, it is a recognition that the events all belong to the realm of story, of imagination" (1953, p. 59).

Those are elements of the formula of folktale. Every voice that speaks the tale adapts and personalizes the formula through pitch and dialect and dramatic emphasis. Occasionally, the printed versions of these tales try to preserve the flavor of the dialect of a particular teller, like this excerpt, the opening of a southern Appalachian tale called "Jack and the Varmints."

> Jack was a-goin' about over the country one time, happened he passed by a place where a man had been rivin' boards, saw a little thin piece and picked it up, started in to whittlin' on it. Jack was so lazy he never noticed much what he was doin' till he'd done made him a little paddle. He didn't know what he'd do with it, just carried it along. Directly he came to a muddy place in the road where a lot of little blue butterflies had lit down to drink. So Jack slipped up right close to 'em and came down with that paddle right in the middle of 'em—*splap!* Then he counted to see how many he'd killed. (Chase, 1943, pp. 58–59)

This passage could be shorter; instead of "started in to whittlin' on it," for instance, the storyteller might have said "began to whittle it." But the words in dialect dance to jiglike rhythm; the beat holds listeners' attention.

TYPES OF FOLKTALES

There are as many variations as there are human voices. But some types of folktales—groups of stories distinguished by a motif—are

Illustrations, like dialect, may help capture the flavor of a tale. (From *The Tailypo, A Ghost Story* by Joanna Galdone, illustrated by Paul Galdone. Illustrations copyright © 1977 by Paul Galdone. Reproduced by permission of The Seabury Press.)

particularly popular with children. Why? The next section of this chapter contains some answers. Meanwhile, see if you can identify the appeal of each of these categories.

Tales of Talking Animals

"The Three Billy Goats Gruff" is a talking animal tale, often called a beast tale. Animals talk and have human feelings, although not as profound as talking animals in modern fantasy. And frequently, folktale animals are caught in competition and depend on cleverness to see them through.

Anansi, for example, is a wily and mischievous spider in West African folktales who enjoys playing tricks on other animals. (Storytellers pronounce his name "ah-NAN-cy," although sometimes it appears in print as "Ananse.") When Turtle comes to visit him just at dinner, Anansi is forced by custom to invite him to stay. Reluctantly, the spider sets out a steaming platter of fish. But as Turtle reaches for a piece, Anansi reminds him to wash his paws because "in my country it is ill-mannered to come to the table without first washing." Turtle complies, but gets his paws dusty as he returns from the stream. Again Anansi sends him to wash, and by the time Turtle has come back to dinner, the spider has eaten all the fish. Turtle thanks him sarcastically for "wonderful hospitality," tells Anansi he must come and visit, and leaves in a huff.

Anansi tries to visit Turtle at the bottom of a river, but has trouble sinking. He fills his jacket pocket with pebbles. The extra weight drags him down to the dinner table. Before he can eat any of the oysters or clams, Turtle announces "in my country it is ill-mannered to come to the table wearing a jacket. Please take it off." Anansi does, and floats slowly away from the feast (Kaula, 1968, pp. 26–31).

Tales That Tell Why

Pourquoi tales (*pourquoi*, pronounced "poor-QUAH", is the French word for why) give imaginative explanations to childlike questions about why things are the way they are. A Native American, for instance, once asked "Why does the wildcat have all those spots?" and the answer, from a Shawnee storyteller, was a pourquoi tale. A wildcat traps a rabbit in a hollow tree, and tells his prey he will wait there until the rabbit gets hungry and comes out. The rabbit knows the bigger animal can outwait him, so he decides that his only hope is to outwit the wildcat. The rabbit convinces the wildcat to build a fire to cook him. When the fire is blazing the rabbit leaps into the flames, scattering coals onto the wildcat's fur where they burn permanent spots. The rabbit escapes (Belting, 1961, pp. 71–73).

"Why do children have short names?" a Chinese child asks. A tale which provides an amusing answer, "Tikki Tikki Tembo," is a favorite with children. When young Chang falls into a well, his older brother gets help quickly because his mother understands immediately when he tells her what happened. But when the older brother falls in the same well, Chang runs out of breath trying to get help for "Tikki tikki tembo-no sa rembo-chari bari ruchi-pip peri pembo." Finally Chang is able to get an old man with a ladder to come to the well by saying that his "brother" is in the well. Short names are used from then on (Mosel, 1968).

ISSUE

SHOULD SEXIST FAIRY TALES BE REWRITTEN?

Sex role stereotypes are also communicated to children through fairy tales. Despite their costumes, girls admire fine ladies, queens, and princesses, female like themselves, who are gentle, helpful, weak and rarely think or act strongly on their own. And likewise, boys admire princes, kings, and knights, male like themselves, who are strong, brave, athletic, and always lead people or protect them from danger. These stories, however, do not leave room for females who are strong and protective or for males who are gentle and caring.

It is simple and fun to retell these fairy tales with a broader range of action and qualities for the females and males in these stories *without* losing their wonderful magic. Here is an example of one way (you can probably think up many other ways, too) to retell "Cinderella" without sex role stereotypes. It is reprinted from Verne Moberg's *A Child's Guide to Equal Reading*, put out by the National Education Association.

Cinderella is a hard-working young woman with a good deal of self-pride. When the pressures put upon her to complete her work become unreasonable, she makes her feelings known to her stepmother and sisters: if this doesn't bring results, she then grows frustrated, venting her anger at the source of her irritation. She takes intiative whenever it is in her own interest to do so. Cinderella is pleasing in appearance, but as she spends much of her time at household labor, her body bears the signs: dishpan hands and flat feet. At the ball, she is interested in meeting as many new and interesting people as she can, and during the evening she dances with many men. Since she knows that the coach will turn into a pumpkin if she doesn't leave before the stroke of twelve, she plans her exit well in advance: the prince was her favorite during the evening, so she bids him goodnight, deliberately yet discreetly leaving her shoe on the step where he will see it (ordinarily, she might simply have arranged a meeting, but this prince is hopelessly romantic). Finally, the prince pays his visit to propose marriage (he has no trouble finding her since she was wearing monogrammed shoes). Cinderella explains that she is flattered by his proposal and will certainly think it over: however, she would need to get to know him better before she made up her mind: on the other hand, she's been reconsidering her options . . . What's really the best way to live happily ever after?

Cohen, Martha. *Sex Role Stereotypes in Elementary Education:*
A Handbook for Parents and Teachers
(Hartford, Connecticut: Travelers Insurance Co., 1974).

Keep Mother Goose and the folktales, too. Look for folktales and myths with female "heroes"; they do exist. But don't distort the others, as did the Russian grandmother in the Charles Adams [sic] cartoon who is telling a bedtime story to her grandchild. "And then Cinderella shot the capitalist prince, established a people's democracy and lived happily ever after." The recent record "Free to Be You and Me" did similar violence to the Atalanta myth. This sort of thing is an unforgivable destruction of our cultural heritage. (p. 536)

Ward, Nancy. "Feminism and Censorship,"
Language Arts, May 1976, pp. 536–537.

Is, as Ward suggests, the retelling of Cinderella a destruction of our cultural heritage? Why or why not? What is gained by the rewriting of a sexist fairy tale? What is lost through such action? In the Moberg article which Cohen quotes, it is suggested that the children compare this version of Cinderella with the one they know. How might this change the impact of the retelling?

Tales of Magic

In every version of "Cinderella," the poor kitchen maid obtains a beautiful gown by magic. In "Snow White," a girl falls asleep and wakes up under terms of a magic spell. A boy named Jack climbs to the sky on a stalk grown from magic beans in "Jack and the Beanstalk." Each of these stories is commonly called a fairy tale, but more accurately each is a tale of magic.

Cumulative Tales

Like songs or poems with refrains, cumulative tales encourage listeners to join in the telling when the words become familiar. Plots are particularly simple. In "All in the Morning Early," as told by Sorche Nic Leodhas (1963), author of many books retelling folktales, a boy named Sandy starts walking to the grinding mill with his sack of corn. He meets people and animals along the way and as each decides to join him, a new line is added to the refrain, which always ends:

> . . . down the road that leads to the mill,
> Where the old mill wheel is never still—
> Clicketty-clicketty-clicketty-clack!
> All in the morning early.

The group with Sandy grows after each refrain until fifty-five people and animals have joined his march to the mill. This odd collection of travelers includes three gypsies, six hares, eight ladybugs, and nine larks, among others.

Silly Folk and Legendary Figures: Tales of Exaggeration

Fools in folktales never change, but they survive, single-minded and simple-minded, against all laws of evolution. Sometimes they prosper.

The American poet and biographer Carl Sandburg told one story of a fool who won a raffle by choosing the number 42.

> And when he won they asked him whether he guessed the number or had a system. He said he had a system, "I took up the old family album and there on page 7 was my grandfather and grandmother both on page 7. I said to myself this is easy for 7 times 7 is the number that will win and 7 times 7 is 42. (1936, p. 91)

An extravagantly foolish daughter apparently lives happily ever after in "The Three Sillies" as told by Margot Zemach (1963). When the girl goes to the cellar to draw beer for herself, her parents, and the young man who is courting her, she sees an ax stuck in one of the beams and develops a morbid worry. What if she and the young man married, had a son, and the son when grown to manhood should come to the cellar for beer, and the ax fell on his head? What then? She becomes so distraught she sits down and cries. Her mother and father come down to see what the matter is, and when she tells them her fear, they cry too. The young man says they are all "sillies" and vows he will not marry the girl until he has found three bigger sillies than they. Without much effort, he finds three new sillies, and returns to marry the girl.

In a story called "The Snow in Chelm," told by Isaac Bashevis Singer (1966), village elders demonstrate their right to rule as "oldest and greatest fools." Snow falls one Hanukkah evening, and the flakes look like silver, pearls, and diamonds in the moonlight. The elders decide it is a treasure, and that all the people must be warned not to walk on it until it can be collected. A problem: The messenger himself may trample the treasure.

The elders have a subtle plan. The messenger will stand on a table, carried by four men. But in the morning, they find that the feet of the four who carried the table have trampled the treasure. Ah, but already they have thought of a solution in case it should snow next

211

The fools of Chelm decide to hold for trial a carp
which slapped Gronom Ox with its tail. (From *Naftali
the Storyteller and His Horse, Sus* by Isaac Bashevis
Singer, illustrated by Margot Zemach. Illustrations
copyright © 1976 by Margot Zemach. Reproduced by
permission of Farrar, Straus & Giroux, Inc.)

Hanukkah: they will employ four others to carry the four who bore
the table which carted the messenger.

The tellers of these tales exaggerate folly. Other stories are amusing because they exaggerate the dimensions of legendary figures.

212

Many of these *tall tales* developed in the United States. Paul Bunyan, for instance, was no ordinary lumberjack. When he has to get the cut trees from Minnesota to the sawmill in New Orleans, he decides the best route would be a river. But there is no river. So after a lunch of 19 pounds of sausage, 6 hams, 8 loaves of bread, and 231 flapjacks—each slathered with a pound of butter and a quart of maple syrup—he digs a river and names it the Mississippi.

Paul was not always such a giant of a man. When the twelve storks delivered him to his mother in Kennebunkport, Maine, "he didn't weigh more than 104 or 105 pounds—and 46 pounds of that was his black, curly beard" (Emberley, 1963).

Again, the telling helps the tale. Parts of Bunyan's story may be hard to swallow; it may also be hard to believe that frontiersman Davy Crockett (1786–1836) rode a bear or that the legendary cowboy, Pecos Bill rode a cyclone from Texas to the West Coast. But the best of storytellers spin out these fantastic details as if they were as real as rain and sun. When the audience raises eyebrows, the teller can soften the exaggeration. If listeners take delight in Bunyan's birthweight, the tale can grow taller in the telling.

Of course there is a limit to acceptable exaggeration. Overblown stories can be boring. What saves exaggeration in many of the tall tales that have survived is clever expression, or an unexpected twist: *The pancakes were so thin, they only had one side. . . . The man was so tall he had to climb up a ladder to shave himself. . . . Mike Fink, a riverboatman, was "half wild horse and half cock-eyed alligator, the rest of him snags and snapping turtle"* (Sandburg, 1936, p. 93).

WHY CHILDREN LIKE FOLKTALES

Why are folktales appealing to children? Psychologists provide one reasonable answer: Young readers or listeners step easily into the roles of the characters, and find comfort there. Bruno Bettelheim, a child psychologist, discusses what Snow White meant to one 5-year-old girl:

> Her mother was cold and distant, so much so that she felt lost. The story assured her that she need not despair: Snow White, betrayed by her stepmother, was saved by males—first the dwarf and later the prince. This child, too, did not despair because of the mother's desertion, but trusted that rescue would come from males. Confident that "Snow White" showed her the way, she turned to her father, who responded favorably; the fairy tale's happy ending made it possible for this girl to find a happy solution to the impasse in living. . . . (1976, p. 16)

213

Bettelheim reports that different children respond differently to the same tale; a 13-year-old, for instance, might unconsciously extract a message from "Snow White" about becoming independent from her mother who is jealous of her youth and beauty.

A contrasting analysis, by the late F. André Favat of Northeastern University, suggests that children are not primarily intrigued by the symbolism in the stories. Favat theorized that children find escape in folktales from the confusions of day-to-day life. The tales call up memories in children of a "world order they once knew" (1977, p. 57) as small children, when magic was real, when trees and rocks seemed alive, when they—like heroes in stories—were at the center of attention, and when parents had the power to make everything come out all right.

Favat and Bettelheim are two of the latest of a long line of people who have interpreted folktales and other traditional literature in terms of how they meet psychological needs. In the 1800s, experts on language development explained traditional stories as attempts by primitive people to penetrate nature's mysteries. Sigmund Freud (1856-1939), a physician who pioneered in methods of investigating mental processes, said many of the tales represented parent-child conflicts. A contemporary of Freud, Carl Gustav Jung (1875-1961), disagreed. He argued that the conflicts of the ancient stories represented conflicts originating within people's minds: between the inner soul (he called it the *anima*) and the personality exhibited to the world (called the *persona*).

Using techniques developed by these and other psychologists, it is possible to disassemble folktales and try to plumb what emotional appeal they have for children. Michael Hornyansky does this light-heartedly in his analysis of "Snow White," a few years before Bettelheim:

> This is one of those myths expressing a truth that dare not be faced directly—here, a clear case of mother-daughter rivalry (and presumably sexual rivalry, though it's presented as a straight beauty contest). The fact that the queen is called Snow White's stepmother shouldn't fool us for a moment. A child hesitates to accuse Mummy of being jealous enough to murder her, so Mummy turns into step-Mummy—which partly explains her behaviour, partly makes it okay for the child to hate *her* . . . . (1965, p. 23)

But this kind of psychological second-guessing can go too far. One major warning: folktales are no panacea for a child's mental distress. Nor should they be presented as therapy, nor should the child's response to a tale be dissected to shake out hidden emotions or problems. Bettelheim himself warns:

> Fairy-tale motifs are not neurotic symptoms, something one is better off understanding rationally so that one can rid oneself of them. Such motifs are experienced as wondrous because the child feels understood and appreciated deep down in his feelings, hopes, and anxieties, without these all having to be dragged up and investigated in the harsh light of a rationality that is still beyond him. (1976, p. 19)

Even without complicated theory, it is easy to see how children can identify with folktale figures. Cartoonist Al Capp once challenged adults: How would you like to be a pygmy in a world run by giants, without a dime to your name? That is the way children sometimes feel. Some children have to learn to cultivate the trickiness of the tiny spider Anansi, or the rabbit cornered by the leopard. Pourquoi tales explain the confusing, giant-dominated world, and cumulative tales suggest that it is possible to live in that world in harmony with others—including friendly animals—who give help and support. Even fools, far more vulnerable than children, survive, if their intentions are good.

The world of giants may have harsh and arbitrary laws ("It's bedtime"), but in folktales, bad laws bend. Magic rights injustice. People are not bound by physical norms, either: Paul Bunyan keeps growing—good news for young children—even though he was full-sized at birth.

Folktales are comforting and informative. And just as important, each of these tales is a good short story. Just as children enjoy fast-paced narrative poems, young readers or listeners like active stories in prose.

WHY READ FOLKTALES TODAY?

A child's enjoyment is one good reason to keep folktales alive in the classroom and home. But there are other positive values.

Folktales Help Foster Imagination

In an age when rational physicists talk about black holes in space and subatomic quarks, folktales can limber up the mind for further imaginative exploration of the real world.

A well-known Russian poet and translator, Kornei Chukovsky, wrote that fantasy is essential to science (1925).

215

Without imaginative fantasy there would be complete stagnation in both physics and chemistry, because the fomulation of new hypotheses, the invention of new implements, the discovery of new methods of experimental research, the conjecturing of new chemical fusions —all of these are products of imagination and fantasy. (1971 edition, p. 124)

Almost every folktale begins with a problem and ends with a solution. Exposure to many tales may encourage children to act to solve their own problems in imaginative ways and keep up hope for a happy outcome.

Folktales Simplify Moral Questions

Folktales also encourage respect for human greatness. A bad troll crumbles under the charge of a single goat, and even the smallest child can cast a stone at an evil giant. Unlike many modern stories, folktales put clear labels on right and wrong and enable a child to simplify moral questions. The abstract battles in folktales, writes Elizabeth Cook, remind us of modern struggles against evil; dragons, for instance, symbolize injustice, corruption, and hatred. That is why, she writes, "it is a great mistake to feel sorry for the dragon, as some adult readers do if they have not been brought up on fairy tales" (1969, p. 4).

Folktales Introduce Foreign Lands and People

Norway itself is an undercurrent of "Billy Goats Gruff," according to Lillian Smith.

The story suggests, but does not describe, the headlong mountain stream rushing under the bridge which gives passage to the steep spruce-clad hillside beyond. The bold, sturdy, headstrong attributes of the characters of the story harmonize with the setting and with out conception of the Norse character. (1953, p. 54)

Costumes and dwellings vary from tale to tale depending on the nationality of the teller. In some folktales, kings or queens reign; in others, chiefs. Such details introduce children to different people, times, and places as well as illuminate emotions and problems that are common to all people.

There are hundreds of stories from dozens of countries to choose from. How do you choose the most valuable?

ISSUE

WHAT HAVE FAIRY TALES GOT TO DO WITH CHILDREN?

But my interest in fairy tales is not a result of such technical analysis of their merits. It is, on the contrary, a consequence of asking myself why, in my experience, children—normal and abnormal alike, and at all levels of intelligence—find folk fairy tales more satisfying than all other children's stories. The more I tried to understand why these stories are so successful at enriching the inner life of the child, the more I realized that these tales, in a much deeper sense than any other reading material, start where the child really is in his psychological and emotional being. They speak about his severe inner pressures in a way that the child unconsciously understands and—without belittling the serious inner struggles that growing up entails—offer examples of both temporary and permanent solutions to difficulties. (p. 6)

Bettelheim, Bruno.
The Uses of Enchantment
(New York: Knopf, 1976).

Among those who still have enough wisdom not to think fairy stories pernicious, the common opinion seems to be that there is a natural connection between the minds of children and fairy stories, of the same order as the connection between children's bodies and milk. I think this is an error; at best an error of false sentiment, and one that is therefore most often made by those who, for whatever private reason (such as childlessness), tend to think of children as a special kind of creature, almost a different race, rather than as normal, if immature, members of a particular family, and of the human family at large.

Actually, the association of children and fairy stories is an accident of our domestic history. Fairy stories have in the modern lettered world been relegated to the "nursery," as shabby or old-fashioned furniture is relegated to the playroom, primarily because the adults do not want it, and do not mind if it is misused. It is not the choice of the children which decides this. Children as a class—except in a common lack of experience they are not one—neither like fairy stories more, nor understand them better than adults do; and no more than they like many other things. (pp. 111-112)

Tolkien, J. R. R. "Children and Fairy Stories,"
in Sheila Egoff, G. T. Stubbs, and
L. F. Ashley (eds.) *Only Connect*
(Toronto, Oxford University Press, 1969).

What evidence can you cite to show that fairy tales do or do not have a special appeal to children? What bearing does the fact that the tales were originally told for adult audiences have on the statements of Bettelheim and Tolkien? Is it possible to reconcile the two positions? If so, how? If not, why not?

EVALUATING THE FOLKTALE

There are two major criteria in evaluating a folktale. Is the content appropriate? And is the story presented well or would another version of the same story better suit the reader or listener?

Is Content Appropriate?

Some stories are too involved to hold the interest of young children. Others fail to appeal to a particular child at a particular time. On the other hand, when content is appropriate, a child may want to hear or read the same story day after day, taking it to bed and poring over it at breakfast.

There is no easy way to choose content. The best strategy is to keep a good stock of stories in the classroom and choose flexibly.

Is the Story Presented Well?

Do modern retellings preserve the flavor and meaning of the tale as traditionally told? Do illustrations complement the tale? Is the story well told?

Preserving the tradition "Why Mosquitoes Buzz in People's Ears" is an African tale retold by Verna Aardema and illustrated by Leo and Diane Dillon (1975). Aardema uses some odd words. An iguana slithers away in the reeds with a "mek, mek, mek." A rabbit bounds across a clearing with a "krik, krik, krik." These words, which do not pretend to be realistic sound effects, suggest the *idea* of moving animals in the same way a child watching a descending leaf says "it's falling downdy downdy down." Words which convey an idea through sound are called *ideophones*, and they are a natural component of original African folktales. Aardema's use of ideophones preserves some of the conventions of the original, besides adding some poetry to the tale, and is best appreciated if the story is told out loud.

ISSUE

IS *THE FIVE CHINESE BROTHERS* A COMIC FOLKTALE, OR A DEROGATORY STEREOTYPE OF THE CHINESE?

The Five Chinese Brothers was published at a time when the Chinese Exclusion Act was in effect, but also a time when some sympathy for the Chinese was being generated due to the sufferings being inflicted on China by the invading Japanese. The book seems, then, to have been in part a response to a new, not necessarily negative, interest in China and the Chinese; but, at the same time, it drew upon the period's popular, extremely negative stereotypes of the Chinese. These stereotypes are reflected in the Kurt Wiese illustrations (Wiese also illustrated *The Story of Ping* [sic] and *You Can Write Chinese*), which are typical of the political cartoons found in the jingoistic U.S. press of the 1930's.

First of all, the drawings jibe with the concept, popular then *and* now, that Asians "all look alike." While it is entirely legitimate for a story to depict five brothers of any nationality as being identical, the Wiese pictures show not only the brothers but all of the characters—brothers, mother, townspeople, judge, etc.—looking exactly alike. Moreover, the characters' appearances are reduced to the common stereotypical denominator of bilious yellow skin, slit and slanted eyes (Asian people's skin is *not* yellow, and their eyes are neither slanted nor slits), queues and "coolie clothes." These caricatures were part and parcel of the perception of Asians and their descendants as subhuman creatures, a perception which led members of the white majority to persecute, ridicule, exploit and ostracize Chinese Americans. (pp. 3-4)

Schwartz, Albert V. "The Five Chinese Brothers: Time to Retire,"
Interracial Books for Children Bulletin, vol. 8, no. 3, 1977, pp. 3-7.

Far from finding the five brothers' yellow skin "bilious," I always thought of artist Kurt Wiese's faces as being the color of sunshine or butter, cheerful and highly appealing. And if Mr. Wiese's heroes are rendered in a broad cartoon style, well, why not? This approach has been used by many a successful children's book artist from Peter Newell to Jack Kent without the intention of demeaning the subjects that are rendered. It is, in fact, a style particularly well-suited to the folktale, a genre which deals in broad truths. We are not concerned with the names, ages, or specific physical features of the characters in a Grimm fairy tale any more that we are in Bishop's confection.

219

The fact of the brothers' being exact look-alikes is the great joke of the book—not a racial joke on the Chinese, but a specific joke on the judge and townspeople in the tale. The great charm of the story, of course, is that the joke is never on us, its child-readers. We know from the very start that "Once upon a time there were Five Chinese Brothers and they all looked exactly alike." . . .

I cannot remember a tale during my childhood that gave me a cozier sense of all being right with the world. Thus, there seems to me to be a danger to the free growth of the human spirit, as well as an element of the ludicrous, in bringing contemporary social sensitivies (many of them entirely justified and commendable) so heavily to bear on books like *The Five Chinese Brothers*. (pp. 90, 91)

Lanes, Selma G. "A Case for The Five Chinese Brothers,"
School Library Journal, October 1977, pp. 90-91.

The Five Chinese Brothers is a retelling of a Chinese folktale. Get a copy of the book and look at the illustrations yourself. Do you think the book presents a negative stereotype of Chinese people, or simply has a broad cartoon style of illustration appropriate for its genre? What do you think accounts for this book's lasting popularity?

Another similar characteristic of spoken African tales is the sing-song repetition of short descriptive phrases to indicate emphasis and depth of feeling. Again, Aardema adopts the convention, and adds a dash of poetry in keeping with original versions. Here is an owl, for instance, who is not merely sad. "All that day and all that night, she sat in her tree—so sad, so sad, so sad." In *A Story, A Story*, by Gail Haley (1970), the Sky God questions Ananse, who in this tale is a Spider Man: "How can a weak old man like you, so small, so small, so small, pay my price?" These are honest retellings that maintain the playful rhythm and music of African storytellers.

Illustrating with full dimension Other modern retellings cut the heart out of traditional stories, although often the authors have good intentions. Walt Disney's version of "Snow White" for instance, transforms the menacing forest of the original tale into a children's zoo of smiling chipmunks, rabbits, and fawns. Snow White smiles too, even when she falls into drugged sleep, so children will not be frightened (Disney, 1975). Compare Disney to Nancy Burkert, who illustrated a version of "Snow White" retold by the poet Randall Jarrell (1972). In a dreamlike scene spread over two full pages, the forest closes in on the delicate girl as she walks over stones. Thorny tendrils reach toward her as a wolf and a bear watch. "Snow White"

Folktales are one way of introducing children to
another culture. (Illustration from *Cricket Boy* by
Feenie Ziner, illustrated by Ed Young. Illustration
copyright © 1977 by Ed Young. Reproduced by
permission of Doubleday & Company, Inc.)

had frightening dimensions, preserved here in mystery-laden illustrations that fascinate children.

Some artists strive to add symbols to illustrations to help tell the
story with all its dimensions. Gerald McDermott, for instance, tells
a story about how he discovered a symbol to support the text of a
story called "Arrow to the Sun." In this Pueblo tale, a boy seeks his
father, the sun. His quest leads him through a landscape tinted gold
by sun and corn, the staff of Pueblo life. When he finds his father, the
boy receives four tasks to perform. He completes each task, emerges
reborn, and returns to his people.

Was there a symbol that would unite sun and corn, underlining
the vital power of solar fire?

221

Yes. One day, as he searched for such a symbol, McDermott turned an ear of corn in his hands.

> Then I broke the ear in half. At that moment, the symbol hidden beneath the surface was revealed. . . . The cross section of the ear of corn, with its concentric rings and radiating rays of kernels, forms a perfect image of the sun. (1975, p. 127)

So the end-on view of an ear of corn becomes a rich symbol in McDermott's book (1974) and in an animated movie he produced at the same time.

Artist Beverly Brodsky McDermott also uses meaningful detail to enhance the illustrations for the old tale called "The Golem." The story is set in medieval Prague. Rabbi Yehuda Lev ben Bezalel dreams that the Jews in the ghetto will be accused of baking matzos with the blood of Christian children, and that an angry mob will storm the ghetto and kill the Jews. The rabbi believes his dream is an omen, so he molds a sacred lump of clay into the Golem, the likeness of a person, breathes life into it, and places the name of god in its mouth.

The dream comes true. Gentiles burn the houses in the ghetto, and the Golem becomes a defender. It grows into a giant and crushes the mob, then continues in wild destruction until Rabbi Lev commands it to stop and to return to dust. The Golem opens its mouth and the name of God falls from it before the giant crumbles. Rabbi Lev gathers the clay and replaces it under the sacred books.

In her book *The Golem* (1976), Beverly McDermott symbolizes the name of God with the letters Y and H, signifying *Yod He* ("the name of God"). Houses shrink next to the immense Golem; the giant's rampage seems to thunder against a background of orange and red. Traditional storytellers could color their voices at climactic moments in their tale; in successful modern versions, color can help supply resounding drama.

FABLES

Fragments of fables endure, and have become part of the currency of everyday language. Where, for instance, did the reference to "sour grapes" come from? A fable:

> One hot summer's day a Fox was strolling through an orchard till he came to a bunch of Grapes just ripening on a vine which had been trained over a lofty branch. "Just the thing to quench my thirst," quoth he. Drawing back a few paces, he took a run and a jump, and just missed the

TELLING WELL

Here are the opening lines of two versions of "Hansel and Gretel." Which do you think tells the story better?

Near a large forest lived a poor woodcutter with his wife and two children. The boy's name was Hansel and the girl's Gretel. The woodcutter had little to eat, and once when a great famine swept the country, he was no longer able to earn even their daily bread. One evening when he was lying in his bed and tossing about and worrying, he sighed and said to his wife, "What's to become of us? How can we feed our poor children when we've nothing left for ourselves?" "Do you know what, husband," answered the wife, "The first thing tomorrow morning we'll take the children out into the densest part of the forest. There we'll kindle them a fire and give each a little piece of bread; then we'll go about our work and leave them there alone; they won't find their way back home, and we'll be rid of them."

(Thompson, 1974, p. 55)

In a little house at the edge of a forest lived a poor woodcutter and his family. For a long time the woodcutter had not been able to find work. Without work, he had no money to buy food. His children, Hansel and Gretel, were always hungry.

The woodcutter had a wife who was very selfish. She was not the children's real mother and she did not care about them. Whenever there was a little food, she complained because she had to share it with Hansel and Gretel. Day after day she blamed her husband for being poor.

The woodcutter did not know what to do. He was very troubled.

One night when there were all in bed, Hansel and Gretel heard the wife talking to their father.

"Listen," she said. "Tomorrow we will take the children into the forest and leave them there. Perhaps someone will find them and feed them."

(Hayward, 1974)

Both are simple to read, but the language in the second is pale next to the first. Compare what the wife says to her husband. In the first, she begins, "Do you know what, husband," as if an evil idea were unfolding in her mind as she spoke. Her murderous plan comes out in measured, rhythmical phrases ("we'll go about our work . . . ; they won't find their way back home"), leading to a cruel conclusion which sounds like a fragment from a taunting children's song: ". . . and we'll be rid of them." In contrast, the wife in the second version is shallow. Her words are conversational, as if she has just poked her sleepy husband in the ribs to talk about plans for a picnic. Her casual tone does not match what she is saying.

There are many ways to tell these tales again; each age will interpret them. But successful modern storytellers hear the echoes of earlier versions as told in great stone halls. In the best retellings, something old and familiar survives despite changing voices and styles.

223

Many of Aesop's fables have become part of our
everyday idiom. (From *Aesop's Fables* edited and
illustrated by Boris Artzybasheff. Copyright © by
Boris Artzybasheff. Reprinted by permission of The
Viking Press, Inc.)

branch. Turning round again with a One, Two, Three, he jumped up, but
with no greater success. Again again he tried after the tempting morsel,
but at last had to give it up, and walked away with his nose in the air,
saying: "I am sure they are sour."

It is easy to despise what you cannot get. (Jacobs, 1894; 1966 edition, pp. 76–77)

Other familiar fables generated the expressions "don't count your chickens before they are hatched" (from "The Milkmaid and Her Pail") and "cry wolf" from "The Boy Who Cried Wolf." Both stories are found in Louis Untermeyer's *Aesop's Fables* (1967).

Most fables are beast tales. But they differ from other folktales in leading the reader toward a lesson, often summarized at the end by a one-line moral. Fables have few characters, more than three is unusual, and few twists of plot. Many of the most familiar today are attributed to Aesop, although—as with folktales—there are many different versions of each fable. And there are entire collections of less well known fables appropriate for children.

No one is sure Aesop really existed, or, if he did, whether he made up fables, or passed them on after hearing the lastest versions of much older Egyptian, Persian, or Hindu tales. Some colorful, perhaps fabulous, stories about Aesop have been passed along over centuries.

The stories depict Aesop as a hunchbacked Greek slave born around 620 B.C. Despite his deformity and menial position, he was clever and composed well-aimed political satires, hiding his barbs in little tales of foxes, dogs, and lions. Perhaps it was his wit that led to his death. As an old man, at about the age of 60, he was sentenced to execution, and hurled from a cliff. His fables survived, first in Greek, then in Latin, and finally translated into English, French, German, and many other languages.

Less well known to Americans is the French poet Jean de la Fontaine (1621-1695) who used Latin versions of Aesop to create his own fables in verse.

La Fontaine also drew on venerable—and long—stories from ancient India. The earliest of these collections is called *The Panchatantra* ("the book of five headings"), a guide in poetry to proper living, laden with philosophical stanzas. Another set of Indian stories, called the *Jatakas*, relates events in the lives of Buddha, the title of the philosopher Gautama Siddhartha who was supposedly born in India at roughly the same time Aesop died in Greece. Buddhist religious belief holds that Gautama Buddha died and was reborn many times in different animal forms. In the *Jatakas*, animals act out lessons of ancient folk wisdom, often so that errant humans will learn.

Aesop (600 B.C.), La Fontaine (A.D. 1650), and the *Jatakas* (exact date unkown) each drew fables from a great cauldron of tales available in their times, and served stories to match adult tastes. Today,

McDermott created the illustrations for this Japanese
fable by using gouache on white paper, then cutting
out and mounting the figures. (From *The Stonecutter*
by Gerald McDermott. Copyright © 1975 by Gerald
McDermott. Reprinted by permission of The Viking
Press, Inc.)

in turn, fables from each of the three have been adapted again for
children. Some of them are so popular, in fact, that there are several
versions, each appropriate for a different child.

"The Hare and the Tortoise," for instance, shows up in Boris Artzybasheff's *Aesop's Fables* (1933), as well as in the *The Hare and the Tortoise*, a one-story book illustrated by Paul Galdone (1962).

Artzybasheff takes his text from two translations of Aesop written in the eighteenth and nineteenth centuries. The words are elegant and antique. The "application" (moral) of the story is "Industry and application to business make amends for the want of quick and ready wit" (p. 31). Fourth-, fifth-, or sixth-graders might get the drift of this, but younger children would probably miss it.

The race is easier to follow in Galdone's book. The conceited hare challenges. The tortoise accepts, and wins after the hare stops to rest and falls asleep. "Slow and steady often wins the race," the tortoise says, and first-graders can understand.

La Fontaine's fable, "The Lion and the Rat," has been interpreted in bold design and vivid color by the British illustrator Brian Wildsmith (1963). The huge lion dominates a lush, dark jungle inhabited by smaller animals, few of them tinier than the lowly rat. By accident one day, the rat walks between the lion's paws, but the haughty lion chooses to overlook the indiscretion. Later, when a netlike trap snares the lion, the rat alone of all the animals is able to free him by gnawing through the net. "So the little rat, by patience and hard work, was able to do what the lion, in all his strength and rage, could not."

Wildsmith's lion stalks double-page spreads early in the book, but after he is caught, he shrinks in the course of several pages to the size of a well-wrapped yellow lump. The book is an appropriate choice for children between the ages of 5 and 7.

Striking illustrations also help to add freshness to an old Indian fable in Marcia Brown's *Once a Mouse . . .* (1961). As the story begins, a white-bearded hermit with magical powers sits in a forest thinking "of big and little" when he sees a mouse running from a crow. He saves the mouse. But then a black cat stalks the mouse, his tail slicing the air like a sword and his whiskers bristling out before him. Threatened by other animals, the mouse is turned into a dog and finally into a vain tiger who "peacocked about the forest" scaring other animals. The hermit chides him, angering the tiger into murderous thoughts. The hermit reads the thoughts, and turns the tiger back into a mouse who runs away into the forest. "And the hermit sat thinking about big and little . . . ."

The *Jataka* tales are the source of another Indian fable, "How to Catch a Fish." The newly married jackal's wife wants fish for dinner. Her husband says he will get it even though he cannot swim. At the water's edge, he finds two otters arguing over who should have the larger portion of a fish they have pulled from the water. The jackal offers to settle the argument if they agree to abide by his decision. They agree. The jackal awards the head to one otter, the tail to the other, and takes the middle for himself. When his wife asks how he got the fish, he smiles and says, "Fighting leads to losses."

The jackal's story appears in *The Talkative Beasts, Myths, Fables and Poems of India* collected by Gwendolyn Reed (1969). The illustrations, photographs of animal sculptures in India, may help introduce children in the fifth and sixth grades to non-Western cultures.

MYTHS

Fables are short, moralistic forms of the beast tale; myths are similar to pourquoi tales. They answer fundamental "why?" questions with stories of gods and natural phenomena.

One Nigerian myth, retold by Elphinstone Dayrell, explains *Why the Sun and the Moon Live in the Sky* (1968). To begin with, Sun and Moon live on earth, with Water. The three get along well, but Water has never visited the house of Sun because the house appears too small. Sun offers to build a structure big enough for Water and all his people. But the new house is still too small, and Water overflows, forcing Sun and Moon into the sky forever.

Like folktales, such stories were passed on by storytellers for centuries before anyone wrote them down. When they were collected and ordered logically, the resulting *mythology* presented an entire universe. Unlike the factual universe, there is no vacuum in the elaborate universe of mythology. The storytellers filled heaven and earth with restless populations of gods and humans, monsters and spirits.

But two of the most famous mythologies—one southern, one northern—do reflect the air and earth of the countries where they developed. Both mythologies are a mother lode of stories, and both have been mined by contemporary writers for fresh retellings.

Greek Mythology: Stories from a Golden Land

Tree branches are heavy with fruit and olives. The sun cuts clear shadows. Nature supplies food and warmth, and leaves time for music and poetry, philosophy and art. Deities live well. Lightning may threaten humans at times, but the gods themselves were created by Heaven and Earth; nature is generally benign.

The Greeks called their universe a *cosmos*—a system that, in the beginning of creation, brought order out of primordial chaos. (*Cos-*

228

This myth explains that when the water's house became too crowded, the sun and the moon were forced to live in the sky. (From *Why the Sun and the Moon Live in the Sky* by Elphinstone Dayrell, illustrated by Blair Lent, Jr. Copyright © 1968 by Blair Lent, Jr. Reproduced by permission of Houghton Mifflin, Company.)

mos is the root of our word "cosmetic," a substance to bring harmony to disorder, or at least to cover it up.) And order is apparent in the home of the gods.

Their home was called Olympus, sometimes described as a

mountain top, and sometimes as a mysterious, unearthly place. But Olympus was secure and elegant. Edith Hamilton described Olympus in her comprehensive survey *Mythology* (1942).

> Wherever it was, the entrance to it was a great gate of clouds kept by the Seasons. Within were the gods' dwellings, where they lived and slept and feasted on ambrosia and nectar and listened to Apollo's lyre. [Apollo was god of light and truth.] It was an abode of perfect blessedness. No wind . . . ever shakes the untroubled peace of Olympus; no rain ever falls there or snow; but the cloudless firmament stretches around it on all sides and the white glory of sunshine is diffused upon its walls. (pp. 22–25)

The god Zeus presided over Olympus with awful power. Zeus was lord of the sky, armed with thunder and lightning and respected by all other gods. He did have weaknesses; one was beautiful women. He constantly angered his wife, Hera, with his infidelity, and to avenge herself she pursued his lovers without mercy. This endeared her to wives in ancient Greece, and her daughter Ilithyia was said to help women in childbirth.

Zeus had two brothers. One, Poseidon, ruled the sea, carrying his three-pronged spear (called a trident), battering waves into submission by riding over the waters in a golden chariot. The second brother, Hades, ruled the dead in a dark underworld kingdom.

The Greek poet Hesiod collected the myths about these and other gods, about 800 B.C. Later, around the time of Christ, the Roman poet Ovid translated the Greek stories into Latin. He changed the names of the characters as he wrote his mythology, called the *Metamorphoses.* In Ovid's version, Zeus became Jupiter; Poseidon, Neptune; Hera, Juno; and Hades, sometimes called Pluto, was named Dis, a Latin word for rich, because he presided over all the gold in the earth.

In all versions the Hades/Pluto/Dis, figure was dour despite his wealth. In one myth, which explains the crop-killing cold that descends each winter, Hades tries to bring something of real value to his kingdom. He spirits away Persephone, the beautiful daughter of the goddess Demeter and makes her live as his wife in the underworld. In fury, Demeter, goddess of fertility and agriculture, commands the trees to wither and the crops to fail. The earth turns gray. To placate Demeter, Zeus sends Hermes, his messenger, to Hades with the command to let Persephone return to her mother, provided she has eaten no food of the dead. Hades complies. But as Persephone is about to leave, an old gardener named Ascalaphus reveals that she has eaten some seeds from the underworld. Again Zeus inter-

According to the Greek myth, Spring comes each year
when Persephone returns from the land of the dead.
(Illustration from *Demeter and Persephone* by
Penelope Proddow, illustrated by Barbara Cooney.
Illustration copyright © 1972 by Barbara Cooney
Porter. Reproduced by permission of Doubleday &
Company, Inc.)

venes with a compromise: Persephone must stay with Hades for one
season, but she may be with her mother the rest of the year. Spring
arrives each year when Persephone emerges from the land of the
dead.

Details in the story change slightly in different retellings. But, more important in selecting writing to match a particular child, the tone and the complexity of language vary widely from version to version.

Penelope Proddow's *Demeter and Persephone, Homeric Hymn Number Two* (1972) tells the story in simple, stately verse. When Demeter learns that Persephone has eaten pomegranate seeds, she proposes what must be done, and explains the coming of spring:

"... you must return
to the land of the dead," said Demeter,
"for one third of the rolling seasons.

"But when you come back
to me
for the other two,
the earth will burst into bloom
with flocks of sweet-smelling, spring flowers—
a great marvel to all men."

At that moment,
Wide-ruling Zeus
sent a messenger—
Rhea
with a golden band in her hair.

"Demeter, my daughter," said Rhea,
"Zeus wishes you
to return to the company of the gods.
Yield to him,
lest you carry your anger
toward dark-clouded Zeus
too far.

"And now,
bestow some nourishing fruit
on mortal men!"

Bright-garlanded Demeter
did not disobey.

In the illustrations by Barbara Cooney, the bright warmth of Persephone's flowing gossamer gown and the colorful wildflowers in spring contrast with grim scenes of starving humans when Demeter in anger keeps all seeds from sprouting. The adaptation is clear enough for third- or fourth-graders.

A straightforward prose version by poet, novelist, and critic Robert Graves covers the same ground in a few clipped sentences. Hades tells Demeter in a matter-of-fact tone that Persephone must return to Tartarus, the land of the dead, because she ate some seeds. Demeter rages:

> "If she goes," screamed Demeter, "I shall never lift my curse from the earth, but let all men and animals die!"
>
> In the end, Zeus sent Rhea (who was Demeter's mother as well as his own) to plead with her. The two at last agreed that Persephone should marry Hades, and spend seven months of the year in Tartarus, one month for each pomegranate seed eaten, and the rest above ground. (1960, p. 30)

The writing is simple enough to appeal to children around the sixth grade. For older students, beginning somewhere around junior high level, British writers Leon Garfield and Edward Blishen have freely translated Greek stories into sophisticated and often passionate language in *The God beneath the Sea* (1971). Hera, in their version of the Persephone story, criticized Demeter for spending time in the fields rather than her home in Olympus, "and declared contemptuously that the hot lady Demeter was overfond of tumbling in the hay with her stone-eyed muddy mortals." Zeus himself, the story continues, "had tumbled in the hay with fair Demeter" (p. 135).

At the end of the tale, springtime comes with an explosion as Demeter rushes to meet Persephone, nicknamed Core:

> "Core . . . Core! Where are you?"
> The bright poppies nodded in the golden field.
> "Core!"
> Then they exploded into a laughing scarlet storm as Core, goddess of the spring, flung herself fiercely into Demeter's arms, once more to be armisticed with kisses.
>
> The world was in summer and the days were long. Demeter smiled, all disaster forgotten in her vast nature and love . . . . (p. 164)

Northern Myths: Stories from a Land of Frost

In Scandanavian countries, by contrast, the air is crystal cold and icy for long winter seasons. Clouds block the sun. The earth seems made of frost, and life, even for gods, is vulnerable.

In northern creation myths, the world we know was made from parts of the great frost giant Ymir. Three brothers, the gods Odin, Vili, and Ve, dismembered Ymir and created the seas from his blood, mountains from his bones, and clouds heavy with hail from his brain. After this violent beginning, the gods fought the other giants in a continual war; eventually the gods died in a final all-out battle.

In contrast to Olympus, the home of the northern gods rings with the disharmonious sounds of armed fighting. The land of the gods is called Asgard. In Valhalla, the great hall of Odin in Asgard, warriors who died bravely in battles on earth continue to fight with each other. They battle for recreation now, slashing each other to pieces, and then miraculously recovering in time for feasting on boar's meat and mead.

Norse myths, as far as we know, came together in a mythology more than a millenium after the Greeks had collected their ancient stories. The *Poetic Edda* is a book of old Norse verse recorded in the tenth and eleventh centuries after Christ. Sometimes this collection of narrative poetry is called the Elder Edda, because a second collection, the younger or *Prose Edda*, was written down by Snorri Sturluson in the early part of the thirteenth century.

These two works are the sources for modern retellings, such as the several versions for young readers of the stories of Loki. Near the beginning of creation, Odin had taken Loki into his family as a brother, and as god of the kindled fire. And since creation, armed with magic and crafty intelligence, Loki had frequently caused trouble between the gods. There was the time, for instance, when Loki coveted the silken gold hair of Sif, the young wife of Odin's son, Thor. The story of Loki's mischief can be told in simple and unadorned prose, as in this passage from Ingri and Edgar Parin d' Aulaire's *Norse Gods and Giants* (1967):

> Great was Thor's horror when he woke up one morning and saw a cropped head next to his! During the night someone had sneaked in and had cut off all of Sif's beautiful hair. There was nothing worse for a woman than the shame of a bald head, and only Loki could have done such an awful deed. In a fury so wild that sparks flew from his beard, Thor stormed at Loki, threatening to break every bone in his body. (pp. 44–45)

This might be read aloud to fourth-graders but is probably better suited to children around sixth grade.

Another version better suited for older children is the retelling by

ISSUE

WAS SOMETHING LOST
IN THE RETELLING?

I particularly remembered being read to by a charming primary school lady called Mrs. Brown. She always read at what seems to me still one of the most desirable moments of the day, that moment when darkness is falling. Among the things she read to us were some of the Greek myths and legends. I remembered vividly how these stories seemed to illuminate, to make clear, what was going on around me in my small and unimportant life. They were about love, to begin with. They were about the desire for power, about jealousy, about triumph and great defeat.
. . . Well, I was saying something like this to Leon Garfield, and he said he'd had very much the same experience. These stories, heard by him at the same period in his own life, had very much the same effect. And the result of this conversation was that Leon said: "Look, do you remember those stories as we were told them? My recollection is that they had a kind of upholstered Victorian quality. . . . I think possibly it's time somebody tried to write these stories for today's children—and perhaps remove some of the upholstering." A phrase that perhaps explains rather well what we've done. (pp. 48-49)

Edward Blishen, discussing the origins of *The God beneath the Sea*
by E. Blishen and Leon Garfield, *Children's Literature in Education*,
vol. 3, November 1970, pp. 48-54.

The editor is to blame as much as anybody. Personal taste is one thing, but *The God beneath the Sea* is quite another; and whoever accepted the manuscript in its published form has rendered a disservice to the authors. Leon Garfield and Edward Blishen have fallen into the trap they tried to avoid. The prose is overblown Victoriana, "fine" writing at its worst, cliché-ridden to the point of satire, falsely poetic, groaning with imagery and, among such a grandiloquent mess, intrusively colloquial at times. Worst of all, the authors are so coy in their efforts to be "frank" about sexuality that only the cumulative absurdity saves them from prurience: ". . . and in a white passion of wings, he quenched his restless heat" (p. 28). "The Titan's daughter was already quick with child" (Ibid.). "Her time was at hand" (Ibid.). "Her gown was torn, her hair awry and everything about her proclaimed her ruin" (p. 140). All that is missing is, "Afterwards, they slept."

Alan Garner, *Children's Literature in Education*,
vol. 3, November 1970, pp. 69-71.

Read the episodes containing the quotes cited by Garner. Is *The God beneath the Sea* weakened by "fine" writing? When does good writing become "fine" writing in Garner's terms? What defense might Blishen offer against Garner's criticism? Why are myths retold by modern writers? What dangers do the writers face?

Cynthia King, *In the Morning of Time* (1970). King's work adds a mysterious, conflicting underside to Loki's character.

> The strange mixture of good and bad had always been Loki's way and Loki's mystery. If God or man had an evil thought, Loki expressed it. If a God had a jealous bent, Loki played on it.
>
> Back in time when Asgard was young and the Gods had not known how to fight the giants, Loki had sat by a clump of yew trees watching Thor's wife, Sif, reading by a river. The mischief-maker looked longingly at her thick yellow hair flowing like a shining liquid over her smooth back . . . . Sif felt the snips too late. She jumped and cried out in misery when she saw her beautiful hair in Loki's hands . . . . (p. 112)

A third version of the same episode appears in *The Children of Odin* (1920), by Irish poet, playwrite, and critic Padraic Colum. Colum's dignified, lyrical prose, suited for children in the sixth or seventh grade or older, covers Sif herself in mystery. Thor returns to Asgard from a trip and finds an empty house. He searches all over Asgard for his golden-haired wife, then returns home.

> When he was coming back to his house he heard his name whispered. He stopped, and then a figure stole out from behind a stone. A veil covered her head, and Thor scarce knew that this was Sif, his wife. As he went to her she sobbed and sobbed. "O Thor, my husband," she said, "do not look upon me. I am ashamed that you should see me. I shall go from Asgard and from the company of the Gods and Goddesses . . . I cannot bear that any of the Dwellers in Asgard should look upon me now." (p. 28)

Loki is captured, and to atone, provides the gods with gifts and Sif with new hair, all made by dwarfs.

Modern versions of myths always depend on earlier sources which were, themselves, once modern. Edward Blishen, coauthor of *The God beneath the Sea*, has written that he and Leon Garfield relied on Robert Grave's work, "partly because Graves tells the stories with such simplicity that we thought we were not likely to be contaminated by them." The two authors also borrowed from Ovid (1970, p. 50).

Three gnomes help Loki earn forgiveness by making a
spear, a ship, and golden hair to replace Sif's.
(Illustration from *Norse Gods and Giants* by Ingri and
Edgar Parin D'Aulaire. Copyright © 1967 by Ingri and
Edgar Parin D'Aulaire. Reproduced by permission of
Doubleday & Company, Inc.)

The sources for modern retellings need not be so familiar; Betty
Baker, a writer in Arizona, drew material for her mythology from
Pima and Papago tribes of southern Arizona and northern Mexico,
and worked them into a continuous narrative called *At the Center of
the World* (1973). This mythology, too, has a creation story; everything began when a powerful figure named Earth Magician came out
of the deep, scraped dust from his chest, patted it flat, danced upon
it, and made the world. The sun and moon are balls of ice, and the
buzzard is a shadow from his left eye.

Baker began with the earliest forms of the stories she could find.
Then, like all creators of myths, she searched her own mind for
other material. "I've added portions of my own," she writes, "a
respectable practice since the originals showed considerable borrow-
ing from the Hopi, pueblo dwellers in northeastern Arizona, as well
as from the people living westward along the Colorado River"
(p. 52).

237

EPICS

The search for the roots of ancient stories is usually quiet and un-heralded. But in the case of the oldest known epic, the search at one point became sensational news.

In 1872, a man in his early thirties named George Smith became interested in an ancient clay tablet at the British Museum in London. Marks in the clay related a story from Assyria. But a piece of the tablet was missing. Smith estimated that the missing fragment was fifteen lines long. He developed a driving ambition to find the missing piece. An account of what happened appears in Anita Feagles's book, *He Who Saw Everything* (1966, pp. 61-62). A London newspaper, the *Daily Telegraph* offered Smith a small fortune for the times—the equivalent of $5,000—to go on a quest for the piece, provided they could print the story of his search. So Smith went to what is now Iraq where the story was first told. With astonishing luck, he found the missing piece in a few days. Smith had made a good guess. The fragment he found was seventeen lines long.

The missing piece completed one of the twelve tablets telling the epic story of a young king named Gilgamesh. First recorded more than 3,000 years before Christ, the story was almost certainly told to the sound of a harp before that.

The tablets in the British Museum preserved in hard clay some of the familiar foundations of all later epics, including the stories of the legendary Greek poet Homer, and epic Indian poems.

Why did the Gilgamesh story have enough stature to last more than 5,000 years? Two characteristics in particular seem significant. First, the hero is close to the gods; the heavens watched his deeds and sometimes intervened. Gilgamesh is similar to the figures in tall tales in that his dimensions are bigger than life. Second, despite his high standing as king and favored son of the heavens, Gilgamesh is vulnerable.

Time and again in great epics, the hero risks his life in tests or battles while the story's audience watches over the shoulders of gods. Battles have great moment partly because heroes are powerful, and partly because the enemy appears even stronger.

An epic hero of northern mythology, Sigurd, is directly descended from the god Odin. But Sigurd is dwarfed by the scaly dragon Fafnir in one suspenseful episode. Colum's *The Children of Odin* tells the story of the confrontation. Sigurd lies in a pit in the ground, practicing sword thrusts, waiting for Fafnir. The shape of the dragon comes over the pit. Fafnir looks down on Sigurd, who drives upward

Beowulf struggles against the Sea-Hag, the mother of
Grendel. (From (retelling) *Beowulf* by Rosemary
Sutcliff. Copyright © 1962 by Rosemary Sutcliff,
illustration © 1962 by The Bodley Head, Inc.
Reprinted by permission of the publishers, E. P.
Dutton)

through the hard scales toward the dragon's heart. Sigurd retreats to avoid a drenching by Fafnir's poisonous blood, and then risks his life again to deliver the death blow.

> He came to him and thrust his sword right through the dragon's neck. The dragon reared up as though to fling himself down on Sigurd with all his crushing bulk and dread talons, with his firery breath and his envenomed blood. But Sigurd leaped aside and ran far off. Then did Fafnir scream his death scream. After he had torn up rocks with his talons, he lay prone on the ground, his head in the pit that was filled with his envenomed blood. (p. 219)

Beowulf, hero of the oldest-known English epic, written down some time in the eighth century after Christ, faces a similar contest with a supernatural, spell-casting monster named Grendel. Beowulf almost loses. Even Robin Hood, the spirited outlaw of the Middle Ages who robs the rich for the sake of the poor, must face death. In Howard Pyle's version, *The Merry Adventures of Robin Hood* (1946), the apparently indomitable Robin is betrayed by a nun, and killed.

All the best retellings preserve the mighty power of the hero as well as the possibility of the hero's death. Here is a closer look at three great epic traditions and recent translations that tell the stories in modern voice without losing ancient force and magic.

Gilgamesh

The gods keep watch over the young king of Uruk (located near the juncture of the Tigis and Euphrates rivers in what is now Iraq). Early in Bernarda Bryson's powerful version, *Gilgamesh* (1967), the elders of Uruk climb to a towering wall of the city to complain to the gods about their king. All he wants to do is build walls, the elders contend. One of the gods answers, speaking, in a primitive way, for all the gods in future epic literature.

> "We ourselves rather like the high walls . . . . We often come and crouch here at night and watch the goings-on of mortals. It's very entertaining!"(p. 14)

Gilgamesh is reminded that he is mortal when his best friend, Enkidu, is killed by an angry goddess. Then, like many later epic heroes, Gilgamesh sets out on a quest, a long and perilous journey. His goal is to find a legendary old man, Utnapishtim, who is said to

Bryson based her illustrations on relics from the time
when this legend was current. (From *Gilgamesh*
written and illustrated by Bernarda Bryson. Copyright
© 1967 by Bernarda Bryson. Reproduced by
permission of Holt, Rinehart and Winston, Publishers.)

hold the secret of life and death. The young king crosses deserts and
rocky land, and overcomes darkness and madness and the temptations of Shamash the sun, before he is able to rest awhile in a beautiful garden. His face burned, his body emaciated, he crosses the deadly Bitter River, whose waters are poison to mortals. Finally he
kneels before Utnapishtim who is lying in a hammock. The old man
looks up at the unkempt king and shouts, "I do not like you at all!"
(p. 76).

The meeting produces scant reward. Utnapishtim reveals that he
has no secret; many years before, he was told to build a ship and take
aboard the "seed of every living thing" (p. 79). He boarded the ship
and survived a worldwide flood, precursor of waters navigated by
Noah in the later Biblical epic. His reward was everlasting life. Gilgamesh arrives back in his walled city without any balm against
death, and finally walks of his own will toward the underground
where Enkidu and all the dead reside. Then:

> He bowed; he fell into the dust among the weeds and bracken and the
> trailing vines of arbutus. Like a worm he lay on his face for seven days
> and seven nights while Enkidu knelt beside him. He was dead, and the
> earth reached up and seized him. (p. 104)

Bryson's watercolor illustrations in red and gold, blue and

241

emerald, show wide-eyed figures that appear to have come alive from decorations on ancient relics.

The Iliad and Odyssey

These two Greek epics, written thousands of years after Gilgamesh, weave dozens of subplots, intrigues between gods, quests, and battles into a labyrinthine narrative. The works are a challenge to modern writers; it is difficult to simplify the story without killing its spirit. Not all versions succeed.

Legend has it that Homer, a blind Greek poet, composed the two works and sang them as he traveled from city to city, some time within the last 1,000 years before Christ. But no one is exactly sure when, or whether Homer was the only author. Somewhere around 1200 B.C., there *was* a battle between Greeks and residents of Troy in the northwestern part of Asia Minor, where Turkey is located today. The war lasted ten years, and generated the epic stories.

According to the *Iliad*, the conflict begins with an abduction. Paris, son of the king of Troy, steals the beautiful Helen, wife of the Greek king Menelaus. The Greeks come by sea to rescue Helen; they lay seige to Troy, and years later enter the city through trickery. They build a wooden horse, hide soldiers inside it, and present it as a gift to the Trojans who admit the horse through their gates. Troy falls. The *Odessey* picks up the story after the Greek victory as one of the warriors, Odysseus, travels home. It takes a decade of grueling tests and temptations—reminiscent of Gilgamesh's quest—before he arrives back in Greece.

Complex as the stories are, they can be told simply. Robert Graves combines the *Iliad* and *Odyssey* in *The Seige and Fall of Troy* (1962). His writing has a contemporary flavor, which is irritating to some readers, but the story is salted with humor and with the suspense of good adventure. Look at the following passage. The Greeks are outside the walls of Troy, and it seems there will be no end to the war.

Athene [goddess of wisdom] now inspired Odysseus to think of a stratagem for getting armed men into Troy. Under his directions, Epeius the Phocian, the best carpenter in camp though a fearful coward, built an enormous hollow horse out of fir planks. It had a concealed trap-door fitted into the left flank, and on the right a sentence carved in tall letters: "With thankful hope of a safe return to their homes after nine years' absence, the Greeks dedicate this offering to Athene." Odysseus would enter the horse by means of a rope-ladder . . . . Coaxed, threatened and bribed, Epeius was forced to sit by the trap door, which he alone could open quickly and silently. (p. 90)

Another version by writer Juliet Mosley, *The Wooden Horse of Troy* (1970), tries to tell children the whole history of the Trojan War in a kind of telegram, less than 100 sentences long. Again, the Greeks are outside the walls of Troy. Suddenly, Odysseus

decided that if a large horse was built of wood, and filled with soldiers, the Trojans might perhaps want to take it right into their city.

Athene is gone. The mystery and danger of the horse are gone. Impersonal soldiers fill it up like gasoline. Passive constructions replace the active language of Graves ("was built" instead of "built"), and other language is weak ("might perhaps" is coy and redundant).

This picture book, aimed at 7- or 8-year-olds, is so simple it becomes confusing. Why, for instance, would the Trojans want to accept a horse filled with enemy soldiers?

Several other versions of Homer's poetry are clear and simple without losing the grandeur of the heroes and without softening the dangers they face. As Odysseus travels home, his ship at one point must pass between Scylla, a six-headed monster, and the swirling waters of Charybdis. In *The Odyssey of Homer* (1952) by Barbara Picard, Odysseus puts on a brave face before his seamen, hiding the danger from them and heightening suspense for readers:

Odysseus went among them with words of encouragement and comfort. "My friends, we have been in many perils together, but we have lived through them all. And indeed, this new danger cannot be worse than the Cyclops [one-eyed monster] in his cave; and yet I brought you out alive from that monster's den. Be guided by me now and we may be saved. Row as you have never rowed before, and look not aside from your oars." Then to the helmsman he spoke, "Steer clear of the churning and thundering around the lower half of the rocks, keep close in beside the tall cliff." But he did not tell them of Scylla in her cave half-way up the rock, lest fear should take the strength from their arms and make them feeble. (p. 44)

A more straightforward and less poetic rendition by Barbara Watson, *The Iliad and the Odyssey* (1966), still maintains the dignity of the original:

The illustrations for this edition of *The Ramayana* were drawn from Indian temple sculpture. (From *The Ramayana* by R. K. Narayan, illustrated by R. K. Laxman. Illustration copyright © 1972 by R. K. Laxman. Reprinted by permission of The Viking Press, Inc.)

Odysseus said nothing to the crew about Scylla. Circe had warned him that there was no escape from her, and he did not want the men to panic and hide, leaving the ship adrift. (p. 75)

Picard's book is appropriate for adolescents; the Watson and Graves books are suggested for children in the sixth or seventh grade.

The Ramayana

This classic Hindu epic somewhat parallels Homer's works. Like Odysseus, the hero, Prince Rama, spends years wandering from adventure to adventure. Like Helen, Rama's wife, Princess Sita, is abducted. In Indian tradition, the villain is an evil giant named Ravana. Rama, who is the god Vishnu in mortal form, allies himself with an army of millions of monkeylike warriors, offspring of the sun, moon, and wind. Sita is rescued, and they return to Ayodya, their home.

An Indian poet named Valmiki collected the legends of Rama into a long Sanskrit epic about four or five centuries before Christ, probably some centuries after Homer had assembled his epics. But it seems certain that the Indian epic was told centuries before Valmiki. It took seven books, containing 24,000 stanzas, to recount this convoluted and complex epic, which includes long descriptions of rites, geneologies, and feasts, as well as the plots of related legends.

A modern English version by Joseph Gaer, *The Adventures of Rama* (1954), brings the story within reach of intermediate-grade students, a feat which writer Gaer likens to trying to reduce a colorful mural to a small black-and-white sketch. But his version preserves the main story line of the Valmiki poem, the godly stature of Rama (Rama means "the great delight"), and the thunder of battle against steep odds. In the following passage Rama has just gravely wounded an evil giant in the final battle with the forces of Ravana. Then, like Sigurd fighting Fafnir, Rama faces a second attack from the giant, named Kumbhakarna:

> Though the blood flowed down his limbs like torrents down a mountainside, Kumbhakarna lifted a hugh mass of rock high above his head to fling at Rama. But the master bowman had raised his bow and placed upon it two crescent-headed arrows given him by his teacher Vishvamitra. He aimed; then let them fly. One pierced the giant's heart, the other tore the giant's head from off his shoulders. For an eerie moment the headless giant remained erect. Then slowly he leaned, like a tower shaken by an earthquake, and crashed to the ground. (pp. 158–159)

Rama survives in India today in dramatic pageants produced each fall. The words of the spoken story seem novel enough to hold audiences in taut suspense. And the lines are familiar enough so that even the youngest listeners can instantly correct actors who muff their parts.

SUMMARY

1 Before the invention of the printing press in the middle of the fifteenth century, stories were passed along out loud from person to person. The theory of *monogenesis* suggests that such stories originated in one society, and then changed as they traveled to other lands. *Polygenesis*, by contrast, suggests that similar stories grew

spontaneously in separate countries because human societies, despite their differences, share the same basic needs and emotions. However stories in the oral tradition began, they changed as they spread. For example, today there are at least 500 versions of "Cinderella" in Europe alone. Many modern versions of traditional literature are appropriate for children.

2 "Cinderella" is an example of a *folktale*, a short story with fast-moving plot, uncomplicated characters, familiar motifs (elements recurring in tale after tale), and happy endings. Many of the hundreds of tales still told today are associated with their collectors. *Charles Perrault* is sometimes credited with inventing Mother Goose. *Jakob and Wilhelm Grimm* sought out stories from uneducated people to try to learn more about early Europeans and their migrations; their stories, like Perrault's, were not printed primarily for children. *Joseph Jacobs* was one of the first to publish tales specifically for young readers.

3 Some categories of folktales are particularly popular with children today: *tales of talking animals; pourquoi tales,* which answer childlike questions about the world; *cumulative tales*, which incorporate into the text recurring passages similar to refrains in songs; and *tales of exaggeration and nonsense.* The same basic story can appear in different forms, but the best of these tales preserve the flavor and meaning of older forms.

4 *Fables* are folktales with morals. Many of the most familiar today are attributed to *Aesop*, who tradition holds was a hunchbacked Greek slave born around 620 B.C. The seventeenth-century poet *Jean de la Fontaine* called on Latin versions of Aesop to create his own fables in verse; La Fontaine also drew his material from two collections of ancient Indian tales, the *Panchatantra* and the *Jatakas*. Like folktales, fables reappear today in different forms, appropriate for different children. *Boris Artzybasheff's* version of "The Hare and the Tortoise," for example, appeals to readers in the fourth through sixth grades, while *Paul Galdone's* retelling of the same fable is more appropriate to first-graders.

5 *Myths* are similar to pourquoi tales: they answer basic questions about why things are the way they are. Two great traditions generated myths that have survived in literature for children today. *Greek mythology* tells of gods in a warm and golden realm called Olympus. Again, different versions of the same myth match the needs and interests of different children; the story of Demeter and Persephone, for example, is currently available in poetry or prose, and at several different reading levels. *Northern mythology* reflects the long winter

seasons in Scandanavian countries. In contrast to generally peaceful Olympus, Asgard—home of northern gods—rings with the sounds of fighting among warriors who died bravely in battles on earth. Like the Greek myths, tales of disharmony among the gods have been retold in many different versions and appeal to a variety of modern readers at different levels.

6 *Epics*, like *Gilgamesh*, are stories of mortal—and vulnerable—heroes whose fates are followed and often determined by the gods. Epic stories frequently involve the hero in a quest, or journey; many epics culminate with a battle setting the hero against a huge and evil creature. *Sigurd*, for example, faces the terrible dragon Fafnir. *Beowulf* contends with a spell-casting monster, Grendel. A Greek epic, the *Iliad*, tells the long story of the ten-year war between Greece and Troy, and the *Odyssey* follows one of the warriors as he travels home in the course of another ten years. Complex as the stories are, they have been retold simply in modern translations appropriate for young readers by authors such as *Robert Graves, Barbara Picard,* and *Barbara Watson. The Ramayana,* an Indian epic that somewhat parallels these Greek epics, follows the adventures of a hero, Prince Rama, as he tries to release his wife, a prisoner of the evil giant Ravana. *Joseph Gaer* has retold the story in a version suitable for intermediate-grade students.

BIBLIOGRAPHY

Recommended Traditional Literature

Folktales

Berson, Harold (ad.). *Kassim's Shoes* (New York: Crown, 1977).
Kassim loves his old shoes, but feels he must throw them away when his neighbors give him new ones. They are not easy to get rid of, however.
Moroccan

Carter, Dorothy Sharp. *Greedy Mariani;* and Other Folktales of the Antilles, illus. Trina Schart Hyman (New York: Antheneum, 1974).
These stories, told in a conversational tone, will be enjoyed for their humor and for the dialogue.
West Indian

Courlander, Harold. *The King's Drum and Other African Stories,* illus. Enrico Arno (New York: Harcourt, 1962).

Courlander captures the humor of the African folktale in his retelling of these twenty-nine brief stories.

De Paola, Tomie. *Strega Nona* (Englewood Cliffs, N.J.: Prentice-Hall, 1975).
Anthony says magic words and Strega Nona's magical pasta pot begins to produce the pasta. But then Anthony cannot stop it, so pasta floods the town.

Italian

De Regniers, Beatrice Schenk. *Little Sister and the Month Brothers,* illus. by Margot Tomes (New York: Seabury, 1976).
Little Sister is kind to the Month Brothers, and her sister is not, so she is rewarded and the sister is lost in a snowstorm.

Slavic

Galdone, Joanna. *The Tailypo,* illus. Paul Galdone (New York: Seabury, 1977).
The old man cuts the tail off a varmint, eats it, and from that time on is harassed by a voice which announces that it has come for its tailypo.

American

Ginsburg, Mirra. *Striding Slippers,* illus. by Sal Murdocca (New York: Macmillan, 1978).
The slippers help a shepherd who made them leap and bound across the fields. But thieves who steal the slippers cannot control them.

Russian

Grimm Brothers. *The Sleeping Beauty,* retold and illus. Trina Schart Hyman (Boston: Little, Brown, 1977).
Hyman's illustrations for this favorite fairy tale are strong in their portrayal of emotion.

Grimm, Jakob Ludwig Karl. *The Complete Grimm's Fairy Tales,* illus. Josef Scharl (New York: Pantheon, 1974).
This standard edition of the Grimm tales was first published in 1944.

Harris, Christie. *Mouse Woman and the Mischief-Makers,* illus. Douglas Tait (New York: Atheneum, 1977).
Mouse Woman was a tiny spirit, called a narnauk, who tried to keep order, and who was very proper. These seven tales are about her attempts, including trickery, to see that everything turns out right.

Indian—Pacific Northwest

Haviland, Virginia. *Favorite Fairy Tales Told in India,* illus. Blair Lent (Boston: Little, Brown, 1973).

This is one of a series of books of folktales grouped by country of origin.

Hogrogian, Nonny. *The Contest.* (New York: Greenwillow, 1976).
Two robbers discover that they are both engaged to the same girl, and so decide to see which of them is the more clever.

Holman, Felice. *The Drac; French Tales of Dragons and Demons,* illus. Stephen Walker (New York: Scribner's, 1975).
Each of the five stories is filled with action, and with careful descriptions of the demons.

French

Jacobs, Joseph. *Munachar and Manachar,* illus. Anne Rockwell (New York: Crowell, 1970).
Munachar and Manachar are leprechauns. Munachar becomes angry because as fast as he can pick raspberries, Manachar eats them.

Irish

Keats, Ezra Jack. *John Henry, An American Legend* (New York: Pantheon, 1965).
Keats' illustrations show the power of John Henry, from birth through his contest with a steam drill.

McDermott, Beverly Brodsky. *The Crystal Apple* (New York: Viking, 1974).
The crystal apple, in which Marusha could see beautiful things, is broken by her sisters, but her father assures her that "imagination is a precious gift." She gazes at water and clouds and realizes she does not need the apple.

Russian

McDermott, Gerald. *The Stonecutter* (New York: Viking, 1975).
The stonecutter keeps wishing to be more powerful, from stonecutter, to prince, to sun, to cloud, to mountain—where he feels another stonecutter chipping at his feet.

Japanese

Minard, Rosemary (ed.). *Womenfolk and Fairy Tales,* illus Suzanna Klein (Boston: Houghton Mifflin, 1975).
These eighteen tales focus on women who are active and decisive—characters such as Molly Whuppie.

Wiesner, William. *Turnabout* (New York: Seabury, 1972).
A man thinks his wife's job is easier than his until they change places and he attempts to run the house.

Norwegian

Ziner, Feenie. *Cricket Boy,* illus. Ed Young (Garden City, N.Y.: Doubleday, 1977).

Scholar Hu's wish, when his cricket defeats that of the Emperor, is that his son will live again. His wish comes true.   Chinese

Fables, Myths and Epics

Bierhorst, John (ed. and trans.). *Black Rainbow: Legends of the Incas and Myths of Ancient Peru,* illus. Jane Byers Bierhorst (New York: Farrar, 1976).
This scholarly volume contains eight legends, seven myths, and five fables, with notes on the sources of each.

Brown, Marcia. *Backbone of the King, The Story of Pakáa and His Son Ku* (New York: Scribner's, 1966).
Brown retells the Polynesian legend of the father and son who are the chief guardians of the king.

Brown, Marcia. *The Blue Jackal* (New York: Scribner's, 1977).
This tale of the jackal who jumps into a vat of indigo dye and then returns to the forest to rule as king until he gives himself away by howling is based on *The Panchatantra.*

D'Aulaire, Ingri and Edgar D'Aulaire. *Book of Greek Myths* (Garden City, N.Y., 1962).
The retellings are fairly brief, with full-color illustrations which aid in their interpretation.

DeRoin, Nancy (ed.). *Jataka Tales,* illus. Ellen Lanyon (Boston: Houghton Mifflin, 1975).
Each of these animal fables concludes with a moral, most relating to how people get along with one another.

Erdoes, Richard (ed.). *The Sound of Flutes and Other Indian Legends,* illus. Paul Goble (New York: Pantheon, 1976).
These tales of the Plains Indians include legends and creation myths.

Gates, Doris. *Two Queens of Heaven, The Story of Demeter and Aphrodite,* illus. Trina Schart Hyman (New York: Viking, 1974).
This is one of several books by Gates which organize the myths related to specific gods and godesses and present them as a single book.

Green, Roger Lancelyn. *The Tale of Thebes,* illus. Jael Jordan (Cambridge: Cambridge, 1977).
This story of the royal family of Thebes is based on the author's wide reading in Greek and Latin literature.

Jablow, Alta. *Gassire's Lute,* illus. Leo Dillon and Diane Dillon (New York: Dutton, 1971).

This epic poem from West Africa tells of Gassire's desire to become a hero in battle, and his eventual loss of his kingdom and all but one son. He renounces his past and becomes a bard.

Narayan, R.K. *The Ramayana,* illus. R.K. Laxman (New York: Viking, 1972).

This is not a translation, but what the author describes as a "literary product" based on the impact of his reading and studying of the Indian epic.

Serraillier, Ian. *Heracles the Strong,* illus. Rocco Negri (New York: Walck, 1970).

This poet has retold several of the Greek myths as single stories. The language is forceful and evocative.

Spriggs, Ruth (Reteller). *The Fables of Aesop; 143 Moral Tales Retold,* illus. Frank Baber (Chicago: Rand McNally, 1976).

The fables are presented in a direct style, illustrated with realistic drawings.

Sutcliff, Rosemary. *Dragon Slayer: The Story of Beowulf,* illus. Charles Keeping (London: The Bodley Head, 1961).

Sutcliff offers a dramatic retelling of this Anglo-Saxon epic.

Synge, Ursula. *Land of Heroes: A Retelling of the Kavevala* (New York: Atheneum, 1978).

This prose version of the Finnish epic poem recounts the competition of three heroes to win the hand of the Maiden of Louhi.

Williams, Jay. *Sword of King Arthur,* illus. Louis Glanzman (New York: Crowell, 1968).

Williams' language is clear and direct, making this version of the tale fairly easy to read.

Adult References

Bettelheim, Bruno. *The Uses of Enchantment* (New York: Knopf, 1976).

Blishen, Edward, Leon Garfield and Charles Keeping. "Greek Myths and the Twentieth Century Reader," *Children's Literature in Education,* vol. 3, November 1970, pp. 48–54.

Chukovsky, Kornei. *From Two to Five,* trans. and edited Miriam Morton (Berkeley: University of California Press, 1971). (1925)

Cohen, Martha. *Sex Role Stereotypes in Elementary Education: A Handbook for Parents and Teachers* (Hartford, Conn.: Travelers Insurance Co., 1974).

Colwell, Eileen. "Folk Literature: An Oral Tradition and an Oral Art," *Top of the News,* vol. 24, pp. 175–180, 1968.

Cook, Elizabeth. *The Ordinary and the Fabulous* (Cambridge, England: Cambridge University Press, 1969).

Egoff, Sheila, G.T. Stubbs, and L.F. Ashley. *Only Connect* (Toronto: Oxford University Press, 1969).

Favat, F. André. *Child and Tale: The Origins of Interest.* (Urbana, Ill.: National Council of Teachers of English, 1977).

Garner, Alan. "The Death of Myth," book review, *Children's Literature in Education*, vol. 3, November 1970, pp. 69–71.

Hornyansky, Michael. "The Truth of Fables," *The Tamarack Review*, Autumn 1965, pp. 19–28.

Kamenetsky, Christa. "The Brothers Grimm: Folktale Style and Romantic Theories," *Elementary English*, March 1974, pp. 379–383.

Lanes, Selma G. "A Case for The Five Chinese Brothers," *School Library Journal*, October, 1977, pp. 90–91.

Larrick, Nancy. *I Heard a Scream in the Street* (New York: Dell, 1970).

McDermott, Gerald. "On the Rainbow Trail, " *The Horn Book*, April 1975, pp. 123–131.

Sandburg, Carl. *The People, Yes* (New York: Harcourt, 1936).

Sawyer, Ruth. *The Way of the Storyteller* (New York: Viking, 1942).

Schwartz, Albert V. "The Five Chinese Brothers: Time to Retire," Interracial Books for Children *Bulletin*, vol. 8, no. 3, 1977, pp. 3–7.

Smith, Lillian. *The Unreluctant Years* (Chicago: American Library Association, 1953).

Thompson, Stith. *Motif-Index of Folk Literature* (Bloomington, Ind.: Indiana University Press, 1955).

Ward, Nancy. "Feminism and Censorship," *Language Arts*, May 1976, pp. 536–537.

Children's Book References

Aardema, Verna. *Why Mosquitoes Buzz in People's Ears,* illus. Leo and Diane Dillon (New York: Dial, 1975).

Artzybasheff, Boris. *Aesop's Fables* (New York: Viking, 1933).

Baker, Betty. *At the Center of the World,* illus. Murray Tinkelman (New York: Macmillan, 1973).

Belting, Natalie. *The Long-Tailed Bear and Other Indian Legends,* illus. Louis Cary (Indianapolis: Bobbs-Merrill, 1961).

Brown, Marcia. *Once a Mouse . . .* (New York: Scribner's, 1961).

Bryson, Bernarda. *Gilgamesh* (New York: Holt, 1967).

Chase, Richard. *The Jack Tales,* illus. Berkeley Williams, Jr. (Boston: Houghton Mifflin, 1943).

Colum, Padraic. *The Children of Odin*, illus. Willy Pogany (New York: Macmillan, 1920).

D'Aulaire, Ingri, and Edgar d'Aulaire. *Norse Gods and Giants* (Garden City, N.Y.: Doubleday, 1967).

Dayrell, Elphinstone. *Why the Sun and the Moon Live in the Sky*, illus. Blair Lent (Boston: Houghton Mifflin, 1968).

Disney, Walt, adapted by Guy N. Smith. *Snow White and the Seven Dwarfs* (New York: Pyramid, 1976). (1975)

Emberley, Barbara. *The Story of Paul Bunyan*, illus. Ed Emberley Englewood Cliffs, N.J.: Prentice-Hall, 1963).

Feagles, Anita. *He Who Saw Everything*, illus. Xavier Gonzalez (New York: Young Scott, 1966).

Gaer, Joseph. *The Adventures of Rama*, illus. Randy Monk (Boston: Little, Brown, 1954).

Galdone, Paul. *The Hare and the Tortoise* (New York: McGraw-Hill, 1962).

Garfield, Leon, and Edward Blishen. *The God beneath the Sea*, illus. Zevi Blum (New York: Pantheon, 1971).

Graves, Robert. *Greek Gods and Heroes* (Garden City, N.Y. : Doubleday, 1960).

———. *The Seige and Fall of Troy*, illus. C. Walter Hodges (Garden City, N.Y.: Doubleday, 1962).

Grimm, Jakob, and Wilhelm Grimm, trans. Edgar Taylor. *King Grisly-Beard*, illus. Maurice Sendak (New York: Farrar, 1973).

———, trans. Randall Jarrell. *Snow White and the Seven Dwarfs*, illus. Nancy Ekholm Burkert (New York: Farrar, 1972).

Haley, Gail. *A Story, A Story* (New York: Atheneum, 1970).

Hamilton, Edith. *Mythology*, illus. Steele Savage (Boston: Little, Brown, 1942).

Hayward, Linda. *Hansel and Gretel*, illus. Sheila Beckett (New York: Random House, 1974).

Kaula, Edna Mason. *African Village Folktales* (Cleveland: World, 1968).

Jacobs, Joseph. *The Fables of Aesop* (New York: Schocken, 1966). (1894).

King, Cynthia. *In the Morning of Time*, illus. Charles Mikolaycak (New York: Four Winds, 1970).

Leodhas, Sorche Nic. *All in the Morning Early*, illus. Evaline Ness (New York: Holt, 1963).

McDermott, Beverly Brodsky. *The Golem* (Philadelphia: Lippincott, 1976).

McDermott, Gerald. *Arrow to the Sun* (New York: Viking, 1974).

Mosel, Arlene. *Tikki Tikki Tembo*, illus. Blair Lent (New York: Holt, 1968).

Mosley, Juliet. *The Wooden Horse of Troy* (London: Watts, 1970).

Pearce, Philippa. *Beauty and the Beast,* illus. Alan Barrett (New York: Crowell, 1972).

Picard, Barbara. *The Odyssey of Homer,* illus. Joan Kiddell-Monroe (New York: Walck, 1952).

Proddow, Penelope. *Demeter and Persephone, Homeric Hymn Number Two,* illus. Barbara Cooney (Garden City, N.Y.: Doubleday, 1972).

Pyle, Howard. *The Merry Adventures of Robin Hood* (New York: Scribner's, 1946).

Ransome, Arthur. *The Fool of the World and the Flying Ship,* illus. Uri Shulevitz (New York: Farrar, 1968).

Reed, Gwendolyn. *The Talkative Beasts, Myths, Fables and Poems of India,* illus. Stella Snead (New York: Lothrop, Lee and Shepard, 1969).

Singer, Isaac Bashevis. *Zlateh the Goat and Other Stories,* illus. Maurice Sendak (New York: Harper, 1966).

Thompson, Stith. *One Hundred Favorite Folktales,* illus. Franz Altschuler (Bloomington, Ind.: Indiana University Press, 1974). (1968)

Untermeyer, Louis (selector and adapter). *Aesop's Fables,* illus. Alice Provensen and Martin Provensen (New York: Golden, 1967).

Watson, Barbara. *The Iliad and the Odyssey,* illus. Alice Provensen and Martin Provensen (Racine, Wis.: Golden, 1966).

Wildsmith, Brian. *The Lion and the Rat* (London: Oxford University Press, 1963).

Zemach, Margot. *The Three Sillies* (New York: Holt, 1963).

CHAPTER
6

MODERN FANTASY

A SMALL STEP FROM REALITY

L loyd Alexander, an American writer whose books are often set in imaginary kingdoms, woke up early one morning worrying about a cloud. In the story he was writing at the time, he had planned to use the cloud to warn a few of the inhabitants of his current kingdom that something terrible was going to happen.

The Muse in charge of fantasy jarred him awake, he reported later.

"I've been meaning to speak to you about that cloud," she said. "You like it, don't you? You think it's dramatic. But I was wondering if this had occurred to you: you only want a few of your people to see the cloud, is that not correct? Yet you have already established a number of other characters in the vicinity who will see it, too. An event like this? They'll do nothing but talk about it for most of the story. Or," she purred, as she always does before she pounces, "did you have something like closed-circuit television in mind?" (1965, p. 144)

Modern writers of fantasy face strict disciplines. Wizards who use magical powers to escape in one scene cannot lose those powers, without good reason, if recaptured in another scene. A mountain range poking the clouds over a magical kingdom early in a book must, barring miracles, be there at the end of the book. If frogs can speak English, there had better be a clear reason why dogs cannot.

Writers of fantasy today, Alexander says, wind up being hard-headed realists: "What appears gossamer is, underneath, solid as prestressed concrete" (p. 142).

Fantasy is made up of elements that do not exist outside of the imagination—one elf, one accelerated trip through time, one child who can fly. Realistic fiction, by contrast, is based on what happened or could have happened.

Much of fantasy literature, however, also *appears* plausible. Characters—even when they are rats or rabbits—behave something like people. Maybe they are able to disappear under certain conditions, or fly, but they cannot escape normal human sadness, longing for love, or other real human emotions.

HOW FANTASY BEGINS:
THE CROW TALKS, THE RADIO CRACKLES

Some writers require an immediate commitment to fantasy from the reader, but give plenty of solid reason to believe.

A crow flapping into the opening scene in Alexander's *The High*

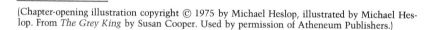

Many fantasies begin with a realistic setting. *Amigo* begins with Francisco wishing he could have a pet. (Reprinted with permission of Macmillan Publishing Co., Inc. from *Amigo* by Byrd Baylor Schweitzer, Copyright © 1963, Garth Williams.)

259

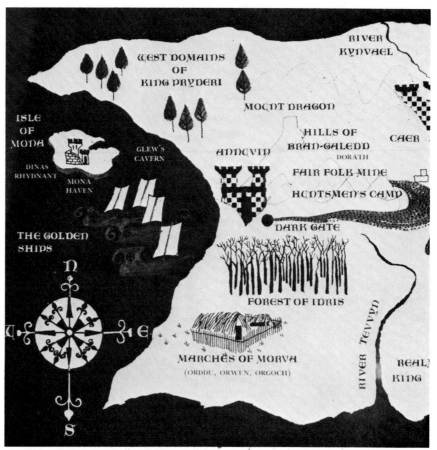

This map shows the mythical land of Prydain where Alexander's *The High King* takes place. (From *The High King* by Lloyd Alexander. Text copyright © 1968 by Lloyd Alexander; map copyright © 1968 by Holt, Rinehart and Winston, Inc. Reproduced by permission of Holt, Rinehart and Winston, Publishers.)

King (1968) croaks to two riders on horseback: "Princess! Home!" The characters are astounded—by the news, not by the fact that the report comes from a crow.

Why do we believe in the talking bird? One reason is that the animal flaps into a scene decked with realistic detail. We know one of the riders wears a "silver-bound battle horn," and that their camp is in a grove of ash trees. We learn that their fire burns in a ring of stones and that when the crow arrives it begins impatiently squawking its news even before landing on an outstretched wrist. Particulars like these overwhelm disbelief.

Other writers don't demand a sudden leap from reality. Author
Susan Cooper lets ominous signs fall gently into a meticulously
drawn description of real English country life, in the early pages of
The Dark Is Rising (1973). Will Stanton, on the eve of his eleventh
birthday, is getting ready to do some humdrum farming work with
his brother. Will pulls on boots and bundles himself against the cold
outside as his sister slices onions and Mrs. Stanton bends red-faced
over a hot oven. Susan Cooper's kitchen scene is believable, down to
the warm music of a symphony orchestra sounding from a table
radio. Fantasy enters in small doses, signs showing that Will has
begun transmitting a mysterious aura. The first sign:

"We're going!" Will shouted back. The radio let out a sudden hideous crackle of static as he passed the table. He jumped. Mrs. Stanton shrieked, "Turn that thing DOWN." (p. 2)

The static could have been caused by weather, but outside, a few minutes later, pet rabbits shy away from him in terror. The ambiguous radio static, the animals' fear—both indicate that Will is no ordinary lad. And in fact within a day, young Will sets off on a quest to try to defeat the forces of evil. Not long after the kitchen scene, he learns to transmit his thoughts. He finds he can ignite wood with his mind and fire bursts of light at the forces of darkness by forming a magic circle with supernatural friends—pure fantasy. But it is believable because its elements—magical powers, mysterious signs—make quiet entrances.

IMAGINARY CHARACTERS AND CURIOUS OCCURRENCES

Once Will Stanton's story departs from the reality of the natural world, Cooper is free to add layer on layer of fantastic detail. The burst of radio static is slightly ominous, although Mrs. Stanton's complaint about the noise tugs the story quickly back down into the kitchen. Within a few chapters, such elements of fantasy become almost as commonplace as the smell of quartered onions. Mysterious figures appear from nowhere. Great carved doors spring up in empty fields. The boy sets fire to a fallen log by willing the flames, and neither he nor the reader is much surprised. These are comparatively minor touches.

Beneath the surface detail, however, the story departs from reality in two major respects: first, Will Stanton is a superhuman person with extraordinary, though limited, powers. And second, the logic of the natural world has been rewritten—odd things keep happening to him.

This chapter focuses mainly on *modern* fantasy and science fiction, although writers today sometimes draw on *traditional* fantasy—myths, legends, folktales, or fairy tales—for form or content. Fantasy clearly cannot be pigeonholed into neat categories.

But one way to try to organize a shelf of such books is to identify the primary element of fantasy. Is it an *imaginary character*—a toy, an animal, a tiny or strange person? Or is the primary departure from the real world a series of *curious occurrences*—do normal people fly, travel through time, or perform inhuman tasks?

Here is a sampling of books to illustrate the use of these two major elements.

Pooh and piglet go hunting, following their own tracks round and round in a circle—until Piglet gets frightened and goes home. (From *Winnie-the-Pooh* by A. A. Milne. Reprinted by permission of the publishers, E. P. Dutton.)

IMAGINARY CHARACTERS: TALKING TOYS AND ANIMALS, TINY PEOPLE, STRANGE PEOPLE IN STRANGE LANDS

Talking Toys

Winnie-the-Pooh (1926) is a stuffed bear and a companion of a little boy named Christopher Robin. Pooh ordinarily lives by himself in a

263

forest, near a pessimistic donkey friend named Eeyore and a homey collection of other stuffed animals including Piglet, Rabbit, Owl, Kanga, and little Roo. The none-too-bright bear is always affable, only mildly surprised at the indignities he continually suffers, often at his own hand. Each chapter in the book by A. A. Milne is a separate story. In one, Pooh leaves home with a birthday gift, a jar of honey, for Eeyore. But he eats the honey on the way, so Eeyore gets instead a Useful Pot to Keep Things In.

Inanimate toys also come alive in Pauline Clarke's *The Return of the Twelves* (1963), a story about an 8-year-old named Max. The boy finds a dozen wooden soldiers under the floorboards of an attic in England. These are no ordinary soldiers. They come to life and tell Max they were once commanded by four children in a famous nineteenth-century literary family: Branwell, Emily, Charlotte, and Anne Bronte. When Max and his sister learn that a foreigner wants to buy the soldiers for an American museum for 5,000 pounds, they decide that the soldiers really belong to the Bronte museum, located nearby. The soldiers agree but insist on a hazardous condition: they will march there themselves rather than be carried like common toys.

Different Animals for Different Ages

Young children readily accept talking toys; it is even easier to accept talking animals. "To the child [before the age of puberty] there is no clear line separating objects from living things," writes psychologist Bruno Bettelheim in *The Uses of Enchantment* (1976). "And whatever has life has life very much like our own. If we do not understand what rocks and trees and animals have to tell us, the reason is that we are not sufficiently attuned to them" (p. 46).

So animal stories have powerful appeal to young children. Such fantasies answer the child's hope (Bettelheim thinks *belief*) that animals can tell us something. The appeal does not end after the first few grades of elementary school. Some of these books win a large audience among adults.

Here is a selection of different animal books for different ages.

Ages 5 to 7 Children of this age enjoy the nonsense in a series of books by Arnold Lobel about a frog and a toad. In *Frog and Toad Are Friends* (1970), Frog bursts into Toad's cozy house, nestled in a green forest of grass. "It is spring!" Frog announces. Still hibernating, Toad replies: "Blah" (p. 4). It is only by changing Toad's calendar that Frog convinces him to get up. In another story—there are five in the book—Frog is the one stuck in bed.

"One day in summer Frog was not feeling well. Toad said, 'Frog,

Jason Everett Bear gives himself gold stars for being so
terrific. Young children understand why his friends are
not impressed, even if Jason does not. (Copyright ©
1977 by Kay Chorao. Reprinted by permission of
Holiday House from *I'm Terrific.*)

you are looking quite green.' 'But I always look green,' said Frog. 'I
am a frog' " (p. 16).

Despite their realistically grimacing expressions and the moist,
root-level scenery, it is easy to forget that these are animals. In a
later story about a swimming expedition, Toad makes Frog hide his
eyes until Toad gets in the water because he says he looks funny in a
bathing suit. Toad's embarrassment arouses the curiosity of several
animals who gather to look and laugh at Toad. And when he
emerges from the water, he *does* look funny in a bathing suit—as
funny as a lot of humans.

Preschool children and youngsters in the early grades also identify
with a young badger named Frances in a series by Russell Hoban. In
A Birthday for Frances (1968), Frances suffers jealousy over birthday
celebrations for her sister, Gloria. She decides to give Gloria a
Chompo bar and four pieces of bubble gum, and buys the presents
with her father at a store. On the way home, wily Frances asks, "Are
you sure that it is all right for Gloria to have a whole Chompo Bar?"
Later, she tries again: "Probably Gloria could not eat more than half

265

of one." Her father finally asks, "You would not eat Gloria's Chompo Bar, would you?" And Frances, continuing to calculate, answers: "It is not Gloria's yet" (p. 17).

The party begins. The group sings Happy Birthday to Gloria—all except Frances, who sings "Happy Chompo to me." Gloria's wish as she blows out the candles is that Frances will be nice to her. And Frances tries, singing "Happy Birthday" again, with the right words, when she gives Gloria the present.

But Frances the badger is still in most respects a human child with love-hate feelings for her sister: between the lines of the song she gives the Chompo bar a little squeeze.

The English writer and illustrator Beatrix Potter (1866-1943) created entire farms of animals with human traits, including the mischievous Peter Rabbit. One of her small books, *The Tale of Jemima Puddle-Duck*, is about a naive duck who trusts a fox intent on roast duck for dinner. The leering fox offers a shed to Jemima as a nesting place and even talks her into bringing him herbs to flavor the roast. A friendly collie and two foxhound puppies save Jemima, but the ending is melancholy. The exuberant puppies cannot be stopped from eating the duck eggs. And when Jemima tries again to sit on a new batch of eggs, only four hatch. "Jemima Puddle-duck said that it was because of her nerves; but she had always been a bad sitter," the book concludes (p. 59); readers can recognize rationalization, even if they cannot name it. And they can feel affection for Jemima, trying hard to be a mother in her shawl and bonnet, even when she fails.

Ages 7, 8, and 9 Children around this age are ready to appreciate a slightly more sophisticated tale such as *Macaroon* (1962), by Julia Cunningham. A smart raccoon lends himself out for adoption each winter; a child cares for him until the cold season ends, when he runs away. This system supports his stomach, but drains his emotions each spring when he hears the cries of the children he leaves behind. His solution is to adopt a child so nasty that he will not mind leaving at the end of winter.

His choice is nasty enough, a gangly girl named Erika, and their first meeting is appropriately disagreeable: he bites her and she squeals "You rotten raccoon!" (p. 20). But during the winter, he learns about her loneliness—her parents leave her in the care of a cook and a governess—and they become close friends. Macaroon grows to learn the lasting value of friendship and discovers that lovable people sometimes hide behind angry masks.

Children in second or third grades can also appreciate the unstated themes flowing as an undercurrent through *The Mousewife*

Charlotte may do the spinning, but Wilbur gets the glory in *Charlotte's Web.* (Illustration by Garth Williams from *Charlotte's Web* by E. B. White. Copyright © 1952 by E. B. White. By permission of Harper & Row, Publishers, Inc.)

(1951) by Rumer Godden. A wife in a family of mice takes care of her husband, but she is troubled by longings for something more than savory cheese. Then she becomes friends with a caged dove. Her fascination with his stories of flight lands her in trouble with her husband.

One day, "She stayed a long time with the dove. When she went home, I am sorry to say, her husband bit her on the ear" (p. 30).

She decides it is time for bold—unmousy—action, and frees the dove by pouncing on the catch of its cage. She is thrilled by the bird's flight, discovers joy in watching stars, and lives a long life. "It has been given to few mice to see the stars," the story says (p. 42). Her courage has made her wise.

267

More sophisticated still—perhaps best understood by children at least 8 years old—is one of the most popular children's books in history, E. B. White's *Charlotte's Web* (1952). Wilbur the runt pig first meets the gray spider, Charlotte A. Cavatica, when she offers to be his friend. She proves the value of her friendship when Wilbur is slated for slaughter. She weaves the words "some pig" into her web, and Wilbur is saved: Who could butcher a special pig under an advertisement like that? One character's comment that the spider seems more special than the pig is ignored, and Wilbur wins a prize at a local fair. He is assured of a long life.

Charlotte, however, lives only long enough to make her egg sac which she entrusts to Wilbur. She dies alone.

White, long a writer with the *New Yorker* magazine, is famous for his clear, deceptively simple style and his love for the New England farm where he lives. *Charlotte's Web* captures the scents and sounds of barnyard living at the same time it explores themes of life and death, friendship and selfishness. Charlotte's lonely death is all the more poignant to children because of their earlier laughter at the terse and silky messages in her web. Though Wilbur makes friends with some of her children the following spring, he will never forget Charlotte. "She was in a class by herself. It is not often that someone comes along who was a true friend and a good writer. Charlotte was both" (p. 184).

There are unforgettable characters, too, in Robert Lawsons's *Rabbit Hill* (1944), including Mother Rabbit, an inveterate worrier, Father, a long-winded southern gentleman, and Uncle Analdas, a filthy bachelor who accepts an invitation to visit the hill even though it means taking a bath. Exciting news reaches the hill: a new family is moving into the nearby house. Will they be hostile to the rabbits? Or will they be "planting folks" with a garden for the animals to harvest? Luckily for the rabbits, the family not only plans a large garden plot without fences but also puts up a sign that says "Please Drive Carefully on Account of Small Animals."

Animal stories against a city backdrop are rare, but an exception, *The Cricket in Times Square* (1960), by George Selden, appeals particularly to fourth- and fifth-graders. Tucker Mouse and Harry Cat, urban animals, make friends with Chester, a cricket who has been transported to New York City from Connecticut in a picnic basket. Chester becomes the pet of Mario Bellini, whose parents run a newsstand in the Times Square subway station.

The stand has fallen on hard times. (Smart city youngsters may wonder if the ridiculously low prices the Bellinis charge for newspapers contribute to their plight; the book was published in 1960 and seems dated on matters of city life in several small respects.) But

Chester, it turns out, has rare musical talent: perfect pitch and a repertoire from hymns to operas. The cricket swells the Bellini coffers by giving regularly scheduled concerts in the station. On his last night in New York, Chester stops traffic with his rendition of the sextet from the opera *Lucia di Lammermoor.* Harry and Tucker help him find a spot on the Late Local Express, and after he is gone, plan a summer vacation at Chester's real home in Connecticut. The story of that trip appears in the sequel, *Tucker's Countryside* (1969).

9 and older Children around the fifth grade often become interested in "true" stories; they ferret out biographies and realistic fiction and some readers never again return to the cozy fox's den, or the warm hearth in the frog's house. The late English novelist C. S. Lewis, once wrote that some adults reject fantasy because they enjoy cloaking themselves—vicariously, by reading—as real heroes. And it is hard to identify, while playing hero, with foxes or frogs. "A story which introduces the marvellous, the fantastic," Lewis writes, "says to the reader by implication 'I am merely a work of art. You must take me as such—must enjoy me for my suggestions, my beauty, my irony, my construction, and so forth. There is no question of anything like this happening to you in the real world'" (1961, p. 50).

There is no good reason, however, why animal fantasy should be put aside, like an old teddy bear, as the child matures. Several good books for older readers touch on human nature in stories as "true"—though often whimsical—as historical or realistic fiction. Among them are the following.

Mrs. Frisby and the Rats of NIMH (1971), by Robert O'Brien. Mrs. Frisby, widowed head of a family of field mice, fears that her home in a garden will be discovered during spring plowing. But her son, Timothy, is too ill with pneumonia to move. An owl suggests that she seek help from a group of special rats living under a rosebush. She learns that they had known her late husband; they had escaped with him from a laboratory named NIMH (based on a real federal facility, the National Institute for Mental Health, in Maryland). Scientists there had given them injections which increased their intelligence and life-span. Taught to read, they had spent the winter after their escape in an empty house, reading the books in its library and practicing writing. They help Mrs. Frisby move her home, and she in turn warns them of government exterminators on their way to kill the rats with poison gas. Almost all the rats escape to a hidden valley where they intend to give up stealing, and farm the soil.

Wind in the Willows (1908), by Kenneth Grahame. Written for Grahame's son, this book of stories has won an enthusiastic following among older children and adults; its appeal has survived genera-

269

Tasha Tudor is one of several artists who have illustrated *Wind in the Willows.* Here Mole, Toad, and Ratty walk to town after Toad's cart has been wrecked. (From *Wind in the Willows* by Kenneth Grahame, illustrated by Tasha Tudor. Illustration copyright © 1966 by Tasha Tudor. Reproduced by permission of The World Publishing Company.)

tions. The main reason is the cast of eccentric animals. There is a bashful mole, exhilarated by springtime, a loyal rat, a faddish but generous Toad, and a wise old badger.

Grahame revealed his feelings about his animals once when he was talking over his book with an illustrator, Ernest Shepard. Grahame, then an old man, listened as Shepard, a young artist, explained how he hoped to illustrate *Wind in the Willows.* Then Grahame said, "I love these little people. Be kind to them" (Shepard, 1954, p. 84).

Here are Mole and Rat during Mole's first boat ride. Rat has just asked his friend to slide a basket under his feet and Mole has asked what it contains.

> "There's cold chicken inside it," replied Rat briefly; "cold tongue ham cold beef pickled gherkins salad french rolls cress sandwidges potted meat ginger beer lemonade soda water—"
>
> "O stop stop," cried the Mole in ecstasies: "This is too much!"
>
> "Do you really think so?" inquired the Rat seriously. "It's only what I always take on these little excursions; and the other animals are always telling me that I'm a mean beast and cut it *very* fine!" (1966 edition, p. 23).

Toad supplies high comedy. Here, he has just given up one fad, a horse-driven cart, and jumped wide-eyed to his next, a motor car.

"All those wasted years that lie behind me, I never knew, never even dreamed! But *now*—but now that I know, I fully realize! O what a flowery track lies spread before me henceforth! What dust clouds shall spring up behind me as I speed on my reckless way! What carts I shall fling carelessly into the ditch in the wake of my magnificent onset! Horrid little carts—common carts—canary-coloured carts!" (p. 50)

Watership Down (1974), by Richard Adams. Curiously, when Adam's 426-page chronicle of a rabbit quest for a new home first appeared in England, it was touted as a children's book, but in the United States it appeared on adult best-seller lists. In some respects it seems written for mature audiences. It offers an elaborate rabbit mythology, and scholarly footnotes on rabbit language. (For example, "tharn" is the rabbit word for the dreaded paralysis that sometimes enfeebles rabbits in the face of attack by weasel or fox.) To a child's question: "How come Peter Rabbit never has to go to the bathroom?" this book has an answer. Its rabbits leave droppings, and mate, and talk about bodily functions in bawdy rabbit language.

The story begins one evening when a rabbit named Fiver has a chilling premonition of danger: a field at sunset appears to him covered in blood. Fiver's older brother, Hazel, respects the premonition but is unable to convince the condescending chief rabbit in the warren to lead his animals to safety. So Hazel sets out on his own with a group of ten other male rabbits including Fiver and Bigwig, a powerful member of the rabbit elite group called "owsla."

Through perilously strange land (a map near the front of the book indicates the rabbits wander over about 50 square miles of countryside), the animals seek a new home. Hazel survives challenges from Bigwig and establishes a new warren at Watership Down. The rabbits raid another warren to rescue some females and then, under Hazel's crafty and maturing leadership, survive a counterattack led by a militaristic rabbit named General Woundwort. Fiver's premonitions of doom turn out to have been correct: the original warren is bulldozed under to make way for a housing development.

Tiny People; Strange People in a Strange Land

Other odd characters in modern fantasy spring from the imagination in minature human form. They are small enough to hide under flowers but big enough to impinge on the world of full-grown people, often without being detected.

There is a long tradition in English literature, for adults, behind these little characters. Elves—small magical people—appear in the

For tiny people like the borrowers, being seen by a
human can be extremely dangerous. (Illustration by
Beth and Joe Krush reproduced from *The Borrowers*,
copyright, 1952, 1953 by Mary Norton, by permission
of Harcourt Brace Jovanovich, Inc.)

play *A Midsummer-night's Dream*, by William Shakespeare (1564-1616). Lilliputians, hand-sized people, overwhelm a sleeping man in *Gulliver's Travels* by the English satirist Jonathon Swift (1667-1745).

In this tradition, *The Borrowers* (1953) are tiny people living under a grandfather clock. The well-dressed little folk, in the story by British writer Mary Norton, squirrel away items they "borrow" from residents of an old but elegant house. They cook soup in a thimble. A chest of drawers is made of matchboxes. Queen Victoria's portrait, hung on a wall, is a postage stamp. Pod and Homily Clock and their daughter Arrietty live comfortably in their quarters under the timepiece, but Arrietty longs to see more of the world. This worries her parents, since the worst thing that can happen to a borrower is to be seen by a human. Humans do not like the little people, and are liable to call in a cat to get rid of them. Arrietty ignores her parents' fears and goes exploring anyway, becoming friends with a boy. The friendship pays off. When the grumpy cook in the house discovers the borrowers and calls in a rat-catcher, the boy helps the Clock family escape.

An American entry in the literary world of little people is *The Gammage Cup* (1959) by Carol Kendall. The Minnipins, or Small Ones, are a race of tiny folk living along the Watercress River in the Land Between the Mountains. Four of the villagers dare to depart from the rigid dress and behavioral codes which require reverence for the society's first family, the Periods. The Laws also require wearing green cloaks and having green doors on all the houses. Walter the Earl keeps searching ancient records to expand Minnipin history; proper Minnipin society thinks he is just "digging holes in the ground."

Curley Green wears a shocking bright red cloak and paints pictures. Gummy roams the hills and makes up jingles. And Muggles sometimes ties her green cloak with an orange sash. When the Gammage Cup, a prize named after the founder of all nearby villages, is offered for the best village, the Minnipins decide that to win they will have to enforce conformity. The four straying citizens along with the town treasurer are banished to the mountains for their eccentricities. Here, they learn that the Minnipins' arch enemies—the Mushrooms—are planning to attack the riverbank village. They hurry home. They sound a warning, and save the society that rejected them. Their welcome-home celebration is so boisterous—with cheering and trumpet calls, banners and flowers—that no one even notices that the judges have awarded the prize to their village.

Both *The Borrowers* and *Gammage Cup* avoid sentimentalizing their little characters. Arrietty goes through growing pains typical of a real adolescent and her parents suffer genuine anxiety. The confining codes of Minnipins are as much the villains as the Mushrooms, and the outlaws in the hills show giant courage in bucking the system and finally correcting it. The characters may be small but they are not cute.

Not all stories within the tradition of tiny people avoid boring preciousness. A famous English author of fantasy, J. R. R. Tolkien writes that some of the best known of the literature is the worst. The English writer Michael Drayton (1563-1631) wrote the *Nymphidia*, with characters so small that one rides an earwig, a tiny insect, and another wears a bracelet of ant eyes. Beneath these arresting details, however, the story is dull. Tolkien says it is "one ancestor of that long line of flower-fairies and fluttering sprites with antennae that I so disliked as a child and which my children in their turn detested" (1965, p. 6).

Tolkien himself wrote a lively adventure story about a moderately small character, Bilbo Baggins (who stands taller than a Lilliputian, but shorter than a dwarf). Baggins is a hobbit, a quiet, retiring resident of Middle Earth who enjoys his regular meals, his pipe, and his cozy hobbit hole. Then Gandolf the wizard appears, and the next day a band of elves. And before he realizes what is happening, Baggins is off on a quest for treasure stolen by the horrible dragon, Smaug. His adventures are chronicled in *The Hobbit* (1938). He finds a wealth of courage in himself, but is pleased to return home, even if he does arrive in the middle of an auction of his household belongings; he has been presumed dead. Tolkien, a professor at Oxford until his death in 1973, continued his sagas about Middle Earth in the three-part *Lord of the Rings*.

Sedentary suburbanites may recognize themselves in Tolkien's portrait of the unassuming Mr. Baggins. And it is easy for readers to place themselves in his company as he travels through Middle Earth; if the vivid descriptions are not enough, there is a full map of Baggin's homeland in the front of the book.

A similar map lends authenticity to Ursula K. Le Guin's *A Wizard of Earthsea* (1968), set in a land of many islands. One of these, Gont, is famous for wizards. A young resident of Gont named Ged discovers one day that he can call animals to follow him. Expanding his powers with a little training in wizardry, he learns enough to repel an attack of enemies by summoning a protective fog to his village. But his powers soon outstrip his ability to control them; in wizard school he boastfully summons a spirit of the dead and then finds himself hounded by a shadow beast. He learns he must face what he has created. So, in the climactic scene, "Ged

The Earthsea trilogy concludes with *The Farthest Shore* in which, after a series of adventures, Ged and the future king Arren are returned to Roke by the dragon Kalessin. (Text copyright © 1972 by Ursula LeGuin. Illustrated by Gail Garraty from *The Farthest Shore.* Used by permission of Atheneum Publishers.)

reached out his hands, dropping his staff, and took hold of his shadow, of the black self that reached out to him. Light and darkness met, and joined, and were one'' (p. 201). Ged names the shadow with his own name and—in a tradition as old as the Bible's Old Testament—finally takes control of it in the naming.

Ged is a character of fantasy. But—even in the author's austere style—he comes alive like all good characters of fantasy: first he is frightened of his own power, then overimpressed, and finally humbled by it. The best of fantastic characters, be they toys, animals, tiny people, or people with strange powers, are never so overwhelmed by the trappings of fantasy that they seem unreal.

Children are likely to recognize themselves or people they know in such characters. Even if they do not, there is great fun in believing for a time that dreams can come true, that children can cast spells, or that dogs can think.

One third-grader finished *Amigo* (1963), by Byrd Schweitzer, about a boy who tames a dog for a friend while the dog simultaneously trains the boy. "I know it's not true," the young reader said, "but I wish it was."

CURIOUS OCCURRENCES:
TRAVELS THROUGH TIME AND ODD TRANSFORMATIONS

The fantastic character is likely to undergo extraordinary experiences. Pod, the borrower, can climb curtains using a hatpin as a kind of piton. Rabbits can share mythology in an evening story hour in *Watership Down*. A toad puts on a bathing suit in one book (*Frog and Toad Are Friends*) and drives a motor car in another (*Wind in the Willows*). But none of these adventures—once the reader's natural inclination to doubt is numb—seems particularly fantastic. Once you accept a talking toad, it is a fairly small step to put it behind the wheel.

In another major class of fantasy, the characters are comparatively normal. The fantastic element is what happens to them, the curious occurrence in which they are carted through time, taught to fly, turned temporarily into someone else, or transported someplace else.

Characters in such books almost always pass through periods of questioning, surprise, and doubt.

What is that strange drumming sound under the ground? In *Earthfasts* (1967), by William Mayne, two bright twentieth-century youngsters, Keith Heseltine and David Wix, work like young scientists to explain the noise.

The drumming seems to come from a mysterious swelling in the middle of a field. Maybe it is a strange echo of the churchbells in Garebrough. But David counts the distinct sounds of the distant bells. There are eight. This sound is a ninth.

Maybe it is underground water. But the ground below the surface is firm.

Maybe the water is pushing a rock up toward the surface; then the rock would insulate the surface from the spring beneath. The boys scratch at the earth to try to find the edges of the rock. The reader's credulity rises as the resonant sound of a drum intensifies. Fantasy emerges:

> The ground stirred. The stirring did not extend beyond the swelling turf. But there was movement, a lot of movement. It was as if someone were getting out of bed. And with the movement came clear drumming. They could hear the stick on the parchment. There was light, increasing light, pure and mild and bleak.
>
> David tried to say that it was the last of the day shining on moving water, but the words would not form themselves, because his jaw was trembling. . . . (p. 6)

All possible explanations for the shifting of the ground have been exhausted. And then an astounding thing happens: a drummer boy emerges from the ground carrying a candle, smiling, and spouting archaic language. Almost immediately, from reading he has done, David realizes that the boy, Nellie Jack John, is an unwitting traveler from a time two centuries ago. The last John remembers, he was searching for King Arthur's resting place and treasure trove in tunnels near an armed castle. He banged the drum to let those on the surface follow his underground progress as he searched.

But now that he is back on the surface, the castle is in ruins, and John's psyche begins to go to pieces. First he is angry. David is a liar, he says. Then he runs away from the two boys, sputtering plans in eighteenth-century English to walk home, visit his girlfriend's house, and find friends. Then,

> They heard his words change to a different sound. When he had come to the edge of the rock, and was casting about for a way to go down, he was no longer speaking and calling them liars and villains and claiming they were mainswearing him, but gasping out sobs. As he went down the rock, clambering and scrambling, his voice grew louder. Anger gave way to fear, and his last cry was one of terror, coming up the rock out of the darkness. (p. 20)

The wild fantasy beneath the earth has risen up to astonish everyone. Eventually, all the boys descend back down into the mystery, encounter King Arthur, and finally walk back together into the twentieth century.

Repeated shifts of time amaze a young boy in another book, *Tom's Midnight Garden* (1959), by Philippa Pearce. Tom has to go live with his Uncle Alan and Aunt Gwen to avoid catching measles from his brother Peter. In his relatives' rented flat, Tom has trouble sleeping and becomes fascinated one night when he discovers that an alley out the back door, "poky, with rubbish bins" (p. 19) by day,

Two children from an earlier century join Kate for *A
Game of Catch* in this recent time-shift fantasy.
(Reprinted with the permission of Macmillan
Publishing Co., Inc. from *A Game of Catch* by Helen
Cresswell, illustrated by Ati Forberg. Copyright ©
1977, Macmillan Publishing Co., Inc.)

has turned into a large lawn with flower beds, fir tree, greenhouse, and path, all bordered by thick yew trees. He also meets a little girl named Hatty.

In repeated night visits to the garden, Tom discovers that seasons in the garden change unpredictably, and so does Hatty's age. But Tom grows to love the garden where it never rains; he does not want to leave when it is time to go home. The whole idyllic scene vanishes. The next day, the elderly lady who owns the house and lives in its attic calls Tom to her side. Her name is Hatty. She has been dreaming each night, summoning up scenes of her childhood, and Tom has been joining her in the timeless world of her dreams.

In other books, the curious occurrence is a fantastic transformation in one or more of the characters. A girl named Charlotte, in Penelope Farmer's *The Summer Birds* (1962), learns how to fly by flapping her arms one day; her coach is a mysterious boy.

"Don't flap wildly like a worried hen," Charlotte's coach tells her as she struggles to take off.

> And quite suddenly she understood. Her movement ceased to be choppy and hurried like a frightened swimmer, but slowed to an easy acceptance of rhythm, the pull of the arms, the turn of the ankles: in, out, together. Soon she was sitting jubilant on the branch of an oak tree, eager for more. She shut her eyes and jumped out again into the sunlight. . . . (p. 23)

Charlotte, her friend Emma, and her entire class at school are normal children in every respect except that they all learn from the boy how to fly. They spend the summer in outings on the wing, without telling adults how they are getting around. Then one day the boy tries to lead the class to a distant island. Charlotte demands to know where they are going, and the boy is forced to tell them who he is: the last surviving member of a species of bird. Anyone who follows him to the island will become one of his race, he explains, never to come back. One girl, an orphan named Maggot, chooses to go. The other children return to home and humdrum living. They can no longer fly.

There has been, it turns out, an ominous risk running throughout the carefree flights of summer. They might all have become birds. Charlotte's courage has prevented the catastrophe of complete transformation.

In *Freaky Friday* (1972), by Mary Rodgers, a complete transformation—at least for a day—does take place, but the premise is funny: a girl named Annabel turns into her mother.

Annabel had always thought adult life sounded like a picnic. However after trying to be her own mother—coping with a broken washing machine, discussing herself with her teacher, and trying to fix dinner for unexpected guests—she changes her mind.

SCIENCE FICTION

If fantasy is hard to classify, science fiction is close to impossible. "It is the literature of pure escapism," writes Sheila Egoff, a teacher at the University of British Columbia "and it may also be the vehicle for biting criticism of contemporary society. . . . If you will, it is often children's literature for adults and it may equally well be the child's easiest entry into speculations that trouble the adult mind" (1969, p. 384).

The field includes stories of monsters stalked by clichés. ("Are you saying, doctor, that that—that *thing* is alive?" "Stay in your houses. Repeat, stay in your houses. The creatures have been sighted on the Los Angeles Freeway." "Run for it, boys; the frog's moving again." . . . Make up your own.) Many earlier entries are distinctly unscientific. Robert Heinlein's *Farmer in the Sky* (1950) has a passage about what happens when a spaceship is punctured by a meteor (a disaster that would cause it to blow up in real space): nothing. A passenger simply plugs the hole with his Boy Scout uniform (p. 75). In Heinlein's *Rocket Ship Galileo* (1947), three high school students and a scentist climb into a homemade backyard rocket and ride it to the moon, silencing one concerned parent who dares question the harebrained project.

Hardly comparable to these howlingly inaccurate tales, another kind of science fiction today makes serious comment on where we are really going in society and what we are likely to be when we get there. Some of this work, too, is unscientific—but deliberately so. One writer of this kind of literature is Sylvia Louise Engdahl, who says she does not like the term "science fiction."

One major aim of writers in the field, she says, is "to suggest real hypotheses about mankind's future or about the nature of the universe. There is nothing inherently 'scientific' in this aim, at least not unless 'science' is defined in the broad but archaic sense of knowledge.' Indeed, like other works of imagination, science fiction is decidely unscientific in that its hypotheses are based not upon systematic analysis, but upon free speculation" (1971, p. 450).

So science fiction, based on free speculation about the future or the nature of the universe, ranges from pure escapism to biting criticism. Broad as the genre is, it is often considered a stepchild of fantasy because its stories revolve around fantastic—unreal by current standards—elements: odd characters and curious occurrences.

A large number of books, often incorporating both of these general elements, are woven around rides in outer space. They range from pleasantly silly escapism to significant social comment.

There are no weighty themes in Louis Slobodkin's series built on his 1952 book, *The Space Ship under the Apple Tree*. Short, punchy chapters, appealing to children in the early grades, tell the story of Eddie Blow who becomes friends with a Martian named Marty. Similarly, Ellen MacGregor's *Miss Pickerell Goes to Mars* (1951) is about what happens when the elderly Miss Pickerell tries to get a spaceship out of her pasture.

Other space stories have serious messages for readers about human nature or society. On one level, Madeleine L'Engle's *A Wrinkle in Time* (1962) is simply a crackling adventure fantasy about a girl named Meg Murry who single-handedly rescues her scientist father and brilliant younger brother, Charles Wallace, from imprisonment on an alien planet, Camazotz. The pathetic inhabitants of this dark planet move in rhythm to the pulsation of an evil brain, called It, enclosed in glass.

But *Wrinkle* is more a story about good and evil than about space travel or electronic control of the brain. After Charles has fallen into the zombielike state imposed by It, Meg battles to free him. She discovers in a climactic scene that It is vulnerable: her own love for her brother, repeated over and over aloud, can break the bonds on Charles Wallace.

Similarly, although the plot of Engdahl's *The Far Side of Evil* (1971) is about a space mission to the planet Toris, one of its themes is about how societies handle nuclear power. Elana and Randil are emissaries from the advanced societies joined in the Federation of Planets. The pair, from the federation's Anthropological Service, visit the Youngling—not yet mature—planet to try to answer a basic question about societies: When they develop nuclear power, why do some use the atom for war and thereby destroy themselves while others call on nuclear power for space exploration?

Society is also a central figure in two trilogies—with earthbound plots—by John Christopher. Both are set in the twenty-first century. In the White Mountain trilogy, future society has become primitive and oppressive. The ruling Tripods, giant three-legged machines, force everyone to wear a steel plate, inserted into their skull at age 14 during a ritualized "capping" ceremony. The metal appliance enslaves almost everyone, but in *The White Mountains* (1967), Will and two friends escape and join a group of free mountain people. In *The City of Gold and Lead* (1967) and *The Pool of Fire* (1968), Will returns to the Tripod-dominated society and eventually defeats the machines and the lizardlike creatures which run them.

Tripods are products of scientific knowledge gone bad. In a second

281

trilogy, Christopher presents a complementary premise: Ignorance of science breeds primitive superstition and suspicion. Society in *The Prince in Waiting* (1970), *Beyond the Burning Lands* (1971), and *The Sword of the Spirits* (1972) is divided into warring, primitive city-states. A series of earthquakes and other natural disasters has destroyed the earlier technological civilization. Now, no one is permitted to make scientific investigations. In the last book, Seers, priests in the city-states, lead the people back into accepting science. The future, however, is not necessarily rosy: as scientific sophistication grows, near the end of the story, so does cynicism.

What happens when society on earth turns away from science is also the concern of Peter Dickinson in *Heartsease* (1969). Residents of a small village in an England of the future reject all machines. They believe in witches, and when an American pilot is downed near the village, they assume he is a witch and stone him. He is saved by two children who refuse to adopt the prejudices of their society, and who help him escape on a boat named Heartsease.

Writers of science fiction have often been credited with the gift of prophecy. The romantic fiction of the Frenchman Jules Verne (1828–1905) was filled with stories of fabulous journeys in vehicles waiting to invented: the airplane, submarine, and moon rocket. Communications satellites appeared in the writing of contemporary British author Arthur C. Clarke before the real thing was on the drawing boards; some scientists scoffed.

But prophecy is not the main stock of science fiction. Like all good fantasy, the best science fiction deals with time-tested, down-to-earth themes about people and their societies, even though plots may range over distant or future worlds.

Again and again in these stories, children out of the future call on long-respected values, such as love and regard for the individual, to help cope with frightening changes in society or the threat of evil technology. The best of these books will survive even if their prophecy fails.

When the first desolate, rocky scenes of Mars flashed back to earth from the Viking lander in 1976, some wrote off the Red Planet as a setting for future science fiction. But they missed the point. For many others, the pictures from space stimulated new and interesting speculation. Was there life there? What happened to it? What is under all those rocks?

Untouched by their countrymen's fear of machines,
Margaret and Jonathan plan to help an American pilot
escape by boat. (From *Heartsease* by Peter Dickinson,
illustrated by Robert Hales. Illustration copyright ©
1969 by Robert Hales. Reproduced by permission of
Gollancz Publishers.)

Until science pries up the rocks, writers are free to make up their own answers to these questions. Isaac Asimov, a famous American writer of science fiction, was one of those exuberant over what Viking had found. "That means a whole new set of stories," he said. "Every advance of science opens up new possibilities for fiction" (1976, p. 29). And every fresh story, besides entertaining, can illuminate the world as it is, can tell us more about ourselves as we are now, and will be.

MODERN MYTHMAKERS

Science fiction often looks toward the future. Another major category of fantasy uses stories drawn from past forms.

Unlike classic tales or myths or epics (described in Chapter 5), narratives from modern mythmakers appear in print before they are widely told. The stories may borrow mermaids, or other motifs, from traditional literature, but they grow out of a known author's own experiences and feelings.

Some of the stories by Hans Christian Andersen (1805-1875), for example, seem to be about him, even though they have the form of the fairy tale. Andersen, who was born into a poor shoemaker's family, grew to become a straggly young man with an oversized nose and ill-fitting clothes. As a teenager in Copenhagen, he sought out well-known artists and entertainers and bored them with his songs and poetry. He was said to have loved several women, among them a famous Swedish singer named Jenny Lind. He never married.

Finally he began to publish plays and poems with some success, but his first fairy tales did not appear in print until he was in his thirties. Then, at last, his reputation began to grow and spread. In his late thirties, he began to invent his own plots.

One of his friends, Edward Collin, said that Andersen told stories to groups of children every day. He made up some of the stories on the spot, and also told well-known traditional tales. The children loved it, Collin reports.

> He gave life even to the driest of sentences: he did not say, "The children got into the carriage and then they drove off," but "Then they got into the carriage, bye-bye daddy, bye-bye mummy, the whip cracked, smick smack, and off they went, gee-up there." (in Cook, 1969, p. 42)

Andersen seems to have put his own life into one of his most famous stories, *The Ugly Duckling*. Duck society mocks the awkward little bird, just as Danish society had spurned Andersen. In the story, the ugly duckling leaves the nest, and meets wild ducks in the marsh.

"What a scarecrow you are," said the wild ducks. "But that won't matter to us, as long as you don't marry into our family." (1965 edition)

There is probably a commentary on Copenhagen society here, just as there is in "The Emperor's New Clothes," another Andersen tale taken from an old Spanish story about a proud emperor who parades before his people in the buff until a small boy has the courage to tell him he is naked.

Other Andersen stories are closer to traditional fairy tales. "The Snow Queen" is made of hearty traditional stock: lost children, a quest, a witch, talking beasts, and magic. The story involves two close friends, Kay and Gerda, who are divided when Kay gets a glass splinter in his eye. The splinter also stabs Kay's heart, turning it cold as ice and making him angry and critical of his friend. He goes to live in the Snow Queen's cold palace where Gerda, after an adventurous quest, finds him and melts the cold and crippling splinter with her tears. Love and courage conquer, just as they do in classic folktales.

Fables appear in modern form, too. Lloyd Alexander wrote *The King's Fountain* (1971) to make a point. In the book, a poor man hears of a king's plan to build a magnificent fountain—which will stop the water from reaching the city. He tries in vain to get someone to speak to the king, first a scholar, then a glib merchant. Next, he asks a brave metalsmith, who wants only to smash the palace windows and crack its walls. So the poor man is forced to see the king himself, and declares, "Majesty—thirst is thirst, a poor man's no less than a king's." The king, impressed by his bravery, cancels plans for the fountain. The language is beautiful and flowing, complemented by full-page illustrations by Ezra Jack Keats. Alexander and Keats produced the book after a discussion they had on the need for individuals to act on their own when situations demand it.

Another modern fable, Leo Lionni's *Frederick* (1967), is about the need for art. Frederick is a mouse who gathers sun rays, colors, and words while other mice pick up corn and nuts, wheat and straw for the winter. Winter descends; food dwindles. The other mice turn to Frederick, asking him to speak of the sun to warm them, to describe the red poppies in yellow wheat, and to tell them poems to help them survive.Groups of children hearing the story often divide over the moral; some argue that poetry can help sustain life, and others contend that Frederick is a freeloader.The issue is fresh; the story is modern despite its traditional garb.

The street experiences of a modern black child in Harlem play against traditional African folktales in Virginia Hamilton's *The Time-Ago Tales of Jahdu* (1969). Where young Lee Edward lives, the air is filled with stories about a mythical character named Jahdu. Lee Edward points to a plot floating in the air, and Mama Luka, who takes care of him after school, grabs the story and tells it. In the last story, Jahdu takes the form of a small black child who stays in the Harlem neighborhood awhile and, like Lee Edward, enjoys living there.

Some of these contemporary stories, of course, will be adopted as personal property by the people who hear them. The original authors will become anonymous. Many of Andersen's tales are no longer associated with him. They are told in the company of Grimm's collected stories as if the oral tradition had generated them.

Jane Yolen, a writer who coined the phrase "modern mythmakers," reports that one of her stories, *Greyling*, is read over British Broadcasting Company radio every year as "a folk tale from the Shetland islands," although she made it up (1976, p. 492).

THE VALUE OF FANTASY

The shelf of fantasy and science fiction we have explored includes an odd collection of talking toys and toads, tiny people, wizards, and a trove of narratives about impossible occurrences. Surprisingly, all of this can be valuable in helping children to understand real life. Some even argue that fantasy is more illuminating than realistic fiction. How is that possible? C. S. Lewis answers:

> I think what profess to be realistic stories for children are far more likely to deceive them. I never expected the real world to be like the fairy tales. I think I did expect school to be like the school stories. The fantasies did not deceive me; the school stories did. (1963, p. 464)

Good fantasy does not deceive; more than that, it tells truths which children could not understand unless coded in imaginary stories. Ten-year-olds may never have talked about human death. But many can understand death as treated in Natalie Babbitt's fantasy, *Tuck Everlasting* (1975), the story of a family that will never die. Tuck, his wife Mae, and two sons, Miles and Jesse, have all looked the same for four score and seven years, since they drank the waters of a mysterious spring. The spring, hidden away in a forest near the house of a 10-year-old girl named Winnie Foster, gives immortality to all who sip it. It remains a Tuck family secret until Winnie, running away from home, encounters the spring and learns the secret. The Tucks carry her away before she has time to tell anyone else. After a hard journey, the family and a frightened Winnie arrive at the Tuck homestead, a dusty little house on the edge of a pond. Tuck takes Winnie for a rowboat ride and explains the family's situation—and death—almost entirely in images.

> "It's a wheel, Winnie. Everything's a wheel, turning and turning, never stopping. The frogs is part of it, and the bugs, and the fish, and the wood thrush, too. And people. But never the same ones. Always coming in new, always growing and changing, and always moving on. That's the way it's supposed to be. That's the way it *is*. . . .
> "We ain't part of the wheel no more. Dropped off, Winnie. Left behind. And everywhere around us, things is moving and growing and changing. You, for instance. A child now, but someday a woman. And after that, moving on to make room for the new children." (pp. 62–63)

The image is too powerful to Winnie and she feels sudden rage and helplessness. She does not want to die. Tuck presses on, calmly: "But dying's part of the wheel, right there next to being born" (p. 63).

At 10, Winnie comes to an understanding that she must die—unless she decides to drink some of the spring water Jesse has given her. In an understated but triumphant ending, the indestructible Tucks return to Winnie's village decades later, and find a tall monument in a cemetery over Winnie's grave. She had lived 78 years, and had been a loving wife and mother. "Good girl," Tuck says aloud.

Winnie learned through images. The reader can, too. "Children need such images quite as much as adults do," writes Penelope Farmer, an author of fantasy, "because so much of what goes on around them, and even more what goes on in their minds and the minds of other people, is totally inexplicable intellectually. . . . Only through images, therefore, can they begin to recognize and understand many of their own feelings and much of their emotional experience, or at least to recognize that they are not alone in it" (1972, p. 32).

So fantasy helps explain the way things really are. It can also help readers explore how things should be.

Look at the ethical choices available to characters in William Sleator's *House of Stairs* (1974). Five 16-year-olds, all living in state institutions, are brought one by one to a strange, windowless building containing an endless maze of stairs.

They find each other, and a red-and-green blinking machine which dispenses food cylinders when they perform. At first, food drops out when they make faces. But the machine keeps changing the rules: making faces fails to work, but dancing does; finally the only way to coax food from the machine is to hurt each other, emotionally and physically. Two of the group, Lola and Peter, go on a hunger strike, climbing away from the others. But Lola cannot maintain her fast. She starts back toward the tyrannical machine and Peter goes with her. His concern about her is greater than his enmity for the machine.

Before they go far, all five are whisked from the house to a hospital to recover. They learn they have been part of a government experiment to provide the President with a group of young people who would follow orders unquestioningly and be constantly cautious and alert. Lola and Peter are failures in the experiment because they continue to think independently, and to hold fast to care and concern for others.

But it is clear that they made what most readers would consider the right ethical choice. As the three "successes" leave the hospital, they come to a blinking traffic light. There, perfectly trained, "Without hesitation they began to dance" (p. 166).

Adolescents may resist philosphical discussions of right and wrong. But they quickly identify with Lola and Peter and agonize over their decisions. They may also begin to grapple with some broader ethical issues: How much power can the state exert over the individual? Can scientists use human subjects without their informed consent? The story is a touchstone for thinking about how things should be.

On the other hand, things will never be the way they are in Roald Dahl's *Charlie and the Chocolate Factory* (1964). The book does treat ethical issues, in a way. Four of five children invited to visit Mr. Willie Wonka's chocolate factory have awful personalities. By contrast, young Charlie Bucket has the Boy Scout virtues of a true hero. One by one, the other children are lost in terrible misfortunes. Only the sainted Charlie survives.

But children like the book for its inventiveness, not for the mock ethical lessons about honesty, bravery, and obedience. The factory's storeroom 77, for instance, contains all the beans: "cacao beans, coffee beans, jelly beans, and has beans" (p. 92). In another passage, a pun makes it possible for square candies to look round. Each has a pink face painted on one side. When Mr. Wonka opens the door suddenly, "all the rows and rows of little square candies looked quickly round to see who was coming in" (p. 114).

Nonsense? Not much more than conventions of real, everyday language. What, for instance, might the portrait of an average family with 2.58 children look like? Norton Juster has an idea, in his book *The Phantom Tollbooth* (1961). A boy named Milo finds a kit for a tollbooth, puts it together, and travels through it to a weird land where, among other odd folk, he meets a child approximately divided in half, lengthwise.

"It's .58 to be precise," the child tells Milo from the left side of his mouth which is also the only side of his mouth.

The boy explains he is part of an average family, "mother, father, and 2.58 children—and, as I explained, I'm the .58."

> "It must be rather odd being only part of a person," Milo remarked.
> "Not at all," said the child. "Every average family has 2.58 children, so I always have someone to play with. Besides, each family also has an average of 1.3 automobiles, and since I'm the only one who can drive three tenths of a car, I get to use it all the time." (pp. 195–196)

The precedent for Milo's trip was set in 1865 with the publication of Lewis Carroll's path-breaking *Alice's Adventures in Wonderland.* Alice's long fall from reality down the rabbit hole brings her to a world where words are often doubletalk, and logic is in limbo. Alice, a proper little girl, tries politely to restore order to Wonderland. But characters like the Mock Turtle—that is the animal you use for mock turtle soup—defeat her at every turn of phrase. What did the turtle study in school, Alice asks primly?

> "Reeling and Writhing, of course, to begin with," the Mock Turtle replied; "and then the different branches of Arithmetic—Ambition, Distraction, Uglification, and Derision." (1971 edition, p. 76)

In another book by Carroll, *Through the Looking Glass* (1871), The Queen of Hearts has her own kind of logic. Alice says that she does not want any jam.

> "You couldn't have it if you *did* want it," the Queen said. "The rule is, jam to-morrow and jam yesterday—but never jam *today*."
> "It *must* come sometimes to 'jam to-day,'" Alice objected.
> "No, it ca'n't," said the Queen. It's jam every *other* day: to-day isn't any other day, you know." (1971 edition, p. 150)

Carroll had a passion for mathematics as well as for telling stories to little girls, and sometimes taking their pictures. His complicated play with words, like mathematical puzzles, does not appeal to everyone.

Some groan at Dahl's puns. And other readers may find Milo's adventures through the tollbooth tiresome. It makes sense to introduce each of these books, and particularly *Alice*, by reading passages out loud and gauging the response. No one should be unwillingly dragged on these imaginary excursions.

ISSUE

IS *ALICE* A "SOURCE OF PLAY," OR IS IT "PLOTLESS, POINTLESS"?

During this centennial year of its publication, it is especially timely to note children's enduring enthusiasm for *Alice's Adventures in Wonderland*. Besides being a source of play and refreshment for children and a pastime for scholars, *Alice* set a precedent in children's books. (p. 133)

MacCann, Donnarae. "Wells of Fancy, 1865-1965," in Sheila Egoff, G. T. Stubbs, and L. F. Ashley (eds.), *Only Connect* (Toronto: Oxford University Press, 1969).

Like *Gulliver's Travels, Robinson Crusoe,* and *Huckleberry Finn, Alice* has joined that curious list of books that librarians call "children's classics" but which are read and relished mostly by grownups. . . . The truth is that, from a modern child's point of view, the Alice books are plotless, pointless, unfunny, and more frightening than a monster movie. (p. 151)

Gardner, Martin. "A Child's Garden of Bewilderment," in Egoff et al (eds.), *Only Connect* (Toronto: Oxford University Press, 1969).

Did you read *Alice's Adventures in Wonderland* as a child? If so, what reaction did you have to it? Do you think it is popular with today's children? What makes you think this? Perhaps you might want to read a selection from *Alice* to several fifth-or sixth-grade children, and see if they consider it "a source of play and refreshment," or "plotless, pointless, and unfunny."

But if listeners enjoy the liberties taken with language—and logic—they are also likely to gain greater power of expression for themselves. The Mock Turtle,"has bean," and the 58-percent boy are fantastic by-products of real language. Children will expand their vocabularies to understand how they exist; readers will find ample fare in such books to help their own imaginations grow.

This short policeman is Office Shrift–Short Shrift. He gives Milo a short sentence, "I am." It is the shortest sentence he knows. (From *The Phantom Tollbooth* by Norton Juster, illustrated by Jules Feiffer. Illustrations copyright © 1961 by Jules Feiffer. Reproduced by permission of Random House, Inc.)

ISSUE

IS *CHARLIE AND THE CHOCOLATE FACTORY* HARMFUL TO CHILDREN?

What I object to in *Charlie* is its phony presentation of poverty and its phony humor, which is based on punishment with overtones of sadism; its hypocrisy which is epitomized in its moral—stuck like a marshmallow in a lump of fudge—that TV is horrible and hateful and time-wasting and that children should read good books instead, when in fact the book itself is like nothing so much as one of the more specious television shows. . . .

If I ask myself whether children are harmed by reading *Charlie* or having it read to them, I can only say I don't know. Its influence would be subtle underneath the catering. . . . Possibly its tastelessness, including the ugliness of the illustrations, is, indeed (whether the author meant it so or not), a comment upon our age and the quality of much of our entertainment. (p. 440)

> Cameron, Eleanor. "McLuhan, Youth, and Literature," part I,
> *The Horn Book*, October 1972, pp. 433–440.

Mrs. Cameron finally asks herself whether children are *harmed* by reading *Charlie and the Chocolate Factory*. She isn't quite sure, but she is clearly inclined to think that they are. Now this, to me, is the ultimate effrontery. The book is dedicated to my son Theo, now twelve years old. . . . So the thought that I would write a book for him that might actually do him harm is too ghastly to contemplate. It is an insensitive and a monstrous implication. Moreover, I believe that I am a better judge than Mrs. Cameron of what stories are good or bad for children. We have had five children. And for the last fifteen years, almost without a break, I have told a bedtime story to them as they grew old enough to listen. That's 365 made-up stories a year, some 5,000 stories altogether. Our children are marvelous and gay and happy, and I like to think that all my storytelling has contributed a little bit to their happiness. The story they like best of all is *Charlie and the Chocolate Factory*. . . . (p. 78)

> Dahl, Roald. "*Charlie and the Chocolate Factory*: A Reply,"
> *The Horn Book*, February 1973, pp. 77–78.

Read *Charlie and the Chocolate Factory*. Do you agree with Cameron that the book is tasteless? It is immensely popular with children. Why do you think this is so? Is Dahl's argument that *Charlie* is popular with his own children a sufficient answer to

Cameron's criticism? What is the relationship, if any, between popularity and literary value?

Do you believe children might be harmed by reading *Charlie*? If so, in what way? If not, why not?

EVALUATING FANTASY: IS IT REAL ENOUGH?

The freedom to take readers on soaring trips, or introduce them to odd characters, does not give writers of fantasy license to write wildly. As Alexander learned in his bout with the Muse, the world of imagination is mined; the farther the writer strays from reality, the greater the risks.

There are, to begin with, the disciplines of all good writing. Good fantasy tells an original story well. But fantasy must meet other tests, too. These are the basic criteria.

The Fantastic Element Must Be Believable

In *Tuck Everlasting*, the story takes its first jog away from reality while Mae Tuck, "a great potato of a woman," is getting dressed—a simple, everyday ritual filled with lulling detail. She puts on three petticoats, a skirt, a cotton jacket, a shawl, and leather boots and winds her hair into a bun, without looking in the mirror.

Why does she not need a mirror? The reason is fantastic. It is also simple. "Her reflection had long since ceased to interest her. For Mae Tuck, and her husband, and (her sons) Miles and Jesse, too, had all looked exactly the same for eighty-seven years" (p. 12). The scene's detail puts the reader's disbelief to rest.

In addition to the details in this credible introduction, the Tuck's varied reactions to their lives everlasting—Jesse is pleased, his father feels useless—lend authenticity throughout the book.

The Elements of Fantasy Must Be Central to the Story

A collection of unrelated happenings, no matter how interesting, is not fantasy. The entire plot in *Tuck*, and its theme of life and death, revolve around the element of immortality.

Details Must Be Consistent with the Fantastic Element

The one touch of fantasy explains details small and large throughout the whole story—why the Tuck's house on the pond is so dusty, why they are afraid to tie themselves emotionally to mortals, and why they fear someone else will find the spring and pass the water around. Jesse hesitates when Winnie asks "How old are you, anyway?" (p. 27) before she knows the Tuck's secret. He cannot answer directly. Mr. Tuck stops in midsentence to ask "Does she know?" (p. 49) before saying anything revealing.

No Matter How Fantastic the Story, Main Characters Must Be Plausible and Familiar

The best characters in fantasy remain humanlike—even when cloaked in animal identities, or when flung into weird lands, or when under magical spells. They are fearful when readers would likely be afraid. They are unpredictable up to a point, just like real people. By refusing to drink the water, Winnie remains vulnerable and mortal, choosing fragile life over the certainty of everlasting existence. We last see her pouring Jesse's gift of spring water on the back of a toad.

Characters in realistic fiction make choices too, of course. They are fearful, sometimes unpredictable, kind, and cruel; and their adventures challenge them. They are believable. But only in fantasy—magic made by just a small step from reality—can a little girl choose to confer immortality on a toad.

SUMMARY

1 *Imaginary characters* such as elves, *curious occurrences* such as time travel—fantasy is made of elements like these. Such things do not really exist, but much of modern fantasy seems plausible because the imaginary elements appear in otherwise realistic settings. Author *Susan Cooper*, for instance, injects fantasy into a meticulously drawn description of real English country life in the early pages of *The Dark Is Rising*.

2 The wide field of *imaginary characters* includes talking toys and animals, tiny people, and strange people in strange lands. Young children tend to enjoy such books as *Arnold Lobel's Frog and Toad Are Friends*, but many stories told about odd characters, such as *Ursula Le Guin's A Wizard of Earthsea*, are more appropriate for older readers.

3 In another major category of fantasy, characters are normal, but they are caught up in *curious occurrences. William Mayne's Earthfasts* is based on the premise that a young drummer boy has traveled in time to the twentieth century from the days of King Arthur. *Penelope Farmer's The Summer Birds* is a story about a girl

who learns to fly. And *Mary Rodgers' Freaky Friday* is an amusing fantasy about a girl who turns into her mother.

4 *Science fiction* uses imaginary characters or curious occurrences or both to tell stories about the future, or reflect on the nature of the universe. The field ranges from escapism, such as *Ellen MacGregor*'s Miss Pickerell series, to social commentary, such as *Sylvia Louise Engdahl*'s *The Far Side of Evil*. Some science fiction is prophetic, but the best of it survives even when actual scientific fact contradicts fiction.

5 Another kind of fantasy draws on the form of stories from the past. *Modern mythmakers*—like *Hans Christian Andersen*, a nineteenth-century Danish author—use the form of traditional stories to write fairy tales. Contemporary writers such as *Lloyd Alexander* have called on the form of fable, myth, or epic to write stories reminiscent of the oral tradition.

6 The best of fantasy is entertaining, but critics and writers argue that stories from the imagination are valuable in other ways as well. Ten-year-olds, for instance, may never have talked about death, but they can understand the concept as treated in *Natalie Babbitt*'s *Tuck Everlasting*, the story of a family that will live forever and the family's encounters with a little girl. Fantasy often reveals life as it is; in some books, however, writers suggest life as it *should* be. Characters in *William Sleator*'s *House of Stairs*, for instance, face difficult ethical choices in a story about government research. Other fantasies, such as *Lewis Carroll*'s Alice books, may be valuable in expanding language as well as imagination.

7 In these and other good fantasies, the fantastic element is easy to believe, and central to the story. Other criteria for *evaluation*: details of plot and setting should be consistent with fantastic elements, main characters should be plausible and familiar, and books must meet basic literary standards.

BIBLIOGRAPHY

Recommended Fantasy

Atwater, Richard and Florence Atwater. *Mr. Popper's Penguins*, illus. Robert Lawson (Boston: Little, Brown, 1938).
   Mr. Popper gets first one penguin, then another so the first will not be lonely, and soon there are ten little penguins, taking over his house.

Babbitt, Natalie. *The Search for Delicious* (New York: Farrar, 1970).
   Gaylen is sent to poll the people in the kingdom, to find what

"delicious" is to them so that the Prime Minister can complete the dictionary he is writing.

Bond, Michael. *Paddington on Top,* illus. Peggy Fortnum (Boston: Houghton Mifflin, 1975).

Paddington, the bear from Peru, continues to get in and out of trouble, a separate adventure for each chapter.

Boston, Lucy. *The Stones of Green Knowe,* illus. Peter Boston (New York: Atheneum, 1976).

A child of the twelfth century finds that he can, through the magic of two ancient stones, see the children who will live in Green Knowe in the future.

Butterworth, Oliver. *The Enormous Egg,* illus. Louis Darling (Boston: Little, Brown, 1956).

When Nate Twitchell's enormous egg hatches, he becomes the owner of a baby triceratops. Feeding such a pet is not an easy task.

Chant, Joy. *Red Moon and Black Mountain; The End of the House of Kendreth* (New York: Dutton, 1976).

Three children find themselves transported to another world which is caught in a struggle between the forces of good and evil.

Christopher, John. *Empty World* (New York: Dutton, 1978).

Neil is one of the few people in the world to survive a plague. Other survivors react to the situation in widely diverse ways.

Cooper, Susan. *Silver on the Tree.* (New York: Atheneum, 1977).

In the last of "The Dark is Rising" series, Will Stanton, Bran, and the Drew children work to vanquish the Dark.

Cresswell, Helen. *A Game of Catch,* illus. Ati Forberg (New York: Macmillan, 1977).

In this time-shift fantasy, two children see a picture of two eighteenth-century children. Later Kate realizes that she can call them into the present.

Dahl, Roald. *The Magic Finger,* illus. William Pène du Bois (New York: Harper, 1966).

The girl who tells the story points her magic finger at the Greggs, who are going hunting, and they are turned into ducks.

Garner, Alan. *The Owl Service* (New York: Walck, 1968).

When Alison and Gwyn find dishes with decorations that look like owls—the owl service—an old Welsh legend begins to be reinacted.

Hoban, Russell. *The Mouse and His Child,* illus. Lillian Hoban (New York: Harper, 1967).

The mouse and his child are wind-up toys. After being repaired by a tramp, they go on to many adventures as they search for a home.

Hunter, Mollie. *A Stranger Came Ashore* (New York: Viking, 1975).

In this tale, the folklore of the Selkies is woven into a full-length story about a young man who appears during a storm and who is suspected of being a seal-man.

Jansson, Tove. *Tales from Moominvalley,* trans. Thomas Warburton (New York: Walck, 1964).

This is one of a series of books about the Moomintroll family. Moomin are creatures who live in a valley with their friends—the stump collector, the Snork, and others—and have some frightening experiences.

Jarrell, Randall. *The Animal Family,* illus. Maurice Sendak (New York: Pantheon, 1965).

The hunter, left alone, makes a family of a mermaid, a bear, a lynx, and a shipwrecked baby.

Jones, Diana Wynne. *Charmed Life* (New York: Greenwillow, 1978).

When Gwendolyn is no longer permitted to use her magical powers, she forces a double from another world to take her place.

Kipling, Rudyard. *Just-So Stories,* illus. Etienne Delessert (Garden City, N.Y.: Doubleday, 1972).

These are Kipling's classic tales about how certain animals ended up with particular characteristics—for instance, how the elephant got its trunk.

Kumin, Maxine and Sexton, Anne. *The Wizard's Tears,* illus. Evaline Ness (New York: McGraw-Hill, 1975).

The old wizard had retired, and the new one did well except that everyone turned into frogs.

Lewis, C.S. *The Lion, the Witch, and the Wardrobe,* illus. Pauline Baynes (New York: Macmillan, 1961).

This is one of seven books about the mythical land of Narnia. All seven are religious allegories, but also good adventure stories.

Lively, Penelope. *The Ghost of Thomas Kempe,* illus. Antony Maitland (London: Heinemann, 1973).

James finds that Thomas Kempe's ghost can be quite annoying, particularly when he insists upon leaving notes, and creating a draft.

Merrill, Jean. *The Pushcart War,* illus. Ronni Solbert (Reading, Mass.: Young Scott, 1964).

The war occurred in New York City and lasted for four months. The combatants were pushcart peddlers and truckers.

Pinkwater, D. Manus. *Lizard Music* (New York: Dodd, 1976).

Victor first sees the lizard band on television, then begins to see lizards everywhere, eventually visiting their island. Filled with puns.

Pope, Elizabeth Marie. *The Perilous Gard,* illus. Richard Cuffari (Boston: Houghton Mifflin, 1974).

In this complex fantasy, set in 1558, Kate is sent to Elvenwood Hall, to the perilous gard, a castle feared by the country folk because of its association with heathen magic.

Saint-Exupery, Antoine de. *The Little Prince,* trans. Katherine Woods (New York: Harcourt, 1943).

The author tells of his meeting with the little prince, and how the prince describes the planet on which he lives—only as big as a house, but with a rose that is unique in all the universe.

Snyder, Zilpha Keatley. *Until the Celebration,* illus. Alton Raible (New York: Atheneum, 1977).

In this third and last book of a series, dissension within both the Erdlings and the Kindar threatens to ruin the celebration of their reunion.

Travers, Pamela L. *Mary Poppins,* illus. Mary Shepard (New York: Harcourt, 1934).

Mary Poppins is the nanny who blows into a London household and takes over, much to the delight of Jane and Michael.

Turkle, Brinton. *The Fiddler of High Lonesome* (New York: Viking, 1968).

Lysander Bochamp goes to live with the Fogles, the only kin he has, but he objects to their killing of animals. They let him stay because he plays the fiddle.

Westall, Robert. *The Wind Eye* (New York: Greenwillow, 1977).

In this time-shift fantasy, three children discover a boat which will take them back to medieval times.

Wrightson, Patricia. *The Ice Is Coming* (New York: Atheneum, 1977).

Wirrun, a young Aborigine, sets out to find the Nargun in order to stop the ancient ice people from taking over the land.

Adult References

Alexander, Lloyd. "The Flat-Heeled Muse," *The Horn Book,* April 1965, pp. 141–146.

Asimov, Isaac. Quoted in *The New York Times,* July 22, 1976, p. 29.

Bettelheim, Bruno. *The Uses of Enchantment* (New York: Knopf, 1976).

Cameron Eleanor. "McLuhan, Youth and Literature," part I, *The Horn Book,* October 1972, pp. 433–440.

Cook Elizabeth. *The Ordinary and The Fabulous* (Cambridge: Cambridge University Press, 1969).

Dahl, Roald. *"Charlie and The Chocolate Factory*: A Reply," *The Horn Book,* February 1973, pp. 77–78.

Egoff, Sheila, G. T. Stubbs, and L. F. Ashley (eds.). *Only Connect:*

Readings on Children's Literature (Toronto: Oxford University Press, 1969).

Engdahl, Sylvia Louise. "The Changing Role of Science Fiction in Children's Literature," *The Horn Book*, October 1971, pp. 449–455.

Farmer, Penelope. " 'Jorinda and Jorindel' and Other Stories," *Children's Literature in Education*, March 1972, pp. 23–37.

Lewis, C.S. *An Experiment in Criticism* (London: Cambridge University Press, 1961).

———. "On Three Ways of Writing for Children," *The Horn Book*, October 1963, pp. 459–469.

Shepard, Ernest. "Illustrating *The Wind in the Willows*," *The Horn Book*, April 1954, pp. 83–86.

Tolkien, J. R. R. *Tree and Leaf* (Boston: Houghton Mifflin 1965).

Yolen, Jane. "The Modern Mythmakers" *Language Arts*, May 1976, pp. 491–495.

Children's Book References

Adams, Richard. *Watership Down* (New York: Macmillan, 1974).

Alexander, Lloyd. *The High King* (New York: Holt, 1968).

———. *The King's Fountain*, illus. Ezra Jack Keats (New York: Dutton, 1971).

Andersen, Hans Christian. *The Ugly Duckling*, illus. Adrienne Adams (New York: Scribner's 1965).

Babbitt, Natalie. *Tuck Everlasting* (New York: Farrar, 1975).

Carroll, Lewis. *Alice in Wonderland* (New York: Norton, 1971). (*Alice's Adventures in Wonderland* first published in 1865; *Through the Looking Glass* in 1871.)

Christopher, John. *The White Mountains* (New York: Macmillan, 1967).

———. *The City of Gold and Lead* (New York: Macmillan, 1967).

———. *The Pool of Fire* (New York: Macmillan 1968).

———. *The Prince in Waiting* (New York: Macmillan, 1970,

———. *Beyond the Burning Lands* (New York: Macmillan, 1971).

———. *The Sword of the Spirits* (New York: Macmillan, 1972).

Clarke, Pauline. *The Return of the Twelves* (New York: Coward-McCann, 1963).

Cooper, Susan. *The Dark Is Rising*, illus. Alan E. Cober (New York: Atheneum, 1973).

Cunningham, Julia. *Macaroon*, illus. Evaline Ness (New York: Pantheon, 1962).

Dahl, Roald. *Charlie and the Chocolate Factory*, illus. Joseph Schindelman (New York: Knopf, 1964).

Dickinson, Peter. *Heartsease* (Boston: Little, Brown, 1969).

Engdahl, Sylvia. *The Far Side of Evil* (New York: Antheneum, 1971).

Farmer, Penelope. *The Summer Birds* (New York: Harcourt, 1962).

Godden, Rumer. *The Mousewife*, illus. William Pène du Bois (New York: Viking, 1951).

Grahame, Kenneth. *The Wind in the Willows*, illus. Tasha Tudor (Cleveland: World, 1966). (1908)

Hamilton, Virginia. *The Time-Ago Tales of Jahdu*, illus. Nonny Hogrogian (New York: Macmillan, 1969).

Heinlein, Robert. *Rocket Ship Galileo*, illus. Thomas Voter (New York: Scribner's, 1947).

———. *Farmer in the Sky* (New York: Scribner's, 1950).

Hoban, Russell. *A Birthday for Frances*, illus. Lillian Hoban (New York: Harper, 1968).

Juster, Norton. *The Phantom Tollbooth*, illus. Jules Feiffer (New York: Random House, 1972). (1961)

Kendall, Carol. *The Gammage Cup* (New York: Harcourt, 1959).

Lawson, Robert. *Rabbit Hill* (New York: Viking, 1944).

Le Guin, Ursula K. *A Wizard of Earthsea*, illus. Ruth Robbins (Berkeley, Calif.: Parnassus, 1968).

Lionni, Leo. *Frederick* (New York: Pantheon, 1967).

Lobel, Arnold. *Frog and Toad Are Friends* (New York: Harper, 1970).

L'Engle, Madeleine. *A Wrinkle in Time* (New York: Farrar, 1962).

MacGregor, Ellen. *Miss Pickerell Goes to Mars* (New York: McGraw-Hill, 1951).

Mayne, William. *Earthfasts* (New York: Dutton, 1967).

Milne, A. A. *Winnie-the-Pooh* (New York: Dutton, 1926).

Norton, Mary. *The Borrowers* (New York: Harcourt, 1953).

O'Brien, Robert. *Mrs. Frisby and the Rats of NIMH* (New York: Atheneum, 1971).

Pearce, Philippa. *Tom's Midnight Garden* (Philadelphia: Lippincott, 1959).

Potter, Beatrix. *The Tale of Jemima Puddle-Duck* (London: Warne).

Schweitzer, Byrd Baylor. *Amigo*, illus. Garth Williams (New York: Macmillan, 1963).

Selden, George. *The Cricket in Times Square*. illus. Garth Williams (New York: Farrar, 1960).

Sleator, William. *House of Stairs* (New York: Dutton, 1974).

Slobodkin, Louis. *The Space Ship under the Apple Tree* (New York: Macmillan, 1952).

Tolkien, J. R. R. *The Hobbit* (Boston: Houghton Mifflin, 1938).

White, E. B. *Charlotte's Web*, illus. Garth Williams (New York: Harper, 1952).

CHAPTER
7

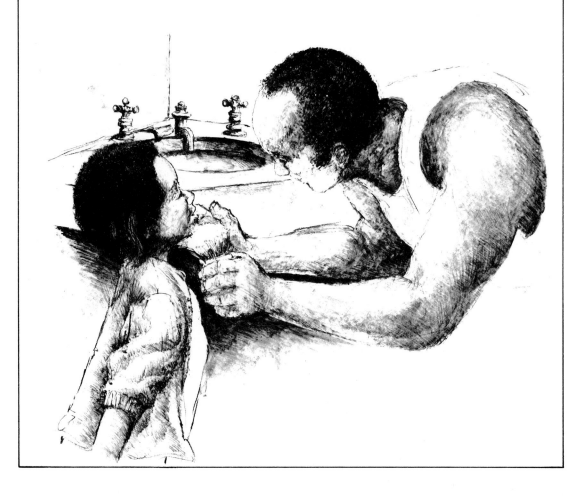

CONTEMPORARY REALISM

FICTION OUT OF FACT

The fact was that a visiting friend of Ivan Southall suggested trapping rabbits one day. "Bunny's good," the friend said. And Southall, an Australian writer, followed quietly as traps were set and covered with dust and leaves and twigs.

At dusk they heard a scream from a trap. They grabbed a hurricane lamp and ax handle to use as a club and ran down a hill. "And that rabbit went on screaming until he saw the light and heard us come," Southall reported in a piece of nonfiction (1974, p. 47). The incident happened in the early 1950s.

The fiction was Southall's *Josh*, published twenty years later in 1971. Two boys named Bill and Rex set a trap. And then, with the boy Josh, they hear a cry "like an agonized baby" (p. 55). The story continues:

> Josh not wanting to look, dreading it, but drawn in despite himself, even pushed on toward it by the pressure of Bill and Rex. A narrow track in the scrub as if made by tiny men, an arch knee-high in wire-grass as if woven for shelter and security, in it a rabbit, brown and white, caught by one foreleg between rusty iron jaws, dragging the trap on a frantic arc, eyes huge with terror but making no cry. . . . (p. 57)

Another modern writer, Felice Holman, plunged into a study of the world underneath New York City. She memorized subway maps, drew her own diagrams, lurked in basements among boilers, ferreted out detail about hidden chambers behind buried walls. Her down-below-earth research (described in Holman, 1976) became the basis for a fictional setting behind a story of a boy who lived below the city. The fiction was called *Slake's Limbo* (1974).

A third writer, Norma Klein, knew a woman who had become pregnant by a man who did not want to marry her. The woman raised the child by herself for several years. Then she met another man and got married.

"Not only was the child's life not ruined, but she developed a strength of character and sense of purpose that I, at least, had not seen in most girls her age," Klein wrote (1975, p. 308). That situation from life was the seed of an idea that blossomed into the theme for a novel called *Mom, the Wolfman and Me* (1972).

Each of these writers began with vivid reality. Each then applied imagination and artistic skill to write fiction. They chose and enlivened facts. They reflected the reality of specific times and places. But they did much more in their fiction. Holman's data about New

York are already as out of date as an old railroad timetable; *Slake's Limbo* lives on.

The best of realistic fiction, in fact, survives because it is more than just a report of problems, fads, or fancies. The best survives as literature.

REALISM BEGINS WITH REFLECTION

Realistic fiction tells a story which could happen, or could have happened in the past. *Josh, Slake's Limbo,* and *Wolfman* are *contemporary realism*: the setting for each is modern. Realistic stories with settings in the past are called historical realism or, more commonly, *historical fiction.* (Chapter 8 surveys the branch of realism with roots in the past.)

Contemporary realism usually reflects the times when the writing was done. So stories are often a kind of weathervane, pointing out directions for winds of change in society.

Here, for instance, are two selections about the first day for a black student in a previously all-white school. The first, *Call Me Charley,*

Male role models have begun to reflect more flexibility. Max (below) enjoys ballet on his way to baseball, and Julius (next page) openly accepts the love and concern of his counselor, Luke. ([a] Reprinted with permission of Macmillan Publishing Co., Inc. from *Max* by Rachel Isadora. Copyright © 1976 by Rachel Isadora. [b] From *Luke Was There* by Eleanor Clymer. Illustrated by Diane de Groat. Illustrations copyright © 1973 by Holt, Rinehart and Winston, Inc. Reproduced by permission of Holt, Rinehart and Winston, Inc.)

(a)

(b)

about a mother's lecture to a young boy named Charley, was written in 1945 by Jesse Jackson.

> It was Monday morning. Charley's mother sat across from him at the breakfast table looking at the letter Mr. Winter had sent her by Charley. She signed it slowly and then looked to make sure she had done it correctly.
>
> "It's all up to you, Charley," she said. "Mr. Winter says here in this letter that you will only be allowed to attend their school for a three months' trial. He says the school you used to go to in the Bottoms wasn't up to the standards of his school. I'll work and see you go to school clean, but you'll have to get the kind of grades it says here in the letter. You'll have to keep out of trouble . . . . First trouble you get into, Mr. Winter will say: 'See, I knew we shouldn't have let that colored boy come here.' . . . . And watch your manners, boy. Good manners go a long way to help a colored boy get along in this world." (p. 54)

The second passage was published in 1966 after two decades of legislative and social change. Robby, the main character in *Lions in the Way*, by Bella Rodman, literally towers over black characters from the 1940s. As he leaves for integrated Carver High School, his mother offers no advice about manners. She asks only if he is afraid.

> He was much taller than she was; he smiled down at her. "I guess one minute I am, and the next, I'm not afraid of anything. But you've got no cause to worry; I can make it all right."
>
> He had to bend down to be kissed, and Mrs. Jones restrained herself from putting her arms around him, knowing that he would not like the babying. (p. 83)

The portrayals of Charley and Robby in these passages tell more than most newspaper reports about what happened to many black people between World War II and the mid-1960s.

Realism for children is not restricted in what it can reflect. Some books are built on familiar feelings, sights, sounds, and smells. Writer Miriam Cohen captures a more common kind of first-day-at-school jitters in a 1967 book for preschoolers called *Will I Have a Friend?* In an inner-city kindergarten, young Jim at first gets the impression that there are not enough friends to go around. No one notices the lumpy man Jim makes of clay. His neighbor at the juice and cookie table stuffs his mouth too full to answer when Jim says something. But after rest time, a classmate named Paul lets Jim hold his tiny truck, with doors that really work. "I have a gas pump," Jim says. "I'll bring it tomorrow."

The situation is as lightweight as the truck, at least for adult taste, but young children know what it means to try to find friends at juice-and-cookie time.

Other contemporary realism reflects darker corners of society that may not be nearly so familiar to most young readers. *Grandma Didn't Wave Back* (1972), by Rose Blue, is a book for intermediate-grade children about senility. A 10-year-old girl named Debbie has become accustomed to waving at her grandmother after school as the girl arrives home. One day, the aging and confused lady fails to return the wave. Later it becomes evident that she needs care in a nursing home. There, once again, she waves when Debbie comes to call. Grandma's apparent comfort in her new home softens the harshness around the agony of her aging.

Some books offer little comfort. Norma Fox Mazer's *A Figure of Speech* (1973), written for adolescent readers, is about an 83-year-old man named Carl shunted aside by all in his family except his grand-daughter, Jenny. Carl runs aways from the family when he learns they are about to put him in a nursing home. Jenny follows as the old man returns to his former home, a farmhouse. Then one morn-ing Jenny awakes to find her grandfather gone. She discovers his body outside. Jenny realizes that he chose to die under the boughs of his apple tree instead of an unfamiliar nursing home. In the book's final scene, Jenny runs from her home to escape overhearing her parents' discussion with friends about how wonderful it was that Carl was never bedridden. To them, he remains a "figure of speech." To Jenny, he was a grandfather, deeply loved.

Once, the topics of death and dying were considered inappropriate in books for children. Today editors encourage writers to deal with a wide range of subjects including death, drugs, divorce, sexual prob-lems, and disabilities. Often, books in these once-forbidden ter-ritories are labeled "new realism," although authors broke some ground on the frontier of these areas decades ago.

In 1958 Margaret Wise Brown published a book about children's reactions to the death of a small animal. *The Dead Bird* focuses on the funeral and burial of the bird, but the fact that the children return to their play at the end of the book serves to underscore the fact that death is a natural part of life. In the mid-1960s, writer Louise Fitzhugh allowed a book character to say "damned." The undeleted expletive was a new idea in 1964, when Fitzhugh's *Har-riet the Spy* was published. (There is more on the book in Chapter 10.) Today, standards of newer realism permit books on homosexu-ality, incest, and child abuse in books for intermediate-grade read-ers, and stories about death and aging for children of all ages.

LITERATURE—OR SLICE OF LIFE?

Good realism must do more than reflect reality, or introduce curious fact lightly cloaked in fiction.

Writer Robert Burch reports that he once went to a widely acclaimed play which presented, with tape-recorder accuracy, the speech patterns of people in New York City. Watching the first act, Burch was astounded.

"The characters on stage are so real," he told himself. "Why, they sound exactly like my neighbors arguing." His boredom rose, however, as the lines continued to sound just like homey chatter. No characters developed, or changed. The plot went nowhere. By the third act, Burch thought he might as well have spent the evening listening out the window to his neighbors.

> But the show was "in" at the moment, it was being talked about at parties, and I wanted to know about it, so I would have gone, even if I had known it would bore me. We adults are like that. I am glad children are not. (1971, p. 258)

Stories that merely reflect reality are not literature, any more than car repair manuals or biology textbooks or books about children's literature are literature. But adults sometimes become entranced by a play or book just because it models life, exactly to scale. Realistic fiction may win favor solely because it introduces readers to real difficulties, such as physical handicaps or sexual disorders. For readers like this, books function as museums or zoos; the readers get to watch realistic people trying to cope with their problems.

On the other hand, adults reading children's books sometimes ignore literary qualities like theme or character development and see only the "slice of life"—the realistic street talk or the setting in the dingy subway. For example, when some critics in the mid-1960s read *Harriet the Spy*, they reduced it to a sliver of life; it became "the book about the girl who says 'damned.'" And some librarians damned the whole book for that one word.

Many of the books discussed in the next two sections of this chapter may be educational about current issues. The realism in others may be objectionable to some tastes. But as you approach each of the books in this chapter, look beneath surface reflections of reality, and try to gauge basic quality. (The second-to-last section of the chapter will suggest more specific criteria for judging realism.)

Norma Klein, author of *Mom, the Wolfman and Me,* makes the same point in a plea for an even greater freedom for writers to deal with contemporary problems. She argues there should be more children's books on sexuality, for instance. But Klein continues:

> I'm not referring to books on sex education, which always bored me out of my mind, though I know they are very useful and important. I still have trouble remembering exactly where and what a uterus is, and I could live perfectly happily without ever seeing another diagram of a tadpole-like sperm swimming happily across the page of a picture book. I'm referring to books concerned with life, books concerned with emotions that all of us have felt, and that our children are feeling right now. These feelings need *literary* expression. (1977, p. 84; italics added)

REALISM FOR DIFFERENT AGES

What children feel right now varies from child to child and place to place. But children do tend to pass through similar stages of growth, and these stages relate roughly to age (see Chapter 1).

In the books that follow, you will find many different children and plots, and several different themes. You can also find *one* child, growing up. In several of the books for youngest readers, the child is allied with a family, although the alliance is sometimes strained by hassles with brothers and sisters or parents. In some of the books for intermediate-grade children, the child crosses family borders, searching for self-identity, leaving one foot behind in the home. In books for adolescents, the child often ventures far from parents, into awesome arenas where battles are fought alone.

Of course, there is really no "typical" child, nor are there exact age ranges. And there is no typical children's book. There *are* signs of a pattern in this selection of books; many of them show a child venturing on a quest for independence, discovering strengths, mastering some part of the world nearby. Watch for that recurring theme. And look for it again in the next section, on special categories of realism.

For Children 5 to 7: the World of the Family

Sam (1967) is the story of a restless boy. He has discovered a way to stand on his head with his body supported between the rungs of an overturned chair. But he wants to play with someone. His mother is angry with him for touching a kitchen knife. His brother outside on the porch yells at him for turning the pages of a book. In Symeon

ISSUE

DOES TELEVISION VIEWING STIMULATE CHILDREN'S INTEREST IN READING THE "NEW REALISM?"

Television is programmed to satisfy adult appetites. Its programming is becoming increasingly frank and sensational. Because most adults are reluctant to keep children away from television, children are, from infancy, exposed to elements of the adult world from which they had been shielded. This is true of situational/fictional programs and of nonfictional presentations. . . .

The *now* children are ready for the new realism. Probably, past ready. They want books that "tell it like it is," or as they suspect it is. They are tired of being lied to and treated like children. "Don't give us that pablum and namby pamby stuff," they say. "Don't lie to us." (p. 22)

> Root, Shelton L. "The New Realism—Some personal Reflections,"
> *Language Arts*, January 1977, pp. 19-24.

There is, I believe, a growing skepticism about the nonliterary criteria by which children's books are evaluated, particularly as the criteria relate to the new realism (sensitive books, junior novels, problem books, whatever). If it is true that such slices of life are being read (as well as having wide circulation), it does seem rather off—for how can children both read avidly and watch television all the hours research would have us believe? Again, and much more puzzling: the ratings would seem to indicate that both older and young people are watching much the same TV programs. But the prime favorites are certainly not serious slices of life, any more than *Peg's Paper* and TV soap operas are. (p. 481)

> Ashley, L.F. "Bibliotherapy, etc."
> *Language Arts*, April 1978, pp. 478-481.

Both writers talk of a relationship between television viewing and reading. How might their differing conclusions about what children want to read be explained? How would you classify prime-time television in terms of "telling it like it is," and as a "serious slice of life"? What evidence do you have that television does or does not affect children's reading habits?

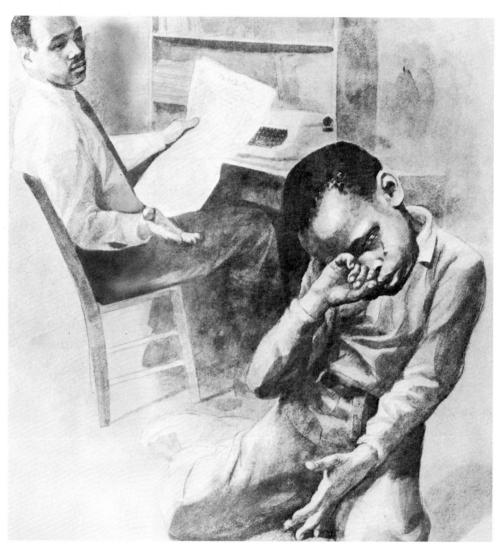

When Sam begins to cry, his family realizes his need for attention. (From *Sam* by Ann Herbert Scott, illustrated by Symeon Shimin. Copyright © 1967 by Ann Herbert Scott and Symeon Shimin. Reproduced by permission of McGraw-Hill Book Company, Inc.)

Shimin's realistic illustrations, Sam droops, eyelids down, holding his hands lightly in front of him. His sister and father also reject him, and his eyes glisten with tears. "Then Sam really did cry. He sat right down on the floor by his father's desk and he cried and cried and cried." The family knows they have neglected him. His crying

ISSUE

HOW CLOSELY SHOULD
LITERATURE MIRROR LIFE?

In a recent study of one hundred randomly selected books, Barnum (1977) found that the aged are discriminated against in young children's literature. They appear less frequently than they should, in view of their proportion in the United States population, and are depicted as disadvantaged in many socioeconomic and behavioral characteristics. (p. 29)

> Barnum, Phyllis Winet. "The Aged in Young Children's Literature,"
> *Language Arts*, January 1977, pp. 29-32.

I would like sexuality to be woven into the texture of books, not dealt with head on, grimly, as the theme, just something kids do and think about while in the midst of family and school situations. . . . Am I saying all books for children should deal with sexuality? My answer would be no. In many books it would be inappropriate or irrelevant. It's just that if one read a thousand books for children and found that trees were never mentioned one would begin to wonder at the reason for this omission. Similarly, the absence of any frank treatment of sexuality in book after book for children of all ages makes one aware that more than just routine selection of topics is going on. (pp. 311-312)

> Klein, Norma. "More Realism for Children,"
> *Top of the News*, April 1975, pp. 311-312.

Both Barnum and Klein use the frequency with which a particular topic appears in books for children as the basis for some conclusions. What is the conclusion of each, and how does the reasoning in the two arguments differ? What, if any, relationship do you think there should be between frequency of a topic in "life," and the frequency of that topic in literature for children? What is the rationale for your position?

rallies the world to his side: he gets to make raspberry tarts with his mother.

Tears also bring relief to a boy named Christopher in Carol Carrick's *The Accident* (1976). The boy and his dog, Bodger, are walking to a lake from their summer cottage when they come to a road. Christopher calls the dog to cross just as a truck approaches. The dog stops to sniff, and the truck hits and kills him. The driver can do nothing to ease Christopher's anger and sorrow, and it is not until his father takes him along in a search for a stone to mark the dog's grave that the boy is able to cry. Crying helps relieve the pain of his loss.

There is another young boy wrestling with emotion in Barbara Williams's humorous *If He's My Brother* (1976). The boy bridles under the rules laid down in his family, and he dreams of freedom as he carries on a philosophical discussion with himself. "If it's my room . . . Why can't I paint it any way I want? If they're my pockets . . . Why can't I put worms in them?" He drones on while this mental dialogue with himself moves to the last question: "If he's my brother . . . Why can't I punch him?" The final illustration answers the question: The younger brother resents being punched, and retaliates by hitting the older boy with a teddy bear.

These books and many others for the youngest readers center around children struggling to understand and cope with their feelings as the smallest members of families. The families need not be traditional. In Jeannette Caines's *Daddy* (1977), for instance, a child tells what it is like to be with her divorced father, on Saturdays only. At the father's apartment, his new wife hugs the girl. Then, in unvarying ritual, the child watches her father shave and makes a game of looking for eyeglasses. During the week, the child says, she worries about her father, getting "wrinkles in my stomach." Those wrinkles disappear on Saturdays when the second half of the family reunites.

In some books for the first few grades, characters begin to move out on their own. A boy named Benje makes his move when his grandmother with whom he lives fails to show up to take him home from school. Granny has never approved of letting young children walk on their own on city streets. But today the boy has waited and waited for her to meet him outside the heavy fence in front of his school. "I don't think Granny's coming," he says. "Well, I'll show her I can go home by myself."

Joan Lexau's *Benje on His Own* (1970) follows him through the maze of city streets marked with illegible signs and inhabited by a snarling dog and bullies in tight pants. Benje's fear that Granny is sick rises as he passes a strange lady, who never smiles, in the window of a second-floor apartment. In Don Bolognese's illustrations, the steps and railings to Benje's fifth-floor apartment seem to

Emi discovers, while picking up her napkin, that Reverend Okura is not the staid sort of adult she had expected—and had feared would ruin her birthday. (Reprinted from *The Birthday Visitor* by Yoshiko Uchida, illustrated by Charles Robinson. With the permission of Charles Schribner's Sons, copyright © 1975 Charles Robinson.)

slow him like a huge spider web. (Look at the way the steps seem to run almost *horizontally*; the drawing heightens suspense.)

Granny is "awful sick," it turns out, and Benje is the only one who can help her, using all the independence he can muster. As ambulance attendants carry her away, he wants to shout: "Wait for me." But with his new-found maturity, he knows crying would only cause more trouble. "Don't worry about me, Granny," he calls after her.

For Children 8 to 11: Exploring the New World of Self

Does Benje's perilous journey home seem familiar? It should. On a small scale, it recalls hazardous voyages in traditional epics (See Chapter 5). It parallels Max's imaginary journey in Sendak's *Where the Wild Things Are* (Chapter 2), and is like many other stories of fantasy about journeying characters ranging from rabbits to hobbits (See Chapter 6). A common feature in all these stories—and in realistic fiction as well—is that those who risk the journey find themselves.

In *The Stone-Faced Boy* (1968), by New York writer Paula Fox, a boy named Gus Oliver is the third and middle child in his family. Gus is so beset on all sides by siblings and other children—one of his

brothers named Simon keeps smashing toy brooms on Gus' head—
that he no longer smiles or scowls. "Stone face," other children have
called him for years. And now, "Gus had begun to fear there would
come a time, soon, when he couldn't close his eyes to sleep, or open
his mouth to eat" (p. 14). When Great Aunt Hattie comes for a visit,
she seems to understand him. She gives Gus a geode, a small hollow
rock with glimmering cystals lining the inside wall.

Gus's journey begins in the middle of a snowy night when his
younger sister begs him to go out in the dark and search for a runaway dog. Are there milk snakes in winter in the clearing by the well?
Will the well overflow and flood the world, the way it did in one of
Gus's worst nightmares? Irrational fears track him as he follows the
howling of the dog, caught in a fox trap. His boots collect the snow.
His mittens are soaked. When he reaches an abandoned shed and
opens the door, something squeaks and moves inside.

"Gus!" he cries near a stone wall, without knowing why.

There are other threats. Gus trudges on. He finds the dog. And—
when he returns home at dawn—he also finds the strength to stop
Simon cold as his brother is about to swing his terrible broomstick.
Gus refuses to break open the geode, even under pressure from his
older brother. The quest in the night has made him bold, and "his
head was bursting with laughter" (p. 102).

By the wall in the snow, Gus called his own name to try to find
himself. Another character about Gus's age, 9-year-old Kelly
O'Brien, learns about himself during explorations of a creek behind
his house. In *Kelly's Creek* (1975), by Doris Buchanan Smith, Kelly
feels stupid and useless. A handicap prevents him from balancing on
a bicycle or catching a ball as classmates can. He is in a special class,
one hour a day, to learn better coordination. But parents and
teachers think he is not trying. In the creek behind the house, however, Kelly becomes a skilled explorer. A college student named
Phillip passes on some of his knowledge of marine biology, and
Kelly begins to win some admiration from classmates for his impressive familiarity with fiddler crabs. Kelly's coordination improves. He draws a square for the first time. He breaks off a friendship with another 9-year-old named Zack who wants to visit the
creek, but only to play games there. Kelly has more serious work in
the marsh: to keep growing and learning, and to discover who he is
and will be.

In dreams about who they might become, intermediate-grade children often look up to someone older. Kelly follows Phillip, for instance. In another book, Virginia Hamilton's *Zeely* (1967), an 11-
year-old girl named Elizabeth Perry chooses a different kind of
model.

Geeder sits in awe as Zeely explains, through stories, that she is not a Watusi queen. (Reprinted with permission of Macmillan Publishing Co., Inc. from *Zeely* by Virginia Hamilton, illustrated by Symeon Shimin. Copyright © 1967 Macmillan Publishing Co., Inc.)

A summer's trip with her brother John to an uncle's farm has given Elizabeth the chance to play beautiful roles. She even chooses a summer name. "I'm going to be Geeder," she tells John on the train. "I am Miss Geeder Perry from this second on. Horses answer to 'Gee,' don't they? I bet I can call a mare to me even better than Uncle Ross!" (p. 9)

To Geeder, in the romance of a summer "fine and sluggish," there is much to look up to in Zeely, one of the hands on a farm. Zeely is more than 6½ feet tall, "thin and deeply dark as a pole of Ceylon ebony" (p. 31). Zeely is a queen. She looks like a magazine picture Geeder finds showing a tall African woman of royal birth. Geeder spreads word of Zeely's royalty throughout the children of the village, and eventually the tales reach Zeely herself. She asks to meet Geeder at the entrance to a forest. There, Zeely is dressed regally in flowing colored silk.

Once, she tells the girl, she imagined herself that she was a queen.

319

Geeder moves closer to her and listens as Zeely tells stately, mysterious stories. One is a kind of myth about her tall ancestors at the beginning of the world. And the other—the one that impresses Geeder most—is about an old cackling woman who discovered Zeely one night as she emerged from a swim in a lake. Zeely hid in blackness between a bush and a tree. The story continues:

> "'Zeely Tayber,' [the cackling woman] said again. She raised her cane right at me, and she was coming toward me. I could see her bow moving in the air. Suddenly, she had me by the arms. She was cackling again—I thought she would never stop.
>
> "At last, she spoke," Zeely said. "'Zeely Tayber,' she said, 'you have made a poor soul happy. You are the night and I have caught you!' . . .
>
> "All at once in my mind everything was as clear as day. I liked the dark. I walked and swam in the dark and because of that, I was the *night!*" (p. 112)

But Zeely's mother broke the dream, the story continues. "She said that since the woman was not quite right in her head, she had decided that I was the night because my skin was so dark. . . . No pretty robe was about to make me more than what I was and no little woman could make me the night" (p. 113).

The story leads Geeder gently back to Elizabeth: the young girl realizes that her mask as a farm girl, and worship of regal Zeely, have been summer games.

> I *was* silly, she thought. I made up myself as Geeder and I made up Zeely to be a queen. (p. 114)

Yet Zeely is as good as a queen. She does not reign over distant kingdoms with servants and diamonds and gold, "like you read in books or hear on the radio." Instead, she is real—a beautiful, skilled, sensitive farmhand. Back at her uncle's farmhouse, Elizabeth gathers all her sparkling necklaces, draped on furniture. Once, earlier in the summer when she had played footloose farm girl, they had made her feel that she rested among stars. Now she packs them away in a box.

Zeely was Hamilton's first book, but she had already nearly mastered the realist's art of making object, places, and people resonate with mystery and truth. Blackness, for instance, is never simply the absence of light. In one moment in Zeely's skilled telling, it is the essence of night, captured by a cackling woman. One moment later it becomes Zeely's own dark skin. A stonelike shadow in the night by Zeely's lake becomes a turtle when the old lady pokes it, and what looks like a fallen twisted branch is really a snake. Reality is not always what it seems. Elizabeth is not who she dreamt she was. She is better, and growing.

There is plenty of lighter fare in books of contemporary realism for third-, fourth-, and fifth-graders. Intermediate-grade children often enjoy meeting Maurice, the single-minded lad in *Maurice's Room*, a 1966 book by Paula Fox (who also wrote *The Stone Faced Boy*). Maurice's passion is junk. He likes his trashy collection of odds and ends so much that when his mother tells him to get everything off the floor, he and a friend and the building janitor manage to hang everything from the walls or ceiling.

His parents try to entice him with real toys. But he would rather play with the old stuff he has. His parents try to distract him with a dog named Patsy. But Maurice is interested only in keeping Patsy from sniffing around his stuff. Then comes a crisis: When the family moves, the trunk containing his things bounces off the van and all is lost. But wait. The new house has a barn, filled with old junk. A new collection begins.

Another funny story tells of a running boy-girl feud. The boy, Thad, has told Maggie Marmelstein that she squeaks like a mouse. She strikes back by called him by his full name, Thaddeus Gideon Smith. Then, in the rising hostility, Maggie obtains what Thad thinks is the equivalent of a bomb: she sees Thad helping her mother make bread pudding. When the time is right, she threatens, she will tell everyone. Thad's only defense is to get something on her. In *Getting Something on Maggie Marmelstein* (1971), by Marjorie Sharmat, Thad goes to great lengths. He even plays frog to her princess in the school play. Danger ever hangs over him that she will blab. But then he learns something to balance her power: Maggie Marmelstein writes letters to movie stars. Finally, he gives her the letter he has swiped, and they declare a truce.

Many intermediate-grade students are in the middle of serious conflicts and competition with children around them. For a time, many toe lines drawn by others their age. In Thad's society, for instance, it is taboo for a boy to make bread pudding. As they turn toward their teenaged years, many children become freer to write their own rules. With growing stature and reasoning power, young teenagers are also freer to take dangerous risks in quests to find out who they are.

For Children 12 and Older: *Let the Balloon Go*

Here are two children near the threshold of adolescence. John Sumner, in Ivan Southall's *Let the Balloon Go* (1968), is a 12-year-old spastic child, prevented by his handicap from running, swinging

321

from ropes, or riding a bike. Doretha, in Eloise Greenfield's *Sister* (1974), is a 13-year-old black girl gripped by fear that she will turn out like her stray 16-year-old sister.

John and Doretha are vastly different children. He is the son of well-educated parents. His mother lectures in a university. She is the daughter of a woman who works in a laundry and a man who parked cars until he died, when Doretha was 10. But they are also fundamentally alike. Each feels trapped, John by his handicap and Doretha by her blood ties to her sister. Each has loving parents. And both break restrictive bonds by what they do alone, in the course of a few critical hours.

When John convinces his anxious, protective mother to leave him alone one day, he remembers once meeting a stranger on a city street. The man had seen John trying to fight spastic trembling. The stranger had lowered his head to speak to the boy.

> "You'll do it son. Don't let anything stop you from being the boy you want to be. The answer's inside you. A balloon is not a balloon until you cut the string and let it go." (p. 47)

Let the balloon go? To John that day, when he is left alone, it means freedom—being like other boys at least in one simple way. John wants to climb a tree.

His agonizing ascent at least 50 feet up a peppermint gum tree draws attention from the whole town. He can hear voices from his high, swaying bough.

> "Where's his mother?"
> "Mrs. Sumner, are you there?"
> "Has he fallen? It's a wonder he held on at all. . . . " (p. 112)

The tree trunk and branches are slippery with rain, but John defies police orders to stay where is until someone can find a ladder. He begins to shinny down the main trunk, "bark like gravel grating across his skin, and hung by forearms and wrists like a mantis praying . . . " (p. 132).

> John went down, from branch to branch and bough to bough, weaker at
> the knees than a child of three, dripping with rain, soaked with sweat,

The solution to Maurice's problem of getting his junk off the floor is not to throw it away but to suspend it from the ceiling. (Reprinted by permission of Macmillan Publishing Co., Inc. from *Maurice's Room* by Paula Fox, illustrated by Ingrid Fetz. Copyright © 1966 Macmillan Publishing Co., Inc.)

smeared with blood, but singing in his heart and sometimes out loud. . . . (pp. 134–135)

Somewhere near the ground, John falls. But injuries are minor and his brave climb has been successful: his father recognizes that John needs to be independent, to take the "knocks and bruises" of life.

Like John, Doretha feels trapped. She feels trapped by the circumstances of being Alberta's sister.

> She couldn't say it, not even to her mother. But she wanted to. She wanted to say, "I'm so scared, Mama. Everybody keeps saying I'm just like Alberta, walk like her, talk like her, look like her. And I know sometimes I feel like her. And I'm scared. Maybe by the time I'm old as she is, I'll stay out late every night or not come home at all. Maybe I'll make you cry, Mama, and put worry lines in your forehead. Maybe I'll even have a fingernail scar like hers curving down the side of my face. (p. 6)

John had a tall tree to take his own measure. Doretha has a book, a journal she has kept for four years of all important things, each written in a different color. One night, waiting for her sister to come home, she reads her book. She remembers hard times written in "hard colors"—the death of her father in the middle of his birthday party, a hateful but smiling teacher in a stiff wig who humiliates her in class. During her wait, she also calls up memories of good times. An aunt, for instance, shows her how to walk down the street past a clump of intimidating boys and say "How you doing?" as if she is not scared. A friend of her father gives her his flute.

> . . . What she would remember most were the good times, the family and friend times, the love times, that rainbowed their way through the hard times. . . .
> She laid her books on the floor beside the bed. "I'm me," she said. "I'm not Alberta, I'm me." (p. 82)

Sister reflects daily life among poor people. News of the arrest of Alberta's best friend drops as casually as a discard into the middle of a card game. The supervisor at the laundry where Doretha's mother works prohibits anyone from talking to employees; but when Doretha arrives to see her mother, the boss upstairs is too busy with slow-motion typing to notice her sneak to the back shop. Everyone becomes afraid when the typewriter stops; the silence signals a threat to job security. Details like these draw readers into reality. At the same time, the story—like *Let the Balloon Go*—is universal: both show children breaking ties that bind them.

Queenie has just demonstrated her skill at throwing
stones by hitting a squirrel from 60 feet away. (From
Queenie Peavy by Robert Burch, illustrated by Jerry
Lazare. Copyright © 1966 by Robert Burch. Reprinted
by permission of The Viking Press, Inc.)

There is a similar theme in a book with a different setting, Robert Burch's *Queenie Peavy* (1966). Thirteen-year-old Queenie, a gangly and bright eighth-grader, is tied by iron loyalty to her father. Mr. Peavy's sentence to the federal penitentiary has left Queenie and her mother alone to cope with the Depression on a farm in the rural South.

In addition to skill with algebra and English, Queenie is a sharpshooter at throwing stones. "The only girl in Cotton Junction who could chew tobacco," she could also spit it with deadly aim. So she is apparently well equipped to stick up for herself and stay faithful to her father when children tease her about him. But she is always in trouble for slinging rocks while throwing tantrums, and finally she is accused of breaking the bell tower windows in the Hilltop Baptist Church.

"Wasn't me," Queenie tells the sheriff, truthfully, but she becomes afraid she will have to go to a reformatory. Then—a surprise—her father comes home. Queenie is convinced that now people in town will not lock her away.

> "They'll know I'll behave just fine from now on. They'll know that most of my trouble has been brought on by folks aggravating me 'cause Pa was in jail and that if he's not there anymore they won't need to worry about me one little bit. My problems are over just like that!" She snapped her fingers to show how quickly her situation had improved. (p. 113)

There is no snap solution, though. Queenie's father does not seem to like her, and does nothing to help. One day, when she meets him carrying a pistol on the way to town, he tells her to mind her own business. As he goes on without her, she realizes that she has been locked up in foolish loyalty,

> . . . loyalty to him and resentment against almost everyone else. Yet she had known all the time, and refused to face up to it, that he had brought on his own troubles. She knew nobody had picked on him and that she must learn to be honest with herself. (p. 143)

Gradually Queenie gains the freedom to control herself. When anger rises after her father breaks parole and disappears once again, she fights off the urge to break one last unbroken pane at the church.

Bette Greene's *Philip Hall Likes Me, I Reckon Maybe* (1974) is the story of another spirited girl who is caught up in a complex relationship. Twelve-year-old Beth Lambert loves eleven-year-old Philip Hall, the cutest boy in the J. T. Williams School. And often, in about every other scene in this lighthearted, episodic book, she also hates him. Philip Hall has made a kind of serf of Beth. She has to clean his

The sign reads: THE ELIZABETH LORRAINE LAMBERT & Friend VEG. STAND

For some reason Philip says the sign for the vegetable
stand is "not fair." (Excerpted from the book *Philip
Hall Likes Me. I Reckon Maybe* by Bette Greene.
With pictures by Charles Lilly. Pictures copyright ©
1974 by The Dial Press, Inc. Reprinted by permission
of The Dial Press, Inc.)

327

barn, for instance, while he strums his guitar. Eventually she recognizes that Philip Hall may be the best student in the school only because she is willing to take second place. When she decides to do her best—to be herself—she beats the pants off him. Even then, Philip admits he likes her, at least sometimes.

ADULT PROBLEMS, ADOLESCENT SOLUTIONS

In modern realism, the adolescent quest to find self-sufficiency and adult strength is often complicated by particular problems such as divorce, the death of a friend, or the mental retardation of a sibling. In several books for fifth-grade or older readers, these tests reveal unkown strengths, as well as limits, in young characters.

It's Not the End of the World (1972), by Judy Blume, is about trying times for 12-year-old Karen Newman, who attempts to undo her parents' divorce. She tries bringing them together by getting sick, and by sending them each an anniversary card after they have separated. Then another crisis strikes. Her older brother, Jeff, runs away. Her mother and father have to deal with his disappearance as a team, but it is soon evident to Karen that the team is wracked by dissension. They argue more fiercely than ever. So she realizes there is no hope for reconciliation; she discovers a limit to what she can do.

In *A Taste of Blackberries* (1973), by Doris Buchanan Smith, a young boy—who tells the story in the first person, without naming himself—has to adjust to the death of his best friend, Jamie. Everyone knows Jamie as the clown of the neighborhood. One day, when Jamie and friends are gathering Japanese beetles off a neighbor's grape vines, he pokes a willow branch down a bee hole. The bees swarm and sting him. His friends think Jamie's writhing is just another act. It turns out, though, that he is allergic to bee stings. He dies. The boy, the narrator, is forced to face his own feelings: guilt for having thought Jamie was faking, desire to keep him alive by trying to deny his death, grief and incomprehension about why his friend had to die. With the help of parents and other adults, the boy meets his emotions. He picks blackberries as he and Jamie had planned to do, and takes one basket of them to Jamie's mother.

Betsy Byar's *Summer of the Swans* (1970) follows a 14-year-old named Sara through a difficult summer. She feels ungainly, especially compared to her older sister, with the "biggest feet" in school and the shoe size of a typical boy. The turning point comes one night when her 10-year-old retarded brother, Charlie, wakes up and decides to wander outside to look for the swans Sara had shown him earlier in a nearby pond. He gets lost. During the search, her arch-

Sara comforts Charlie, her 10-year-old retarded
brother, after he has been lost in the woods near their
home. (From *The Summer of the Swans* by Betsy
Byars, illustrated by Ted CoConis. Copyright © 1970
by Betsy Byars. Reprinted by permission of The Viking
Press, Inc.)

enemy Joe Melby offers to help, and she learns she has misjudged
him. She finds Charlie, unhurt, in a ravine. She also discovers a good
person under her own awkward exterior.

329

The book captures the roller-coaster upswings and dips of adolescence, from high elation to sickening depression. *Summer of the Swans* is also sensitive to the feelings of retarded children. Sara discovers a vivid analogy one night, looking at stars:

> "I was thinking about the sky one night and I was looking up at the stars and I was thinking about how the sky goes on forever, and I couldn't understand it no matter how long I thought, and finally I got kind of nauseated and right then I started thinking, Well, this is how Charlie feels about some things. You know it makes him sick sometimes to try to print letters for a long time. . . ." (p. 101)

SPECIAL CATEGORIES OF REALISM

A few topics in realism are so popular they sometimes earn their own displays or special shelves in libraries. Many of the books in the special categories of sports, animals, and mystery are good literature; like other works of contemporary realism, they deal with significant themes such as the child's drive for independence. Others on these special shelves are escapist fare: flat characters beat all odds or outwit bumbling adults in the course of precut plots.

Sport Stories

Many sports stories suffer from formula writing. The main character frequently faces impossible odds in the last seconds of the big game. The clock is running . . . the crowd is on its feet . . . the ball/hockey puck is in the air . . . *touchdown!/goal!/basket!* The game ends with a bang or a buzz, and readers seldom get to see the losers' locker room.

Some sports-story writers use tired, cliché-ridden language. In *Football Fugitive* (1976), Matt Christopher, a prolific author of sports stories, writes about the "sweet taste of victory" (p. 118), and about a player with "legs churning like pistons" (p. 116). At one point in the narration, Christopher manages to team up two clichés in the same sentence: "Larry, plowing through like a wild buffalo, picked up the ball, carried it for eight yards and was dropped like a sack of potatoes" (p. 114).

The book includes several diagrams for football plays that are given to Larry's team in the story by Green Bay Packers' player Yancey Foote. Foote is a client of Larry's lawyer father in a court case. There are no surprises. Larry's team wins on the field. Foote wins in court.

Many of Christopher's stories are simple to read—on a second- or

In typical sports-story style, Zan wins the final game
for her team. (Book jacket by Richard Cuffari for
Zanbanger by R. R. Knudson. Published by Harper &
Row, Publishers, Inc.)

third-grade level—while the action is interesting to readers in intermediate grades. So many of the books appeal to older students
with reading problems.

Two other writers of sport stories keep action levels high while avoiding clichés. Both give explanations of games and their rules so those who have never played or watched before know what is happening. Beman Lord, in *Shrimp's Soccer Goal* (1970), tells the story of a new teacher at school who is under pressure from her class. It wants a football team. She explains that she does not know much about football, but would be happy to coach soccer. She starts in cold with the class in explaining the game, and readers learn too, kick by kick.

Marion Renick, in *Take a Long Jump* (1971), uses the character of a coach to explain running and jumping techniques to a boy named Jay, who has just joined the track team. The language in *Long Jump* is fresh and original, although the book packages several of the most common—and somewhat stale—themes found in sports stories for young readers. The *need for fair play*, for instance, emerges from an incident in which a boy who cheats at a cross-country race is discovered and discredited. The *importance of team work* is exemplified in the scene where Jay's family runs together in a special race. In one or two other passages, the book turns preachy, for instance, when the coach delivers a short talk against drug abuse.

Alfred Slote's books, written for fifth- and sixth-graders, are enriched by depth of characterization and development of theme. *Matt Gargan's Boy* (1975), for instance, draws a lively portrait of the 11-year-old son of a catcher for the Chicago White Socks. Danny Gargan keeps hoping his parents will get back together. He even tries to keep eligible men away from his mother. When she starts dating Herb Warren and Herb's daughter tries out and makes Danny's baseball team, he quits. He hopes that by resigning from the team, he will discourage his mother from coming to the field, at least with Herb. But she goes to the games anyway. Danny learns that his father plans to remarry. Finally, he has to accept the unsettling changes in his family. These serious threads of plot keep the action on the field from dominating the book, although there is a climactic game and Danny is the winning pitcher.

Another of Slote's books, *Hang Tough, Paul Mather* (1973), focuses so much on the personal story of Paul that often it is not classified as a sports story. Paul is an excellent pitcher, and baseball is his prime interest in life. But Paul has leukemia. He is not supposed to play baseball anymore. When he does, he is injured and hospitalized. With the help of an understanding doctor, he accepts the likelihood of death, although his hope remains high. Paul is permitted to leave the hospital in a wheelchair to watch one more game, and as the book ends he still hopes to live. Readers know that his chances are slim.

The book has the action of good sports stories, but Paul's disease overshadows the field. In fact, Paul's acceptance of his disease and his conversations with his doctor are far more believable than his instant feeling of team spirit with a group of boys he has just met.

Animal Stories

Paul is an exception. Most children in sports stories win their major battles, showing up disbelievers and taking further steps toward adulthood. Children in believable stories about animals often show similar control over the world around them. In books for children from prekindergarten to grade two, animal stories often depict a child who wants a pet, convinces parents, and becomes master or mistress. Mary Jo, for instance, wants a puppy and promises to take care of it. In *What Mary Jo Wanted* (1968), by Janice Udry, the puppy turns out to be demanding, but the little girl takes the responsibility, even sleeping in the kitchen so the dog will stop crying at night.

Another dog story, one with unusual twists, is *A Dog So Small* by Philippa Pearce, published in 1962. Like Mary Jo, Ben desperately wants a dog. His grandfather promises him one. Grandfather's gift, however, turns out to be just a picture of a Chihuahua. Ben is bitterly disappointed. After a short time, he loses the picture, but not his wish for a dog. The story turns a corner toward fantasy. Ben dreams about the tiny dog in the picture. He dwells on how brave and obedient it is. His dreams begin to block out real life, and one day a car strikes him as he steps into the street, imagining a dog so small he could see it with his eyes closed. After he recovers, Ben finally gets a real dog—a dog so large it cannot fit into earlier dreams. He can no longer call the tiny dog to mind, and he realizes "you couldn't have impossible things, however much you wanted them. He saw that if you didn't have the possible things, then you had nothing" (p. 142).

Horses provide more of a challenge than dogs for young owners, but several nearly classic books show children taking the reins. C. W. Anderson's stories about a horse named Blaze and his owner, Billy, are simple enough for children in the first few grades. The series begins when Blaze is a pony, named after a star marking on its forehead, and other Blaze books take readers through fast-paced adventures laced with carefully researched detail on the care of horses.

Marguerite Henry has also done careful research for her durable stories of horses and children. *Stormy, Misty's Foal* (1963) is an engrossing book about how a horse survives a flood on the island of Chincoteague off the Virginia coast.

In some animal stories, humans play minor roles. *The Incredible*

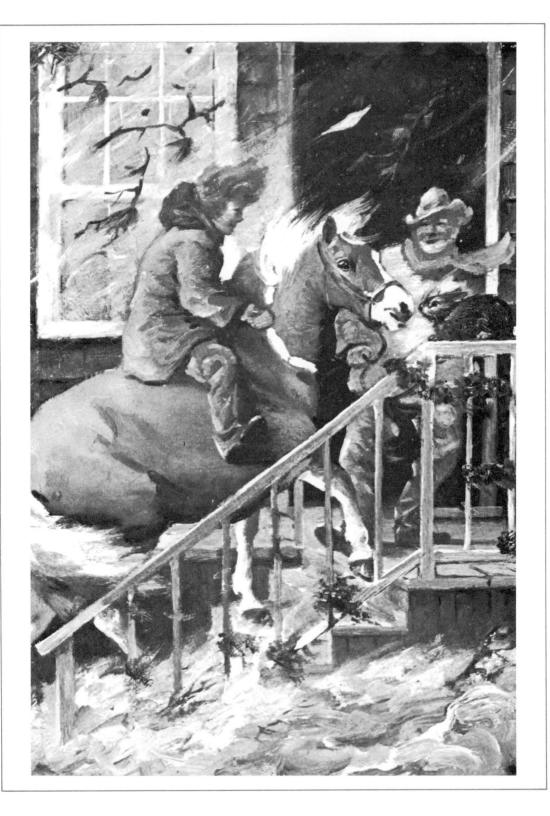

Journey (1960), by Sheila Burnford, centers on two dogs and a cat who travel 250 miles through the Canadian wilderness to find their way home after being left in the care of their owner's friend. Carol and Donald Carrick tell a story about a seagull in *Beach Bird* (1973), but the book's matter-of-fact description of who eats whom almost qualifies it as nonfiction.

Mysteries

Like sports stories, mysteries often combine action with suspense about how things are going to come out. Who outsmarts whom? Again, the child character has a major effect on the outcome, sometimes confounding adults with deft deduction. Again, children reading the stories can find young heroes or heroines who master the world of their neighborhoods.

The dearly loved Nancy Drew, who appears in book after bestselling book, has become a caricature of mystery-book characters. The stories are always roughly the same. Nancy, a one-dimensional character, unravels a mystery that baffles adults, never doubting she can do it.

The final page of a typical Nancy Drew book is filled with praise for the young detective, as well as publicity for another Drew book, like this clumsy passage on the last page of *The Clue of the Black Keys* (1951):

> Laughing, Nancy said she was glad that the case had ended so happily. The thought flashed through her mind as to when a new mystery would present itself—a strange puzzle which later came to be called *The Mystery at the Ski Jump.* (p. 214)

Another perennial Drew mystery centers on the writing itself. Who done it? You never know. "Carolyn Keene"—the author credited on title pages—is a pseudonym for many different writers hired to fill out outlines supplied to them.

In contrast to Nancy, 13-year-old Thomas Small in Virginia Hamilton's *The House of Dies Drear* (1968) is continually puzzled and frightened, and much more believable. Thomas and his family move to an old house in Ohio where his father has taken a college teaching position. Once, the house was a station on the underground

Grandpa and Maureen bring Misty into the house for shelter as the residents of Chincoteague Island prepare to evacuate. (Illustration by Wesley Dennis from *Stormy, Misty's Foal* by Marguerite Henry. Copyright 1963 by Rand McNally & Company.)

railroad. Dies Drear, an abolitionist, built the house to aid escaping slaves. Legend says that ghosts of two slaves killed by a bounty hunter, and Dies Drear himself, haunt the house.

> Deep down, Thomas didn't believe in ghosts. But when night fell, when he was in the dark, he feared he might see one. And if there were haunts in the new house, he wanted to be sure he had everything straight in his mind about them. (p. 18)

Thomas's father is irritated at the boy's questioning. But that does not stop Thomas from exploring the secret passages in the house, tracking strange noises.

Thomas and his family are sure there is an explanation for everything, but they are hard pressed to find it. When finally the family finds out what is happening in an underground cave, the moment of discovery is dramatic. It is also believable. The scene in the cave pulls together all the strands of evidence that run throughout the story.

Not all young sleuths follow spooky trails. Some mysteries are funny. Crosby Bonsall's *The Case of the Hungry Stranger* (1963) is an easy-to-read account of the mirthful adventures of Wizard. He is a private eye which, he explains, means he finds things. With his friends Tubby and Skinny, and little brother Snitch, he tries to help Mrs. Meech discover who has stolen one of her blueberry pies. Following footprints leads nowhere. Neither does tracking along a trail of crumbs: they turn out to be from a cookie Tubby is eating. Finally Wizard and company decide to check for blue teeth, and the culprit is found. For those who cannot stand the suspense—the dog did it.

Authors Scott Corbett and Donald Sobol write for slightly older readers. Corbett's hero is Roger Tearle, who appears to be about 10 or 11. He refers to himself as Inspector Tearle. In *The Case of the Silver Skull* (1974), Roger, his sister Shirley, and his friend Thumbs Thorndyke overhear plans for a robbery, and help in apprehending the thieves. One of several light touches is the fact that Roger's office is a tree house in his backyard, and is continually bombarded by starlings. The pesky birds disappear whenever Shirley yells at them, but mighty detective Roger is totally ineffective in getting them to go away. He has to walk to work under an umbrella.

Author Donald Sobol writes about Encyclopedia Brown, a 10-

Roger nearly gets caught in his spying but hides just in the nick of time. (From *The Case of the Silver Skull* by Scott Corbett, illustrated by Paul Frame, by permission of Little, Brown and Company. Copyright © 1974 by Scott Corbet.)

337

year-old whose real name is Leroy Brown, son of the Idaville chief of police. Young Brown has his own detective agency, charging 25 cents a day plus expenses for his work. Each case takes about six pages, and the reader is let in on all the facts needed to solve the case. Encyclopedia puzzles out solutions, and the reader is asked "How did he know?" There are answers at the back of the book.

HUMOROUS REALISM

A pleasant collection of credible nonsense offers an alternative to the serious themes underlying most modern realism. *How to Eat Fried Worms* (1973), by Thomas Rockwell, for instance, does not say much about the quest for independence or the search for self, but it does have the power to make readers wriggle. A boy named Billy makes a bet that he can eat fifteen worms, one a day for fifteen days. The payoff will be $50, from his friend Alan, or about $3.33 a worm. Billy begins with workaday seasonings such as mustard, ketchup, salt, pepper, and lemon, and then samples more advanced cuisine, such as his mother's own "Whizbang Worm Delight," made by stuffing ice cream cake with a single worm. (Go ahead; have a bite. Author Rockwell told us in an interview that his research showed worms were very good for you. "They're about 70 percent protein, low in calories, and high in minerals," he said, although he added that he had so far not actually eaten one himself.)

Another funny and popular book is Judy Blume's *Tales of a Fourth Grade Nothing* (1972). Peter Hatcher, a fourth-grader, must contend with his younger brother, 2-year-old Fudge. Each chapter relates a complete adventure. One day, for instance, Peter is unable to find his pet turtle Dribble. Where, Peter asks Fudge, is Dribble?

> No answer from Fudge. He banged his pots and pans together again. I yanked the pots out of his hand. I tried to speak softly. "Now tell me where Dribble is. Just tell me where my turtle is. I won't be mad if you tell me. Come on, Fudge . . . please."
> Fudge looked up at me. "In tummy," he said. (pp. 109–110)

Fudge has eaten Dribble. And much to Peter's disgust, all the adults seem to be concerned more about the boy than the turtle in his stomach. Fudge survives Dribble, with the help of some castor oil, and Mr. Hatcher gives Peter a dog—a hound Mr. Hatcher assures Peter is too large for Fudge to swallow.

Much of humor for children depends on exaggeration. Pippi Longstocking, a creation of author Astrid Lindgren, carries independence to an extreme. She lives with her horse and pet monkey and

Fudgie's delight in having swallowed a turtle is not
shared by his mother and brother. (From *Tales of a
Fourth Grade Nothing* by Judy Blume. Copyright ©
1972 by Judy Blume, illustration © 1972 by E. P.
Dutton. Reprinted by permission of the publishers,
E. P. Dutton.)

does what she wants with no adult interference. Her self-sufficiency was assured when her father, a sea captain turned king of cannibals, left her a supply of gold pieces. In *Pippi Goes on Board* (1957), Pippi goes shopping with a style most children envy. She buys candy, for instance, in 36-pound lots.

Another favorite is Robert McCloskey's episodic *Homer Price* (1943), the story of a boy in the small town of Centerburg whose father runs a tourist camp and the gas station. In one chapter, Uncle Telly and the sheriff argue over which of them has the larger ball of string. Both collect little pieces of string, and both have wound string balls approximately 6 feet in diameter. They decide to have a contest, unwinding the string at a fair. The winner will be able to pursue Miss Terwilliger, whom both have been courting, without interference from the other. But then Miss Terwilliger enters the contest herself, and wins. Only a few of the spectators notice how she does it: she unwinds her knit dress.

In humorous books for younger readers, illustrations are often a major source of the humor. The text of Ellen Raskin's *Nothing Ever Happens on My Block* (1966), for instance, just quotes young Chester Filbert as he grumbles, sitting on a curb, that while some places are exciting, nothing ever happens on his block. Behind him, though, something is up. At one house alone, children ring the doorbell, and then hide when the lady of the house answers. After two futile trips down to the door, she pours water from her upstairs window—all over the postman. Another house catches fire. Firemen put out the blaze and owners rebuild the damaged part, which is then struck by lightning. A parachutist lands. A car crashes into an armored truck, spilling money all over the street. A crow on a weathervane flies to another rooftop. Chester misses it all.

In Judy Barrett's *Animals Should Definitely Not Wear Clothing* (1970), ·the illustrations alone provide most of the humor. What would happen if animals *did* wear clothes? The pictures tell the story. The snake loses trousers. The opossums wear everything upside down, and the hen gets an egg caught in her slacks.

EVALUATING REALISM:
WHAT MAKES GOOD FICTION OF FACT?

Writer Don Freeman wrote *Mop Top* (1955) when short hair was the fashion. It is about a little boy who does not want a haircut. When his head gets shaggy, other children call him Moppy, and when he gets a haircut, the text tells how trim, neat, and tidy he looks. But children in the late 1970s think Moppy is much better looking with hair hanging halfway down his ears.

This illustration shows clearly why one animal should
not wear clothing. (Drawings copyright © 1970 by
Ron Barrett. All rights reserved. From *Animals Should
Definitely Not Wear Clothing* by Judi Barrett. Used by
permission of Atheneum Publishers.)

Hair styles and dress lengths change like the tide. Books that
merely reflect current styles go in and out of fashion as fast as
fashions change.

One trap in evaluating contemporary realism is accepting accuracy for quality. A book may be on the mark in conveying current
dress styles, for instance, but its very accuracy may date it and kill it
within a few years as hemlines drop or rise—unless the book is good
literature.

So the first criterion is literary quality. Good realism must meet
basic standards for plot, characterization, setting, theme, and style.
(Chapter 1 outlined general criteria for evaluating books.)

There are other considerations.

341

Style Must Be Fresh, Not Faddish

Rules of style in realism have changed. Today's authors are freer than writers even twenty-five years ago to experiment with new sentence structures, to match dialogue to what they hear on city streets or classrooms. Accuracy, however, can be a trap. Author Robert Burch writes that he once read an article in *Look* magazine arguing for new forms of speech, including a "low, glottal hum, like the purring of a cat, to indicate contentment." Such hums, the article said, could represent "a compressed overlay of facts and sensations and moods and ideas and images" (Jan 13, 1970, p. 48). Burch reports, tongue in cheek, that this "advanced" form of speech had already come to his house.

> One of my nephews, a high-school junior, often answers me with something of a grunt or a groan, and occasionally a more contented sound. I had accused him of being lazy in his speech, but I suppose he is merely advanced. He is not mumbling; he is giving me a compressed overlay of facts and sensations and images. (1971, p. 259)

Good writing today need not always follow the conventions of so-called standard English. For instance, incomplete sentences, used with care (as in the paragraph from *Josh* which opened this chapter), can establish mood or character artistically. However, certain standards must be met. Does the style fit the story? Does it consistently match the characters? Does it convey feelings? Does it illuminate the truth behind the book? If style meets these tests, then the more experimental it is, the better. Editor Jean Karl argues:

> In the end, it is the experimental book that is more likely to be truly literate than the one that slavishly follows an old pattern. Yet not all experiments are valid by any means. (in Painter, 1970, p. 12)

Content Should Be Free Of Cliché

Clichés can weaken individual sentences; there are examples in the section on sports books. It is also possible for an entire story to be stale, even when wrapped in a modern setting.

Writer Norma Klein describes one kind of cliché, prevalent in books about sex.

> A kind of book that still exists all too frequently is what I would call the "and so she turned to" book. I'm sure you know the kind. His mother was an alcoholic and so he turned to homosexuality. Her parents weren't giving her enough attention and so she turned to sex. His parents were getting divorced and so he turned to masturbation. . . . (1977, p. 82)

Another common cliché in realism is the adult-lecture scene authors sometimes drop in near the end of the book. The lecturer is sometimes a parent, although pep talks about drugs or how to live right can come from coaches or understanding family doctors.

Books Should Avoid Didacticism

The temptation to teach something beckons many writers of children's literature (and has for centuries; see Chapter 10). For writers of contemporary realism, the temptation often seems to be irresistible.

Didacticism in literature begins with the assumption that books can be used to seed messages in young minds, planting ideas or philosophies that may come to full flower as the child grows. Author Natalie Babbitt says the temptation is strongest in writers for adolescents. Authors of books for young adults, she writes, "have a kind of last-chance-for-gas-before-the-thruway feeling that now is the moment to drum away, because obviously their personalities are not formed and they are desperately in need of moral instruction" (1972, p. 33).

In fact, there is little research showing how much and in what ways reading affects attitudes, beliefs, and behavior. One study by a doctoral student at Boston University explored whether white children could be influenced in attitudes toward blacks by reading books about them. Researcher Joyce Woodward Lancaster tested white fifth-grade students for racial preference. She measured preference by the child's stated willingness to join groups, some integrated, in a set of pictures. Then for six weeks in special reading periods, children chose from a collection of books whose characters were black. The racial-preference test was repeated after the 6-week period. The conclusion was that books generally did not reverse biases one way or the other, although they did firm up existing attitudes. Lancaster reported that "The impact of books would seem to operate as a booster to one's attitude rather than as a change agent" (1971, p. 97).

Results of the study may not apply to other social concerns. Can contemporary realism stop drug abuse, for instance? Does literature reduce—or increase—violence in society? There are no certain answers to questions like these. For ethical reasons, researchers have never exposed children to a steady diet of violent stories to see if subjects would become more violent. And such an experiment would not prove that books alone caused violent behavior unless subjects could be prevented from watching TV, reading newspapers or magazines, and talking to other children. The isolation of subjects necessary for a valid study of the question—even if such a study

343

were ethically possible—might be enough in itself to drive children to violent fits.

Adults are often quick to draw conclusions about what books teach. But the Lancaster study seems to indicate that books alone do not always have the power attributed to them. Studies designed to show whether books encourage odious behavior have not been done, and probably never will be.

The Lancaster study does show, however, that books can have *some* effect on attitude. In this research, books hardened preconceptions. And it is reasonable to assume that books do teach something, although it may difficult to predict what a particular book will teach to a particular child.

Some teachers and librarians working under this assumption conscientiously choose books to help children with problems. The technique of prescribing books as a treatment for social or emotional disturbances is called *bibliotherapy*. Trained bibliotherapists might suggest books on death, for example, for children having difficulty coping with the death of a parent or brother or sister.

But bibliotherapy can be risky. It can help for a child to identify with a character in a book, suffering through the same agonies as the reader. It can also make the problem worse, particularly if untrained teachers do not know how to deal with feelings and emotions released by reading.

Adult have always used children's literature to try to improve the reader, hoping that readers will then improve society. Sermons and fiction-coated pills, however, do not survive nearly as well as literature. British author John Rowe Townsend writes:

> It is not irrelevant that a book may contribute to moral perception or social adjustment or the advancement of a minority group or the Great Society in general; but in writing there is no substitute for the creative imagination, and in criticism there is no true criterion except literary merit. (1967, p. 164)

Children tend naturally to agree with Townsend. They choose books that do not try too hard to teach. If a story is good, they are even willing to daydream through an adult-lecture scene, provided the writer eventually climbs off the soapbox and tells them how everything comes out.

DEALING WITH CENSORSHIP

Book evaluation and selection should be based primarily on literary quality. Censorship is based on other criteria.

ISSUE

WHAT'S IN A NAME?
THE *SOUNDER* CONTROVERSY

Why is no one in the sharecropper's family identified by a name, except the dog, Sounder? The mother is simply "mother," the father, "father," and the youth, "boy."

This would be an acceptable literary device in the hands of a Black author. For a white author to resort to it immediately raises the issue of white supremacy. Within the white world, deep-seated prejudice has long denied human individualization to the Black person. At the time of the story's historical setting, white people avoided calling Black people by their names; usually they substituted such terms as uncle, auntie, boy, Sambo; or they called every Black person by the same name. The absence of name helped to avoid the use of the polite salutation.

In *Sounder*, did the Black storyteller really narrate the the story without names, or was the unconscious racism of the white transcriber of the tale actively at work? (pp. 90–91)

Schwartz, Albert V. "*Sounder*, A Black or a White Tale?"
(in Donnarae MacCann, and Gloria Woodard (eds.),) *The Black American in Books for Children* (Metuchen, N.J.: The Scarecrow Press, Inc., 1972).

Some of the charges made against *Sounder* seem obviously misguided: the fact that the sharecropper's family are referred to as the father, the mother, the boy, rather than by name is surely not because "within the white world, deep-seated prejudice has long denied human individualization to the black person." It must have been the author's intention that his characters should appear universal, not tied down to a local habitation and a name. A charge of lack of authenticity is hard to evaluate; it depends on what you mean by authenticity. To me it has always seemed that truth in a novel is truth to the enduring, underlying realities of human nature; and that these enduring realities are recognizable whatever the context. It is not necessary or desirable that writer or critic be restricted to what he knows from direct experience; otherwise no man would write about women, no middle-aged person could write about old age; no one at all could write about the past. It is the task of the creative imagination to leap across such frontiers. (p. 275)

Townsend, John Rowe. *Written for Children* (rev. ed.)
(Philadelphia: Lippincott, 1975).

William Armstrong, the author of *Sounder*, is a white man. In the author's note at the beginning of this Newbery Award book, he states that this story of a black sharecrop-

345

per and his family was told him by a black man who had come to their community from farther south.

Would Schwartz have any objections to the book had the author been black? What makes you think this? Some people believe that only blacks can write about black experience. How could this position be supported? Townsend contends that writers should not be restricted to what they know from direct experience. What rationale supports this position?

Read *Sounder* yourself. Does the namelessness of the characters seem to you to deny them individualization, or to give them a more universal quality?

School board members in the Island Trees district on Long Island were not thinking of literary quality, for instance, when they removed nine books from local junior and senior high school libraries in 1976. The local board president told a newspaper reporter that the books had been banned because they were "vulgar, anti-Christian, anti-Semitic or [they] degraded women" (*The New York Times,* March 21, 1976). Among the books were several works of contemporary realism well received by critics, including *The Fixer* (1966), by author Bernard Malamud, and an anthology, *The Best Short Stories by Negro Witers* (1967), edited by poet Langston Hughes.

There have been censors as long as there have been books (Chapter 10 is filled with examples), and censorship was still very much alive in the 1970s. In 1971, a school district in Queens, New York, banned Piri Thomas's *Down These Mean Streets* (1967) from school shelves, objecting to four-letter words and descriptions of heterosexual and homosexual acts. (The ban was lifted four years later.) In 1975, a school district in Butler, Pennsylvania, voted unanimously to burn 140 copies of a paperback anthology of short stories after a parent complained that some passages were offensive. (On reconsideration, the board reversed itself by a 5 to 4 vote.) The same year, Dallas, Texas, officials ordered several books removed from public school libraries, including Peter Benchley's *Jaws,* following a schoolboard's decision that the books were obscene.

The frank and explicit nature of some realism today means that the problem of censorship is likely to arise again and again. Contemporary fiction will continue to offend some people; and some books—sexist or racist stories, for instance—will offend many people. But every time a group succeeds in banning a book that offends it, other books are threatened. Where censorship takes hold, opposing groups can claim with equal authority the right to decimate school shelves.

Librarians can take one simple precaution against such purges:

ISSUE

IS THE CONCEPT OF BIBLIOTHERAPY VALID?

When a teacher or librarian helps a pupil find a book that might help the pupil solve a personal problem, develop skills needed for living and/or bolster self image, bibliotherapy has taken place. It might be a teacher recommending that a student read a book; it could be making (and exposing pupils to) a topical bibliography, a bulletin board or book display. Whatever the method, it is guiding pupils toward helpful books. . . .

A teacher or librarian is in an ideal situation to see what a particular child's problem might be. In daily contact with the child a teacher can observe the child's interactions with others and note his or her self image. The teacher will also be in contact with the library and librarian and have access to many books. Working together, these two people should be able to find some potentially helpful materials for pupils. (pp. 569, 570)

> Shepherd, Terry, and Lynn B. Iles. "What is Bibliotherapy?"
> *Language Arts,* May 1976, pp. 569–571.

To my mind we have here stories perceived in much the same way as *prescriptions*, that is, as blendings of ingredients to be administered or taken for some ailment or other. This granted, it is not unreasonable to assume that the teaching of literature may sometimes have been little more than a dispensing of moral or spiritual medication—as perhaps it may be again if the swing I referred to earlier goes far enough. Somewhere a teacher might mutter, "How can I help Sally get over this terror of snakes? Let's see," looking along the shelves, "Ah, Here we are! *Tales of a Snake-Charmer.* That should do the trick." (p. 479)

> Ashley, L. F. "Bibliotherapy, etc.,"
> *Language Arts,* April 1978, pp. 478–481.

What is the basic difference of opinion between these writers? How does the tone of writing in each reinforce the particular position? What cautions might you suggest for a new teacher who plans to use bibliotherapy with his or her students?

establish a clear policy for dealing with complaints before they arise. The National Council of Teachers of English suggests printing a form for complainants to fill out, with space to specify objections. The form asks for recommendations about what should be done. It also asks whether the complainant has read the whole book. The form clarifies objections and weeds out frivolous gripes, and helps ensure that the book's accuser will be aware of the context around offensive passages. Completed forms can be referred to a committee of concerned parents and school personnel. Many schools take the position that parents may prohibit their own children from reading certain books, but that they have no authority over what other people's children can read.

In some cases, censorship defeats itself. A few weeks after the Island Trees board acted against the nine books, a librarian offended by the action displayed the banned literature prominently in the nearby Merrick Public Library under a sign: "Have You Read These Books?" Merrick Library Director Selma W. Finnel said the board's action had stimulated unusual interest in the books. Most of them, she said, were on a waiting list.

SUMMARY

1 *Realistic fiction* tells a story which could happen or could have happened in the past. Books such as *Josh, Slake's Limbo,* and *Mom, the Wolfman and Me* are *contemporary realism*: their setting is modern. Realism reflects society, and writers today are free to explore many subjects—drugs, sexual problems, divorce—once considered taboo in children's literature. Books in these once-forbidden territories are often labeled *new realism*, although some stories dealing with sensitive subjects are now decades old.

2 A selection of contemporary realism shows signs of a pattern. Many books show a child venturing on a quest for independence, discovering strengths, mastering part of the world. Frequently, in books for children 5 to 7, the "world" is the home, and stories often center on problems of getting along with other family members. In several books for children 8 to 11, such as *The Stone-Faced Boy*, by *Paula Fox,* characters set out from home on their own, trying to discover who they are outside the family's protection. *Zeely*, a book by *Virginia Hamilton,* tells the story of a young girl who idealizes a woman she meets on a summer trip away from home, and then learns to accept herself, and her model, as they really are. *Let the Balloon Go* and *Sister*, books appropriate for children 12 and older, detail struggles of young adolescents in overcoming fears and restrictions, and claiming some independence.

ISSUE

HOW CAN SCHOOLS AND LIBRARIES BE RESPONSIVE TO PUBLIC CONCERNS ABOUT BOOK SELECTION?

REQUEST FOR RECONSIDERATION OF MATERIALS

Title _____ ☐ Book ☐Periodical ☐Other _____
Author _____
Publisher _____
Request initiated by _____
Address _____
City _____State _____Zip _____Telephone _____

Do you represent:
☐Yourself

☐An organization (name) _____

☐Other group (name) _____

1. To what in the work do you object? (Please be specific. Cite pages or sections).
   _____

2. Did you read, view, or hear the entire work? _____
   What parts? _____
   _____

3. What do you feel might be the result of exposure to this work? _____
   _____

4. For what age group would you recommend this work? _____
   _____

5. What do you believe is the theme of this work? _____
   _____

6. Are you aware of judgments of this work by literary or other critics? _____
   _____

7. What would you like your library/school to do about this work?
   ☐Do not assign/lend it to my child.
   ☐Return it to the staff selection committee/department for re-evaluation.
   ☐Other. Explain _____

349

8. In its place, what work would you recommend that would convey as valuable a
picture and perspective of the subject treated? _____

Signature _____

Date _____

Source: *Language Arts,* February 1978, p. 238
It has been the experience in most communities that the very existence of a form
such as this one will discourage parents from pressing their concerns. However,
that is not the point of the form. The point is to get parents to state clearly what
they find offensive, why they find it to be so, and what they would recommend as
suitable alternative materials for their children. This allows parents to feel involved with schools and libraries, not to be in control of them. (p. 237)

NCTE Committee. "Censorship: Don't Let It Become an Issue in Your Schools,"
Language Arts, February 1978, pp. 230-242.

In my opinion, the psychology of complaint forms is all wrong. I know some librarians delight in seeing people back down when faced with filling them out.
What those librarians don't seem to think about is that when you intimidate
another person you have made an enemy, and when those you have intimidated
step into the polling booth and vote no on the library budget, they are achieving a
small measure of revenge for having had their concerns treated with contempt. (p.
331)

Broderick, Dorothy M. "Racism, Sexism, Intellectual Freedom, and Youth Librarians," *Top of the News*, Summer 1977, pp. 323–332.

What are the merits of a complaint form such as the one reproduced above? Why
might it discourage some people from pressing complaints? Do you feel Broderick's
point about making enemies is valid? Why or why not? If you think such a form is
inappropriate, what other procedures might you advocate for dealing with complaints?

3 In some contemporary realism, adolescent characters are drawn
into adult problems such as divorce or the death of a friend. In books
such as *It's Not the End of the World* by *Judy Blume*, characters are
strengthened by grappling with adult crises at the same time they
learn limits of their abilities to solve problems.
4 Some categories of realism—*sports stories, animal stories,
mysteries*—are popular enough to earn their own special shelves in
libraries. *Beman Lord,* author of *Shrimp's Soccer Goal,* and *Alfred
Slote,* author of *Matt Gargan's Boy,* avoid the clichés that weaken

some sports stories. In these and many other sports books, young children grow toward adulthood as they compete athletically. In many animals stories, too, children grow as they learn to care for and control pets. *Janice Udry's What Mary Jo Wanted,* appropriate for young readers, is the story of a little girl who takes responsibility for a puppy. *Marguerite Henry* backs her stories about horses with solid research about equine care and feeding. Mysteries—such as *Virginia Hamilton*'s *The House of Dies Drear*—often center on children as young detectives.

5 Some mysteries are amusing, for instance, *Scott Corbett*'s *The Case of the Silver Skull.* The field of realism includes many other humorous books, such as *Thomas Rockwell*'s *How to Eat Fried Worms* or *Robert McCloskey*'s classic, *Homer Price.*

6 Even when the premise is funny, or the setting foreign to most readers, realistic books generally reflect what *is* or what *was.* Good realism, however, is more than reflection or reportage. *Evaluation* of realistic books requires measuring them against basic literary standards. Other considerations are that the style should be fresh while avoiding faddishness, and content should be free of clichés and didacticism.

7 Often, realistic fiction is evaluated on other grounds, and "offensive" works are banned or censored. Where censorship takes hold, opposing groups can claim with equal authority the right to decimate school shelves. As a precaution against book banning, schools should establish a clear policy for handling complaints before they arise.

BIBLIOGRAPHY

Recommended Realistic Fiction

Bonham, Frank. *Mystery of the Fat Cat,* illus. Alvin Smith (New York: Dutton, 1968).
   The Boys Club was to receive a large sum of money, left to it by a wealthy woman. It was to be paid after her pet cat died, but since the cat is twenty-eight years old, the boys began to think the caretaker may have made some substitutions.
Byars, Betsy. *The Pinballs* (New York, Harper, 1977).
   Three foster children learn to accept and care for each other, gaining some control over their lives.
Cleary, Beverly. *Ramona and Her Father,* illus. Alan Tiegreen (New York: Morrow, 1977).
   Ramona's campaign to get her father to stop smoking is not appreciated at a time when he has just lost his job.

Cleaver, Vera and Bill Cleaver. *Queen of Hearts* (Philadelphia: Lippincott, 1978).

Wilma takes care of her grandmother after the old lady has suffered a minor stroke, and gains in compassion as she recognizes her grandmother's fear that she is no longer self-sufficient.

Coerr, Eleanor. *Sadako and the Thousand Paper Cranes,* illus. Ronald Himler (New York: Putnam, 1977).

When 11-year-old Sadako Sasaki discovers she has leukemia as a result of the bombing of Hiroshima, she begins making a thousand paper cranes, which according to legend will make her well again.

Corcoran, Barbara. *A Dance to Still Music,* illus. Charles Robinson (New York: Atheneum, 1974).

Margaret, having lost her hearing from an ear infection, fears being sent to a school for the handicapped. She runs away, and learns from Josie that she can attend a high-quality university school.

Cormier, Robert. *I Am the Cheese* (New York: Pantheon, 1977).

As three stories merge into one, the reader begins to see what has happened to Adam Farmer. Suspenseful.

Cunningham, Julia. *Come to the Edge* (New York: Pantheon, 1977).

Gravel Winter gradually begins to build trust in himself and in others after he runs away first from a home for foster children, and then from Mr. Paynter, who had taken him in.

Donovan, John. *I'll Get There, It Better Be Worth the Trip* (New York: Harper, 1969).

After Davy's grandmother dies, he goes to live with his divorced mother in New York. He must cope with her alcoholism, and with his own feelings of guilt after some sexual experimentation with his friend Altschuler.

Dunnahoo, Terry. *This Is Espie Sanchez* (New York: Dutton, 1976).

Esperanza lives in Los Angeles with her foster mother. As a member of an auxiliary law enforcement group, she is involved in a number of cases.

Fleischman, Albert Sidney. *McBroom and the Beanstalk,* illus. Walter Lorraine (Boston: Atlantic—Little, Brown, 1978).

This humorous tale begins when McBroom's family suggests that he enter a contest for liars.

Fox, Paula. *How Many Miles to Babylon?* illus. Paul Giovanopoulos (New York: Macmillan, 1968).

James is kidnaped by a gang of boys and forced to help them in their racket of stealing dogs.

Greene, Constance. *Getting Nowhere* (New York: Viking, 1977).

Mark refuses to accept his new stepmother, and after he changes his attitude, he finds that acceptance is not easily won.

Gripe, Maria. *The Night Daddy*, trans. from the Swedish by Gerry Bothmer, illus. Harald Gripe (New York: Delacorte, 1971).
The night daddy is a young writer who babysits for Julia while her mother works the night shift as a nurse. Fatherless, Julia comes to love the night daddy.

Haywood, Carolyn. *Eddie's Valuable Property* (New York: Morrow, 1975).
Eddie makes several attempts to get rid of some of the junk he has collected before the family moves. The story continues after the move as Eddie makes new friends.

Holland, Isabelle. *The Man Without a Face* (Philadelphia: Lippincott, 1972).
Charles goes to Justin McLeod, whose face is scarred terribly, for tutoring. Justin fills a need in his life, and Charles comes to love him.

Houston, James. *Frozen Fire* (New York: Atheneum, 1977).
Matthew Morgan and Kayak, a classmate at the Baffin Island School, set out on a snowmobile to find Matthew's father who has disappeared while prospecting.

Kerr, M. E. *Gentlehands* (New York: Harper, 1978).
Buddy Boyle must reassess his feelings for his Grandfather Trenker when a news reporter writes that the old man is a Nazi war criminal.

Konigsburg, E. L. *From the Mixed-up Files of Mrs. Basil E. Frankweiler* (New York: Atheneum, 1967).
Claudia runs away to the Metropolitan Museum of Art, planning to stay away long enough for her parents to appreciate her, and taking her younger brother Jamie with her because he has some money.

L'Engle, Madeleine. *Meet the Austins* (New York: Vanguard, 1960).
Told by 12-year-old Vicki, the story centers on the Austin household, a home filled with love and openness.

Little, Jean. *Take Wing*, illus. Jerry Lazare (Boston: Little, Brown, 1968).
Laurel takes care of her mentally retarded younger brother, realizing more than her parents are willing to admit that James has special problems.

Maher, Ramona. *Alice Yazzie's Year*, illus. Stephen Gammell (New York: Crowell, 1977).
In her eleventh year, Alice, a Navaho girl, is keenly aware of the beauty around her.

Mathis, Sharon Bell. *The Hundred Penny Box*, illus. Leo and Diane Dillon (New York: Viking, 1975).
Aunt Dew keeps a box with one penny for each year of her life.

When she picks out a penny, she can tell Michael about her life during that year—a story time they both enjoy.

Mazer, Norma Fox and Harry Mazer. *The Solid Gold Kid* (New York: Delacorte, 1977).

In this suspenseful story, five adolescents are kidnaped, though only one is the intended victim.

Paterson, Katherine. *Bridge to Terabithia,* illus. Donna Diamond (New York: Crowell, 1977).

Jess grows in the company of Leslie, and when she is killed going to their special place, he is strong enough to want to share some of the magic they had with his younger sister.

Peck, Richard. *Are You in the House Alone?* (New York: Viking, 1976).

It is as much the reaction of the police and the community as the rape itself that frightens and frustrates the young victim.

Platt, Kin. *The Boy Who Could Make Himself Disappear* (Radnor, Pa.: Chilton, 1968).

Treated cruelly by his mother at home, and ridiculed because of his speech at school, Roger Baxter begins to withdraw, reaching total autism after the death of a woman who was a special friend to him.

Robertson, Keith. *Henry Reed, Inc.* illus. Robert McCloskey (New York: Viking, 1958).

In this humorous story, Henry and his friend Midge set up a research firm in an old barn, beginning with a few animals for sale.

Smucker, Barbara C. *Wigwam in the City,* illus. Gil Miret (New York: Dutton, 1966).

Susan Bearskin and her family are Chippewa Indians who leave the reservation and move to Chicago, making some difficult adjustments.

Werbsa, Barbara. *Tunes for a Small Harmonica* (New York: Harper, 1976).

J. F. McAlister, whose mother says she looks like a teenaged cab driver, gets a crush on her poetry teacher and spends a year giving him gifts and trying to earn enough money to pay his way to England to complete his dissertation.

Adult References

Ashley, L. F. "Bibliotherapy, etc." *Language Arts,* April 1978, pp. 478–481.

Babbitt, Natalie. "Between Innocence and Maturity," *The Horn Book*, February 1972, pp. 33–37.

Barnum, Phyllis Winet. "The Aged in Young Children's Literature," *Language Arts,* January 1977, pp. 29–32.

Broderick, Dorothy M. "Racism, Sexism, Intellectual Freedom, and Youth Librarians," *Top of the News,* Summer 1977, pp. 323–332.

Burch, Robert. "The New Realism," *The Horn Book,* June 1971, pp. 257–264.

Holman, Felice. *"Slake's Limbo*: In Which a Book Switches Authors," *The Horn Book*, October 1976, pp. 479–485.

Klein, Norma. "More Realism for Children," *Top of the News,* April 1975, pp. 307–312.

———. "Growing up human: The Case for Sexuality in Children's Books," *Children's Literature in Education,* Summer 1977, pp. 80–84.

Lancaster, Joyce Woodward. "An Investigation of the Effect of Reading Books Which Include Black Characters on the Racial Preferences of White Children" unpublished doctoral dissertation, Boston University, 1971.

MacCann, Donnarae, and Gloria Woodard (eds.). *The Black American in Books for Children* (Metuchen, N.J.: The Scarecrow Press, 1972).

NCTE Committee. "Censorship: Don't Let It Become an Issue in Your Schools," *Language Arts,* February 1978, pp. 230–242.

Painter, Helen W. (ed.). *Reaching Children and Young People through Literature* (Newark, Del.: International Reading Association, 1970).

Root, Shelton L. "The New Realism—Some Personal Reflections," *Language Arts,* January 1977, pp. 19–24.

Shepherd, Terry, and Lynn B. Iles. "What is Bibliotherapy?" *Language Arts,* May 1976, pp. 569–571.

Southall, Ivan. "Call It a Wheel," *The Horn Book*, October 1974, pp. 43–49.

Townsend, John Rowe. "Didacticism in Modern Dress," *The Horn Book*, April 1967, pp. 159–164.

———. *Written for Children,* rev. ed. (Philadelphia: Lippincott, 1975).

Children's Book References

Barrett, Judi. *Animals Should Definitely Not Wear Clothing,* illus. Ron Barrett (New York: Atheneum, 1970).

Blue, Rose. *Grandma Didn't Wave Back,* illus. Ted Lewin (New York: Watts, 1972).

Blume, Judy. *Tales of a Fourth Grade Nothing,* illus. Roy Doty (New York: Dutton, 1972).

———. *It's Not The End of The World* (New York: Bradbury, 1972).

Bonsall, Crosby. *The Case of the Hungry Stranger* (New York: Harper, 1963).

Brown, Margaret Wise. *The Dead Bird*, illus. Remy Charlip (Reading, Mass.: Young Scott, 1958).

Burch, Robert. *Queenie Peavy*, illus. Jerry Lazare (New York: Viking, 1966).

Burnford, Sheila. *The Incredible Journey*, illus. Carl Burger (Boston: Little, Brown, 1960).

Byars, Betsy. *Summer of the Swans*, illus. Ted CoConis (New York: Viking, 1970).

Caines, Jeannette. *Daddy*, illus. Ronald Himler (New York: Harper, 1977).

Carrick, Carol. *The Accident,* illus. Donald Carrick (New York: Seabury, 1976).

———, and Donald Carrick. *Beach Bird* (New York: Dial, 1973).

Christopher, Matt. *Football Fugitive*, illus. Larry Johnson (Boston: Little, Brown, 1976).

Cohen, Miriam. *Will I Have a Friend?* illus. Lillian Hoban (New York: Macmillan, 1967).

Corbett, Scott. *The Case of the Silver Skull,* illus. Paul Frame (Boston: Little, Brown, 1974).

Fitzhugh, Louise. *Harriet the Spy* (New York: Harper, 1964).

Fox, Paula. *Maurice's Room*, illus. Ingrid Fetz (New York: Macmillan, 1966).

———. *The Stone-Faced Boy*, illus. Donald A. MacKay (Englewood Cliffs, N.J.: Bradbury, 1968).

Freeman, Don. *Mop Top* (New York: Viking, 1955).

Greene, Bette. *Philip Hall Likes Me. I Reckon Maybe,* illus. Charles Lilly (New York: Dial, 1974).

Greenfield, Eloise. *Sister*, illus. Moneta Barnett (New York: Crowell, 1974).

Hamilton, Virginia. *Zeely* (New York: Macmillan, 1967).

———. *The House of Dies Drear*, illus. Eros Keith (New York: Macmillan, 1968).

Henry, Marguerite. *Stormy, Misty's Foal*, illus. Wesley Dennis (Chicago: Rand McNally, 1963).

Holman, Felice. *Slake's Limbo* (New York: Scribner's, 1974).

Hughes, Langston (ed.). *The Best Short Stories by Negro Writers* (Boston: Little, Brown, 1967).

Jackson, Jesse. *Call Me Charley*, illus. Doris Spiegel (New York: Viking, 1945).

Keene, Carolyn. *The Clue of the Black Keys* (New York: Grosset, 1951).

Klein, Norma. *Mom, The Wolfman and Me* (New York: Pantheon, 1972).

Lexau, Joan. *Benje on His Own,* illus. Don Bologuese (New York: Dial, 1970).

Lindgren, Astrid. *Pippi Goes on Board*, trans. Florence Lamborn, illus. Louis Glanzman (New York: Viking, 1957).

Lord, Beman. *Shrimp's Soccer Goal*, illus. Harold Berson (New York: Walck, 1970).

Malamud, Bernard. *The Fixer* (New York: Farrar, 1966).

Mazer, Norma Fox. *A Figure of Speech* (New York: Delacorte, 1973).

McCloskey, Robert. *Homer Price* (New York: Viking, 1943).

Pearce, Philippa. *A Dog So Small*, illus. Antony Maitland (Philadelphia: Lippincott, 1962).

Raskin, Ellen. *Nothing Ever Happens on My Block* (New York: Atheneum, 1966).

Renick, Marion. *Take a Long Jump*, illus. Charles Robinson (New York: Scribner's, 1971).

Rockwell, Thomas. *How to Eat Fried Worms*, illus. Emily McCully (New York: Watts, 1973).

Rodman, Bella. *Lions in the Way* (Chicago: Follett, 1966).

Scott, Ann Herbert. *Sam*, illus. Symeon Shimin (New York: McGraw-Hill, 1967).

Sharmat, Marjorie. *Getting Something on Maggie Marmelstein*, illus. Ben Shecter (New York: Harper, 1971).

Slote, Alfred. *Hang Tough, Paul Mather* (Philadelphia: Lippincott, 1973).

———. *Matt Gargan's Boy* (Philadelphia: Lippincott, 1975).

Smith, Doris Buchanan. *A Taste of Blackberries,* illus. Charles Robinson (New York: Crowell, 1973).

———. *Kelly's Creek,* illus. Alan Tiegreen (New York: Crowell, 1975).

Sobol, Donald J. *Encyclopedia Brown and the Case of the Dead Eagles,* illus. Leonard Shorthall (Camden, N.J.: Nelson, 1975).

Southall, Ivan. *Let the Balloon Go*, illus. Ian Ribbons (New York: St. Martin's Press, 1968).

———. *Josh* (New York: Macmillan, 1971).

Thomas, Piri. *Down These Mean Streets* (New York: Knopf, 1967).

Udry, Janice. *What Mary Jo Wanted*, illus. Eleanor Mill (New York: Whitman, 1968).

Williams, Barbara. *If He's My Brother*, illus. Tomie DePaola (New York: Harvey House, 1976).

CHAPTER
8

HIS
TORICAL
FICTION

LITERATURE'S LIGHT ON THE PAST

The young characters in *Mist over Athelney* (1958), a book by historical novelist Geoffrey Trease, meet a hermit and sit down with him to eat rabbit stew for dinner.

Trease saw nothing wrong with *that* when he wrote the passage in his book set in ninth-century England, and publishers and reviewers let it pass. It took an 11-year-old reader to find the problem. There were no rabbits in England, the reader wrote Trease, in the ninth century (Trease, 1972, p. 9).

The story illustrates one of the major problems faced by writers of historical fiction. Like other fiction, such stories grow from the author's imagination. Unlike other fiction, the stories are set against a historical backdrop and depend on the setting. So historical fiction demands special commitment from its authors. Their research must be exhaustive. What did people wear? What were they afraid of? Did they eat rabbits?

At its worst, historical fiction requires readers to stumble over words such as "zounds!" and "gadzooks!" and other archaic language stuck into characters' speech to bamboozle readers into believing there is research behind the tale. Such phony language is sometimes called "gadzookery."

At its best, historical fiction demands that the reader do some imaginary traveling to a different place and time. Sometimes it will put readers on horseback, cantering through the green forests of England. Sometimes it will carry them to the pitching deck of a Viking ship. Historical fiction can require the reader to feel what it was like to be a young Jewish inmate of a German concentration camp. It can offer the exhilaration of rolling down a Vermont hill in a barrel. Like any form of travel, historical fiction often demands adjustment to new surroundings and strange faces. Like travel, it can lead to new understandings about similarities and differences between people.

HISTORY REMEMBERED, HISTORY RESEARCHED

Some historical fiction is written from memory. Robert Newton Peck's *Soup* (1974), for instance, recreates Vermont when Peck was a boy, when admission to a movie cost a dime for a double feature including a Stan Laurel and Oliver Hardy comedy "that had a gorilla and a piano in it."

Perhaps the best known of such memory-based books are those in the *Little House* series by Laura Ingalls Wilder. These stories are

(Chapter-opening illustration from *The Year of the Three-Legged Deer* by Ethel Clifford, illustrated by Richard Cuffari. Copyright © 1972 by Ethel Clifford Rosenberg. Reprinted by permission of Houghton Mifflin Company.)

Richard Peck uses memory more than research for his
novels about life in Vermont several decades ago.
(From *Soup* by Robert Peck, illustrated by Charles C.
Gehm. Copyright © 1974 by Robert Newton Peck.
Used by permission of Alfred A. Knopf, Inc.)

based on her life, starting when she was 6 in Wisconsin (in *Little
House in the Big Woods*, 1932). Later books take the family through
difficult moves, and the last in the series, *The First Four Years*
(1971), describes what happened after her marriage in 1885.

But most historical fiction grows out of research. Archaic church
records, diaries, tombstones, crumbling newspapers, accounts by

eyewitnesses long passed away—all provide a backdrop of fact for realistic fiction set in the past.

Sometime research produces a heavy flow of fact, enough to help writers know the daily schedules of kings who lived centuries ago, and even guess at their emotions. At other times, authors find that research trickles out or teases, leaving the writer to stab in the dark at what might have been.

"History can often be most unobliging," wrote F. N. Monjo, an editor and author who also wrote historical fiction and biography.

> . . . It will tell us precisely what Mrs. Lincoln wrote to her bonnet-maker about the shade of lavender ribbon she wanted on her hat. But it will not tell us one word about whether or not Lincoln's young son, Tad, ever talked with his father about the Emancipation Proclamation. . . . No, history goes its wayward, uncooperative way; dumps its jumble of facts at our feet. . . . (1976, p. 258)

The process of picking up the facts, and making literature from them, is difficult and sometimes frustrating work.

THE EXTRAORDINARY DEMANDS ON THE WRITER

Hester Burton, a British author of historical fiction, writes that one goal of research is to become so deeply involved with the material that there is no need to look anything up when it comes time to write.

At the end of research, she can envision real houses and clothes and carriages owned by her fictional characters. "I should know what food they eat, what songs they sing when they feel happy, and what are the sights and smells they are likely to meet when they walk down the street" (in Haviland, 1973, pp. 299–300).

But tracking the colors and sounds, emotions and philosophies, of a different age is not as easy as Burton makes it seem. Research may answer questions that have not been asked, or fail to answer other critical questions. Sometimes it becomes difficult for an author to know when to stop searching and start writing.

Geoffrey Trease, author of some sixty children's books, thought he knew every fact he needed to write *Thunder of Valmy* (1960), a book about the French Revolution. He had read or skimmed about fifty books. He had just finished writing a scene in which deputies are locked out of the hall at Versailles and have to move to the tennis court. Trease's characters walked out into the court under the sparkling sunshine of a June morning.

Hester Burton's careful research adds authenticity to
this story of the English civil war. (Illustration by
Victor G. Ambrus from *Kate Ryder* by Hester Burton.
Copyright © 1974 by Hester Burton. First published in
Great Britain as *Kate Rider* by the Oxford University
Press. By permission of Thomas Y. Crowell.)

And then in the public library I'd come across the fifty-first book, the one
I hadn't seen before, the memoirs of the American ambassador at that
time, and he'd noted what a miserable wet morning it had been. It
changed the feeling so completely that I had to rewrite the whole passage. And I said to myself, if this is going to happen all through the story,
I'm going to give it up. I'll switch to a period where there aren't so many
damn documents. (1972, p. 9)

Writers John and Patricia Beatty tell another story about agonizing over accuracy. One of their novels, *Campion Towers* (1965), had
been written in the first person. The action was narrated by a young

363

resident of the Massachusetts Bay Colony in 1651. After thorough research, the Beattys sent their fictional heroine, Penitence Hervey, on a trip to England, then embroiled in a civil war. They completed the book. The publisher accepted it, asking only that it be cut.

While the Beattys sat down to the disagreeable task, they were suddenly struck by an even more disagreeable thought. What if Penitence, in telling her own story, used words that did not exist in 1651? The standard set by the authors was total accuracy. They wanted a perfect reflection—as true as possible—of the age in which Penitence lived. That meant they had to review every word in the book, tracing the history of any word they thought might not have existed in the seventeenth century. There were many surprises. The word "mob" for instance did not exist in 1651; it was not invented until 1688. "Aisle" and "amazing" were not used during the period, neither were "bewildering," "chunk," "clump," "carefree," or "complete." Penitence's little sisters played with "poppets" but not with "dolls."

Some authors of historical fiction might argue that this is going too far. But most would agree that the best historical fiction arises out of the writer's intense involvement with known facts of the period used in this book. A writer of a historical novel needs to know what might have been around every corner of the old cities and streets used as story settings. Faded maps—whether authentic or reconstructed—will affect the movement of all the characters in the story.

EVALUATING HISTORICAL FICTION

A single misplaced rabbit in a land without rabbits may not doom a book to failure, but major contradictions with known historical facts will vastly reduce a book's interest or usefulness. Accuracy, a particular concern for the writer of historical fiction, is one criterion used to judge the writer's work.

Historical research, however, never seems to come up with all the answers. After the writer has plunged into the period as deeply as possible, there remains a second responsibility: to tell a good story. Historical fiction must meet the standards for all fiction. It needs a well-constructed plot, developed characters, and a basic theme. In serving both masters—accuracy and good storytelling—authors frequently run into conflicts. How well they resolve them, determines the success of the book.

These are the major areas of conflict.

Fact versus Invention

Jill Paton Walsh, a well-known writer of historical fiction, distinguishes two different definitions of "not true"—"not true" meaning "known not to be true" and "not true" meaning "not known to be true." The writer is free to use whatever is "not known to be true" to move the story onto what Walsh calls the "thrilling quagmire of the 'might have been' " (1972, p. 20).

Writer C. Moreau Barringer makes extensive use of the "what might have been" in his story of the Stone Age, *And the Waters Prevailed* (1956). The story traces the life of Andor, a tribesman, from the eve of his first solo hunt until he is an old man. Early in his life, Andor wanders far west from his village in a valley. He discovers the Atlantic Ocean and—filled with awe and fear—realizes that the valley is lower than sea level. If the earth dam holding back the ocean should fail, the valley will be flooded. He returns to his village. Others in the tribe scoff at the prophecy of a flood, and only members of his family are willing to learn the routes to higher grounds. The waters do rise, when Andor is too old to follow his family on the long trip to safety. In the final scene, Andor walks toward the advancing water, no longer hearing the cries of others trapped on a small piece of land. He concentrates on the moon and strides to meet his wife, Bardis, and friend, Kelan, who have already traveled to the land of the dead. Here is the book's last page:

The last line of text in Barringer's book appears above this illustration: "And when the people sought him, with cries of terror and reproach and helplessness, they found him not" (p. 186). (From *And the Waters Prevailed* by D. Moreau Barringer. Copyright © by E. P. Dutton. Reprinted by permission of the publishers, E. P. Dutton.)

In a concluding note, Barringer writes that the book is a story, before all else. It is not a thinly disguised study of the roots of the human race. "I believe that people have not changed much in these latest few thousand years of man's million year history," Barringer writes. "And that they *might* have lived and acted as the people in my story did" (p. 187). No research by historians or other scholars flatly contradicts the fictionalized history Barringer created.

In a few books, invention carries historical fiction all the way into the realm of fantasy. E. L. Konigsburg, for example, imposes fantasy on a historical backdrop in *A Proud Taste for Scarlet and Miniver* (1973). Historical fact provides the foundation for this story, which is centered on Eleanor of Aquitaine (1122?-1204). The basic facts—she was queen consort to Louis VII of France and later married Henry II of England and gave birth to two future English kings—are real. But much of the setting for the story is fantastic. At one point, Eleanor frets in heaven, waiting impatiently to see if Henry will be admitted. "Henry was due Up long before this," Eleanor tells the spirit of a priest as they hover over treetops. "But it had taken almost eight hundred years to get enough lawyers Up to make a case." "Yes," Abbot Suger agreed, "in Heaven lawyers are as hard to find as bank presidents" (p. 8).

As the queen waits, spirits from her past reminisce with her, each telling a part of her vigorous life on earth. Through their stories, readers glimpse twelfth-century England and France.

The setting for Don Freeman's *Will's Quill* (1975) is England a few centuries after Eleanor, in the time of Shakespeare (1564-1616). But again, the fiction is tinged with fantasy: the main character is a goose who goes to London because he wants to be useful. Fantastic invention is also found in Robert Lawson's *Mr. Revere and I* (1953), about a horse fiercely loyal to the British when she is transported to Boston in 1768. Then the horse, Sherry, is passed on to the revolutionaries and slowly becomes converted to the colonial cause. Finally she carries Revere on his famous ride to warn of the approaching British.

Each of these books is a hybrid of fantasy, realism, and biography, but each is fundamentally honest: the backdrop of historical fact is accurate, even when the foreground has been taken over by angels or talking animals.

Facts versus Facts

Which historian do you read? In writing *Johnny Tremain* (1943), Esther Forbes chose mainly to follow historians who believed in the

Left^{nt} *Sir Cedric Noel Vivian Barnstable*

The style of Lawson's illustrations is appropriate for
his blend of historical fiction and fantasy in the text.
(From *Mr. Revere and I* by Robert Lawson, by
permission of Little, Brown and Co. Copyright © 1953
by Robert Lawson.)

American Revolution as a just uprising against a tyrant, King George
III. There is token sympathy for the Tory struggle: in one scene an
English doctor says, "You remember that *we* don't like being here in
Boston any better than you like having us" (p. 133). But most of the
book, written during World War II at a time of intense national
pride, celebrates the glory of the revolution. One character, James
Otis, explains the idealism behind the fight: "We fight, we die, for a
simple thing. Only that a man can stand up" (p. 180).

On the other hand, Christopher Collier and his brother James
Lincoln Collier told their story of the war, *My Brother Sam Is Dead*
(1974), from an English Tory point of view. So the Colliers' book can
be read as an antiwar statement. As the narrator puts it, "There

367

might have been another way, beside war, to achieve the same end"
(p. 211).

There are historians enough to support both points of view.
Christopher Collier himself writes that there are at least three different groups of historians who have written about the American
Revolution. Each group fights the war all over again with its particular marshaling of facts. *Whig* writers support the American patriots.
Imperialist historians focus on the loyalty to England of nearly half
the American colonies while small-minded revolutionaries went to
war. *Progressive* historians argue that the war was fought for the
economic gain of revolutionary leaders (Collier, 1976).

It would be impossible for a writer to accept all these historical
factions. The Colliers chose to emphasize the progressives; Esther
Forbes sides with the Whigs. The authors' conscious decision to rest
the story on one set of facts gives each of the books focus. Now the
reader is left to judge whether the author's choice of historical allies
was reasonable and fair.

Fact versus Stereotype

When is historical fiction "unfair"? One way to misrepresent history is to base story and characters on stereotypes rather than on
fact. Until the early 1970s, for instance, Native Americans were
usually villains in children's books. Members of Indian tribes appeared either as blood-loving warriors, simpering sidekicks to white
masters, or noble but naive savages. When the one-dimensional Indian in these stories had to choose between living with the tribe or
joining white civilization, the "right" choice was to go with the
whites.

Then several books from the early 1970s began presenting more of
the truth about Native Americans in factually based fiction. One is
Scott O'Dell's *Sing Down the Moon* (1970), the credible story of a
young Navaho girl named Bright Morning. In 1864, she tends sheep
as she dreams of her approaching marriage with Tall Boy, another
member of the tribe. Before the marriage, she is kidnapped by
Spanish slavers, forced to be a servant in a Spanish home, and escapes. She returns to her canyon. Once again soldiers drive her away
from home. This time, they burn her village and all the Indian crops,
and eventually she is taken prisoner again and marched to Fort
Sumner. As wards of white soldiers, the Indians lose initiative—
except Bright Morning, who prods her husband into trying to escape
once again.

Told in the first person, the story reads something like a diary
written in lean prose. Tall Boy may be brave, haughty, and stubborn,

ISSUE

SHOULD A WRITER PRESENT MORE THAN ONE POINT OF VIEW?

To present history in simple, one-sided—almost moralistic—terms, is to teach nothing worth learning and to falsify the past in a way that provides worse than no help in understanding the present or in meeting the future. (p. 138)

Collier, Christopher. "Johnny and Sam: Old and New Approaches to the American Revolution," *The Horn Book*, April 1976, pp. 132–138.

When I come to describe the historical situation which I have chosen, I try to view it through the limited vision of a single character or group of characters. I am not all-wise or all-knowing as the historian is; but neither, it is well to remember, were the people actually taking part in the historical event I am describing. They had no access to state papers; they could merely use their eyes. Not only is it a wise caution for the writer of historical novels to limit his range of vision but it is also much better art. (p. 300)

Burton, Hester. "The Writing of Historical Novels," in Virginia Haviland, *Children and Literature, Views and Review* (Glenview, Ill.: Scott, Foresman, 1973).

Both Collier and Burton write historical fiction for children. Which do you feel makes the more valid point? Should a historical novel present more than one point of view? Is "limited vision" a falsification of history, or better art?

but he can also be lazy. Bright Morning loves him, but she is independent enough to scold him ["Are you an old woman . . . a woman who eats a lot and dozes beside the fire?" she asks (p. 122)], and she dreams of owning a horse of her own someday so she can ride while her husband walks. Characters like these help break down stereotypes about Navahoes.

Sing Down the Moon is usually recommended for children in intermediate grades. Another book, Nathaniel Benchley's *Small*

Wolf (1972), is comprehensible to children in the first few grades. Again, it challenges preconceptions and prejudice. Small Wolf is a boy who discovers the Dutch settlement in Manhattan one day while hunting. His father tells him that the settlers are harmless if you leave them alone. But as the story ends, the whites need more and more land, and the Indians are forced to move again, and again, and again.

Another Benchley book, *Only Earth and Sky Last Forever* (1972), presents two perspectives. The story, aimed at adolescent readers, is about Dark Elk, a Cheyenne struggling to prove his bravery after growing up in a family supported by a government Indian agency. Who is the villain? The answer is blurred. White soldiers shoot women and children in a village, but Indians later crisscross over the silent battlefield, stripping clothing off white soldiers and cutting off their genitals. The facts indict both sides, and challenge black-and-white conclusions about history.

Solid Setting versus Distracting Detail

Authors are not required to include all the facts. Some of the dullest books bulge with their research; the authors seem to hope a hidden history lesson will sneak up on the reader.

Here, for instance, is a passage extracted by Sheila Egoff, a teacher at the University of British Columbia, from a book about the Northwest Mounted Police.

> "Why is it called the Dawson Road, Sergeant Major?" Sam asked. Coyne was unable to answer that question, but Ensign Stewart Mulvey could. "Dawson is the name of an engineer who laid it out a few years ago," he explained. "It really isn't a road; it's more of a trail where a road could be built. It roughly follows the old trade route of the Nor'westers. It starts at Prince Arthur's Landing, near Fort William, and follows the Kaministik-wia River west and north past the Kakabeka Falls to the Junction of the Sehbabandowan."
>
> "Then west to the Matawin and Oskandagee Creek," Big Neil continued. "From there. . . . " (in Egoff, 1967, p. 82)

The young reader, of course, was lost somewhere back near the Kaministikwia River.

Accurate Dialogue versus "Flavor"

The Beatty's check of 10,000 words was unusual and extreme. Other authors have chosen to let characters talk in currently used English.

ISSUE

SHOULD HISTORICAL FICTION PRESENT YESTERDAY'S VIEWS OR TODAY'S OUTLOOKS?

Perhaps the most flagrant violation of ethnic pluralism is the extreme examples of lack of respect for the Indian culture, which resulted in the Indian-white conflict of the past centuries, with its policy of annihilation of the Indians. To rationalize such a policy, not only was the culture considered devoid of value but the Indian individual too was stripped of respect. The stereotyped, depraved savage was the result. A number of books present this outlook of the Indian and his culture. While this probably was a historical viewpoint common among whites, and books exhibiting it have some value as historical examples of the limited white viewpoint, still, children's books showing Indians killed so joyously may grate on our sensitivity. . . .

"I shot an Indian . . . I did, with Pa's old musket!" is the happy shout of a child in Steele's *The Buffalo Knife*. Although Steele has several fine books about Indians, in this one, in the *Flaming Arrows,* and in *Year of the Bloody Sevens* the Indians are considered savage and bandy-legged, have cruel, unwinking eyes, and are comparable to rattlesnakes. (p. 195)

> Herbst, Laura. "That's One Good Indian: Unacceptable Images in Children's Novels," *Top of the News*, January 1975, pp. 192–197.

When I write from the viewpoint of the pioneer boy as the hero, he is naturally going to be against Indians because all the pioneers were against Indians. The best Indian then was a dead Indian. And they were considered as savages. I do get a lot of flack on that. On the other hand I have written from the Indian's viewpoint, although I haven't written as many Indian books as I have pioneer books. (p. 72)

> Steele, William O. Quoted in Reese Wells, and Gena Davidson, "Censorship and the Authors' Viewpoint," *Journal of Research and Development in Education,* vol. 9, no. 3, Spring 1976, pp. 69–75.

Herbst and Steele agree on the basic facts of his writing. At what point do their opinions diverge? What evidence suggests that it is or is not possible to write a book of literary merit from the viewpoint of a pioneer without grating on our sensitivity for its portrayal of Native Americans? Which do you think is more important, presenting how a major character may have felt about a particular group of people, or presenting that group of people from a broader perspective? Why?

There are several arguments on their side. The reader can better identify with characters who do not say things like "poppets" to mean "dolls." Secondly, using archaic words today adds a strange and foreign tone to communications between characters. The real people on whom such characters are based did not speak strange words to each other. They conversed in the language currently in use in their times.

Rosemary Sutcliff, a famous British author of historical fiction, suggests a compromise. "I try to catch the rhythm of a tongue, the tune that it plays on the ear," she writes (in Haviland, 1973, p. 307). You can feel several rhythms in the words of Marcus, a character in Sutcliff's *The Eagle of the Ninth* (1954), set in Britain when it was under Roman rule. "Esca, I should never have asked you to come with me into this hazard when you were not free to refuse. It is like to prove a wild hunt, and whether or no we shall come back from it lies on the knees of the gods" (1970 edition, p. 107). The language is clear, but much more evocative than it might have been if translated into modern English: "I shouldn't have asked you to come when I knew you couldn't say no. It's probably going to be rough, and lord only knows whether we'll make it." Read both versions aloud.

Happy Ending versus Tragic Ending

Once, authors believed that all books for children should end happily, or at least on a note of hope. But history, as Monjo wrote,

> doesn't know the meaning of a happy ending. . . . It is not enough that the great French chemist Lavoisier, the discoverer of oxygen, must lose his head on the guillotine. No, somebody must add: "La republique n'a pas besoin de savants" ("The French republic has no need of learned men"). Why does history tell us that? What sort of moral uplift is that supposed to provide? It is mean-spirited and barbaric. But it happened. (1976, p. 261)

Today, the author has a lot more freedom to *say* that it happened. Hans Peter Richter's *Friedrich* (1961), for example, tells of the growing oppression of the Jews in Nazi Germany. In the book's last scenes, Friedrich is not allowed in a bomb shelter during a raid because he is Jewish. He dies sitting "in the shadow of the stoop. His eyes were closed, his face pale" (p. 138).

Books no longer have to "come out all right." The main criterion is that they convey the spirit of the times and the minds and motives of the people, while meeting all other tests for good fiction.

These woodcuts match the stark and lonely life of the Vikings they portray. (From *Hakon of Rogen's Saga* by Erik C. Haugaard, illustrated by Leo and Diane Dillon. Copyright © 1963 by Erik Christian Haugaard. Reprinted by permission of Houghton Mifflin Company.)

Evaluating Illustrations

The woodcuts by Leo and Diane Dillon in *Hakon of Rogen's Saga* (Haugaard, 1963) are appropriate for the story of the stark and lonely life of the Vikings and the bold struggle made by Hakon as he seeks his birthright. In contrast, the drawings for Marguerite De Angeli's *The Door in the Wall* (1949) are soft and gentle. They complement the medieval English setting behind the story of a young boy crippled by a strange disease. (There is more on the book in Chapter 1.) The illustrator has the same responsibility for accuracy in pictures as the author has in the text. Props in pictures must be accurate, but the whole illustration has to support the spirit the author is trying to convey. Illustrations become critical, of course, in picture books. Peter Spier's illustrations for songs add a lot of historical data to the words. In *The Erie Canal* (1970), Spier shows us the cargo of barrels, bottles, and produce on the boat. He tells us about society, too: a woman does washing atop the deckhouse of one boat while another boat carrying wealthy gentry passes by.

373

HISTORICAL FICTION FOR DIFFERENT AGES

Picture books for youngest children convey history in tightly constructed stories, many centered on simple family life in another era. Books for older children—with fewer illustrations—add dimensions to the picture of history. For adolescent readers, stories of the past become a complex tapestry whose patterns are not always easily discerned.

For Children 5 to 7: What Counts Is the Story

There are few books of historical fiction for children 5 to 7 years old. Perhaps one reason is authors realize that children at this age are mainly interested in themselves. They generally have no concept of historical time. For a 5-year-old, parents explain that some events, like the beginning of the United States, were "a long time ago," and prehistoric times were "a long, long time ago." What really counts to a child of this age is the story. It is possible for the child to see differences and similarities between their lives and the lives in the story. A dose of where-and-when history, however, will draw blank faces.

Some of the best books for this age are in Brinton Turkle's *Obadiah* series. Young Obadiah Starbuck is a member of a Quaker family living on Nantucket. The family's Quaker customs and speech may be different from ours, but they seem natural, and children quickly identify with Obadiah. In *The Adventures of Obadiah* (1972), he exaggerates, like many small children. He also suffers teasing from brothers and sisters, again like many small children, as a gull follows him in *Thy Friend, Obadiah* (1969). When he tells about dreams of seeing Cape Horn (in *Obadiah the Bold*, 1965), his father comforts and supports him: "Father put his hand on Obadiah's shoulder. 'I expect thee will,' he said." Young children can feel the warmth.

Some books for young children succeed because of their rollicking language. Arnold Lobel's *On the Day Peter Stuyvesant Sailed into Town* (1971) tells the story of Stuyvesant's arrival in New Amsterdam in 1647. He is dismayed and angered at the condition of the settlement and issues laws and proclamations to improve things. Young children enjoy the nimble poetry:

The governor slipped in the the mud and the mire,
And he said, "Things are not at all well here.
I am standing in garbage right up to my knees,
And the air has a very bad smell here.
Yes, the air has a very bad smell here."

Jouett saddles his horse in preparation for his ride to Charlottesville. (From *Jack Jouett's Ride* by Gail E. Haley. Copyright © 1973 by Gail E. Haley. Reprinted by permission of The Viking Press, Inc.)

Older children can understand Stuyvesant's dream, also expressed in verse, in which he hears a rumble and roar and sees tall buildings clustered together.

For Children 8 to 11: History with Several Dimensions

Children from 8 to 11 have a much wider range of reading interests and abilities than younger children. Even books for the youngest of these readers can deal with thorny contemporary issues. F. N. Monjo's books, for instance, are easy to read, but never talk down. Monjo's *The Drinking Gourd* (1970) is the story of a young boy and his father who help slaves escape on the underground railroad. The book does not back away from the issue: father and son discuss the breaking of an unjust law.

With the same honesty, Nathaniel Benchley's account of the opening battles of the Revolutionary War, in *Sam the Minuteman* (1969), includes a report on the number of minutemen killed, and an account of the pain when Sam's friend John is hit in the leg.

Both books are suited for 8- or 9-year-old children. So are some picture books. Gail Haley's *Jack Jouett's Ride* (1973), for example, tells a suspenseful revolutionary war story in picture-book form. The illustrations show Jouett in 1781 racing to Charlottesville to warn Thomas Jefferson and other Americans that the British Tarleton's Raiders are after them.

Children in grades three and four are able to understand complex characters. Heroes and heroines need not be one-dimensional, all good or bad. Luke, a character in Clyde Bulla's *White Bird* (1966), at first appears to be a man of compassion as he rescues a baby boy from a flood and raises him. But when the baby has grown to boyhood, Luke lets a stranger passing through their valley take the boy's pet bird. What kind of man would do that to his son? Children 8 and 9 years old can begin to discuss the question.

A wide bookshelf of historical fiction is available for children ages 10 and 11, and some of these books, too, raise vexing questions. Jethro Creighton, 9, at first finds the thought of the American Civil War exciting. Then, in Irene Hunt's *Across Five Aprils* (1964), family and friends begin enlisting. One of Jethro's brothers joins the Southern forces. Other brothers and his teacher join the North. The thrill of war dies in the suffering of divided loyalties. Jethro—and those who read about him—emerge with more sensitivity to the tragedy of war.

For Children 12 and Older: The Complexity of the Past

Children 12 to 14 have developed a concept of time and can put character and events into an intellectual framework. They can perceive cause-and-effect relationships and use abstract reasoning. Authors writing for this age are free to leave issues unresolved. Occasionally they can even use sophisticated devices such as irony: What happens is different from what is expected.

The hero of *One Is One* (1966), by Barbara Picard, is a boy, Stephen de Beauville, who lives in medieval England. At age 7, Stephen is considered a coward because he fears dogs. His family considers him a misfit and sends him to a monastery where he is miserable. He has artistic skills. But no one encourages him and finally he runs away. Now on his own, this "coward" learns the skills for knighthood and, ironically, becomes a knight. The irony deepens when Stephen discovers he dislikes being a knight and returns to the monastery where he can be a quiet painter. Here the book ends with a sense of hope. Young adolescents can identify with Stephen's situation even though the setting is centuries old.

Many books for older readers do not end so hopefully. James Foreman's *Ceremony of Innocence* (1970) is the story of Hans and Sophie Scholl, arrested by the Gestapo for distributing leaflets

376

Children learn about the values and life style of the
Quakers on Nantucket as they read about Obadiah.
(From *Thy Friend, Obadiah* by Brinton Turkle.
Copyright © 1969 by Brinton Turkle. Reprinted by
permission of The Viking Press, Inc.)

against the Nazis in 1943. The book opens with the arrest, flashes
back to incidents leading to the arrest, and ends with the unjust
execution of the Scholls.

THE VALUE OF HISTORICAL FICTION

What use is it for modern readers to know about the Scholls, or of
Stephen's quest for himself? Beyond the enjoyment of a simple adventure story, what does a 9-year-old pick up from Jack Jouett's
breakneck ride to Charlottesville?

For one thing, like some kinds of travel, reading historical fiction
provides the experience of living somewhere else, with strangers,
smelling exotic foods over wood fires, seeing flashes of color in
costume and personality. These are alien sensations. Sampling alien
worlds is one value of historical fiction. Another value is the readers' discovery during the exploration that there are similarities between characters populating historical fiction and characters we all
live with—and are—today. They are not strangers after all.

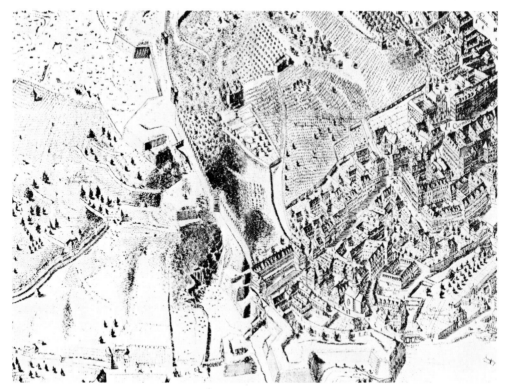

The endpapers for this book give readers a view of
Prague in the 1550s. (From *A Boy of Old Prague* by
Sulamith Ish-Kishor, illustrated by Ben Shahn.
Copyright © 1963 by Sulamith Ish-Kishor. Used by
permission of Pantheon Books, Inc.)

Illustrating Differences

Obadiah and his Quaker family go to meetings where they sit and
worship on wooden benches—men on one side, and women on the
other. One job for the children is filling the woodbox. After a few
pages of living with the family, readers of the Obadiah books begin
to feel at home despite these generally unfamiliar patterns of living.
Recognition of the different life-style—along with growing
familiarity—encourages understanding that all societies are not
alike and that there are values in each. Similarly, following the Civil
War through Jethro Creighton's eyes makes it apparent that serious
questions can have more than one answer.

   Different family structures, different systems of child raising—

378

readers of historical fiction can savor such variations in social custom and by extension learn more about what forces affect people today. Misfits are no longer sent to monasteries, as Stephen de Beauville was. They are, however, still cast out of society today: rejected at school, sent to institutions, or, in more subtle ways, excluded from "in" groups.

Fourth-graders reading about Sarah Noble in Alice Dalgliesh's *The Courage of Sarah Noble* (1954) can see why Sarah's father has to leave her in the care of Indians. It was 1707; he had brought her with him to find a homesite in the wilderness of Connecticut. Now he was going to return to Massachusetts for the rest of the family, and the trip would take a long time. So he entrusted his daughter to Tall John, a friendly Indian, knowing she would be safe. The reader learns to accept Father's decision to leave Sarah, just as she does. With Sarah, the reader learns that the Indian ways can be as comfortable as the moccasins on her feet.

379

Similarly, the sixth-grader reading *Dragonwings* (1975) can see the white population of San Francisco through the eyes of Moon Shadow, an 8-year-old Chinese boy who has come to join his father, Windrider. It is the early 1900s, and the residents of Chinatown refer to the whites as "Demons" and to English as the "Demon tongue." During the course of the story, Moon Shadow comes to know and respect one of the "Demons." The experience may not be foreign to modern readers moving into a new neighborhood or school. The book by Laurence Yep raises challenging questions about turn-of-the-century America: What is different? What is the same?

Illustrating Similarities

The best historical fiction never seems dated, partly because themes do not go out of style. The question of whether to break an unjust law—one theme in Monjo's *Drinking Gourd*—is as relevant within the past twenty years as it was to the time following the Civil War. Emotions do not go out of style, either, although ways of showing them may. In Henry Treece's *Viking's Dawn* (1956), a Viking leader Thorkell Fairhair goes blind. His men show their love for him by competing to comfort him. A seaman named Wolf begins:

> "I will be your eyes, Thorkell Fairhair," he said. "You have lost nothing."
> "I will be your right arm, Thorkell Fairhair," said Aun. "You have gained something."
> "I will be your spellmaster, Thorkell Fairhair," said Horic, crying a little as he said it. "You will gain everything." (p. 173)

It is easy to feel the sense of loss and compassion behind these bold pledges.

Problems recur. They may be as simple as how to cope with the teasing of brothers and sisters as Obadiah must; they may be as complex and difficult as Stephen's realization that he must be brave enough to be himself, different from others.

The problem may be social—prejudice, for instance. Sulamith Ish-Kishor's *Boy of Old Prague* (1963) is set in the 1550s. A young peasant boy, Tomas, steals a chicken to feed his sick mother. He is caught by the feudal lord, and his punishment is the most horrendous he can imagine: he is to be a servant to an old Jewish man, and live in the ghetto with the Jews. Only when he gets to know the Jewish family does he realize that they are gentle, loving people, and that the stories he had heard about the Jews were untrue.

War is another recurring social problem. Some books go beyond the immediate sounds of battle and the colors of the uniforms to convey the universal agony of soldiers and civilians. Jaap ter Haar's *Boris* (1970), focuses on a 12-year-old boy in Leningrad during World War II, but illuminates issues of forgiveness and mercy. The Germans have laid siege on the city, and people are starving. Boris's father drowned while trying to bring food and supplies to the city, and now the boy lives alone with his mother.

There is some food in no-man's land, his friend Nadia tells Boris; potatoes grow in the area between German and Russian lines. The two risk their lives to try to gather a secret harvest. But Nadia collapses during the mission, and Germans capture them. Will they be shot? No, the enemy shows mercy and eventually Boris returns to his mother. The siege is broken. German prisoners march through Leningrad. In the climactic scene, Boris—remembering the mercy shown him—offers a chocolate bar to one of the prisoners. The Russian crowd murmurs in anger. One old woman speaks for Boris. "What use is freedom to us if we still live in hate?" she asks.

> There was a pause, then most people nodded. Because those who have suffered much, can forgive much. (p. 149)

Like all good historical fiction, the scene accurately reflects a past event at the same time it imparts truth about who we are today.

SUMMARY

1 Historical fiction is realistic fiction set in the past. Some books, like *Robert Newton Peck's Soup,* are written from memory, but most historical fiction is based on research, sometimes exhaustive. *John and Patricia Beatty*, for example, made a complete check of 10,000 words in one of their books, *Campion Towers*, to edit out words that did not exist in the seventeenth century. They wanted a perfect reflection of the age in which their main character lived.

2 Writers of historical fiction strive for accuracy, but they also have a responsibility to tell good stories that meet basic literary criteria. *Evaluation* of historical fiction requires examining how well authors deal with common problems of writing in the genre.

3 Sometimes facts of history are sparse. Then the writer is free to invent scenes and dialogue from what *Jill Paton Walsh* calls the "thrilling quagmire of the 'might have been.' " Another problem is that sometimes historians disagree about the facts. *Esther Forbes* chose to follow one group of historians who supported the American Revolution when she wrote *Johnny Tremain; Christopher and James Lincoln Collier* followed another group, one with an antiwar focus, in writing *My Brother Sam Is Dead*.

4 Writers are challenged to avoid stereotypes, about Native Americans for example, in their search for facts. Good historical fiction also avoids overloading the story with historical detail, or clogging dialogue with so much "authentic" language that readers lose interest.

5 There is enough good historical fiction to appeal to children from preschool age to adolescence, although there are fewer books for youngest readers, who generally have difficulty understanding historical time. Young children do find a character they can identify with in *Brinton Turkle*'s *Obadiah* books, which are about a Quaker child on Nantucket.

6 Children 8 to 11 have a wider range of reading interests; they can understand *F. N. Monjo*'s books (*The Drinking Gourd*) or *Nathanial Benchley*'s easy-to-read historical fiction (*Sam the Minuteman*). Readers 12 and older can comprehend more complex stories such as *Barbara Picard*'s *One is One* or *James Foreman*'s *Ceremony of Innocence.*

7 Good historical fiction gives readers a sense of different value systems and an appreciation of diverse cultures. *Alice Dalgliesh*'s *The Courage of Sarah Noble*, for example, introduces Native American customs as seen through the eyes of a young girl. At the same time, such books explore timeless themes, such as the agony of war (in *Boris*) or the cruelty of prejudice (in *Boy of Old Prague*).

BIBLIOGRAPHY

Recommended Books of Historical Fiction

Bacon, Martha. *In the Company of Clowns,* illus. Richard Cuffari (Boston: Little, Brown, 1973).
    Gian-Piero is a foundling who joins a group of traveling players in eighteenth-century Italy, and has a series of adventures.

Beatty, Patricia. *How Many Miles to Sundown* (New York: Morrow, 1974).
    In a story set in the Southwest in the 1880's, three children hunt for a place, Sundown, mentioned by the father of one of them before he died.

Behn, Harry. *The Faraway Lurs* (Cleveland: World, 1963).
    Heather, a member of the Stone Age Forest People, and Wolf Stone, a member of the Bronze Age Sun People, fall in love despite each tribe's fear of the other.

Burton, Hester. *Kate Ryder,* illus. Victor G. Ambrus (New York: Crowell, 1975). (1974)
    In a story set during the English Civil War (1642–1651), Kate at 13

is not happy about the pressures of caring for the farm in her father's absence. As the war gets closer, both her father and her brother fight, on different sides.

Chukovsky, Kornei. *The Silver Crest; My Russian Boyhood,* Trans. Beatrice Stillman (New York: Holt, 1976).

Chukovsky recalls his boyhood, with emphasis on his schooling, particularly the year in which he was expelled from the gymnasium (school), ostensibly for being a bad influence on a classmate.

Clapp, Patricia. *I'm Deborah Sampson; A Soldier in the War of the Revolution* (New York: Lothrop, 1977).

Deborah tells about her childhood, and about her experiences disguised as "Robert Shurtlieff" in the Continental Army.

Clifford, Eth. *The Year of the Three-Legged Dear,* illus. Richard Cuffari (Boston: Houghton Mifflin, 1971).

Jesse Benton's life with his Lenni Lenape wife and his two children is shattered by the racial hatred of others.

Colver, Anne. *Bread and Butter Indian,* illus. Garth Williams (New York: Holt, 1964).

Because she does not understand why adults are afraid of the Indians, Barbara offers to share the bread and butter from her tea party with one, and makes a friend.

DeJong, Meindert. *The House of Sixty Fathers,* illus. Maurice Sendak (New York: Harper, 1956).

A young Chinese boy, Tien Pao, is separated from his parents when the country is invaded by the Japanese, but is adopted by a squadron of American airmen.

Eckert, Allan. *Incident at Hawk's Hill,* illus. John Schoenherr (Boston: Little, Brown, 1971).

Six-year-old Ben relates to animals easily, and when he gets lost he is cared for by a badger, living underground for several weeks. Based on a real incident.

Fritz, Jean. *Early Thunder,* illus. Lynd Ward (New York: Coward-McCann, 1967).

Set in Salem, Massachusetts, in 1775, the story presents Whig and Tory viewpoints as 14-year-old Daniel West decides on his position.

Gauch, Patricia Lee. *This Time, Tempe Wicke?* illus. Margot Tomes (New York: Coward, McCann, 1974).

Tempe Wicke is a physically strong girl with a mind of her own. When two Revolutionary soldiers, part of a group which has mutinied, try to take her horse, she hides it in her bedroom, fending off their suspicions determinedly.

Garfield, Leon. *Black Jack,* illus. Antony Maitland (New York: Pantheon, 1968).

This adventure story, set in mid-eighteenth-century England, begins when a hanged man comes back to life.

Greene, Bette. *The Summer of My German Soldier* (New York: Dial, 1973).

Patty Bergen, a 12-year-old Jewish girl living in Arkansas, admires a German prisoner of war who comes into her father's store. Her help in his escape is eventually discovered.

Griese, Arnold A. *The Way of Our People,* illus. Haru Wells (New York: Crowell, 1975).

Set in the village of Anvik, in Alaska in 1838, this is the story of Kano, an Indian boy who fears that he will shame his family because he is afraid to be alone in the woods. The patterns of village life are a natural part of the tale.

Haugaard, Erik Christian. *A Messenger from Parliament* (Boston: Houghton Mifflin, 1976).

A young English boy, named after Oliver Cromwell, is caught in the conflict between those who support the king and those who support parliament in the mid 1600s.

Hautzig, Esther. *The Endless Steppe* (New York: Crowell, 1968).

Esther learns that she can survive the dismal housing and the forced labor in the Siberian camp where she and her family are sent by the Russians after the invasion of Poland.

Hickman, Janet. *The Stones,* illus. Richard Cuffari (New York: Macmillan, 1976).

It is easy for Garrett, living in a small midwestern town during World War II, to believe that an eccentric old man is an enemy because of his German background.

Holm, Anne. *North to Freedom,* trans. L. W. Kingsland (New York: Harcourt, 1965).

David, having lived in a concentration camp since he was a baby, escapes at age 12, and must learn how people live on the outside.

Hunter, Mollie. *The Ghosts of Glencoe* (New York: Funk & Wagnalls, 1969).

In this story based on the Massacre of Glencoe in the seventeenth century, Ensign Robert Stewart must decide if he will follow orders to kill the residents of the town where the army had been billeted.

Jones, Weyman. *Edge of Two Worlds,* illus. J. C. Kocsis (New York: Dial, 1968).

Calvin, the sole survivor of an attack on a wagon train, needs the help of Sequoyah to find his way, and the Indian needs Calvin to travel with him for protection from hostile whites. The two cross the prairie together.

Kerr, Judith. *When Hitler Stole Pink Rabbit* (New York: Coward McCann, 1972).
Nine-year-old Anna and her family leave Germany just prior to Hitler's election, and live as refugees going to Switzerland, then France, and then England.

Lampman, Evelyn Sibley. *Squaw Man's Son* (New York: Atheneum, 1978).
Billy Morrison, the son of a white man and an Indian woman, and not fully accepted by either group, views the conflict between Indian and white from a Native American perspective.

Reiss, Johanna. *The Upstairs Room* (New York: Crowell, 1972).
Annie and her older sister spend the war years hidden in an upstairs room of a farm family in Holland to escape the Germans.

Speare, Elizabeth. *The Bronze Bow* (Boston: Houghton Mifflin, 1961).
Daniel bar Jamin has sworn revenge against the Roman soldiers who occupy his homeland, and who killed his parents, but begins to change his mind after hearing Jesus speak.

Steele, William O. *The Perilous Road,* illus. Paul Galdone. (New York: Harcourt, 1958).
Chris Brabson's sympathies are entirely with the Confederacy, even though his brother has joined the Union army. However, his opinions change as he gains more experience and sees both sides in action.

Sutcliff, Rosemary. *The Witch's Brat,* illus. Richard Lebenson (New York: Walck, 1970).
A small crippled boy with knowledge of medicinal herbs makes a bargain which ends in the building of St. Bartholomew's hospital.

Taylor, Theodore. *Teetoncey,* illus. Richard Cuffari (New York: Doubleday, 1974).
Ben and his mother care for a young girl who was the only survivor of a shipwreck in which Ben's father and brother were killed. Set in 1898.

Tunis, John. *His Enemy, His Friend* (New York: Morrow, 1967).
A German soldier, part of the occupation, makes friends with the residents of the small French village, but is then forced to permit the killing of six hostages. Years later he meets the son of one of the hostages in a world championship soccer game.

Walsh, Jill Paton. *Toolmaker,* illus. Jeroo Roy (New York: Seabury, 1974).

In this Stone Age story, Ra learns that he can trade the tools he makes for food.

Adult References.

Collier, Christopher. "Johnny and Sam: Old and New Approaches to the American Revolution," *The Horn Book*, April 1976, pp. 132-138.

Egoff, Sheila. *The Republic of Childhood* (Toronto: Oxford University Press, 1967).

Field, Elinor Whitney (ed.). *Horn Book Reflections* (Boston: The Horn Book, 1969).

Haviland, Virginia. *Children and Literature, Views and Reviews* (Glenview, Ill.: Scott, Foresman, 1973).

Herbst, Laura. "That's One Good Indian: Unacceptable Images in Children's Novels," *Top of the News*, January 1975, pp. 192–197.

Monjo, F. N. "The Ten Bad Things about History," *Childhood Education*, March 1976, pp. 257-261.

Trease, Geoffrey. "The Historical Novelist at Work," *Children's Literature in Education*, vol. 7, 1972, pp. 5-16.

Walsh, Jill Paton. "History is Fiction," *The Horn Book*, February 1972, pp. 17-23.

Wells, Reese, and Gena Davidson, "Censorship and the Authors' Viewpoint," *Journal of Research and Development in Education*, vol. 9, no. 3, Spring 1976, pp. 69-75.

Children's Book References

Barringer, D. Moreau. *And the Waters Prevailed*, illus. P. A. Hutchinson (New York: Dutton, 1956).

Beatty, John, and Patricia Beatty. *Campion Towers* (New York: Macmillan, 1965).

Benchley, Nathaniel. *Sam the Minuteman*, illus. Arnold Lobel (New York: Harper, 1969).

———. *Only Earth and Sky Last Forever* (New York: Harper, 1972).

———. *Small Wolf*, illus. Joan Sandin (New York: Harper, 1972).

Bulla, Clyde. *White Bird*, illus. Leonard Weisgard (New York: Crowell, 1966).

Collier, James Lincoln, and Christopher Collier. *My Brother Sam Is Dead* (New York: Four Winds, 1974).

Dalgliesh, Alice. *The Courage of Sarah Noble*, illus. Leonard Weisgard (New York: Scribner's, 1954).

De Angeli, Marguerite. *The Door in the Wall* (New York: Double-day, 1949).

Forbes, Esther. *Johnny Tremain*, illus. Lynd Ward (Boston: Houghton Mifflin, 1943).

Foreman, James. *Ceremony of Innocence* (New York: Hawthorn, 1970).

Freeman, Don. *Will's Quill* (New York: Viking, 1975).

Haar, Jaap ter. *Boris*, trans. Martha Mearns, illus. Rier Poortuliet (New York: Delacorte, 1970).

Haley, Gail. *Jack Jouett's Ride* (New York: Viking, 1973).

Haugaard, Erik. *Hakon of Rogen's Saga*, illus. Leo and Diane Dillon (Boston: Houghton Mifflin, 1963).

Hunt, Irene. *Across Five Aprils* (Chicago: Follett, 1964).

Ish-Kishor, Sulamith. *A Boy of Old Prague*, illus. Ben Shahn (New York: Pantheon, 1963).

Konigsburg, E. L. *A Proud Taste for Scarlet and Miniver* (New York: Atheneum, 1973).

Lawson, Robert. *Mr. Revere and I* (Boston: Little, Brown, 1953).

Lobel, Arnold. *On the Day Peter Stuyvesant Sailed into Town* (New York: Harper, 1971).

Monjo, F. N. *The Drinking Gourd*, illus. Fred Brenner (New York: Harper, 1970).

O'Dell, Scott. *Sing Down the Moon* (Boston: Houghton Mifflin, 1970).

Peck, Robert Newton. *Soup*, illus. Charles. C. Gehm (New York: Knopf, 1974).

Picard, Barbara. *One Is One* (New York: Holt, 1966).

Richter, Hans Peter. *Friedrich*, trans. Edite Kroll (New York: Holt, 1971). (1961)

Spier, Peter. *The Erie Canal* (New York: Doubleday, 1970).

Sutcliff, Rosemary. *The Eagle of the Ninth*, illus. C. Walter Hodges (London: Oxford University Press, 1970). (1954)

Trease, Geoffrey. *Mist over Athelney* (New York: Macmillan, 1958).

———. *Thunder of Valmy* (New York: Macmillan, 1960).

Treece, Henry. *Viking's Dawn*, illus. Christine Price (New York: S. G. Phillips, 1956).

Turkle, Brinton. *Obadiah the Bold* (New York: Viking, 1965).

———. *Thy Friend Obadiah* (New York: Viking, 1969).

———. *The Adventures of Obadiah* (New York: Viking, 1972).

Wilder, Laura Ingalls. *Little House in the Big Woods*, illus. Garth Williams (New York: Holt, 1932).

———. *The First Four Years*, illus. Garth Williams (New York: Harper, 1971).

Yep, Laurence. *Dragonwings* (New York: Harper, 1975).

CHAPTER 9

BIOGRAPHY AND INFORMATIONAL BOOKS

FACTUAL PORTRAITS AND EXPLORATIONS

Back in the 1930s, editor F. N. Monjo wrote, society foisted black-and-white biographical portraits on young readers, life stories of great people who were "desperately single-minded, antiseptic, humorless, and perfect" (1975, p. 435). Biography was supposed to teach ponderous lessons so young readers would grow up to equally dry perfection. Students learned to pigeonhole great people: George Washington was honest. So was Abe Lincoln. Ben Franklin was the one who flew the kite. . . .

The forerunners of today's informational books for children were often equally dull. Here, for instance, is a lesson on telescopes from a book called *The Child's Guide to Knowledge,* published in 1832, by "A Lady."

> *Q.* What is a telescope?
> *A.* It is an optical instrument of many glasses which brings objects at a great distance close to view.
> *Q.* Who has the honour of the invention?
> *A.* This is not exactly known; but Galileo was the first who brought it to any degree of perfection. . . .
> *Q.* What did he become from great study, and the constant use of his glasses?
> *A.* Quite blind. (pp. 137–138)

In recent years, biography and informational books have changed. Writers have gained the freedom to show biographical subjects accurately, even when the picture is ambiguous or puzzling. And modern informational books have become much livelier. The best of them stimulate curiosity, rather than pretending to offer all the answers.

Recently published science books, for example, "have tended more and more to be open-ended in that theories are carefully labeled as theories . . . and they have tended to leave the reader with the feeling that there is still more to learn," writes Mary K. Eakin, a teacher of children's literature (in Haviland, 1973, p. 320).

Informational books are often grouped with biography, and both are labeled members of the family of nonfiction. There are, however, major differences.

Biography is a story centering on a person who actually existed or exists. The story may be partially fictionalized or abridged, like historical fiction (see Chapter 8).

Informational Books center on topics of nonfiction—how babies

ISSUE

ARE NONFICTION BOOKS WIDELY USED IN TODAY'S CLASSROOMS?

Informational books have been tagged with the label "nonfiction" for many years. This creates a connotation that these books are not as desirable as fiction, that they are "non-" books in some way. This label might account for the lack of use of these books in the average classroom. A change in attitude might promote a change of use. (p. 498)

> Greenlaw, M. Jean. "Information, Please! Books and Their Many Many Uses,"
> *Language Arts*, April 1978, pp. 498–500.

I also know that informational books for children have never been more important. This is true because of the intensive demands of today's curriculum, the decreasing dependence upon textbooks in the several subjects, and the many investigative "research" and "independent study" projects children are encouraged to undertake. (p. 61)

> Egoff, Sheila. "Informational Books for Children,"
> *Instructor*, May 1973, pp. 61–62.

Think of classrooms you have visited within the last five years. Did you see informational books in use? If so, in what ways? If not, how would you explain their absence? Which of the two positions seems to you to present the stronger argument? Why?

are conceived, for instance, or how Romans built cities—and need not tell a story.

Despite their roots in nonfiction, both biography and informational books may be evaluated by the same standards for good writing used to evaluate fiction. Techniques of character development used by writers of biography are often the same ones used by novelists. Is the main character haughty, irritable, lusty? Biographers writing for children today are freer than ever before to say so.

BIOGRAPHY: LIFE STORIES
NEED NOT BE STORIES TO LIVE BY

Monjo's *Poor Richard in France* (1973) presents an uncommon portrait of Ben Franklin, drawn from the perspective of Franklin's 7-year-old grandson, Benny Bache. "All the ladies in Paris want to kiss Grandfather," young Bache reports.

> But Grandfather says it isn't so easy to kiss French ladies. Here's why you can't kiss them on the lips. It's impolite. And you can't kiss them on the cheeks, either, because they wear big bright circles of rouge there. That means you have to kiss them on the neck! So that's what Grandfather does. (p. 27)

Franklin leaps from the story as a spritely old man, a grandfather whom many mothers would not want their children to emulate.

Of course biographers will go on portraying important people—men and women whose lives can stir ambitions, perk interest in the period when they lived, raise ideals. The subjects of biography, however, need not be paragons.

"To see a person whole," says Frances Clarke Sayers, a well-known critic of children's literature, "is to recognize the flaws in his character and to weigh them as best one can against the traits that give greatness to the subject and make him a personality" (1972, p. 450).

There are many ways to write biography, and not all of them depend on presenting a "whole" person.

BIOGRAPHY IN MANY FORMS

Biographers are not required to tell every known fact about a subject from birth to death. They can choose to focus on a few years in their subject's life, and may fictionalize part of the account of those years. They may even write in the first person, creating a narrative as if told by the subject. Some biographies deal with one person; others present the lives of several people grouped around a single theme. So biography may be sorted out in several ways:

Use of Factual Data

Nonfictional biography Virginia Hamilton's *Paul Robeson, The Life and Times of a Free Black Man* (1974), has reliable sources for all its information. The book presents, for the adolescent reader, Robeson's early years, his career as an actor and singer, his realization of injustice for blacks in America. It details his persecution by the American government for his political ideology. Like all nonfictional biography, the book is verifiable page by page with solid source material. The author even provides footnotes for quotations.

Children between the ages of 8 and 11 enjoy W. J. Jacob's nonfictional *William Bradford of Plymouth Colony* (1974). Jacobs's text is well researched. Illustrations are reproductions of documents, maps, and drawing of facsimiles of writings produced during the time of the Pilgrims. *William Bradford* is one of a series of "visual biographies" published by Franklin Watts. Every entry in the series uses authentic illustrations, as well as documented text.

Fictionalized biography The most common type of biography for young readers, fictionalized biography, is similar to historical fiction: the author is bound by what is known from historical research—and may not change these facts. But the writer does create some scenes, dialogue, or thoughts to mesh reasonably with what is known. Author Jean Lee Latham, for example, helps readers identify with a mathematician, the subject of *Carry On, Mr. Bowditch* (1955), by inventing dialogue.

In one scene, Bowditch's future wife Elizabeth comes to his store to buy a present for her father, a sailor. A few lines of their conversation help bring Bowditch's personality into focus:

> Nat studied. "Parallel rulers might be nice."
> "Do you suppose Father has them already?"
> Nat exploded. "Of course! What sort of sailing master do you think he is?" Then he apologized quickly. "I'm sorry. I didn't mean to bark at you."
> "I know. I'm just like a chair you stumble over in the dark," Elizabeth said. "It isn't the chair's fault, but you kick it anyhow."
> Nat blinked. "What are you talking about?"
> "Your brain. It's too fast. So you stumble on other people's dumbness. And—you want to kick something." (p. 82.)

The discovery books, published by Garrard, and the Crowell biography series for children in the middle grades are all fictionalized biography; so are the "I Can Read" books, published by Harper, for younger children. Some books of biography are almost totally fictional, although the story centers on a famous person. Robert Lawson's *Ben and Me* (1939), for example, is Ben Franklin's biography as told by a mouse who lives in the American statesman's hat and counsels him.

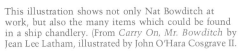

This illustration shows not only Nat Bowditch at work, but also the many items which could be found in a ship chandlery. (From *Carry On, Mr. Bowditch* by Jean Lee Latham, illustrated by John O'Hara Cosgrave II.

Fantasy like this is the basic material for some fictionalized biography, but other works—while fabrications—are stories that could have happened. Anne Rockwell's *The Boy Who Drew Sheep* (1973) is a realistic portrait of the Italian painter Giotto. However, historians are uncertain even about Giotto's birthdate, and there are so few facts available that Rockwell's story is almost entirely fiction. The author's assumptions seem reasonable, and the use of Giotto's paintings as illustrations adds authenticity (although they are reproduced in black and white). But for the most part the book is not based on fact.

Stage of Life

Childhood It was once widely held that children do not like to read about adults, that young readers cannot understand what is happening in books about grownups. So biographies usually told stories about great people as children. Some of what resulted was lopsided and trivial. Lincoln was depicted as no more than honest, hardworking, and, occasionally, funny. Some of what resulted was myth. George Washington, in fact, never chopped down the cherry tree.

Recently that view has changed, and children can now choose understandable stories about adult life of interesting people. Some good books, however, still focus on the subject as a child. Edith Fisher Hunter's *Child of the Silent Night* (1963), tells the story of a young girl born in 1829 and attacked by scarlet fever at age 2. As a result the girl, Laura Bridgman, loses sight and hearing; the disease also weakens her senses of taste and smell. Her only link to the world is her sense of touch. For six years after the disease, Laura lives at home. Walking with a neighbor, Asa Tenney, nourishes her mind. Then she goes to the Perkins Institution in Boston, where Dr. Samuel Howe teaches her to read, a breakthrough enabling her to communicate with others. (Laura Bridgman's story was told earlier by English novelist Charles Dickens. His account inspired the parents of Helen Keller, who was herself deaf and blind from infancy, to get help from the Perkins Institution.)

Child of the Silent Night centers on Laura Bridgman's childhood because that was the most dramatic period in the subject's life, not because of a dictate—now out of date—that children only want to know other children.

Adulthood *Amos Fortune Free Man* (1950), by Elizabeth Yates, begins when Amos is 15, a logical starting place because Amos was 15 when slave traders captured him in his African village and took him

ISSUE

CAN CHILDREN IDENTIFY WITH ADULT FIGURES IN BIOGRAPHY?

Biographies extend the child's opportunity for identification, not only with those who are great today but with those who have lived greatly in the past.

Biography fulfills children's needs for indentification with someone "bigger" than they are. In this day of mass conformity, it may give them new models of greatness to emulate or suggest new horizons of endeavor. (p. 555)

Huck, Charlotte S. *Children's Literature in the Elementary School* (New York: Holt, 1976).

Children will undoubtedly make many mistaken interpretations of the activities of adult subjects in the biographies they read. Exemplifying their limited ability to understand the adult world was Freeston's (1945) finding that at age eleven only two-thirds of children had an objective or realistic conception of adult work or occupations. The question remains, then, as to how much, what per cent, of other more complex or sophisticated behavior of adults as depicted in biographies would children understand? . . . There is no evidence to substantiate the contention that they can identify with the adult figures in biographies written for them. (p. 614)

Groff, Patrick. "How Do Children Read Biography about Adults?" *The Reading Teacher*, April 1971, pp. 609–615.

What does "identifying" with a character in a book mean? Why does it happen? Can children identify with adult problems and concerns? On the basis of your own experience which of the above statements would you support?

to Boston. There is little information on his earlier years. Fortune himself is the only source of information and as he aged, his memory weakened. The story of his adult life is astounding enough. He purchased his freedom at age 60, and then set up his own tannery. He was married three times—each time purchasing the freedom of his wife—and spent his life supporting the helpless.

The biography of Laura Bridgman concentrates on her
life as a child because it was then that she learned to
communicate, even though deaf and blind. (From
Child of the Silent Night by Edith Fisher Hunter,
illustrated by Bea Holmes. Copyright © 1963 by Edith
Fisher Hunter. Reprinted by permission of Houghton
Mifflin Company.)

Complete or nearly total life-span Complete biographies trace the
most significant events in a subject's life from birth to death. They
enable readers to see such things as the effects of a harsh childhood,
and to understand the complex forces that shape personality as a
person matures. The selection of milestones is critical. Today's authors may include material once thought unsuitable for young read-

ers, particularly in books for upper elementary and adolescent readers.

Olivia Coolidge's *Gandhi* (1971), for instance, candidly details the disastrous marriage of India's Mahatma Gandhi when he was 13. The marriage convinced the future spiritual leader that sex used up energy which should be directed toward more positive goals. This complete biography allows adolescents to see the stirrings of Gandhi's religious awareness and to understand how he was affected by his father's death. The book concludes with Gandhi's murder and funeral.

Partial biography Partial biography offers only a portion of the subject's life, giving readers a taste and stimulating their appetite for more. Books of partial biography cover a few years in the subject's life, or relate a few incidents grouped around one theme. Jean Fritz's *Why Don't You Get a Horse, Sam Adams?* (1974) is based on Adams' refusal to ride horseback, even when he has to escape from the British at Lexington. John Adams argues that great statesmen of great nations have always ridden horses, and since Sam is a great statesman of a great nation, he ought to get a horse, too. Sam Adams does, and rides it, and along the comparatively short and humorous trail the reader travels through some of the events leading to the revolution.

Single or Collective Biographies

Some biographical books comprise stories of several subjects—great women athletes, for example, or war heroes. Elizabeth Levy's *Lawyers for the People* (1974) is a series of sketches of nine lawyers who work for clients unable to afford legal help.

Point of View

First person Most first-person biographies for young readers are told by young observers. F. N. Monjo's *Me and Willie and Pa* (1973), for instance, is a fictionalized partial biography—a first-person story of what it was like to be Abe Lincoln's son between 1860 and 1865. One fictionalized detail: Tad asks his father to explain the Emancipation Proclamation, Lincoln's declaration freeing slaves. The scene is fictionalized because there is no historical evidence that Tad wanted to know about the Proclamation.

Other first-person accounts are autobiographies; but these are rarely written for young readers. Adolescents may enjoy *The Young*

Jean Fritz has written several partial biographies of figures in American history, giving insight into foibles as well as strengths. (Illustration reprinted by permission of Coward, McCann & Geoghegan, Inc. by Trina Schart Hyman from *Will You Sign Here, John Hancock?* by Jean Fritz. Copyright © 1976 by Trina Schart Hyman.)

Ardizzone (1970), an autobiography of writer Edward Ardizzone, particularly if they read his books as young children.

Third person The narrator of an autobiography is free to tell a tale without qualification or credential. "I was there" usually replaces research. The narrator of a nonfictional *third*-person story has to reflect the historical record, and sometimes let the reader know when the record has blank pages. Thaddeus Stevens, an American political leader who led the movement for the impeachment of President Andrew Johnson, never married. Why? Perhaps the fact that he had a misshapen foot contributed. But his biographer, Milton Melt-zer, wrote the authentic *Thaddeus Stevens and the Fight for Negro Rights* (1967) in the third person and had to indicate that he did not know.

"Perhaps," Meltzer says, "his lameness dammed his emotions. He may have been so sensitive to his physical defect that he could not believe any woman would marry him for himself alone. Or perhaps he dreaded fathering children who might have his defor-mity" (p. 20).

EVALUATING BIOGRAPHY

Accuracy and Honesty

By letting the reader know that he did not have all the answers about Thaddeus Stevens, Meltzer was supporting the authenticity of his book. For the same reason, most authors of good biography list sources, and often tell which parts of the story, if any, are fiction. This allows readers to judge the accuracy of a book themselves.

There is more to accuracy than supporting detail, however. Indi-vidual costumes may look right, and there may be several witnesses to what was said, but the overall picture may be flawed, sometimes by what is left out.

The central character in *Kit Carson* (1963), by Nardi Reeder Campion, for instance, is a brave Indian fighter who in 1853 be-comes an Indian agent in Taos and then does "great work helping the whites to understand the Indians" (p. 75). After seven years, Carson fights in the Civil War. He is glad when the conflict is over so he can go back to his humanitarian work—much praised in the book—with the Indians.

Kit Carson fails to mention that in June of 1863 Carson, under orders from the United States government, invaded the Navaho country of northeastern Arizona. He destroyed crops and livestock and killed Indians who fought back.

Real people have faults. And for the sake of honesty, biographers have a responsibility to present these faults.

Writer Jean Fritz is a master at breathing life into characters using small, sometimes irreverent, details. The point is not to malign great men and women, she argues, or puncture ideals.

"I am not laughing at John Hancock," she writes, "when I quote his letter to his wife after his triumphant entry into Philadelphia with the Massachusetts delegation to the Continental Congress. 'No person,' he wrote proudly, 'could possibly be more noticed than myself.' Well, I cannot help smiling at John Hancock; moreover I

401

This biography presents both a recent history of
Vietnam and the chronology of Ho Chi Minh's life.
(Reprinted with permission of Crowell-Collier
Publishers from *Ho Chi Minh, Legend of Hanoi* by
Jules Archer. Copyright © 1971 by Jules Archer. Photo
supplied by Black Star Photo Agency.)

want to share this small, amusing insight into his character" (1976,
p. 196).

Good biography does not eulogize, but it does not demean, either.
Many American readers might have accepted an unfavorable portrait of Ho Chi Minh, former president of North Vietnam. But Jules
Archer's *Ho Chi Minh, Legend of Hanoi* (1971) presents several
facets. Ho had the power to keep his country from becoming a satel-
lite of either Communist China or the Soviet Union. He was a hero
to his people. Yet he could be ruthless, and his plans cost bloodshed
and devastation.

Accuracy and Honesty in Illustration

Illustrators share some of the responsibility for accuracy. Details must be correct. The contrast between the plain dress of the Quakers and the frills of the rich shows clearly in the drawings by Aliki (a pseudonym for Aliki Brandenburg) for *The Story of William Penn* (1964), for instance. The artist's pictures of the rolling ship Penn rode across the Atlantic help propel the narrative.

Accurate details alone are not enough. To be outstanding, the illustrations have to support the spirit of the writing. Trina Schart Hyman, for instance, drew a funny picture of Sam Adams thumbing his nose at a portrait of King George hanging outside "Ye George" tavern in *Why Don't You Get a Horse, Sam Adams?* Buildings, wharves, and the dress of Boston residents appear as quiet background, just as historical detail flavors the humorous text by Jean Fritz. In contrast, Margot Tomes's illustrations for Fritz's *And Then What Happened, Paul Revere?* (1973) lack the humor and the detail of the writing, although they are adequate.

Quality of Writing

Accuracy does not count for much if the writing is second-rate. A good story is much more important to a young reader than the weight of the research or the number of footnotes or even the name of the subject.

Writer Mary Hays Weik's grandfather was a baker who came to the United States in 1848 wanting to be an American citizen. In his lifetime, he helped on the underground railroad, married twice, and built a house in Indiana where Mary Weik grew up. He was no statesman, scientist, or superstar, but Weik's biography, *A House on Liberty Street* (1973), tells his story so vividly that most readers will never forget him. Here is the tantalizing opening of a scene in which her grandfather, Louis, steps off the stagecoach in a new home town:

> Louis arrived in Noblestown on a golden October day. He dropped off the dusty Cincinnati–St. Louis stage at the old Tanner Inn on East Washington Street, a carpetbag hanging from one arm, his rolling-pin under the other: his heart full of hope for a new life, new friends. He found on the long front porch of the Tanner Inn a line of chill and hostile faces, drawn up like an enemy battery, repelling him with the silence of their welcome.
>
> "You the Dutchman from Cincinnati?"
>
> "I'm from Cincinnati—yes," said Louis stiffly, though he caught the unfriendly ring of the word "Dutchman."

403

Biographies of contemporary figures are popular with
many young readers. (Excerpted from the book
Barbara Jordan by James Haskins. Copyright © 1977
by James Haskins. Used by permission of The Dial
Press, Inc.)

"How long you aim to stay?"
"Depends," said Louis in his now-easy English, "on how I like it."
"Think you'll like it?"
"I couldn't say," said Louis cautiously. . . . (pp. 40–41)

By contrast, the subject of *Joe Namath, The King of Football*

(1974), by James T. Olsen, is well known to many young readers, but the book's writing sometimes falls into melodrama and the character seems flat.

One of Namath's black friends is refused service in a pizza parlor, and author Olsen quotes Namath as saying, "That was the first time I ran into prejudice." The passage continues: "Joe didn't like prejudice then, and he certainly doesn't like it now. That's the kind of man Joe Namath is" (p. 18).

Many biographies of sports heroes are well written. Julian May's *Bobby Orr, Star on Ice* (1973) avoids stilted dialogue and the sort of hero worship that distorts facts. May describes Bobby as a child:

> But soon Bobby learned to skate well. When he was five, he could keep the puck away from much older boys. Sometimes his father, Doug Orr, would come down to watch his little son play. He smiled as Bobby went sailing through a yelling crowd, handling his stick like an expert.
> "Bobby is a natural," Doug Orr thought. (p. 8)

Theme

Good writing page to page supports a central theme taken from the life of the subject. Without the theme—running through the narrative as sharply as an arrow—biography can become a boring chronology.

The theme arises from the material. "It is only too easy to decide on a thesis and then start looking for the material that will support it," writes Marchette Chute in describing how she wrote a biography of Shakespeare, "but it is a method that never results in a good biography. The material must all be collected first, and if the work has been done properly the thesis will eventually emerge" (in Field, 1969, p. 104).

Pursuing her unknown theme, she arrived every day at the New York Public Library 2 minutes before it opened and ran up the steps to the third-floor reading room. She read account books from Shakespeare's time, lawsuits, parish records, government reports, diaries, prison records. Sometimes she raced through twenty-five books in a single morning. Eventually she discovered how she would have to focus her book: "The key to Shakespeare's life was the theatre. . . . It was against a theatre background that the silhouette of Shakespeare would have to emerge . . ." (p. 105). After reading some 10,000 books and articles, she wrote two books—*Shakespeare of London* (1949) and, especially for young readers, *The Wonderful Winter* (1954).

405

THE VALUE OF BIOGRAPHY

One adolescent finished a biography of Rear Admiral Robert Peary, the arctic explorer, and decided he had found his life's work. He slept on the floor on a sleeping bag with windows open to let in subzero air. He persuaded a university research team to sign him on for a summer in the Arctic Circle. The book had called him to decide who he was; and he had answered: "arctic explorer" (Carlsen, 1967, p. 155).

Good biography can provide models, and shape ideals. It can stimulate readers to copy heroes and heroines. Many children in the 1950s who heard a biographical song about American frontiersman Davy Crockett, for instance, talked their parents into buying them coonskin caps—authentic except for the snap-on tail.

Many young readers believe that adopting heroes like Crockett is a good thing. In a survey Jean Fritz took of students in Westchester County, New York, 84 percent thought having heroes was fine. One student said it was good to have someone to pattern yourself after (1976, p. 195).

But biography does not have to generate authentically capped young Crocketts to be valuable. Several articulate students in the survey, in fact, argued that hero worship was a bad idea. "I found myself in whole-hearted agreement," author Fritz reported, "with the girl who believed that people should concentrate on fulfilling their own personalities. 'Too much worship,' she added, 'keeps people from being themselves' " (ibid.).

The reader does not have to adopt John Hancock's bold handwriting or his occasional vanity to profit from his biography. It is probably valuable enough that readers meet him, foibles and all. Sam Adams was eccentric in refusing to ride a horse. Gandhi had some extraordinary ideas about sex. But the experience of close contact with these strangers can help readers better understand their own lives. It can dramatize the possibilities for human choice, and show the constraints of human society. It can show how human emotions are constant through changing times and customs.

Jean Fritz talks about biographies as if they are charts revealing hidden countries we may never actually see. "In actual experience," she writes, "we are able to see so few lives in the round and to follow them closely from beginning to end. I for one need to possess a certain number of relatively whole lives in the long span of history" (1976, p. 193).

Biography is also useful as a bridge for young readers between stories read strictly for fun and teaching texts. The life story of an atomic scientist, for example, might dress the researcher in a lab coat and let the reader follow an experience step by step until the climactic moment when the scientist sees the foggy trails of atomic particles in a cloud chamber. The same material—minus the scientist—might appear in a chemistry textbook. Readers reluctant to do battle with the textbook will probably find it easier to get interested once they have experienced the sights, sounds, and smells of the lab where the textbook knowledge originated. Biographies of Ben Franklin may spur young students into wanting to know more about the American Revolution—or about electricity or early American newspapers or Congress or French-English enmity in the eighteenth century. . . .

It is, of course, impossible to predict the ways in which vivid portraits of people might affect the lives of people reading the portraits. And there is little the author or teacher can do to mold biographical data or historical fact into plastic, moralistic lessons. The material of biography is as untidy as the unsifted facts of history. It often defies the writer's efforts to make sense of it, and often leaves the reader curious and questioning. What could be more valuable than that?

INFORMATIONAL BOOKS: UNSETTLING EXPLORATIONS

A 5-year-old boy was playing with a compass when he realized that he did not understand the world. He knew that animals moved by themselves, and that objects moved when pushed. But the compass needle was odd: it was an object that appeared to move on its own. Faced with this wonder, the boy suddenly recognized a world of forces "deeply hidden." And so young Albert Einstein began to revise and invent. As an adult, he went on to make spectacular contributions to physics.

Einstein's contact with the compass stimulated and challenged him in a way that no lecture on magnetism could. It raised questions he felt he had to answer. [Einstein himself described the experience (in Schilpp, 1951, p. 9).] Similarly, the best informational books—like good biography—often raise as many questions as they answer.

Millicent E. Selsam, one of the best writers of science books for children, suggests in a story what a good informational book should do. A little girl kept visiting her and bringing along caterpillars the girl had found. Mrs. Selsam and the girl kept the wormlike animals in jars, with twigs and leaves, and soon the caterpillars began to spin

407

Young children may want to learn more about the "olden times" after seeing photographs such as the ones in *Grandpa Had a Windmill*. (From *Grandpa Had a Windmill, Grandma Had a Churn* by Louise A. Jackson, photographs by George Ancona. Photographs copyright © 1977 by George Ancona. Used by permission of Parents' Magazine Press.)

cocoons. The child and the grownup were excited because both had taken roles—as collector and observer—in the event.

A good book simulates the direct experience, Mrs. Selsam writes. "The role of the writer is to write the book so that a child can feel he is *participating* in an observation or a discovery. It should send him out looking for his own caterpillars immediately" (in Fenwick, 1967, p. 96).

Informational books present facts. They may also report generalizations or concepts. Chapter 3 introduced a small collection of concept books with pictures; all of them are informational books.

ISSUE

HOW SHOULD ECOLOGICAL PROBLEMS BE PRESENTED IN BOOKS FOR CHILDREN?

In general, juvenile books in the area of environmental control should in one way or another instill certain broad concepts, or perhaps "approaches" would be the better word. One is ecological, the idea that for every gain something is lost and must ultimately be returned. The idea of man as ultimate consumer without giving anything represents the frontier rather than the ecologic approach.

Where appropriate, books should indicate what the reader can do as an individual and what he can do as a member of a group. Whether it be picking up his own trash, or planting trees, or feeding birds, or making the most self-sacrificing decisions, such as forgoing automobile transportation when not absolutely essential, the reader should feel that in some manner he is involved in the problem and can contribute to its solution. For a writer to cry doom to an audience still politically helpless is not only sadistic but pointless. (p. 45)

Heylman, Katherine M. "The Little House Syndrome vs. Mike Mulligan and Mary Anne," *School Library Journal*, April 1970, pp. 44-50.

Children may need books to make them fully aware of the danger of losing a part of their natural heritage. So along with the books of beautiful color photographs of nature, in its smallest manifestations—insects, hummingbirds, a single flower, let them also see picture books of the devastated earth, of limbered and burned over areas; of birds dying in the oil slicks along the coasts; of fish gasping for air in lakes so polluted that they can no longer sustain any life except algae; of skies lost to sight in the smog over cities, and children in those same cities wearing gas masks.

Some people will say that such subjects are too grim, too disturbing, and too strong fare for young children. That they will create fears which will cause children unnecessary anxiety and possibly even result in some children becoming so depressed about the future of the world and of their own lives that they will completely withdraw, emotionally or through suicide. It is, or course, true that problems created by science and technology can be presented to children in such a manner that there seems no hope for the world. However, it does seem that writers should be able to achieve a balance between the Pollyanna attitude of the past (All is for the best in this best of all possible worlds) and complete resignation to a future of such insurmountable problems that no one will be able to solve them. (p. 320)

Eakin, Mary K. "The Changing World of Science and the Social Sciences," in Virginia Haviland, *Children and Literature, Views and Reviews* (Glenville, Illinois: Scott Foresman 1973), pp. 316-322.

How would Heylman assess a book for children which showed "skies lost to sight in the smog over cities, and children in those same cities wearing gas masks"? What might Eakin look for in such a book? How would you assess it?

They may deal with rudimentary knowledge, the shapes of numerals for example. Or they may cover arcane subjects, foreign to most adults, such as atomic research or Indian art.

There are more of these fact-based books than any other kind of writing for children. Of the 40,000 children's books listed in *Subject Guide to Children's Books in Print*, the clear majority are nonfiction. Their number is so large that it is impossible to be familiar with all the best informational books.

But what facts do these books present, and how? Do they pelt the reader with facts, or do they draw the reader in as a participant, stimulating questions and suggesting ways that readers themselves can find out more? It is possible to develop general principles for evaluating the thousands of informational books. Children themselves can use some of the principles to judge what they read.

EVALUATING INFORMATIONAL BOOKS:
THE QUALITY OF EXPLORATION

Good informational books launch readers on a kind of exploration. They offer a clear idea—with their own kind of markers—of where the journey is going before the reader sets off. They carry children straight along, accurately charting what is known and unknown. They rouse interest in further exploration. Illustrations—comparable to colorful vistas opening up to travelers—add to the excitement of the trip; sometimes they are the reason for going.

An overall plan, truthfulness, a stimulating style, illustrations to extend the text—do these criteria sound familiar? They should. They are closely related to standards used to evaluate fiction. Look at them one by one.

Where Is the Book Going?

First of all, most good informational books are generous with information about themselves.

Unless an informational book is short—a beginning concept book, for instance—it should map itself out in a table of contents. And in an index it should give detailed data on what it offers. From the title and table of contents alone, readers should know whether the book surveys a broad field. Scanning the index gives a more detailed idea of the scope. Most informational books center on one clearly defined territory. Books for younger readers seldom offer a table of contents, but most of these books are so short that the plan and scale of the book are apparent after brief skimming.

Dorothy Hogner's *Good Bugs and Bad Bugs in Your Garden* (1974), for intermediate-grade readers, has limited its scale to backyard ecology. The table of contents shows the boundaries of the book. After an introduction, there is material on harmful bugs, then on beneficial ones, but only those found within the borders of a typical yard. There follows a section on pest control. Each topic takes up about two pages. The markers are clear:The book's plan is to present concise information on a specific set of bugs.

And that is what the text does. Here is the heart of the section on mosquitoes:

> In order to breed, mosquitoes must have water. The females, which are the bloodsuckers, lay their eggs in water or on damp ground that has been flooded. The wrigglers (larvae) that hatch from the eggs live in water.
>
> So the first thing in mosquito control around the home is to get rid of standing water. . . . (p. 16)

Here are two more bug books, these for younger children.

A Dog's Book of Bugs (1967), by Elizabeth Griffen, has a brief text about the kinds of bugs that a dog might encounter. Part of the fun for readers in the first few grades is watching the curious, shaggy dog react to discoveries about crawling and flying things around it. When a click beetle flies end over end into the air in front of the dog, the dog flips in surprise and then sits back suspiciously on its haunches as the beetle hurries away. The plan and scale are clear from skimming: The book will survey a number of bugs familiar enough to come nose to nose to a family pet.

Ladybug, Ladybug, Fly Away Home (1967), by Judy Hawes, has a more limited scope: it is restricted to information about one insect. But it does tell a lot about that insect. A full-page drawing by Ed Emberley, for instance, shows the parts of a ladybug's body, reveal-

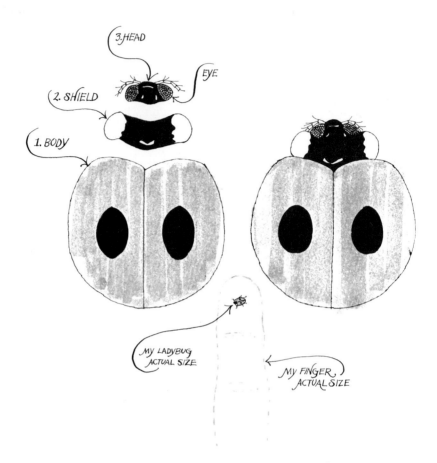

Emberley's drawing clearly indicates the size of a
ladybug, and the names of its body parts. (Illustration
by Ed Emberley from *Ladybug, Ladybug, Fly Away
Home* by Judy Hawes. Illustrations copyright © 1967
by Ed Emberley. By permission of Thomas Y.
Crowell.)

ing that what youngsters might have thought were eyes are really
part of a shield behind the head (p. 3). To avoid confusion, Emberley
adds a drawing of a finger with a ladybug perched on the tip to give
an idea of the bug's real size.

Glancing through these books, or skimming the table of contents
on longer books, tells about the scale of the exploration. Does the
child want a microscopic view of one insect? Or is there interest in
finding out what animals share backyard play areas, and how they
get along? Assessing the scope of the book can help teachers match
it to readers' current interests in exploration.

Most books provide other indications, easily checked, about how good the exploration will be.

The *copyright date*, for instance, can reveal quickly whether the material is likely to be dated. Sometimes the date is irrelevant: books of history, for instance, have a better chance at long-range survival than books about atomic physics. Dates on the bug books may not matter if the reader is interested in what mosquitoes or ladybugs or click beetles look like. Data on pesticides, on the other hand, are perishable. Theories about what to use to kill pests without harming the environment change from year to year. So the date of the book might be a clear warning sign to doubt some of the information. Children themselves should learn to look at the book's age and try to decide how time might have affected accuracy.

The *author's qualifications* are sometimes another clue to the quality of the exploration. Can you trust the information in Millicent Selsam's *Peanut* (1969), a book about how nuts grow, flower and reproduce? Yes, you probably can, because a note at the back of the book reports that Selsam majored in biology, holds a master's degree in botany, has taken all course work for a doctorate, and has taught biology in high school for ten years. Another reassurance is that the author and photographer express thanks to the head curator at the New York Botanical Gardens for checking text and photographs. Selsam's *How Puppies Grow* (1971) gains credibility from a note reporting that the National Science Teachers Association has judged the book "outstanding."

Notes, copyright date, table of contents, index, even the title—all are signs pointing to the direction the book will take, partially answering whether the exploration will be worthwhile. Further evaluation depends on reading the text and studying illustrations.

Does the Exploration Stray?

A collection of verifiable facts does not necessarily give an accurate view of a subject, any more than a jet flight over the Grand Canyon gives insight into the life of former cave dwellers there. Facts can be simplified, abridged, fogged, or disguised until they are meaningless or misguiding.

There is a problem, for example, in a book titled *War and Weapons* (National Army Museum, 1977). The book is only forty-eight pages long. But it tries to cover the entire history of warfare, as well as theories of human aggression and war, what it feels like to be a soldier, treatments for the wounded, technological advances, guerrilla warfare, and, according to a description from the publisher, "much more."

How can this be done in forty-eight pages? The answer is that the book takes misleading shortcuts. Human aggression, for instance, is explained in four paragraphs, including this one:

> Konrad Lorenz, the famous Austrian naturalist, has pointed out that animals seldom kill other animals of the same species. Men also have no in-built desire to kill other men. But man's weapons have become so powerful that his natural urge not to kill has been overruled. (p. 4)

What is left out? One major omission is that Lorenz suggested a theory, not a proven fact. Secondly, his theory is based almost totally on studies of animals, not humans. Finally, no support is given for the controversial conclusions that humans have no in-built desire to kill, or that weapons have "overruled" natural tranquillity.

By contrast, writer Shirley Glubok, in *The Art of the Woodland Indians* (1976), suggests that there are limits to what is known about her subject. There are no shortcuts in this book, which is written for intermediate or adolescent readers. Difficult and alien words are used, but they are defined clearly. She writes that snowshoes "were made by stretching webs of babiches, thongs made from the skin or muscle of the moose or caribou, over a wooden frame" (p. 5). The description adds an authentic flavor to the text.

But Glubok cannot answer all questions about Indian artifacts. There is some mystery, for instance, surrounding winglike polished stones with holes in the center. They are called bannerstones, she explains, and "are thought to have been used as handles or weights" attached to devices to help Indians throw spears. The explanation continues, next to a picture: "The butterfly-shaped bannerstone at right is made of banded slate" (pp. 10–11). The "thought to" statement, acknowledging the fact that even experts are not sure of everything, adds credibility to the "is" statement about what the bannerstone is made of.

She goes a step farther in describing two bannerstones: "It is not known who made these two, nor when they were made" (p. 11). When the facts run out, candor makes the book more believable.

Glubok even anticipates where readers might stray toward unwarranted conclusions. On one page, an illustration shows an Algonquian chief wearing a deerskin apron-skirt. The text cautions that the dress would be different in colder areas and that jewelry and body decorations varied as well. The warning helps prevent the reader from forming stereotyped pictures of Indian dress or concluding that all Native Americans look alike.

Other books stray from accuracy by trying to dress up facts in a misguided attempt to make them more appealing to children. Two

Photography is a particularly appropriate medium for illustration in a book about art objects. (Reprinted by permission of Macmillan Publishing Co., Inc. from *The Art of the Woodland Indians* by Shirley Glubok, Photographs by Alfred Tamarin. Copyright © 1976 by Shirley Glubok.)

common errors in informational books are called *anthropomorphism* and *teleology*.

Anthropomorphism means giving human characteristics to things that are not human. For instance, writer Peter Mayle and illustrator Arthur Robins turn human sperm into puffy-cheeked, smiling creatures in a book called *Where Did I Come From?* (1973). Text about "the romantic sperm" says that these happy little animals make their way up the vagina, "hoping to find . . . one of the eggs that the woman produces inside her every month."

The next page shows another goggle-eyed sperm in a top hat, sniffing a rose and wearing a bow tie on its tail. "How could an egg resist a sperm like this?" the text asks.

But sperm do not have eyes, nose, mouth, top hat, bow tie, or hope. All these touches of anthropomorphism might be appropriate and fun in a fantasy. But they are misleading and confusing in a book subtitled "The Facts of Life, Without Any Nonsense. . . ."

The word *teleology* refers to the belief that there is an overall design or plan in nature. Teleological explanations assume that all of nature (or Mother Nature) knows the plan and works toward certain ends or goals. For example, in one book by Victoria Cox and Stan Applebaum, called *Nature's Flying Janitor* (1974), a turkey vulture talks like a civil service worker following orders.

"I just wait around to do my part in Nature's Sanitation Corps," the vulture explains. "I help to keep the landscape tidy. You could call me a 'flying janitor,' but my name is Turkey Vulture." The vulture's job description goes a step beyond anthropomorphism: not only does the animal think like a human; it also acts according to a grand scheme of Nature. Again, the assumptions might pass in fiction, but they befog books of fact.

Does the Book Propel the Reader to Turn the Page?

The beginning of Clyde Watson's *Binary Numbers* (1977) uses references to common household items to thrust readers into unfamiliar territory. The book opens with clear directions:

> Take a ball of string and a ruler. Measure off 1 foot of string and pinch the 1-foot mark between your thumb and index finger. (Mark it with a felt pen if you want to.)
>
> Now double this length of string. To do this, fold the string at the 1-foot mark. Make a new mark even with the loose end. Pinch the new mark between thumb and finger, and then straighten out the new length.
>
> How long is the new length? Measure and see.
>
> Double the length again. How many feet long is it now? Guess before you measure. Were you right? (pp. 1–3)

Moving from simple tasks like these to more complicated experiments, the book accurately develops the concept of binary numbers, numbers with a base of 2 rather than a base of 10. (The decimal

Think of it this way: You could set up a row of
light bulbs and write numbers with them. Each
bulb would stand for a number in the binary
sequence, just as the strips did:

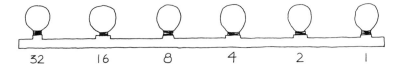

For whatever number you wanted to write, you
would turn certain bulbs **on** and others **off**. On
would mean **yes** and off would mean **no**. The
number five would look like this:

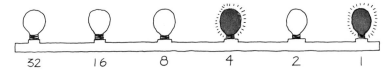

This diagram, set within the text of the book, clarifies
the concept being presented. (Illustration by Wendy
Watson from *Binary Numbers* by Clyde Watson. A
Young Math Book. Illustrations copyright © 1977 by
Wendy Watson. By permission of Thomas Y. Crowell.)

system is a base-10 system.) But *Binary Numbers* does more than
convey accurate facts. It also propels readers forward, stimulating
participation and encouraging independent discovery. It puts a child
in touch with string, ruler, and marking pen, and later with rods and
weights.

There are other ways to draw readers into an exploration. A
question-and-answer style enlivens Ann McGovern's *If You Lived
in Colonial Times* (1964). *"Were there doctors in colonial days?"* an
italicized question at the top of the page asks.

The answer follows immediately: "There weren't many doctors.
If you were very sick, your neighbor might be sent to get the nearest
doctor. Your neighbor might have to ride all day before he found a
doctor" (p. 32).

This kind of "dialogue" seems natural for books like this. Other
informational books encourage continuing interest by using tried-
and-true techniques of good writing style. Writer Joe Lasker, for
instance, uses a direct, personal tone to report medieval wedding
customs. His book, *Merry Ever After* (1976), focuses on two wed-

dings. One is between a merchant's daughter and a nobleman's son and the other between a blacksmith's daughter and a plowman's son. In this passage, Lasker launches readers into what could have been a dry and brittle discussion:

> Anne was only ten years old when her father told her she would marry Gilbert, who was eleven. Anne had never met Gilbert. She would not meet him until her wedding day, when she would be fifteen. Anne was not upset to find out that she was betrothed to Gilbert. In fifteenth-century Europe it was the custom for parents to arrange a marriage for their children.

The stories of Anne and Gilbert are not excursions off the main road of fact. Their stories are the central route of exploration.

Do Illustrations Improve the View?

Real-life examples—the stories of Anne and Gilbert—are more than rest stops in informational books. Examples add information. So do good illustrations. Like a new view opening up as a hiker rounds a bend, a good illustration gives a sense of where you are in a way that words cannot.

"Maybe it shows scale, in relation to a child," writes Jeanne Bendick, an illustrator and author. "Maybe it locates and labels parts. Maybe it simply shows something or somebody as part of the world—growing or being alive, enjoying and being enjoyed" (1973, p. 20).

Drawings, paintings, or photographs in informational books should stand on their own as good art. Illustrations should also blend with the text, capturing the same joy of discovery that propels text readers from page to page.

That means, to begin with, that illustrations should be near passages they illustrate or extend. They should be accurate, like the text, when drawings show scientific detail such as the designs on a ladybug's back. And the media and style of the artwork should match the nature of the material.

Do fact-based books always require realistic illustrations, preferably photographs? No, sometimes abstract drawings are more appropriate.

Of course some books profit from photographic realism. Selsam relied on photographs for the most part to illustrate *Peanut*. Many of the photos are magnifications, giving readers precise information about the Spanish peanut. On one page, a sequence of photographs shows the growth of a plant from a smooth bud to a plump nut with

Lasker's illustrations evoke the style of medieval artists while accurately portraying the customs of the period. (From *Merry Ever After* by Joe Lasker. Copyright © 1976 by Joe Lasker. Reprinted by permission of The Viking Press, Inc.)

its patterned shell. Looking at the three photographs gives an exciting sense of watching active growth a few inches from where it is happening (p. 38).

But often, photographs cannot give as good a view of a subject as a

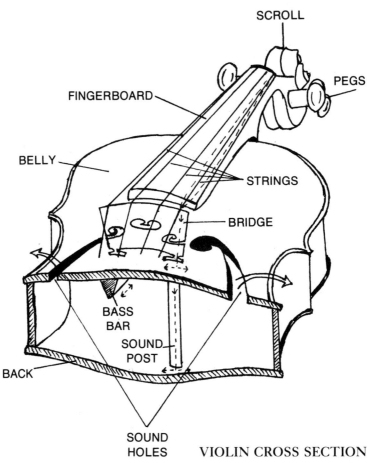

This cutaway technique gives perspective on the
construction of a violin. (Reprinted by permission of
the publisher, Thomas Nelson, Inc. From the book
The Instruments of Music. Copyright © 1977 by Guy
L. Luttrell.)

diagram or painting. A simple sketch in Jeanne Bendick's *The First
Book of Airplanes* (1976), for instance, shows how aircraft approaching landing move from one stacking level to another to avoid colli-
sion. The silhouetted, abstract plane appears at four stacking levels
along with arrows to show how it descends step by step toward a
trim—and abstract—airport. Simple lines clarify a complicated idea
(p. 29).

On the other hand, abstract designs or diagrams would never have
captured the flavor of Lasker's text for *Merry Ever After*. Lasker's
illustrations, in full color, evoke the style of fifteenth- and

sixteenth-century artists while accurately conveying the costumes and customs of the period when the weddings took place.

The illustrator's basic responsibility is not much different from the obligation of writers. Art and text in informational books act something like the compass Einstein played with as a boy. Sometimes the books are unsettling. Often they raise questions and point in new directions. They encourage readers to look down foreign roads, and move toward startling discoveries.

SUMMARY

1 *Informational books* and *biography* are often grouped under the category of *nonfiction*. But biography, a story centering on a person who actually existed or exists, may be partially fictionalized or abridged, like historical fiction. And informational books—centering on nonfictional topics such as Roman construction techniques—may be evaluated by some of the same literary standards used to evaluate fiction.

2 Biography takes many forms. *Virginia Hamilton's Paul Robeson, The Life and Times of a Free Black Man* has reliable sources for all its information; every line is nonfiction. More commonly, biography is fictionalized; it includes believable scenes and dialogue to mesh with known fact. For example, invented dialogue helps readers understand the main character, a mathematician, in *Jean Lee Latham's Carry On, Mr. Bowditch.*

3 Biographies differ in scope. Some, like *Edith Fisher's Child of the Silent Night*, center on the subject's childhood; others, like *Elizabeth Yate's Amos Fortune, Free Man* introduce subjects as adults. *Olivia Coolidge's Gandhi* traces the entire life-span of the Indian spiritual leader, while other books are based on a single incident in the subject's life. Some books comprise several biographies grouped around a single theme, such as women athletes.

4 Stories of real people may be told from several points of view. *F.N. Monjo's Me and Willie and Pa*, for example, is told in the first person, while *Thaddeus Stevens and the Fight for Negro Rights* is written in the third person by biographer *Milton Meltzer.*

5 *Evaluation* of biography requires more than checking facts in books against historical records. Some books are inaccurate because of what is left out; *Nardi Reeder Campion's* flattering portrait in *Kit Carson*, for instance, omits information about Carson's role in a brutal raid on Native Americans. Good biography for children presents whole characters, including their flaws. Accurate illustrations support the spirit of the writing (as in *The Story of William Penn* with drawings by *Aliki*). And the writing itself is more important to

421

young readers than the weight of research or even the name of the subject.

6 Biography can act as a bridge for young readers between stories read strictly for fun and teaching texts. Good biography also brings readers closer to an understanding of the complexity of human nature, to what writer *Jean Fritz* calls "lives in the round."

7 Similarly, good informational books suggest the complexity of a subject without pretending to offer all answers. *Millicent Selsam*, one of the best-known writers of science books for children, suggests that informational books should stimulate readers to want to continue explorations begun in the books, to search for more information.

8 *Evaluation* of informational books requires examining the quality of the exploration. Specifically, readers should look at features such as the *table of contents, index, copyright date,* and *author's qualifications*; each is a sign pointing out the direction the book will take. As in biography, accurate facts alone do not ensure accuracy. Good informational books also indicate the boundaries of current knowledge, often leaving some questions open. Facts themselves are presented interestingly, without *anthropomorphism*—giving human characteristics to nonhuman things—or *teleology*—the assumption of an overall design or plan in nature to explain behavior or other observable occurrences. Finally, illustrations—as in fictional books—should stand on their own as art, as well as propel readers along from page to page and stimulate their curiosity.

BIBLIOGRAPHY

Recommended Informational Books

Adler, David A. *Redwoods Are the Tallest Trees in the World,* illus. Kazue Mizmura (New York: Crowell, 1978).
Appropriate for primary grade children, this book presents facts about the growth of redwoods, in a clear and simple text.

Asimov, Isaac. *Mars, The Red Planet,* illus. Giulio Maestro (New York: Lothrop, Lee and Shepard, 1977).
Asimov gives detailed descriptions of the physical aspects and movement of Mars, as well as a history of theories and discoveries related to it.

Baker, Betty. *Settlers and Strangers; Native Americans of the Desert Southwest and History as They Saw It* (New York: Macmillan, 1977).
Baker's narrative focuses on how various peoples lived in the

Southwest, how they responded to the environment, and how they coped.

Bendick, Jeanne. *The Mystery of the Loch Ness Monster* (New York: McGraw-Hill, 1976).

Bendick includes discrepancies in evidence as well as corroborating evidence for the existence of some sort of creature in Loch Ness.

Berger, Melvin. *Jigsaw Continents,* illus. Bob Totten (New York: Coward-McCann, 1978).

Intermediate grade students will find this explanation of plate tectonics understandable; the illustrations help to clarify meanings.

Bitter, Gary G. *Exploring With Pocket Calculators,* illus. Thomas H. and Jeffery T. Metos (New York: Messer, 1977).

History and uses of calculators are described, and a few "tricks" are shown.

LeShan, Eda. *Learning to Say Good-by; When a Parent Dies,* illus. Paul Giovanopoulos (New York: Macmillan, 1976).

This account describes the emotions common to children when a parent dies. Brief anecdotes illustrate specific points.

Luttrell, Guy L. *The Instruments of Music* (Nashville, Tenn.: Nelson, 1977).

The book presents the history of various instruments, how they operate and how they sound. The emphasis is on orchestral instruments.

Macaulay, David. *Castle* (Boston: Houghton Mifflin, 1977).

Maccaulay's meticulous drawings provide information on medieval life as well as the construction of a Welsh castle.

McClung, Robert M. *Peeper, First Voice of Spring,* illus. Carol Lerner (New York: Morrow, 1977).

The stages in the life of a peeper, and the ecology of its environment, are clearly explained.

Meltzer, Milton. *Remember the Days; A Short History of the Jewish American,* illus. Harvey Dinnerstein (New York: Doubleday, 1974).

Meltzer describes Jewish life and culture, and focuses on the problems of Jewish immigrants in the United States, in this historical account.

Pringle, Laurence. P. *The Gentle Desert; Exploring an Ecosystem* (New York: Macmillan, 1977).

Clear explanations of ecosystems within deserts are enhanced by photographs and maps.

Silverstein, Alvin, and Virginia B. Silverstein. *Itch, Sniffle & Sneeze; All About Asthma, Hay Fever and Other Allergies,* illus. Roy Doty (New York: Four Winds, 1978).

Allergic reactions, substances which may cause them, and medical care are discussed.

Simon, Hilda. *Snails of Land and Sea* (New York: Vanguard, 1976).
Beautiful drawings make reading this book an esthetic and informative experience.

Weiss, Harvey. *What Holds It Together?* (Boston: Atlantic—Little, Brown, 1977).
This book describes how nails, screws, cement, glue and the like work, and gives advice about using them.

Recommended Biographies

Brandenburg, Aliki. *The Many Lives of Benjamin Franklin* (Englewood Cliffs, N.J.: Prentice-Hall, 1977).
In this biography for primary readers, Aliki touches on the major events in Franklin's life.

Burchard, Marshall. *Sports Hero: Pete Rose* (New York: Putnam, 1976).
For primary readers, this book focuses on Rose's career, his skill at hitting and his enthusiasm for baseball.

Clapp, Patricia. *Dr. Elizabeth* (New York: Lothrop, Lee and Shepard, 1974).
Clapp uses the first person to tell the story of Elizabeth Blackwell, the first woman to receive a medical degree in the United States.

Coolidge, Olivia E. *The Statesmanship of Abraham Lincoln* (New York: Scribner's, 1977).
A well-researched document for mature readers, this biography centers on Lincoln's years in office.

Fritz, Jean. *Can't You Make Them Behave, King George?* illus. Tomie de Paola (New York: Coward-McCann, 1977).
In this biography of King George III, the reader receives an English view of the American Revolution.

Faber, Doris. *Bella Abzug* (New York: Lothrop, Lee and Shepard, 1976).
Abzug's life and career, and other people's reaction to her, are candidly portrayed.

Gauch, Patricia Lee. *The Impossible Major Rogers,* illus. Robert Andrew Parker (New York: Putnam, 1977).
Robert Rogers' leadership of a band of rangers during the French and Indian War, and some of his misdeeds, are narrated in a conversational writing style.

Goodsell, Jane. *Daniel Inouye,* illus. Haru Wells (New York: Crowell, 1977).
This biography of Inouye, for young readers, is frank about race

relations in Hawaii as it describes discrimination he encountered because of his Japanese heritage.

Haskins, James S. *The Story of Stevie Wonder* (New York: Lothrop, Lee and Shepard, 1976).

The life of this popular musician is presented in a style that will appeal to intermediate and adolescent readers, whether they know his music or not.

Hovey, Tamara. *A Mind of Her Own; A Life of the Writer George Sand* (New York: Harper, 1977).

For adolescent readers, this biography relies on original sources for the dialogue.

Johnston, Johanna. *Harriet and the Runaway Book; The Story of Harriet Beecher Stowe and Uncle Tom's Cabin,* illus. Ronald Himler (New York: Harper, 1977).

In smooth, clear style, appropriate for intermediate grade children, Johnston shows how Stowe's life experiences led her to write *Uncle Tom's Cabin.*

Monjo, Ferdinand N. *Letters to Horseface,* illus. Don Bolognese and Elaine Raphael (New York: Viking, 1975).

The letters are from Mozart to his sister, and describe his journey through Italy when he was 14.

Terry, Walter. *Frontiers of Dance; The Life of Martha Graham* (New York: Crowell, 1975).

The author's experience as a dance critic adds dimension to a study of Graham and her work.

Tobias, Tobi. *Isamu Noguchi: The Life of a Sculptor.* (New York: Crowell, 1974).

Many photographs of Noguchi's work illustrate this book, which develops the sculptor's isolation and loneliness, his feeling of belonging neither to the Japanese nor the American culture.

Walker, Alice. *Langston Hughes, American Poet,* illus. Don Miller (New York: Crowell, 1974).

For primary grade readers, this biography is direct in its presentation of Hughes' early life and his father's bitterness.

Adult References—*Biography*

Carlsen, G. Robert. "Biography—The Bridge between Fact and Fiction," *Books and the Teen-Age Reader* (New York: Harper, 1967), pp. 153–163.

Egoff, Sheila. "Informational Books for Children," *Instructor,* May 1973, pp. 61–62.

Field, Elinor Whitney (ed.). *Horn Book Reflections* (Boston: The Horn Book, 1969).

Fritz, Jean. "George Washington, My Father and Walt Disney," *The Horn Book*, April 1976, pp. 191–198.

Groff, Patrick. "How Do Children Read Biography about Adults?" *The Reading Teacher*, April 1971, pp. 609–615.

Greenlaw, M. Jean. "Information Please! Books and their Many Many Uses," *Language Arts*, April 1978, pp. 498–500.

Huck, Charlotte S. *Children's Literature in the Elementary School* (New York: Holt, 1976).

Monjo, F. N. "Great Men, Melodies, Experiments, Plots, Predictability, and Surprises," *The Horn Book*, October 1975, pp. 433–441.

Sayers, Frances Clarke, and Carolyn Horovitz. "Remembrance and Re-Creation: Some Talk about Writing a Biography," *The Horn Book*, October 1972, pp. 444–451.

Informational books

Bendick, Jeanne. "Illustrating Science Books for Children," *Science and Children*, April 1973, pp. 20–21.

Fenwick, Sara Innis. *A Critical Approach to Children's Literature* (Chicago: The University of Chicago Press, 1967).

Haviland, Virginia. *Children and Literature, Views and Reviews* (Glenview, Ill.: Scott, Foresman, 1973).

Heylman, Katherine M. "The Little House Syndrome vs. Mike Mulligan and Mary Anne," *School Library Journal*, April 1970, pp. 44–50.

Schilpp, Paul Arthur. *Albert Einstein: Philosopher-Scientist*, 2d ed. (New York: Tudor, 1951).

Subject Guide to Children's Books in Print, vol. 2 of *Children's Books in Print* (New York: Bowker, 1977).

Children's Book References—*Biography*

Archer, Jules. *Ho Chi Minh, Legend of Hanoi* (New York: Crowell, 1971).

Ardizzone, Edward. *The Young Ardizzone, An Autobiographical Fragment* (New York: Macmillan, 1970).

Brandenberg, Aliki. *The Story of William Penn* (Englewood Cliffs, N.J.: Prentice-Hall, 1964).

Campion, Nardi Reeder. *Kit Carson*, illus. Shannon Stirnweis (Champaign, Ill.: Garrard, 1963).

Chute, Marchette. *Shakespeare of London* (New York: Dutton, 1949).

———. *The Wonderful Winter*, illus. Grace Golden (New York: Dutton, 1954).

Coolidge, Olivia. *Gandhi* (Boston: Houghton Mifflin, 1971).

Fritz, Jean. *And Then What Happened, Paul Revere?* illus. Margot Tomes (New York: Coward-McCann, 1973).

———. *Why Don't You Get a Horse, Sam Adams?* illus. Trina Schart Hyman (New York: Coward-McCann, 1974).

Hamilton, Virginia. *Paul Robeson, The Life and Times of a Free Black Man* (New York: Harper, 1974).

Hunter, Edith Fisher. *Child of the Silent Night*, illus. Bea Holmes (Boston: Houghton Mifflin, 1963).

Jacobs, W. J. *William Bradford of Plymouth Colony* (New York: Watts, 1974).

Latham, Jean Lee. *Carry On, Mr. Bowditch*, illus. John O'Hara Cosgrove II (Boston: Houghton Mifflin, 1955).

Lawson, Robert. *Ben and Me* (Boston: Little, Brown, 1939).

Levy, Elizabeth. *Lawyers for the People* (New York: Knopf, 1974).

May, Julian. *Bobby Orr, Star on Ice* (Mankato, Minn.: Crestwood House, 1973).

Meltzer, Milton. *Thaddeus Stevens and the Fight for Negro Rights* (New York: Crowell, 1967).

Monjo, F. N. *Me and Willie and Pa*, illus. Douglas Gorsline (New York: Simon and Schuster, 1973).

———. *Poor Richard in France*, illus. Brinton Turkle (New York: Holt, 1973).

Olsen, James T. *Joe Namath, The King of Football*, illus. Montie Salmela (Mankato, Minn.: Educreative Systems, 1974).

Rockwell, Anne. *The Boy Who Drew Sheep* (New York: Atheneum, 1973).

Weik, Mary Hays. *A House on Liberty Street*, illus. Ann Grifalconi (New York: Atheneum, 1973).

Yates, Elizabeth. *Amos Fortune Free Man*, illus. Nora S. Unwin (New York: Dutton, 1950).

Informational books

Bendick, Jeanne. *The First Book of Airplanes*, rev. ed. (New York: Watts, 1976).

Cox, Victoria, and Stan Applebaum. *Nature's Flying Janitor*, illus. Jo Polseno, (New York: Golden Press, 1974).

Glubok, Shirley. *The Art of the Woodland Indians*, illus. Alfred Tamarin (New York: Macmillan, 1976).

Griffen, Elizabeth. *A Dog's Book of Bugs,* illus. Peter Parnall (New York: Atheneum, 1967).

Hawes, Judy. *Ladybug, Ladybug, Fly Away Home,* illus. Ed Emberley (New York: Crowell, 1967).

Hogner, Dorothy. *Good Bugs and Bad Bugs in Your Garden*, illus. Grambs Miller (New York: Crowell, 1974).

Lady, A (anon.). *The Child's Guide to Knowledge.* (London: Simpkin and Marshall, Hurst, Chance, and Co., Harvey and Darton, 1832).

Lasker, Joe. *Merry Ever After* (New York: Viking, 1976).

Mayle, Peter. *Where Did I Come From?* illus. Arthur Robins (Secaucus, N.J.: Lyle Stuart, 1973).

McGovern, Ann. *If You Lived in Colonial Times*, illus. Brinton Turkle (New York: Scholastic, 1964).

National Army Museum. *War and Weapons* (New York: Watts, 1977).

Selsam, Millicent. *Peanut,* illus. Jerome Wexler (New York: Morrow, 1969).

————. *How Puppies Grow*, illus. Esther Bubley (New York: Four Winds Press, 1971).

Watson, Clyde. *Binary Numbers*, illus. Wendy Watson (New York: Crowell, 1977).

CHAPTER 10

LITERATURE SINCE 1600

WHO IS THE CHILD BEHIND THE BOOK?

M rs. Sarah Trimmer, an English writer and editor in the late 1700s, was certain she knew what children should not read.

Her credentials as critic were impeccable. Her father had tutored the Prince of Wales, who later became King George III. She grew up in the company of famous writers and artists in bustling London. She married at 21, and raised six girls and six boys, finding time to write between nursing, teaching, and sewing. At 61, she began editing the *Guardian of Education . . . A Copious Examination of Modern Styles of Education. . . .* This thick journal contained essays—copious indeed at sixty to eighty pages each—on what children should read, and shun. She considered sleep a waste of time, rose at 5 A.M. and sometimes 4, never used an assistant to edit the *Guardian,* and died at her desk in 1810.

What books are fit for children's eyes? Mrs. Trimmer told England. Selections from scripture won her approval. So did ancient and some modern histories, natural history, poetry, fables, and gardening books. "But books of Chemistry and Electricity and all that might lead [children] prematurely to making philosophical experiments we would still keep from them," she wrote (in St. John, 1970, p. 23). "Novels certainly, however excellent, should not be read by young persons," she argued (in Maxwell, 1974, p. 48). The story of Cinderella "paints some of the worst passions that can enter into the human breast, and of which little children should, if possible, be totally ignorant; such as envy, jealousy, a dislike of mothers-in-law and half sisters, vanity, a love of dress . . . " (p. 49). And as for *Robinson Crusoe,* by Daniel Defoe, the story of a shipwreck survivor on a tropical island, Mrs. Trimmer warned that "it might lead children into an early taste for a rambling life, and a desire of adventure." And she told of a lady who had been so frightened at seeing her little boys trying to copy Crusoe that she had become ill and died (in Avery, 1973, p. 18).

There have always been critics like Mrs. Trimmer who judge books on other than literary criteria. They are respected in this century. Bruno Bettelheim, a famous child psychologist and author of the well-received *The Uses of Enchantment* (1976), wrote like Mrs. Trimmer in 1969 when he reviewed Maurice Sendak's *Where the Wild Things Are* (1963). The story of a boy's dream after being sent to bed without supper, Bettelheim said, would frighten children. What Sendak had failed to understand, he contended, "is the incredible fear it evokes in the child to be sent to bed without supper" (Bettelhein, 1969, p. 48). He had not actually read the book, he said.

(Chapter-opening illustration courtesy of Thomas Y. Crowell Company.)

What some would consider a Trimmer approach to books for children also appears in parts of *Free to Be . . . You and Me*, a 1974 book produced by the Ms. Foundation. "There are messages within the merriment," writes Letty Cottin Pogrebin, one of the editors, in a note at the beginning of the book. And there is no doubt that messages support the nonsexist cause. Take just one example: " . . . Two or three selections redefine fairy tales so that Sleeping Beauty can stay awake and look at her life with her eyes wide open, and the brave prince can relax and enjoy *his* life without continually having to prove his 'manhood' " (p. 12). Mrs. Trimmer would have shunned the Ms. "messages," but she would have agreed that old fairy tales were not suitable for children.

For centuries, adults have used some books—and censored others—to advance current causes. Often, children in the books—or characters appealing to children—have been the teachers. Here is a nineteenth-century lecture on sin, for instance, from a little girl named Elsie Dinsmore to an adult friend of her father named Travilla. [The passage comes from *Elsie Dinsmore* (1867), by Martha Farquharson.]

> "O Mr. Travilla!" she said, looking up at him in great surprise, "surely you know that there is no such thing as a *little sin*; and don't you re-member about the man who picked up sticks on Sabbath-day? . . . God commanded that he sould be stoned to death, and it was done. . . ." (p. 243)*

Most of such well-meaning, earnest texts have brief life-spans. Writes Gillian Avery, an English author, "The melancholoy fact is that the higher the reputation of the book with educationalists and moralists of the time, the flatter it falls with the children of succeeding generations" (1973, p. 10).

Children themselves in every age from the seventeenth century on have decided for themselves what they liked, sometimes agreeing with adults about what they should read, sometimes not. Often, they have appropriated books written for adults; despite the fatality reported by Mrs. Trimmer, Robin Crusoe has survived. Often, they have fastened on fairy tales or fantasy considered too violent or frightening by adult critics. "Cinderella" lives, and *Wild Things* has become a favorite. When parents barred certain books from the home, children hid them in closets or tree trunks and traded them back and forth in secret for marbles or frogs.

This and several other excerpts in this chapter appear in Yankee Doodle's Literary Sampler of Prose, Poetry and Pictures *(1974) edited by Haviland and Coughlin. The* Sampler *reproduces original pages from rare children's books. Where applicable, references will cite the original source* and *the page number from the* Sampler. *This excerpt is from* Sampler, *p. 236.*

Elsie Dinsmore has just fainted, having refused to sing
on the Sabbath and been forced to stay seated at the
piano. (Courtesy of Thomas Y. Crowell Company.)

Over the past three centuries, publishers have come to recognize
a market in catering to children's tastes. The Trimmers continue
to call: teach and train them. But some editors of children's books

today go to classrooms to test book ideas on young customers them-selves, without consulting parents or guardians.

WHY EXPLORE TRENDS?

The tension between teaching and entertaining began almost as soon as there were printed books, back in the fifteenth century. There has been no resolution of the tension, although throughout the intervening centuries a number of critics have urged that chil-dren's books should do both—instruct *and* delight. It is worth fol-lowing the lines of the old debate over how books should be used, because the arguments recur century after century. School boards and teachers, librarians and parents, continue to takes sides today. It also helps in judging the quality of new books—and using them in the classroom—if modern writing is held against the backdrop of the past few centuries. Is the literature fresh? Will children like it? Will it help them? Will it change their thinking, and if so, how? Those are everyday questions for teachers and librarians; there are some answers in the arguments between the Trimmers and the dime-novel publishers, between the tellers of fairy tales and the teachers of hard fact.

The second major section of this book, beginning with the next chapter, will describe techniques of using children's literature day by day. But before studying specific tools that can be used to bring literature alive for children, go back to the central question posed in the first chapter of this book: Who is the child?

The answers adults have given over the centuries have helped define how *they* used literature in their times. Changing patterns of use, in other words, can be traced by exploring how adults in each age—from the invention of the printing press on—viewed their children.

It is possible to chart at least four different philosophies over the past few centuries about who the child is. Young readers have been seen in many lights, some dark, some bright. Puritans viewed their offspring as sinners headed for hell. In later ages, unspoiled goodness and humor came to dominate the portraits of young people. Today many observers have adopted what is in some ways an earlier view: the child is again like an adult in facing heavy social problems.

Ideas about children, of course, do not suddenly change at mid-night on a specific day. The dates used here to mark philosophies are somewhat arbitrary. They indicate merely that a group of people in that time viewed their daughters and sons in a certain way. And their identification of their children strongly affected what young people got to read, just as your concept of your students today will determine what books you offer them.

Inevitably your own philosophy will be shaped by the thinking of people in other eras. As you explore the thinking of the last few centuries, see if you can recognize fragments of earlier philosophies in your own feelings about children today. Imagine the child you will teach. Ask: Who are you?

Here are some answers.

THE CHILD IN NEED OF SALVATION: 1671

About the time the printing press was invented in Germany in the mid-fifteenth century, children were seen as little adults. They were dressed like adults, sat in on adult parties in the great halls of kings in the late Middle Ages, and listened to the old, sometimes bawdy stories told by wandering minstrels.

But then in the early seventeenth century, strong religious forces in England and the American colony put a dark cloak on the child. The Puritans in England believed that children were born sinners. Their beliefs traveled to America with early New England settlers.

In the harsh new land, children frequently died young. The pressing danger, however, was not dying, but eternal damnation. So out of love and concern for their children's souls, Puritan parents decided that they should be saved as soon as possible. Books favored by the Puritans warned constantly of brimstone, extolled the joy of death after a sinless life on earth, and tried literally to scare hell out of young readers.

The warnings in *A Token for Children*, published by an English minister named James Janeway about 1671 (and in many later editions), were typical. As in most books of the age, the actual title covered almost half a page and previewed the contents: *An Exact Account of the Conversion, Holy and Exemplary Lives, and Joyful Deaths of Several Young Children*. There are about a dozen stories of children in Janeway's book, each child a diminutive preacher and moralist, each dwelling on death and the release it will provide.

Printers in Boston adapted the book in the eighteenth century, adding passages Puritans thought important for New England children. An edition dated 1771, for instance, warned that children themselves would rise against sinful peers.

If the Children of New-England should not with an Early Piety, set themselves to Know and Serve the Lord JESUS CHRIST, the GOD of their Fathers, they will be condemned, not only by the Examples of pious Children in other Parts of the World, the publish'd and printed Accounts

ISSUE

IS LITERATURE A MEANS OR AN END?

Goals and Targets

In an age of great and necessary upheaval, new educational materials—including children's books—must be developed. Failure to do so would be a betrayal of our children, for it would leave them stranded and lost in a changing world, unprepared to relate to that process of change. We propose that children's literature become a tool for the conscious promotion of human values that will help lead to greater human liberation. We are advocates of a society which will be free of racism, sexism, ageism, classism, materialism, elitism, and other negative values. We are advocates of society in which all human beings have the true, not rhetorical, opportunity to realize their full human potential. We therefore frankly advocate books that will help achieve such a society and help prepare children for such a society. (p. 4)

Council on Interracial Books for Children. *Human and Anti-Human Values in Children's Books, A Content Rating Instrument for Educators and Concerned Parents* (New York: Racism and Sexism Resource Center for Educators, 1976).

It is natural if you feel strongly as most decent people do about racial discrimination to welcome books that give it short shrift; but to assess books on their racial attitude rather than their literary value, and still more to look on books as ammunition in the battle, is to take a further and still more dangerous step from literature-as-morality to literature-as-propaganda—a move toward conditions in which, hitherto, literary art has signally failed to thrive. (p. 164)

Townsend, John Rowe. "Didacticism in Modern Dress," *The Horn Book*, April 1967, pp. 159–164.

What is the basic difference in attitude toward books for children represented by these two statements? What dangers might there be in following the policy recommended by the Council on Interracial Books for Children? Would any of these dangers apply to Townsend's position as well? What is your own position on assessing books in terms of the social values they present?

437

whereof have been brought over hither; but there have been Examplary Children in the Midst of New England itself, that will rise up against them for their Condemnation. . . . (p. 107; *Sampler*, p. 12)

In order to frighten children away from sin with such material, the Puritans had to teach reading skills. So one result of conservative Puritan discipline was progressive legislation designed to ensure literacy. Seventeen years after the founding of Boston, in 1647, legislators passed a law about reading in Massachusetts. The law mandated that where schools were lacking, parents were required to teach "their children and apprentices prefectly to read the English tongue." And any town of 100 families had to set up a grammar school.

The foremost book of instruction in reading was the *New England Primer*. Primers were originally books of private prayer, but the *New England Primer*, first published some time before 1690, included a section on the alphabet with rhymes for each letter (except, for unknown reasons, I and V, which were omitted) and a catechism—a summary of religious belief in question-and-answer form. (The catechism was lifted from an earlier tome by John Cotton called *Spiritual Milk for Boston Babes in Either England Drawn from the Breasts of Both Testaments for Their Souls' Nourishment*.) Children had to memorize the answers. Even the alphabet section of the *Primer* taught the faith:

> A.
> In Adam's fall
> We sinned all.

Another version was:

> A.
> Adam and Eve
> Their God did grieve.

Forms of the primers, like Janeway's *Token*, lasted decades. For a while in the eighteenth century, a picture of King George III appeared on the frontispiece. After the revolution he was deposed in American primers and replaced by George Washington. The lessons inside remained unflaggingly religious despite minor changes in wording.

Puritan schoolchildren used another device to learn to read, called a hornbook, although it was neither a book nor a horn. It was a single sheet of paper glued to a piece of wood cut in the shape of a

N.
Nightingales sing
In time of Spring.

O.
The Owl at night
Hoots out of sight.

P.
Peter denied
His Lord, and cry'd.

Q.
Queens & kings must
Lie in the dust.

R.
The Rose in bloom
Sheds sweet perfume.

S.
Samuel anoints
Whom God appoints

7

T.
Time cuts down all,
Both great and small.

U.
Urns hold, we see,
Coffee and tea.

W.
Whales in the sea
God's voice obey.

X.
Xerxes the great
Shar'd common fate.

Y.
Youth should delight
In doing right.

Z.
Zaccheus, he
Did climb the tree
His Lord to see

The New England Primer was the foremost book of instruction in reading for Puritan children. (Courtesy of Thomas Y. Crowell Company.)

small paddle, about 3 inches wide by 5 inches long. A transparent shaving of animal horn covered and protected the paper. Thin brass strips held the horn in place. Again, the contents blended religion with basic skills needed for reading: the paper displayed the alphabet and the Lord's Prayer.

Ballads and fairy tales were banned by unwritten law in Boston and all over the new colonies. But the religious fare of the seventeenth century occasionally offered some adult-approved adventure and excitement to young readers. The most popular author of the century among children was probably John Bunyan (1628–1688), a Puritan preacher in England who grew up tormented by nightmares about hellfire. Bunyan was jailed because of his nonconformist sermons, and began to write his famous *Pilgrim's Progress* (1678) in a cell. The story grew out of his own dramatic dreams, forged into a story by his prison experience.

The book was about Christian, a pilgrim on an epic journey through life. Like all epics, there were snares and battles along the way, including lions, a monster named Apollyon, a jail cell in Doubtful Castle, and a happily-ever-after destination, the glimmering gate of the King's Palace. Bunyan was apparently so encouraged by young readers' responses to *Pilgrim's Progress*—which he had written for adults—that he then produced what he thought was a genuine children's book with short, preaching poems about birds and insects. Bunyan called it *Divine Emblems* (1686). But it was not *Progress*, and children avoided it.

The view of the child as sinner in need of emergency instruction lasted well into later centuries. Lessons to save souls, however, got lively competition—at least in England—from several sources.

One was the small-time salesman called the chapman, who carried his goods with him as he wandered, peddling necklaces, trinkets, beads—and inexpensive books. These chapbooks (*chap* comes from an Old English word meaning "trade"; *chapbook* means "trade book") were published to appeal to large audiences. They were printed like modern newspapers, with no binding, and—like newspapers—they put into print what people were talking about: some of the tales that had come down through the Middle Ages in the voices of storytellers. The earliest known printed version of "Tom Thumb," for one, is a chapbook dated 1621 (Avi, 1977, p. 150).

In contrast to most of the Puritan's tracts, chapbooks brought adventure, fantasy, and humor to children who had never seen books before.

In the middle of the seventeenth century, a Moravian educator named John Amos Comenius came up with another idea extraordinary for the times. Comenius's *Orbis Pictus* (meaning "illustrated world"), first published in 1657, was a book of facts for children. As far as we know, no one before Comenius had devoted a book to teachings about the world. Almost half of each page was a woodcut, marked with numbers. The text below told what was happening, more or less accurately, in English and Latin. For instance:

A Wind *under Ground*, 5.   Ventus *subterraneus*
causeth an *Earthquake*.   excitat *Terrae motum.*
  An Earthquake causeth   Terrae motus facit
gapings of the Earth,   Labes (& ruinas.) 6.
(and falls of Houses.) 6.

(Comenius, 1887, p. 10)

The pictures made this pleasurable reading in an age when adults put little stock in pleasure.

But toward the end of the seventeenth century, there were signs

This illustration is from a chapbook edition of the
Dick Whittington folktale. (From *Pictures and Stories
from Forgotten Children's Books* by Arnold Arnold.
Copyright © 1969, Dover Publications, Inc.)

of change. Puritan influence began to fade. Children passed chapbooks between them; some of the little unbound books were snuck aboard ships to the colonies. In 1693, a widely respected English philosopher named John Locke seemed to put his blessing on reading for fun. In *Some Thoughts Concerning Education*, Locke said that children should begin to learn to read as soon as they begin talking. "Great care is to be taken that it be never made as a business," he wrote. Locke also suggested: "There may be dice and playthings, with the letters on them to teach the children the alphabet by playing; and twenty other ways may be found, suitable to their particular tempers, to make this kind of learning a sport to them" (1947, pp. 332–333).

By the end of the century, American children still toted their hard hornbooks, memorized their religious catechism, and probably suf-

441

fered nightmares about hell. But then other books and new ideas—Locke's among them—began drifting into the colonies. Over the next century, children's literature changed. By 1800 on both sides of the Atlantic, writes librarian Carolyn A. Allen, children were getting "growing encouragement to play, not pray" (1976, p. 129).

Many adults during the 1700s came to agree with Locke. That, of course, meant a change in the adult view of the child. Children might be sinners, but adults no longer had to drum salvation into them. Children had some inherent ability to learn even when acting like children, and having fun.

THE CHILD AS SENSIBLE STUDENT: 1765

The Business and Pleasure of John Newbery

In 1765, *The History of Little Goody Two-Shoes* came off the press of a London printer, writer, businessman, patron of writers, and promoter of cure-all medicines. His name was John Newbery.

Newbery was a farmer's son born in 1713, twenty years after Locke published his benediction on pleasure in education. Newbery took over a business by marrying the widow of a printer. At 30 he moved to London and soon afterwards his shop, called The Bible and Sun, began issuing books written expressly for children. The first of these, *A Little Pretty Pocket-Book* (1744), laid down principles Newbery was to follow in all his path-breaking books. *Pocket-Book,* the title page announced, was "intended for the Instruction and Amusement of Little Master Tommy and Pretty Miss Poll, with an agreeable Letter to read from Jack the Giant killer...." Like seventeenth-century publications, the book was meant to teach. But breaking with Puritan philosophy, Newbery intended his books to amuse and be agreeable at the same time, just as Locke had suggested. [An American version of *A Little Pretty Pocket-Book* (1787), appears in *Sampler*, pp. 68–79.]

Newbery was one of the first to recognize the possibilites for profit in children's books. He was a master of selling techniques. The *Pocket-Book*, for instance, was a package deal. The book cost sixpence; for just twopence more, you could get a cushion to tote up children's good and bad deeds by sticking pins in one side or the other. In one of his ads in 1755, Newbery as huckster offered a *free* book for boys called *Nurse Truelove's New Year Gift*. All boys had to do was buy the binding, twopence a book.

Newbery also owned a profitable side business, the selling rights to Dr. James's Fever Powder, one of many cure-alls in a line of patent medicines. The powder, based on the element antimony, was sold until World War II, when its formula was destroyed in the London blitz. "In its heyday two centuries ago it had the confidence of the highest in the land," reports author John Rowe Townsend. "It also cured distemper in cattle" (1965, p. 32).

Newbery probably wrote many books himself. He enjoyed making up tripping titles and funny names, such as Peregrine Puzzlebrains and Giles Gingerbread. He also employed a stable of writers to turn out bound books and chapbooks. Among them was Oliver Goldsmith (1728–1774), the English poet, dramatist, and novelist. It is Goldsmith who often gets credit for Newbery's most famous publication, *The History of Little Goody Two-Shoes* (1765).

Modern children find *Goody Two-Shoes* melodramatic and overly moralistic. But in its time, the story seemed believable, and its morals were disguised a bit by a fast-paced plot.

In an 1855 edition (*Sampler*, pp. 93–102), a little girl named Margery Meanwell loses her father when he dies of "care and discontent." Margery's mother dies of a broken heart a few days later, leaving the little girl and her brother Tommy alone in the world with just three shoes between them. Tommy goes off to sea to seek his fortune. A kindly gentleman gives Margery two new shoes to replace her one. She gets her nickname from showing them off, and makes not a misstep from then on. She takes joy in teaching playmates to read, lectures adults on the value of going to bed early, dispenses advice to a squabbling couple (if you feel angry, count to twelve before you speak), and becomes a beloved school teacher. She is about to marry a rich gentleman when a stranger interrupts the ceremony: it is Tommy, back from sea with a fortune. He wants to be sure his sister is marrying the right man. Margery faints on recognizing her brother, recovers, is married after all, and lives for many years. Death is no longer the occasion for joy it was in the Puritan's books. Margery's "life was the greatest blessing, and her death the greatest calamity that ever was felt in the neighborhood."

Newbery's books began infiltrating the American colonies around the time of the American Revolution. His importer was a Massachusetts printer, Isiah Thomas of Worcester. Thomas piously passed on Newbery's moral lessons ["Know this (which is enough to know)/ Virtue is Happiness below"] while picking the Englishman's *Pocket-book*. Some 135 years later, Newbery officially won the credit Thomas had failed to give him in America. In 1922, Frederic G. Melcher, a publisher, set up an annual award in Newbery's name for the best children's writing by an American author.

Newbery was not the only publisher to produce books for

In this 1855 edition, Goody Two-Shoes is shown
teaching neighborhood children to read. (Courtesy of
Thomas Y. Crowell Company.)

amusement as well as instruction; nor was he the first (Author John
Rowe Townsend, 1965, lists earlier child-oriented publishers). But
he was the best known of his time and probably did more than any
other person to establish children's books as a separate, flowering
field. No longer—in Newbery's view—was the child a minature
adult corrupted by sin, headed toward damnation. Now children had
time to be children, even though they still had much to learn.

The Legacy of Jean Jacques Rousseau: Moral Tales

About the time *Goody Two-Shoes* appeared, French philosopher Jean Jacques Rousseau (1712-1778) added his voice in support of the view that children were different from parents, and had their own needs. In *Emile*, published in 1762, Rousseau argued that children learn for themselves through experience and activity. *Emile* is the story of a boy mostly without books; he reads only *Robinson Crusoe* and learns with enthusiasm by following natural inclinations, his thinking shaped by a lone teacher.

Rousseau might not have been pleased to see what came of his thinking toward the end of the century. His philosophy helped to spawn a whole series of somber books written to teach moral customs. These "moral tales," writes Avi, a modern author of children's books,

> . . . had a number of easily recognized elements: an all-knowing tutor (teacher, parent, elder sister or brother), a contrasting pair of children (good and bad), and a story which depicted the child discovering happiness through his or her own good acts. Such books rested firmly upon a rational empirical premise. Children should not be told what is right or wrong, but should, using their *own* good sense (with guidance) discover universal truths for themselves. (1977, p. 151)

Sandford and Merton (1783), by Britisher Thomas Day (1748–1789), was a typical moral tale. Tommy Merton, the spoiled son of a rich man, and Harry Sandford, son of a farmer, are 6-year-olds educated together. But where Harry is righteous and smart, Tommy is stubborn and ignorant. A series of long conversations with Mr. Barlow, the boys' clerical tutor, remakes Tommy into Sandford's mold.

Toward the end of the eighteenth century, educators competed for the attention of the sensible child of the day with barrages of instructive books, both religious and secular.

Textbooks on arithmetic, geography, and spelling appeared for the first time in American schools. In England, Mrs. Trimmer and a contemporary, Mrs. Letitia Barbauld, condemned fairy tales and Mother Goose. Sarah Trimmer produced a book herself titled *Fabulous Histories, or, The Story of the Robins* (1786), which taught children to be kind to animals and learn domestic virtues. The lesson was heavily sweetened; the main characters were talking robins named Robin, Dicky, Pecksy, and Flapsy. In a typical syrupy scene, Pecksy doubts her ability to learn to sing like other robins, although she is willing to try. Her father, Mr. Robin, then gives her a lesson, like a real robin popping a worm into its baby's mouth: "I do not doubt that you will apply yourself to what your mother requires of you: and she is an excellent judge both of your talents and of what is suitable to your station in life" (in Avery, 1973, p. 16).

The messages were easy to take, in keeping with the belief that the child needed playful handling and should not be frightened into learning. But not everyone agreed about *what* should be taught. Mrs. Trimmer, for example, thought Day's *Sandford and Merton* contained "great danger of sowing the seeds of democracy and republicanism in the youthful breast" (in St. John, 1970, p. 24). She thought Rousseau was a dangerous radical, and even criticized some of Mrs. Barbauld's moral tales that did not sufficiently stress religion.

There were plenty of other sermonizing authors around who did propound the Gospel. Hannah More, for one, another Englishwoman, turned from playwriting to producing conservative religious lessons—"Cheap Repository Tracts," as she called them—for children. Her upright lessons about obeying authority and maintaining class lines appeared in the form of tales issued twice a month. They cost little or nothing, and were aimed at Sunday School readers.

The Legacy of England: American Literature Almost Comes of Age

Early in the 1800s, for the first time, American literature began to set off on its own, breaking with English domination. But the writings of the two countries had been so closely allied for centuries that the first steps toward independence were taken with many backward glances.

In 1822, a young American named Samuel Goodrich was having a bad year. His wife died. His business ventures were failing. He fell off a horse, and was lamed. When he decided to go to Europe to try to relax—and also to search for books he might import to America—his bad luck held. Storms lashed the ship, and Goodrich got violently seasick.

Then his luck changed. He made a pleasant tour of Europe and then traveled to Bristol, England, where he met 79-year-old Hannah More. She was a small woman, with penetrating eyes and a cheerfulness that radiated through the wrinkles on her face. Goodrich told More that he had grown up admiring her writing. The two talked of how authors could use fiction to convey truth and good moral conduct. They agreed there was little value in imaginative stories of giants, fairies, and monsters.

Goodrich traveled on, meeting other British writers, including Sir Walter Scott, the poet and historical novelist, whom he described as

Young readers were shown how Peter Parley
supposedly looked, and many of them took the
description quite literally. (Courtesy of Thomas Y.
Crowell Company.)

tall, gray-haired, freckled, and weather-beaten. Then he went home,
married an English woman from Boston, and began to translate
some concepts of More and other Britishers into American idiom.

In 1827, still inspired by More's philosophy, he wrote the first of
what would become a series of books about America. It was called
The Tales of Peter Parley, and it began:

> Here I am. My name is Peter Parley. I am an old man. I am very grey and
> lame. But I have seen a great many things, and had a great many adven-
> tures, and I love to talk about them. . . . (p. 5; *Sampler*, p. 50)

Parley went on about how New England was settled and about the
war with British. He also told Indian stories, at times with direct
honesty. The white man, Goodrich wrote,

> . . . killed the children of the red men, they shot their wives, they burned
> their wigwams, and they took away their lands. . . . The red men were

beaten. They ran away into the woods. They were broken-hearted, and they died. They are all dead or gone far over the mountains, except a few. . . . (p. 20; *Sampler*, p. 56)

The Parley books were so popular that they were pirated—Newbery's revenge—by English printers. In America, there were many imitators and even some who dressed like Parley and gave lectures.

Once, Goodrich himself was introduced as Parley and tried to give a talk to a group of children. But he did not at all resemble the pictures of the old man in his books. His audience thought he was a phony, and walked out.

Peter Parley was meant to teach lessons, and Goodrich's English counterparts continued to turn out their didactic tales as the nineteenth century began. Another American writer, New Englander Jacob Abbott, carried on the tradition in a series about an American boy named Rollo. In early books, published from 1834 on, Rollo learned to talk and read; he then set off on travels, picking up a heavy load of moral instruction wherever he went.

Another angelic American character, young Elsie Dinsmore, was created by Martha Farquharson (a pseudonym for Finley) in 1867.

Elsie is so pious in *Elsie Dinsmore* that she refuses her father's order to play the piano on the sabbath. In a battle of wills, she sits silently at the piano for hours. Finally, she faints, hitting her head on the piano on the way down. She might have died, the reader learns. Her father relents. He carries her to bed, but she refuses to lie down until she has said her prayers (pp. 236-253; *Sampler*, pp. 229-246).

America may have won the revolution, but for the first half of the nineteenth century, at least, much of children's literature was still tied to the mother country.

Not everyone in the eighteenth and nineteenth centuries was pleased with the view of the child as sensible student. Newbery had added some whimsy to his lessons, but as the nineteenth century ended, he had been gone for more than thirty years. Children's literature seemed to have awakened from Newbery's comparatively amusing dreams into an age of sugar-coated reason.

Where were Giles Gingerbread and Peregrine Puzzlebrains?

Charles Lamb, an English essayist at the turn of the century, grumbled about what had happened. On October 23, 1802, he wrote a complaint about the times to the English poet Samuel Taylor Coleridge.

Goody Two-Shoes is almost out of print. Mrs. Barbauld's stuff has banished all the old classics of the nursery; and the shopman at New-

This is one of the original illustrations created by John
Tenniel for the two books about Alice. (Reprinted
with permission of Crowell-Collier Publishers from
Alice's Adventures in Wonderland by Lewis Carroll,
illustrated by Sir John Tenniel. Copyright © 1962 by
Crowell-Collier Publishers.)

bery's hardly deigned to reach them off an old exploded corner of the
shelf. . . . Mrs. B's and Mrs. Trimmer's nonsense lay in piles
about. . . . Science has succeeded in Poetry no less in the little walks of
children than with men. Is there no possibility of averting this sore evil?
Think what you would have been now, if instead of being fed with Tales
and old wives' fables in childhood, you had been crammed with geography and natural history?

Damn them!—I mean the cursed Barbauld Crew. . . . (1935, p. 326)

449

Lamb himself decided to do something. Four years after his letter to Coleridge, he and his wife Mary published *Tales from Shakespeare*, retelling the stories of many of the plays with such imagination that the book became an immediate success. Two years later, in 1808, Lamb brought out his version of Homer's *Odyssey* in *The Adventures of Ulysses*. The old tales—and the imaginative dreams behind them—were beginning to make a comeback. Astonishingly for the times, it was hard to find the lessons in them.

THE CHILD OUT OF SCHOOL: 1865

The signs of change during the nineteenth century are easy to read in Lewis Carroll's *Alice's Adventures in Wonderland*, first published in 1865. There was no moral instruction in this story. Not only that, there was no tutor or wise guardian to help the little girl through Wonderland. About her only guides were a harried rabbit and a sometimes-invisible cat. Carroll's book even made fun of authors he thought had loaded their writing with lessons.

In 1715, an English poet and author of hymns named Isaac Watts had written a poem about industry in a book called *Divine and Moral Songs for Children*. In one scene of *Alice*, she tries to remember the old Watts song, written 150 years before. But it comes out garbled. Here is the way Watts wrote it and as Alice recalled it:

Watts (1715)	*Alice (1865)*
How does the busy little bee	How doth the little croc-
Improve each shining hour,	odile
And gather honey all the day	Improve his shining tail,
From every opening flower.	And pour the waters of the
	Nile
How skillfully she builds her cell!	On every golden scale!
How neat she spreads her wax!	
And labours hard to store it well	How cheerfully he seems
With the sweet food she makes . . .	to grin
	How neatly spreads his
	claws,
	And welcomes little fishes
	in,
	With gently smiling jaws.

(Carroll, 1971, p. 17)

The view of the child had softened. The moralistic writings of Watts had turned into odd images that seem like remnants of a dream.

Children were still regarded as students: there were plenty of books around to instruct them in morals, manners, and science. But now there were respectable alternatives. Authors like Carroll seemed to want to give children books to entertain them when school was out. The new child of the nineteenth century—many adults thought—was free to dream a little.

There were at least two kinds of dreams in the nineteenth century. Some dreams were fantastic: folktales had come alive again, in print, and several new stories of fantasy appeared, including *Alice*.

Other new dreams were based on what was happening in the world. Factories began encroaching on farmland on both sides of the Atlantic. Americans were moving, encountering adventures and freedom from many of the Puritan restrictions. The first railroad in the United States was built in 1827; by 1840, there were close to 3,000 miles of track. The first wagon train arrived in California in 1841, and seven years later, 100 dragoons and the United States Navy claimed California.

In 1800, just 3 percent of the American population lived in urban areas. By 1860, the percentage had more than tripled. In the course of migrations, children began to gain freedom to dream up adventures for themselves. Struggles at the frontier, battles to survive in the burgeoning cities—real life generated romantic stories to rival fairy tales in action and suspense.

Folktales and Fairy Tales

Charles Lamb helped to start the movement back to old, imaginative tales partly to combat the "sore evil" he saw in seventeenth-century children's literature. Ironically, others who explored traditional literature were probably encouraged by the same cold scientific spirit that irked Lamb.

Jakob and Wilhelm Grimm in Germany, for instance, were historical linguists. They studied language scientifically hoping to find clues about the migrations of Europeans. The brothers collected and published folktales for adults. They worked like archeologists to dig up fragments of folk art and preserve them for future study.

But the Grimms also recognized that many of the stories had been told to children, and so they called their collections *Kinder und Haus Märchen (Children and Household Tales)*.

Whatever the Grimms' intention, children claimed the tales for themselves. Right after they were published, a translator named Edgar Taylor presented them to young readers with the title *Household Tales*, and soon they fit into English—and American—households as naturally as a kitchen table.

The door was open; other European writers and translators fol-

451

lowed the Grimms. In the 1850s, several new versions of Greek legends were published in England. In 1859, Sir George Dasent brought English readers the wintery Scandanavian folklore in *Popular Tales from the Norse*.

In America, later in the century, Joel Chandler Harris collected and published folktales from southern plantations, many of which had roots in traditional folklore from other parts of the world. The stories of how a clever rabbit tricks his enemies time and time again are like similar stories about clever animals found in African and Native American folklore.

The narrator of Harris's *Uncle Remus, His Songs and His Sayings* (1881) was an old black slave, Uncle Remus, who speaks in southern slave dialect (insulting to some modern readers concerned with breaking old stereotypes about blacks). In one of the stories, "The Tar Baby," Uncle Remus explains to a little boy that a tar baby is a rabbit-sized figure made of tar and turpentine. Brer Fox sets the Tar Baby in the road, then hides in the bushes to wait for Brer Rabbit to come along. Here is a sample of the dialect:

> ...Bimemby here come Brer Rabbit pacin' down de road—lippity-clippity, clippity-lippity—dez ez sassy ez a jay-bird. Brer Fox, he lay low.... (pp. 23–24; *Sampler*, pp. 274–275)

Brer Rabbit greets the Tar Baby, then turns angry when the figure does not respond. His anger comes to blows, but his fists and finally his head get stuck in the tar. The fox saunters out of hiding. "You look sorter stuck up dis mawnin'," he says (p. 25), and rolls on the ground laughing.

Where is the moral? There is none. There is not even a definite ending to the original. Did the fox eat the rabbit? the boy asks. "Dat's all the fur de tale goes," Uncle Remus replies (p. 25).

Other nineteenth-century writers took off from traditional literature to write wholly new imaginative stories. In Denmark, the young Hans Christian Andersen gathered material for his later writing: he grew up listening to tales told by old women in a poorhouse where his grandmother gardened. Then he wrote—and spoke—his own stories, including *Ugly Duckling* and *The Little Mermaid*. Mary Howitt translated them in England in 1846; they have appeared in new translations every few years since then.

The first *Alice* book came out less than a decade after Howitt's translation, and *Through the Looking Glass*, another of Lewis Carroll's fantastic trips, was published in 1871. The same year Alice jumped into her first journey down the rabbit hole—1865—the Frenchman Jules Verne took readers on a submarine ride, *Twenty*

UNCLE REMUS

HIS SONGS AND HIS SAYINGS

THE FOLK-LORE OF THE OLD PLANTATION

By JOEL CHANDLER HARRIS

WITH ILLUSTRATIONS BY FREDERICK S. CHURCH AND
JAMES H. MOSER

NEW YORK
D. APPLETON AND COMPANY
1, 3, AND 5 BOND STREET
1881

The title page shows Joel Chandler Harris's Uncle
Remus, teller of plantation legends, proverbs, songs,
and sayings. (Courtesy of Thomas Y. Crowell
Company.)

Thousand Leagues under the Sea, generally considered the first book of science fiction.

And that is just a sampling. By the 1870s and 1880s, on both sides of the Atlantic, there were some new rules of writing for children. Two women, one American and one English, presented some of the rewritten standards in separate critical essays.

"Stop preaching"—that was the call that began to sound in America a decade after the Civil War. In 1873, *Scribner's Magazine* put forth the new approach in an unsigned piece written by Mary Mapes Dodge, an author and editor. Children's magazines of the day, she wrote, were sometimes a "milk and water" version of adult journals.

> But, in fact, the child's magazine needs to be stronger, truer, bolder, more uncompromising than [adult magazines]. Its cheer must be the cheer of the bird song, not of condescending editorial babble. . . . No sermonizing either, no wearisome spinning out of facts, nor rattling of the dry bones of history. . . . The ideal child's magazine is a pleasure ground. (in Lanes, 1971, p. 18)

Shortly after her article appeared, she began editing a new children's magazine, *St. Nicholas*. It lasted until 1940 and drew contributions from generations of well-known imaginative writers. Joel Chandler Harris, inventor of Uncle Remus, was among the *St. Nicholas* authors. Children wrote for *St. Nicholas* also; and contributors included Robert Benchley, who grew up to be a famous humorist, and E. B. White, who would later spin *Charlotte's Web*.

"Beguile, amuse"—that was what Charlotte Yonge, an Englishwoman, asked of children's books when she compiled *What Books to Give and What to Lend* in 1887. An outspoken Christian in the tradition of Mrs. Trimmer, Yonge boldly parted company with the critics of the early years of the century. Young readers *must* be exposed to fairy tales, she argued, and that includes modern stories by Andersen and Carroll. Adventure is good for boys, and romance refines girls—even without an overt Christian message. With recommendations like these—doughty Mrs. Trimmer would have been apoplectic over them—it is no wonder Yonge found that "many stories have become obsolete." For instance, "the stories of the good children who are household supports and little nurses, picking up chance crumbs of instruction, have lost all present reality" (in Avery, 1973, p. 17).

Didactic literature had not died by any means. There were still plenty of lessons, sometimes lurking in newly mined fantasy. For instance in 1887—the same year Charlotte Yonge compiled her booklist—the American Tract Society published *Mother Goose for Temperance Nurseries*, which included this verse:

> Ding, dong, bell!
> Paddy's in the well!
> What threw him in?
> Half a glass of gin. (in Coughlin, 1977, p. 138)

But by the early part of the twentieth century, many adults thought that the real Mother Goose, Alice, and legendary Greek and Norse heroes had become respectable companions for children.

Realism

Some adults were not quite so sure Mark Twain's *Tom Sawyer* (1876) and *Huckleberry Finn* (1884) were respectable. These stories about believable Missouri boys—both of them rebels against repressive or disreputable adults—were intially banned in some libraries as trashy and dangerous. After the Booklyn Public Library removed Huck Finn, Twain—the name is a pseudonym for Samuel Clemens—responded with pretended indignation that anyone should have considered *Huck* a children's book. In a letter sent in 1905 to Asa Dickinson at the Brooklyn library, he contended:

> I wrote Tom Sawyer and Huck Finn for adults exclusively, and it always distresses me when I find that boys and girls have been allowed access to them. The mind that becomes soiled in youth can never again be washed clean; I know this by my own experience, and to this day I cherish an unappeasable bitterness against the unfaithful guardians of my young life, who not only permitted but compelled me to read an unexpurgated Bible through before I was 15 years old. . . . I wish I could say a softening word or two in defence of Huck's character, since you wish it, but really in my opinion it is no better than those of Solomon, David, Satan, and the rest of the sacred brotherhood. . . . (Clemens, 1924, pp. 335–336)

Twain's warm, funny, suspenseful portrayals of growing up in the American Midwest triumphed over the censors.

Some adults grumbled against other realistic books, such as Louisa May Alcott's *Little Women* (1868). The story of the March family as told by Jo, one of four affectionate but sometimes willful daughters, was based roughly on the plot of *Pilgrim's Progress*—but not enough to suit critics who thought the adventures of Jo were not religious enough.

But the critics could not restrain the nineteenth-century authors who wrote realistic stories of frontier adventures, modern war epics,

455

and rags-to-riches sagas. A century before, chapbooks had brought fantasy to young readers. Now the new *dime novel*—written for adults, read by children—brought "true life" stories that in some ways were just as dreamy. But the chapmen of 1860s were more sophisticated. Instead of hawking their wares on the street, they put ads in the newspapers.

One appeared June 7, 1860, in New York *Tribune*. "BOOKS FOR THE MILLION!" the ad's headline said. The idea for the ad was not new. Within the previous decade or so roughly the same headline had been used to sell clothing, dry goods, and coffee, all "for the million!" The ad went on:

A DOLLAR BOOK FOR A DIME ! !
128 Pages complete, only Ten Cents ! ! !
BEADLE'S DIME NOVELS NO. 1
MALAESKA:
the
Indian Wife of the White Hunter
By Mrs. Ann S. Stephens
128 pages, 12 mo., Ready SATURDAY MORNING, June 9
IRWIN P. BEADLE & CO. Publishers . . .

(in Johannsen, 1950, p. 31)

Malaeska, the first of the dime novels, came out in an orange wrapper that became characteristic of the vastly successful Beadle books.

One man who had been a boy in 1860s told in an *Atlantic Monthly* article in 1907 what it had been like when the books hit the streets, one book every two weeks. Charles M. Harvey rhapsodized:

> How the boys swarmed into and through stores and newsstands to buy copies as they came hot from the press! And the fortunate ones who were there before the supply gave out—how triumphantly they carried them off to the rendezvous, where eager groups awaited their arrival! What silver-tongued orator of any age or land ever had such sympathetic and enthusiastic audiences as did the happy youths at those trysting places, who were detailed to read those wild deed of forest, prairie and mountain! (in Avi, 1977, pp. 155–156)

Perhaps none of the Beadles ever actually sold a million copies, but the most popular sold in the hundreds of thousands (Johannsen, 1950, p. 33). At a dime a book, that was more than enough to make a booming profit for publisher Beadle. More expensive ($1 each), but

RAGGED DICK SERIES

BY

HORATIO ALGER JR.

RAGGED DICK.

In Horatio Alger's stories, the hero goes from poverty
to great wealth. (Courtesy of Thomas Y. Crowell
Company.)

457

also mass-produced, were the rags-to-riches books of Horatio Alger, Jr., set in the *other* frontier of the nineteenth-century, the city.

Alger (1834–1899), son of a Unitarian minister, graduated from Harvard and proceeded under family pressure to divinity school. But after a year's work in Brewster, Massachusetts, he quit the ministry, went to New York, and stored up impressions for a book whose theme he trotted out again and again in more than 100 books.

Ragged Dick (1868) is a 14-year-old bootblack; he is honest and hardworking, although sometimes he spends his meager earnings on theater, oyster stew, liquor at two cents a glass, and cigars.

A Sunday School teacher changes his life, encouraging him toward greater self-discipline and more reading. One afternoon, he is riding on the Staten Island Ferry when the son of a rich man falls overboard. Ragged Dick plunges to the rescue, and comes up with riches.

The realists of the late nineteenth century presented an exciting world, and created adventurous children to explore it. But much of the mass-produced realism—Alger's work, for instance—was built of clichés and shallow thinking. Ragged Dick's extraordinary luck was as implausible as a visit from a fairy godmother. It was not until the twentieth century that the honest realism pioneered by Twain and a few others matured. At the same time, new lines were added to the portrait of the child.

CHILDREN OF THIS CENTURY:
FROM SCAMPS TO VALUED CUSTOMERS, YOUNG ADULTS

By the turn of the century, childhood had become golden. Many adults looked with longing at the carefree years of their youth. Compared with the stiff model child of Mrs. Trimmer's day, children in the early twentieth century seemed younger. Gillian Avery, a writer who has closely studied nineteenth-century literature and children, said the new ideal in 1900 was "the little friend of all the world,"

> . . . the innocent child who might do deliciously naughty things, but who was sound at heart, since he looked up at scolding elders with brave, fearless eyes and never flinched an instant from the truth. "Madcaps," "scamps," "pickles," these children were variously called by their creators . . . [And by the 1920s,] we have now reached the era when the child is emancipated from his elders. (1973, p. 12)

But in the course of the twentieth century, views of the child became much more complicated. For one thing, children and their literature now got much more attention. In 1880, fewer than 300 books were written for children. By 1930, the number of children's books produced each year had tripled, to about a thousand. (These figures come from Johnson, 1971, p. 68.) In the 1870s, editors aimed *St. Nicholas*, the children's magazine, at an audience from 6 to 16. Then, as the one-room schoolhouse yielded to schools with many rooms, books and magazines began to specialize. There were books for 2-to-4-year-olds, easy-to-read books for early grade-school children, books with near-adult sophistication for older children, and—at the height of specialization—a magazine called *Seventeen*. (Lanes, 1971).

Children themselves had become specialities. Sigmund Freud (1856–1939), the founder of modern psychoanalysis, spawned generations of experts on children with his theories that childhood deeply affected adulthood, often unconsciously. Child psychologists took posts next to teachers; teachers themselves specialized in children of particular ages; libraries set apart children's rooms. And, for the first time, publishing houses took on editors whose only job was trying to reach the rapidly growing children's market.

The Child as Valued Customer: 1919

Louise Seaman Bechtel was working in the advertising office at the Macmillan Company, publishers, at the end of World War I when she was offered a department of her own. The company astutely recognized that post-war prosperity would stimulate interest in children's books. So in 1919 Bechtel was assigned a secretary and a budget and told to run the country's first children's department.

From then on, she recalled in 1969, fiftieth anniversary of her promotion, "my secretary—Gertrude Blumenthal—and I were the entire department.

> Alone we accomplished everything: editing, manuscript reading, bookmaking, interviewing artists, laying out books, advertising, preparing catalogues. From the beginning we usually received fifty to one hundred unsolicited manuscripts a week....
>
> One discovered books in many places. Of course, one such place was the children's room of a public library. At the New York Public Library children's room on 42nd Street, I found ten little boys absorbed in a book in Italian, "the big Pinocchio." So we sent to Italy to have it printed for us in English; and it was a great success. (in Silberberg and Donovan, 1969, p. 704)

Early editors set high standards for children's writing. Louise Bechtel recalls meeting many of the best authors of the day as they came and went from the Macmillan offices, writers such as John

459

Masefield, poet laureate in England, and William Butler Yeats, Irish poet and playwright. Encounters with them encouraged her to seek the best from authors and artists for children.

Over the next decade, a comradeship devoted to quality began to grow between editors. Alice Dalgliesh, who became children's editor at Charles Scribner's Sons in 1935, recalls that even during the Depression of the 1930s, when editors thought twice before taking new books, they kept faith "that if it was a *good* book it would sell" (p. 706). By the 1950s, children's editors no longer felt like stepchildren in the publishing house.

There were other people behind the improved quality of children's books in the early twentieth century. Anne Carroll Moore became head of the children's room at the New York Public Library in 1906. Amid stacks of papers and books in room 105, editors and authors and illustrators came to talk about children's books and how they might be better. Anne Moore also set stringent literary standards in a regular column in the *New York Herald Tribune*.

Meanwhile, Franklin K. Mathiews, librarian of the Boy Scouts of America, convinced publisher Frederic G. Melcher to institute a National Children's Book Week in 1919 to encourage adults to recognize good books for children. A few years later, in 1922, in an era when several publishers were beginning to agree with John Newbery that children's literature could stand on its own, Melcher led the Children's Book Council to establish the Newbery Award. It was the first of many prizes established in this century to encourage quality. The Caldecott Award—named after the witty nineteenth-century artist Randolph Caldecott—was begun in 1938 for the best illustrations by an American artist. Specialization had crept into the world of prizes; in 1977, the National Council of Teachers of English gave their first annual children's poetry award, to David McCord.

Committed editors, publishers, and librarians, as well as the incentive of the marketplace—these helped to boost interest in children's books in the first few decades of the century. Fortunately at the same time a growing group of talented writers and artists chose to work in the children's field. Of course many popular books in the 1920s and 1930s had been written decades before. Alcott's *Little Women* remained a favorite, for instance; so did Twain's books. But after World War I, new authors on both sides of the Atlantic began producing works that would be classics.

The Englishman A. A. Milne created the simple-minded teddy bear, *Winnie-the-Pooh*, for his son in 1926. Two years later, Wanda Gág told the still-popular story of the man who went out to get his wife a cat, could not settle on which was best, and came home with

Gág's *Millions of Cats*, first published in 1928, is still popular today. (Illustration reprinted by permission of Coward, McCann & Geoghegan, Inc., from *Millions of Cats* by Wanda Gág. Copyright © 1928 by Coward-McCann, Inc.; renewal copyright © 1956 by Robert Janssen.)

Millions of Cats. In the early 1930s, the American writer Laura Ingalls Wilder wrote the first in a series of books about log-cabin life in Wisconsin, *Little House in the Big Woods*.

American children benefited after World War I from an influx of authors and artists from Europe who crossed the ocean seeking artistic freedom; many turned to children's books. Padraic Colum from Ireland, who was to provide elegant retellings of Greek and Norse myths, was one. Kurt Wiese from Germany, who was to illustrate the story of a runaway duck in Marjorie Flack's *The Story about Ping*, was another.

Other publishers and writers after the turn of the century were less interested in quality for young customers than cash. The newest successor to the chapman was a writer and business genius named Edward Stratemeyer (1862–1930). Educated on dime novels—he grew up on Alger's stories and never went to college—he wrote his first story on a brown wrapping paper while working at a tobacco store and sold it for $75. It was a lick of sweet profit. In a short time, equipped with pen name Arthur M. (for "Million") Winfield, he began selling stories to children's magazines as fast as he could write them. He then turned to dime novels signed with other pseudonyms, such as Jim Bowie, Nat Woods, and Jim Daly.

Stratemeyer's biggest break came when Admiral George Dewey routed the Spanish fleet in Manila Bay in May, 1898. At the time, Stratemeyer's latest book—about boys on a battleship—was lying fallow in a safe at a Boston publishing house, Lothrop, Lee and Shepard, where Stratemeyer had submitted it. After Dewey's victory, an editor at the house remembered the manuscript and asked the author to rewrite it with Dewey at the helm. The request was no real challenge for plot-wise Stratemeyer; in a few days he produced *Under Dewey at Manila*, which sold out edition after edition.

In a few more years, Stratemeyer had set up his own syndicate to turn out books. He sat in a small New York office, dictated plot outlines, hired hack writers to turn them into books, and sold the manuscripts to publishers. The Rover Boys, Tom Swift, the Hardy Boys, Nancy Drew—all sprang from Stratemeyer's dime-novel mind. All sold—and sell today—at prices children can afford without asking parents for the money, or approval, to read them.

At his death in 1930, he had conceived or written more than 800 books, and he left an estate of $1 million (Egoff, 1969, pp. 41–61). His characters outlived him; in the late 1970s, the Hardy Boys and Nancy Drew books were selling at the rate of 5 million copies a year (*Publishers Weekly*, Feb. 28, 1977), and Nancy and the boys had their own TV show.

Was it literature? No, Stratemeyer did not add a jot to the library of good literature that was built in this century. Profit was his passion, and the mass market was the way to profit. His work was not far removed from the industry that has grown in the past few decades, manufacturing what writer and editor Selma Lanes calls "products in book form" (1971, p. 113). Chapmen used to display their books next to trinkets, and department stores today sell booklike items next to plastic-wrapped toys at check-out counters. Scratch-and-sniff books, shape books, touch-and-feel books—none of them relies on good writing or illustration; all depend on marketing opinions about what will sell at the supermarket.

"What can follow 3-D storybooks, pop-ups supreme, books that double as blocks, and others with magnetic pages?" Selma Lanes wonders. "It is possible that some publisher will eventually take the mordant remark of one British author of juveniles as a challenge: 'Kids like bangs. What about a book that explodes?' " (p. 127).

In 1964, Harriet's use of the word "damned" caused
the book to be removed from some library shelves.
(Illustration from *Harriet the Spy*, written and
illustrated by Louise Fitzhugh. Copyright © 1964 by
Louise Fitzhugh. By permission of Harper & Row,
Publishers, Inc.)

The Child as Young Adult: 1964

The field of children's books exploded in the twentieth century. By
1976, the number published for children each year had risen to
2,222, more than four times the number published annually at the
turn of the century. Who was the child in these books?

There were many. Psychologists and teachers alike spread the
word in the course of the century that each child was different, and
that childhood itself divided into many phases. Some, like children

463

in the Wilder *Little House* books, grew up in a family nest. Others, like Mark Twain's Tom Sawyer and Huck Finn, rebelled against family and struck out on their own. And others, particularly in the 1960s, appeared on the page as young adults, often independent of their parents, facing real social problems with no magic sword or Sunday School lessons to save them.

The benchmark for such books is *Harriet the Spy* (1964), by Louise Fitzhugh, the story of a New York City girl. Harriet's parents are so busy they entrust their daughter to a nurse. By the time she turns 11, Harriet has settled on a career plan: she wants to be a writer. She begins by keeping observations about people she knows in a notebook. She writes honestly, and alienates classmates when they find her notebook and read about themselves.

Harriet was too real for some adults. At one point, Harriet says "I'll be *damned* if I'll go to dancing school" (p. 83). Even though her mother reprimands her, that *"damned"* revived an old-fashioned uproar. In some libraries, the book was kept off the shelf. Other libraries required a note from home before children could read the book. The furor settled down, and within the next few years, books on sex, drugs, divorce, racial discrimination, and death followed Harriet into the thicket of what came to be called "new realism."

There was nothing new about the controversy over new realism. Twain's books had faced similar attempts at censorship about sixty years before. A century before that, Mrs. Trimmer had given uncompromising directions about what children should not read. School boards today often debate what books are fit for children's eyes, arguing from cultural or religious criteria just the way the Puritans did. Parents today pull out well-worn threads of argument from John Newbery's time about whether books should enlighten or entertain.

Today's teachers and librarians are often caught in the middle. There, sometimes, they may be tempted to turn censor themselves. At other times they might find themselves cheering at the jocular rallying cry of Margaret Coughlin of the Library of Congress, who writes: "Intellectual freedom and children's books have a sandy path to travel; the best way to fight clear of the boggy mire is to hang the censors, and hold onto the books with both hands" (1977, p. 147).

But that might lead to a lot of hangings. Friends as well as prudes and bigots might be executed. A more realistic cry might be: hold on to common sense about who the child is. Find the censor in yourself—that little voice that commands you to teach something at the very sight of a child—and tell the voice to keep quiet in the presence of a new book, at least until the child in you can say how good it is.

ISSUE

IS THE "NEW DIDACTICISM" DIFFERENT FROM THE OLD?

"Stories for free children," designed to attack racism and unequal treatment for sexes, began appearing in books and papers produced by feminist publishers in the late 1960's and in periodicals like *Ms* by 1971. . . .

Rather than reinforcing the prevailing views of morality and social order, as didactic writers for children have always done, authors of these contemporary stories deliberately challenge the existing standards and established institutions and stimulate the young reader to search for alternative understandings of moral issues. Social commentators and political theorists from Plato through Hitler have addressed the cultural impact of children's fiction, but they have always assumed that literature for children should reinforce conservative positions held by adults. Because the didacticism in stories for free children encourages children to question the teachings of the church, school, and law, as well as the personal relationships within their home, the aims of the writers of this new fiction are decidedly different from those of didactic writers for children throughout the centuries. (pp. 41–42)

McDowell, Margaret B. "New Didacticism: Stories for Free Children," *Language Arts*, January 1977, pp. 41–47.

It came as no surprise when, in an attempt to correct misconceptions, fill vacuums, and present the liberated woman's point of view, feminist writers rushed into the children's book field. . . .

These books (whose purpose is social activism rather than an aesthetic experience) are just as surely tracts in their own way—offering codes that tell the child how to act, what to know, and what to value—as were the manners-and-morals sermons of the past. They are just as noncreative, stultifying, limiting, and pat.

Any literature written for a specific social-activist purpose to serve special interests, whether women's liberation or whatever is not literature. Ultimately, such propaganda hurts the cause; more importantly, it hurts children. (p. 256)

Bingham, Jane M., and Grayce Scholt. "Books for Special Experiences," *Top of the News*, April 1976, pp. 253–260.

Do you think the aims of "stories for free children" are different from those of earlier didactic writers? Why or why not? Is the way in which they are written different? Perhaps you might want to compare a current "story for free children" with one of the "manners-and-morals sermons of the past."

SUMMARY

1 For centuries, critics like *Sarah Trimmer*, a British writer and editor who died in 1810, have judged children's books by what the books taught. During the same centuries, children themselves have often been able to read books that entertained them, even when books failed to teach currently popular ideas. Arguments over the uses of literature—frequently over whether books should *teach* or *entertain* or both—recur century after century. Tracing the lines of debate can be useful for teachers and librarians today.

2 At the heart of debates about children's literature is the question raised in Chapter 1: Who is the child? It is possible to chart at least four different answers which have been offered over the past few centuries. Adults today may find it useful to look at their own views of children and see how those views may have been influenced by philosophies from previous ages.

3 *The child in need of salvation.* Seventeenth-century Puritans believed that children would go to hell unless they lived a sinless life on earth. So the Puritans' extraordinarily didactic books preached the joy of death after faultless living according to stringent standards. *James Janeway's A Token for Children*, published about 1671, was typical in telling stories of exemplary children who died happily. Ballads and fairy tales were banned by unwritten law in the new colonies, but the preachy books aimed at saving souls got some competition—at least in England—from *chapbooks*, inexpensively printed editions of adventure, fantasy, and humor, often picked up from traditional literature.

4 *The child as sensible student.* Late in the seventeenth century, English philosopher *John Locke* suggested that learning could be pleasurable. The idea gained currency in the early eighteenth century as Puritanism faded. In the changing climate, publisher *John Newbery* produced books "for the Instruction and Amusement" of children, including the moralistic—but action-filled—*History of Little Goody Two-Shoes*. Around the time of the American Revolution, Newbery's books began infiltrating the colonies, pirated by a Massachusetts printer named *Isiah Thomas*. At the same time, another philosopher, *Jean Jacques Rousseau*, suggested that children were inherently sensible and could learn for themselves through experience and activity. The philosophy spawned dozens of *moral tales* aimed at training children to be good. American writers such as *Samuel Goodrich* (who wrote about Peter Parley) and *Jacob Abbott* (who related the adventures of Rollo) loaded their tales with lessons.

5 *The child out of school.* In the course of the nineteenth century,

however, children's books changed. *Lewis Carroll*'s *Alice's Adventures in Wonderland*, first published in 1865, exemplifies what had happened: the story has no moral, and even mocks earlier writers who insisted on teaching lessons in literature. The nineteenth century saw the renaissance of folktales and fairy tales, stimulated by the linguistic studies of *Jakob and Wilhelm Grimm* and others. At about the same time, *Mark Twain* produced realistic stories—*Tom Sawyer* and *Huckleberry Finn*—about believable and rebellious Missouri boys. *Dime novels*—frontier adventures, modern war epics—flourished, as did the cliché-filled rags-to-riches stories of *Horatio Alger Jr.*

6 *Children of the twentieth century*. Views of the child became much more complicated in the twentieth century. The number of titles increased, magazines began to specialize, *Sigmund Freud* suggested that childhood had a profound influence on adulthood, and publishing houses took on editors whose sole job was acquiring books for the growing children's market. After World War I, an influx of authors and artists from Europe to America—including *Padraic Colum* and *Kurt Wiese*—contributed to growing quality in the literature. By the 1960s, there were many views of children; childhood itself appeared to be divided into many phases. In one perspective, exemplified in *Louise Fitzhugh*'s *Harriet the Spy*, the child has gained a measure of independence from parents and from strict social codes of behavior. Harriet is in some ways a young adult.

7 Many views of children that were held in other times survive today. The particular view of the child held by teachers, librarians, school board members, or parents may sway their choice of books or even lead them to support censorship. *Margaret Coughlin* suggests, "Hang the censors." Short of that, teachers and librarians can be aware of their own views of children, and at least try to measure books by sound literary standards as popular tastes change.

BIBLIOGRAPHY

Adult References

Allen, Carolyn A. "Early American Children's Books at the American Antiquarian Society," *The Horn Book*, April 1976, pp. 117–131.

Avery, Gillian. "Fashions in Children's Fiction," *Children's Literature in Education,* vol. 12, pp. 10–19, 1973.

Avi. "Children's Literature: The American Revolution," *Top of the News*, Winter 1977, pp. 149–161.

Bettelheim, Bruno. "The Care and Feeding of Monsters," *Ladies Home Journal*, March 1969, p. 48.

————. *The Uses of Enchantment* (New York: Knopf, 1976).

Bingham, Jane M., and Grayce Scholt. "Books for Special Experiences," *Top of the News*, April 1976, pp. 253–260.

Clemens, Samuel L. *Autobiography*, vol. 2 (New York: Harper, 1924).

Coughlin, Margaret. "Guardians of the Young," *Top of the News*, Winter 1977, pp. 137–148.

Council on Interracial Books for Children. *Human and Anti-Human Values in Children's Books, A Content Rating Instrument for Educators and Concerned Parents* (New York: Racism and Sexism Resource Center for Educators, 1976).

Egoff, Sheila, G. T. Stubbs, and L. F. Ashley (eds.). *Only Connect: Readings on Children's Literature* (New York: Oxford University Press, 1969).

Johannsen, Albert. *The House of Beadle and Adams and Its Dime and Nickel Novels*, vol. 1 (Norman, Okla: University of Oklahoma Press, 1950).

Johnson, Janice (ed.). *The Bowker Annual of Library and Book Trade Information* (New York: R. R. Bowker, 1971).

Lamb, Charles, in E. V. Lucas (ed.), *Letters of Charles Lamb* (New Haven: Yale University Press, 1935).

Lanes, Selma. *Down the Rabbit Hole* (New York: Atheneum, 1971).

Locke, John. *On Politics and Education* (Roslyn, N.Y.: Walter J. Black, 1947). (*Some Thoughts Concerning Education* was first published in 1693.)

Maxwell, Margaret. "The Perils of the Imagination: Pre-Victorian Children's Literature and the Critics," *Children's Literature in Education*, vol. 13, pp. 45–52, 1974.

McDowell, Margaret B. "New Didacticism: Stories for Free Children," *Language Arts*, January 1977, pp. 41–47.

St. John, Judith. "Mrs. Trimmer—Guardian of Education," *The Horn Book*, February 1970, pp. 20–25.

Silberberg, Sophie C., and John Donovan. "Fifty Years of Children's Book Week: Fifty Years of Independent American Children's Book Publishing," *The Horn Book*, December 1969, pp. 702–711.

Townsend, John Rowe. *Written for Children* (Philadelphia: Lippincott, 1965).

————. "Didacticism in Modern Dress," *The Horn Book*, April 1967, pp. 159–164.

Children's Book References

Alcott, Louisa May. *Little Women.* (Boston: Little, Brown, 1868).

*Alger, Horatio. *Ragged Dick* (Boston: Loring, 1868).

Carroll, Lewis. *Alice in Wonderland* (New York: Norton, 1971). (*Alice's Adventures in Wonderland* was first published in 1865; *Through the Looking Glass* in 1871.)

Comenius, John Amos. *Orbis Pictus* (Syracuse, N.Y.: C. W. Bardeen, 1887). (Reissued by Singing Tree Press, Detroit Mich., 1968.)

*Farquharson, Martha (pseudonym for Martha Farquharson Finley). *Elsie Dinsmore* (New York: M. W. Dodd, 1867).

Fitzhugh, Louise. *Harriet the Spy* (New York: Harper, 1964).

Flack, Marjorie. *The Story about Ping*, illus. Kurt Wiese (New York: Viking, 1933).

Gág, Wanda. *Millions of Cats* (New York: Coward-McCann, 1928).

*Goodrich, Samuel Griswold. *The Tales of Peter Parley about America* (Boston: S. G. Goodrich, 1827).

*Harris, Joel Chandler. *Uncle Remus, His Songs and His Sayings*, illus. Frederick S. Church and James H. Moser (New York: D. Appleton and Co., 1881).

Haviland, Virginia, and Margaret N. Coughlin (eds.). *Yankee Doodle's Literary Sampler of Prose, Poetry and Pictures* (New York: Crowell, 1974).

The History of Little Goody Two-Shoes (New York: H. W. Hewet, co. 1855).

*Janeway, James. *A Token for Children* (Boston: Z. Fowle, 1771).

A Little Pretty Pocket-Book (Worcester, Mass.: Isaiah Thomas, 1787).

Milne, A. A. *Winnie-the-Pooh*, illus. Ernest Shepard (New York: Dutton, 1926).

Ms. Foundation. *Free to Be . . . You and Me* (New York: McGraw-Hill, 1974).

Sendak, Maurice. *Where the Wild Things Are* (New York: Harper, 1963).

Twain, Mark (pseudonym for Samuel Clemens). *The Adventures of Tom Sawyer* (New York: Harper, 1876).

————. *The Adventures of Huckleberry Finn* (New York: Harper, 1884).

Wilder, Laura Ingalls. *Little House in the Big Woods*, illus. Garth Williams (New York: Harper, 1953). (1932)

---

*Excerpts of this book appear in Haviland and Coughlin's *Yankee Doodle's Literary Sampler of Prose, Poetry and Pictures* (New York: Crowell, 1974).

PART TWO

How do children encounter good books? How do they respond to what they read, and how can adults enhance their responses? Those are some of the questions explored in Part Two. Later chapters suggest how to group books into units and techniques for relating literature to other subjects. With Part One as a backdrop, these chapters are a guide to exploring and working with books and children, day to day.

LITERA-
TURE
AND
CHILDREN
TO-
GETHER

CHAPTER 11

PRESENT-ING

LITERA-TURE

BRINGING CHILDREN IN TOUCH WITH BOOKS

Dolores Vogliano, a New York City librarian, had taken *Harry the Dirty Dog* (Zion, 1956) to Central Park one day when she ran into trouble with a stray German shepherd.

It was the first of a series of summer story-reading sessions in the park, and seventy-five preschool children had turned out. In addition, half a dozen newspaper reporters had been taking notes on her and *Harry,* and a television crew had hung a microphone around her neck and kept reminding her to look at the camera. Distractions tugged at her like a yapping puppy on a short leash. In a loud voice, she began reading the story, about a white dog with black spots who gets so dirty that his family does not recognize him.

Then, suddenly, a real German shepherd wandered into the crowd of seated children. He rambled toward Mrs. Vogliano. In an instant, he had challenged *Harry's* hold over the children's interest. He had also badly frightened Mrs. Vogliano, who was terrified of real dogs.

She froze. She knew that if she got hysterical, the children might get hysterical. The dog ambled up to her and sniffed.

What would you have done?

Mrs. Vogliano looked down at the frightening dog and took a deep breath. "Hello, Harry," she said. The children laughed. The dog trotted away, and Mrs. Vogliano returned to the book.

It was an unusually chaotic situation. But teachers, librarians, and parents who have tried to present good books to children will recognize familiar elements. Even in well-controlled classrooms or library situations, there are distractions. It begins to snow outside, or someone has to go to the bathroom, or someone has heard the book before and wants everyone to know it.

No one can stop all the distractions. Some, like Mrs. Vogliano, are so involved with the literature that not even intruding hounds can cripple their presentation.

Others, less skilled or involved, can become part of the problem, whether reading or telling stories. Joan Cass, a British educator, describes one storytelling session she observed where the teller strayed far from the material.

> I remember once seeing a story-teller mount a chair and stand on tiptoe to try to convey to a group of children how high the trees were in the forest she was describing; the children, sitting breathless with astonishment, were obviously waiting for her to fall off. (1967, p. 68)

Skillful presentation of books by adults can lead children to a love of good literature. (Nancy Hays/Monkmeyer Photo Service.)

Unlike most literature for adults, books for children often need a skillful broker—an adult to lead young readers to good writing. It takes more than common sense or good taste about literature to do it well. Common sense, for instance, might suggest that bold, dramatic gestures make storytelling more interesting to children. But most good tellers today avoid grandstanding gestures while presenting tales.

Chapters 1 to 10 of this book introduced the literature—to adults. The next few chapters suggest practical ways to introduce the literature to children.

THE IMPORTANCE OF PREPARATION

The key to a good presentation of literature, as suggested through all these chapters, is preparation. Mastering the material before you introduce it provides the freedom to present it well. Good presentation frees you to ride out distractions, to be aware of children's reactions, to change the program on the spot when necessary, to make literature fresh and new.

It may seem paradoxical: how can studying a book or poem or story until it is second nature help you present it as if for the first time?

A famous storyteller, Ruth Sawyer, suggests an answer in a story about an actor and a little boy.

> I knew an elderly man once who took his small grandson to see his friend Joseph Jefferson in a performance of *Rip Van Winkle*. It was toward the end of Jefferson's life and he must have given more than a thousand performances of that one part. The following Sunday Mr. Jefferson was invited to the family dinner that the little boy might never forget this truly great artist. "What night did you see the play?" Mr. Jefferson asked. And the answer provided the old actor with one of the greatest tributes of his career: "I saw you on the night you went to sleep on the mountains and woke up after twenty years, a very old man."
>
> To the little boy that was the one night that particular incident could have happened. On other nights the play must have been quite different. (1970, p. 145)

The material meant so much to the actor that he could present it freshly each night. Mrs. Sawyer's advice to people who want to be storytellers is: Make the story "live for you to the point that you can make it live for others" (pp. 144-5).

Of course, the actor or actress has a stage, props, costume, and lights to help bring a role to life. But those who present literature usually have control over the setting, too. Even before you enter the scene, the way a room is set up can nurture interest in good books or stories.

Setting Up to Stimulate Interest

Visualize two classrooms.

In one, the teacher has set aside a corner for books and magazines. Oversized pillows on the floor make this reading center comfortable, and books are arranged informally—their covers showing—on shelves and tables used to divide the corner from the rest of the room. Time for informal reading is built into the daily plan, and the teacher regularly reads books aloud.

In the other, the teacher also reads to the class, and children get encouragement to read at home. But individual reading for pleasure

An inviting book display encourages children to read.
(Kenn Goldblatt/Design Photographers International,
Inc.)

does not take up class time. Nor is there space in the classroom for
bookshelves or displays.

Which classroom nurtures more interest in literature? The
teacher in the second classroom may be conscientious about presenting books, and certainly pays lip service to the importance of reading. But the setting does not indicate that the teacher puts high
value in literature. In the first room, there is space for books. The

477

covers are far more inviting than the books' spines that children see when they look at a row of close-packed books on the teacher's desk. Allowing the children to talk in the reading center permits them to read passages they enjoy to other children, the way adults do when they find literature they particularly like.

Teachers or librarians can set up a reading center in the course of a few hours. From then on, an adult should tend the center regularly to keep children's interest alive. Here are some techniques that have been used to make centers attractive for young readers.

In many centers, a bulletin board on one wall provides room for readers' written comments on books they like or dislike. There is space as well for children's drawings and paintings inspired by books.

Teachers often encourage children to select and take out books from centers on their own. Children are given a simple rule of thumb to decide whether they will have a hard time with unfamiliar words. The child is told to try reading one or two pages, and to count the unfamiliar words on each page. If there are more than five on a page, the book may be too difficult for now. This quick test should not prevent any child from taking out a difficult book. Nor should children be discouraged from choosing books below the reading level of books used in formal instruction.

The collection of books in the center changes regularly to offer varied fare. The teacher or librarian can display several books on the same subject, or several works by the same author. (Chapter 13 suggests strategies for grouping several books into a small collection.) In any case, the center regularly offers new material.

A reading center invites children toward books. Similarly, controlling the setting when reading aloud or telling stories or using audiovisual material helps bring children closer to literature you present.

New ideas on how to arrange a room when presenting a book have led in recent years to more comfort and informality. At one time, for example, administrators of the New York City Library system suggested that all children hearing stories should sit in chairs. Now, listeners often sit on stools. Students in school once sat in military rows, their desks screwed to the floor. In modern classrooms, desks are freestanding so children are freer to change positions. Sometimes they sit on carpeted floors or mats or cushions. Teachers themselves often sit on lower chairs to face children at their level.

Even the most informal setting, however, has to be carefully planned to keep distractions from intruding. Whenever possible, for instance, children should sit facing away from diversions like bright lights, other children in movement, or other backgrounds that siphon away interest. If you are working in a park near an attractive statue, resist the impulse to turn the statue into a backdrop for your presentation. Place children between you and the statue. In a classroom, when possible, face the window so children can focus on you and the literature instead of the scene outside.

Creating the proper setting is often a matter of common sense about small detail. But small detail can often make the difference between fascination or boredom with literature.

Several teachers were grumbling one day as they took an advance look at some filmstrips based on books. The color was dull, they complained. The films could not be used in the classroom. After the showing, they met other teachers who argued that in an earlier showing, the strips had been fine. After a long discussion, the two groups of teachers recognized what had gone wrong. It was a problem of petty detail—of setting—but it was enough to make the pictures pale: the grumblers had been projecting the filmstrips onto a yellow wall. A slight change of setting, projecting onto a white wall, brought the colors back.

MASTERING MATERIAL

Experienced teachers do not begin to present literature to a group of children—even in a relaxed, well-planned setting—without getting themselves set as well. Before considering means of presentation—filmstrip, reading aloud, storytelling—they weigh the quality of the literature.

A story chosen for presentation to children, for instance, "must be one the storyteller likes to live with, one she or he enjoys so much he wants others to enjoy it too. No good storyteller will bother with anything that is cheap or mediocre," writes veteran storyteller Ruth Tooze (in Cohen, 1972, p. 42). And books chosen for reading aloud should be excellent literature: the time it takes to speak should not be wasted on commonplace material.

Chapter 1 suggests other general criteria for evaluating children's books, and subsequent chapters present criteria for judging quality in each genre of the literature.

Choosing and Previewing Books

Apart from quality, the choice of books to read aloud depends largely on the children.

To begin with, does the selection offer good literature that chil-

Teachers often read books aloud to children who
cannot read themselves but who enjoy hearing them,
such as the books about Ramona. (Illustration from p.
53 by Alan Tiegreen in *Ramona and Her Father* by
Beverly Cleary. Copyright © 1977 by Beverly Cleary.
By permission of William Morrow & Co., Inc.)

dren might not choose on their own? If a group of third-graders has
just finished E. B. White's *Charlotte's Web* (1952), for instance,
maybe they would be interested in hearing a quite different spider
story. A teacher could select *Anansi the Spider* (1972), a retelling of
an African folktale by Gerald McDermott, or another African tale,
Joyce Cooper Arkhurst's *The Adventures of Spider* (1964). Another
possiblity is *The Web in the Grass* (1972), which is realistic fiction
about a spider by Berniece Freschet, with captivating illustrations by
Roger Duvoisin. Teachers can also read aloud books that children
would not choose because of their difficulty, but might enjoy because of their subjects.

In addition to providing literary variety, do books you select offer
some familiar elements? Are there people or emotions the children

will recognize? Robert Peck's *Soup* (1974), for instance, a recollection of rural Vermont when Peck was a boy, serves up familiar feelings about what it is like to accept a dare. City children have no trouble identifying the feeling. Suburban or rural children, meanwhile, recognize the situation in Ezra Jack Keats's *Goggles!* (1969) when two young boys in a vacant city lot are threatened by older boys. Settings for fantasy or folktales may also be far away from the child's time and place, but the actions and feelings of characters should seem close to home.

Some books set off a special flash of recognition at certain seasons. Fourth-graders, for instance, like to hear Rebecca Caudill's *A Certain Small Shepherd* (1965) around Christmas time. First-graders enjoy listening to Edna Mitchell Preston's *One Dark Night* (1969) just before Halloween.

These books are well received by most children when read aloud. If you have not yet tried out a book on children, sometimes you can get a feeling for whether it will capture their interest by reading passages to yourself and imagining your students' reactions. Does the style offer some change of pace for reading aloud, or are there long sections unrelieved by dialogue, or description unrelieved by narrative action? Is it clear in passages of dialogue who is speaking? Are sentences too involved to permit you to catch your breath?

It is also important to consider the size of the group that will hear the reading.

One preschool teacher picked up Brian Wildsmith's *Puzzles* (1970) in the school library and considered how she would introduce it to her class of ten children. The splashy illustrations in the book are bold enough to be visible to a large group. But *Puzzles* calls on readers to solve small mysteries contained in the pictures—and that requires getting a close view of each page and having a chance to try to answer the questions in the text. One illustration shows an Eskimo fishing through the ice in front of a group of igloos. His footprints lead back to one of the icy houses. "Can you find his home?" the text asks. In planning her presentation, the teacher realized that the book would fare far better in a small group. She decided to read the book to just two children at a time.

She was right. During the reading, a 5-year-old boy listened to the question about the Eskimo's house, and pointed at the biggest igloo. Footprints, however, led to another igloo. In a large group, the boy's answer might have been dismissed quickly as other children competed for a chance to respond. Working with the pair of children, the teacher had time to ask the boy why he had made his choice.

"Because it's the biggest house," he said.

"Why did he live in the biggest house?" the teacher asked.

"To have room for all his furniture," the boy said.

The interchange gave the teacher new insight into the boy's reasoning processes and imagination, and gave the child pleasure in expressing what he saw in the book. *Puzzles* had been a good choice for a small group.

Sometimes the size of the book suggests the size of the group for which it is appropriate.

William Steig's *The Amazing Bone* (1976) is big enough—9 by 11 inches—for reading to a group of twenty children, if they are seated closely. They could pick out detail in drawings showing the kidnapping of Pearl, a pig, by a fox. And they could see her joyous expression after a magic bone she has found has shrunk the fox to the size of a mouse.

Another book about a fox with alarming dinner plans is Beatrix Potter's *The Tale of Jemima Puddle-Duck*. Illustrations play a major role in telling this story about a "bushy long-tailed gentleman"— the fox—whose plans to make a meal of Jemima are foiled by a stout-hearted farm dog. But the pages measure just 4 by 6 inches; the dimensions make the book a poor choice for reading to more than one or two children at a time.

In sum, selection of books to read aloud depends first on literary quality, but other considerations should sway your choice: What are children reading on their own—and can you provide variety? Will actions and feelings of characters seem close to home? Is the group too large for the book?

Careful selection alone, however, does not ensure a good presentation. Suppose you had chosen Mary and R. A. Smith's *Long Ago Elf* (1968) for your class of first-graders. Now try reading this part of it aloud as if your class were listening:

> By blue-white shimmer
> Through thorn bush shiver
> By firefly glimmer
> Through tall grass quiver. (p. 17)

Many who have not read this passage before lose their tongues in the thorn bush or tall grass. The point is that preparation also requires reading material through to yourself, preferably aloud, to avoid annoying surprises.

Watch out for Italian words, for example, in *Watch Out for the Chicken Feet in Your Soup* (1974) by Tomie de Paola. Those who have not read ahead may trip over the greetings of a woman to her grandson: "Joey, mio bambino!" Reading ahead of time can ease you

The title of this book is expressed in this illustration. (From the book *Watch Out for Chicken Feet in Your Soup* by Tomie De Paola. Copyright © 1974 by Tomie DePaola. Published by Prentice-Hall, Inc., Englewood Cliffs, N.J. 07632.)

over individual words that might otherwise obstruct your presentation.

Studying de Paola's book before introducing it to children also turns up an important discovery about its format. In most books, the story begins after the title page. But here there is important text before the title page, when Joey tells his friend:

> "Now listen, Eugene, my grandma is nice. But she pinches my cheeks a lot and her house is full of funny old stuff. She's always cooking and she talks funny, too. And, Eugene, . . ."

Then comes the title: *Watch Out for the Chicken Feet in Your Soup*. Grandmother greets the two boys on the following page and offers them soup. Eugene discovers the chicken foot in his bowl soon after the book begins. The significance of his find rests on material presented before the title page.

Other surprises may await readers far into a book. The back cover of the paperback edition of Judy Blume's entertaining *Then Again, Maybe I Won't* (1971) reports that the story is about Tony Miglione and his problems when his family moves to an affluent community on Long Island. One problem is a friend who shoplifts. And, the cover blurb continues, "there were the growing-up problems that all boys must face." It takes a reading of the book to discover that among the problems is embarrassment over an unwanted erection one day when Tony stands at a blackboard in front of the whole class. The scene will distract some preteenaged listeners so much that their attention can be scarcely be recovered. For other groups, Tony's problem may stimulate discussion. In either case, the teacher needs to be prepared, and the first step is a close reading.

But reading out loud requires more than a clear understanding of the material. A lackluster voice or breakneck reading rate can spoil even the best stories. A clear, expressive voice can add life to literature and encourage children to ask for more. Speaking well also requires practice, but since it is often hard for people to hear their own voices, you may want to ask for help from friends or classmates in finding strengths and weaknesses.

One way to get a clear idea of how you sound to others is to read one or two books—one picture book, say, and an excerpt from a junior novel—out loud to half a dozen adults. Ask them to rate your reading frankly on copies of a chart like this:

	Excellent	Satisfactory	Needs improvement (specify the problem)
Rate			
Volume			
Enunciation			
Expression			
Eye contact			
Showing of illustrations (if appropriate)			

Your evaluators need not sign their names. Look for patterns when you read the charts, and then make an effort to correct weak points. Practice. Recording yourself when you read to children, and later listening to the tape, may also give surprising insight on how you could be a better reader. Even experienced teachers find that tapes can turn up irritating quirks of expression. (A transcript of such a tape appears at the end of the chapter.)

Ciardi's poem about Sylvester, whose proposal of marriage was received by a kangaroo, demonstrates that poetry requires preparation to be read well. (From *The Man Who Sang The Sillies* by John Ciardi, drawings by Edward Gorey. Copyright © 1961 by John Ciardi. Used by permission of J. B. Lippincott Company.)

Choosing carefully, previewing what you have chosen and practicing aloud—all these preparations make it easier to maintain children's interests in books you present.

Preparing for Poetry Reading

John Ciardi's poem "Sylvester" (in *The Man Who Sang the Sillies*, 1961) contains a challenge for anyone who chooses to read it aloud. Try it:

> Sylvester wrote to Mary Lou.
> Said, "Will you marry me?"
> Replied a Lady Kangaroo,
> "My darling, I agree."

485

"Agree to what?" Sylvester cried.
"I've never before seen *you*!"
"Well, no," the Kangaroo replied,
"But though *that's* perfectly true,

Here is your letter sent to me."
"To *you*! Don't be absurd!"
"Don't tamper with the mails," said she,
"A man must keep his word!"

"My letter was sent to Mary Lou!"
"It came to *me*!" "Agreed.
But you saw it wasn't addressed to you!"
"How could I?—I can't read."

"Then how could you read the letter
But not how it was addressed?"
'I could say your writing got better,
Or I could say I just guessed.

The point is," said the Kangaroo,
"—And the mailman will agree—
Whatever you wrote to Mary Lou,
The letter came to *me*.

You must either learn to write what you mean
Or to mean what you write!" she cried.
"And though I'd rather not make a scene
I insist you must make me your bride!"

"We'll just see about that," said Sylvester.
  "No doubt
We will," said the Kangaroo.
—And how do you think it all turned out?
—I only wish I knew. (p. 21)

The challenge is how to indicate who is talking. One solution is
to use a slightly higher voice for Kangaroo, and a slightly lower and
gruff voice for Sylvester, but it should be obvious from trying to read
the poem cold that switching voices takes practice. Even after two
or three attempts, some readers still find themselves playing Sylvester when they mean to be a Lady Kangaroo.

The point is that many poems require at least as much practice as
prose before reading aloud. Studying and reading poems before class
can help prevent clumsy presentations that cloud meaning. Here, for
instance, is a poem—Judith Thurman's "Pretending to Sleep" (in

Flashlight and Other Poems, 1977)—with another kind of potential
problem for readers.

> Pretending to sleep
> in the back seat
> I squeeze my eyelids
> like the wings
> of a caught moth.
> They flutter—
> but I breathe deep.
>
> I suck my cheeks in
> So I can't grin
> when they whisper,
> *"We won't wake her."*
> I'm a good faker. (p. 15)

Teachers or librarians who have not read the poem before presenting it to children might tend to stop at the end of lines, producing
odd fragments such as "like the wings," which would baffle young
listeners.

In addition to practicing poetry they plan to read, some teachers
find it helpful to memorize lines that they can call up at appropriate
moments. Short verses can enhance a child's joy at the first snow-
fall, or give support when a friend moves away, or add magic to
everyday objects. For instance, Shel Silverstein's "Magical Eraser"
(1974) turns an ordinary pencil into a fantastic wand.

> She wouldn't believe
> This pencil has
> A magical eraser.
> She said I was a silly moo,
> She said I was a liar too,
> She dared me prove that it was true,
> And so what could I do—
> I erased her! (p. 99)

There are other examples of poems to match children's everyday
experiences in Chapter 4.

The Hours before Story Hour: Preparation for Storytelling

Preparation for storytelling should never involve line-by-line
memorization. "It is extremely improbable that anyone who
memorizes will be able so to abandon word-by-word commitment as

A book which relies on its illustrations to tell part of the story is better read than told. (Reproduced with the permission of Farrar, Straus & Giroux, Inc. from *The Judge: An Untrue Tale* by Harve Zemach, illustrated by Margot Zemach. Text Copyright © 1969 by Harve Zemach, pictures copyright © 1969 by Margot Zemach.)

to lose all evidence of it, and be able to give back the story with that perfect art of seeming improvisation,'' writes Ruth Sawyer (1970, p. 142).

Storytellers convey action, dialogue, and colorful scene without using the exact words of books or scripts in their presentation. Often, however, storytellers begin with printed stories. Some books translate to spoken stories better than others. Written stories that adapt well for telling have concise, action-filled plots. They begin boldly, and build toward a climax. They offer drama and emotional appeal.

There are other considerations in choosing stories. Here are three action-filled tales, well liked in book form, all told and illustrated by Harve and Margot Zemach.

Only one is appropriate for a beginning storyteller.

The Judge (1969) tells a story in verse about five prisoners brought to court. Each reports seeing a horrible monster coming closer. The haughty judge throws each in jail. As prisoner number five is carted away, the monster appears in the window behind the judge. The creature invades the courtroom and, in the final pictures, gobbles up the old man.

Is this a good story for telling? No, the story is better read and shown than told. For one thing, the illustrations carry the tale to its conclusion. For another, the verses lose force if translated into prose and retold in "seeming improvisation."

Duffy and the Devil (1973) is the story of a country maiden named Duffy who makes a pact with the devil. He will help her with spinning and knitting clothes for her employer, a squire. But at the end of three years, if she cannot guess the devil's name, he will take her away. At the last moment, she learns the name and the devil disappears—but so do all the things the devil has helped to spin and knit, including the clothes on the squire's back.

489

The story could be told without the illustrations, although they enrich the text. But the way the story is told is critical to its communication.

Here is one passage, when Squire Lovel is looking for a maid to help his old housekeeper. Try reading it aloud and then retelling it in your own words.

> On his way into the town he suddenly heard an awful screeching and hollering. The door of a cottage flew open and out ran a blubbering, bawling girl chased by an old woman who was clouting her with a broom and shouting, "You lazy bufflehead, you!"
>
> "What's all this about, auntie?" cried the squire. "What's the cause of this confloption with you and Duffy?"
>
> "Oh, your honour!" wailed the old woman. "What am I to do with this gashly girl? She gallivants with the boys all day long and never stops at home to boil the porridge, not knit the stockings, nor spin the yarn!"
>
> "Don't believe a word she says, your honour," spoke up the girl, dabbing at her teary eyes with a corner of her dusty apron. "I do all the work, I spin like a saint, I knit like an angel, and all I get for it is clouts and clumps."

Most beginning storytellers cannot convey the flavor of the language in their own words.

A Penny a Look (1971) is the shortest of the three books. It has few characters. While the illustrations and writing are well crafted, neither is essential to the story. The plot is interesting in itself. The book is good material to adapt for storytelling.

Once the teacher or librarian has chosen a story, the work of mastering it begins. Many storytellers use cards to help them recall tales they want to tell. Here, for example, is a set of cards for *A Penny a Look*.

1 Opening. "Once there were two brothers." One was "red-headed rascal" who everyone thought would get rich. Other was "lazy good-for-nothing" who everyone thought would never amount to much.

2 Red Head tells Lazy he's found map showing where one-eyed people live. Wants to capture one, bring him home, put him in cage, charge a penny a look, get rich. Insists Lazy go with him.

3 Two start on trip with map and rope. Go 500 miles in car. Lazy asks what one-eyed people eat. Red says scraps and crumbs.

4 Wade stream. Lazy asks if one-eyed person will be in cage all the time. Yes, Red says. One-eyed person won't try any tricks. "Don't worry," Red says.

5 Climb fence. Lazy asks if person will like being stared at. Red says he won't be able to do anything about it. "Don't worry," Red says.

6 Fly over desert in a balloon. Lazy says can't help feeling it's not right. Red says to forget worries and think about pennies.

7 Arrive at strange land. See one-eyed man. Run to catch him. Another appears, and then a whole group of one-eyed people.

8 Brothers are captured by the one-eyed men. They put Red in a cage. They charge a penny a look to see a two-eyed man with red hair.

9 Conclusion. Lazy is ignored because they can see he'll never amount to much. "So they let him collect the pennies. He didn't mind."

Storytellers might memorize the opening and concluding sentences of the tale. Occasionally, they memorize phrases from the body of the story, particularly when the words are repeated. Like the beginning and closing bars of a jazz composition, these sentences and phrases provide a set frame around improvisation in the middle of the piece. But like jazz-note variations, the words in the body of the tale will vary with each telling. The composition will remain the same, but the story will sound fresh each time it is told.

Finally, after careful preparation, the story becomes second nature. Then a storyteller is ready to present it as if no one had ever told it before.

One experienced librarian explained in an interview how she takes control of a story.

> I read a collection of folklore and see what appeals to me. If I find something, I read it over eight to ten times, then read it aloud and then try to tell it aloud. The first attempt without the book tells me what sections I'm weak in. I keep trying to tell it without the text. When I feel I have the flow, I go back to the text and pick up words that give the story its flavor.
>
> But I'm not memorizing. I cannot do that. It terrifies me. I'm sure if I memorized, I'd go cold. I'd freeze right in the middle of the story, worrying that I might forget the words.

Her method is similar to one suggested by Ruth Sawyer, "that of learning incident by incident, or picture by picture. Never word by word" (1970, p. 142).

PUTTING CHILDREN IN TOUCH WITH BOOKS AND TALES

Careful preparation eases the presentation of literature, freeing you to transmit your own enthusiasm and enjoyment of books, poetry, and stories. There are a few techniques to help you read books and tell stories while tailoring your presentation to a particular audience.

491

Reading Aloud

A third-grade teacher had won friends for author Beverly Cleary by reading *Henry Huggins* (1950) to her class. They liked the funny, realistic tale about a boy, a dog, and one episode in which guppies stage a population explosion in his mother's mason jars. About a month after the class had met Henry, the teacher introduced another Cleary character by calling on their previous experience with a book.

> I have a new book for you today. Its title is *Ramona the Pest*. It's by Beverly Cleary. She's the author who wrote about Henry Huggins, and you may be surprised to find that there are some people in this book you already know—like Henry Huggins.

This brief introduction stirred the same shivery anticipation children feel when they see a well-wrapped birthday present. The class was prepared to like what they found inside the covers: the story of one of Henry's younger neighbors and her rocky kindergarten career.

In a story continued for several days, a teacher can introduce a new installment with one or two sentences telling where the story left off. In intermediate grades, children themselves can explain what happened in the last segment. It is not necessary to recap the entire story each day; after several days of reading, a full retelling would require too much time.

During the reading itself, make sure all the children in your class have a chance to see any pictures. Some teachers and librarians are adept at reading upside down; they can hold the book in front of them and look over the top. Others hold the book to one side so the illustrations show while they are reading. A third technique—not quite as smooth and not quite as rewarding to children but more comfortable for some adults—is to alternate reading the text and showing the illustrations.

When a crowd of children fans out in front of you, move the book slowing in an arc from your right to your left so that every child can look.

Good preparation means that you should be familiar enough with the material so that as you read and show the book, you can maintain eye contact with many of the listeners. Observations of your audience allow you to gauge the reaction of your students, and to spot potential trouble—one child who is just beginning to wiggle, or another who has just pulled her scissors out of her pocket. A look from you may draw the child back into the story without stopping the reading. A nod of the head or twinkle in the eye can acknowledge stray comments without distracting the whole class.

ISSUE

DO GOOD STORIES NEED
NO INTRODUCTION?

When a new book is first introduced to the children, be sure to give the title of the book and the author's name. If the book immediately captures the fancy of the listeners, some children may wish to find in the library other books by the same author, or books containing similar contents. Many children will be already familiar with certain authors, and mention of a familiar name will set the youngsters to comparing the present story with ones read previously. The book jacket may present interesting information about the author and illustrator. These tidbits may be shared with the class, and they do much to make the story more meaningful and enjoyable for the children. (pp. 98–99)

> Whitehead, Robert. *Children's Literature: Strategies of Teaching*
> (Englewood Cliffs, N.J.: Prentice-Hall, 1968).

Never announce, "Today's story will be. . . ."As soon as the children know what story you are telling, they will comment, "Oh, I know that one, who wants to hear it again," or something similar. At the end of the story, you can give its name, but in any case, begin in a straightforward manner and end the same way. (p. 123)

Sivulich, Sandra Stroner. "Strategies for Presenting Literature," in Bernice E. Cullinan and Carolyn Carmichael (eds.), *Literature and Young Children* (Urbana, Ill.: National Council of Teachers of English, 1977).

How might you give the title and author following the telling or reading of a story and still capture children's interest? How could you announce them first and cope with a possible "I've heard that before" comment? Which procedure are you more likely to follow? Why?

How many animals can you see in this picture?

Some books call for participation during reading. (From *Brian Wildsmith's Puzzles* written and illustrated by Brian Wildsmith. Copyright © 1970 by Brian Wildsmith. Used by permission of the publisher, Franklin Watts, Inc.)

In many situations, on the other hand, teachers *want* students to speak up—about the literature. Young children get more involved in picture stories, for example, when they are given a chance to say what they see in illustrations, rather than merely listening to a teacher's description of what shows on the page. Some books call on children to chant, sing, or move (there are several examples in the next chapter). And children's spontaneous movements during reading can provide valuable clues about how they like what they are hearing.

One teacher gauges response by the movement and angle of her children's heads. "If they're interested, their faces look up at you," she said in an interview. "If they're bored, the heads nod, or turn to the side, or point toward the hair of the child in front of them."

The same teacher uses an interesting technique at the end of reading sessions to encourage children to seek out the books themselves. The idea works particularly well with 8- to 10-year-olds, she said. At the end of a reading, instead of passing books around, she puts them back in the reading center with their covers showing conspicuously. "The class gets curious," she said. "It may take a day or so, but sooner or later children visit the center looking for the books."

Telling Stories

Experienced teachers read their audiences while reading aloud. So do storytellers.

Virginia L. Swift, a librarian in New York City, learned the importance of reading an audience when she was telling a story in a city park one day. The setting was unusual. She was facing a pool, and tiny drops of fountain water drizzled on her and her audience of 12-year-old children. The story was scary: "Molly Whuppie," an English tale (in Jacobs, pp. 130–135) about a girl and an evil giant.

Miss Swift knew the story well enough to tell it while studying every face in the crowd of seated children. She soon noticed that one girl on the edge of the group was terrified. "She had blond hair and I imagine her complexion was usually pale," Miss Swift said in an interview. "But at that moment her face was white with fear."

What would you have done?

Miss Swift never stopped the tale. As she continued the story, she walked casually closer to the girl, smiled, and put her hand on the girl's shoulder. The girl relaxed and smiled back. Miss Swift's sensitivity to her listener had turned an unpleasant experience into a warm encounter with spoken literature.

Awareness of listeners' responses also enables storytellers to

ISSUE

SHOULD STORIES
BE CHANGED FOR TELLING?

A story, of course, should not be altered to suit a particular group of children. If it is felt to be too difficult, too sad, to contain incidents which the adult feels embarrassed telling, then it should be left untold until the children are older. Not only is it unfair to the creator of the story to alter it but later on, if children hear the correct version, they feel both confused and cheated. (p. 63)

> Cass, Joan. *Literature and the Young Child*
> (London: Longmans, 1967).

A book will often prove to be excellent read-aloud fare except for a few long descriptive passages interspersed throughout the text. An example of a book in which such passages are to be found is *The Adventures of Tom Sawyer*. As the teacher rereads this book, she will want to "blue pencil" the long repetitive descriptions of the Mississippi River. . . . Deleting the descriptive passages should not be viewed as censorship or watering down a story. On the contrary, it gives the story more vitality and movement as a read-aloud tale. (pp. 99–100).

> Whitehead, Robert. *Children's Literature: Strategies of Teaching*
> (Englewood Cliffs, N.J.: Prentice-Hall, 1968).

Do you think deleting parts of a book as you read is ever justified? If not, why not? If so, when and why?

adapt material on the spot. If an audience gets fidgety, many storytellers abridge their tales, skimming over incidents and moving to another story. Editing as you go is a matter of controversy among experts on children's literature (see "Issue: Should Stories Be Changed for Telling?"). But no one argues in favor of prolonging a tale that children do not want to hear.

Even storytellers who occasionally shorten tales know that certain elements in every story are essential. Cinderella, for example, must lose her glass slipper. Her coach has to turn into a pumpkin. She and the prince must marry. If any of these or other elements is left out, some children feel cheated and angry.

Practicing the same story with many different groups of children helps tellers understand how to shape the material to match the listeners. Practicing also improves technique. A change in the pitch of the voice, for instance, might help establish one character compared with another. In dialogues, a slight turn of the head from one side to the other can indicate that the speaker has changed. Gestures should be used sparingly, however, or they will siphon interest away from the material.

Similarly, aids to presenting literature—audiovisual media, for instance, based on books—should be used only when they focus attention on the literature itself.

USING AIDS TO ENHANCE MATERIAL

Morton Schindel, president of a company that produces audiovisual material, sensed a problem one day while he was observing a library story hour.

There were about thirty children on a carpet in front of a librarian, who was reading Beatrix Potter's *The Tale of Peter Rabbit*. Schindel could tell that the librarian liked the story, and she presented it well, first reading a page and then holding the book toward the group so everyone could see the picture. But the children in the large group were restless, Schindel wrote,

> . . . first as they were deprived of the sight of the picture while the librarian read, then as the flow of words stopped while she held the book high so that those in the back row could see. (1968, p. 46)

Schindel's experience in reading to his own children had convinced him that "no medium speaks more directly and intimately to a child than a book" (ibid.). But his observations at that story hour, and conversations with other librarians, convinced him that sound films made from books might be useful for story sessions involving large groups.

So Schindel, president of Weston Woods Studios, began to produce films. His cameras, fitted with close-up lenses, hovered over the pages of books. The cameras roved from characters' faces to details of setting. With this moving-camera method, called *iconographic technique,* he simulated a child's experience with a book.

High-quality media based on children's books offer opportunities for presenting literature to children. (George S. Zimbel/Monkmeyer Photo Service.)

He added a recorded reading, some quiet background music, and subtle sound effects.

The point was not to replace books with films. The point was, Schindel wrote in an article aimed at school librarians, that

> ... given materials artfully prepared, you have at your disposal many ways to share with the rising tide of eager children more of the thoughts and feelings that you, yourself, have discovered between the covers of good books. (ibid., p. 47)

A Wealth of Media

Films and filmstrips, recordings, and videotapes haved poured into school media centers, classrooms, and libraries in almost flood proportions in recent years. Many children have become accustomed to using individual sound filmstrip projectors, casette recorders, and closed-circuit TV tapes in addition to more traditional audiovisual material such as classroom movies, records, and slides. Library media specialists consult with teachers on many ways to present literature and other arts through sound and picture. Sometimes they also offer camera and recording equipment, art prints, and advice on multimedia approaches to books.

This wealth of media can help communicate literature to large groups of children. And individual recorders or filmstrip machines can enrich a single child's experience with books. Weston Woods' *Poetry Parade*, for example, is a two-record album on which poets

David McCord, Harry Behn, Karla Kuskin, and Aileen Fisher read some of their poems, providing distinctive rhythm and accent. The sound helps students listening to the poets to like their poetry more, and to understand its meaning.

Other useful media materials show students something *about* literature. *How a Book Is Made*, for example, is a filmstrip by Media Plus about how illustrator Ann Grifalconi created the pictures for *The Ballad of the Burglar of Babylon* (Bishop, 1968), and about the printing and binding of the book. Miller-Brody has produced a series of filmstrips called *Meet the Newbery Author* in which authors such as Natalie Babbitt, Susan Cooper, and Lloyd Alexander talk about their lives and work.

Evaluating Audiovisual Material

The editors of one selection guide for films, filmstrips, and recordings based on children's books write that audiovisual material has improved in recent years. But editors Ellin Greene and Madalynne Schoenfeld warn that many filmstrips, among other media, are still second-rate. Too often, artwork "verges on stereotype cartoon images. Original artwork, even when technically good, often is not appropriate in mood or feeling for the story illustrated" (1977, p. xi).

Like adults who try to tell stories without first mastering the material, poor audiovisual presentations distract audiences and prevent them from getting acquainted with good literature. Just as practice is important to the storyteller or reader, previewing is vital for the teacher who wants to use audiovisual material to bring books and children together.

One second-grade teacher had no time to preview the filmstrip she had chosen to show near Thanksgiving. She had picked out one about Pilgrims, and had begun to show it when she realized that some of the characters looked familiar. Then several frames focused on witchcraft, and she developed an odd feeling that she knew what was going to happen. Stranger yet, some of the children also seemed to know the story: one boy explained that a lady accused of being a witch had been playing around with her accuser's husband. It was a phony charge, the second-grader explained. He added that he knew because he had watched the film on TV two nights before. He was right. The filmstrip had been made from an old full-length feature exhumed only for occasional TV late shows.

Previewing would have avoided wasting time. It would also have afforded the teacher a chance to look for high-quality material instead of rerun fodder. A few basic criteria can be used in choosing audiovisual material:

Is the material based on good literature? Filming or recording a story or poem which lacked literary merit in the original is unlikely to result in anything better.

Is the medium appropriate to the story?

Does the material have esthetic integrity, whether or not it deviates from the original?

Is technical quality high? For example, are voices of characters clear and easy to understand? Do music or sound effects blanket voices? In movies, are voices and lips synchronized, or do mouths flap open sometimes without emitting sound? Is photography creative? Are prints clear?

Is the presentation authentic? If there is dialect, for instance, is it accurately spoken? Is the setting in a film or filmstrip authentic to the time and place represented?

Is the material appropriate? Even high-quality material may not match the needs of a particular group of children. The film version of *Johnny Tremain* (Buena Vista, Walt Disney Productions), for instance, has enough action to hold the interest of first-graders, but fifth- or sixth-graders are usually far better equipped to understand and appreciate it. Can the film be used to accelerate the growth of literary appreciation in first-graders? No. Force-feeding "great books" through films usually fails to rouse interest in reading, particularly when the original book is too advanced for the audience.

As a final step before presentation, teachers or librarians should understand the equipment. They should, for example, puzzle out how film threads through a projector, and they should know what to do when film breaks.

Other Aids

In one classroom, a translucent bead set in a bed of sand presented a fascinating foreground for a display of Byrd Baylor Schweitzer's *One Small Blue Bead* (1965). The book tells a story set in prehistoric times in which the bead becomes a reminder that there are many tribes of people in the world. Seeing and touching a bead drew students to the story. In another elementary school classroom, a teacher papered the walls of the reading center with 6-foot-square posters by artist Ezra Jack Keats about school, home, and community. (The set of posters is available from Franklin Watts.) Another

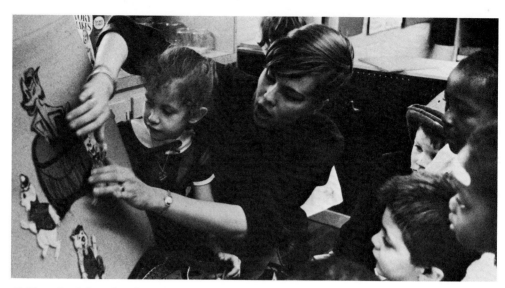

Children often help in the telling of a flannelboard story. (Grete Mannheim/Design Photographers International, Inc.)

teacher in a seventh-grade classroom combined clay figures of characters from a C. S. Lewis book with a map of the author's fictional world, Narnia. (The map is available from Macmillan.)

These aids helped establish a stimulating setting for good books. Other aids help in the formal presentation of literature. There are many options, from puppets to pictures to flannelboard. But again, the choice of aid requires forethought and preparation. In telling a story, for instance, visual aids are not an end in themselves. Joseph A. Wagner, an educator, suggests that visual aids should be used in storytelling only "to enhance the material being presented and thereby assist in the realization of a story's objective." And he warns:

> The use of puppets, flannel board objects, chalkboards, artifacts and pictures are justifiable to the extent that they clarify a story's content, and do not detract from it. (1970, p. 85)

Sometimes small details determine whether aids add to a child's experience with a book or story.

Consider flannelboard, for instance, an aid often used in storytelling. The equipment for a flannelboard is made by covering a board of wood or stiff cardboard with flannel, other cloth, or indoor-

ISSUE

SHOULD CHILDREN RETELL THE TALE?

Having children tell back a story is an excellent means of reinforcing the tale. This may be done by outright recall by various members of the group or the teacher may show pictures from a well-illustrated book and let the pictures remind the children of the story's sequence. Another feedback technique is to give flannel board objects appropriate to a story to members of the group. As the story is retold, the children will apply their objects to the flannel board at the proper moment. (p. 49)

Wagner, Joseph A. *Children's Literature through Storytelling.* (Dubuque, Iowa: Wm. C. Brown, 1970.)

Be cautious about reviewing the story, once it has been told. After all, we don't sit in an audience after a concert, humming the music back to the conductor to verify the fact that we've been listening. Generally the same should be true of the storyteller. He gives the gift of the story, and there the matter rests. (pp. 49–50)

Ross, Ramon R. *Storyteller* (Columbus, Ohio: Merrill, 1972).

What do you see as advantages of having children retell a story? What do you see as disadvantages? What factors might influence your decision about whether to have children retell a story in the same way? Why do you consider each of these factors to be important?

outdoor carpeting. The board becomes the background for the story. During the presentation, characters and bits of setting cut from felt (or paper, backed with felt or sandpaper) are placed on the board, where they adhere if the board is set up properly.

The challenge is inclining the board at the right angle. If it leans too far back, children will miss the display. If the board stands straight up, they will lose the thread of the story in the excitement of watching characters and pieces of setting tumble to the floor.

503

Use of the flannelboard, like gestures or quirks of voice, can add to the meaning of the story, or detract from it. Again, careful preparation will improve the chances that the medium will enhance children's experience with literature.

Preparation begins with careful selection. Stories that can be enhanced by using flannelboard have simple settings, few characters, and fairly uncomplicated plots. One such story is *Bear's Picture* (1972), by Manus Pinkwater. All the action takes place in one setting, and there are only three characters, the bear and two gentlemen.

The plot is simple. The bear sets up his easel and begins to paint. He starts with an orange squiggle, and then adds dabs of color. The gentlemen enter the scene and begin arguing with the animal. Bears should not paint pictures, they contend. The bear disagrees, and the men turn to criticism of the painting. No one can tell what it is supposed to be, they argue. The bear says he can tell, and continues painting while the gentlemen try to guess what the picture is. Finally, the bear tells them it is a picture of a honey tree, a cold stream in the forest, a hollow log filled with soft leaves for a bear to keep warm, among other things. But it does not *look* like those things, the men complain. The bear says it does not have to, since it is his picture. The men leave, grumbling, and the bear remains to look happily at what he has made.

To tell the story with flannelboard, teachers or librarians cut pieces and stack them in the order in which they will be used. The board is anchored firmly, at such an angle that children can see and flannel figures will cling.

The storyteller begins by applying the bear and his easel to the board. No background is necessary. Scraps of felt are added to the bear's painting, bit by bit, and then the gentlemen enter to one side. As the conversation continues, more colors appear on the easel. The teacher can create a different "painting" each time the story is told. Finally the gentlemen leave, but new colors continue to fill the easel. After the storytelling session, pieces are removed and stored in order in a folder, along with a sheet of paper containing a short synopsis of the story for later use.

THE CHICK AND THE DUCKLING:
A CASE STUDY OF A PRESENTATION

In the following actual presentation, a librarian uses a puppet to introduce a book to a group of five 3-year-old children and two teachers. The presentation, in a city library one rainy morning, is a good example of how to use an aid to enhance children's appreciation of a book.

When the children entered and sat down on stools, the librarian produced a large shoulder bag. Inside where children could not see there was a simple hand puppet and a book. The puppet was a sock with buttons for eyes and a long, trailing red ribbon on top of its head. The book was Mirra Ginsburg's *The Chick and the Duckling* (1972), with simple, large illustrations by Ariane and Jose Aruego. The children had visited the library before, and knew the routine, as you can see in the beginning of the transcript.

Later, the librarian listened to the tape of the session. Her reaction, as well as a general critique, appear to the left of the transcript.

The puppet has been popular in previous sessions, but the librarian heightens expectations by keeping the puppet and the book hidden for a few moments.

One of the librarian's major goals was encouraging a response from the children. She begins before she produces the book, encouraging children to speak up.

CHILD: I want to see the puppet.

LIBRARIAN: What's the puppet's name, do you remember?

CHILD: I don't know.

ANOTHER CHILD: Patty.

LIBRARIAN: That's right, Patty. She's here. And you know what? She's here, and she's got a new hair ribbon.

CHILD: I want to see it.

LIBRARIAN: Okay, Patty's in here. And she's going to come out. But you have to ask her to come out. Okay? I'm going to say "One, two, three," and when I say "three," you say, *"Come out, Patty."*

I have to wake her up. She wanted to stay in bed this morning, it was so wet and nasty. Did *you* want to stay in bed? (A few children nod.)

Ready to come out, Patty?

We're going to say *one, two, three,* and now you say—

The puppet need not have a voice.

LIBRARIAN AND CHILDREN: Come . . . out . . . Patty. (Puppet appears and whispers in librarian's ear.)

505

*There is more encouragement
to respond, and the librarian
shows genuine personal interest
in the children. All are en-
grossed in the situation.*

LIBRARIAN: (Explaining what
puppet is saying) She wants to
know where the other children
are. Where are the other children? Where's Toby?

CHILD: She went far away, to
Florida.

LIBRARIAN: I bet it's not raining
there. And who else?

CHILD: And Ruthy's sick. (Puppet coughs.)

LIBRARIAN: Now come on,
Patty, *you* don't have a cold.
Open your mouth. Open it up.
Open your mouth and let me
see down your throat. (Puppet
opens mouth wide.) You're all
right.
   (Puppet whispers in librarian's ear.) Oh. She asked if you
saw her new hair ribbon.

CHILDREN: Yeah.

LIBRARIAN: That's nice, isn't it?
She got a new one for the
holidays. See what color it is?

CHILDREN: Red. (Puppet laughs.)

LIBRARIAN: She's pleased with
herself. (To puppet:) Did you
find a book for the children?
Would you go down in your
sack and find that book? (Puppet plunges into sack; librarian
looks down into puppet's
"house.") What a mess down
there! You should clean up
your house one of these days.
(Patty appears with a book in
her mouth.) What have you
found? Oh. This is a good one,
I think. You go sit in the sack
and listen to me read the story
to the other children. You'll be
able to hear when I read to

The librarian introduced the book at a leisurely pace, lingering over the cover and title page.

She anticipated a point of confusion. However, here and at several other points in the presentation, she might have heightened interest more by questioning the children more fully on what they know or what they saw in the book, rather than quickly supplying answers.

The librarian opened to the first page, holding the book to her side. The children's curiosity about the pictures had risen before she turned to the text.

"I was surprised the children didn't know about how eggs hatch," the librarian said later. Her suggestion here was really aimed at the teachers who were sitting with the children. The 3-year-olds did not understand the word "incubator." The idea might better have been saved until after the session.

them. Okay? And you might pick up some of that paper on the floor when you're down there. (Puppet goes reluctantly back into the sack.)
This is called *The Chick and the Duckling.* You know what a duckling is?

CHILD: I don't know.

LIBRARIAN: It's a baby duck, a little duck.

CHILD: Where's the mother?

LIBRARIAN: Well, the mother must be inside because the baby chick and the baby duck are outside playing.
    A chick is a baby chick, and a duckling is a baby duck. See? Here they are. This is what the words say: "A duckling popped out of a shell. 'I'm out,' he said."

CHILD: A *duck?* Ducks can't live in a shell.

LIBRARIAN: Baby ducks come out of shells, yes.

CHILD: Just like crabs.

LIBRARIAN: No, not just like crabs.

CHILD: Snails come out of shells.

LIBRARIAN: Snails do come out of shells. But this is a different kind of shell. Chickens come out of eggs. Did you all know that? Chickens do come out of eggs. One time maybe you can go get an egg and incubator and that would be great fun.
    Look who else comes out of an egg. Remember I told you? The chicken.

507

*Here, the librarian began
building a pattern of repetition,
saying "Me too" in the same
pitch and rhythm.*

*The pattern was well
established . . .*

*. . . so here the librarian tried
for a response. "If I can get
them to participate, they'll listen to much longer stories," she
commented later. "They won't
sit still for a five-minute dissertation."*

*Here is another attempt to
draw a response: the librarian
broke away briefly from the
story to ask a question. She
soon returned to the material.*

*"Oh no!" the librarian said
when she heard the tape. She
said her tone of voice was condescending.*

"'Me too,' said the chick.
'I'm out of the egg.'
"'I am talking and walking,'
said the duckling.
"'Me too,' said the chick.
"'I am digging a hole,' said
the duckling.
"'Me too,' said the chick."

CHILD: Heh heh.

LIBRARIAN: "'I found a worm,'
said the duckling.
"'Me too,' said the chick.
"'I caught a butterfly,' said
the duckling."
(Whispered:) What did he
say? What did he say?

CHILD: "Me *too*."

LIBRARIAN: "'Me *too*,' said the
chick.
"'I am going for a swim,'
said the duck."
Can chickens swim? Do you
know? Do they swim?

CHILDREN: Nooo.

LIBRARIAN: Nooo, they can't.
But you know what?

CHILD: What?

LIBRARIAN: The baby chicken
didn't know that. So when the
duck said, "I'm going for a
swim," the chicken said, "*Me
too*," and look what happened.
He jumped into the water. He
couldn't swim.
"'I am swimming,' said the
duckling.
"'Me too,' cried the chick."
(Librarian speaks with pursed
lips, simulating child's speech.)
But look at the poor chicken!
(Picture shows a sinking chick.)
But here comes the duck. He
comes down and gets the

chicken. The duckling pulled the chick out of the water.

"'Aah,' said the chick."

"'I am going for another swim,' said the duckling."

Know what the chicken said this time?

"'Not me.'"

And he stayed right there and watched the duck go for a swim. And that's the story of the chicken and the duck.

CHILD: (Pleading:) One more story?

Another question about the story stimulated involvement. The children were fascinated by the change in the chick's response. They wanted more.

What happened in this session? First of all, the puppet led the children to the book, and then literally dropped out of sight in the bag: the session focused on the book, not on a puppet show. The book had been well-chosen. It had a repetitive pattern the children enjoyed. It offered action. The librarian made a few errors: talking over the children's heads at one point, and at another point, using a trick voice which later struck her as unnatural. She was also too quick to explain what she saw in the book without first encouraging children to try to say what was happening.

But overall, she had mastered the material well enough so that distractions—the confusion over where chicks come from, for instance—never derailed the children's trip through the book.

Her enticing introduction and her interaction with the children as she presented the book seemed to indicate that she liked and valued literature. And so at every step of the presentation, the children responded with rapt attention and eager faces that seemed to say, "Me too."

SUMMARY

1 Children often need a skillful adult to lead them to good literature, and teachers, librarians, and parents who take on the job need more than common sense. The successful presentation of books, or stories told without reading, depends on preparation involving several specific steps.

2 The way the classroom is set up can stimulate—or stifle—interest in literature. A *reading corner*—a section of the room set aside for books and magazines—stimulates readers to become involved with books on their own. In well-designed reading corners,

bulletin boards display children's work, children are encouraged to take books out, and the selection changes regularly. In general, classroom settings are more informal today than they used to be, but teachers are still required to plan seating arrangements carefully before introducing books or stories out loud.

3 Preparation for reading aloud also includes careful *selection* and *previewing* of books to be presented. The *complexity* and *size* of a book determine how big a group will be able to appreciate it when an adult reads it aloud. *Brian Wildsmith*'s *Puzzles,* for instance, is too complex to permit every member of a large group to respond, and *Beatrix Potter*'s books are too small; these books are best presented to one or two children at a time. Previewing material uncovers tongue-twisters, unfamiliar words that might otherwise impede presentation, and passages that may require extra teacher preparation, such as the scene in *Judy Blume*'s *Then Again, Maybe I Won't* in which a boy is embarrassed in class over an unwanted erection. Previewing also enables adults to practice reading in a clear, expressive voice.

4 Preparation for *storytelling*—presenting tales without using the exact words of books or scripts—also involves careful selection. A book such as *A Penny a Look* translates well into a spoken story because if offers a *fast-moving plot* and *few characters*, and *does not depend essentially on illustrations or specific writing style*. After selection, many storytellers transfer elements of specific tales to cards, each displaying key words.

5 During book reading, teachers use one of several techniques to show pictures: turning the pages toward children and reading upside down, over the top; holding the book to one side; or alternating reading with displays of the picture. Preparation frees adults to watch children frequently during reading to gauge reactions.

6 During storytelling, adults can adapt material on the spot to match children's interests. They can also change the pitch of their voices to indicate that different characters are speaking, or turn slightly to indicate that the speaker has changed; but gestures should be used sparingly or children become distracted.

7 Similarly, *audio visual media* and other aids can draw children closer to literature, although poor selection or misuse can drive potential readers away. Some media, Weston Woods Studio filmstrips for example, can help teachers to present books to large groups of students. Recordings give students a chance to hear writers read in their own voices, and other audio visual material presents information about how writers work and how books are made.

8 But not all media materials are useful. Films based on books and

other material should be judged by several criteria, including whether the material is based on good literature.

9 Other aids, such as flannelboard, puppets, or map displays, can heighten interest in literature, provided they are used after careful preparation. Telling a story with *flannelboard*, for instance, requires choosing a story with a simple setting, few characters, and uncomplicated plots. In the case study at the end of the chapter, a librarian uses a hand puppet to introduce a book, but quickly puts away the puppet and focuses children's attention on the literature itself.

BIBLIOGRAPHY

Adult References

Cass, Joan. *Literature and the Young Child* (London: Longman's, 1967).

Cohen, Monroe (ed.). *Literature with Children* (Washington: Association for Childhood Educational International, 1972).

Cullinan, Bernice E., and Carolyn Carmichael (eds.). *Literature and Young Children* (Urbana, Ill.: National Council of Teachers of English, 1977).

Greene, Ellin, and Madalynne Schoenfeld. *A Multimedia Approach to Children's Literature* (Chicago: American Library Association, 1977).

Ross, Ramon R. *Storyteller* (Columbus, Ohio: Merrill, 1972).

Sawyer, Ruth. *The Way of the Storyteller* (New York: Viking, 1970). (1942)

Schindel, Morton. "The Picture Book Projected," *School Library Journal*, February 1968, pp. 46–47.

Wagner, Joseph A. *Children's Literature through Storytelling* (Dubuque, Iowa: Wm. C. Brown, 1970).

Whitehead, Robert. *Children's Literature: Strategies of Teaching* (Englewood Cliffs, N.J.: Prentice-Hall, 1968).

Children's Book References

Arkhurst, Joyce Cooper. *The Adventures of Spider*, illus. Jerry Pinkney (Boston: Little, Brown, 1964).

Bishop, Elizabeth. *The Ballad of the Burglar of Babylon*, illus. Ann Grifalconi (New York: Farrar, 1968).

Blume, Judy. *Then Again, Maybe I Won't* (Scarsdale, N.Y.: Bradbury, 1971).

Caudill, Rebecca. *A Certain Small Shepherd*, illus. William Pène du Bois (New York: Holt, 1965).

Ciardi, John. *The Man Who Sang the Sillies*, illus. Edward Gorey (Philadelphia: Lippincott, 1961).

Cleary, Beverly. *Henry Huggins*, illus. Louis Darling (New York: Morrow, 1950).

————. *Ramona the Pest*, illus. Louis Darling (New York: Morrow, 1968).

De Paola, Tomie. *Watch Out for the Chicken Feet in Your Soup* (Englewood Cliffs, N.J.: Prentice-Hall, 1974).

Freschet, Berniece. *The Web in the Grass*, illus. Roger Duvoisin (New York: Scribner's, 1972).

Ginsburg, Mirra (trans.). *The Chick and the Duckling*, illus. Ariane and Jose Aruego (New York: Macmillan, 1972).

Jacobs, Joseph. *English Fairy Tales*, illus. John D. Batten (New York: Putnam's).

Keats, Ezra Jack. *Goggles!* (New York: Macmillan, 1969).

McDermott, Gerald. *Anansi the Spider* (New York: Holt, 1972).

Peck, Robert Newton. *Soup*, illus. Charles C. Gehm. (New York: Knopf, 1974).

Pinkwater, Manus. *Bear's Picture* (New York: Holt, 1972).

Potter, Beatrix. *The Tale of Jemima Puddle-Duck* (London: Warne).

Preston, Edna Mitchell. *One Dark Night,* illus. Kurt Werth (New York: Viking, 1969).

Schweitzer, Byrd Baylor. *One Small Blue Bead*, illus. Symeon Shimin (New York: Macmillan, 1965).

Silverstein, Shel. *Where the Sidewalk Ends* (New York: Harper, 1974).

Smith, Mary, and R. A. Smith. *Long Ago Elf* (New York: Follett, 1968).

Steig, William. *The Amazing Bone* (New York: Farrar, 1976).

Thurman, Judith. *Flashlight and Other Poems*, illus. Reina Rubel (New York: Atheneum, 1977).

White, E. B. *Charlotte's Web*, illus. Garth Williams (New York: Harper, 1952).

Wildsmith, Brian. *Puzzles* (London: Oxford University Press, 1970).

Zemach, Harve, and Margot Zemach. *The Judge* (New York: Farrar, 1969).

————and————. *A Penny A Look* (New York: Farrar, 1971).

————and————. *Duffy and the Devil* (New York: Farrar, 1973).

Zion, Gene. *Harry the Dirty Dog*, illus. Margaret Bloy Graham (New York: Harper, 1956).

CHAPTER 12

A CHILD'S RESPONSE

DRAWING A RUMPUS AND OTHER REACTIONS TO BOOKS

A second-grade boy drew the creature on page 514 after he had heard a teacher read Maurice Sendak's *Where the Wild Things Are* (1963). Sendak's monsters set up such a rumpus in the boy's imagination that, without prompting, he invented his own monster. (Two pages of Sendak's Wild Things—the inspiration for the boy's drawing—appear in the color insert in Chapter 2.)

In another classroom, a group of fourth-graders sat uncommonly still as their teacher read a passage from Roald Dahl's *Charlie and the Chocolate Factory* (1964). Charlie Bucket, the young hero of the book, was about to unwrap a candy bar that could change his life. If he found a gold ticket under the wrapper, he would win a tour of Willy Wonka's chocolate factory, and an endless supply of candy. Charlie took off the wrapper. He found the gold ticket. The class broke into cheers and applause.

Those are two responses to children's books. In both instances, the teacher had mastered and presented the literature well, in a controlled classroom setting. The responses, however, were unpredictable and individual. Cheers and drawings, rapt silence, tears, exuberant discussion—none of these can be mastered or programmed. But adults *can* create activities to encourage response to literature. And the planned activities and the spontaneous way children plunge into them can fix books in their minds, enhance their enjoyment and understanding, help them to speak and write clearly, and broaden their interest in literature.

THE WIDE RANGE OF RESPONSE

No one can count the ways children will respond to books. One girl rewrote the ending to E. B. White's *Charlotte's Web* (1952) because she did not want Charlotte, the spider-heroine, to die. Some children listen to the original ending in silence because they want no one to know about the tears beginning to well up. Others are angry. Many forces other than the book itself affect the way children feel and act about the literature.

In one study of teenagers, for instance, investigator James R. Squire discovered that adolescents are swayed by widespread conventions about how stories should come out. One such convention is that if adults and adolescents are in conflict, the adults are almost always wrong. Teenagers in the study felt that when adult characters in one story accused a boy of shoplifting, the adults must have been wrong. Many of the young readers held to this belief even after

(Chapter-opening illustration: A child's drawing of a Wild Thing)

Some children prefer to read by themselves while others like to experience books in a group situation. (Illustration by Erik Blegvad from *Someone New* by Charlotte Zolotow. Illustrations copyright © 1978 by Erik Blegvad. By permission of Harper & Row, Publishers, Inc.)

the boy admitted the crime. Students were also certain that adolescents are not responsible for their own actions, and that children in trouble do not have a healthy home life. They believed that wealth and happiness are incompatible, and that adults should avoid punishing their children. In many cases, these stock assumptions about life determined young readers' reactions to stories. Squire concluded:

> In responding to worthwhile literary selections, readers who rely on [stock assumptions] are often led to distortions of character and situations and thus are prevented from grasping the full intent of the author. (1964, p. 41)

In other instances, immediate reactions from a class or a teacher about a book shape the individual's response to literature. A doctoral candidate, Ann Petry, asked 5- and 7-year-old children whether they liked to look at a humorous book alone or with other people. Most children (55 percent) said they liked to experience books by themselves, but several who said they preferred to be in a group reported that the group itself sometimes made books seem funnier. One answer was, "If I think it's not funny, and other people laugh,

then I think it's funny." Another child said, "Someone looks at you,
and they make you laugh" (1978, p. 32).

A college student in his twenties bitterly remembers a fifth-grade
teacher who ridiculed him because he cried during a story the
teacher was reading to the class. "I decided then that I would never
again show how I felt about a story," he said.

So social pressures in a classroom—from peers and adults—may
affect the way children feel about books and how they express those
feelings. But a child's response is also styled and tailored by who the
child is. Alan C. Purves, an educational researcher and editor, surveyed a half century of studies into how children react to books. The
research shows, he writes (1975), that differences in responses between children reading the same book

> . . . can be accounted for by the experiential, psychological and concep-
> tual baggage that the reader already has before picking up the book or
> scanning the poem. It is what the reader brings to the text as much as the
> text itself that determines the nature of the response. (p. 463)

In research of his own, Purves also found wide differences between children depending on their age. Third-graders tended to respond to books on a literal level, retelling tales in their own words
but following the story faithfully. These third-graders made statements like "It's about a rock," and "He got a whole bunch of cats."
Fourth-graders discussing books tended to compare themselves with
characters, although their response was still literal. In the sixth
grade, children began to interpret stories, drawing conclusions and
raising questions beyond the text, particularly about characterization. And by senior year in high school, readers responded primarily
in terms of interpretation. They related books they were reading to
broad themes such as "alienation" and "searching for themselves"
(pp. 465–466).

In sum, even before the teacher, librarian, or parent presents a
book, a child is set to respond in certain ways. Adults, classmates,
and setting also help shape the response. Of course the book itself
also determines how children will react to it, but Purves, Squire, and
others suggest that the literature is only one of several causes for the
cheering, crying, drawing, role playing, babbling, or other responses
to books.

Many of these responses are surprising. Classrooms sometimes
explode into laughter or fall into reverential silence when adults
least expect it. Other responses are the result of adult stimu-
lation—teachers encourage student expression because the expression itself enriches the child's experience with literature.

THE USES OF RESPONSE

One girl confused the word "arbor" in a story she was reading with the word "harbor." Later, she solemnly reported to researcher Squire that in one scene of the story, a young couple had met under water.

One boy, having misread the word "musician" in another story, reported that a father wanted his son to become a concert magician (Squire, 1964, p. 38). Another boy fell into laughing fits at odd moments while reading a story about a pig and a stick. His teacher discovered later why he thought sentences like "The pig took the stick into the house" were funny. He had been reading "stink" for "stick."

In these instances, young readers held tenaciously to mistaken beliefs about what stories say, even when beliefs led to bizarre twists of plot. So one good reason for trying to get children to express their responses is to help uncover and clear up confusions.

But garnering responses gives much more than a check of reading accuracy. Here are some other reasons why teachers try to draw out reactions to good literature.

Responding Increases Enjoyment of Literature

In discussion, drama, or other activities based on books, students experience again the passages they liked on first reading. In many projects, such as drawing a picture of a favorite character, they are allowed to pass on to others what they have found in a book. Most children enjoy responding as much as sharing a secret or telling a riddle. They come to associate the pleasure of expressing or interpreting a story with the story itself.

Increased enjoyment of books heightens interest in future trips to the library or reading corner. But there is another good reason for enhancing enjoyment: understanding good literature *requires* emotional involvement with the material. Students may be able to recite accurately what happened—"the couple met at the arbor"—but unless readers also feel the heartbeat of the literature, the emotions contained in the words, they cannot understand the major dimensions of a good book. One interesting finding in Squire's research is that readers who were most involved with stories were also most inclined to want to evaluate literary qualities (p. 51).

Responding to Literature Can Develop Literary Taste

Critic and writer Northrop Frye suggests that basically there are two kinds of responses to literary experience. One occurs while reading a book or watching a play.

519

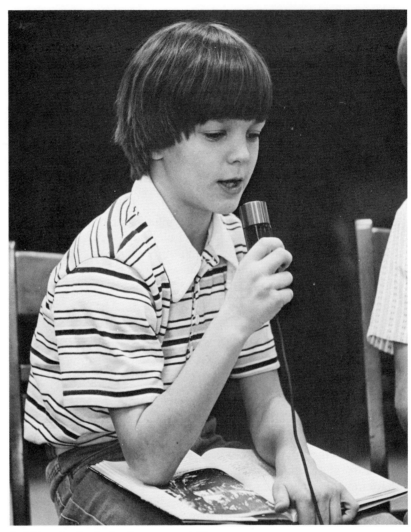

Activities related to books often increase children's
interest in and enjoyment of literature. (Bruce
Roberts/Photo Researchers, Inc.)

"If our experience is limited, we can be roused to enthusiasm or
carried away by something," he writes (1964). The second kind of
response occurs later: "the conscious, critical response we make
after we've finished reading or left the theatre." Frye argues that
practicing this second response makes the first response "more sen-

sitive and accurate, or improves our taste" (p. 104). Discussion or other activities after reading can provide perspective for readers of all ages. First-graders can learn early to express like or dislike of what they have read. Children around 11 or 12—in fifth or sixth grade—are old enough to begin to evaluate books on the basis of form or structure, testing, for instance, how well plot supports theme.

But classroom activities need not involve criticism to sharpen taste. Students who savor a scene from a book, interpret it in spontaneous play or lively discussion, are obliged to look back on what they have read. Is the scene as exciting as it first seemed? What elements made it work or fail? What books do others in the class like, and why? Answering questions like these requires taking a hard, second look at the literature—a look that can reveal flaws and strengths.

Responding Builds Skill at Communication

All the activities suggested in the following sections of this chapter call on children to express themselves. Practice in speaking, writing, acting, singing, or painting improves a child's ability to organize thought and convey it clearly. Ideally, activities also call for practice in comprehending other students' points of view.

Those are some of the major reasons for stimulating students to express themselves about literature: *heightening enjoyment and understanding, sharpening literary taste, improving communication skills.* Teachers may focus on one goal over another depending on their children. In elementary schools, for example, teachers ordinarily concentrate on enhancing enjoyment and providing a chance to practice communication skills. Students before the intermediate grades can pick up differences in authors' styles, and decide what they like and dislike. Later, around the sixth grade, teachers call increasingly for discussions or other projects to improve literary taste and broaden understanding of universal themes.

The time-worn reason for calling on students to respond to books was to make sure they had completed reading assignments. Today teaching goals have expanded, and, consequently, activities to support those goals have changed. Boring book reports have yielded to imaginative letter writing. Dull catechisms between class and teacher (Question: "What was the boy's name in *Wild Things?*" Answer: "Max") have given way to discussions between students, often as the teacher stands aside.

Abel, a rather sophisticated mouse, makes an attempt
to get off the island where he is marooned.
(Reproduced with the permission of Farrar, Straus &
Giroux, Inc. from *Abel's Island* by William Steig.
Copyright © 1976 by William Steig.)

MANY ACTIVITIES AROUND ONE BOOK

A single book can generate many activities to support different
teaching goals. Take William Steig's *Abel's Island* (1976), for example. The story itself—with a kind of Robinson Crusoe ring to it—is
strong enough to generate interest, daydreams, and playacting
among children who hear it. A teacher who plans activities to

heighten response can fix the story in children's minds so that it is nearly indelible.

The story is about a mouse named Abel—his full name is Abelard Hassam di Chirico Flint—and his bride Amanda. The couple have gone on a picnic. Lunch includes sandwiches of pot cheese and watercress, hard-boiled quail eggs, onions, olives, caviar, and chilled champagne.

But rain spoils this repast, and drives the two aristocratic mice to a cave. Amanda peers out to see the downpour and loses her scarf in the wind. Abel chases and catches it, but the wind hangs him up on a nail sticking out of an old board, and soon he is awash on a frothy river. The board floats far away, to an island. Abel soon learns it will not be easy to get home, and, like Crusoe in Daniel Defoe's book, sets up camp. He is lonely, fearful of a local owl, buffeted by winter winds, plagued by a bout with a high fever. Crusoe had his Bible; Abel has *Sons and Daughters*, a book left behind by picnickers, and he takes his reading in small doses to make it last.

Crusoe had his man Friday; months after Abel's arrival, he is joined by an old frog named Gower Glackens. Glackens promises to give messages to Amanda when he leaves the island, but disappears without a trace. Finally, Abel takes advantage of an August drought to cross the river while the water is slack, barely making it home. He dresses in silk shirt and velvet jacket, and leaves the scarf in Amanda's hall as a sign of his return. The two are reunited.

Most sixth-graders like this book. Activities to enrich their experience with it depend on teaching goals.

Discussions and Drawings Interpreting the Book

Suppose, for instance, the goals include enhancing enjoyment, understanding, and communication skills. What activities support those goals? For one, students can pair off and improvise a conversation between Gower and Abel. In preparation, the class talks about the characteristics of the mouse and the frog, and perhaps lists subjects they might discuss. The conversations themselves last about five minutes, and then one member of each pair reports on what was said (or croaked or squeaked). One way to practice communication might be to have students break into small groups to make missing-person posters like those hanging in post offices. The job is to make a picture of Abel showing what he was wearing when he disappeared, and to write a paragraph under the picture telling when he was last seen by Amanda and other animals.

This poster was created by a fifth grader
after hearing Steig's *Abel's Island*.

Students could also write a letter to Gower Glackens from Abel after the mouse comes home. Does he forgive Glackens's forgetfulness? In the book he is understanding; and students can be encouraged to be consistent with what they know of the mouse. How would Abel sign his letter? How would he seal the envelope, and reach the mail slot? Students can draw on what they know of the mouse from the book to invent plausible solutions.

Each of these activities is closely dependent on Steig's story. Each develops material that could fit into the plot. Each adds expression to Steig's ideas—carrying the plot forward logically or extrapolating dialogue from what the author has made of a character.

Taking a Step Away from the Story

Other activities require students to take a step or two away from the story. For example, to help students understand Abel's personality and to appreciate how writers bring characters to life, a teacher might encourage students to close the book and think about themselves. In *Abel's Island*, the mouse talks about his "private star," a kind of spirit in the air that hears his needs and offers security. Abel called on his star when he was young, and needed it again when the storm stranded him on the island. Do the students remember what objects—such as teddy bears or blankets—gave security when they were young? Again, the class can pair off and talk. But in this instance, most of the initial discussion will center on personal experiences, not literature. Each pair is asked to draw up a list, and after the discussions, the class can try to find similarities in the lists. Are group members relaxed with each other? If so, they might also volunteer to talk about what helps them to feel more secure now. Then the discussion can return to Abel: "How is he different from you? How is the mouse like you?

A teacher with the same goal—helping readers to understand Abel—might suggest that students are stranded on an island with nothing but an old cabin and some canned food. Their task is to make a list of all the things and people they would miss. What three things would they miss the most? Again, they can talk about the list, to explore how their feelings differ from the mouse's.

In these two activities, literature is a springboard for launching explorations that go beyond the book; in fact, the students could carry on their discussion without having heard of Abel. But the projects can give students added perspective on what they have read, helping them to identify with a major character and others like him.

Some activities begin by centering on the book, and then move

Dear Gower,

It's Abel! How come you didn't send help? Well anyway I'm home safely. Amanda was so happy, she almost fainted when I walked in the door. Mom and Dad <u>DID</u> faint. I told all about you and the island. They said that someday we will get a ride on one of those big boats that across the river to the island, and that you would meet us there. As I was telling Amanda about the I came to the part about the staues, she said that she would love to see it, so, I made one out of clay of her. She talked me into starting a staue shop. I opened up Tuesday. Bussnus is great. Remember, anytime your in Mossvillee, come and see me.

Love,
Abel

Dear Gower,

What happened? You were supposed to bring someone back to rescue me. I waited and waited but nobody came. Well I'm home safely now. No thanks to you! I was happy to see my wife. Did you get back safely? I'm curious to know why you didn't bring someone back to rescue me. My trip back wasn't very good. After I got across the river and onto the land I met a cat. He kept catching me but then I would escape. Finally I got away. Then I came home.

Yours truly,
Abel

These students' letters (in rough draft form) suggest what Abel might have said to Gower had he written to him after getting home.

toward peripheral explorations. Sixth-graders, for example, are just entering the period of formal operations. This stage of growth, described by psychologist Jean Piaget, is discussed in Chapter 1. At around 11 or 12, children begin to understand the form of thought as well as content, Piaget reported. Teachers in earlier grades might ask a content question, such as: What were Abel's bravest acts? Teachers at the sixth-grade level might try a question concerning literary form: How did William Steig develop the mouse into a believable character?

A Child's
Response

Abel Flint
89 Bank St.
Mossville

Dear Gowr,

What happened to you? I thought you? Were going to rescue me after you got home. I waited and waited but you never came.

Finally I figured out how to get off the island without your unreliable help. But if you still want to be friends I'm willing to forgive and forget. I really hope this won't end our friendship, but if it does just remember that I'm forgiving you.

Your friend,
Abel

Dear Gower Glackens,
Do you rember me? I'm Abel the mouse you met on the island. I returned home safely, did you? Did you forget to send somebody back for me? Thanks a whole lot! I kept waiting and waiting for you! Boy do you have a awful memarey! Do you know what it is like to spend a whole year on a island! Well, I just wanted to write and say thanks a whole lot for forgetting me!

Your angry friend,
Abel Flint

In this case, the activity might start with a discussion of the book itself. The teacher asks: What adjectives describe Abel? The words are listed on the blackboard as they are called out. The teacher makes no effort to evaluate their accuracy.

Then the teacher reviews the list, word by word, asking how students know that the word applies. As students justify their responses, they will be stating methods an author uses to draw characters: the words arise from what the character does, says, and thinks; from what others say about the character; and from direct description. (Chapter 1 also discusses methods authors use to reveal character.)

Some words will drop off the list as students find they cannot support them. Others will stay on, backed up by passages students

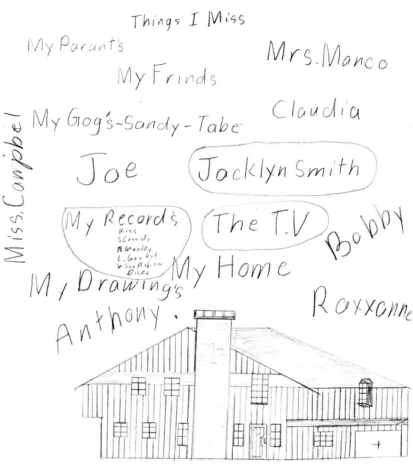

Things I Miss

My Parant's

My Frinds

Mrs. Manco

Claudia

My Gog's-Sandy-Tabe

Miss, Campbel

My Gog's-Sandy-Tabe

Joe

Jacklyn Smith

My Records
Kiss
S. Cassidy,
B. Manley,
L. Gar hit,
V. Sue Robien
Disea

The T.V

Bobby

My Drawing's

My Home

Anthony.

Roxxanne

In preparation for a discussion, this student listed
what he would miss if he were stranded on an island.
He circled the things he would miss the most.

recall from the book. By the end of the activity, students are working
primarily with general principles—techniques used by authors in
many books, not just *Abel's Island*.

The teacher should begin planning each of these activities by
defining a goal: enhancing enjoyment, for example, or developing
critical ability. Then the plan turns to specifics. What projects will
help students respond directly to the book? What activities related
to the book—discussions about universal themes, for instance—can
add perspective? Teachers should use several criteria to evaluate
ideas.

Practicality Does the activity call for readily available or inexpensive materials? Will the teacher be required to be in the front and the back of the classroom at the same instant? Or can the project run almost entirely on its own, freeing the teacher to circulate and give support to students?

Challenge Is the project challenging without surpassing the capabilities of students? Are participants likely to succeed, or will most come away with a sense of frustration? Will the whole class understand directions?

Relevance Does the activity depend directly on the book, or does it take off in a different—perhaps inappropriate—direction? Does the project revolve around an idea in the story?

Individuality Does the project offer some options so that students themselves take responsibility for some of the decisions made?

See if you can relate these guidelines to two teaching situations:

One teacher with a class of thirty first-graders read *The Surprise Party* (1969) by Pat Hutchins, a funny story showing how a group of animals garbled a message as they passed it on.

To enhance students' enjoyment of the book, the teacher decided to start a message at one end of the classroom and tell students to whisper it to a neighbor. Then they would see, she said, how it came out on the other end.

Problems began within a few seconds when one boy who had forgotten the directions told the girl next to him she was a "dum dum" instead of passing on what he had heard. "You're not supposed to say *that*," the girl complained. Students nearby giggled. Others across the room grew bored waiting for the teacher to straighten things out.

What had gone wrong? The project was relevant to the book, and offered ample responsibility to the students. But it was far too difficult—requiring sustained silence while doing nothing—for first-graders. It called for constant attention from the teacher.

Another teacher using the same book broke the class into small circles of six children each and whispered a message to one child in the circle. This activity took about three minutes instead of ten. The small-group approach ensured that no child had to wait very long before doing something. Groups of interested children managed themselves without teacher intervention, and later, one member of each group reported on the funny way the message had been messed up. The activity provided a realistic challenge, designed in a practical way.

The guidelines are not meant to be restrictive. With practice, teachers or librarians can come up with several spirited activities for each book, some close to the text, some several steps away. The examples that follow cluster around four kinds of activities: *oral, dramatic, written, and artistic.* Each example should spawn other ideas of your own.

ORAL EXPRESSION: GIVING VOICE TO LITERATURE

Children sway in their seats, nod their heads, thump hands on their desks as a teacher reads a counting rhyme with pulsing rhythm:

> ... "Run," said the mother,
> "We run," said the two;
> So they ran and were glad where the tall
> grass grew.

Within three verses, first-graders have caught the pattern and begun, without coaching, to chant key words: *"We run ... So they ran ... glad ... tall grass grew."* The poem used in this classroom is *Over in the Meadow*, a traditional rhyme (available in book form from John Langstaff, 1957). Mother Goose rhymes such as "Pease Porridge Hot" and "Pat-a-cake" also stimulate young children into lending their own voices to literature.

The activity has elements of a community sing. Several other children's books are designed specifically for actual singing. Peter Spier's *The Fox Went Out on a Chilly Night* (1961), for example, includes notes at the back so adults introducing the book can learn the melody before encouraging children in the first few grades to join in. John Langstaff's *Frog Went A-Courtin'* (1955) and Aliki Brandenburg's *Hush Little Baby* (1968) also provide the music. For teachers uneasy about their singing voices, Weston Woods Studios offers filmstrips of each of these books along with a soundtrack recorded by a professional singer.

Another book based on song, John W. Ivimey's *Complete Version of ye Three Blind Mice*, contains all thirteen verses of the old lyrics. A modern author and artist, Maurice Sendak, wrote words for *Really Rosie*; a popular singer, Carole King, set them to music and recorded the songs (on Ode Records, Hollywood).

Even beginning readers can become deeply involved in books by speaking words aloud, and each of these books and recordings makes

This song is fully illustrated with the music provided
at the end of the book. (From the book *Hush Little
Baby* by Aliki Brandenburg. Copyright © 1968 by
Aliki Brandenburg. Published by Prentice-Hall, Inc.,
Englewood Cliffs, N.J. 07632.)

it easy to participate. Children in the first few grades also find it fun
to embellish stories read to them by making sound effects or by
telling the story of a wordless picture book.

Sound effects enhance lighthearted books whose stories refer frequently to noises. One such book is Jan Wahl's *Crabapple Night*
(1971). It is the story of "mean grouchy crabby Louella Fink" who
has not been herself since her husband disappeared. Louella is at war
with neighborhood children because they think she has poisoned a
local Scotch terrier. As they play tricks on her, the story refers to

531

sounds of owl hooting, sirens, snoring, yawning, gunfire, and weird
music. (Mr. Fink returns in the end; Louella makes crabapple pies,
and the children learn she did not poison the dog.)

A teacher reading the story can conduct the sound effects. One
way to proceed is for the teacher to touch the top of the book when
he or she wants the children to get set to supply sounds. Then, when
the teacher's hand rises, they begin background noise, building in
crescendo as the hand rises and quieting as it falls. It helps to practice difficult sounds before the story begins. *Crabapple Night*, for
example, refers to the sound of corn tossed in handfuls against
Louella's window. What sort of noise is that? Children can try to
invent it before the reading begins.

Storytelling based on wordless picture books is most effective
when the pages are visible to all the children. Weston Woods Studios
has produced a package of filmstrips made from wordless picture
books. After viewing a story once, students take parts to add
dialogue, or they volunteer to tell what happens on the screen.

Books with text can be adapted for children's storytelling as well,
provided the pictures tell the tale on their own. Teachers may want
to prepare their own slides of books, although copyright laws require
that the copyright holder—usually the publisher—grant permission
in advance, even when copies are made only for use in one classroom.

Voices in Chorus

Chanting what they can of nursery or counting rhymes prepares
children for later choral reading—reading a poem out loud, in a
group.

There are several ways to do it, but all rely on careful selection of
good poems children like. (Chapter 4 suggests criteria for evaluating
poems.) A class could begin with a simple poem, such as this one,
untitled, by Beatrice Schenk de Regniers:

> Scare me easy
> Scare me slow
> Scare me gentle
> Don't let go
> > my hand. (1977, p. 16)

Another appropriate poem for choral reading is Eve Merriam's
''Bam Bam Bam'' (1966):

> Pickaxes, pickaxes swinging today.
> Plaster clouds flying every which way.

Workmen are covered with white dust like snow,
Oh, come see the great demolition show!

Slam, slam, slam,
Goes the steel wrecking ball;
Bam, bam, bam,
Against a stone wall.

It's raining bricks and wood
In my neighborhood.
Down go the houses,
Down go the stores,
Up goes a building
With forty-seven floors.
Crash goes a chimney,
Pow goes a hall,
Zowie goes a doorway,
Zam goes a walk.

Slam, slam slam,
Goes the steel wrecking ball;
Bam, bam, bam,
Changing it all. (1966, pp. 12–13)

Starting with these or other poems, choruses can chant in unison, everyone reciting at the same time. Several variations are possible. One child can read part of a poem—one line or one section—alone, and the rest of the class can then respond with the next line or section, in chorus. Or each child can take one line. Teachers can also divide classes into two groups, to recite parts of the poem back and forth in a kind of dialogue.

There should be room for experiment and interpretation. One interesting technique is the use of *obbligato*. Obbligato is a spoken accompaniment to choral reading, a background of words or sounds made by one group while a second group reads the poem. For example, half the class might chant "tick, tock, tick, tock" while the other half speaks the words to "Hickory Dickory Dock." A more involved obbligato, suggested by educator John Stewig (in Cullinan and Carmichael, 1977, p. 26) for older children, is built on Lewis Carroll's "Jabberwocky" in *Alice in Wonderland*. Some children read the poem while others supply sounds of Carroll's imaginary beasts. What do toves, borogroves, and jubjub birds sounds like? Again, those supplying the accompaniment should decide before the reading.

533

The Variety of Discussion

Creating an obbligato requires moving a short step from the poem and adding a personal stamp to the way it is interpreted. Discussion, another activity involving an oral response to literature, offers students the chance to take several steps away from the book or poem, and to talk about their own responses.

But discussion is more than a series of statements from students about what they think—or what their teacher wants them to think. It is a two-way conversation. Participants can state opinions, but they are also called to respond to what others say. Some discussions are led by teachers, but many others in modern classrooms are run by students themselves.

For both kinds of discussion, small groups promote participation better than large crowds. In intimate circles of three to six persons, no one needs to raise a hand for attention. No one who wants to talk needs to wait long. Students uncomfortable about speaking up in front of the whole class often find it much more comfortable to respond in a small circle.

Backdrop for Discussion

A teacher has just finished reading Betsy Byars's *The 18th Emergency* (1973) to a class of intermediate-grade students. The teacher's goal now is to help students learn some new critical skills, as well as to practice communication and to enhance the students' enjoyment of the book.

The class likes the story. They talk about it in lunch lines in the cafeteria, and during recess. The plot they discuss naturally among themselves is about a sixth-grade boy named Benjie Fawley, known as Mouse to his friends.

Benjie and one of his friends, Ezzie, have dreamed up escapes from seventeen emergencies that might befall jungle explorers. If a lion attacks, for example, you just wait until it is upon you and then jam your arm down its throat, choking it to death. The boys have also drawn up simple escape plans for situations ranging from an attack by a boa constrictor to a charge by mad elephants.

The eighteenth emergency, however, is closer to home. The trouble begins one day when Mouse adds a piece of graffiti to a chart hung on a hallway wall. Next to a picture on the chart of Neanderthal man, Mouse pencils in the name "Marv Hammerman," a dreaded sixth-grade bully in Mouse's school. Mouse turns from his work to find Marv himself watching. The eighteenth emergency: how to keep Marv from beating up Mouse.

ISSUE

SHOULD CHORAL READING BEGIN WITH UNISON WORK?

Successful beginnings are heavily dependent upon simplicity of execution. This means that much satisfying unison work should be done before commencing more complicated work with solo and choir parts. Unison speaking keeps the weight of the individual perfection from resting too heavily on the consciousness of young speakers. If one should forget a line or make a word substitution, he can continue without the embarrassment of having seriously interrupted the group effort. (p. 27)

Root, Shelton R. "Doing Choral Speaking," in Leland B. Jacobs (ed.), *Using Literature with Young Children* (New York: Teachers College Press, 1965).

Unison is the most difficult choral speaking to direct because of the problems of coordinating timing and inflection. Therefore small children should not be given a heavy dose of unison experience. In all instances, brief poems should be utilized. (p. 123)

Whitehead, Robert. *Children's Literature: Strategies of Teaching* (Englewood Cliffs, N.J.: Prentice-Hall, 1968).

If you were beginning choral reading with a group of second-graders, would you begin with unison work? Why or why not? How might you use the advice of both Root and Whitehead in your planning?

First, Benjie fakes illness to avoid a brawl. Finally, he faces the problem. He finds Hammerman and fights. Benjie receives five solid blows, and lands none, but Hammerman gains respect for him. In the encounter, Benjie also learns that he hurt Hammerman by insulting him—as much as it hurts Benjie to be called Mouse. Because he survived the fight, Benjie also wins greater respect from his friends. No more a Mouse, he gets his real name back.

The emergency Benjie had not planned for was being
stalked by Marv Hammerman. (From *The 18th
Emergency* by Betsy Byars, illustrated by Robert
Grossman. Copyright © 1973 by Betsy Byars.
Reprinted by permission of The Viking Press, Inc.)

DISCUSSION OR DISPLAY?

Students in one Rhode Island school had invited parents and other outsiders to hear what the teacher called a "discussion" about World War II. The third- and fourth-graders had completed Katherine Savage's *The Story of World War II*, and then practiced their presentation for two weeks, using detailed scripts about the book. On the day of the performance, scripts were replaced with a brief outline because, one child explained, "we were reading too much from the papers." During the presentation itself, children occasionally jumped ahead of the "discussion" order. Other children shushed them. (The activity was reported by Bert Wade in the *Providence Journal*, Apr. 19, 1972.)

Was it a real discussion? James Moffett of Harvard University suggests that the heart of discussing is "picking up ideas and developing them; corroborating, qualifying, and challenging; building on and carrying each other's sentences, statements, and images." Moffett suggests that questioning should arise from students themselves. And the teacher, he writes, "should be relieved from the exhausting, semi-hysterical business of emceeing" (1973, p. 46).

In what ways did the "discussion" about the Savage book depart from the standards suggested by Moffett? What skills did children gain in preparing and putting on the display for their parents? What other skills does discussion build? How could the teacher have reconstructed the activity to strengthen those skills?

Categories of Question

In informal discussions about this book, students tend to recall scenes to each other. ("Remember the part where Marv catches Mouse on the school stairway?") They savor passages they like.

In planning a more formal discussion of the book, teachers can invent questions based on memory to begin a small-group discussion. There are, however, other, more useful, categories of questions. These categories, developed by educator Norris M. Sanders,* can remind people planning a discussion that there are many vantage points for viewing books. The first three categories face the writing head on; the others call for standing away and viewing with more perspective.

Memory. One line of questioning encourages students to recall what they have read.

"What was Mouse's real name?"

Translation. Some questions—or assignments—require students to go a step farther than simple recall. They direct readers to translate an idea in the book into a different form, sometimes in the students' own words, sometimes in a drawing or other activity.

---

*Sanders's categories (1966) are built on previous work by Benjamin S. Bloom (1956).

*"Based on descriptions in the book, draw a picture of Marv
Hammerman."*

Interpretation. To answer questions of interpretation, students
process information in the book. They compare facts, or find im-
plicit causes for what happens, or draw inferences about how
characters felt.

*"Why do Benjie's mother and Mr. Stein (his teacher) have differ-
ent opinions of Benjie's illness?"*

Application. Stepping slightly away from the book, students answering questions of application apply ideas from the book to a
separate situation.

*"How might you use the idea of honor as Benjie saw it to explain
an argument you have had?"*

Analysis. Other questions require the student to respond with
conscious knowledge of literary form or reasoning processes. Do
characters think and act logically? What literary devices does the
author use to tell readers about Marv? Both questions require
analysis.

*"The author often uses humor in Benjie's statements about his
problem. For example, the author says that if Ezzie and Mouse
fought Hammerman, Hammerman would probably bang them together like cymbals, and they would twang for forty-five minutes.
How does humor like this change the tone of the story?"*

Synthesis. These questions call on students to put given pieces
of information together in a new way, drawing data from the story.
There may be many answers to questions requiring synthesis.

*"What do you think Benjie would say if he were to describe his
encounter with Hammerman to his father?"*

Evaluation. There are two parts to answering every evaluation
question: (1) What standard do you use to judge the merit of an idea
or literary work? (2) How well does the material match the standard?

*"In comparing the hard cover edition of the book (published by
Viking in 1973) with the paperback version (published by Camelot,
1974), which cover better matches the story? Why?"*

Teacher-Led Discussion

Teachers at all grade levels can ask those *kinds* of questions, representing different ways of looking at books. But in a specific teacher-
led discussion, the set of questions above seems haphazard. As far as
students are concerned, they could be asked in any order.

To give direction to a discussion, the first step is choosing a focus
for questioning based on teaching goals.

One teacher planning to lead a discussion on *The 18th Emergency*

Compare this cover with the one shown on page 536.
How would you answer the evaluation question?
(From *The 18th Emergency* by Betsy Byars, Illustrated
by Robert Grossman. Copyright © 1973 by Betsy
Byars. Reprinted by permission of Camelot Books in
cooperation with The Viking Press, Inc.)

considered several options. The class could have explored the use of humor in the book. Another alternative would have been a discussion on whether fighting could settle arguments, or on Benjie's courage, or on family relationships reported in the book.

Instead, the teacher chose to try to develop understanding of one theme: facing problems. With this focus, the teacher wrote a set of about a dozen questions, then eliminated some and rearranged the others so one question led to another. Here is the final list, along with a parenthetical note identifying the type of question. See if you can explain the rationale for the order in which they appear.

1 Do you think "Mouse" was a good nickname for Benjie during the first part of the story? Why or why not? (Interpretation)

2 Benjie's mother doesn't understand why other children call her son Mouse. Why doesn't she? (Interpretation)

3 Why is it important that both his friends, and Benjie himself, refer to him as Benjie rather than Mouse at the end of the story? (Interpretation)

4 Why do you suppose Benjie did not stop and get Ezzie to go with him when he went to meet Hammerman? (Interpretation)

5 How might the story have been different if Benjie had managed to tell his mother or his father what his problem was? (Synthesis)

6 Why did Benjie feel so good after the fight? (Interpretation)

7 Do you think Benjie would have felt the same way if Hammerman had caught him after school? Why or why not? (Synthesis)

8 Has there ever been a time when you felt as relieved as Benjie felt after the fight? When? (Application)

9 Do you think Benjie will ever have a nineteenth emergency? Why or why not? (Synthesis)

During the discussion, the teacher relies on these questions as guides, adding other questions or comments for clarification. Do students stumble over question 5, requiring more than just interpretation? Then the teacher can return to the level of interpretation for a moment with a question like "How much did Benjie's mother understand about his problem?"

If questions requiring interpretation bring on blank faces, the teacher can intersperse other kinds of questions. Here is one, for instance, that requires only remembering the story: "What did Benjie say to Ezzie after he encountered Hammerman?" As Sanders classifies the questions, each level calls on students to use some of the same skills in answering as lower levels required. The answers to memory questions, for instance, help in finding answers to questions of interpretation.

It is important, however, for adults to avoid tossing in a second question while students are still struggling with a first. Teachers

Children can begin to learn discussion skills by working in pairs and recording their responses. (Leima Druskis/Editorial Photocolor Archives, Inc.)

may be tempted to try to help with leading questions or hints. Some of the best discussions are punctuated by stumbling over words, hesitations, or silences. Each is a sign of hard work in progress.

Student-Led Discussion

In other discussions, teachers initiate conversation, but then back away, letting students pick their own paths. In student-centered discussions, however, adults can still control a few crucial variables: *group size, length of discussion,* and *complexity of the task.*

Second-graders may have to begin learning how to carry on their own discussions by working in pairs, a few minutes at a time, on simple questions. They could explore the theme of friendship by drawing up a list of things they like to do with friends, one list per pair. A time limit, say four minutes, should be set. Children a few years older would work in groups of three on a slightly more complicated task; for example, answering the question: What *is* friendship? The threesomes could be given six or seven minutes to interpret what characters in a book thought about friendship. Then the students would have to write a definition satisfying every member of

541

the group. They would also have to choose someone to report how the group felt.

Students with more experience in group work might be assigned to groups of five to weigh the question: "Should friends always tell each other the truth?" Again, they might begin with interpretation of characters in a story, and then move to application—calling upon their own experiences with situations where they had to juggle tact and truthfulness. Twenty minutes is an appropriate time limit for this activity.

In each of these discussions, students begin with a specific task. Vague directions—"Discuss courage"—generate superficial reports. Specific instructions—"Decide whether Benjie was a courageous person, and produce evidence to support your decision"—stimulate students to probe deeper into books, and to test and sharpen their own reactions to them.

DRAMATIC EXPRESSION:
THE CLASSROOM AS PRIVATE THEATER

In one kindergarten classroom, students take turns playing Jack jumping over a candlestick as a teacher reads "Jack Be Nimble."

A fourth-grader takes the role of a book character in trouble and trembles as she tells her story out loud, in a scene that never appeared in the book.

In these two instances, children used drama to extend their experience with books. They became actors and actresses without an audience or formal scripts, using body movements or dramatic voice or both to express literature and to learn as they performed.

There is a constellation of projects for dramatizing good books. This section suggests just four as a sample: *interpreting* a story dramatically, *improvising, role playing,* and *puppetry*. Like the oral activities discussed in the previous sections, these explorations in drama permit children to respond to writing on a literal level— jumping over the candle just like Jack—or to make up scenes based only loosely on the text provided by the book.

Interpreting

On the first level, *interpreting* a story or poem means following the story line literally while presenting it dramatically. Interpretation, however, never depends on speaking the author's words. An adult can read the book, while children pantomime the story, or add only occasional fragments of dialogue.

Stories with repeating patterns lend themselves well to interpre-

These children are extending their experience with
books by interpreting a story dramatically. (Mimi
Forsyth/Monkmeyer Photo Service.)

tation by children just learning dramatic expression. A book like
Miles Miska's *Chicken Forgets* (1976) also provides parts for many
children. In the story, Mother Hen sends Chicken to hunt wild
blackberries. "Get wild blackberries," the chicken mutters to himself so he will be able to remember his marching orders. But animal
after animal on the way stops to talk, and Chicken keeps forgetting
what he is supposed to be after. Finally, a robin mentions berries,
and leads the chick to a patch of wild blackberries where he fills his
basket. Back home, his mother praises him for not forgetting.

In interpreting the story, one child plays the chicken, wandering
through a group of children playing other animals. Each supplies a
single sentence, as the chicken's confusion grows. The adult adds
narration.

Second-graders with some experience in drama may be ready to
put on an entire production without adult intervention during the
play.

One class, for example, has just finished reading *The Little Red Hen*, by Paul Galdone (1973), a folktale with a repetitive pattern. The main character is a hard-working hen who gets no help from her friends. Other animals answer "Not I" every time she requests aid on jobs like planting wheat. After reading the story, children review it in a teacher-led discussion. The class names the major characters in the story—Hen, Dog, Cat, and Mouse. During the discussion, children interpret how different animals feel, and make a preliminary try at acting out boredom, or sleepiness. Some slump. Some snore and yawn. Then the class plans a set; children move desks, tables, and chairs to make an imaginary farm, with a house made out of a desk and crops of boots.

The teacher casts the show after asking what parts children want to play, but no child becomes type-cast. After the first performance, there are two other performances with different actors in each role. (In one variation, the teacher chooses the players by recognizing one child and asking "What role do you want to play?" and then moving in set order through the class. For the next show, the order is reversed so different children get first choice of roles.)

After children complete each show on their own, the teacher leads another discussion about what happened. What was funny about the way the dog drooped lazily? How can you avoid the problem next time of all the animals speaking up at once? Then the play begins again, with actors themselves as the only audience. Each version will be slightly different.

Improvising

Children who are interpreting a story use the books' story lines as a basis for the impromtu script they make up as they act. Another dramatic activity, *improvisation*, involves more of a departure from the story: much of the material comes from the actors themselves, inspired by the story as a kind of premise.

Material in the previous section on the kinds of discussion questions suggests different ways of planning improvisation. What would happen to the hen, for instance, if she needed help on yet another project? In making up a new story, children in the first few grades would be practicing *application* as they chose parts and made the story unfold in a new way. Fourth- to sixth-graders might use *analysis* to dissect the structure of *The Little Red Hen*, extracting a premise: one character always does all of the work, but others want to share rewards. To improvise on that premise, children pick a new setting, new characters, and even a new plot: a dramatic activity requiring *synthesis* of what they have read.

In the original, the industrious hen kept the rewards for herself. In improvisation, the main character may decide to share rewards, or win no reward at all. One of the other characters might decide to help after all, leaving the other slackers to quibble about whether they should join too. The direction depends on the participants, but in following their own impulses, children get a better sense of how they compare and contrast with the hen in the original tale.

Role Playing

Some improvisation focuses on finding solutions to a problem expressed in the literature. In *role playing*, students first decide what the problem is, and then take the roles of characters to explore what is wrong and what can be done. Seventh-graders could read Willo Davis Roberts's *Don't Hurt Laurie!* (1977), for example, and examine the problem of child abuse from the main character's perspective.

Laurie cannot understand why her mother beats her, and knows she will be in trouble if she reports the abuse she takes. She assumes no one would believe her, anyway. In role playing, one student might play Laurie and another could be her stepfather, or the stepfather's mother. The task for the student playing Laurie is to try to tell her relative. The child playing the relative has latitude in responding. In one variation, a child might take the role of a doctor explaining to Laurie why her mother beats her. (The book provides some explanation.) Laurie's role in this improvisation is to ask questions to help her understand. A third variation might have Laurie discuss her problem with her stepbrother, seeking a way out. After each role-playing session, students should have a chance to say how they felt living in Laurie's shoes. The activitiy can put them in close touch with a character at the same time they delve into a theme.

Puppetry

Another dramatic activity, *puppetry*, can be used to interpret literature or to improvise on it. Some children find it easier to manipulate a puppet than to face a class themselves as actors. Puppets provide a kind of cloak or disguise, freeing students to concentrate on dramatizing what they have read, or taking off from it in shows made up on the spot.

Hand puppets or stick puppets work better than marionettes requiring dexterous string pulling. Puppets without strings are easily made from paper bags, from cylinders of all kinds, from socks, or even from tattered shirts. Children should make them themselves,

A table serves as a stage for this puppet presentation.
(Bruce Roberts/Rapho/Photo Researchers, Inc.)

adding hair and features. For stick puppets, children first draw
characters, then cut out their drawings and paste them on heavy
construction paper or cardboard and paste the cardboard to a
stick—a ruler, a straw, a popsickle stick. As in all dramatic
activities—whether they interpret or improvise on literature—
children produce their own dialogue, without working from scripts
or memorizing lines. Generally, the actors and actresses perform
only for themselves, with the simplest of props and setting. There is
no need for an elaborate stage, curtain, or spotlight. The activity
spotlights the literature itself and the children's reactions to it.

That is just a sampling of activities, based on books, that help
children respond by speaking out or acting. Many of these activities
also adapt to children's writing about books.

WRITTEN EXPRESSION: BEYOND THE BOOK REPORT

"Read a book, and write a report of 100 words about it, including the title and name of the author." For decades, this dreaded and vague assignment has led children to write dull prose, rehashing the plot until the required number of words has been reached. ("Do you get to count your name and your teacher's name in the 100 words?" is a child's question from the depths of boredom.)

Today there are so many successful alternatives to this style of old-fashioned book report that teachers have no excuse for assigning tedious written responses to literature. As with oral and dramatic activities, some written work calls for translation or interpretation of the text; some requires using the book as a springboard into other territory. Some written work is only a few words long—an imaginary telegram from one character to another, for example. Some writing tells a story; some describes a character or scene; some argues; some entertains. A classroom should be open enough to accommodate all kinds of writing, not just reports.

Variations in the *content* and variations in the *form* of writing both help to make writing more fun for students, and lead them closer to understanding what they have read.

Content

John S. Goodall's *The Surprise Picnic* (1977) is an action-filled tale about a mother cat and two kittens who row over to an island for a picnic. The rock on which they spread their food turns out to be a turtle, who wanders away with their lunch and eats it himself. Their boat drifts out to sea, and wind and rain make travel via umbrella and baskets unpredictable. Finally they land at the home of another cat, where they have their picnic after all. All this is told without words.

One assignment is to write words, narrating the story told in pictures. Another wordless picture book, *OOPS* (1977), by Mercer Mayer, shows the feelings of characters through facial expressions and body language. It offers the chance for students to write dialogue as the main character, Ms. Hippo, drives her car into a stoplight, nearly hitting an alligator policeman. Ms. Hippo drives herself into several other predicaments. She picks a piece of fruit from a vendor's cart, for instance, causing the stack to tumble. What does the vendor say? When a fly lands on the leg bone of a dinosaur at a museum, she whops the leg with her purse, dismantling the dinosaur. What does she think? What is the policeman planning to do with her? Student writing on these two books can interpret and extend the author's material.

547

Taking another imaginative step, students could write what the alligator told his wife about Ms. Hippo and the stoplight after he got home from work. Or they would write a description of Benjie's difficulties as they were seen by Ezzie in *The 18th Emergency.*

The contents of student writing, in other words, can and often should go beyond retelling what authors have written.

Fourth- or fifth-graders, for example, enjoy continuing the story of a lovable bear in Michael Bond's *Paddington Takes the Air* (1971). What might happen if Paddington, a bumbler despite good intentions, came to the classroom? What if he became school custodian?

Younger children can try to imagine what happens next after reading a series of books by Carol Carrick about a boy named Christopher and his dog, Bodger. In *Lost in the Storm* (1974), Bodger disappears overnight during a fierce storm. The dog is killed in the next book in the series, *The Accident* (1976), but in *The Foundling* (1977), Christopher adopts a stray puppy. What happens when the puppy grows up? Children could write brief, original episodes, or dictate their own stories about Christopher to older students.

Material for new stories also grows out of changes in plots of stories children have read. What if Bodger had not been killed, but injured badly enough that Christopher had to nurse him back to health? Teenagers could imagine what might have happened to Harriet, in Louise Fitzhugh's *Harriet the Spy* (1964), if her classmates had never found her notebook containing embarrassing observations about them. And what if Robin, the crippled boy in Marguerite De Angeli's *The Door in the Wall* (1949), had been captured by the enemy as he limped through the fog on his mission to get help for a besieged castle?

Some books build plot from a pattern. Students can adopt the pattern—a recurring phrase, for instance, or stylistic device—to generate fresh pieces of writing.

The pattern in Jeri Marsh's *Hurrah for Alexander* (1977), for example, is easy to apply to different situations. Alexander wants to be an inventor. Each page contains one line about one of his inventions, and a second line about what happens to it.

> Once he invented a way to keep his baby
> sister from getting into things.
> But his mother made him untie her.

Students could describe their own inventions in one sentence, and add a second, "But . . .," sentence.

Other books may suggest writing projects whose content is only loosely based on the original book. A biography of a famous civil

This illustration shows how Alexander invented a way
to clean his room in a hurry. (Reproduced from
Hurrah for Alexander, copyright © 1977 by
Carolrhoda Books, Inc. Used by permission of the
publisher.)

rights crusader, *Martin Luther King, Jr., Man of Peace* (1969), describes the freedom crusade in Birmingham, Alabama, in May 1963,
when marchers were struck down with water from fire hoses, and
arrested. "The scenes in Birmingham, pictured in newspapers and
on television, filled the nation with horror. Hearts changed, even
hearts in Birmingham," writes author Lillie Patterson (pp. 71-72).
The account may be history to children, but many adults remember
the pictures. Young readers can explore the impact television had
during the early 1960s by interviewing several adults on what they
remember and how they felt. Interview notes become the basis for a
short article.

549

Hurrah for Alexander

Once Alexander Invented a way to
scare away Monsters but, his sister
washed off her make up.

① Once he invented a way to save ...

Was he ... near it ...

② Once he invented a way to keep the bugs
out of the garden
But his father didn't use it

Once Alexander invented a family size table. But the family didn't
like the dishes always sliding.

These new Alexander-type inventions were created by
middle-school students.

Most students in all grades enjoy developing their own material.
They also like exploring different *ways* of writing about what they
have found.

Form

Children out of school encounter dozens of different kinds of
writing every day. People write newspapers, magazines, TV titles,
letters, diaries, memos, awards. They scribble graffiti on subways,
scratch poems into tables, and furrow love notes into sand. Students
can present their material in any of dozens of forms.

Suppose a class of sixth-graders has just heard *Alan and the Animal
Kingdom* (1977), by Isabelle Holland. In the story, 12-year-old
Alan has been shuttled from one relative to another. His latest home
is with a great aunt named Jessie who has a heart attack early in the
story and dies in a hospital.

No one at the hospital can identify her, and Alan offers no help
because he has no faith that adults will take care of him and the pets

his aunt permitted him to keep in her apartment. He tries to live by himself. He puts off Jessie's friends who wonder why she does not return calls or go to church. But it becomes more and more difficult to keep up the pretense. Eventually, Alan confides in Betsy, a classmate, and in Dr. Harris, a vet who helps when Alan's cat is ill. Then the headmaster of Alan's school learns what has happened, and takes Alan into his home. The animals board with friends. Alan begins to regain trust in people.

A teacher trying to heighten students' enjoyment and involvement with Holland's book might begin planning by listing the forms of writing found in a daily newspaper. Student writing could follow several forms.

Headlines would tell major events in the story in a few words. How many headlines should there be for the whole book? Students could be asked to decide which major events rated a headline. Then the task would be to fit as much information as possible into the least number of words—say thirty letters per line for two lines.

Obituaries for Jessie could be written from Alan's point of view right after her death. Or teachers could ask students to take the viewpoint of a hospital official seeking help in identifying the deceased woman.

Help-wanted ads by Alan could outline what he needs after his aunt dies; the number of words might be limited to thirty.

Editorials could weigh the pros and cons of putting children's pets to death when the children become wards of the state. Writers would have to take a stand.

Starting with several ideas for possible forms, the teacher pares down the list to projects supporting specific teaching goals. Short forms—headlines, ads—call for clear, concise expression. Longer forms require development of an idea through several stages, building an argument step by step in an editorial, for example.

Some writing projects become even more interesting to students when combined with artistic expression such as drawing, painting, photography, and three-dimensional constructions.

ARTISTIC EXPRESSION: PERSPECTIVE BEYOND WORDS

Artistic expressions inspired by literature are more than decorations for classroom or library walls.

Like other activities suggested in this chapter, student artwork can help readers recall, translate, or interpret what they have read, turning a line of plot directly into lines of an action-filled drawing, or an author's character sketch into a painted portrait. Work in different media can help students appreciate how artists create picture books. Chapter 2 contains descriptions of major media. Water colors, collage, crayon, and opaque paint are easy to use in the classroom. Students can also make pictures of characters or book settings in scratchboard by coloring paper with heavy wax crayon, painting over the crayon with thick tempera, letting the paint dry, and scratching the surface to reveal the crayon beneath.

Books can also influence the way students draw a classroom scene, color a painting of a school yard, or shade a sketch of a friend. As with other activities, student artists can use a book as a springboard into fresh experiments with self-expression.

Literature as Artistic Subject

In some artistic activities, literature is the subject. Students cast an artist's eye on literary elements such as plot or characterization or setting and then reproduce what they see.

One simple project is to retell a story in a series of drawings within frames on a roll of paper. Like scenes in a slide show, episodes come into view as the roll is unwound. Students can construct a box to hide the roll, with a hole cut in the side to see the drawings. Inside the box, the roll unwinds like a scroll, from one stick to another. Boxes can be as small as a snapshot camera, or as large as a TV set. Making a roll requires interpretation and analysis of plot; writing a script to accompany the show is an excercise in communication skills.

In another project, a group of students teams up to create a large mural based on books. Students in one class made a large painting of rats and mice from literature. The painting brought to one canvas such characters as Templeton and Stuart Little, from books by E. B. White, and Mrs. Frisby, from Robert O'Brien's *Mrs. Frisby and the Rats of NIMH* (1971). The mural also included Tucker, the Broadway mouse in George Selden's *The Cricket in Times Square* (1960), and Abel, the storm-tossed mouse in William Steig's *Abel's Island*. Working together on the rodent-filled mural required the students to talk about each of the books and relate them to a single setting they invented themselves.

Some books on fantasy—Richard Adams's *Watership Down* (1974), for example—provide maps of their imaginary kingdoms. Students can draw similar maps based on verbal descriptions in books such as *Abel's Island*. What did the island look like? Once students have drawn their own charts, they could be asked to plot with a dotted line the route Abel took to escape when the river waters abated. Taking a step past the plot, they could also sketch a summer house for Abel and his bride, assuming the mouse wanted

After hearing *Two Hundred Rabbits,* this first grader
drew a rabbit's eye view of his classroom.

to return to the island for vacations.

Abel's house could also become the focal point for a *diorama*, a
miniature scene with model figures and props standing before a
painted background. Abel's refuge could be built into a box, like a
tiny stage setting, with house and characters made of scraps of plastic foam, milk cartons, yarn, foil, or buttons.

Literature as Vantage Point

In other activities, books give students fresh perspective for viewing
the world around them artistically.

Some books suggest offbeat ways of looking at things. One illustration in *Two Hundred Rabbits* (1968) by Lonzo Anderson and
Adrienne Adams, shows the world as it appears to a rabbit (p. 29).
How would the classroom appear to a rabbit or a mouse or a giant?
As another example, on one page of Ezra Jack Keats's *Goggles!*
(1969), a boy named Archie peers through a hole in a board to secretly observe some boys chasing him. There is some security behind the board. Children could make drawings of what other frightening things—bullies or trolls, for instance—might look like

553

through a peephole. Students who try to find out by making their own drawings gain insight into Archie's feelings as he hides.

Students who crouch near the floor to sketch their desks from rabbit height may find it easier to identify with the main characters in *Two Hundred Rabbits*. Intermediate-grade students might also find it easier to discuss artistic technique in these books—how Keats uses collage, for example—after trying the techniques themselves.

Another book, Byrd Baylor's *We Walk in Sandy Places* (1977), is a powerful inspiration for some students to tell stories of their own—with photography. Baylor's book shows interesting textures in tracks left in the desert. Students can search for and photograph tracks on their own in sand, mud, or snow, following an artistic trail suggested by the book.

ENCOURAGING RESPONSE BEFORE READING

The activities outlined in this chapter—from photography to chanting in unison—intensify response during or following reading. Teachers or librarians should also consider drawing a reaction from students even before they have begun reading a book.

One teacher asked students to write their definition of hero. She collected the responses, and then read *The Book of Three* (1964), by Lloyd Alexander. Alexander's main character, Taran, is an uncommon candidate for hero. As the book opens, he is an assistant pig keeper, dreaming of glory. His stature grows in the course of the story, as he tries to defend the Kingdom of Prydain from evil. But he makes mistakes, like an ordinary person. After the reading, students got their definitions back. They compared responses in small group discussions centered on the question: can we find a definition of "hero"? The activity before reading enhanced interest in Taran's attempt to become a champion. The discussion also sharpened students' responses after they had closed the book.

A teacher in another class of sixth-graders brought a drum to school one day and asked students to move in time with its rhythm. They were told to wave one hand first, and then both hands, and then to breathe in time with the drumming from the front of the class. Then they walked in time, with the rhythm unchanged.

"Now keep on moving," said the teacher, "but don't follow the drum's rhythm. Make your own time." The steady sound continued for a minute or two, and then the class stopped and talked about how they had fought the sound, and tried to move out of synchronization with the drum.

Some were unable to beat the rhythm. One or two moved in

A book may provide the inspiration for children to create artistic photographs of their own. (Reprinted by the permission of Charles Scribner's Sons from *We Walk in Sandy Places* by Byrd Baylor, illustrated by Marilyn Schweitzer, copyright © 1976 by Marilyn Schweitzer.)

double time. Some thought of something else to block out the noise. A couple of children gained control by jerking arms and legs in random motion.

After the discussion, the teacher introduced Madeleine L'Engle's *A Wrinkle in Time* (1963). In the book, the teacher said, a smart young boy is captured on the evil planet of Camozotz. All the inhabitants of the planet are controlled by the steady, throbbing pulse of a monstrous force called IT. The boy's sister, Meg Murry, has to find a way to release her brother from IT's grasp without becoming a slave herself to its evil rhythm.

Like all well-planned activities based on books, the pulsing dance

to the teacher's drum was more than a pastime or classroom entertainment. It led students straight to the heart of the literature.

SUMMARY

1 Planned activities before or after presentation can heighten children's enjoyment and understanding of books as well as help them
to speak and write clearly and broaden their interest in literature.

2 A book is only one of many factors affecting how children respond
to literature. *James R. Squire* discovered that teenagers are swayed
by stock assumptions about how stories should come out. *Ann Petry*
reports that 5- and 7-year-olds reading humor in a group are sometimes influenced in what they think is funny by what others in the
group think is funny. *Alan C. Purves*, another researcher, writes that
differences in responses between children reading the same book can
be accounted for by the "experiential, psychological and conceptual
baggage that the reader already has." Purves also found wide differences in response depending on age.

3 Encouraging children to speak or write about literature provides
teachers with a test of student comprehension. There are several
other reasons for encouraging reactions from readers. Responding to
books increases involvement, and *Squire's* research shows that students most involved with literature were also most inclined to want
to evaluate literary qualities. Discussion and other activities also
develop literary taste and build communication skills.

4 One book can generate many activities, depending on teaching
goals. *William Steig's Abel's Island*, for example, can stimulate discussions or drawings designed to enhance enjoyment and understanding and to give children practice in communication skills.
Some activities involve interpreting the book. Others use literature
as a springboard into explorations of literary form or personal experience outside the range of the book. These peripheral explorations
can give readers new perspective on what they read. Specific ideas
for activities should be measured against several criteria including
practicality, challenge to students, relevance, and the opportunity
for individual expression and decision making.

5 Examples in this chapter center around four kinds of activities:
oral, *dramatic*, *written*, and *artistic*. Books provide impetus for a
wide variety of oral activities, from singing to sound effects,
storytelling based on wordless books, chanting, and discussion. In
planning a discussion, teachers should consider using many different kinds of questions. *Norris M. Sanders* suggests seven categories
of questions (based on work by *Benjamin S. Bloom*), including
memory, translation, interpretation, application, analysis, synthe-

sis, and *evaluation*. Specific questions depend on teaching goals. Students can also run their own discussions, even in primary grades, although the teacher should control group size, length of discussion, and complexity of the task.

6 The most effective dramatic activities—whether *interpreting* a book dramatically, *improvising*, *role playing*, or *using puppets*—are not based on formal scripts; rather, classroom productions give students a chance to express in their own way what they have found in books.

7 Stock book reports have been superseded in many classrooms today by writing activities allowing variations in *content* and *form*. Wordless picture books provide students the opportunity to write narratives matching pictures. Another activity calls on students to write scenes extending stories they have read, or to use a stylistic device or recurring phrase to make up new stories. Teachers can assign writing exercises in any of dozens of forms, such as newspaper editorials or headlines.

8 In some artistic activities, literature is the subject as students interpret plot, character, or setting in drawings, paintings, photographs, or dioramas. In other artistic projects, books provide a fresh perspective for viewing the world around the student: the scene through a knothole in *Goggles!,* for instance, can stimulate students to view other subjects through peepholes, and to appreciate why and how artist *Ezra Jack Keats* used the technique.

9 Readers' experiences with books are often enhanced by participating in an activity *before* reading. Writing about heroism before reading *Lloyd Alexander*'s *The Book of Three,* for instance, helped one class understand the attempts of one character to become a champion. Like all well-planned activities, the writing led students to a deeper understanding of the literature.

BIBLIOGRAPHY

Adult References

Bloom, Benjamin S. (ed.). *Taxonomy of Educational Objectives* (New York: Longmans, 1956).

Cullinan, Bernice, and Carolyn Carmichael (eds.). *Literature and Young Children* (Urbana, Ill.: National Council of Teachers of English, 1977).

Frye, Northrop. *The Educated Imagination.* Bloomington, Ind.: (Indiana University Press, 1964).

Jacobs, Leland B. (ed.). *Using Literature with Young Children* (New York: Teachers College Press, 1965).

Moffett, James. *A Student-Centered Language Arts Curriculum, Grades K-6: A Handbook for Teachers* (New York: Houghton Mifflin, 1973).

Petry, Ann. *Responses of Young Children to Three Types of Humor*, unpublished doctoral dissertation, University of Connecticut, 1978.

Purves, Alan C. "Research in the Teaching of Literature," *Elementary English*, April 1975, pp. 463–466.

Sanders, Norris M. *Classroom Questions: What Kinds?* (New York: Harper, 1966).

Squire, James R. *The Responses of Adolescents While Reading Four Short Stories* (Champaign, Ill.: National Council of Teachers of English, 1964).

Wade, Bert. "John Howland Readers Share Ideas," *Providence Journal*, Apr. 19, 1972.

Whitehead, Robert. *Children's Literature: Strategies of Teaching* (Englewood Cliffs, N.J.: Prentice–Hall, 1968).

Children's Book References

Adams, Richard. *Watership Down* (New York: Macmillan, 1974).

Alexander, Lloyd. *The Book of Three* (New York: Holt, 1964).

Anderson, Lonzo, and Adrienne Adams. *Two Hundred Rabbits* New York: Viking, 1968).

Baylor, Byrd. *We Walk in Sandy Places*, illus. Marilyn Schweitzer (New York: Scribner's, 1977).

Bond, Michael. *Paddington Takes the Air*, illus. Peggy Fortnum (Boston: Houghton Mifflin, 1971).

Brandenburg, Aliki. *Hush Little Baby* (Englewood Cliffs, N. J.: Prentice-Hall, 1968).

Byars, Betsy. *The 18th Emergency*, illus. Robert Grossman (New York: Viking, 1973).

Carrick, Carol. *Lost in the Storm*, illus. Donald Carrick (New York, Seabury, 1974).

———. *The Accident*, illus. Donald Carrick (New York: Seabury, 1976).

———. *The Foundling*, illus. Donald Carrick (New York: Seabury, 1977).

Dahl, Roald. *Charlie and the Chocolate Factory*, illus. Joseph Schindelman (New York: Knopf, 1964).

De Angeli, Marguerite. *The Door in the Wall* (Garden City, N. Y.: Doubleday, 1949).

De Regniers, Beatrice Schenk. *A Bunch of Poems and Verses,* illus. Mary Jane Dunton (New York: Seabury, 1977).

Fitzhugh, Louise. *Harriet the Spy* (New York: Harper, 1964).

Galdone, Paul. *The Little Red Hen* (New York: Seabury, 1973).

Goodall, John S. *The Surprise Picnic* (New York: Atheneum, 1977).

Holland, Isabelle. *Alan and the Animal Kingdom* (Philadelphia: Lippincott, 1977).

Hutchins, Pat. *The Surprise Party* (New York: Macmillan, 1969).

Ivimey, John W. *Complete Version of Three Blind Mice,* illus Walton Corbould (London, Warne).

Keats, Ezra Jack. *Goggles!* (New York: Macmillan, 1969).

Langstaff, John. *Frog Went A-Courtin,* illus. Feodor Rojankovsky (New York: Harcourt, 1955).

———. *Over in the Meadow,* illus. Feodor Rojankovsky (New York: Harcourt, 1957).

L'Engle, Madeleine. *A Wrinkle in Time* (New York: Farrar, 1963).

Marsh, Jeri. *Hurrah for Alexander,* illus. Joan Hanson (Minneapolis, Minn.: Carolrhoda Books Inc., 1977).

Mayer, Mercer. *OOPS* (New York: Dial, 1977).

Miska, Miles. *Chicken Forgets,* illus. Jim Arnosky (Boston: Little, Brown, 1976).

O'Brien, Robert C. *Mrs. Frisby and the Rats of NIMH,* illus. Zena Bernstein (New York: Atheneum, 1971).

Patterson, Lillie. *Martin Luther King, Jr. Man of Peace* illus. Victor Mays (New York: Dell, 1969).

Roberts, Willo Davis. *Don't Hurt Laurie!* illus. Ruth Sanderson (New York: Atheneum, 1977).

Selden, George. *The Cricket in Times Square,* illus. Garth Williams (New York: Farrar, 1960).

Sendak, Maurice. *Where the Wild Things Are* (New York: Harper, 1963).

Spier, Peter. *The Fox Went Out on a Chilly Night* (Garden City, N. Y.: Doubleday, 1961).

Steig, William. *Abel's Island* (New York: Farrar, 1976).

Wahl, Jan. *Crabapple Night,* illus. Steven Kellogg (New York: Holt, 1971).

White, E. B. *Charlotte's Web,* illus. Garth Williams (New York: Harper, 1952).

CHAPTER 13

BUILDING UNITS

INTRODUCING THE FAMILY OF LITERATURE

orothea teaches a single class of twenty-six fifth-graders, but frequently she feels more like an umpire settling disputes between several competing clubs.

Girls sit together on one side of the room, most of them taller and physically stronger than most of the boys. Like bothersome younger brothers, the boys try to compensate for their smaller physical stature by taunting the girls. One girl who might pass for a seventh-grader is a particularly vulnerable target. But when one of the bigger boys tells her "You belong in the category of reptiles," she is not above throwing herself into a quick and bloodless hallway fight.

A few years before, these children looked to adults for acceptance and approval. No longer. Now, a few weeks after school has opened, boys and girls alike turn to people their own age for support. Within the group of boys, several in one small gang wear the same kind of khaki pants to school every day, fearful of rejection if they break a rigid dress code they have set for themselves. Several of the girls who wear armbands as members of the school's hallway patrol do not talk or play with the other girls.

There have been several studies of forces within such peer groups. In classic research published in 1950, R. W. Berenda tested ninety children between the ages of 7 and 13. The experimenters measured the childrens' ability to distinguish between the lengths of lines printed on a card. Test subjects in one run-through were placed one at a time in a room with eight other children who had been coached to give the wrong answer before the test subject was allowed to respond. The results indicated the power of peer pressure. Only 54 percent of the 10- to 13-year-old children answered the simple questions right when others gave the wrong answer first.

One 11-year-old—the age of children in Dorothea's class—summed up her experiences during the embarrassing test, and at the same time described common emotions of many fifth-graders:

> I had a funny feeling inside. You know you are right and they are wrong and you agree with them. And you still feel you are right and you say nothing about it. (1950, p. 232)

Despite the fears and pressures, Dorothea's class also shows potential. Their interest in books, for example, has broadened impres-

(Chapter-opening illustration from *Peter and Veronica* by Marilyn Sachs, illustrated by Louis Glanzman. Copyright © 1969 by Marilyn Sachs. Reproduced by permission of Doubleday & Company, Inc.)

sively within the past two years. Many of the children are now opening books seventh- and eighth-graders are reading. They enjoy hearing such books read to them. Some of the children have discovered that they like an author or series well enough to read several related books in a row. In the armband clique, battered copies of Nancy Drew books—stock and predictable mystery stories—circulate among girls as fast as comic books pass from hand to hand among the boys.

Reading abilities have developed at different rates, and tastes are beginning to diverge. The challenge to Dorothea is to introduce good literature to the whole class, despite its divisions and diversity.

Her solution to the problem is to present several related books in a unit. Using aids available to all teachers, she plans to build a small collection of books around a central issue of interest to her students: peer groups.

Case studies in this chapter illustrate how Dorothea and other teachers constructed and used units. Each case weaves strands of several teachers' experiences into one composite story. Each study shows that units can help teachers meet specific teaching goals, and lead students to a deeper understanding of literature as a whole.

THE UNIT: A SET OF BOOKS, A SINGLE THREAD

A *unit* is a small set of books—usually about five titles—related by theme, style, story situation, or other common element. There are good reasons for building units. A well-designed unit offers a variety of reading experiences for a diverse class. At the same time, the thread tying the books in the unit together will also unify the group of children: boys in khakis and girls in armbands may enjoy different books in the unit, but in activities following the reading, the two groups will come together to explore a common subject. Comparing and contrasting books on the same subject will sharpen students' understanding of the individual titles.

A unit can also enhance enjoyment. If students like one book, they will be more receptive to a second book when the teacher introduces it as "another story about someone with the same kind of problem."

Finally, creating a unit makes sense because the field of literature itself comprises related books. "There is one story and one story only," writes the poet Robert Graves (1955), and while individual books mark out separate plots, even preschool children can begin to see that these plots are situated on common ground.

Critic Northrop Frye offers one rationale for grouping books together rather than presenting and responding to them merely as a stack of separate titles. Frye suggests that all themes, characters, and stories in literature belong to "one big interlocking family." He continues:

> You can see how true this is if you think of such words as tragedy or comedy or satire or romance: certain typical ways in which stories get told. You keep associating your literary experiences together: you're always being reminded of some other story you read or movie you saw or character that impressed you. For most of us, most of the time, this goes on unconsciously, but the fact that it does go on suggests that perhaps in literature you don't just read one novel or poem after another, but that there's a real subject to be studied, as there is in a science, and that the more you read, the more you learn about literature as a whole. This concept of "literature as a whole" suggests something else. Is it possible to get, in however crude and sketchy a way, some bird's eye view of what literature as a whole is about: considered, that is, as a coherent subject of study and not just a pile of·books? (1964, pp. 48–49)

Frye's answer is yes. He suggests that all modern stories relate to primitive tales, and ultimately to one tale about a hero "whose adventures, death, disappearance and marriage or resurrection are the focal points of what later became romance and tragedy and satire and comedy in fiction . . ." (p. 55).

But Dorothea need not lead her fifth-graders in a search for ancient literary roots to give the students a sense of the family of literature and a framework for understanding other books they read. She can begin simply, by introducing some closely related members of the family. Then her students can discover their relationships.

What are these relationships? There are as many as there are in human families. Some books grow out of ancient themes involving such human emotions as fear or jealousy, although their plots— matching interests of a current generation—may be quite contemporary. Some groups of books spring like siblings from the same author or illustrator. Perhaps you have noticed other relationships between books as you read Part One. It is evident, at least, that books fall naturally into different groups depending on their genre. One simple approach for Dorothea is to build a unit based on books with the same situation—a situation reflecting what is happening day by day in her classroom.

But what books should be chosen, and how should they be intro-

Planning a literature curriculum means being aware of children's differing tastes in reading. (Kenneth Karp.)

duced? In human families, children are more likely to feel at ease in a playroom full of cousins than in a study full of great-uncles. In choosing books for her unit, Dorothea has to call on what she knows of her children's interests and abilities, as well as her own critical skill in evaluating literature. Then she needs other skills in presenting books in her unit and drawing a response from her students.

Overall, the task is many times more complex than picking titles at random from a list of recommended books and giving them to children one by one. But the unit approach offers many more rewards, as students discover patterns in literature.

"I know this story," says a child in the third grade starting a new book, because the book falls in the context of a unit. Many units and years later, the adolescent may discover the "one story, and one story only" that lies beneath all literature.

A BRIEF GUIDE TO UNIT BUILDING

The case studies in this chapter show how several teachers in different settings constructed units. Each of the teachers begins by weighing particular interests and abilities in the classroom. Each defines teaching goals, and then calls for help in building a good unit from a variety of sources.

As a starting point, the following chart contains a thumbnail sketch of children's reading interests and abilities in different age ranges. The ranges are listed horizontally, across the top of the chart. (There is more material in Chapter 1 on how children grow and learn.) The generalizations about children lead naturally to suggestions about grouping books into units; some of the ways are listed vertically to the left of the chart.

Please note that each of the units suggested in the chart is only a sample, and the generalizations are not the last word on children or on the literature they will like. Information in the chart is meant to stimulate preliminary thought about particular young readers whose needs may be quite different from most children their age.

The chart contains almost ninety titles; ninety others might have been chosen to replace them. Perhaps you can think of half a dozen replacement titles off the top of your head, based on your reading in Part One.

A contemporary book such as *Sounder* may present an ancient theme, such as courage or loyalty. (Illustration by James Barkley from *Sounder* by William H. Armstrong. Illustrations copyright © 1969 by James Barkley. By permission of Harper & Row, Publishers, Inc.)

567

SITUATION
: The child is particularly interested in subjects close to home.

Unit: Bedtime*
Babbitt, Natalie. *The Something.*
Crowe, Robert L. *Clyde Monster.*
Hoban, Russell. *Bedtime for Frances.*
Kraus, Robert. *Milton the Early Riser.*
Sharmat, Marjorie. *Goodnight Andrew, Goodnight Craig.*
Waber, Bernard. *Ira Sleeps Over.*

THEME
: An egocentric outlook—putting the self at the center of all experience—makes it difficult for children to understand more than one point of view.

Unit: Jealousy over a new baby
Alexander, Martha. *Nobody Asked Me If I Wanted a Baby Sister.*
Greenfield, Eloise. *She Come Bringing Me That Little Baby Girl.*
Hoban, Russell. *A Baby Sister for Frances.*
Keats, Ezra Jack. *Peter's Chair.*
Klein, Norma. *If I Had My Way.*

GENRE
: Children are in the process of developing concepts of real versus make-believe.

Unit: Fantasy versus realism
Freeman, Don. *Bearymore.*
Freschet, Berniece. *Little Black Bear Goes for a Walk.*
Sendak, Maurice. *Pierre.*
Sharmat, Marjorie. *I Don't Care.*

AUTHOR OR ILLUSTRATOR
: These Keats books are some of his simplest; they were chosen to match pre-schoolers' short attention span.

Unit: Ezra Jack Keats
Dreams.
Over in the Meadow.
Pet Show!
The Snowy Day.
Whistle for Willie.

OTHER COMMON ELEMENT
: Children at this age enjoy the interplay of imagination with reality.

Unit: Books whose illustrations show both the real and the imagined parts of a story
Alexander, Martha. *Blackboard Bear.*
Krauss, Ruth. *A Very Special House.*
Zolotow, Charlotte. *The Unfriendly Book.*

*Units marked with an asterisk are described in detail in this chapter's case studies.

SITUATION Children understand and empathize with family situations different from their own.

Unit: Divorced families
Eichler, Margaret. *Martin's Father.*
Lexau, Joan. *Me Day* and *Emily and the Klunky Baby and the Next-Door Dog.*
Newfield, Marcia. *A Book for Jodan.*
Thomas, Ianthe. *Eliza's Daddy.*

THEME Awareness of right and wrong increases.

Unit: Honesty
Cohen, Miriam. *The New Teacher.*
Duvoisin, Roger. *Petunia, I Love You.*
Marshall, James. *George and Martha.*
Ness, Evaline. *Sam, Bangs & Moonshine.*
Zemach, Harve. *The Tricks of Master Dabble.*

GENRE Children quickly pick up, and continue to enjoy, patterns in language and story.

Unit: Cumulative folktales
Jacobs, Joseph. *Munachar and Manachar: An Irish Story.*
Jameson, Cynthia. *The Clay Pot Boy.*
Kent, Jack. *The Fat Cat: A Danish Folktale.*
Lazarus, Keo F. *The Billy Goat in the Chili Patch.*
Leodhas, Sorche Nic. *All in the Morning Early.*

AUTHOR OR ILLUSTRATOR Appropriate poetry helps to expand language during a period of rapid growth.

Unit: Karla Kuskin (poet)*
Any Me I Want to Be.
A Boy Had a Mother Who Bought Him a Hat.
In the Flaky, Frosty Morning.
In the Middle of the Trees.
Near the Window Tree.

OTHER COMMON ELEMENT Taste in humor runs to riddles and slapstick.

Unit: Human foibles
Hutchins, Pat. *Clocks and More Clocks* and *Don't Forget the Bacon!*
MacGregor, Ellen. *Theodore Turtle.*
Merriam, Eve. *Epaminondas.*
Ryan, Cheli Duran. *Hildilid's Night.*

SITUATION

Children are more concerned now about gaining acceptance from others who are their age.

Unit: Peer groups *
Fitzhugh, Louise. *Harriet the Spy.*
Greene, Constance C. *The Unmaking of Rabbit.*
Griffiths, Helen. *The Greyhound.*
Sachs, Marilyn. *Peter and Veronica.*

THEME

The child can empathize with a variety of book characters, readily understanding emotions—such as fear—in others.

Unit: Courage
Armstrong, William H. *Sounder.*
Byars, Betsy. *The 18th Emergency.*
Dalgliesh, Alice. *The Courage of Sarah Noble.*
Hautzig, Esther. *The Endless Steppe.*
Sperry, Armstrong. *Call It Courage.*

GENRE

Careful selection and presentation can nurture appreciation of good poetry at a time when some children lose interest.

Unit: Humorous narrative poetry
Nash, Ogden. "Adventures of Isabel."
Silverstein, Shel. "Sarah Cynthia Sylvia Stout."
Starbird, Kaye. "Eat-It-All Elaine."

AUTHOR OR ILLUSTRATOR

Many children enjoy building collections, of model cars, for example, or of books by the same author.

Unit: Jean Fritz
Brady.
The Cabin Faced West.
Early Thunder.
Who's That Stepping on Plymouth Rock?
Will You Sign Here, John Hancock?

OTHER COMMON ELEMENT

Interest sometimes outstrips reading ability. This sample unit of engrossing stories, for instance, contains dialect which children may find difficult to read on their own. They enjoy hearing the books, provided the teacher has practiced reading the dialect beforehand.

Unit: Regional dialect—Appalachia
Caudill, Rebecca. *Did You Carry the Flag Today, Charley?*
Chaffin, Lillie D. *John Henry McCoy.*
Chase, Richard. *The Jack Tales.*
Cleaver, Vera, and Bill Cleaver. *Where the Lillies Bloom.*
Turkle, Brinton. *The Fiddler of High Lonesome.*

SITUATION	Young adolescents often develop idealistic concern about the plights of other people.

Unit: Physical disability
Corcoran, Barbara. *A Dance to Still Music.*
Haar, Jaap ter. *The World of Ben Lighthart.*
Neuffeld, John. *Twink.*
Resnick, Rose. *Sun and Shadow.*
Sutcliff, Rosemary. *The Witch's Brat.*

THEME	They search for their own set of standards and values.

Unit: Individuality
Conford, Ellen. *The Alfred G. Graebner Memorial High School Handbook of Rules and Regulations.*
Cunningham, Julia. *Come to the Edge.*
Kendall, Carol. *The Gammage Cup.*
Picard, Barbara. *One Is One.*

GENRE	In defining who they are, young readers sometimes seek models in literature.

Unit: Biography
Campion, Nardi Reeder. *Ann the Word; The Life of Mother Ann Lee, Founder of the Shakers.*
Coolidge, Olivia E. *The Statesmanship of Abraham Lincoln.*
Faber, Doris. *Bella Abzug.*
Hamilton, Virginia. *Paul Robeson.*

AUTHOR OR ILLUSTRATOR	Tastes diverge, but many at this age level enjoy fantasy and science fiction.

Unit: Ursula Le Guin
The Farthest Shore.
The Tombs of Atuan.
A Wizard of Earthsea.

OTHER COMMON ELEMENT	Adolescents can understand the form of literature apart from the content of the story; they can discuss myths, short stories, novels, and the forms of poetry.

*Unit: Symbolism**
Arkin, Alan. *The Lemming Condition.*
Cunningham, Julia. *Dorp Dead.*
Steele, Mary Q. *Journey Outside.*

Suppose you faced a blank chart, with no specific titles in mind other than a few unrelated books you happen to recall. How would you fill out the chart with books that relate to each other as well as to the needs of children at each age?

How to Find Appropriate Titles

Teachers sometimes begin with one or two titles they know well, and then ask other teachers or librarians for help in finding other books to fill out a unit. Journals about children's books also suggest new titles. Among the most useful journals are the following.

The Horn Book Magazine (585 Boylston Street, Boston, Mass., 02116) contains reviews of children's books as well as an interesting variety of articles about literature in each issue.

Language Arts (National Council of Teachers of English, 1111 Kenyon Road, Urbana, Ill., 61801), like *The Horn Book,* evaluates writing for children on literary grounds. *Language Arts* also offers articles focusing on a different theme—creative writing, for example—each month.

The Bulletin of the Center for Children's Books (Graduate Library School, University of Chicago Press, 5801 Ellis Avenue, Chicago, Ill., 60637), contains reviews only, with a rating system from "R" for recommended books to "NR" for not recommended. The *Bulletin* is particularly useful to librarians and teachers trying to decide what new books to buy.

The Web (Center for Language, Literature and Reading, College of Education, Ohio State University, room 200, Ramseyer Hall, 29 W. Woodruff, Columbus, Ohio, 43210) contains reviews and suggests potential units. The Fall 1977 issue, for instance, has a section on books about nature and how to use them in the classroom.

Reviews in these journals often compare books with similar books, providing foundations for units based on recent writing for children. Journals, however, do not cover a large number of books per issue. A typical *Horn Book,* for instance, reviews only about forty to fifty titles. By contrast, a large volume, *Subject Guide to Children's Books in Print 1977–1978,* published by Bowker, lists 39,250 titles. Bowker's book, however, provides no reviews; all information, including age recommendations, comes from the publishers of the titles.

In addition, there are dozens of easy-to-use book lists that provide you with plot synopses, thumbnail reviews, and even ready-made

SOME SELECTION GUIDES

Here is a sampling of selection guides. Each has distinctive features; look at the differences between them.

Adventuring with Books (1977), edited by Pat Cianciolo, lists 2,500 titles, chosen on literary grounds, for children from preschool to eighth grade. The table of contents contains books grouped under general categories such as animals, books without words, fantasy, mystery, and fine arts. Two or three sentences describe each title and often evaluate the books. Entries include age recommendations. There is an author and title index.

The Best in Children's Books, 1966–1972 (1973), edited by Zena Sutherland, provides one-paragraph reviews, evaluating books on literary grounds, from *The Bulletin of the Center for Children's Books.* This guide has fewer titles than *Adventuring with Books* (1,400 compared with 2,500), but its index is particularly useful. Books are listed not only by subject but also by several other categories that might be helpful to teachers trying to plan units, such as developmental values, curricular use, reading level, and type of literature (legends, songbooks, historical fiction, for example). Reviews themselves are arranged alphabetically by author.

The Bookfinder (1977), edited by Sharon Spredemann Dreyer, lists even fewer titles than the first two guides (1,031). Books listed here were chosen on the basis of their potential in helping children to "cope with the challenges of life" (p. ix). *The Bookfinder* also has a distinctive system to help readers locate what they want: the index is a book in itself, bound in at the top of the volume. Synopses of children's books with age recommendations and evaluations are in a separate book below the index, sharing the same spine. This arrangement lets readers look for titles while leaving the index open.

A Multimedia Approach to Children's Literature (1977), compiled and edited by Ellin Greene and Madalynne Schoenfeld, differs from other guides in listing films, filmstrips, records, and tapes that could be used to complement units. The guide gives brief descriptions of 550 books, 225 films, 300 filmstrips, and 375 recordings. These include recordings of authors reading or talking about their work. Again, compilers developed their own criteria for selection. All material was tested on children, and their responses helped determine what was listed. The book includes rental and purchase prices, but unlike other guides, it does not make age- or reading-level recommendations.

Reading Ladders for Human Relations (1972), edited by Virginia Reid, is a selection of 1,500 books that deal in some way with human relations. There are four general categories: creating a positive self-image, living with others, appreciating different cultures, and coping with change. Within each, books are listed by age, from "primary" to "mature," suggesting a ladder running from beginning books to books for young adults.

Any of these books can help build a unit, but you should choose the selection guide most likely to contain the information you need. To find a list of all the books published by one author, for instance, you would probably look first at *Children's Books in Print* because it contains by far the largest number of titles. *Books in Print,* however, would yield no evaluations of literary quality. For books related to a specific emotional problem, you might begin with *The Bookfinder* and then check *Adventuring with Books* or *The Best in Children's Books* to get perspective on literary quality. Finally, of course, proper selection depends on your own reading of suggested titles coupled with your understanding of the children you work with.

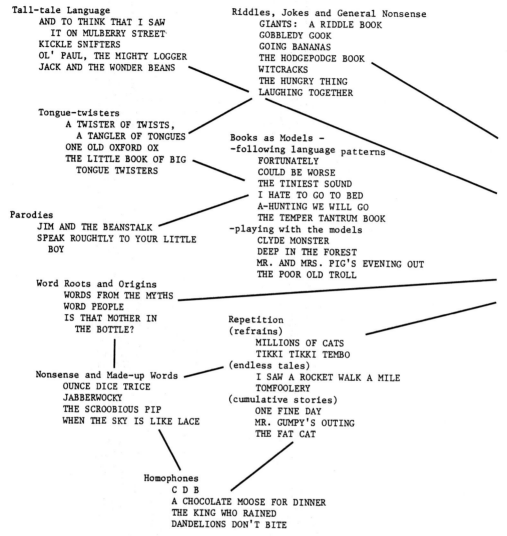

Tall-tale Language
    AND TO THINK THAT I SAW
      IT ON MULBERRY STREET
    KICKLE SNIFTERS
    OL' PAUL, THE MIGHTY LOGGER
    JACK AND THE WONDER BEANS

Riddles, Jokes and General Nonsense
    GIANTS: A RIDDLE BOOK
    GOBBLEDY GOOK
    GOING BANANAS
    THE HODGEPODGE BOOK
    WITCRACKS
    THE HUNGRY THING
    LAUGHING TOGETHER

Tongue-twisters
    A TWISTER OF TWISTS,
      A TANGLER OF TONGUES
    ONE OLD OXFORD OX
    THE LITTLE BOOK OF BIG
      TONGUE TWISTERS

Books as Models -
-following language patterns
    FORTUNATELY
    COULD BE WORSE
    THE TINIEST SOUND
    I HATE TO GO TO BED
    A-HUNTING WE WILL GO
    THE TEMPER TANTRUM BOOK
-playing with the models
    CLYDE MONSTER
    DEEP IN THE FOREST
    MR. AND MRS. PIG'S EVENING OUT
    THE POOR OLD TROLL

Parodies
    JIM AND THE BEANSTALK
    SPEAK ROUGHTLY TO YOUR LITTLE
      BOY

Word Roots and Origins
    WORDS FROM THE MYTHS
    WORD PEOPLE
    IS THAT MOTHER IN
      THE BOTTLE?

Repetition
(refrains)
    MILLIONS OF CATS
    TIKKI TIKKI TEMBO
(endless tales)
    I SAW A ROCKET WALK A MILE
    TOMFOOLERY
(cumulative stories)
    ONE FINE DAY
    MR. GUMPY'S OUTING
    THE FAT CAT

Nonsense and Made-up Words
    OUNCE DICE TRICE
    JABBERWOCKY
    THE SCROOBIOUS PIP
    WHEN THE SKY IS LIKE LACE

Homophones
    C D B
    A CHOCOLATE MOOSE FOR DINNER
    THE KING WHO RAINED
    DANDELIONS DON'T BITE

units. There is a sampling of some of these books about books on page 573.

    These guides and others like them enable teachers to draw up a

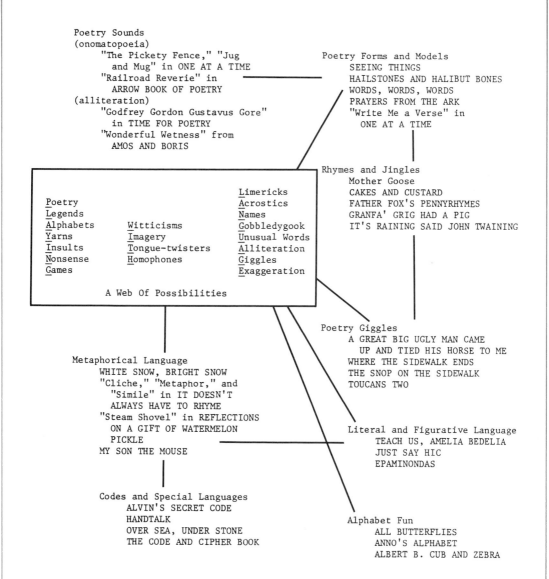

Poetry Sounds
(onomatopoeia)
     "The Pickety Fence," "Jug
       and Mug" in ONE AT A TIME
     "Railroad Reverie" in
       ARROW BOOK OF POETRY
(alliteration)
     "Godfrey Gordon Gustavus Gore"
       in TIME FOR POETRY
     "Wonderful Wetness" from
       AMOS AND BORIS

Poetry Forms and Models
     SEEING THINGS
     HAILSTONES AND HALIBUT BONES
     WORDS, WORDS, WORDS
     PRAYERS FROM THE ARK
     "Write Me a Verse" in
       ONE AT A TIME

Poetry		Limericks
Legends		Acrostics
Alphabets	Witticisms	Names
Yarns	Imagery	Gobbledygook
Insults	Tongue-twisters	Unusual Words
Nonsense	Homophones	Alliteration
Games		Giggles
		Exaggeration

A Web Of Possibilities

Rhymes and Jingles
     Mother Goose
     CAKES AND CUSTARD
     FATHER FOX'S PENNYRHYMES
     GRANFA' GRIG HAD A PIG
     IT'S RAINING SAID JOHN TWAINING

Poetry Giggles
     A GREAT BIG UGLY MAN CAME
       UP AND TIED HIS HORSE TO ME
     WHERE THE SIDEWALK ENDS
     THE SNOP ON THE SIDEWALK
     TOUCANS TWO

Metaphorical Language
     WHITE SNOW, BRIGHT SNOW
     "Cliche," "Metaphor," and
       "Simile" in IT DOESN'T
     ALWAYS HAVE TO RHYME
     "Steam Shovel" in REFLECTIONS
       ON A GIFT OF WATERMELON
       PICKLE
     MY SON THE MOUSE

Literal and Figurative Language
     TEACH US, AMELIA BEDELIA
     JUST SAY HIC
     EPAMINONDAS

Codes and Special Languages
     ALVIN'S SECRET CODE
     HANDTALK
     OVER SEA, UNDER STONE
     THE CODE AND CIPHER BOOK

Alphabet Fun
     ALL BUTTERFLIES
     ANNO'S ALPHABET
     ALBERT B. CUB AND ZEBRA

list of related books in just a few minutes of cross-checking between
index and book descriptions. The next step in building a unit is
paring down the list to a handful of books.

Criteria for Paring Down the List of Titles
In part, of course, selection depends on what is available in a school
or local library, or what can be obtained. Final choice is also swayed
by how much time there is for a unit. Many school libraries, for

instance, require the return of all books a week or two before the end of the year. It would be impractical in such schools to begin a unit of five novels a month before summer vacation. Teachers have little control over these conditions.

Once the conditions have been met, however, it takes creative judgment to choose a group of books to match a particular class.

Will the readers understand each of the books?
Will they be interested?
Will the selection extend their experience with literature?

All the criteria for selecting individual titles come into play when creating units.

Beyond these criteria, teachers should be concerned with matching each book to other *books* in the unit.

Does the collection provide variety within itself, even though all entries relate to a common theme?
Can books be compared and contrasted to sharpen perspective on each title?
Do the books naturally generate different activities to enhance the students' response to the literature?

Those are some of the key questions teachers in the following case studies have to face.

CASE STUDY: A FIFTH-GRADE TEACHER, A UNIT ON PEER RELATIONSHIPS

Dorothea has a basic idea—peer groups—and has decided to try to put together a unit. Since her main teaching goal now is to foster enjoyment of good literature, she plans to read the unit aloud. That will give her freedom to choose highly interesting books that would be too difficult for some in her class if they tried to read on their own. Her other teaching goals are to improve her children's speaking and writing abilities with engrossing activities related to the books.

Use of selection guides

What books should she use? Her first step in the search for titles is consulting *The Bookfinder's* index—the top half of the book—under "Peer Groups." Under an entry for "Peer Relationships," she finds subheads for "Avoiding Others, Cliques, Clubs, Gangs, Identification with Peers, Isolation, Jealousy, Ostracism. . . ." She leaves the index open at the top and thumbs through the book descriptions at the bottom, quickly finding two interesting books referred to under "Peer Relationships."

One is *The Unmaking of Rabbit* (1972), by Constance C. Greene. The entry reports:

380

Greene, Constance C.
The Unmaking of Rabbit
The Viking Press, Inc., 1972.
(125 pages)

BELONGING
Appearance: concern about
Friendship: meaning of
Grandparent: living in home of
Parental: absence
Parental: rejection
Peer relationships: rejection
Self, attitude toward: accepting

Paul, eleven, has lived unhappily with his grandmother for nine years, ever since his father disappeared. Paul's mother promises him that he can come to live with her when she finds a larger apartment or marries a man who wants Paul too. The boy has no friends at school. The other children put pencil shavings in his lunch box, call him Rabbit because his ears stick out, and mock him because he stutters. Paul tells himself that their teasing does not matter, because he will soon be leaving to join his mother. On his next visit with her, however, he realizes that they probably never will be reunited. He also discovers, after placing himself in danger in a desperate attempt to win the acceptance of his classmates, that he does not want their type of friendship after all. Some time later, he finally experiences true friendship with the son of one of Gran's acquaintances.

At the beginning of the story, Paul waits for his mother to want him and for the boys at school to accept him. He constantly tries to please his mother, but since she never seems to appreciate him and seldom even pays attention to him, he finally realizes that she is concerned only with herself and decides that living with Gran is better after all. As the story progresses, Paul develops a more positive sense of self-worth, which enables him to reach out for genuine friendship.

Ages 10-13

Also available in:
Braille — *The Unmaking of Rabbit*
Library of Congress
Paperbound — *The Unmaking of Rabbit*
Dell Publishing Company, Inc. (Yearling Books)

The second is *Harriet the Spy* (1964), by Louise Fitzhugh, with this synopsis and age recommendation:

320

Fitzhugh, Louise
Harriet the Spy
Black/white illustrations by the author.
Harper & Row Publishers, Inc., 1964.
(298 pages)

MATURATION
Friendship: keeping friends
Peer relationships: avoiding others
Separation anxiety

Eleven-year-old Harriet Welch wants to be a writer. To "train her powers of observation," she keeps a notebook in which she writes down her thoughts about people she knows. Ole Golly, Harriet's governess, encourages Harriet to write but, oddly enough, never reads the girl's notebook. Harriet is devoted to Ole Golly and feels that no one understands her as well as her governess does. She hopes Ole Golly will never leave. But Ole Golly departs to get married. Shortly after her governess "deserts her," Harriet's classmates find the notebook and read what Harriet has written about them. The notebook contains many frank and unkind observations, for Harriet seems to have observed and described her peers at their most unflattering moments. Her classmates retaliate by refusing to speak to her and by playing cruel tricks on her. Harriet tries to stay home to avoid her "friends." Mr. and Mrs. Welch force her to attend school, but she misbehaves there and runs back home. Her parents now see that they really do not know their daughter and have no idea how to help her. So they take her to a psychiatrist and ask her teachers to help change her attitude. The psychiatrist suggests that Harriet's parents write to Ole Golly and ask her to correspond with Harriet. Before receiving a letter from Ole Golly, Harriet is kept out of school for six days. When she receives the letter, it instructs her to begin writing something besides notes in her notebook, to apologize to her friends, and to be more kind in her observations of others, even if that requires her to tell small lies. After this letter, and after she is appointed editor of the sixth-grade page in the school newspaper, Harriet regains friends and comes to be at peace with herself.

Harriet's blunt manner of writing hurts others' feelings, and they react by rejecting her friendship and badgering her. Harriet tries to escape the situation instead of face it. She feigns illness so that she will not have to go to school. When this does not work, she fights and runs away. The book explains that her bad behavior results from her governess's departure. Harriet again appears in Louise Fitzhugh's *The Long Secret*.

Ages 10-12

Also available in:
Large Print — *Harriet the Spy*
Harper & Row Publishers, Inc.
Talking Book — *Harriet the Spy*
Library of Congress

After browsing in *The Bookfinder* for a few minutes, Dorothea turns at the suggestion of the school librarian to another promising-looking index, *Reading Ladders for Human Relations.* The second topic in the table of contents, "Living with Others," appears to relate to Dorothea's unit. And under it, she finds a subheading that raises expectations: "Peer Relationships." *Reading Ladders,* she discovers, offers much shorter entries about books, grouped according to age level. Under the section for readers in intermediate grades, thirty-one books are listed, including *Harriet the Spy.* Two other books in the group attract her attention: *The Greyhound* (1964), by Helen Griffiths, and *Veronica Ganz* (1968), by Marilyn Sachs. Griffiths' book is described like this:

> GRIFFITHS, HELEN. *The Greyhound.* il. by Victor Ambrus. Doubleday, 1964, $3.50. Jamie becomes deeply involved with a gang when he borrows money from the leader in order to buy food for his dog. Forced to help in robberies, his relationship with his mother becomes tense and strained. All ends well, but not without a struggle as Jamie attempts to determine which values should guide his actions.

And here is the annotation for *Veronica Ganz:*

> SACHS, MARILYN. *Veronica Ganz.* il. by Louis Glanzman. Doubleday, 1968, $3.95 (P/WSP, $.60). Thirteen-year-old Veronica's automatic response to being teased about her height is to bully the teaser. One day she realizes that Peter actually admires her and instead of bullying him, she giggles. The story is complicated by the fact that Veronica and her sister live with their mother and stepfather and visit their father with decreasing frequency.

On the basis of the descriptions, both books look like strong entries in the unit. But Dorothea decides to take her exploration one step further. The notes on *Veronica Ganz* have reminded her that many of the peer problems in the classroom seem to revolve around conflicts between boys and girls. The class has grown in awareness of sex differences, and some of the taunting and teasing is probably an early kind of flirting, although currently the class is strictly segregated according to sex. She wonders if there are other books about the relationships between the sexes. She returns briefly to *The Bookfinder* to a major heading: "Boy-Girl Relationships." There, again, is *Veronica Ganz.* Nearby, however, is another book by the same author that complements the unit better. The book is *Peter and Veronica* (1969), and *The Bookfinder* has this to say about it:

762

Sachs, Marilyn

Peter and Veronica

Black/white illustrations by Louis Glanzman.
Doubleday & Company, Inc., 1969.
(174 pages)

FRIENDSHIP: Meaning of
PREJUDICE: Religious
    Boy-girl relationships
    Inferiority, feelings of
    Jew

Peter Wedemeyer, twelve years old, is an intelligent and well-liked boy who expects to do well in Hebrew school. His schoolmate and friend Veronica Ganz is clumsy, sloppy, and large for her age. To hide her feelings of inferiority and shyness, Veronica often is aggressive and belligerent. Peter is her only friend. Their friendship is frowned upon by both their mothers because of religious differences. Peter argues and fights with his family for weeks before his Bar Mitzvah because he wants to ask Veronica, a gentile, to the celebration. When she finally is invited, Veronica dreads having to mingle with other people and decides not to go. Later, when she apologizes for turning down the invitation, Peter is so angry that he mocks her and refuses to accept her apology. His anger lasts most of the summer. When school begins, Peter approaches Veronica, wanting to be friends again. Before he can say anything, Veronica says, "I didn't owe you an apology. You owed me one... You were thinking about you... It had nothing to do with me." Peter admits the truth of her accusations and they resume their friendship.

The problems of prejudice and friendship are conveyed sensitively through the main characters' realistic, often humorous, dialogue. The characterizations of Peter and Veronica give the book, a sequel to *Veronica Ganz*, a lively quality. The third book in this series is *The Truth about Mary Rose*.

Ages 10-12

Also available in:
Paperbound — *Peter and Veronica*
Dell Publishing Company, Inc. (Yearling Books)
Talking Book — *Peter and Veronica*
Library of Congress

Other books in the unit—*The Unmaking of Rabbit, Harriet the Spy,* and *The Greyhound*—have told stories about individuals and their peer problems with entire groups. *Peter and Veronica,* by contrast, focuses on a relationship between just two people.

The two reference guides to selection alone have suggested dozens of books on peer groups. Assembling potential titles has primarily involved winnowing down the list of suggestions. This process of elimination has resulted in a balanced collection, small enough for Dorothea to present the unit in about five weeks, the time between two vacations.

Matching the unit to time available for presentation

Now she reads each of the four books in the unit, and plans all activities supporting her teaching goals.

Here is what happens over the next month and a half.

First Week

Just back from their first vacation of the year, the children in Dorothea's class are receptive to an idea that does not sound like work. Before she picks up the first book in the unit, she asks students to write down short descriptions of typical arguments people have, in school or at home. No one will have to share the descriptions unless they want to, Dorothea announces. But after fifteen minutes of writing, several want to read what they have written. Two examples are "Some boys always butt in line in front of me," and "My sister stole three erasers from me and we had a big fight."

Dorothea jots notes on these and other conflicts on the blackboard, and then asks the class which one or two arguments

they would like to try acting out, now, in class. A few students
volunteer to role-play, and Dorothea assigns them to take the parts
of two quarreling people. These dramatized tiffs take only a few
minutes to act out. Then the whole class is encouraged to talk about
what happened. Why was there a disagreement? Was the argument
resolved? Why or why not?

Finally, Dorothea picks up the first book in the unit: *Peter and
Veronica.* "We've talked about the kinds of arguments people have,"
she begins. "Now here's a story about two people who get angry
with each other. Watch how the argument begins."

Dorothea reads the book aloud in installments for several days
without further discussion with the class. Peter, preparing for his
bar mitzvah, lays down an ultimatum. If his friend Veronica cannot
come, he will not go through with the ceremony. She is invited, but
mysteriously does not come after all. The day after the disappoint-
ing bar mitzvah, she comes to Peter's house, carrying a gift and
prepared to explain why she did not show up. . . .

Here (around page 145), Dorothea pauses in the reading for an
activity to enhance interest in the book, and to give students more
practice in speaking up in class. One student takes the part of Peter,
coming downstairs in his apartment house and meeting Veronica,
played by another student. What do they say to each other? Several
pairs have a chance to act out the scene before Dorothea continues
with the actual scene of the battle in the book. She completes her
reading of the book in two or three days.

Second, Third Weeks

In *Harriet the Spy,* by comparison with the first book in the unit, the
conflict broadens. It becomes Harriet against her world. The book
will take about two weeks to read aloud. But early in the reading,
after students understand how Harriet keeps her diary, Dorothea
again pauses for a day for an activity to sharpen interest in the book,
and give practice in writing.

This time, she asks her class to imagine they were invisible spies
this morning. "Pretend you were someone else and no one could see
you," she suggests. "And your assignment was to watch and take
notes on—*you.*" The task calls on the class to write about their day
in the third person, from the time they got up.

Phil got out of the wrong side of bed.
Susan sat with Charlene on the bus.
Mike was almost late. His mother made him put on boots.

Harriet's classmates are reading her comments about them in her notebook. (Illustration from *Harriet the Spy*, written and illustrated by Louise Fitzhugh. Copyright © 1964 by Louise Fitzhugh. By permission of Harper & Row, Publishers, Inc.)

"Now," Dorothea suggests, "turn back into *you*. Pretend that the spy made a mistake and dropped the notes on a sidewalk near where you live. You find the notes and read them. Now you know someone has been watching every move you make. How do you feel? Write down how you feel." Next, Dorothea leads the activity back to the book again: "Thinking about what you wrote, do you think it was OK for Harriet to keep notes on everybody in her class? Why? Why not?"

She raises the same question at the end of the two weeks spent with *Harriet*.

Fourth Week

The Unmaking of Rabbit takes just a few days to read, presenting a portrait of Paul, the class outcast because of his prominent ears and occasional stutter. (She would not have chosen the book if her class included anyone who stuttered, or had prominent ears, or "Rabbit" as a nickname.)

Another writing activity follows the reading. Half the students

imagine they are Rabbit, writing a letter to a newspaper advice column about how to get rid of an unwanted nickname. The other half
of the class has to answer the letters with some written suggestions.
The work supports two teaching goals: heightening involvement
with the book, and providing practice in communication skills.

The following day, Dorothea introduces another project to help
the class find a common pattern in separate books. She begins a
discussion with the questions: "How did the way other kids act and
think change the way Paul and Harriet acted?" "Which one handled
the problem better, and why?" After this preliminary discussion,
she hands out blank sheets of paper and asks students to write how
they are affected by what others think and do, by clothes others
wear, or opinions they hold. She explains before they begin that no
one else will see or hear what they have written. At the end of
writing, they can keep the sheets as the start of a diary, like Harriet's, or they can tear them up.

Fifth Week

After their experiences with other books in the unit, the story in *The
Greyhound* sounds remarkably familiar to Dorothea's fifth-graders.
Like Paul, Jamie is caught up in a plan to commit robbery; unlike
Paul, he goes through with it, and his threat to reveal who commit-
ted the crime lands him in deep trouble with his peers and con-
spirators.

This time, the discussion following the reading ranges over four
books, beginning with the story of Jamie. "How much of Jamie's
problem was the fault of the other boys around him? How much was
his own fault, and why?" Students have the background to answer,
with precedents from the story about Paul. In the brisk discussion,

one or two students make the connection between the two characters without any prompting. Dorothea picks up the point from
them. "Thinking over the other stories you have heard, were Peter
or Veronica, Jamie or Paul, or Harriet forced to act the way they did
by other people? How?" Finally, she asks a series of questions calling on her class to apply what they have read to their own lives.
"How are people you know pushed into saying or acting certain
ways by other people?" "What can they do to get more control over
their lives?"

At the end of the unit, the reading and discussion have not broken
the pattern of peer pressure in Dorothea's classroom. But therapy
was not among Dorothea's goals. The unit has accomplished her
major aims. The books have suggested several writing projects, and
stimulated participation in discussions from every corner of the

Given guide questions by their teacher, these intermediate-grade students discuss several books they have read. (Miriam Reinhart/Photo Researchers, Inc.)

classroom. Even the slowest readers in the class have encountered good literature that provided several fresh perspectives on their own lives.

In discussions, Dorothea's class was able to deal with four books simultaneously. Younger children may have difficulty holding that many titles in mind at the same time. But even preschool teachers can use units to achieve teaching goals, as the next case study shows.

CASE STUDY 2: A KINDERGARTEN TEACHER, A UNIT ON BEDTIME

Michelle, a teacher in an Ohio suburb, met her class of twenty kindergarten children a few days ago and wonders how she can help make them feel more at ease. Several of the children still linger around the classroom door each morning, watching their parents leave. Most of the children sit quietly during the day, apparently too shy to speak out in class. Although one little girl can read whole short sentences, most in the class have difficulty identifying all the alphabet letters. Few pick up books when given the chance to play with anything in the classroom.

Michelle has several goals relating to literature during these early days of fall. She wants students to be at home with good books. She wants them to recognize that books tell stories about familiar experiences, and she wants them to be able to match experiences they have had to what happens to characters in books. Like all kindergarten teachers she wants to expand children's ability to use language.

Teaching goals

583

She also wants her class to begin to compare one story with another—two books at a time—to enhance enjoyment and to build a foundation for critical skills. As a practical classroom matter, she wants to display books well, and to draw as much interest in literature as in the classroom's gerbil cage or building blocks.

A group of books set out informally on a central table, with their covers showing, will rouse curiosity, she realizes. Her choice of related books will help students begin to see similarities and differences in the way writers deal with the same experience. A small collection will also lead to many different activities tied to one issue of interest to her children.

But what issue should she choose? What books? As Michelle begins planning a unit one afternoon, she makes a list of topics that she knows will engross her children. "Home," she writes, "brothers, sisters, kinds of food, holidays with parents, bedtime." The last entry reminds her immediately of two books: one is Russell Hoban's *Bedtime for Frances* (1960), about a badger reluctant to go to bed. She has read that book before as a single title, and knows children like it.

The second is a more recent story, *Clyde Monster* (1976), by Robert L. Crowe. Michelle first heard about the book by skimming reviews supplied by the Ohio Teachers and Pupils Reading Circle (1456 N. High Street, Columbus, Ohio, 43201). The Circle produces an annual free bulletin suggesting a selection of children's books, and offers a discount on books it selects. The bulletin had this report on *Clyde Monster:*

> 6. **CLYDE MONSTER** by Robert L. Crowe. Clyde was a nice little monster. He was a little more clumsy than average, but otherwise lived an almost happy normal monster life in the forest with his father and mother. But why was Clyde afraid when night came and he was supposed to go to bed -- in the dark!?

The two books are about bedtime, but their plots diverge. Frances the badger puts off bedtime with a series of tried-and-true ploys: needing a glass of milk, making sure she has kissed everyone goodnight, shuttling back and forth between bedroom and living room with reports of frightening things she has seen in the dark. ("There is a giant in my room. May I watch television?") Clyde lives with a family of monsters, and fears people when it is time for him to go off to his cave at night. He convinces his parents to leave the rock ajar a little.

These two related books become the anchor of a kindergarten unit on bedtime. To fill out the list, Michelle confers with the school librarian, who suggests three other possibilities. *Goodnight*

Father's patience begins to wear thin as he hears one more of Frances' reasons for not staying in bed. (Illustration by Garth Williams from *Bedtime for Frances* by Russell Hoban. Illustrations copyright © 1960 by Garth Williams. By permission of Harper & Row, Publishers, Inc.)

Andrew, Goodnight Craig (1969), by Marjorie Sharmat, is realistic fiction about two boys who delay going to sleep by trading silliness between the levels of their bunk beds. [" 'Pleasant nightmares to you,' said Andrew.'And a big bowl of spaghetti' " (p. 8).] Ruth Sonneborn's *Friday Night Is Papa Night* (1970) is the story of a little boy named Pedro who waits with his brothers and sisters for his father to come home from work. But Papa does not come, and finally the disappointed family goes off to bed. Pedro is the first to greet Papa later when he arrives—after he has helped a sick friend to get home.

Both are good books, but the first relates more to the theme of bedtime than the second. *Goodnight Andrew, Goodnight Craig* has something else to recommend it. Its realism complements the fan-

585

tasy in *Bedtime for Frances.* So Michelle tucks Sonneborn's book into her memory for later use, perhaps in a unit on fathers and their work. The librarian also suggests Natalie Babbitt's *The Something* (1970). Pen-and-ink drawings by the author introduce a toothy and shaggy creature named Mylo who is as scared of the dark as Clyde or Frances. But there is a twist in Babbitt's book: Mylo is frightened of a Something which turns out to resemble a little girl in a nightie. Mylo tries sculpting the Something in clay, and he wishes that the Something would appear so he could make a good statue. Eventually he meets her in a dream and discovers that the Something is not frightening after all.

"I'm not afraid of you either," the Something tells Mylo. "But I wish you'd get out of my dream." This is more fanciful than any of the other books, and suggests an activity—modeling dream figures in clay. This bonus—as well as the curious plot—ensures that the book will join the unit.

A first-grade teacher later reminds Michelle of two other books. Bernard Waber's *Ira Sleeps Over* (1972) is realistic fiction about a boy invited for the first time to a friend's house for the night. Should he take his teddy bear, named Tah Tah, to his friend's house? "He'll laugh," says the boy's sister (p. 14). When darkness falls, secrets emerge: Ira's friend has a teddy bear, too, named Foo Foo.

The teacher also proposes *The Gorilla Did It* (1974), by Barbara Shook Hazen, about a child visited at bedtime by a disruptive gorilla who helps the boy mess up his room. The child's mother misses seeing the gorilla, but notices the mess. "The gorilla did it," the boy explains.

Michelle adds *Ira Sleeps Over* to improve the balance in her collection between fantasy and realism, and decides to postpone reading *The Gorilla Did It:* the small set of books already includes several imaginary bedtime creatures.

The five books remaining in the unit are short enough to read out loud in about ten minutes each. They revolve around the same topic, but they complement each other with a balance of genre, setting, and situation. Michelle reads each book aloud to herself and plans a full week's activities based on the books, before the children hear the first story.

Monday

On Monday, the presentation begins without major fanfare. After the careful balancing of the unit, Michelle does not explain her rationale for selection to her class. Nor does she try to point out

Babbitt's book naturally leads to modeling dream figures in clay. (Reproduced with the permission of Farrar, Straus & Giroux, Inc. from *The Something* by Natalie Babbit. Copyright © 1970 by Natalie Babbit.)

differences and similarities between the books. Her strategy for the week is inductive: to introduce children to a group of related books they will probably like, and to let them draw connections and conclusions from day-to-day listening experiences.

Michelle reads *Bedtime for Frances* while the children relax on a large rug. Then she leads a brief discussion, calling on students to interpret what they have read and to apply Frances's situation to their own lives. "Do you think Frances is afraid to be alone in her room? Why do you think so?"

In answering, some begin retelling parts of the story. Michelle moves on. "What do you do if you want to stay up late? Does it work?"

These questions require application of the book to life at home. (An explanation of these and other kinds of discussion questions appears in the previous chapter.)

The introduction to Frances closes with a pantomime exercise: several children take turns acting out what they do to get ready for bed, while others try to guess what they are doing.

Activity relates to teaching goals

587

Michelle leaves *Bedtime for Frances* in the center of a table in the classroom where children pick it up and point at the pictures for the rest of the day.

Tuesday

"Remember Frances?" Michelle asks. The class is back on the carpet, more at ease today, and speaking up. They remember. "Frances was a little animal who could talk, and the story was make-believe. Today you're going to hear another story. It's about two boys. Maybe afterward you'll tell me whether it's make-believe."

Michelle does not introduce the words "fantasy" and "realism" to her kindergarten class. A question or two after reading, however, will help the children to draw contrasts between the two books. In the course of the week, she will never ask the class to compare more than two books at a time: at age 5, her children have difficulty holding one story in mind while hearing another.

Michelle reads a page or two of *Goodnight Andrew, Goodnight Craig* when she realizes that the book is a bit too small—at 6 by 7 inches—for the whole class to see. It takes extra time to move it slowly by the faces of her children, and she makes a mental note to divide the class into two groups the next time she uses the book.

After the reading—it takes about ten minutes—she asks just one question, requiring children to synthesize their experience with two books. "How was Frances's father like Andrew and Craig's father?" One child suggests, "They both yelled." Many others look puzzled. Michelle nods at the child's not entirely accurate response, and does not answer her own question. A brief lecture comparing and contrasting the two male figures would have filled the silence at the moment, but it might well have led to longer silences throughout the rest of the year.

Two researchers who have examined how classroom groups work suggest what can happen when teachers take over discussions:

> The teacher who dominates discussions develops students who don't initiate. The student who is ignored in discussions for a week may stop speaking the next week, and may be ignored for much of the rest of the year. (Schmuck and Schmuck, 1971, p. 90)

Goodnight Andrew joins *Bedtime for Frances* on the book table.

After school on Tuesday, the librarian comes to Michelle's classroom with several other suggestions for rounding out the unit. One is *Bunk Beds* (1972), by Elizabeth Winthrop, a poetic mixture of fantasy and realism about a brother and sister who turn their bunk beds into a ship, a house, and a car as they try to ignore bedtime. The book's situation is reminiscent of *Goodnight Andrew, Goodnight Craig,* and might substitute for it in a future unit. Michelle decides not to present it now.

The librarian also proposes two other titles for variety: both relate to waking up in the morning. One is Myra Cohn Livingston's "Morning":

> Everyone is tight asleep,
> I think I'll sing a tune,
> And if I sing it loud enough
> I'll wake up someone—soon! (1958)

The second title is Robert Kraus' (1958) *Milton the Early Riser* (1972) with large and lavish illustrations by Jose and Ariane Aruego. Milton is an early-rising panda who is disappointed to find the whole colorful world asleep. He goes into bored contortions watching test patterns on TV, and then jumps up and down on a little brown hillock. But everyone sleeps on. Finally he "sang up a storm," loud enough to shake mountains and trees, and all the animals are tossed out of bed in a whirlwind.

The book and poem seem to match perfectly, and the two titles provide a kind of ending for the unit on bedtime. Michelle decides to save them for the following Monday.

Wednesday

The next two days introduce two similar books of fantasy; on each of the days, Michelle will ask children to relate the stories to their own lives. She is hoping to see more willingness to speak up, but she takes satisfaction in the way children now recognize the two books on the book table and "read" through them on their own by looking at the pictures.

On Wednesday morning, she reads *Clyde Monster.* Then she moves a large sheet of blank newsprint paper in front of the crowd on the carpet. "Why is Clyde afraid of the dark?" she asks. "He's afraid of people," someone answers. "Why are some people afraid of the dark?" Now several students speak up. "Ghosts." "Witches." "Spooky things." "Monsters."

"What could you do if you're afraid of the dark?" Michelle asks. As children respond, she begins writing what they say on the newsprint. The responses come faster than she can write.

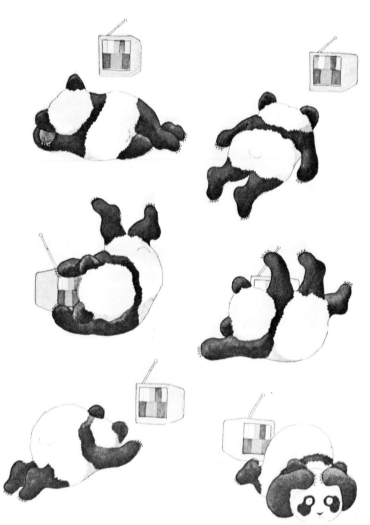

Milton finds that he must entertain himself when he
is the first to awaken. (From *Milton the Early Riser* by
Robert Kraus, illustrated by Jose and Ariane Aruego.
Illustrations copyright © 1972 by Jose Aruego. By
permission of Windmill Books, Inc.)

You could call your mommy.
Scream.
You could ask Daddy to leave the hall light on.
Tell God, He might help you.

Without evaluating any of the suggestions, Michelle records them
all. Several of the shyest children are now willing to speak in front of

590

the group for the first time; every one of their ideas will be respected in her classroom as a treasure.

Although it was not one of her teaching goals to help children overcome their nighttime jitters, Michelle is aware that children between the ages of 2 and 6 harbor a great number of new fears. And she is aware that "the best ways to help children overcome their fears—which they are usually quite eager to shed—involve activity on the part of the children themselves. Children are most successful when they become more competent in finding practical methods of their own to deal with what they fear . . ." (Papalia and Olds, 1975, p. 366).

Clyde joins Frances and Andrew and Craig on the reading table. The newsprint chart hangs nearby.

Thursday

Warned by her experience with the size of *Goodnight Andrew,* Michelle breaks the class into two groups for her reading of Natalie Babbitt's *The Something* (whose pictures are hardly bigger than a postcard). While one group crayons pictures of their bedrooms, the other hears the story about Mylo and his fear of the Something who looks like a little girl. When the whole group has heard the book and seen the pictures, Michelle asks just one question, tying the book to the rest of the unit: "Was the story make-believe, or could it really happen?" Many of the class are able to recognize the difference. Then, she asks the class to close their eyes, and imagine a Something of their own. Finally, children get small lumps of clay to mold their own statues—which wind up near the books, on a shelf under the chart.

<small>Controlled set-
ting enhances
presentation</small>

Friday

Michelle has borrowed *Bedtime for Frances* and *Clyde Monster* from the book table, and holds them both open to a page showing that Frances and Clyde go to bed with dolls or toys. Now she reads *Ira Sleeps Over,* another book focusing on children's almost universal desire for something to snuggle with at night. There is no planned activity after the reading, but Michelle encourages children to bring in toys they sleep with.

Monday

About half the children remember and bring a collection of bears and cloth babies and other toys to school. Michelle admires them

barlene

I like to watch television
and hold my puppies

A kindergarten child drew what she does when she
wakes up early, and she dictated the sentence for her
teacher to write.

individually, and then reads the Livingston poem to the class.
"What do you do when you wake up before anyone else?" she asks.
The children crayon new pictures to illustrate what they say, and
those who wish to hold up and describe the pictures for others to
see. Then Michelle reads the story about Milton the panda, and adds
it to the other books.

The drawings, chart, and clay figures now heighten children's
interest in looking at the table, which now has half a dozen books.
All the stories bring an experience from home into the classroom,
helping children to feel more at ease. The children have begun to
express themselves, and for the first time, Michelle is beginning to
arbitrate between students who want to talk at the same time. Some
of the children have already begun to understand that books can
treat the same subject in different ways. Interest generated in
Frances has helped enhance interest in hearing other stories about
bedtime, throughout the week. And the unit as a whole has stimulated curiosity about books. Michelle now plans to capitalize on that
curiosity in her plans for the rest of the year.

Michelle's classroom—and Dorothea's—are organized conventionally, with a single class in a single room. Today, many schools are using different classroom setups. The next case study illustrates how a teacher created a unit in one such classroom.

CASE STUDY 3: A THIRD-GRADE TEACHER, A UNIT ON POETRY

Hal teaches third grade in a large room reminiscent in some ways of the old-fashioned Little Red Schoolhouse.

But several features distinguish the arrangement from a one-room school. Hal's room is nicknamed the Green Pod because within its pale green walls are three grades, each with its own teacher. The grades, separated by bookcases and movable bulletin boards, work independently most of the time. Individual students from each grade, however, frequently cross the token borders. A few advanced second-graders, for instance, often join Hal's class for a reading lesson. Some third-graders are helping first-graders make papier-mâché models of dinosaurs. Each of the students in the room gets a chance from time to time to use the records or filmstrips on hand in an adjoining media center.

The Green Pod nurtures individual students, and encourages teachers to intertwine their curriculum plans. Hal is pleased with the system, except for one problem; there is a little too much distraction. Hal's reading of *Charlotte's Web*, for example, was punctuated several times by laughter from the first- or second-graders at inappropriate moments. Some of Hal's students have trouble concentrating, even when the lower grades are quiet. Like many third-graders, several students also have a kind of blind spot about books. Even after Hal told them that the author of *Charlotte's Web* was E. B. White, a few of the students assumed White was just another fictional character lurking around the barnyard in the book.

Hal would like to sharpen his class's concentration, and he has several other teaching goals related to literature. He wants his students to understand that real people write books. He wants to boost language development, and he is aware of the study by educator Dorothy H. Cohen showing that elementary school students' ability to read is enhanced when teachers read aloud to them. (The Cohen study, published in 1968, is described in Chapter 1.)

Teaching goals

What should he read? Poetry is a strong possibility, Hal realizes. Listening to poetry calls for high concentration, but for short periods of time. Hal will be able to present a poem in a few minutes, and immediately gauge whether students are picking it up despite distractions. The rhythm and rich sound of poetry should demonstrate the power of language, and good poems will complement the long prose selection he has just completed. Finally, using poetry, he can introduce students quickly to a substantial body of different works by a single author. In a single, short unit, the class should sense contrasting moods as well as stylistic similarities. In other words, they should be able to pick up a personality behind the poetry, to recognize that writers are real people.

Hal is aware that *A Multimedia Approach to Children's Literature* (Greene and Schoenfeld, 1977) might also help introduce authors as people. This selection guide includes listings of recorded readings by authors as well as interviews with them about how they work. Before checking this reference, however, Hal explores the card catalogue in the school library under the names of two or three writers he knows have produced many poems for children: Aileen Fisher, Karla Kuskin, and Myra Cohn Livingston. There are a few books from each poet, but one small volume in particular catches his attention. Karla Kuskin's *Near the Window Tree* (1975) alternates poems with italicized comments by the author. For instance, Kuskin writes:

> There are those days when it is damp and cold and grey. Then everything is the same grey color: the sky, the tree, the wall at the end of the yard. I feel that same grey feeling inside of me.
>
> You can write about anything. You can write about things or feelings. When I have feelings that make me sad or angry I try to write them down to get them outside myself. (p. 14)

This kind of material can help Hal approach one of his teaching goals: to make students more aware of writers as real people.

A check of *A Multimedia Approach* shows that Kuskin has been recorded, on tape and record, reading her own poetry. Hal can obtain a record to complement the unit through an interlibrary loan.

Near the Window Tree becomes the foundation for the unit, and the library offers five other Kuskin books with a good variety of poetry. In final planning for a two-week unit, Hal decides not to introduce one of the five, *The Bear Who Saw the Spring* (1961). The poetry in this book—a conversation between a bear and a dog—is about seasons. Hal knows that his students have covered the subject thoroughly in first and second grades; the Green Pod walls near the second-grade area are currently decorated with pictures of trees in all four seasons. Hal passes the book on to the second-grade teacher, reads the remaining books carefully, and plans a full two weeks' schedule of presentations and follow-up activities.

Here is a chronological account of what happens.

Monday The unit begins after lunch with a kind of riddle game. The children sit on the carpeted floor. Hal reads from Kuskin's *Any Me I Want to Be* (1972).

> I do not understand
> ARF
> How people
> ARF
> GROWL
> BARK
> Can walk around on two
> ARF
> Legs.
> I see them in the park
> BARK
> And all around the town.
> They walk around on just two legs
> Without
> BARK
> Falling Down!
> ARF

The game is to guess who or what was talking. The class has no trouble figuring out that the first Kuskin poem is about a dog. After the class has agreed unanimously, Hal shows them Kuskin's picture of a dog, and then asks how they knew. "The barking," several students answer. One or two bark. Hal moves on to a harder poem.

An activity introduces the unit

> I am softer
> And colder
> And whiter than you.
> And I can do something
> That you cannot do.
> I can make anything
> Anything
> Beautiful:
> Warehouses
> Train tracks
> An old fence
> Cement.
> I can make anything
> Everything
> Beautiful.
> What I touch,
> Where I blow,

595

Even a dump filled with garbage
Looks lovely
After I've fallen there . . .

Because he has read all the poems in advance, Hal knows that to play the riddle game, he will have to leave out the last line, "I am the snow," until children have guessed. This time no one is able to answer, so Hal reads the poem again. After the second hearing, several students guess "snow!"

They have little trouble recognizing a dragon in another poem, but a fourth riddle is puzzling:

Steel wheels
I have those.
Gears that whrrr and grind in rows.
(No nose.)
Buttons click quick quickly
Lights flashing
Red green green red.
(No head.)
Nuts, bolts, valves, pipes, screws
Fuses
Placed precisely each and every part.
Latches, levers, springs
A thousand metal things
That run as one.
(No heart.)

A motor? A machine? A robot? Any of these answers applies to the poem, and an accompanying picture shows intriguing lights, meters, switches, and cogwheels running as one for no apparent reason.

The reading has taken about fifteen minutes, bracketed at the beginning and end with a brief introduction pointing out that Karla Kuskin is the writer.

Tuesday By contrast with the short riddles presented the first day, Tuesday's poem fills an entire book. But because it is a cumulative story—passages are repeated, like choruses, throughout the poem—no one has trouble following what is happening. The story, *A Boy Had a Mother Who Bought Him a Hat* (1976), begins:

A boy had a mother who bought him a hat.
He loved it so much that whatever he did
    or whatever he said,

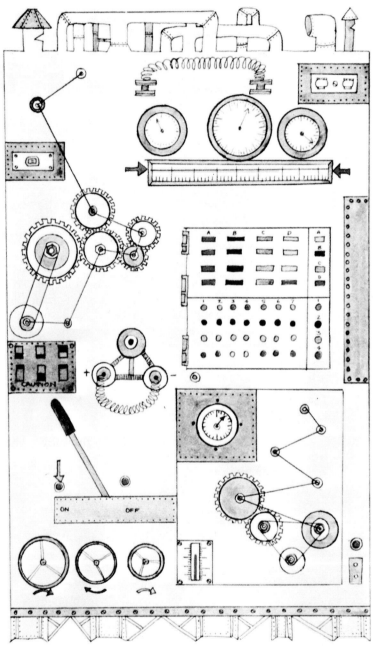

This illustration accompanies Kuskin's poem which begins "Steel wheels . . ." (Illustration for poem 18 from *Any Me I Want to Be*, written and illustrated by Karla Kuskin. Copyright © 1972 by Karla Kuskin. By permission of Harper & Row, Publishers, Inc.)

He wore his new hat
Which was wooly and red.
He stood in the wood in his hat on his head.
So then she went out and she bought him a
    mouse,
Sniffing and squeaking and seeking and peeking.
He loved it so much that whatever he did,
Whatever he said, dressed in his hat which
    was wooly and red,
He included his mouse
And he built it a small very comfortable house
Which he painted sky blue . . .

The bountiful mother adds shoes, black boots, skis, a Halloween mask, a cello, and finally an elephant to the boy's hat and mouse.

To heighten enjoyment of the poem, and to build language skills, Hal rounds out the reading with an activity. Each child receives five blank squares of paper. Hal tells the class to draw gifts on each blank sheet, and then to write the name of the gift under the picture. The gifts can be as funny as the ones in the book, he suggests. During the drawing, Hal circulates around the class and helps with spelling. Then all the cards go into a hat, and each child draws five new cards. Then the task is to draw one picture of a person using all five gifts, similar to Kuskin's illustrations in the book. These illustrations decorate the bulletin board near a table with the first two books in the unit.

Wednesday Kuskin's *Flaky, Frosty Morning* (1969) is a narrative poem about the rise and fall of a snowman, as told by the snowman. "In the flaky, frosty morning, some mittens made a start," the poem begins. "They rolled cold snow together and they built my bottom part. After that they made my middle, with pushes, slaps and punches, and then they left me headless and went in to eat their lunches. . . ."

Eventually sun makes the elegant snow figure droop. "The sun will set on snowman soup," the poem concludes.

Now, after the reading, Hal begins to tie the unit together. "You answered riddles the first day, heard the story about the boy and the hat yesterday, and heard about a snowman today. Which poem was the funniest?" And then: "Why was it so funny?" The discussion supports all the teaching goals. It calls on students to review several different poems by the same author. In reporting what was funny, they return for a second look at Kuskin's well-crafted language while practicing their own skill at speaking.

Hal allows time each day for students to visit the book table; he encourages the third-graders to read aloud to each other. Several of his students also get the opportunity—after Hal has consulted with the other two teachers in the room—to read poetry to younger children.

Thursday The poems read on the first three days have been light-hearted. Humorous poetry seemed appropriate to start the readings because many research studies show children are most likely to enjoy poems that make them laugh.

"Humor, more frequently than any other poetic characteristic, seems to influence students' choices," reports Ann Terry, a children's literature specialist at the University of Houston, in a study of children's preferences. "If a poem is funny, children like it" (1974, p. 47. The study is cited extensively in Chapter 4).

On the fourth day, Hal adds two more short, funny poems from another book (*In the Middle of the Trees*, 1958) by Kuskin. One is called "Catherine":

Catherine said "I think I'll bake
A most delicious chocolate cake."
She took some mud and mixed it up
While adding water from a cup
And then some weeds and nuts and bark
And special gravel from the park
A thistle and a dash of sand.
She beat out all the lumps by hand.
And on the top she wrote "To You"
The way she says the bakers do
And then she signed it "fondly C."
And gave the whole of it to me.
I thanked her but I wouldn't dream
Of eating cake without ice cream.

The other, "Lewis Has a Trumpet," is about a boy with a "loud proud horn" that his parents think is awful. The poem concludes:

. . . But
Lewis says he loves it
It's such a handsome trumpet
And when he's through with trumpets
He's going to buy a drum.

There is no activity following this reading. By now, students are interested enough in Kuskin to pursue the books on their own.

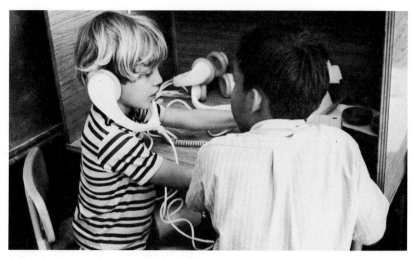

A listening center makes it possible for children to
hear their favorite poems and stories several times.
(Vivienne/Photo Researchers, Inc.)

Friday The climate is right in Hal's class to add some serious
poetry, rounding out the unit, and to capitalize on interest in Kuskin's writing by formally introducing the writer. So, after four days,
Hal returns to the book that led him to Kuskin in the first place:
Near the Window Tree. Many of these poems are tinged with sadness. All have comments by Kuskin next to the poetry, like this:

Some feelings stay the same
no matter how old you get
or how much you change.
Until I was nearly through
high school I was very
small. I looked younger
than all my friends. I'm
an ordinary-sized adult
now, but that
feeling of being smaller
comes back at times and
I still don't like it. (p. 20)

Okay everybody, listen
   to this:
I am tired of being smaller
Than you
And them
And him
And trees and buildings.
So watch out
All you gorillas and adults
Beginning tomorrow morning
Boy
Am I going to be taller. (p. 21)

"How are these poems different from the ones you have been
reading?" Hal asks. "How did the poet feel when she wrote this? Do
you ever feel the way the poet probably felt?"

Hal closes the first week with two activities. To practice language
skills, his class writes short poems about things that make them feel

600

ISSUE

HOW SHOULD CHILDREN LEARN ABOUT SIMILES AND METAPHORS?

Children should become aware of the logic of metaphorical language in literature, not by collecting similes and metaphors as if they were so many colorful pebbles, but by seeing for themselves, as they read and write, the worth and value of using concrete and sensory imagery to express ideas. Children employ metaphor in their natural expression and are skilled users of slang, which might be called the poetry of everyday speech. (p. 62)

Sloan, Glenna Davis. *The Child as Critic*
(New York: Teacher's College Press, 1975).

As the teacher previously made the children aware of poetic rhyme, so she should now introduce the concepts of simile and metaphor. Contrary to the opinion of some others who have written on this subject, I think that students should also be taught the terms simile and metaphor because it seems to help them if they can describe exactly what they have found in a poem, or they have the security of knowing exactly what the teacher wants if she asks for a certain kind of comparison. Once again, the pupils should be given ample opportunity to hear this kind of figurative language read and to imitate it. One activity which children enjoy in this regard is to have one child make up the first half of a simile and then call on someone else to complete it. (pp. 845–846)

Cline, Sister Deborah. "Developing Middle-Grade Children's Creativity through Poetry,"
Elementary English, November 1971, 843–848.

If you were to plan a lesson based on Sloan's philosophy, what sorts of things might you have the students do? What philosophy underlies Cline's suggestions for introducing metaphors and similes? Which approach seems better to you for helping children write and appreciate poetry? Why?

sad or frustrated. To bring them closer to Kuskin, he shows pictures of her on the backs of the books as part of an introduction to the Weston Woods record of her readings. Hal plays one or two poems the students have already heard because he knows students often require one or two hearings before they appreciate a poem. Then he replaces all the books on the reading table, beneath the student drawing and poetry, and provides a record player and earphones on a jack for those who want to hear more.

Second Week

Hal continues to read a poem or two every day, repeating many of the poems introduced the first week. One final activity supports teaching goals: he introduces the form of letter writing, and then tells his class to write someone a letter about what has been happening in school. "You could write Karla Kuskin," he suggests. When several students do, he mails the letters to her, in care of the publisher.

By the end of the second week, Hal's class has become familiar with many poems—as listeners and readers. They have practiced written skills, and discussions and artistic activities have drawn them closer to the poetry. The literature has called on them to concentrate. But there has been a natural reward in the daily discipline of listening hard: the children have enjoyed the poetry. The unit has laid a solid foundation for further poetry reading over the next few years.

In the course of those years, students' interests and reading skills would diversify dramatically. The next and final unit illustrates how a teacher can use the unit approach to introduce one concept to students of widely varying abilities.

CASE STUDY 4: AN EIGHTH-GRADE ENGLISH TEACHER, A UNIT ON SYMBOLISM

Tony faces several problems in teaching English to a class of twenty-eight eighth-graders in a city school. His class includes students reading at several different levels. Some have difficulty with books that most sixth-graders find easy. Others are reading books from the young-adult shelf, picking out the same titles as tenth-graders. Each child's taste is different, and each child is growing at a different rate.

Partly because of these differences, an undercurrent of self-consciousness runs through the class, making students particularly sensitive to personal remarks from the teacher or peers and setting up interference patterns which Tony must try to penetrate.

Describing a typical eighth-grade class, one textbook on children's development sketches a picture of "startling contrasts":

> We see flat-chested little girls next to full-bosomed, full-grown young women. We see scrawny little boys next to broad-shouldered, mustached young men. This individual variability is normal. (Papalia and Olds, 1975, p.554)

The class shows little inclination to read on its own. And Tony meets the group for just fifty minutes a day before students move to different classes and different teachers.

Despite these difficulties, Tony has planned to introduce several C. S. Lewis books in the Narnia series. Lewis's series explores a fantastic world, Narnia, where four children are swept up in conflict between the good lion Aslan and an evil witch. Younger readers like the action in the first of the series, *The Lion, the Witch and the Wardrobe* (1961); the story stands on its own even if readers fail to understand that the battles in fantasy between the lion and the witch represent human spiritual struggles. But Tony has decided his students may be ready to appreciate the Narnia books on a different level. Each is allegorical: each element in the imaginary story parallels and illustrates a deeper meaning. The Wicked Snow Queen, for instance, can be taken as a symbol for evil.

Tony's Teaching Goals

One of Tony's teaching goals is to help students recognize symbolism when it appears in other books. More generally, he wants students to be sensitive to different levels of meaning in literature.

Are his students ready to consider such questions of form? Tony thinks they may be. According to psychologist Jean Piaget's theories (elaborated in Chapter 1), children gain the ability to understand formal concepts somewhere around the age of 12. Now, in what Piaget called the stage of *formal operations*, "thought no longer proceeds from the actual to the theoretical, but starts from theory so as to establish or verify actual relationships between things" (1957, p. 19). Tony's class should be old enough.

Evidence that they are old enough comes during a conversation Tony has with the woman who teaches mathematics to the same students. With few exceptions, she reports, the eighth-graders have no trouble with elementary algebra. Tony recognizes that manipulating algebraic symbols requires "formal," abstract thought: letting the letter X, for example, represent a number. A social studies teacher adds that Tony's students have seemed intrigued with the concept of freedom as they have become involved with the concrete historical fact of the American Revolution. It seems probable that they will be able to grasp literary abstraction as well.

Tony has several other teaching goals. He wants to foster fluency in speaking to complement other work involving writing. As a backdrop for all that he does, he wants to guide students to good books they will enjoy reading.

Presenting a unit is a sensible path toward these goals. Students should find it easier to understand the concept of symbolism if they discover examples of it in several books, rather than in a single title. If Tony uses three related titles, he can divide the class into three small groups and assign one book to each group. Each of the groups can report orally to the others about what they have read; the similarities in the readings will enhance the climate for communication and mutual understanding. If students like one of the books, they will be more likely to enjoy others in the series than they would be if they encountered the Narnia stories as separate titles.

But Tony's plans for unit a based on C. S. Lewis change a few days before the unit is to begin when he reads a set of writing samples from his class. He has asked the class to use dialogue in creating a scene between a child and a parent, and the students' writing is revealing: most of the dialogues are arguments. There are fights over hanging around with the wrong friends, staying up too late, putting off homework. The papers suggest a pattern of friction between the generations. Suddenly, the religious symbolism of the Narnia series seems a bit irrelevant to the interests of Tony's students. Are there other books that might seem more resonant to them?

Tony puts off starting his unit for several days.

In seeking substitute books, Tony consults several introductory textbooks of children's literature, browsing through descriptions of realistic fiction as well as fantasy and looking up "allegory" in the indexes. Two other books based on symbolism emerge from this checking, focusing on the theme of friction between older and younger.

Dorp Dead (1965), by Julia Cunningham, is the realistic story of Gilly Ground, an ll-year-old orphan whose guardian, Kobalt, offers security at the price of freedom. Kobalt, a ladder-maker, bolts the doors and windows of his house, and holds Gilly a virtual prisoner in a world where every ladder must be precisely in place, like the strands of a spider's web. One day Gilly finds a cage Kobalt has apparently built for him, and he decides he must run away. He

604

Kobalt is furious when Gilly disturbs one of his
ladders. (From *Dorp Dead* by Julia Cunningham,
illustrated by James Spanfeller. Copyright © 1965 by
Julia Cunningham. Used by permission of Pantheon
Books.)

escapes by climbing one of Kobalt's ladders out the chimney. Kobalt pursues. Gilly escapes and returns to Kobalt's house where he scrapes "Dorp Dead" on the door, not noticing his spelling error in the exuberance of his freedom.

In *Journey Outside* (1969), by Mary Q. Steele, the rift between old and young widens early in the story. A young boy named Dilar does not believe the bland assurances of his family that the raft they are riding on an underground river is headed for a "Better Place." Dilar knows the river is circular and leads nowhere. He jumps off the raft. Rats force him into a crevice, and eventually he claws his way to the open ground above. Here, like a character in an epic quest, he encounters different societies. The People Against the Tigers, for instance, are a generous group who share all belongings but never plan for the future. Finally, Dilar meets an old man named Vigan, who explains that Dilar's people originally lived on the surface until danger scared them into fleeing underground. Dilar decides he wants to lead his people away from their runaround river and back to their home, despite the danger. Vigan encourages him: "No matter what I've said, it is a fine thing to want to show other people the light of day and the loveliness of green growing things," Vigan says (p.149).

In reading both books, Tony decides that they are not too difficult for most of his class. Nor will most of his students find their length oppressive: *Journey* has 149 pages, and *Dorp*, 88.

The reading has reminded him of another book he read on his own several years before, *The Lemming Condition* (1976), by actor Alan Arkin. He remembers it as a kind of long short story, and now he requests it from the school library to complement the other two books.

Before adding it to the unit, he rereads Arkin's book. Like Dilar, the main character in *The Lemming Condition* is troubled by the direction of adult society. Bubber, a young lemming, does not understand plans to march into the sea, and other characters increase his apprehension. A crow, for instance, asks if he can swim and when Bubber raises the point with his father, the older lemming tells him to forget about crows. After all, Bubber's father lectures as he avoids explanation, such questions are "exactly the kind of thing you come to expect from crows." Another lemming, named Arnold, seems to make more sense to Bubber: "The only thing I know," Arnold says, "is why the hell would anybody jump into the ocean if they can't swim?" (p.18).

Eventually, Bubber avoids being swept along with the mass suicide, and walks back to the plain where a few baby lemmings who slept through the march are waiting to grow up and follow the

His conversation with a crow causes Bubber to question the plans of the other lemmings. (Illustration by Joan Sandin from *The Lemming Condition* by Alan Arkin. Illustrations copyright © 1976 by Joan Sandin. By permission of Harper & Row, Publishers, Inc.)

same self-destructive path. Bubber keeps walking, and when other lemmings call after him, he answers that he is not a lemming any more.

Arkin's book parallels the other two, but its shorter length—fifty-seven pages—makes it more suitable for readers who have trouble sustaining interest. Now, with a group of books, he can divide his class according to his estimate of their interests and abilities.

Tony's teaching strategy involves two steps: fixing the book in the readers' minds and helping them share what they have read with others.

Enhancing the Reading Experience

Two weeks after the books are assigned, each student has read one of the three stories. Now Tony separates the three groups into different parts of the classroom, depending on which book the members have read.

Tony gives each student a list of characters from the book the student has read. For *Journey Outside,* for instance, the list includes the Raft People, People Against the Tigers, Vigan, Dilar and two or three other characters. Students are asked to put the numeral "1"

Ranking characters requires reviewing their roles in books

607

beside the character or characters on the list they think has the best
outlook on life. A "2" goes next to the character with the second-
best outlook, and so on.

Students in each group discuss and agree on a rank order for
characters in their books. The time limit for the discussion is
twenty minutes. Then, in the remaining time, new groups are
formed, the members armed with their ranking sheets and with
fresh memories of what they have read.

Helping Readers to Share Experiences

Each new group comprises students who have read different
books—three or four familiar with *Dorp,* three or four familiar with
Journey, and three or four familiar with *Lemming Condition.* In the
new groups, students will first describe the plot of their book and
then share the information on the lists about the characters. As the
period ends, students have begun to sense for themselves the
similarities in the books.

During the next period, Tony assigns his class to the same groups
and—in the final fifty minutes on the three books—helps students
examine the unit as a whole.

Volunteers in each group set off discussion by reading a brief
passage from each of the books.

Lemming Bubber has just asked Uncle Claude if they really have
been able to swim all along, and whether the lemmings' plans are
just a joke.

> "There's no joke, son," said Claude. "There just isn't any joke at all." He
> looked long and hard at his nephew and found himself feeling great pity
> for this misfit relative. He remembered back to his own time of question-
> ing. Like the rest of his kind, he had outgrown it, and settled finally into a
> wistful acceptance of himself and the condition of his people. It hadn't
> exactly filled him with any peace or joy, but there were other things in
> life. A feeling of solidarity with his kind, a tenuous belief in the future,
> and a semblance of order. Seeing Bubber's confusion, panic and isolation,
> he was sure now that his path was the right one.
>
> Bubber returned his uncle's stare, and what he saw was something old,
> lost and worn-out: no longer a relative nor anything else that he could
> communicate with. He turned and ran off. (pp. 26–27)

Dorp Gilly goes into Mr. Kobalt's house for the first time.

> I am in the middle of a little palace! But before I have the chance to do
> more than get a fuzzed impression of the polished wood and velvet and

the sculptured fireplace, the man speaks and I have to strain a little to catch the low, cello-pitched words. "When you address me, and let this be only when strictly necessary, you will call me Master Kobalt. I shall give you, this first day, one hour to know my house. I live in lanes of time; each hour is channeled. You will fit into these grooves. Your job will be to plane the wood I use for my ladders but you are never to touch any part of my work or tools. I am now going to buy the day's food and will return at the end of your hour."

I murmur, "Yes, sir," and he treads the floor so heavily going to the door that I can feel the vibrations even under the thick carpeting.

"It's quiet here," he adds as he starts to shut the door on himself. "I wish it so." The door clicks shut and I hear a key lock it tight. I wonder why but only until I inspect the double-plated glass windows and see that they, too, are fastened, with tiny padlocks.

I start to grin. Well, if I am a prisoner, at least I am a royal one.

This is a house like a very detailed drawing that someone has sketched and resketched, placed and replaced for hundreds of evenings until it is, down to the box of matches on the exact center of the mantel, perfect. And there is a feeling in the exactitude of every table, chair, picture, and kitchen canister, that no carelessness or rearrangement will ever be permitted. And it strikes me, though my experience only takes in my grandmother's one-chair, one-bed, one-plate-apiece kind of interior, that Master Kobalt has not created this shiny, absolute precision out of love but because it creates safety for him." (pp. 27–29)

Journey Vigan is explaining to Dilar how the Raft People came to be.

"Now the fishermen knew about the underground river that ran beneath the mountains and coiled back upon itself and made a great slow circle through caves and tunnels. During the storms of winter they occasionally fished on that river, for it was full, oh, full of fish. But getting in and out of the entrance was hardly ever possible because of snow and ice and high winds and tides.

"And then there was a particularly savage season and many of the people died, and some niddy goat among them said, 'Let us build rafts and go and live on the underground river, where there are always fish, where storms and winter never come, where we will never be in danger again.' And so they did. All the people went in the entrance and began to go around and around and around and around, endlessly, in the rock tunnels.

"Who knows what happened? Perhaps they forgot where the entrance was. Or perhaps the earth moved and closed it up. Or perhaps they simply did not care any longer to admit to themselves how foolish they had been. At any rate, they started telling themselves that they were headed for a Better Place to live and work, that the tunnel did not swallow its own tail, but led them towards some marvellous goal. And now most of

609

them believe this to be the truth and those who do not believe it are
ashamed to say so." (pp. 142–143)

After the readings, each group wrestles with questions that move
students closer to the heart of literary symbolism: "How are these
excerpts alike?" "How are they different?" "What are the authors
saying about how some people behave and what they believe?"

Tony suggests other questions that tie the books together and
help reveal their underlying truths: "How are Bubber's father and
mother like some people you know?" "Do you know anyone like
Bubber?" "Do you know anyone like Master Kobalt?" "Have you
encountered groups of people who acted like the groups Dilar encountered?"

Finally, Tony's questions to each of the groups relate directly to
the use of symbolism in literature. "Sometimes parts of a story, or
the whole story, may have more than one meaning," he suggests to
all three groups. "Why do you suppose these authors used a story to
communicate their meaning instead of a simple, straightforward
paragraph? Think of the characters and the setting for each story.
Why were they appropriate for conveying what the author wanted to
say?"

The major teaching goals have been met. Tony's students have
encountered three samples of symbolism. The unit has required
students to depend on other students for information; each has had
to speak up, and to listen. The discussions have stimulated some of
the students to go on and read other books in the unit; slow readers,
particularly, have received encouragement to pick up longer books
because they already know something about them.

And finally, Tony's careful selection of good books has stimulated
some interest in other books outside the unit. Some of his students
will go on to read the Narnia series after all. Almost all his students
have a stronger sense of patterns in stories, of common elements
that relate books to each other and to the family of literature.

SUMMARY

1 A *unit* is a set of books related by theme, style, story situation, or
other common element. Well-planned units offer a variety of reading experiences for a diverse class while illustrating relationships
between books. Critic *Northrop Frye* suggests one rationale for
grouping books: literature, he writes, is a "family" with roots in
ancient stories. There are many apparent associations between
books today.

2 The chart on pages 568 to 571 displays five kinds of relationships

between books: *story situation, theme, genre, author or illustrator,* and a *miscellaneous* category (for instance, books containing dialect). In addition to finding relationships, teachers constructing units need to be aware of specific children's needs and interests and to weigh each title against literary standards.

3 *Selection guides* generate titles for potential units. Each guide has distinctive features. *Adventuring with Books,* for example, contains 2,500 titles chosen on literary grounds, while Bowker's *Children's Books in Print* includes more than 39,000 titles, listed without regard to literary merit. Once teachers have made a preliminary list of good literature, they pare the list by judging which books are most appropriate to their class and by deciding where each book fits in the structure of the unit.

4 The first case study centers on a fifth-grade teacher constructing a unit on peer relationships. *The Bookfinder* and *Reading Ladders for Human Relations* suggest titles, and the teacher plans all activities relating to teaching goals before beginning her presentation. During the fourth week of the five-week unit, the teacher begins leading the class to find connections between the books, asking students in a discussion to compare book characters. At the end of the unit, discussion ranges over all four books.

5 Preschool children may have difficulty holding several titles in mind at the same time. But kindergarten teachers can use units to lay a foundation for later critical skills and to meet several other teaching goals. The teacher in the second case study begins planning a unit by listing student interests. Then, after skimming book reviews and talking with teaching associates, she draws up a list of five books related to bedtime. In the course of the week-long unit, these books are presented with appropriate activities. No more than two books are compared at a time.

6 The teacher in the third case study works in the same room with two other teachers and two other grades. The unit on poetry is designed to heighten his third-grade students' concentration in this somewhat distracting setup, as well as increase their awareness that real people write books. Poems of *Karla Kuskin* also help him to meet language-development goals by giving the students a sense of rich and powerful language. Another selection guide, *A Multimedia Approach to Children's Literature,* suggests recordings of authors reading their work. Actual presentation begins with humorous poetry (in part because studies by *Ann Terry* and others show children are most likely to enjoy humorous poems). Serious poetry is added later, along with audiovisual material introducing the poet.

7 As students mature, individual differences become more evident. The final case study shows how a teacher uses a unit to introduce

the concept of symbolism to eighth-grade students of widely varying ability. Reports from mathematics and social studies teachers indicate that the class is capable of understanding literary *form*—of comprehending the concept of symbolism, for example. Textbooks, and the teacher's own reading in children's literature, suggest three books of varying length that will match student interests. The class is divided into three groups according to ability, and each group gets one of the three books to read. Then the students are divided into three new groups to compare the books they have read. In the process they are able to recognize the common element of symbolism, and they gain a stronger sense of the family of literature.

BIBLIOGRAPHY

Adult References

Berenda, R. W. *The Influence of the Group on the Judgments of Children* (New York: King's Crown Press, 1950).

Cianciolo, Pat. *Adventuring with Books* (Urbana, Ill.: National Council of Teachers of English, 1977).

Cline, Sister Deborah. "Developing Middle-Grade Children's Creativity through Poetry," *Elementary English,* November 1971, pp. 843–848.

Dreyer, Sharon Spredemann (ed.). *The Bookfinder* (Minneapolis: Circle Press, American Guidance Service Inc., 1977).

Frye, Northrop. *The Educated Imagination* (Bloomington, Ind.: Indiana University Press, 1964).

Graves, Robert. *Collected Poems.* (New York: International Authors, 1955).

Greene, Ellin, and Madalynne Schoenfeld (compilers and eds.). *A Multimedia Approach to Children's Literature* (Chicago: American Library Association, 1977).

Papalia, Diane E., and Sally Wendkos Olds. *A Child's World* (New York: McGraw-Hill, 1975).

Piaget, Jean. *Logic and Psychology* (New York: Basic Books, 1957).

Reid, Virginia (ed.). *Reading Ladders for Human Relations,* 5th ed. (Washington, D. C.: American Council on Education, 1972).

Schmuck, R. A., and P. A. Schmuck. *Group Processes in the Classroom* (Dubuque, Iowa: Wm. C. Brown, 1971).

Sloan, Glenna Davis. *The Child as Critic* (New York: Teacher's College Press, 1975).

Subject Guide to Children's Books in Print 1977-1978 (New York: R. R. Bowker, 1977).

Sutherland, Zena. *The Best in Children's Books, 1966-1972* (Chicago: University of Chicago Press, 1973).

Terry, Ann. *Children's Poetry Preferences* (Urbana, Ill.: National Council of Teachers of English, 1974).

Children's Book References

Alexander, Martha. *Blackboard Bear* (New York: Dial, 1969).

———. *Nobody Asked Me If I Wanted a Baby Sister* (New York: Dial, 1971).

Arkin, Alan. *The Lemming Condition,* illus. Joan Sandin (New York: Harper, 1976).

Armstrong, William H. *Sounder,* illus. James Barkley (New York: Harper, 1969).

Babbitt, Natalie. *The Something* (New York: Farrar, 1970).

Byars, Betsy. *The 18th Emergency,* illus. Robert Grossman (New York: Viking, 1973).

Campion, Nardi Reeder. *Ann the Word: The Life of Mother Ann Lee, Founder of the Shakers* (Boston: Little, Brown, 1976).

Caudill, Rebecca. *Did You Carry the Flag Today, Charlie?* illus. Nancy Grossman (New York: Holt, 1966).

Chaffin, Lillie D. *John Henry McCoy,* illus. Emanuel Schongut (New York: Macmillan, 1971).

Chase, Richard. *The Jack Tales,* illus. Berkeley Williams, Jr. (Boston: Houghton Mifflin, 1943).

Cleaver, Vera, and Bill Cleaver. *Where the Lillies Bloom,* illus. Jim Spanfeller (Philadelphia: Lippincott, 1969).

Cohen, Miriam. *The New Teacher,* illus. Lillian Hoban (New York: Macmillan, 1972).

Coolidge, Olivia E. *The Statesmanship of Abraham Lincoln* (New York: Scribner's 1977).

Corcoran, Barbara. *A Dance to Still Music,* illus. Charles Robinson (New York: Atheneum, 1974).

Crowe, Robert L. *Clyde Monster,* illus. Kay Chorao (New York: Dutton, 1976).

Cunningham, Julia. *Dorp Dead,* illus. James Spanfeller (New York: Pantheon, 1965).

———. *Come to the Edge* (New York: Pantheon, 1977).

Dalgliesh, Alice. *The Courage of Sarah Noble,* illus. Leonard Weisgard (New York: Scribner's, 1954).

Duvoisin, Roger. *Petunia, I Love You* (New York: Knopf, 1965).

Eichler, Margaret. *Martin's Father,* illus. Beverly Maginnis (Chapel Hill, N. C.: Lollipop Power, 1971).

Faber, Doris. *Bella Abzug* (New York: Lothrop, Lee and Shepard, 1976).

Fitzhugh, Louise. *Harriet the Spy* (New York: Harper, 1964).

Freeman, Don. *Bearymore* (New York: Viking, 1976).

Freschet, Berniece. *Little Black Bear Goes for a Walk,* illus. Glen Rounds (New York: Scribner's, 1977).

Fritz, Jean. *The Cabin Faced West,* illus. Feodor Rojankovsky (New York: Coward-McCann, 1958).

———. *Brady,* illus. Lynd Ward (New York: Coward-McCann, 1960).

———. *Early Thunder,* illus. Lynd Ward (New York: Coward-McCann, 1967).

———. *Who's That Stepping on Plymouth Rock?* illus. J. B. Handelsman (New York: Coward-McCann, 1975).

———. *Will you Sign Here, John Hancock?* illus. Trina Schart Hyman (New York: Coward-McCann, 1976).

Greene, Constance C. *The Unmaking of Rabbit* (New York: Viking, 1972).

Greenfield, Eloise. *She Come Bringing Me That Little Baby Girl,* illus. John Steptoe (Philadelphia: Lippincott, 1974).

Griffiths, Helen. *The Greyhound,* illus. Victor G. Ambrus (Garden City, N.Y.: Doubleday, 1964).

Haar, Jaap ter. *The World of Ben Lighthart,* trans. Martha Mearns (New York: Delacorte, 1977). (1973)

Hamilton, Virginia. *Paul Robeson* (New York: Harper, 1974).

Hautzig, Esther. *The Endless Steppe* (New York: Crowell, 1968).

Hazen, Barbara Shook. *The Gorilla Did It,* illus. Ray Cruz (New York: Atheneum, 1975).

Hoban, Russell. *Bedtime For Frances,* illus. Garth Williams (New York: Harper, 1960).

———. *A Baby Sister for Frances,* illus. Lillian Hoban (New York: Harper, 1964).

Hutchins, Pat. *Clocks and More Clocks* (New York: Macmillan, 1970).

———. *Don't Forget the Bacon!* (New York: Greenwillow, 1976).

Jacobs, Joseph. *Munachar and Manachar: An Irish Story,* illus. Anne Rockwell (New York: Crowell, 1970).

Jameson, Cynthia. *The Clay Pot Boy,* illus. Arnold Lobel (New York: Coward-McCann, 1973).

Keats, Ezra Jack. *The Snowy Day* (New York: Viking, 1962).

———. *Whistle for Willie* (New York: Viking, 1964).

———. *Peter's Chair* (New York: Harper, 1967).

———. *Over in the Meadow* (Based on original version by Olive A. Wadsworth.) (New York: Scholastic, 1971).

———. *Dreams* (New York: Macmillan, 1974).

Kendall, Carol. *The Gammage Cup,* illus. Erik Blegvad (New York: Harcourt, 1959).

Kent, Jack. *The Fat Cat: A Danish Folktale* (New York: Parents', 1971).

Klein, Norma. *If I Had My Way,* illus. Ray Cruz (New York: Pantheon, 1974).

Kraus, Robert. *Milton the Early Riser,* illus. Jose and Ariane Aruego (New York: Dutton, 1972).

Krauss, Ruth. *A Very Special House,* illus. Maurice Sendak (New York: Harper, 1953).

Kuskin, Karla. *In the Middle of the Trees* (New York: Harper, 1958).

———. *The Bear Who Saw the Spring* (New York: Harper, 1961).

———. *In the Flaky Frosty Morning* (Harper, 1969).

———. *Any Me I Want to Be* (New York: Harper, 1972).

———. *Near the Window Tree* (New York: Harper, 1975).

———. *A Boy Had a Mother Who Bought Him a Hat* (Boston: Houghton Mifflin, 1976).

Lazarus, Keo F. *The Billy Goat in the Chili Patch,* illus. Carol Rogers (Steck-V, 1972).

Le Guin, Ursula. *A Wizard of Earthsea,* illus. Ruth Robbins (Emeryville, Calif.: Parnassus, 1968).

———. *The Tombs of Atuan,* illus. Gail Garraty (New York: Atheneum, 1971).

———. *The Farthest Shore,* illus. Gail Garraty (New York: Atheneum, 1972).

Leodhas, Sorche Nic. *All in the Morning Early,* illus. Evaline Ness (New York: Holt, 1963).

Lewis, C. S. *The Lion, the Witch and the Wardrobe,* illus. Pauline Baynes (New York: Macmillan, 1961).

Lexau, Joan. *Me Day,* illus. Robert Weaver (New York: Dial, 1971).

———. *Emily and the Klunky Baby and the Next-Door Dog,* illus. Martha Alexander (New York: Dial, 1972).

Livingston, Myra Cohn. *Whispers and Other Poems,* illus. Jacqueline Chwast (New York: Harcourt, 1958).

MacGregor, Ellen. *Theodore Turtle,* illus. Paul Galdone (New York: McGraw-Hill, 1955).

Marshall, James. *George and Martha* (Boston: Houghton Mifflin, 1974).

Merriam, Eve. *Epaminondas,* illus. Trina Schart Hyman (Chicago: Follett, 1968).

Nash, Ogden. *Many Long Years Ago* (Boston: Little, Brown, 1936).

Ness, Evaline. *Sam, Bangs and Moonshine* (New York: Holt, 1966).

Neuffeld, John. *Twink* (New York: Phillips, 1970).

Newfield, Marcia. *A Book for Jodan,* illus. Diane de Groat (New York: Atheneum, 1975).

Picard, Barbara. *One Is One,* illus. Victor G. Ambrus (London: Oxford University Press, 1965).

Resnick, Rose. *Sun and Shadow* (New York: Atheneum, 1975).

Ryan, Cheli Duran. *Hildilid's Night,* illus. Arnold Lobel (New York: Macmillan, 1971).

Sachs, Marilyn. *Veronica Ganz,* illus. Louis Glanzman (New York: Doubleday, 1968).

———. *Peter and Veronica,* illus. Louis Glanzman (New York: Doubleday, 1969).

Sendak, Maurice. *Pierre* (New York: Harper, 1962).

Sharmat, Marjorie. *Goodnight Andrew, Goodnight Craig,* illus. Mary Chalmers (Harper, 1969).

———. *I Don't Care,* illus. Lillian Hoban (New York: Macmillan, 1977).

Silverstein, Shel. in William Cole (ed.), *Beastly Boys and Ghastly Girls* (Cleveland: World, 1964).

Sonneborn, Ruth. *Friday Night Is Papa Night,* illus. Emily A. McCully (New York: Viking, 1970).

Sperry, Armstrong. *Call It Courage* (New York: Macmillan, 1940).

Starbird, Kaye. *Don't Ever Cross a Crocodile* (Philadelphia: Lippincott, 1963).

Steele, Mary Q. *Journey Outside* (New York: Macmillan, 1969).

Sutcliff, Rosemary. *The Witch's Brat,* illus. Richard Lebenson (New York: Walck, 1970).

Conford, Ellen. *The Alfred G. Graebner Memorial High School Handbook of Rules and Regulations* (Boston: Little, Brown, 1976).

Thomas, Ianthe. *Eliza's Daddy,* illus. Moneta Barnett (New York: Harcourt, 1976).

Turkle, Brinton. *The Fiddler of High Lonesome* (New York: Viking, 1968).

Waber, Bernard. *Ira Sleeps Over* (Boston: Houghton Mifflin, 1972).

Winthrop, Elizabeth. *Bunk Beds,* illus. Ronald Himler (New York: Harper, 1972).

Zemach, Harve. *The Tricks of Master Dabble,* illus. Margot Zemach (New York: Holt, 1965).

Zolotow, Charlotte. *The Unfriendly Book,* illus. William Pène du Bois (New York: Harper, 1975).

CHAPTER 14

BUILDING CURRICULA

YEAR-LONG PROGRAMS OF LITERATURE

Fifth-graders in one class followed Harriet, the main character in *Harriet the Spy,* as she secretly followed her classmates. The students refought the Peter versus Veronica arguments in another book, *Peter and Veronica,* and they empathized as another character named Paul shed an unwelcome nickname in the *The Unmaking of Rabbit.* While reading a set of books in a unit constructed by their teacher, Dorothea, they came to know several different lives, in literature.

At the same time, however, the students became aware of a single thread tying the books together: the subject of peer relationships. (The unit is described in Chapter 13.)

A full thirty-six-week school year offers the same potential as the single unit, but on a wider scale. Careful planning by teachers can introduce a broad variety of literature while deepening student awareness of the close relationship between books.

In some ways, a unit is a model for the full year's work. Alan C. Purves, professor of English at the University of Illinois, writes that a single unit of literature can

> . . . exemplify the aims of a whole semester or year, because the objectives of each unit epitomize those of the course . . . While the content might shift, there is usually a repetition of what goes on from unit to unit. Each unit seeks to build on the skills mastered in the preceding unit, to deepen and strengthen them, so that the objective of a unit is both the mastery of the work at hand and the mastery of the skills of reading and responding to that work so that one is able to read and respond to the next work. (In Bloom, Hastings, and Madaus, 1971, p. 716)

Dorothea's full year program—spelled out in a later section of this chapter—does provide for frequent *shifts of content* mentioned by Purves. In the course of a typical nine-month school year, her students would encounter five units, comprising about twenty-five books. They would read a small collection of fantasy to complement the realism in a unit like the one on peer groups. They would hear poetry regularly. Two of the units would tie in with other areas of study: the class would read several books related to the American Revolutionary War, supporting concurrent work in social studies, and they would become familiar with the folktale format in preparation for the mythology they would read as sixth-graders.(Material in the second half of this chapter will provide suggestions for matching literature to several other subjects.)

The variety within the peer-group unit, in other words, would parallel the much wider variety of literature presented in the course of the year.

But at the same time, Dorothea's program would incorporate some *repetition from unit to unit.* Activities to enhance response, for example, would tend to follow similar lines: discussions, dramatic exercises, written work, and artistic work would heighten interest and involvement. After several units, students would develop a stronger understanding that books—members of the family of literature—are related by such things as theme, subject, and genre. Moving from unit to unit—and encountering single titles between units—they would gain a surer sense that stories in different books sometimes tend to follow the same patterns, and that traditional styles survive in fresh forms.

CURRICULUM: LITERATURE THROUGHOUT THE YEAR

A literature *curriculum* is a course of study including a set of books—often divided into units and single titles—and a set of activities related to these books. In written form, a complete curriculum comprises a book list, brief descriptions of how titles will be used, a suggestion for sequencing material, a rationale behind the choice of topics and materials, a statement of goals, and suggestions for evaluating whether the goals have been met.

But many curricula do not contain all these data. Elementary school teachers ordinarily receive a general curriculum guide for all subjects within their grade level. This guide underscores certain topics, and sets goals, but frequently the choice of individual titles rests with the teacher.

Goals of the Literature Curriculum

Goals of literature teachers vary from school to school, and change with the times. Seventeenth-century Puritans, for example, expected children's books to help frighten their children into sinless living so that their souls would go to heaven. As outlined in Chapter 10, teachers in later eras called on books to hammer home lessons in subjects from manners to mathematics. Within this century, Purves reports, general goals of instruction have shifted several times. Under one set of goals, prevalent in the early decades of the century, literature was used for *literacy, oratory, and moral training.* Pursuing different goals, teachers later in the century wrote curricula using literature to *implant a cultural heritage* in students, passing on the history and tradition of the country in storybook form. Other

621

educators thought of literature as a *socializing force;* they considered stories an aid to understanding life and adjusting to society. A fourth approach—one current today—was that literature could be used to *train critical faculties* and instill a habit of scientific analysis of what is read (in Bloom, et al, 1971, p. 699).

A contrasting set of goals arose out a conference of scholars from Great Britain and United States in 1966. The Anglo-American Seminar on the Teaching of English—popularly known as the Dartmouth Seminar—concluded that the main goal of literature programs should be "to get the child actively 'involved' or 'engaged' in a work of literature" to develop such positive attitudes toward books that reading would become a lifetime habit (Muller, 1967, p. 79). The conference, in effect, made pleasure reading an acceptable curriculum goal. Suggestions from the seminar have been influential: "enjoyment" frequently appears on today's curriculum guidelines.

In general, these goals tend to fall under three major categories.

Content Those teachers earlier in the century who wanted to pass on history through literature were concerned that their children learn names, dates, the position of armies, the politics of colonialism, or other facts from books. Modern teachers still expect literature to help young readers apprehend meaningful facts. "How did people find food during the settling of the West?" "Who signed the Declaration of Independence?" "How far is the earth from the moon?" Literature, particularly realistic fiction and informational books, often provides factual answers.

Process Educators who hoped literature would equip students to adjust to society, or approach other literature with critical tools, wanted students to learn general techniques or processes of thought. Teachers today sometimes have similar goals. Children reading literature can learn to classify, generalize and infer, compare, analyze, and make hypotheses or predictions. "How are these two books on astronomy alike?" "Do you think the men who signed the Declaration of Independence realized at the time the import this document was to have? Why or why not?" The answers to these questions require independent thinking; they call on children to use thinking processes that can be used in the analysis of dozens of different books.

Values and attitudes Teachers once used books to impose rules of conduct or morality on children. Today, books are still used to explore questions of personal value and attitude, although students

Informational books such as this one may be chosen
for the content they provide. (Illustration by Albert
Michini from *Wufu, The Story of a Little Brown Bat*
by Berniece Freschet, reprinted by permission of G. P.
Putnam's Sons. Illustration copyright © 1975 by
Albert Michini.)

today are freer to reflect on and express their own value system, even when it contrasts with what they read. Books, in other words, can sharpen *subjective*—individual and personal—value systems. In other cases, literature calls on students to take an *objective* attitude, to try to evaluate writing by holding it against critical standards, just as a scientist tries to take a dispassionate and objective attitude toward experiments.

Subjective and objective attitudes sometimes merge, and sometimes conflict, in characters from literature and in readers trying to talk about books. For instance, value systems are clashing in the reader who argues, "This may be great writing, but I hate it." And values merge in the character who subordinates conscience to the demands of a corrupt and powerful politician. Work with values and attitudes today, in other words, involves investigating values expressed *in* literature and *about* literature.

Diverse goals in many curricula fit into the categories of content, process, and values and attitudes. All the goals of the teachers in the case studies in Chapter 13, for example, are related to one of these general categories or some combination of them. The categories are particularly useful because they parallel commonly used curriculum goals in several other subjects—social studies, science, and mathematics—as a later section of this chapter will show.

The Importance of Planning a Curriculum

Individual titles alone—or individual units—can move students closer to these or other curriculum goals, but teachers who merely present one book or one unit after another without planning ahead can run afoul of school schedules, or miss natural opportunities.

By planning a curriculum, teachers can achieve the kind of balance they strive for in planning a unit. A full year's program will comprise realism as well as fantasy, time-honored books as well as new titles, poetry to balance prose, humorous and serious stories, and nonfiction as well as fiction.

Now don't you hit me

(a)

(b)

Because of Dorothea's planning, students in her classroom recognize that reading is not a haphazard activity used to fill an extra hour now and then. They know that literature will be a basic component of the school day, the whole year long.

PLANNING THE LITERATURE CURRICULUM

Dorothea's school has provided her with a mimeographed curriculum guide covering all subject areas she is to teach in the course of a year. It spells out specific goals in math and social studies, even naming the textbooks she is to use. It calls for arithmetic lessons in division and fractions. It lists concepts to be taught relating to the American Revolutionary War.

The guide is not nearly so specific about the literature program, a section under the broad category of language arts. The curriculum guidelines she has been given for literature are typical of those for elementary schools today. In the course of the year, the guidelines specify, students are to:

1 Read broadly in literature.

2 Understand at least on a literal level books covered during the course.

3 Respond to those books in a variety of activities to enhance enjoyment of good literature and to improve critical skills.

The first two of the guidelines deal with content; the third relates to processes and student attitudes. She is not given specific titles, or told what activities to use with books.

A Backdrop for Planning

Dorothea approaches her planning armed with some general knowledge about children and books. There are, for example, the studies of developmental psychologists—Piaget, Kohlberg, and others, whose work is described in Chapter 1—to provide broad-brush portraits of children at different ages. She also has a working knowledge of criteria to help her choose good literature, criteria discussed in each of the chapters of Part One. She knows how to call on selection aids such as Zena Sutherland's *The Best in Children's Books 1966–1972*. And she is at ease with some basic tests of plot, theme, characterization, setting, and style. Every title in her curriculum will stand on its own as good literature, and every title will conform with Dorothea's understanding of her children's abilities and interests. Finally, she has experience with several units—including the set of books on peer groups—she knows will support curriculum goals.

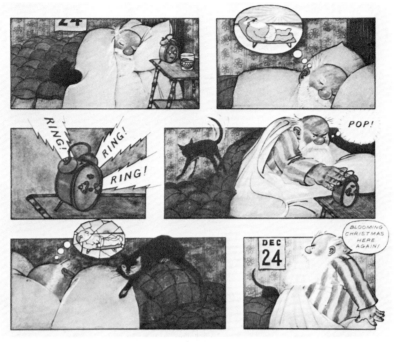

Some books rely heavily on the illustrations for their
humor. (From *Father Christmas* by Raymond Briggs.
Copyright © 1973 by Raymond Briggs. Used by
permission of Hamish Hamilton Children's Books,
Ltd.)

The Core of the Curriculum

Turning to the specifics of planning, Dorothea tentatively decides to
begin the following school year with the peer group unit that was
successful with her current class. The problem of peer pressure, she
realizes, is likely to afflict her next class, and to arise perennially.
(All the titles she plans to use during the year are listed on page 628.)

There are other "given" elements of the curriculum. In reviewing
the school calendar, Dorothea marks off two holiday seasons, Halloween and Christmas/Chanukah, and quickly develops sets of
books on each, using principles outlined in the previous chapter. A
unit on poems about ghosts and nightmares matches Halloween.
She plans to read aloud a set of three books about the December
holidays, mostly to enhance the joy of the season. But two of the
books, *Father Christmas* and *A Chanukah Fable for Christmas*, are
lighthearted stories relying heavily on pictures for their humor. She

Using a previ-
ously successful
unit is one way
to open the
year's program;
checking the
school calendar
suggests other
possible units

627

BOOKS FOR A YEAR: A SAMPLE LIST OF CURRICULUM MATERIALS

I. Units

    A. Peer Relationships

        Fitzhugh, Louise. *Harriet the Spy.*

        Greene, Constance. *The Unmaking of Rabbit.*

        Griffiths, Helen. *The Greyhound.*

        Sachs, Marilyn. *Peter and Veronica.*

    B. Poems on Spooky Topics

        Hopkins, Lee Bennett (ed.). *Hey-How for Halloween!*

        Moore, Lilian, and Lawrence Webster (eds.). *Catch Your Breath: A Book of Shivery Poems.*

        Moore, Lilian. *See My Lovely Poison Ivy.*

        Prelutsky, Jack. *Nightmares. Poems to Trouble Your Sleep.*

    C. Time Fantasy

        Boston, L. M. *The Children of Green Knowe.*

        Cresswell, Helen. *A Game of Catch.*

        Ormondroyd, Edward. *Time at the Top.*

        Pearce, Phillippa. *Tom's Midnight Garden.*

    D. Revolutionary War Period

        Collier, James Lincoln, and Christopher Collier. *My Brother Sam Is Dead.*

        Fritz, Jean. *Early Thunder.*

        Gauch, Patricia Lee. *This Time, Tempe Wick?*

        Johnny Tremain. Buena Vista, 1957. 16-millimeter color film.

    E. Modern Stories in Folktale Format

        Alexander, Lloyd. *The King's Fountain* and *The Truthful Harp.*

        Andersen, Hans Christian. *The Nightingale; The Steadfast Tin Soldier; The Ugly Duckling.*

        Grahame, Kenneth. *The Reluctant Dragon.*

        Myers, Walter Dean. *The Dragon Takes a Wife.*

        Yolen, Jane. *The Girl Who Cried Flowers and Other Tales.*

II. Individual Books

    A. For the December Holiday Season

        Briggs, Raymond. *Father Christmas.*

        Caudill, Rebecca. *A Certain Small Shepherd.*

        Coopersmith, Jerome. *A Chanukah Fable For Christmas.*

    B. Light Reading

        Rockwell, Thomas. *How to Eat Fried Worms.*

makes a note that if her class has trouble understanding the stories, there may be a need for more exposure to picture books in the course of the year, requiring revisions in the curriculum.

Building Curricula

Other blocks in the curriculum fall into place as a result of planning in other subjects. Her guidelines require her, for instance, to teach certain basic concepts about the American Revolutionary War, so Dorothea plans to combine a unit of literature with a social studies unit. Both will begin in March, and run concurrently in the classroom.

Course work in other subjects ties in with a unit of literature

Discussions with sixth-grade teachers during her planning alert Dorothea to the fact that they normally present a unit on mythology early in the year. Partly to prepare students for more advanced forms of traditional literature, Dorothea decides to include a unit some time after Christmas/Chanukah on simpler folktales—specifically, modern stories in folktale format. Two of the books in this unit, *The Truthful Harp* and *The Dragon Takes a Wife,* depend for their appeal on sparkling illustrations. Dorothea can put special emphasis on these two if her students show during the reading of the December books that they have difficulty apprehending detail in pictures.

Discussions with teachers lead to plans for another unit

All these plans leave plenty of room in the curriculum for other books and activities.

Rounding Out the Curriculum

To balance the realism in the peer relationship unit, Dorothea creates a four-book unit of fantasies, all of them about shifts in time and time travel. She also includes Thomas Rockwell's *How to Eat Fried Worms* as a single title on her curriculum list because it has been popular with previous classes; it can be introduced at any time for a change of pace.

Additions to the core of the curriculum add balance and variety

In the course of the year, as she comes to know her newest pupils, Dorothea will add other units and single titles, depending on student interest. If several members of her class are interested in horses, for example, she may consult a selection guide index to find titles about riding and raising horses. Several guides would suggest books about horses by Marguerite Henry, for instance, or Helen Griffith's *The Wild Heart* (1963).

Reviewing her tentative list of literature, Dorothea also plans many of the activities she will introduce during the coming year. The unit on folktales, for example, will be accompanied by an exercise calling on students to write their own tales, in classical form.

Before school begins, Dorothea has drawn up a comprehensive curriculum that goes far beyond meeting the general—and some-

The curriculum may include single titles which have
been popular with other students in previous years.
Incidentally, that is a worm—actually two glued
together—on the plate. (Illustration by Emily McCully
from *How to Eat Fried Worms* by Thomas Rockwell.
Illustration copyright © 1973 by Emily McCully.
Used by permission of the publisher, Franklin Watts,
Inc.)

what vague—guidelines given to her. Her planning proceeded in
several steps:

As a backdrop for curriculum building, she reviewed principles of
child development, as well as basic criteria for evaluating literary
quality. Every choice she made in building her curriculum was held

against two standards: Is the material good literature? Is it likely to match the interests, abilities, and special needs of the class?

She constructed a core curriculum after checking the school calendar, noting the requirements in other subjects and discussing plans with teachers in other grades.

She rounded out her curriculum to ensure balance and variety in the year's program.

Evaluating the Literature Program

Dorothea begins evaluating her curriculum plan during the early days of the following fall, even before the shine on the school's hallway floors has begun to fade. Evaluation will continue day to day throughout the year. When the school year ends and Dorothea again begins planning for the following year, she will look back and evaluate the entire plan.

Evaluation, in other words, is both short-and long-term.

Short-term evaluation   One approach to evaluation involves careful observation of what students actually do in class.

Using this approach, Dorothea decides in advance that one objective in teaching the unit on folktales is to enable her children to write a story which follows a pattern found in modern tales. The writing itself is a specific action, a *behavior* that can be observed. Stating a literary theme in one sentence, drawing a picture of a character in literature, writing a letter to an author—each is a behavior that teachers might hope students would exhibit. To aid evaluation of a curriculum, a teacher could list such possible and desirable student behaviors in advance, during planning. The list is a set of *behavioral objectives.*

Then, after the year begins, Dorothea could gauge the success of her unit by whether students actually responded with a specific behavior on the list of objectives—whether they actually wrote the story she expected them to.

Evaluation based on behavioral objectives requires no teacher guesswork or intuition about what students think or feel about the literature. Some psychologists praise the approach for its built-in precision; other educators suggest that students may perform skillfully on a specific task, and still miss major components of a subject.

Educators V. Perrone and W. A. Strandberg write that competence in basic skills—the ability to write, for instance—is only one of several important teaching objectives.

631

We would not want to suggest that basic skills are unimportant. They are fundamental, but they must be seen in relation to the more encompassing need to nurture in children a higher level of personal motivation and involvement in learning. The skills of literacy—reading, writing, speaking, and thinking—develop more effectively when they are not treated as academic exercises which exist in a vacuum. (1972, pp. 352–353)

In responding to literature by writing, for example, students ought to be increasing their enjoyment of good books and developing habits of reading that will remain with them all their lives. Enhancing pleasure in reading is one of Dorothea's key goals. But she cannot make precise measurements of enjoyment, or determine definitely what her students' lifelong reading habits will be.

So in addition to setting concrete goals about student behavior, Dorothea will call on her own sensitivity to children as young people, and her own critical skill in evaluating the quality of their work. Is one of her fifth-graders shy because she looks young for her age? Then the number of times she speaks up in a discussion about *Harriet the Spy* may provide little useful data about her involvement with literature. Has a boy in the class recently heard his father read a collection of modern fables by the late author James Thurber? Then his experience with literature at bedtime might give him an edge over classmates in writing a folktale, although in general he may be far behind others in his class in reading or writing ability. The point is, behavioral criteria alone cannot fully measure the success of a curriculum; knowledge of a child gained over months of contact is also essential in evaluating the literature program.

Long-term evaluation In the course of the year, Dorothea will watch for other behaviors to indicate that her curriculum is successful, while remaining sensitive to interests and abilities of her individual class. In general, the following behaviors indicate growing appreciation and enjoyment of literature:

Students choose to read on their own.
They recommend books to each other.
Children make drawings based on picture books.
They reread books they have heard the teacher read, or request a book to be read again.

Children's interest in reading on their own is one indication of a successful literature program. (Copyright © 1978, E. Trina Lipton.)

Children use the library or media center.
They mention characters or ideas from literature in a new setting.

Each of these behaviors may be an indication that the curriculum is succeeding in its broad goals, although, again, each must be evaluated in the broad context of the classroom. A girl's request to go to the media center, for example, may be an attempt to put distance between her and a boy who has teased her on the playground. Again, teachers need to weigh what they observe against what they learn about individual children in the course of the year.

MATCHING LITERATURE WITH OTHER SUBJECTS

One elementary school art teacher who works with children from grades one to six keeps a collection of good picture books handy for her students and their parents to borrow. Some of the books on teacher Ellie Menard's shelf in a Rhode Island school provide information about her subject. Donald Stacy's *Experiments in Art* (1975) describes a variety of media. Other children's books in the collection, like Jack Prelutsky's *Circus* (1974), stimulate children's imagination as they scout for possible artistic subjects. One spread in this book, for example, shows a crowd of clowns—one disguised as a teapot, one plugging his ears as a firecracker sizzles on his head—which reminds children of what they have seen at circuses, and helps stimulate ideas about what they would like to draw.

Other elementary school teachers have incorporated literature into their science, math, or social studies curricula. Intermediate and high school English or language arts teachers have taken advantage of interest generated by other teachers to create units of literature related to lessons in other fields.

There are several good reasons for crossing curriculum lines and melding different subjects. First, students in Ellie Menard's class are learning to see that literature overlaps many areas of knowledge; it is not isolated, or irrelevant to other work they do. Second, her students come to recognize that literature, while often imaginative, can be constructed from fact; students in a class studying the history of the American Revolution, for instance, can better understand the research behind a book like *My Brother Sam Is Dead* (1974), and may find it easier to discern its point of view. Third, the perspective of a writer of literature is different from that of a writer of textbooks, and may sharpen a student's understanding of other subjects. A well-written and illustrated informational book, for example, can supplement a textbook on basic concepts in math or science. Finally, children's trade books may be more up to date than classroom textbooks, which generally require more time to produce.

Combining Curricula with Care

Combining curricula makes sense, but teachers planning to match literature with other subjects have to be careful to avoid two mistakes.

Misusing literature "Mark all the verbs in this passage from *Stuart Little.*" This deadly instruction, from a language arts teacher trying to combine literature with a lesson on the parts of speech, vastly reduced student interest in reading or hearing the book. Similarly, turning literature into a source of vocabulary words to be memorized, or carving up paragraphs to show how to find the topic sentence, or testing students on the dates that appear incidentally in historical fiction—each of these practices in a misuse of literature.

Mismatching literature Some children's books can undermine teaching goals in other subjects. For example, a process-oriented science program would include student-run experiments to give practice in the processes—the general techniques—of scientific inquiry. The results of the experiments are less important in such a program than the approaches students take to get results. Consequently, a book about science experiments that explains what will happen, and why, can lessen the incentive for the child to discover the process behind the experiment.

A respect for the literature and an understanding of goals in other subject areas are prerequisites to bringing children's books into the broad school curriculum.

GOALS IN OTHER SUBJECT AREAS

Goals in the literature program, as outlined in an earlier section, cluster around three general categories: *content, process,* and *values and attitudes.* Standard curriculum goals in several other subjects fall into similar categories. And these similarities make it easier to intertwine literature programs with courses in social studies, mathematics, and science.

Edwin Fenton, an educator whose field is social studies, reviewed objectives in many modern social studies programs and discovered that groups of objectives fit under three general headings:

635

. . . the development of inquiry skills (sometimes called critical thinking
or the use of a mode of inquiry), the development of *attitudes and values*
and *the acquisition of knowledge.* (1967, p. 11)

Fenton's first category is close to Dorothea's goal of developing
critical skills. Enhancing enjoyment of literature is a goal related to
student attitudes and values. And Fenton's "acquisition of knowledge" matches Dorothea's guidelines calling for broad reading and
comprehension of content on a literal level.

Remarkably similar kinds of goals appear in studies of curricula
in mathematics and science. Here is a comparison of three goals of
literature programs with goals suggested by educators in other
fields:

LITERATURE	SCIENCE	MATHEMATICS
	(These categories were adapted from a definition of science by educators Arthur A. Carin and Robert B. Sund, 1975, p. 4)	(These categories were adapted from long-range goals of math instruction at the elementary school level suggested by educator Klaas Kramer, 1975, p. 5)
Content: Students gain a literal understanding of books they read.	*Products:* Students of science acquire facts, prin- ciples, laws, and theories, for example, the scientific principle that metals ex- pand when heated.	Courses should develop in the student an *under- standing* of the structure of the real number system and functional *knowledge* of quantitative terms and symbols.
Process: Literature stu- dents should learn tech- niques or processes of thought used to approach literature critically.	*Processes or methods:* Sci- ence students should learn ways of investigating problems, for example, making scientific hypoth- eses and evaluating data.	*Skill in thinking critically:* Mathematics students should learn to appraise the correctness of acquired results and apply tech- niques intelligently in verbal problems.
Attitudes and Values: Students sharpen aware- ness of their own and other values, and learn to value good literature.	*Attitudes:* Students be- come acquainted with sci- entific values, opinions, and beliefs; for instance, the value of suspending judgement until enough data have been collected.	Favorable *attitudes* toward mathematics support an awareness of the place and importance of mathematics in life.

The wording and emphasis may differ in each of these subjects, but the sets of goals appear to be compatible with each other. They suggest among other things that literature can be more than just a source of content to accompany topics in math, science, or social studies.

The following case studies—each a composite of several teachers' classroom experiences—show that in fact literature can be woven into the fabric of the total curriculum to help educators meet several goals.

CASE STUDY 1:
SCIENCE AND LITERATURE IN THE SECOND GRADE

Michael, a second-grade teacher, plans to present *The Quicksand Book* (1977), by Tomie de Paola, to his class as a single title they will enjoy. But he has other teaching goals besides enjoyment; the book can also be used to teach scientific *processes* as well as some basic scientific facts, or *content.*

The story is simple and lighthearted. A jungle girl falls in quicksand when the vine she is swinging on breaks. A boy and a monkey encounter her standing in the sand.

"My goodness, you look very unhappy," the boy says. "Is it because you have fallen into quicksand?" Boy and monkey swing into action, in a way. The monkey produces some chart paper, and the boy begins a long dissertation about quicksand. While the girl sinks deeper into the mire, he tells her what quicksand is, where and how it forms, how certain animals react when they fall into it, and what to do if you fall in while carrying a stick. After delivering this information, the boy helps the girl out of the sand, trips on a turtle, and falls in himself. Now, the tables turned, the girl sits down to a table of cake, cookies, and tea. "Remember what you told me!" she calls to the sinking boy. "Just keep calm, lie on your back, and float. I'll pull you out when I finish my tea." The last page of the book gives directions for making quicksand. (Squirt a stream of water underneath sand in a bucket, simulating loose soil covering an underground spring.)

Teaching Content

Students listen to the book primarily for its humor and story, but *The Quicksand Book* also contains specific content about real quicksand. Before presenting this material as fact, Michael calls on his class to verify information in the book. First, after reading the book, he asks the class to name all the facts they can recall about quicksand. He lists these facts on newsprint, and assigns each item on the list to a different student. Next, he asks students to listen for their assigned facts as he reads two entries from encyclopedias about quicksand. Students are then asked to report on whether their particular facts were confirmed in standard references.

Content-related
activities re-
quire applica-
tion of facts as
well as straight
recall from
memory

In a second activity requiring students to remember what they have heard and to apply material to another situation, he asks several student volunteers to pretend that the carpeted floor is quicksand and that they have just fallen in. In one dramatic activity, the victim is required to escape from the sand, while explaining how escape is possible. In another, the class calls out ideas to the person on the carpet who has to report whether the ideas work. For a final content-related activity, he provides sand, buckets, and hoses to several teams of students and allows them to make their own quicksand, following instructions in the book.

Presenting Processes

Michael is aware that by following "cookbook" instructions, his students learn little about general patterns of thinking behind scientific experiments. To learn a process, students proceed without step-by-step instructions, propelled by curiosity about what their work will turn up.

To learn proc-
esses, students
seek facts with-
out knowing
answers in ad-
vance

To simulate more accurately the way scientists approach their explorations, Michael lets students make another batch of quicksand—with different directions. "What do you think will happen if you use less water in the bucket? What would happen if you used heavy rocks instead of sand?" The second-graders set off to find out. While mixing new ingredients, they are learning more than the answers to Michael's questions. They are also picking up some general techniques scientists use, no matter what the question.

Sharpening Values and Attitudes

Later in the school year, Michael looks to children's literature for books to complement a science unit he has planned on plants. A school librarian introduces him to *The Amazing Dandelion* (1977), by Millicent E. Selsam and Jerome Wexler, respected authors of informational books.

One of Michael's teaching goals in the science unit is to stimulate children's curiosity and to develop in them an objective attitude of

Books such as this one may help stimulate children's curiosity. (Illustration on p. 31 by Jerome Wexler in *The Amazing Dandelion.* Copyright © 1977 by Millicent E. Selsam and Jerome Wexler. By permission of William Morrow & Company, Inc.)

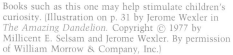

interest and open-mindedness about the natural world. The book by Selsam and Wexler can help him approach that goal. But Michael does not begin activities supporting the goal until he is sure his second-graders are clear on the content of the book.

A simple activity helps fix the facts given in the book in his children's minds. "How do they spread so quickly?" the book asks

639

(p. 7), introducing an explanation of how dandelions propagate by releasing seeds into the air. After the children have heard the book read aloud and had a chance to look at the illustrations, Michael asks them to draw a series of pictures of their own to answer the question.

Then classroom work turns toward development of attitudes, starting with a discussion. "The book says some people think the dandelion is a pest," Michael begins. "Why do they think that? Do you agree with them?"

In answering, children recall passages in the book, about how dandelions crowd out other garden plants, for example. The discussion calls for a clear expression of *subjective* values and reactions. But Michael is also interested in increasing awareness of general *objective* attitudes scientists assume in approaching experiments. "Even if dandelions are pests," he asks, "why do you think people try to find out about them? Can you think of other plants you might think are pests, but would like to know more about?"

The activity is not an occasion for a lecture on scientific detachment. If children fail to react to the second set of questions—about objective attitudes—Michael will not provide answers. He may, however, raise similar attitude questions in other science units, questioning students about what they observe about the way scientists—as depicted in fiction or reported in nonfiction—approach their research.

Michael finds it easy to integrate children's books into the total curriculum because he teaches all other subjects to the same group of children. In later years, when children move from classroom to classroom in the course of a day, teachers may sometimes have to make an extra effort to find out what the total curriculum is and how literature can be melded with other courses. But the effort is worthwhile. In the next two case studies, consultations with other teachers and discussions with students about what is happening in mathematics and social studies courses heighten student involvement with literature.

CASE STUDY 2:
MATHEMATICS AND LITERATURE IN THE SIXTH GRADE

Charlotte, a language arts teacher in the sixth grade, shares her students with three other teachers, each with different curricula. There are, however, several ways to find out what is happening in the other classrooms before integrating literature into the total curriculum. Charlotte can, of course, consult the curriculum guide, although curriculum guides are often vague about teaching plans for a specific day. More useful are discussions with teachers, who are pleased that Charlotte will be using literature to support their teaching goals, and informal talks with students who are pleased with Charlotte's interest in books they are carrying from classroom to classroom.

Charlotte's own curriculum for the year does not call for her to integrate literature with the mathematics curriculum, but one of the single titles she wants to introduce—Norton Juster's *The Phantom Tollbooth* (1961)—takes off from the logic of mathematics to tell its amusing story. (The book is described in Chapter 6.) On rereading it before presentation to her students, Charlotte wonders whether they have enough background in mathematics to understand Juster's humor.

In a middle school, a review of the curriculum guide, talks with teachers and students precede plans for matching literature to other courses

Discussions with a mathematics teacher indicate that the sixth-graders have developed basic skills in decimal fractions, and are working to sharpen ability with multiplication and division. Charlotte reviews several passages in Juster's book with the teacher, including the episode where Milo meets .58 of a child, the smallest member of an average family with 2.58 children. The mathematics teacher suggests that the students would be more likely to understand the story after some preliminary work using an informational book, such as Jane Jonas Srivastrava's *Averages* (1975).

A suggestion for a complementary book comes from a mathematics teacher

The book, part of the Young Math Book series published by Crowell, explains three kinds of averages: mode, median, and arithmetic mean. (*Mode* means "most common"; if there are ten apples, five oranges, and seven pears, apples are the modal fruit. *Median* means the "middle of a group when it is arranged in order"; if five teachers earn $100, $50, $44, $26, and $5 an hour, respectively, the median hourly rate is $44. The *arithmetic mean* is a computed average obtained by adding each measurement and then dividing by the number of measurements; the mean hourly rate of the figures given above is $45.)

The book would be easy for average sixth-grade readers, but Charlotte will read it aloud anyway so that all the students will learn its concepts at the same time. Then she can move quickly to activities. She can complete her reading in about twenty minutes.

Her first teaching goal in presenting the book is related to its content. She hopes students will pick up some facts about averages to help them better understand a fictional book. Additionally, she wants her language arts students to practice certain processes of expression by writing something every day, and by recording actions and observations accurately. And finally, she wants to focus attention on attitudes, in this case the attitudes of authors toward their subjects.

Teaching goals relate to content, process and attitudes

This factual book may be used to help students gain information that will help them to understand a fictional book better. (Illustration by Aliki from *Averages* by Jane Jonas Srivastava. Illustrations copyright © 1975 by Alike. By permission of Thomas Y. Crowell Company.)

To approach the first two goals, Charlotte assigns activities described in *Averages.* These require students to count actual objects, or record events, and then compute or determine the kinds of averages. Then Charlotte asks her classes to write paragraphs describing what they did. The exercises help children understand the concept at the same time they practice written expression. Again, as in the previous case study, content provides material for learning process.

After this preparation, Charlotte reads *The Phantom Tollbooth* and moves toward her final objective. Both books, she points out briefly, use ideas from mathematics. Now she leaves it to the students to recall facts or content from both books, and then go through the process of comparing the two. Content comes first. "I'd like you to think back on what you remember from both books, and write down three ways mathematics is used in Juster's book and three ways it's used in *Averages*," she says. Students write independently, then share what they have written with the class. The next activity emphasizes process: "How do the uses overlap?" To answer, students are required to go beyond content and apply simple techniques of comparison.

This activity provides a good backdrop for a final exercise, on another day, requiring recognition and comparison of attitudes.

To introduce the activity and remind them of the books, Charlotte begins by presenting two pages, one from each book.

In the first, from *The Phantom Tollbooth*, the character named Milo asks for the biggest number there is, and another character called the Mathemagician appears with a gigantic numeral "3" (p. 189). Picking up *Averages*, Charlotte displays cartoon characters speaking to each other. "How was your day?" asks a little girl, rushing to greet her father. "Mode, thank you," he replies (p. 5).

A discussion following the reading centers on the attitudes the authors have about their common subject. "What do you think each of the authors feels about mathematics? How is the way they approach math different from the way people usually think about math?" Charlotte follows every response from students with further questions asking them to suggest passages in the books to support their positions. Once again, students discussing attitudes are required to recall content, and to apply some evaluative processes to what they have read.

Charlotte's teaching goals were spread among all three objectives in the mathematics and language arts curricula. In the next and final case study, the teacher focuses on teaching goals related to attitude and value systems, although by now it should be clear that a good grasp of literary content and skill in using critical processes are often important components in understanding attitudes.

CASE STUDY 3: SOCIAL STUDIES
AND LITERATURE IN THE EIGHTH GRADE

Roy, a junior high school English teacher, sees several groups of students each day, spending no more than an hour daily with each group. His students are taught by two social studies teachers, and in each of their classrooms, students are involved with different projects.

But by talking with members from each of his classes, Roy is able to spot a pattern in the social studies curriculum: each of the teachers is leading studies of societal change in countries and cultures. After confirming the broad outlines of the curriculum used in

Miyax is caught between traditional Eskimo life and modern American culture. (Illustration by John Schoenherr from *Julie of the Wolves* by Jean Craighead George. Illustrations copyright © 1972 by John Schoenherr. By permission of Harper & Row, Publishers, Inc.)

other classrooms, Roy decides to assemble a unit of literature dealing with the theme of cultural change.

Teaching goals
Several teaching goals shape his unit: Roy wants his students to encounter a variety of good literature, and—because all his students are old enough to deal with questions of literary form—he wants to introduce an awareness of the way authors develop literary charac-

ters. His ultimate goals, complementing the social studies curriculum, are to lead an exploration of several value systems in different societies and to challenge students to consider their own attitudes and values.

Roy already knows of one book matching the aims of his unit, *Julie of the Wolves* (1972), by Jean Craighead George. This Newbery-Award-winning book tells the story of a young Eskimo girl who longs for the survival of venerable Eskimo customs and resents the encroachments of modern American culture into her life. One of the social studies teachers suggests another title, Margaret Craven's *I Heard the Owl Call My Name* (1973). Craven's book describes changes in the society of the Tsawataineuk Tribe in British Columbia, while it relates the story of a young vicar, with a terminal disease, assigned to work with the tribe. Where would Roy look for books to complement these two? The common element of tribal society in the first two books suggests looking for titles about Native American tribes. By flipping through the card catalogue under "Indian," and browsing on the fiction shelf, Roy finds two other appropriate books. Theodora Kroeber's *Ishi, Last of His Tribe* (1964) centers on the remnants of the Yahi tribe in northern California, the last survivors of attacks from white settlers. *Bear's Heart, Scenes from the Life of a Cheyenne Artist of One Hundred Years Ago with Pictures by Himself* (1977), by Burton Supree, reproduces pencil and crayon drawings by an actual Cheyenne tribesman. The fictionalized text tells of his imprisonment at Fort Marion in Florida, his release from prison, his education at the Hampton Institute, and his eventual return to his tribe.

Roy's teaching strategy is to familiarize the class with the content of each of the four books, then compare them and lead the classes toward a general discussion of attitudes toward change based on all the reading they have done in the unit.

Roy begins the unit by reading *Bear's Heart* aloud to his classes. The book provides a quick introduction to the unit: it can be completed in one period. The next time each of his classes meets, Roy leads a discussion designed to fix the content of the story firmly in his students' minds by requiring them to recall, interpret, and analyze what they have heard. (Behind Roy's planning of his preliminary discussion are the categories of discussion question developed by educator Norris Sanders; the categories are discussed in Chapter 12.) Thumbing back through the pages in the book, Roy asks students to look at many of the drawings. He asks several basic questions: "How well do the pictures match the written story?" "In what ways does the story—written recently—depart from or add to the drawings made more than a century ago?" "Do you get a differ-

Even preliminary discussion requires more of students than just recalling what they have read

645

Catching a Shark July 1875

How would you describe this picture by Bear's Heart?
What inferences might you make based on the content
of the picture? (From *Bear's Heart* by Burton Supree,
with Ann Ross, pictures by Bear's Heart. Illustrations
copyright © 1977 by The Museum of the American
Indian—Heye Foundation. Used by permission of J. B.
Lippincott Company.)

ent feeling about the characters in the story from the pictures than
from the text?''

Midway through the period, the discussion turns toward value
systems expressed in the book. ''What was Bear's Heart's attitude
about his captivity and about the white man?'' After listening to
several opinions, Roy adds some information to the discussion by
reading the book's afterword:

Like many Indians prior to the present day, Bear's Heart was too trusting
and too amazed by the white man's power to see what was being done to
him. Therefore no rage or resentment is found in his bright, enchanted

pictures. . . . The innocent cannot believe in the ugliness of our world and that is perhaps what makes them so vulnerable and so unbearably tragic. (pp. 62–63)

Roy's students have a chance to agree or challenge the afterword; if they agree, they are asked to express what makes a picture "bright, enchanted"; if they disagree, they are asked to express dimensions they find in the pictures.

Roy's next series of questions extends the discussion from an analysis of one character to an analysis of entire societies. "What Indian ways were important to Bear's Heart?" he asks. "Why were they so important? What white ways became important to him? Why do you think this happened?" A final set of questions challenges students to compare the attitudes of contemporary society with those of a century ago. The questions concern another character in the book, Lt. Pratt, a soldier who wanted fair treatment for the Indians, but who also wanted them taught what they needed to know to get along in the white man's world.

"How would Lt. Pratt have been regarded in his own time?" Roy asks. "How would he be regarded today, and if there is a difference, how would you account for it?"

In a carefully constructed series of discussion questions, Roy has led his students through a review of the content of the book, and required them to use content to practice interpretation and analysis—literary processes—on the content. Finally, he has brought them to a discussion of several kinds of attitudes. They have explored the philosophies of Bear's Heart and Lt. Pratt, as well as the general climate of attitude at the time the two lived. And they have examined how attitudes change over time, all without lectures from Roy.

The rest of the books build on the groundwork laid during two class hours. Roy assigns his students to read one of the other books, asking them to watch as they read for details of custom and belief important to characters. They are also asked to make note of changes in custom, and how characters react to change.

A week after this assignment, students break into small groups to describe the books they have read. The groups will be mixed so that after the discussions, every student will be roughly familiar with the content of every book. A follow-up discussion will build on this content: "How were the plights of the main characters in these books different from each other?" "Did the differences in their situations make a difference in the way they responded to changes in society?"

Part of this discussion centers on literary form: "How does the

author let you know how a character feels?" "What other ways do
writers have of conveying their characters' feelings besides just telling readers how they feel?"

And the final part of the discussion turns to the students' own
attitudes. The entire class considers several questions. "Do you
think old ways *can* be preserved?" "Do you think they should be?"
"What customs or values do you think should be changed?" "How
would society today react to the change?" "How would you react to
the change?"

Roy's teaching has called on all of the skills and techniques described in Part Two of this book. In his presentation of four works,
and in question after question, Roy has challenged students to see
literature as more than a source of stories. The questions have encouraged a range of responses, from simple recall and interpretation
of what students have found in books to expressions of how they feel
about themselves and society. The unit has marked out common
ground between different books, and connected different subjects.
And students themselves have found that the work they have done
in two classrooms has led them to discoveries in one broad field of
knowledge.

SUMMARY

1 A full thirty-six-week program of literature offers the same potential as a unit, but on a broader scale, as students meet a diversity of
books and come to recognize common elements. Whether the potential is attained depends on planning a *curriculum,* a course of
study based on a set of books and an accompanying set of related
activities.

2 Goals of curricula in literature have varied over the years. *Alan C.
Purves* reports that early in this century, literature was used for
literacy, oratory, and *moral training.* In later decades, teachers used
books to implant a *cultural heritage* and as a *socializing force.* More
recently, educators have used literature to *train critical faculties.* In
1966, the *Dartmouth Seminar* concluded that the main goal of literature programs was to promote children's active *"involvement"
with literature.*

3 These and other goals tend to fall under three major categories.
Teachers who expect students to learn facts from books have set
content goals. Books can also be used to teach *process* skills—
classifying or comparing books, for instance. Finally, literature is
used to explore *values and attitudes.*

4 Guidelines supplied by schools are often vague about literature
programs, providing freedom for teachers to use what they know of

books and children to draw up specific plans. One way to approach the task is to set down certain elements of the curriculum on a calendar. A previously successful unit opens the year, for example, and another unit on holidays is scheduled for the Christmas/Chanukah season. Planning in other subjects and discussions with other teachers suggest other blocks in the curriculum. When these are in place, teachers can round out the year's program, balancing realistic fiction with fantasy, for instance.

5 Once underway, the literature program should be evaluated regularly. Using *behavioral objectives,* a teacher would look for specific student responses to see if the program were succeeding. But teachers also need to call up what they know of children to evaluate the quality of responses—to understand that a girl's reluctance to speak up in class, for example, may be caused by shyness, not by a lack of understanding or involvement with literature.

6 Children's books can be used in teaching other subjects—mathematics, science, or social studies, for instance—to enhance the literature as well as to support teaching goals in these subjects. There are several good reasons for combining curricula: to show that literature overlaps many areas of knowledge, to illustrate that good fiction is often constructed from fact, to give students a different perspective on another subject, and to introduce more up-to-date information than is available in standard textbooks.

7 Standard curriculum goals in social studies, mathematics, and science closely match the *content, process,* and *attitude* goals underlying many literature programs. The similarity suggests that literature can be more than a source of content or fact to accompany topics in at least these three subjects.

8 In the first case study, a second-grade teacher uses *Tomie de Paola*'s *The Quicksand Book* to teach scientific processes as well as facts: students learn to make quicksand according to the book's instructions, but also learn general methods scientists use to explore such natural phenomena as quicksand. After reading a second book, *The Amazing Dandelion,* the teacher leads a discussion to explore subjective and objective attitudes.

9 A sixth-grade language arts teacher in the second case study discusses *Norton Juster*'s *The Phantom Tollbooth* with a mathematics teacher before introducing it to her class because understanding some of the humor in the book requires a knowledge of averages. The other teacher suggests an informational book to complement the fiction. Using these two books together helps the teacher to approach content, process, and attitude goals in the literature program.

10 In the third case study, a junior high school English teacher

builds a four-book unit on cultural change to match course work in other classrooms. The unit of fiction complements social studies course work on societal change, but it helps the teacher meet goals of the literature program: to introduce a variety of good literature, to explore characterization in literature, and to use literature to challenge students' values and attitudes. The teachers in each of the case studies use skills discussed throughout Part Two: presenting books well, encouraging students to respond, organizing books into units, and organizing units into programs of literature.

BIBLIOGRAPHY

Adult References

Bloom, Benjamin S., J. Thomas Hastings, and George F. Madaus. *Handbook on Formative and Summative Evaluation of Student Learning* (New York: McGraw-Hill, 1971).

Carin, Arthur A., and Robert B. Sund. *Teaching Science through Discovery* (Columbus, Ohio: Merrill, 1975). (1964)

Fenton, Edwin. *The New Social Studies* (New York: Holt, 1967).

Kramer, Klaas. *Teaching Elementary School Mathematics* (Boston: Allyn and Bacon, 1975). (1966)

Muller, H. J. *The Uses of English* (New York: Holt, 1967).

Perrone, V., and W. A. Strandberg, "A Perspective on Accountability," *Teachers College Record,* February 1972, pp. 347–355.

Sutherland, Zena. *The Best in Children's Books, 1966-1972* (Chicago: University of Chicago Press, 1973).

Children's Book References

Alexander, Lloyd. *The King's Fountain,* illus. Ezra Jack Keats (New York: Dutton, 1971).

———. *The Truthful Harp,* illus. Evaline Ness (New York: Holt, 1971).

Andersen, Hans Christian. *The Nightingale,* trans. Eva Le Gallienne, illus. Nancy Ekholm Burkert (New York: Harper, 1965).

———. *The Ugly Duckling,* trans. R. P. Keigwin, illus. Adrienne Adams (New York: Scribner's 1965).

———. *The Steadfast Tin Soldier,* illus. Monika Laimgruber (New York: Atheneum, 1971).

Boston, L. M. *The Children of Green Knowe,* illus. Peter Boston (New York: Harcourt, 1955).

Briggs, Raymond. *Father Christmas* (London: Hamish Hamilton, 1973).

Caudill, Rebecca. *A Certain Small Shepherd,* illus. William Pène du Bois (New York: Holt, 1965).

Collier, James Lincoln, and Christopher Collier. *My Brother Sam Is Dead* (New York: Four Winds, 1974).

Coopersmith, Jerome. *A Chanukah Fable for Christmas,* illus. Syd Hoff (New York: Putnam's 1969).

Craven, Margaret. *I Heard the Owl Call My Name* (Garden City, N.Y.: Doubleday, 1973).

Cresswell, Helen. *A Game of Catch,* illus. Ati Forberg (New York: Macmillan, 1977).

De Paola, Tomie. *The Quicksand Book* (New York: Holiday House, 1977).

Fitzhugh, Louise. *Harriet the Spy* (New York: Harper, 1964).

Fritz, Jean. *Early Thunder,* illus. Lynd Ward (New York: Coward-McCann, 1967).

Gauch, Patricia Lee. *This Time, Tempe Wick?* illus. Margot Tomes (New York: Coward-McCann, 1974).

George, Jean Craighead. *Julie of the Wolves,* illus. John Schoenherr (New York: Harper, 1972).

Grahame, Kenneth. *The Reluctant Dragon,* illus. Ernest Shepard (New York: Holiday, 1938).

Greene, Constance. *The Unmaking of Rabbit* (New York: Viking, 1972).

Griffiths, Helen. *The Wild Heart,* illus. Victor G. Ambrus (Garden City, N.Y.: Doubleday, 1963).

———. *The Greyhound,* illus. Victor Ambrus (Garden City, N.Y.: Doubleday, 1964).

Hopkins, Lee Bennett (ed.). *Hey-How for Halloween!* illus. Janet McCaffery (New York: Harcourt, 1974).

Johnny Tremain. Buena Vista, 1957. 16-millimeter color film.

Juster, Norton. *The Phantom Tollbooth,* illus. Jules Feiffer (New York: Random House, 1961).

Kroeber, Theodora. *Ishi, Last of His Tribe,* illus. Ruth Robbins (Berkeley, Calif.: Parnassus, 1964).

Moore, Lilian, and Lawrence Webster (eds.). *Catch Your Breath: A Book of Shivery Poems,* illus. Gahan Wilson (Champaign, Ill.: Garrard, 1973).

Myers, Walter Dean. *The Dragon Takes a Wife,* illus. Ann Grifalconi (New York: Bobbs-Merrill, 1972).

Ormondroyd, Edward. *Time at the Top,* illus. Peggy Bach (Berkeley, Calif.: Parnassus, 1963).

Pearce, Phillippa. *Tom's Midnight Garden,* illus. Susan Einzig (Philadelphia: Lippincott, 1959).

Prelutsky, Jack. *Circus* (New York: Macmillan, 1974).

————. *Nightmares. Poems to Trouble Your Sleep,* illus. Arnold Lobel (New York: Greenwillow, 1976).

Rockwell, Thomas. *How to Eat Fried Worms* (New York: Watts, 1973).

Sachs, Marilyn. *Peter and Veronica,* illus. Louis Glanzman (New York: Doubleday, 1969).

Selsam, Millicent E., and Jerome Wexler. *The Amazing Dandelion* (New York: Morrow, 1977).

Srivastrava, Jane Jonas. *Averages,* illus. Aliki Brandenberg (New York: Crowell, 1975).

Stacy, Donald. *Experiments in Art* (New York: Four Winds Press, 1975).

Supree, Burton, with Ann Ross. *Bear's Heart: Scenes from the Life of a Cheyenne Artist of One Hundred Years Ago with Pictures by Himself* (Philadelphia: Lippincott, 1977).

Yolen, Jane. *The Girl Who Cried Flowers and Other Tales,* illus. David Palladini (New York: Crowell, 1974).

CHAPTER
15

TOWARD THE FUTURE

CHILDREN'S LITERATURE IN A CHANGING WORLD

*C*hildren's book author Rumer Godden once imagined what would happen if a greedy modern-day editor could get in touch with the ghost of Beatrix Potter (1866–1943) about reissuing her book, *The Tale of Peter Rabbit.*

In an article that has become something of a classic comment on publishing, Godden presented imaginary correspondence between the editor, Mr. V. Andal of the De Base Publishing Co. Inc., and Miss Potter. In the opening letter, the avaricious Mr. Andal reports that he wants to include one of Miss Potter's books in a series under the general title, "Masterpieces for Mini-Minds."

The De Base plan—outlined in several letters—is to discard Miss Potter's superb watercolors and replace them with "outline drawing," less expensive to reproduce. Text will be rewritten, following suggestions from "experts," to make the story of the young rabbit who strays into Mr. McGregor's garden more salable for sensitive children and slow readers. The De Base edition will be bigger than Potter's petite original ("it must be enlarged—people like to get their money's worth"), and simpler to read. Clearly, Andal is more concerned with making money than publishing good literature. The first letter in Godden's imaginary correspondence concludes: "I send you Hans Andersen's 'Ti-ny Thum-my' to see. (Originally issued as 'Thumbelina,' and I think now much improved)" (1963, p. 5).

Godden's fantasy draws on fact. Children's literature today has reached a high plateau of excellence, but writers and editors are still vulnerable to social and economic pressures that have the power to shape what they do. Editors sometimes suggest rewriting to make books match current taste in the marketplace. Cutbacks in government funds produce deficit budgets in libraries, which in turn engender nervousness in publishing houses and hard times for freelance writers.

Of course what happens in children's book publishing depends to a great degree on what individual writers and artists have to say and illustrate. People like Potter, artist Randolph Caldecott, and publisher John Newbery—each of these individuals shaped the work of others in children's literature. But trends in publishing also depend on such capricious factors as sexual mores, or the cost of color printing.

"Many good books die today," writes children's book editor Jean Karl, "spiked on the need for full-color pictures" (1967, p. 37). Books that successfully pass modern cost-analysis tests still face chal-

(Chapter-opening illustration from *The Tale of Peter Rabbit* used by permission of the publisher Frederick Warne & Co., Inc.)

lenges on their suitability for children. Writer Mary Steele, for instance, was once working on a story about twins of the opposite sex. She wrote her editor to ask if the twins could sleep in the same bedroom. "[The editor] wrote back and said, 'Get those twins into separate bedrooms even if you have to add a wing to the house.' So I did," the writer reports (in Wells and Davidson, 1976, p. 73).

No one can predict precisely what kinds of books will be published in the 1980s and beyond. But it seems clear from a glance back at recent years that trends outside of literature will influence directions in publishing. In an article about the future of children's books, British author John Rowe Townsend writes: "Actually it is not as easy as one might suppose to separate literary from economic and technological trends. If we picture literature as a plant, it is obvious that the way the plant grows will be enormously affected by its environment" (1977, p. 352).

Material in this chapter focuses on two related elements of the "environment" that will certainly continue to impinge on children's book publishing in the years ahead: *economics* and *social attitudes.*

An awareness of these outside factors can help adults choosing books for children to recognize compromises with literary standards. Teachers and librarians who hold fast to those standards can become an outside force of their own in shaping the future of the literature.

THE ECONOMIC ENVIRONMENT OF LITERATURE

The ghost of Beatrix Potter, in Godden's correspondence, objects to editor Andal's plan to rewrite *Peter Rabbit* in simpler language, basing the changes on the recommendations of "modern language experts." She has already written plain and simple language, she argues, using the Old Testament as a model of good style. Andal responds:

> I really must enlighten you to the fact that the Old Testament, as reading, is almost totally out of date, not only for children but adults. It has been replaced by the epic screen pictures which, sequestered as you are in your native Cumberland, you may not have seen. These movies are money-spinners, which is heartening as it endorses our belief that there is life in old tales yet—if properly presented. . . . Publishing nowadays is such a costly business that we need expert advice. Properly handled, in attractive wrappers, perhaps packaged with one or two others, and well advertised, books for juveniles can become really big business . . . .

And Miss Potter answers him:

657

(a)

"Stopping by Woods on a Snowy Evening" by Robert Frost.

Advertisements give some clues as to how publishers
regard their books, and who their buyers may be. ([a]
Advertisement from *Time Magazine,* October 22,
1973. Reprinted by permission of Rand McNally and
Company; [b] From *Small Rabbit* by Miska Miles,
illustrated by James Arnosky. Text copyright © 1977
by Miska Miles, illustrations copyright © 1977 by
James Arnosky. By permission of Little, Brown and
Co.)

Your publishing would not be so costly without all these "experts" and elaborate notions; indeed, your last letter reads as if you were selling grocery, not books. (Godden, 1963, p. 7)

Today even editors highly concerned with literary quality—as Andal is not—are forced to spend some of their time thinking about books as products. Editors weigh strengths and weaknesses of competing books on the subject. They consider costs of illustrating proposed books. They study ways to cut production expenses, make suggestions on marketing and advertising, and pay attention to trends in the national economy and government aid to education. Any editor who worked in the children's field during the late 1960s is aware that federal spending alone can have a major effect on what is published for children. The 1960s, in fact, are a case study of how economic influences affect what children are given to read.

Case Study: The Boom Market in Children's Books, 1965–1969

On April 11, 1965, the late President Lyndon B. Johnson signed a $1.3 billion aid to education bill at an old Texas school where he had first been taught. The bill, the Elementary and Secondary Education Act, contained among its provisions several designed to stimulate school construction and teacher hiring. But the provision that most raised the hopes of librarians and children's book publishers was the section called Title II, authorizing federal grants to the states to boost school library budgets. Money under Title II—$100 million the first year of the bill alone—was to supplement spending in public and private school libraries for books and other materials.

Sitting on a bench next to his first school teacher, Johnson said the act he was signing would "put into the hands of our youth more than thirty million new books, and into many of our schools their first libraries."

There are no figures to show whether Johnson's target of thirty million books was ever reached, but the immediate results of the act were impressive. More than 3,600 new public school libraries were established in the first year of the program alone. On a national basis, the average per-pupil expenditure for library books almost doubled—from $2.70 to $5 in elementary schools (National School Public Relations Association, 1968). High levels of spending under Title II continued for several years, stimulating a boom in children's books as publishers scrambled to meet requests from libraries.

"Nineteen sixty-seven through 1969 were special years," said Olga Litowinsky, an editor of Viking Junior Books, who worked for a different publishing house during the first heady years of Title II. "I don't think we'll see the like of them again. Almost anyone who could put together an outline could get a book contract." Even in publishing houses highly concerned with literary standards, she recalled in an interview, editors were told, "Go out and get product [books]." The focus of attention was on curriculum-related nonfiction, such as science books, she said. Inevitably, this "product" was not always high quality.

"But even though some of the books produced weren't worthwhile," she said, "the federal spending gave a chance to a lot of young artists and writers to get started. The money also made available a lot of nonfiction that would not be done today. If you wanted to introduce a biography of Lord Byron in the 1960s, for instance, it would have been done. But no one would touch it today, because it would sell only a few thousand copies."

The funds stimulated well-established publishers to use more color in their book illustrations, to take risks with young writers, and to increase staff. Title II money also attracted entrepreneurs with no previous experience in literature who wanted to ride the wave of interest in children's books.

"That vast amount of money encouraged people to come into the field," said the late F. N. Monjo, who was an editor and writer, "even people who should not have come in. They cared about nothing at all except the bottom line of their financial statements."

After several flourishing years, the bottom line began to look bad. At the beginning of the boom, in 1965, publishers were producing 2,895 books a year, and the number remained at well over 2,000 for several years. Then, shortly after Richard M. Nixon was elected President in 1968, he began a concerted drive to cut federal spending and the size of government programs in an effort to reduce inflation. Title II appropriations dropped by 50 percent between 1968 and 1969—from $99.2 million to $50 million.

Publishing reacted sharply to this cut, and to rising costs. In the last year of the decade, the number of children's book titles published had dropped to less than half the number published in 1965—from 2,895 to 1,406. (The figures are from Steckler, 1967, p. 45 and Johnson, 1971, p. 70.)

Editorial staffs were trimmed, and raises were pared to a minimum for the survivors. Many publishing houses that had routinely ordered 15,000 copies of new titles from printers in 1967 were left with thousands of unsold books in 1969. Press orders declined steadily.

Overall, what was the effect of President Johnson's dream, the elaborately staged signing ceremony, the dramatic pledge of more than 30 million new books? Children's book editor Margaret K.

Some excellent stories, such as *The Egypt Game*, were
published during the book boom of the sixties.
(Copyright © 1967 by Zilpha Keatley Snyder. From
The Egypt Game by Zilpha Keatley Snyder. Used by
permission of Atheneum Publishers.)

McElderry concludes that the advent of federal funding for education "brought about the largest dislocation in the children's book
world in fifty years."

Had President Johnson's dream of "The Great Society" been sustained
and Federal funds for schools and libraries continued, the country would
have had a chance to achieve real mass literacy. As it happened, there
was too much, too fast, and then—too suddenly—almost complete
withdrawal. Publishers rushed to supply what was needed, often with
quantity instead of quality. When the bubble burst, they were overex-
tended on inventory and, to a degree, on staff; and some painful adjustments were necessary. For authors, too, the sudden glorious increase in

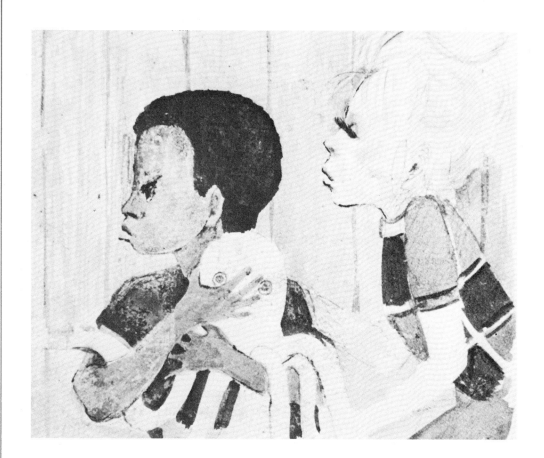

royalties was followed by an equally sudden plunge to a lower level of income. (1974, pp. 91–92)

How Economics Affects Books Today

After retrenching in the late 1960s, publishers began to recover in the 1970s. But the general economic climate of rising costs for materials and labor continued to affect what was produced for children, and economics is likely to remain a factor in publishing in the future. What does that mean to teachers, librarians, and children themselves? People who work in publishing disagree over the question.

On one hand, some argue that increased costs of publishing have led to a decline in the quality of production. "In the old days," one editor said in an interview, "we used reinforced bindings on most of our books. Now we use them only in picture books for very young children. Our covers used to be cloth; now they're paper. The quality of production has gone down."

The same editor contended that cutting costs also cuts opportunities for new, pioneering writers or artists to enter the field.

On the other hand, some in publishing argue that difficult economic conditions have improved the content of books. John Rowe Townsend reports that publishers today may have to be more selective about what they buy, and work harder to sell it well.

> Two or three years ago, a British publisher of children's books told me that he saw hard times coming for the B-plus author. These times have now arrived and look as if they could be here to stay. It may be that hard times will mean some useful pruning, since it is generally agreed that for some years past too many indifferent books have been published on the children's lists. (1977, p. 350)

Editors and publishers are in agreement that one result of economic stringency has been an increase in international *copublishing*. Copublishing means that two or more book companies in different countries share the initial publishing expenses to bring out a book which each house sells in its home country.

The practice is flourishing. Viking Junior Books, for instance, offers many of its titles to British publishers. And of the eighteen books on Viking's fall 1978 list, more than half were copublished, the highest number to date, according to editor Olga Litowinsky.

Under one typical copublishing plan, a book company in New York sends artwork and text for a forthcoming book to an English publisher, who makes the editorial decision to join the publishing venture by taking on 8,000 copies. The American publisher had decided initially to print 20,000 copies of the book, but now the print order is increased to 28,000. When 20,000 copies have been produced, the printer stops the presses and changes one black-ink plate, removing the American publisher's name and replacing it with the imprint of the British publisher. There is a slight extra charge for this plate substitution, but overall the costs are much lower than they would be if the printer had to gear up for two separate books.

Among other advantages, the system permits publishers to take on picture books that otherwise might be too expensive to produce. Some editors in the late 1970s, in fact, were looking forward to a resurgence in the number of full-color picture books as a direct result of international publishing.

There is some disagreement, however, on whether copublishing improves the quality of the literature. Some suggest that interna-

ISSUE

SHOULD ADAPTATIONS BE MADE WHEN BOOKS ARE TRANSLATED FOR DISTRIBUTION IN ANOTHER COUNTRY?

In order to relate translated works to the lives of the children who will read them, certain adaptions to their needs and understandings are necessary. Illustrations, names, place references, descriptions of everyday situations must be changed so that the author's original intention is made comprehensible to children of different cultures and backgrounds. In biography collections, a frequent procedure is to substitute or add the lives of some well-known figures of the particular country. (p. 52)

> Stein, Ruth. "Launching the New Literate," *School Library Journal*, November 1966, pp. 51–53.

Tailoring children's books to their new country takes various forms. When a book comes through an English translation to an American edition, additional adjustments are made to make it conform to our national taste and style. I question whether all such changes are necessary to accommodate English editions to America or, for that matter, American editions to England. Perhaps we are being overly self-conscious in removing distinctive national language that helps create the real atmosphere of the book. (p. 39)

> Batchelder, Mildred L. "Learning about Children's Books in Translation," *ALA Bulletin*, January 1966, pp. 33–42.

Does it seem to you that many adaptations would be needed for American children to understand a book originally published or translated in England? What makes you think this? What are the advantages and disadvantages of adapting a book to the national taste and style of its new country?

PERIWINKLE,

Ermine,   Katydid,   Hawk,

This book was copublished, which means that two or more companies in different countries shared the cost of publishing. (From *A Peaceable Kingdom: The Shaker Abecedarius* illustrated by Alice and Martin Provensen. Illustrations copyright © 1978 by Alice and Martin Provensen. Reprinted by permission of The Viking Press, Inc.)

tional publishing is a healthy trend because it acquaints children with life-styles in other countries and enables the sharing of good books. Others argue that copublishing sometimes leads to undesirable extremes. Philippe Schuwer, deputy director of the children's division of Hachette, a French publisher, asserts that international editions sometimes satisfy one country's interests at the expense of foreign readers. For example, in some picture books about nature, photographs "were shot especially for a book and included only species native to the author's own country of origin and, often, only the rare ones at that." At the other extreme, the international movement, Schuwer writes, can breed blandness. Trying to appeal to an international audience, for example, a publisher might produce a handbook containing a complete census of plants from many countries. Most of the entries would be "of little interest to the youthful searcher in the woods and fields. . . . And the publisher,

666

eager for a large audience, doesn't always have the honesty to reveal the encyclopedic nature of the work" (1976, p. 74).

Schuwer's concern is a useful warning for adults choosing among books published simultaneously in separate countries. Does the book turn bland in trying to please an international audience? Or is it so parochial that it will appeal more to readers in a foreign country? Those are basic tests to apply as publishers continue to form partnerships across national borders.

The Effect of the Children's Book Market

In addition to knowing general economic conditions, publishers today are required to watch market trends in book buying. For hardbound books, that means gauging what teachers and librarians purchase for children, since approximately 80 percent of hardcover children's books sold are bought by adults in schools and libraries on behalf of young readers (Miele, 1974, p. 178). Marketing rules change for the expanding paperback market, however, because children themselves buy soft-cover editions, frequently on the basis of the cover alone. British editor Anthony Kamm explains how the market affects the appearance of books:

> The majority of hardback children's books are bought by adults, particularly those which will go to schools and libraries. They are also reviewed by adults. While the jacket design of a hardback book must appeal to its potential readers, it is impossible to avoid taking into account its effect on adults. With a children's paperback the appeal is direct to the child, which is why very few children's paperbacks have the same cover design as the original edition. (1970, p. 38)

Awareness of the market also means that if a genre of literature is particularly popular, writers and publishers tend to follow success with more entries in that genre. For instance, according to publishers we interviewed, in the late 1970s, contemporary realism continued to have strong appeal for young American readers while young adult novels of historical fiction seemed more difficult to sell. Publishers' knowledge of such trends can affect what is produced in the immediate future.

"I recently wrote a hard-cover historical novel," one writer told us, "and my publisher tried to sell paperback rights, and nobody bought it because it was historical. My next book is going to be contemporary fiction, you bet."

The market itself, in other words, sometimes impinges on the

667

(a)

(b)

Harper publishes two paperback editions of *Little House on the Prairie,* one with the illustrations by Garth
Williams and the other with a photo insert from the television series. ([a] Illustration by Garth Williams
from *Little House on the Prairie* by Laura Ingalls Wilder. Copyright © 1953 as to pictures by Garth
Williams. By permission of Harper & Row, Publishers, Inc.; [b] from *Little House on the Prairie* by Laura
Ingalls Wilder. Copyright © 1935 by Laura Ingalls Wilder. Photos courtesy of the National Broadcasting
Company, Inc.)

kinds of books published for children. What does this mean for teachers and librarians?

For one thing, it means that children who are put off by the appearance or size of a hardcover book may enjoy the same story in a soft-cover edition with a cover aimed at them, a price they can afford, and a size they can carry around in their pockets. At the same time, adults should be aware that paperback illustrations often fail to match the quality of reproduction in the hard-cover edition, printed on better paper. While encouraging children to build a personal library of paperbacks, teachers all through the school years should continue to present hardcover books with high-quality, well-reproduced art.

Another implication is that adults working with children bear at least some of the responsibility for broadening children's interests in literature. If publishers are producing more contemporary realism than any other genre, teachers planning literature programs should be more than ever aware of the necessity for balance between the kinds of books used in the classroom. Can interest in contemporary realism be used to stimulate interest in historical fiction? Are children given a chance to enjoy fantasy and poetry, to read classics as well as contemporary writing?

Economics and marketing concerns will continue to sway the direction of children's book publishing all through the 1980s; government spending to aid disabled children, for instance, may result in dozens of new titles about children with special problems.

Looking Ahead: More Books about Disabilities?

A review of what happened in the wake of Title II suggests that more and more books about people with disabilities will be published in the years ahead. One major impetus is a 1975 bill (federal law 94-142) mandating that every disabled child must be educated in the "least restrictive environment"—meaning that children with special needs must be integrated (or "mainstreamed") into regular classrooms as much as possible. Some education experts anticipate that federal spending to put this far-reaching law into affect will approach $3.5 billion by 1982. (The figure comes from Hewett and Forness, 1977, p. 568.)

Practically, the law means that in the 1980s, regular classroom teachers will need special training and teaching materials to meet the needs of disabled children sitting next to nondisabled students. Teachers will also require help in answering questions, and breaking down stereotypes, about disabilities.

A few children's books in recent years have focused on the

problems—as well as the strengths—of disabled children; more can be expected as the law takes hold.

Joan Fassler's *Howie Helps Himself* (1975) is about a boy with cerebral palsy who cannot walk without something to hold on to. The simple text tells how Howie learns to maneuver his wheelchair, finally achieving enough skill to turn it around by himself and racing triumphantly across a room to his waiting father. Jeanne Whitehouse Petersen tells a realistic story about another disability in *I Have a Sister, My Sister is Deaf* (1977). The book stresses all the things a young deaf girl can do: dance, march in line, climb to the top of monkey bars, laugh, and swing. Outside in a grassy yard, the older sister explains, "I am the one who listens for small sounds. She is the one who watches for quick movements in the grass."

In the years ahead, teachers will probably have more selection guides and other materials to help them work with disabled children. One useful book is *Expectations,* an anthology of children's literature produced annually in Braille by the Braille Institute. The 1977 edition (edited by Betty Kalagian) includes William Steig's *The Amazing Bone,* poetry by Aileen Fisher, pictures outlined in Braille—and even Potter's *Peter Rabbit.* The collection is free to any blind child.

Federal money will provide impetus for more such material in the years ahead, but obviously money alone will not be responsible if authors and editors write and publish books about disabilities. A major factor in recent years has been hard and courageous efforts by disabled adults and by parents of disabled children to focus attention on discrimination and stereotypes (for instance, that disabled people are sinister, or amusing, or pathetic). The disability rights movement is one of the latest in a series of social movements that have shaped the direction of children's literature and will continue to affect it in the future.

THE SOCIAL ENVIRONMENT OF LITERATURE

The imaginary Mr. Andal has now received a copy of the original *Peter Rabbit* from the ghost of Beatrix Potter, and lectured her about how his publishing house will get the venerable *Rabbit* to the literary marketplace in a modern wrapper. Miss Potter's replies to Andal's letters show increasing alarm about his plans for her book. But the De Base editor plunges on in subsequent letters with details for updating the classic. He writes: "As you will see, apart from some words in the text, some details of plot, new illustrations, fresh names and a larger size for the book, very little has had to be changed" (Godden, 1963, p. 8).

Expectations is an anthology of children's literature published annually in Braille. (Credit: From *Expectations* by The Braille Institute of America, edited by Betty Kalagian. Copyright © 1977 Braille Institute of America, Inc. Used by permission of the Braille Institute Press.)

Why does the plot need to be changed? Andal explains:

The De Base Publishing Company has decided to use a certain "thought limitation" so that parents may entrust their children's reading to us with complete confidence. **In this** connection:

p. 10   We do not think father should have been made into rabbit pie.

Mr. McGregor is altogether a too Jehovah-like figure. We want children to *like* people rather than have that out-of-date respect. They must not be left thinking that a little rabbit can be blamed for trespassing and stealing: it was, rather, that he was deprived of lettuce and radishes. Mr. McGregor must be made a sympathetic figure. (Godden, 1963, p. 9)

For centuries, as material in Chapter 10 indicates, educators and other adults have viewed literature as a means to desirable social change; sometimes they have urged "thought limitation." That trend continues today, and will affect some of what is written and published in the years ahead, although the social causes may change.

Some of the causes may strike most modern readers as frivolous or irrelevant. Andal's concern about how Mr. Rabbit was turned into rabbit pie has a familiar ring: the fictional editor sounds like a real modern museum official who criticized British writer Jill Paton Walsh for allowing one of her characters to kill a snake. (Her recollection of the incident opens Chapter 1 of this book.) Some causes that may seem extraordinary now, however, may be taken quite seriously in the future. John Rowe Townsend writes, "It is not beyond the bounds of possibility that graphic accounts of the enjoyment of lavish meals may come to be thought obscene; and, still more, the feeding of high-protein diets to domestic pets" (1977, p. 353).

Other social causes, backed by articulate and hard-working groups, have won widespread respect today and have some effect on what is published for children.

Blacks, and women of all races, have uncovered patterns of repression against them. Many have rejected the "American Dream" in favor of new dreams of a pluralistic society built on respect for a diversity of life-styles and cultures.

The force for change from these and other groups (Chicanos and Native Americans are involved in similar struggles) grows out of many individual efforts. During the 1960s, the courageous freedom marches of the late Rev. Dr. Martin Luther King Jr., for example, focused attention on cruel discrimination against blacks. As early as 1848, Elizabeth Cady Stanton, Lucretia Mott, and others drafted a "Declaration of Sentiments" protesting the enforced inequality of women in America.

Slowly, legislators responded to these individual cries for recognition. For the first time since the end of the Civil War, Congress passed a civil rights bill in 1957; five others were signed between then and 1970, including the 1964 Civil Rights Act prohibiting discrimination on the basis of race, sex, or national origin in public accommodations and in federally assisted programs. In recent years, children's book publishers have also begun to take these groups in society seriously and to make some modifications in what they publish.

Uncovering Insensitivity in Children's Books

Apart from these general trends, publishers have come under specific pressure in recent years from analysts who have performed a simple technique: reading children's books and recording on a kind of scorecard the values that the books appear to support.

In this book, adults explain ideas to children, supporting a central theme of pride in being Chicano. (From *We Are Chicano* by Rose Blue, illustrated by Bob Alcorn. Illustrations copyright © 1973 by Franklin Watts, Inc. Used by permission of Franklin Watts, Inc.)

One such study, published by Nancy Larrick in 1965, is some-times given major credit in alerting the public at large to racism in children's books. Her article, in *Saturday Review,* reported results of a survey of 5,206 books published in 1962, 1963, and 1964, years when the civil rights struggle was a searing issue of national conscience.

Did the issue affect what children were given to read? Larrick concluded that it did not. She discovered that 4,857 of the books—more than 93 percent of the sample—contained no black characters. Most of the publishers presented at least a scattering of blacks in their books, but eight of the sixty-three publishers introduced none at all. Furthermore, even when publishers claimed to have published works including "one or more Negroes," illustrations in many of these books "leave the reader wondering whether a delicate shadow indicates a racial difference or a case of sunburn" (1965, p. 64).

The article concluded: "White supremacy in children's literature will be abolished when authors, editors, publishers, and booksellers decide that they need not submit to bigots."

In the same year that the Larrick article appeared, a group of editors, writers, educators, and parents formed a group called the Council on Interracial Books for Children to promote changes in books and other media. "Council programs are designed to promote learning materials that embody the principles of cultural pluralism," a book from the council reports (1976, p. vii).

Among other material published on children's books, the council put out a guideline called *Human (and Anti-Human) Values in Children's Books* (1976). It briefly analyzes 257 titles published in 1975. Each analysis is accompanied by a checklist, scoring books on racism and sexism, as well as literary quality.

Articles such as the Larrick investigation and materials from the council are a form of social pressure on modern publishers. Do these or other pressures—the general social climate, for example—lead to changes in the kinds of children's books publishers produce?

How Publishing Responds to Changing Social Attitudes

Several studies made during the 1970s indicated that children's literature was changing, apparently as a result of changing social attitudes.

In one research project published in 1976, Thomas D. Yawkey and Margaret L. Yawkey, educators, carefully analyzed fifty-two picture books published before and after 1965 (the year, incidentally, when the Larrick article appeared). They asked four questions at the outset:

674

1 Are there any significant differences between new and old picture books for young children in the *races* of the main characters in these texts?

2 Are there any significant differences between old and new picture books on the *sexes* of the characters in these picture books?

3 Are there any significant differences between old and new picture books on differences in *location* of the settings of these stories?

4 Are there any significant differences between old and new picture books relating the *socio-economic status* of the characters in the stories? (1976, p. 546, italics added)

The study showed that there were some significant differences between books published before and after the middle of the decade. In examining *race,* the authors found that newer picture books included a greater number of people from black, Chicano, Native American, and Chinese racial groups; newer books were also more likely than older books to portray members of these groups in roles equal to whites. *Locations* changed significantly, the study found; 90 percent of the older books were set in the country, but the percentage dropped to approximately 55 percent in new books as urban settings became more popular. Main characters from newer books also included a significantly greater mixture of *socioeconomic levels.*

But the authors found no significant change in one respect. In both the pre-1965 books and the later books males generally played dominant roles while women appeared in secondary positions in the stories, often as homemakers.

Another study, by educators John Warren Stewig and Mary Lynn Knipfel, found some change in the 1970s in the presentation of women in picture books. But the researchers concluded that the changes were slight.

Stewig and Knipfel analyzed 100 picture books published between 1972 and 1974 to explore how realistically recent publications dealt with women's roles. They wrote:

With the increasing emphasis on women's rights and on more realistic presentation of roles in instructional materials, one might assume that trade books would by now feature women, particularly those outside the home, in a wide variety of roles. Instead of finding Mother working happily at the stove, we should now expect to find her busy in the lab solving nuclear problems, or on the site supervising building construction, or in the auditorium leading a symphony. Is such the case? (1975, p. 151)

In the sample, researchers found sixty-eight books that included women in some roles. The vast majority—68 percent—showed

This book has been praised for its nonstereotypic portrayal of the girl, and criticized for its portrayal of the grandmother. (Picture excerpted from the book *Mandy's Grandmother* by Liesel Moak Skorpen with pictures by Martha Alexander. Pictures copyright © 1975 by Martha Alexander. Used by permission of The Dial Press, Inc.)

females in homemaking roles while 32 percent showed women in professional roles (teachers, singers, x-ray technicians, theater jobs, for example). None of the books in the sample was without male characters, while almost 10 percent included no women. (Male roles portrayed in literature, however, hardly seemed to reflect the real world: males in picture books were more likely to work in circuses or on the farm than in any other job.)

ISSUE

WHAT MAKES A PERSON INTELLECTUALLY FREE?

In the name of intellectual freedom we defend materials that perpetuate attitudes that hinder the growth of individuals who are intellectually free. No racist is intellectually free. Try as I may, I can see no issue of intellectual freedom involved in a request to remove *Epaminondas and His Auntie* from library shelves. Except for research libraries, the process known as weeding the collection should have eliminated the book years ago. But the library remains what it was when founded: a reflection of white ruling class values. As long as it is black people being offended we invoke intellectual freedom and tell blacks that bigots have rights, too. . . .

The whole concept of social responsibility implies value judgments—some things are right and some things are wrong and it is that simple. (pp. 65-66)

Broderick, Dorothy. "Censorship—Reevaluated,"
in *Issues in Children's Book Selection*
(New York: Bowker, 1973), pp. 61-66

These contemporary efforts to rid libraries of objectionable children's materials, under the guise of reevaluation, are not much different in substance from traditional efforts. In some instances, the identity of the censors and the means they use have changed, but the motivation remains the same. The *superficial* motivation involved in such efforts has always been one of moral values, whether the subject matter was sex, politics, religion, race, or drugs. . . .

The roots of contemporary and traditional censorship efforts, however, go deeper than the surface issues of moral values and value judgments. At the core of the problem in schools and libraries is a confused and potentially dangerous definition of education. Rather than viewing education as the development of the ability to think critically about social issues, some consider education to be the learning of a prescribed body of knowledge. This brand of education is a thinly disguised, refined form of propaganda. (p. 69)

Harvey, James A. "Acting for the Children?" in *Issues in
Children's Book Selection* (New York: Bowker, 1973), pp. 67-72.

How do you think Broderick would define intellectual freedom? How would Harvey define it? How would the practice of social responsibility differ for the two of them? Which position seems the more acceptable to you? Why?

The authors concluded that there had been some change. In a previous study they made in 1972, 17 percent of books they looked at included women in professional roles—half the percentage they reported in the 1975 study. In newer books, they summarized: "Mother is out of the kitchen and in the world, but only in some parts of it. Picture books for young children have made some progress in portraying women, but much remains to be done" (p. 151).

A slightly more recent study closely examined the content of 214 picture books published in 1973, 1974, and 1975. In a doctoral dissertation at New York University, Marjorie R. Hendler confirmed conclusions of the other studies that males are more likely than females to be portrayed as main characters. However, the sexes were equally represented as secondary characters, she discovered. Hendler also reported "some surprises" in looking for trends between 1973 and 1975. Previous studies, for one thing, had shown that boys in books were depicted as hardheaded realists, while girls were more often depicted as dreamers, engaged in fantasy. Hendler discovered that in her sample, a higher percentage of boys than girls were shown fantasizing in 1973, and both girls and boys fantasized equally in books published in 1974 and 1975. Another surprise was that in the Hendler sample of books from the 1970s, boys were spectators more often than girls. (Studies of older books had shown that boys were usually active while girls watched.) In the 1975 books, in fact, men were shown as less aggressive than women (Hendler, 1976).

Editors and publishers at established publishing houses are clearly aware today of changing social attitudes, and concerned about past insensitivity to large groups of people in American society. In interviews with us, however, some expressed frustration over trying to find books reflecting current trends while meeting basic literary criteria.

"Just because a movement becomes important doesn't mean that someone will come along with a marvelous manuscript on the subject," said editor and writer F. N. Monjo. "You can't really commission fiction. Just because you would like to be able to publish a book about women's liberation, for instance, or any other subject, doesn't mean that you're going to find a good one."

Monjo's comment raises a question of prime importance to adults choosing books for children today: Can a book supporting a cause—whether you agree with the cause or not—be good literature? What makes it literature? It is a question that adults working with children will be called to answer frequently, on a book-by-book basis, in the years ahead.

Can Books That Support a Cause Be Literature?

Charlotte Zolotow's *William's Doll* (1972) is the story of a little boy
who wants a doll with curly eyelashes, a long white dress and bonnet, and eyes that make a little click when they close.

"Creepy," says his brother. "Sissy, sissy, sissy!" says the boy next
door, and even his father thinks a doll is not a proper plaything for a
boy. "How would you like a basketball?" his father asks (p. 12).

Only his grandmother understands. During a country walk, William tells her what he really wants.

> "Wonderful," said his grandmother.
> "No," William said.
> "My brother says
> it will make me a creep.
> And the boy next door
> says I'm a sissy
> and my father
> brings me
> other things instead."
> "Nonsense," said his grandmother. (p. 26)

She buys him a doll. William loves it, but his father objects that
he already has a basketball and electric train and workbench. "Why
does he need a doll?"

> William's grandmother smiled.
> "He needs it," she said,
> "to hug
> and to cradle
> and to take to the park
> so that
> when he's a father
> like you,
> he'll know how to
> take care of his baby
> and feed him
> and love him
> and bring him the things he wants,
> like a doll
> so that he can
> practice being
> a father." (pp. 30–32)

Clearly, *William's Doll* has an antisexist message. One critic,
editor Selma Lanes, argues that the message overwhelms literary

679

quality. Incidentally, she applauds the message that it is normal for
boys to want dolls, and in the years since the book was written, the
idea has gained increased acceptance in society. But Lanes contends
that a flaw in characterization takes the book out of the category of
literature.

> The book itself fudges in a major way in order to put its lesson across to
> the widest possible audience. The author makes it quite clear that Wil-
> liam is a regular little boy in all the other respects that fathers, and even
> mothers, would be likely to approve. He enjoys playing with model trains
> and is a first-rate basketball player. Still, he would like a doll, too. But
> what of those little boys who would like dolls and are perfect duds at all
> or most so-called masculine activities? A book about such a hero that
> could also win over a large audience might possible attain the status of
> literature because it would have to come to grips with a complex human
> being, rather than an obvious, if well-meaning, idea. (1974, p. 186)*

A book, or course, is made of other elements besides
characterization—plot, setting, theme, and style. Each of these
components contributes to overall quality, and so does the way the
components combine to form a complete piece of writing.

Chapter 1 contains criteria for evaluating these elements of literature, and puts the criteria to work in evaluating one book. Does
William's Doll match the criteria? Look at the elements in the book
and—as a review exercise—make your own decision on literary
value.

Plot Zolotow's story has a progressive plot, growing out of the first
line: "William wanted a doll" (p. 5). That, at least when the book
was written, is something of a problem, and within a few pages, his
desire for a doll brings him in conflict with his brother and the boy
next door. At the same time, in other action growing out of the first
line of the story, William's father goes on a small shopping binge to
give his boy a basketball, net, electric trains and cardboard
stations—all "masculine" toys.

A courageous Grandma drops into the plot something like a fairy
godmother, but her arrival does not automatically ensure a happy
ending for the boy and his doll. First she has to reassure William
(who does not think his idea about a doll is "wonderful" after the
taunting he has taken) and then face William's father in a final
confrontation.

---

*Another opinion of *William's Doll* comes from critic Melinda Schroeder. "The neat, delicate
watercolor illustrations depict an unmistakably normal, healthy, fashionably shaggy-haired child,
and the long-awaited realistic handling of this theme makes a landmark book," she writes (1972,
p. 2943).

William's brother and the boy next door tease him about his wanting a doll. (Illustration by William Pène du Bois from *William's Doll* by Charlotte Zolotow. Pictures copyright © 1972 by William Pène du Bois. By permission of Harper & Row, Publishers, Inc.)

What are the strengths and weaknesses of this plot? Does the action in the story build naturally? Toward what scene does the action build? Does the ending provide adequate resolution for the problem expressed in the beginning of the book?

Setting Lush and gentle watercolors by William Pène du Bois help establish the country setting for the story. And the text tells more about place: there is a garage at William's house, with room enough in the driveway for a pick-up basketball game.

What other clues in the text or illustrations establish the life-style of William's family? Is the setting appropriate to the story? Does it make the plot more believable? Why or why not?

Theme Lanes argues that the theme is merely a moral: that boys can own and play with "feminine" toys. It might also be argued, however, that the book makes the more complex point that children

681

need not be bound by social conventions, particularly when those conventions prevent their growth toward adult roles, for instance, fatherhood. In good literature, themes never overwhelm plot; significant commentary on life emerges naturally through plot, characterization, and setting.

Is Zolotow's theme significant, or, in Lanes's phrase, does it express an "obvious, if well-meaning idea" (1974, p. 186)? How well is the theme expressed?

Style The story could have been told in other ways. Curiously, it *is* retold in an adaptation by Sheldon Harnick, who turned Zolotow's text into song lyrics for a section in *Free to Be You and Me* (Ms. Foundation, 1974). Harnick's lyrics begin:

> When my friend William was five years old
> He wanted a doll to hug and hold.
> "A doll," said William, "is what I need
> to wash and clean and dress and feed;
> A doll to give a bottle to—
> And put to bed when day is through;
> And any time my doll gets ill,
> I'll take good care of it," said my friend Bill.
> (pp. 78–79)

Compare the quality of Harnick's version with the original:

> William wanted a doll.
> He wanted to hug it
> and cradle it in his arms
> and give it a bottle
> and take it to the park
> and push it in the swing
> and bring it back home . . . . (pp. 5–6)

Obviously Harnick and Zolotow were writing for different purposes. But the contrast between the two versions helps to clarify Zolotow's style, which has a rhythm of its own and a tone of understatement.

What stylistic differences do you find between the two versions? Which style better matches the story, and why? What are the strengths and weaknesses of Zolotow's language? Does the language distract readers, or draw them deeper into the story? How?

Characterization Lanes's major objection to the book is that William himself is stock and flat. Two other characters in the book—

William's father and Grandma—also play major roles. Each of the three important characters in the story is revealed by what they do as well as by what they say; the illustrations also establish separate personalities.

In what specific ways is character revealed? Would the book be better literature if William were a "perfect dud" at "masculine" activities such as basketball or running electric trains? Do characters change in the course of the story, and if so, in what way?

Overall, are these elements melded successfully so that setting, characterization, plot, and style combine well to support an important theme?

Any book supporting a cause should be analyzed by these literary criteria. Good literature can advocate a principle, point out an injustice, even present society as it should be rather than as it is. But books promoting desirable social values are not necessarily literature.

In the midst of dramatic social and economic change, it is not easy today to write, illustrate, edit, or publish good books for children. Fortunately, scores of adults in recent years have accepted the challenge. They have produced books that shun easy lessons about current society in favor of more difficult truths about humanity as it was and will be.

Sometimes writers have had to overcome current social taboos to express truths they had to tell. Madeleine L'Engle, for one, received stacks of rejection letters in the late 1950s when she showed publishers *Meet the Austins*, because the book opened with a death. She refused to remove the material publishers thought too sensitive for children, and eventually sold the book. It was published in 1960. Since then, death has become a more acceptable topic in children's literature.

The best of the literature today, in fact, seems to survive in its own timeless realm, apart from changing goals about what must be taught, or fluctuations in bookstore sales. Charlotte the spider has died, but comes to life each year as a new group of children grows up enough to meet her. Frog and Toad continue to slosh through their overgrown and sometimes dangerous world as friends forever. Peter Rabbit hops toward trouble in Mr. McGregor's garden despite warnings that literature can seed violence in young minds. These characters live on because writers, editors, and publishers have had the courage to let them be.

In Godden's fictional correspondence between the ghost of Beatrix Potter and editor Andal, the author of *Peter Rabbit* has finally heard enough of plans to repackage and censor her little story for modern readers. She cables Andal:

RETURN PETER RABBIT AT ONCE

Andal returns the book, but tries once more to explain:

Dear Miss Potter:

We are sorry you have taken this attitude, which I confess seems to us
unrealistic and does not take into account public opinion (supported by
our own careful poll statistics) . . . . We can only tell you that it is our
opinion, formed by expert advice, that in its present form, parents,
teachers and children will not buy, nor understand, nor like "Peter Rabbit."

And Miss Potter has the last word:

Seven million have. I rest in peace. (Godden, 1963, pp. 9–10)

SUMMARY

1 Publishing is affected by *social* and *economic* pressures that will
continue to influence books for children in the future.

2 The 1960s are a case study of how *economics* impinges on what is
published. Children's books flourished after passage of the $1.3 bil-
lion *Elementary and Secondary Education Act* in 1965 because the
act contained a provision—*Title II*—authorizing federal grants to
states to boost public and private school library budgets. High levels
of spending under Title II continued for several years, stimulating
publishers to increase output, particularly in nonfiction
curriculum-related areas. Federal funds encouraged publishers to
take risks with unknown artists and writers, but editors today
suggest that the quality of books was not uniformly high. Then,
after 1968, Title II funds were cut in half, ending the boom.

3 Rising costs today make it comparatively more difficult for new
writers and artists to enter the field. On the other hand, author *John
Rowe Townsend* argues that "it may be that hard times will mean
some useful pruning" in reducing the number of "indifferent" books
for children. In any case, economic considerations have stimulated
international *copublishing*—joint publishing by two or more companies in different countries—which has helped cut costs. Copublishing may permit publishers in the years ahead to produce more
full-color picture books, ordinarily the most expensive kind of children's book to publish. Copublishing may also stimulate a greater
interchange of information across national borders about different

life-styles. But it can also be argued that copublishing breeds blandness as writers try to appeal to an extraordinarily broad audience.

4 Market trends also affect what is published. Publishers of hardbound books pay particular attention to what librarians and teachers are buying, because approximately 80 percent of the hardcover books are bought for children by adults in schools and libraries.

5 A review of publishing in the wake of Title II suggests that more books about people with disabilities will be published in the years ahead. One major reason is a 1975 law mandating that every disabled child must be educated in the "least restrictive environment." This means that children with special needs must be integrated ("mainstreamed") into regular classrooms, where teachers will need special skills and teaching materials. Federal spending to put the law into effect is expected to reach into the billions in the early 1980s. Several books on disabilities are already available, such as *Jeanne Whitehouse Petersen*'s *I Have a Sister, My Sister is Deaf,* but more can be expected as the law takes hold.

6 The economics of publishing are sometimes affected by the *social climate.* The civil rights movement in the 1960s and growing concern over sexism have led to some changes in what is published for children. *Thomas D. Yawkey* and *Margaret L. Yawkey* discovered significant differences between books published before and after 1965; later books portrayed a greater diversity of racial groups and socioeconomic levels, and urban settings became more popular. *John Warren Stewig* and *Mary Lynn Knipfel* found slight changes in the presentation of women in picture books published in the early 1970s. A more recent study, by *Marjorie R. Hendler,* reported "some surprises" about books from the mid-1970s; in books she studied that were published in 1975, for instance, women were portrayed as more aggressive than men.

7 Books supporting a good cause, however, are not necessarily good literature. *Charlotte Zolotow*'s *William's Doll* supports some antisexist values, but adults considering the book should also apply basic literary criteria before selection for children, evaluating the book on the basis of its plot, setting, theme, style, and characterization.

8 Here are some final questions on *social attitudes* toward literature. The Hendler study examined secondary as well as primary characters in exploring sexism in children's books. What other aspects of a book might future researchers examine to determine the values inherent in the book? How would you design a study to

685

determine whether racist or sexist literature promotes racism or
sexism? What policy would you suggest for a school library under
attack for lending a book that has been criticized as sexist although
praised on literary grounds? What responsibility does the literature
teacher bear for the social attitudes of students in the class? To what
degree do standards used by groups promoting social causes coincide
with literary criteria?

9 And here are some important questions for consideration on the
economic climate as it affects children's books. Should the federal
government commit funds to support local libraries to the extent
that it did in the mid-1960s? What are the risks in such a commitment? What would be the likely impact of such a commitment on
the quality of books, the chances for new writers, the paperback
market, the number of publishers in the field, the ratio of fiction to
nonfiction? Why? Using leverage in the marketplace, how could
teachers and librarians affect the literary quality of children's books?
Assuming favorable economic conditions, what kinds of books are
likely to be published in the years ahead? Assuming unfavorable
economic conditions, what kinds? If you were a publisher address-
ing your editors, what guidelines would you give them for selecting
manuscripts for publication? To what extent would your suggestions be swayed by economic considerations? If you were a teacher
or librarian with $100 to spend on books for a library, how would
you spend it? How would you justify your choices?

BIBLIOGRAPHY

Adult References

Council on Interracial Books for Children, Inc. *Human (and Anti-
Human) Values in Children's Books* (New York: Racism and
Sexism Resources Center for Educators, 1976).

Batchelder, Mildred L. "Learning about Children's Books in Translation," *ALA Bulletin*, January 1966, pp. 33–42.

Broderick, Dorothy. "Censorship—Reevaluated," in *Issues in Children's Book Selection* (New York: Bowker, 1973), pp. 61–66.

Godden, Rumer. "An Imaginary Correspondence," *The Horn Book*,
August 1963, pp. 4–10.

Harvey, James A. "Acting for the Children?" in *Issues in Children's
Book Selection* (New York: Bowker, 1973), pp. 67–72.

Hendler, Marjorie R. "An Analysis of Sex Role Attributes, Behaviors, and Occupations in Contemporary Children's Picture Books," unpublished doctoral dissertation, New York University, 1976.

Hewett, Frank M., and Steven Forness. *Education of Exceptional Learners*, 2d ed. (Boston: Allyn and Bacon, 1977). (1974)

Johnson, Janice (ed.) *The Bowker Annual of Library and Book Trade Information* (New York: Bowker, 1971).

Kamm, Anthony. "Children's Book Publishing and the Educational Market," *Children's Literature in Education*, November 1970, pp. 30-40.

Karl, Jean. "A Children's Editor Looks at Excellence in Children's Literature," *The Horn Book*, February 1967, pp. 31-41.

Lanes, Selma. "On Feminism and Children's Books," *Library Journal*, Jan. 15, 1974, pp. 23-27.

Larrick, Nancy. "The All-White World of Children's Books," *Saturday Review*, Sept. 11, 1965, pp. 63-65.

McElderry, Margaret K. "The Best of Times, the Worst of Times— Children's Book Publishing, 1924-1974," *The Horn Book*, October 1974, pp. 85-94.

Miele, Madeline (ed.). *The Bowker Annual of Library and Book Trade Information* (New York: Bowker, 1974).

National School Public Relations Association. *The New ESEA* (Washington, D.C., 1968).

Schuwer, Philippe. "Problems and Opportunities in International Copublication of Children's Books," *Publishers Weekly*, Feb. 23, 1976, pp. 74-75.

Schroeder, Melinda. Review of *William's Doll* by Charlotte Zolotow in *Library Journal*, Sept. 15, 1972, p. 2943.

Steckler, Phyllis (ed.). *The Bowker Annual of Library and Book Trade Information* (New York: Bowker, 1967).

Stein, Ruth. "Launching the New Literate," *School Library Journal*, November 1966, pp. 51-53.

Stewig, John Warren, and Mary Lynn Knipfel. "Sexism in Picture Books—What Progress?" *The Elementary School Journal*, December 1975, pp. 151-155.

Townsend, John Rowe. "Peering into the Fog—The Future of Children's Books," *The Horn Book*, June 1977, pp. 346-355.

Wells, Reese, and Gena Davidson. "Censorship and the Authors' Viewpoint," *Journal of Research and Development in Education*, Spring 1976, pp. 69-75.

Yawkey, Thomas D., and Margaret L. Yawkey. "An Analysis of Picture Books," *Language Arts*, May 1976, pp. 545-548.

Children's Book References

Fassler, Joan. *Howie Helps Himself,* illus. Joe Lasker (Chicago: Albert Whitman & Co., 1975).

Kalagian, Betty (ed.). *Expectations* (Los Angeles: The Braille Institute of America, Braille Institute Press, 1977).

L'Engle, Madeleine. *Meet the Austins* (New York: Vanguard, 1960).

Ms. Foundation Inc. *Free to Be You and Me* (New York: McGraw-Hill, 1974).

Petersen, Jeanne Whitehouse. *I Have a Sister, My Sister Is Deaf,* illus. Deborah Ray (New York: Harper, 1977).

Zolotow, Charlotte. *William's Doll,* illus. William Pène du Bois (New York: Harper, 1972).

APPENDIX

A. BOOK SELECTION AIDS
B. CHILDREN'S BOOK AWARDS
C. PUBLISHERS OF CHILDREN'S BOOKS

APPENDIX A
Book Selection Aids

Annotated Bibliographies

Each of these entries presents brief annotations of books and/or media. Most categorize the material by subject or theme and indicate age-level recommendations.

AAS Science Book List for Children, comp. by Hilary J. Deason, (Washington, D.C.: American Association for the Advancement of Science, 1972). (Includes both science and mathematics books.)

About 100 Books: A Gateway to Better Intergroup Understanding, Ann G. Wolfe (New York: The American Jewish Committee, 1972).

Adventuring with Books: A Booklist for Pre-K-Grade 8, Patrcia Cianciolo (ed.) (Urbana, Ill.: National Council of Teachers of English, 1977).

African-Asian Reading Guide for Children and Young Adults, comp. by Jeanette Hotchkiss (Metuchen, N.J.: Scarecrow, 1976).

American Historical Fiction and Biography for Children and Young People, comp. by Jeanette Hotchkiss, (Metuchen, N.J.: Scarecrow, 1973).

And All the Dark Make Bright Like Day: Christmas Books, 1960–1972 (Boston: *The Horn Book,* 1972).

Behavior Patterns in Children's Books: A Bibliography, comp. by Clara J. Kircher (Washington, D.C.: Catholic University Press, 1966).

The Best in Children's Books: The University of Chicago Guide to Children's Literature 1966–1972, Zena Sutherland (ed.) (Chicago: The University of Chicago Press, 1973).

Bibliography of Books for Children, Association for Childhood Education International (Washington, D.C.: ACEI, 1977).

The Black Experience: Books for Children, comp. by Ruth M. Hays (Boston: Boston Public Library, 1971).

The Black Experience in Children's Books, selected by Barbara Rollock (New York: New York Public Library, 1974).

The Black World in Literature for Children: A Bibliography of Print and Non-Print Materials, comp. by Joyce White Mills (Atlanta: Atlanta University Press, 1975).

Book List 1976–1977 (Glenview, Illinois: Center

on Deafness, 1977). (Includes children's books in sign.)

The Bookfinder: A Guide to Children's Literature about the Needs and Problems of Youth Aged 2-15, Sharon Spredemann Dryer (Circle Pines, Minn.: American Guidance Service, 1977).

Books for Elementary School Libraries: An Initial Collection, comp. and ed. by Elizabeth D. Hodges, (Chicago: American Library Association, 1969).

Books for Friendship, 3d ed., Mary Ester McWhirter (ed.) (Philadelphia: American Friends Service Committe, 1962). (Supplement, 1968.)

Books for the Teen Age (New York: New York Public Library, 1976).

Books to Help Children Cope with Separation and Loss, Joanne Bernstein (New York: Bowker, 1977).

Building Ethnic Collections; An Annotated Guide for School Media Centers and Public Libraries, Lois T. Buttlar and Lubomyr Wynar (Littleton, Colo.: Libraries Unlimited, 1977).

Canadian Books for Children (Livres Canadiens pour Enfants), comp. by Irma McDonough (Toronto: University of Toronto Press, 1976).

Children and Poetry: A Selective, Annotated Bibliography, comp. by Virginia Haviland and William Jay Smith (Washington, D.C.: Government Printing Office, 1970).

Children's Book Showcase, Children's Book Council (New York: Children's Book Council, 1977).

Children's Books, comp. by Virginia Haviland and Lois B. Watt (Washington, D.C.: Government Printing Office, 1974).

Children's Books in Print (New York: Bowker, 1977).

Children's Books of International Interest 2d ed., Virginia Haviland (ed.) (Chicago: American Library Association, 1978).

Children's Books of the Year (New York: The Child Study Association of America, 1977).

Children's Books Too Good to Miss, 6th ed., May Hill Arbuthnot et al. (Cleveland: Western Reserve University Press, 1971).

Children's Catalog, 13th ed. (Bronx, New York: Wilson, 1976).

European Historical Fiction and Biography, comp. by Jeanette Hotchkiss (Metuchen, N.J.: Scarecrow, 1972).

Films Kids Like, Susan Rice (ed.) (Chicago: American Library Association, 1973).

Folklore: An Annotated Bibliography and Index to Single Editions, comp. by Elsie B. Ziegler (Westwood, Mass: Faxon, 1973).

Folklore of the North American Indians: An Annotated Bibliography, comp. by Judith C. Ullon (Washington, D.C.: Government Printing Office, 1969).

Gateways to Readable Books, comp. by Dorothy Withrow, Helen Carey, and Bertha Hirzel (Bronx, N.Y.: Wilson, 1975).

Good and Inexpensive Books for Children, Association for Childhood Education International (Washington, D.C.: ACEI, 1972).

Good Reading for the Disadvantaged Reader: Multi-ethnic Resources. comp. by George D. Spache (Scarsdale, N.Y.: Garrard, 1970).

Good Reading for Poor Readers, comp. by George D. Spache (Scarsdale, N.Y.: Garrard, 1972).

Growing Up with Books (New York: Bowker, 1977).

Growing Up with Paperbacks (New York: Bowker, 1977).

Growing Up with Science Books (New York: Bowker, 1974).

A Guide to Non-Sexist Children's Books, comp. by Judith Adell and Hilary Klein (Cambell, Calif.: Academy Press, 1976).

Her Way: Biographies of Women for Young People (Chicago: American Library Association, 1976).

Independent Reading Grades One Through Three: An Annotated Bibliography with Reading Levels (Williamsport, Pa.: Bro-Dart, 1975).

Junior High School Library Catalog, 2d ed. (Bronx, N.Y.: Wilson, 1970).

Juniorplots: A Book Talk Manual for Teachers and Librarians, John T. Gillespie and Diana L. Lembo (New York: Bowker, 1967).

Let's Read Together: Books for Family Enjoyment, Committee of National Congress of Parents and Teachers and Children's Services Division, American Library Association (Chicago: American Library Association, 1969).

The Liberty Cap; A Catalogue of Non-Sexist Materials for Children, Enid Davis (Cambell, Calif.: Academy Press, 1977).

Libros En Español: An Annotated List of Chil-

dren's Books in Spanish, Mary K. Conwell and Pura Belpré (New York: New York Public Library, 1971).

Literature by and about the American Indian, Anna Lee Stensland (Urbana, Ill.: National Council of Teachers of English, 1973).

Little Miss Muffet Fights Back, rev. ed., comp. by Feminists on Children's Media (Whitestone, N.Y.: Feminist Book Mart, 1974).

More Films Kids Like, Maureen Gaffney (Chicago: American Library Association, 1977).

More Juniorplots, John T. Gillespie (New York: Bowker, 1977).

A Multimedia Approach to Children's Literature, 2d. ed., Ellin Greene and Madalynne Schoenfeld (Chicago: American Library Association, 1977).

Music Books for the Elementary School Library, comp. by Peggy Flanagan Baird (Washington, D.C.: Music Educators National Conference, 1972).

Notable Children's Books, Association for Library Service to Children (Chicago: American Library Association, 1977).

Notes from a Different Drummer: A Guide to Juvenile Fiction Portraying the Handicapped (New York: Bowker, 1977).

Paperback Books for Children, comp. by the Committee on Paperback Lists for Elementary School of the American Library Association (Englewood Cliffs, N.J.: Citation Press, 1972).

A Parent's Guide to Children's Reading, Nancy Larrick (ed.) (New York: Bantam Books, 1975).

Picture Books for Children, Patricia Cianciolo (ed.) (Chicago: American Library Association, 1973).

Reading Ladders for Human Relations, 5th ed., Virginia Reid (ed.) (Washington, D.C.: American Council on Education, 1972).

Reading with Your Child through Age 5, Children's Book Committee of the Child Study Association with the staff of the Child-Study-Project Head Start (New York: Child Study Press, 1972).

RIF's Guide to Book Selection (Washington, D.C.: Reading Is Fundamental, 1973).

The School Library Media Center: A Force for Educational Excellence, Ruth Ann Davis (ed.) (New York: Bowker, 1974).

Starting Out Right: Choosing Books about Black People for Young Children, Bettye Lattimer (ed.) (Madison: Wisconsin Department of Public Instruction, 1972).

Subject Guide to Children's Books in Print (New York: Bowker, 1977).

We Build Together: A Reader's Guide to Negro Life and Literature for Elementary and High School Use, Charlemae Rollins (ed.) (Urbana, Ill.: National Council of Teachers of English, 1967).

The Wide World of Children's Books: An Exhibition for International Book Year comp. by Virginia Haviland (Washington, D.C.: Government Printing Office, 1972).

Young People's Literature in Series: Fiction, an Annotated Bibliographical Guide, Judith K. Rosenberg and Kenyon C. Rosenberg (eds.) (Littleton, Colo.: Libraries Unlimited, Inc., 1972).

REVIEWS OF NEW BOOKS AND MEDIA

These journals regularly include reviews of new children's books and/or media.

Appraisal: Children's Science Books, Children's Science Book Review Committee, Longfellow Hall, 13 Appian Way, Cambridge, MA 02138.

Book Review Digest, The H. W. Wilson Company, 950 University Ave., Bronx, NY 10452

Bookbird, Richard Bamberger (ed.), International Board on Books for Young People, Package Library of Foreign Children's Books, Inc., 119 Fifth Ave., New York, NY 10003.

The Booklist, American Library Association, 50 East Huron St., Chicago, IL 60611.

Book World, 230 41st St., New York, NY 10036.

The Bulletin of the Center for Children's Books, Graduate Library School, University of Chicago Press, 5801 Ellis Ave., Chicago, IL 60637.

Childhood Education, Association for Childhood Education International, 3615 Wisconsin Ave., N.W., Washington, DC 20016.

The Horn Book Magazine, Horn Book, Inc., 585 Boyleston St., Boston, MA 02116.

The Instructor, Instructor Publications, Inc., Instructor Park, Dansville, NY 14437.

Interracial Books for Children, Council on Interracial Books for Children, Inc., 1841 Broadway, New York, NY 10023.

Language Arts, National Council of Teachers of English, 1111 Kenyon Rd., Urbana, IL 61801.

Media and Methods, North American Publishing Company, 134 N. 13th Street, Philadelphia, PA 19107.

The New York Times Book Review, New York Times Company, Times Square, New York, NY.

Previews. R. R. Bowker Company, 1180 Avenue of the Americas, New York, NY 10036.

Publisher's Weekly, Spring and Fall specials, R. R. Bowker Company, 1180 Avenue of the Americas, New York, NY 10036.

Ripples, Newsletter of the Children's Literature Assembly of the National Council of Teachers of English, University of Georgia Duplicating Services, Athens, GA 30602.

School Library Journal, R. R. Bowker Company, 1180 Avenue of the Americas, New York, NY 10036.

Science Books, A Quarterly Review, American Association for the Advancement of Science, 1515 Massachusetts Ave., N.W., Washington, DC 20005.

Science and Children, National Science Teachers Association, 1201 16th St. N.W., Washington, DC 20036.

Teacher, Macmillan Professional Magazines, Inc., 22 West Putnam Avenue, Greenwich, CO, 06830.

Top of the News, Association for Library Services to Children and Young Adult Services Division of the American Library Association, Publication Office, 1201-05 Bluff St., Fulton, MO 65251.

The Web, Center for Language, Literature, and Reading, The Ohio State University, Room 200 Ramseyer Hall, 29 West Woodruff, Columbus, Ohio 43210.

Wilson Library Bulletin, The H. W. Wilson Company, 950 University Ave., Bronx, NY 10452.

INDEXES

The following references may be useful in locating specific print and nonprint materials.

Book and Non-book Media: Annotated Guide to Selection Aids for Educational Materials, Flossie L. Perkins (Urbana, Ill.: National Council of Teachers of English, 1972).

Children's Literature: A Guide to Reference Sources, comp. by Virginia Hamilton, et al. (Washington, D.C.: Government Printing Office, 1966). (Supplement, 1972.)

Guide to Children's Magazines, Newspapers, Reference Books, Judy Matthews and Lillian Drag (Washington, D.C.: Association for Childhood Educational International, 1974).

Index to Fairy Tales, 1949-1972, Including Folklore, Legends and Myths in Collections, comp. by Norma Olin Ireland. (Westwood, Mass.: Faxon, 1973).

Index to Poetry for Children and Young People: 1964-1969, 1972 ed., comp. by John E. Brewton, Sara W. Brewton, and G. Meredith (Bronx, NY: Wilson, 1972).

Index to Young Reader's Collective Biographies, 2d. ed., Judith Silverman (ed.) (New York: Bowker, 1975).

Paperback Books for Young People: An Annotated Guide to Publishers and Distributors, 2d ed., John T. Gillespie (ed.) (Chicago: American Library Association, 1977).

Periodicals for School Libraries: A Guide to Magazines, Newspapers, and Periodical Indexes, rev. ed., comp. by Marian H. Scott (Chicago: American Library Association, 1973).

Reference and Subscription Book Reviews 1976-1977 (Chicago: American Library Association, 1978).

Subject Index to Poetry for Children and Young People 1957-1975, comp. by Dorothy B. Frissell Smith and Eva L. Andrews (Chicago: American Library Association, 1977).

APPENDIX B
Children's Book Awards

The awards listed in this appendix are all given on the basis of the literary and/or artistic merit of the work, and all but one are United States awards. Readers interested in lists of other awards, such as children's choices or awards given in other countries, can find a complete listing in *Children's Books: Awards and Prizes,* published biennially by the Children's Book Council.

THE NEWBERY MEDAL

The Newbery Medal has been awarded annually since 1922. It is named in honor of John Newbery, the eighteenth-century British bookseller who was the first to publish books for children. The award is given to the author of the most distinguished contribution to literature for children published in the United States during the preceding year. To be eligible an author must be either a United States citizen or a permanent resident of the United States. The award was donated by the Frederic G. Melcher family; the winner is selected by a committee of the Association for Library Services for Children (formerly the Children's Services Division) of the American Library Association. The following list includes both the winners of the award and the runners-up, or Honor Books.

1922 *The Story of Mankind* by Hendrik Willem van Loon, Liveright
Honor Books: *The Great Quest* by Charles Hawes, Little; *Cedric the Forester* by Bernard Marshall, Appleton; *The Old Tobacco Shop* by William Bowen, Macmillan; *The Golden Fleece and the Heroes Who Lived before Achilles* by Padraic Colum, Macmillan; *Windy Hill* by Cornelia Meigs, Macmillan
1923 *The Voyages of Doctor Dolittle* by Hugh Lofting, Lippincott
Honor Books: No record
1924 *The Dark Frigate* by Charles Hawes, Atlantic/Little
Honor Books: No record

1925 *Tales from Silver Lands* by Charles Finger, Doubleday
Honor Books: *Nicholas* by Anne Carroll Moore, Putnam; *Dream Coach* by Anne Parish, Macmillan
1926 *Shen of the Sea* by Arthur Bowie Chrisman, Dutton
Honor Book: *Voyagers* by Padraic Colum, Macmillan
1927 *Smoky, the Cowhorse* by Will James, Scribner's
Honor Books: No record
1928 *Gayneck, The Story of a Pigeon* by Dhan Gopal Mukerji, Dutton
Honor Books: *The Wonder Smith and His Son* by Ella Young, Longmans; *Downright Dency* by Caroline Snedeker, Doubleday
1929 *The Trumpeter of Krakow* by Eric P. Kelly, Macmillan
Honor Books: *Pigtail of Ah Lee Ben Loo* by John Bennett, Longmans; *Millions of Cats* by Wanda Gag, Coward; *The Boy Who Was* by Grace Hallock, Dutton; *Clearing Weather* by Cornelia Meigs, Little; *Runaway Papoose* by Grace Moon, Doubleday; *Tod of the Fens* by Elinor Whitney, Macmillan
1930 *Hitty, Her First Hundred Years* by Rachel Field, Macmillan
Honor Books: *Daughter of the Seine* by Jeanette Eaton, Harper; *Pran of Albania* by Elizabeth Miller, Doubleday; *Jumping-Off Place* by Marian Hurd McNeely, Longmans; *Tangle-Coated Horse and Other Tales* by Ella Young, Longmans; *Vaino* by Julia Davis Adams, Dutton; *Little Blacknose* by Hildegarde Swift, Harcourt
1931 *The Cat Who Went to Heaven* by Elizabeth Coatsworth, Macmillan
Honor Books: *Floating Island* by Anne Parrish, Harper; *The Dark Star of Itza* by Alida Malkus, Harcourt; *Queer Person* by Ralph Hubbard, Doubleday; *Mountains are Free* by Julia Davis Adams, Dutton; *Spice and the Devil's Cave* by Agnes Hewes, Knopf; *Meggy Macintosh* by Elizabeth Janet Gray, Doubleday; *Garram the*

Hunter by Herbert Best, Doubleday; *Ood-Le-Uk the Wanderer* by Alice Lide and Margaret Johansen, Little

1932 *Waterless Mountain* by Laura Adams Armer, Longmans

Honor Books: *The Fairy Circus* by Dorothy P. Lathrop, Macmillan; *Calico Bush* by Rachael Field, Macmillan; *Boy of the South Seas* by Eunice Tietjens, Coward; *Out of the Flame* by Eloise Lownsbery, Longmans; *Jane's Island* by Marjorie Allee, Houghton; *Truce of the Wolf and Other Tales of Old Italy* by Mary Gould Davis, Harcourt

1933 *Young Fu of the Upper Yangtze* by Elizabeth Foreman Lewis, Winston

Honor Books: *Swift Rivers* by Cornelia Meigs, Little; *The Railroad to Freedom* by Hildegarde Swift, Harcourt; *Children of the Soil* by Nora Burglon, Doubleday

1934 *Invincible Louisa* by Cornelia Meigs, Little

Honor Books: *The Forgotten Daughter* by Caroline Snedeker, Doubleday; *Swords of Steel* by Elsie Singmaster, Houghton; *ABC Bunny* by Wanda Gág, Coward; *Winged Girl of Knossos* by Erik Berry, Appleton; *New Land* by Sarah Schmidt, McBride; *Big Tree of Bunlahy* by Padriac Colum, Macmillan; *Glory of the Seas* by Agnes Hewes, Knopf; *Apprentice of Florence* by Ann Kyle, Houghton

1935 *Dobry* by Monica Shannon, Viking

Honor Books: *Pageant of Chinese History* by Elizabeth Seeger, Longmans; *Davy Crockett* by Constance Rourke, Harcourt; *Day on Skates* by Hilda Van Stockum, Harper

1936 *Caddie Woodlawn* by Carol Brink, Macmillan

Honor Books: *Honk, the Moose* by Phil Stong, Dodd; *The Good Master* by Kate Seredy, Viking; *Young Walter Scott* by Elizabeth Janet Gray, Viking; *All Sail Set* by Armstrong Sperry, Winston

1937 *Roller Skates* by Ruth Sawyer, Viking

Honor Books: *Phebe Fairchild: Her Book* by Lois Lenski, Stokes; *Whistler's Van* by Idwal Jones, Viking; *Golden Basket* by Ludwig Bemelmans, Viking; *Winterbound* by Margery Bianco, Viking; *Audubon* by Constance Rourke, Harcourt; *The Codfish Musket* by Agnes Hewes, Doubleday

1938 *The White Stag* by Kate Seredy, Viking

Honor Books: *Pecos Bill* by James Cloyd Bowman, Little; *Bright Island* by Mabel Robinson, Random; *On the Banks of Plum Creek* by Laura Ingalls Wilder, Harper

1939 *Thimble Summer* by Elizabeth Enright, Rinehart

Honor Books: *Nino* by Valenti Angelo, Viking; *Mr. Popper's Penguins* by Richard and Florence Atwater, Little; *"Hello the Boat!"* by Phyllis Crawford, Holt; *Leader by Destiny: George Washington, Man and Patriot* by Jeanette Eaton, Harcourt; *Penn* by Elizabeth Janet Gray, Viking

1940 *Danel Boone* by James Daugherty, Viking

Honor Books: *The Singing Tree* by Kate Seredy, Viking; *Runner of the Mountain Tops* by Mabel Robinson, Random; *By the Shores of Silver Lake* by Laura Ingalls Wilder, Harper; *Boy with a Pack* by Stephen W. Meader, Harcourt

1941 *Call It Courage* by Armstrong Sperry, Macmillan

Honor Books: *Blue Willow* by Doris Gates, Viking; *Young Mac of Fort Vancouver* by Mary Jane Carr, T. Crowell; *The Long Winter* by Laura Ingalls Wilder, Harper; *Nansen* by Anna Gertrude Hall, Viking

1942 *The Matchlock Gun* by Walter D. Edmonds, Dodd

Honor Books: *Little Town on the Prairie* by Laura Ingalls Wilder, Harper; *George Washington's World* by Genevieve Foster, Scribner's; *Indian Captive: The Story of Mary Jemison* by Lois Lenski, Lippincott; *Down Ryton Water* by Eva Roe Gaggin, Viking

1943 *Adam of the Road* by Elizabeth Janet Gray, Viking

Honor Books: *The Middle Moffat* by Eleanor Estes, Harcourt; *Have You Seen Tom Thumb?* by Mabel Leigh Hunt, Lippincott

1944 *Johnny Tremain* by Esther Forbes, Houghton

Honor Books: *These Happy Golden Years* by Laura Ingalls Wilder, Harper; *Fog Magic* by Julia Sauer, Viking; *Rufus M.* by Eleanor Estes, Harcourt; *Mountain Born* by Elizabeth Yates, Coward

1945 *Rabbit Hill* by Robert Lawson, Viking

Honor Books: *The Hundred Dresses* by Eleanor Estes, Harcourt; *The Silver Pencil* by Alice Dalgliesh, Scribner's; *Abraham Lincoln's*

World by Genevieve Foster, Scribner's; *Lone Journey: The Life of Roger Williams* by Jeanette Eaton, Harcourt

1946 *Strawberry Girl* by Lois Lenski, Lippincott

Honor Books: *Justin Morgan Had a Horse* by Marguerite Henry, Rand; *The Moved-Outers* by Florence Crannell Means, Houghton; *Bhimsa, the Dancing Bear* by Christine Weston, Scribner's; *New Found World* by Katherine Shippen, Viking

1947 *Miss Hickory* by Carolyn Sherwin Bailey, Viking

Honor Books: *Wonderful Year* by Nancy Barnes, Messner; *Big Tree* by Mary and Conrad Buff, Viking; *The Heavenly Tenants* by William Maxwell, Harper; *The Avion My Uncle Flew* by Cyrus Fisher, Appleton; *The Hidden Treasure of Glaston* by Eleanore Jewett, Viking

1948 *The Twenty-one Balloons* by William Pène du Bois, Viking

Honor Books: *Pancakes-Paris* by Claire Huchet Bishop, Viking; *Li Lun, Lad of Courage* by Carolyn Treffinger, Abingdon; *The Quaint and Curious Quest of Johnny Longfoot* by Catherine Besterman, Bobbs; *The Cow-Tail Switch, and Other West African Stories* by Harold Courlander, Holt; *Misty of Chincoteague* by Marguerite Henry, Rand

1949 *King of the Wind* by Marguerite Henry, Rand

Honor Books: *Seabird* by Holing C. Holling, Houghton; *Daughter of the Mountains* by Louise Rankin, Viking; *My Father's Dragon* by Ruth S. Gannett, Random; *Story of the Negro* by Arna Bontemps, Knopf

1950 *The Door in the Wall* by Marguerite de Angeli, Doubleday

Honor Books: *Tree of Freedom* by Rebecca Caudill, Viking; *The Blue Cat of Castle Town* by Catherine Coblentz, Longmans; *Kildee House* by Rutherford Montgomery, Doubleday; *George Washington* by Genevieve Foster, Scribner's; *Song of the Pines* by Walter and Marion Havighurst, Winston

1951 *Amos Fortune, Free Man* by Elizabeth Yates, Aladdin

Honor Books: *Better Known as Johnny Appleseed* by Mabel Leigh Hunt, Lippincott; *Gandhi, Fighter Without a Sword* by Jeanette Eaton, Morrow; *Abraham Lincoln, Friend of*

the People by Clara Ingram Judson, Follett; *The Story of Appleby Capple* by Anne Parrish, Harper

1952 *Ginger Pye* by Eleanor Estes, Harcourt

Honor Books: *Americans Before Columbus* by Elizabeth Baity, Viking; *Minn of the Mississippi* by Holling C. Holling, Houghton; *The Defender* by Nicholas Kalashnikoff, Scribner's; *The Light at Tern Rock* by Julia Sauer, Viking; *The Apple and the Arrow* by Mary and Conrad Buff, Houghton

1953 *Secret of the Andes* by Ann Nolan Clark, Viking

Honor Books: *Charlotte's Web* by E. B. White, Harper; *Moccasin Trail* by Eloise McGraw, Coward; *Red Sails to Capri* by Ann Weil, Viking; *The Bears on Hemlock Mountain* by Alice Dalgliesh, Scribner's; *Birthdays of Freedom*, Vol. 1 by Genevieve Foster, Scribner's

1954 *. . . and now Miguel* by Joseph Krumgold, T. Crowell

Honor Books: *All Alone* by Claire Huchet Bishop, Viking; *Shadrach* by Meindert DeJong, Harper; *Hurry Home Candy* by Meindert DeJong, Harper; *Theodore Roosevelt, Fighting Patriot* by Clara Ingram Judson, Follett; *Magic Maize* by Mary and Conrad Buff, Houghton

1955 *The Wheel on the School* by Meindert DeJong, Harper

Honor Books: *The Courage of Sarah Noble* by Alice Dalgliesh, Scribner's; *Banner in the Sky* by James Ullman, Lippincott

1956 *Carry on, Mr. Bowditch* by Jean Lee Latham, Houghton

Honor Books: *The Secret River* by Marjorie Kinnan Rawlings, Scribner's; *The Golden Name Day* by Jennie Lindquist, Harper; *Men, Microscopes, and Living Things* by Katherine Shippen, Viking

1957 *Miracles on Maple Hill* by Virginia Sorensen, Harcourt

Honor Books: *Old Yeller* by Fred Gipson, Harper; *The House of Sixty Fathers* by Meindert DeJong, Harper; *Mr. Justice Holmes* by Clara Ingram Judson, Follett; *The Corn Grows Ripe* by Dorothy Rhoads, Viking; *Black Fox of Lorne* by Marguerite de Angeli, Doubleday

1958 *Rifles for Watie* by Harold Keith, T. Crowell

Honor Books: *The Horsecatcher* by Mari Sandoz, Westminster; *Gone-Away Lake* by Elizabeth Enright, Harcourt; *The Great Wheel* by Robert Lawson, Viking; *Tom Paine, Freedom's Apostle* by Leo Gurko, T. Crowell

1959 *The Witch of Blackbird Pond* by Elizabeth George Speare, Houghton

Honor Books: *The Family Under the Bridge* by Natalie S. Carlson, Harper; *Along Came a Dog* by Meindert DeJong, Harper; *Chucaro: Wild Pony of the Pampa* by Francis Kalnay, Harcourt; *The Perilous Road* by William O. Steele, Harcourt

1960 *Onion John* by Joseph Krumgold, T. Crowell

Honor Books: *My Side of the Mountain* by Jean George, Dutton; *America Is Born* by Gerald W. Johnson, Morrow; *The Gammage Cup* by Carol Kendall, Harcourt

1961 *Island of the Blue Dolphins* by Scott O'Dell, Houghton

Honor Books: *America Moves Forward* by Gerald W. Johnson, Morrow; *Old Ramon* by Jack Schaefer, Houghton; *The Cricket in Times Square* by George Selden, Farrar

1962 *The Bronze Bow* by Elizabeth George Speare, Houghton

Honor Books: *Frontier Living* by Edwin Tunis, World; *The Golden Goblet* by Eloise McGraw, Coward; *Belling the Tiger* by Mary Stolz, Harper

1963 *A Wrinkle in Time* by Madeleine L'Engle, Farrar

Honor Books: *Thistle and Thyme* by Sorche Nic Leodhas, Holt; *Men of Athens* by Olivia Coolidge, Houghton

1964 *It's Like This, Cat* by Emily Cheney Neville, Harper

Honor Books: *Rascal* by Sterling North, Dutton; *The Loner* by Ester Wier, McKay

1965 *Shadow of a Bull* by Maia Wojciechowska, Atheneum

Honor Books: *Across Five Aprils* by Irene Hunt, Follett

1966 *I, Juan de Pareja* by Elizabeth Borden de Trevino, Farrar

Honor Books: *The Black Cauldron* by Lloyd Alexander, Holt; *The Animal Family* by Randall Jarrell, Pantheon; *The Noonday Friends* by Mary Stolz, Harper

1967 *Up a Road Slowly* by Irene Hunt, Follett

Honor Books: *The King's Fifth* by Scott O'Dell, Houghton; *Zlateh the Goat and Other Stories* by Isaac Bashevis Singer, Harper; *The Jazz Man* by Mary H. Weik, Atheneum

1968 *From the Mixed-Up Files of Mrs. Basil E. Frankweiler* by E. L. Konigsburg, Atheneum

Honor Books: *Jennifer, Hecate, Macbeth, William McKinley, and Me, Elizabeth* by E. L. Konigsburg, Atheneum; *The Black Pearl* by Scott O'Dell, Houghton; *The Fearsome Inn* by Isaac Bashevis Singer, Scribner's; *The Egypt Game* by Zilpha Keatley Snyder, Atheneum

1969 *The High King* by Lloyd Alexander, Holt

Honor Books: *To Be a Slave* by Julius Lester, Dial; *When Shlemiel Went to Warsaw and Other Stories* by Isaac Bashevis Singer, Farrar

1970 *Sounder* by William H. Armstrong, Harper

Honor Books: *Our Eddie* by Sulamith Ish-Kishor, Pantheon; *The Many Ways of Seeing: An Introduction to the Pleasures of Art* by Janet Gaylord Moore, World; *Journey Outside* by Mary Q. Steele, Viking

1971 *Summer of the Swans* by Betsy Byars, Viking

Honor Books: *Kneeknock Rise* by Natalie Babbitt, Farrar; *Enchantress from the Stars* by Sylvia Louise Engdahl, Atheneum; *Sing Down the Moon* by Scott O'Dell, Houghton

1972 *Mrs. Frisby and the Rats of NIMH* by Robert C. O'Brien, Atheneum

Honor Books: *Incident at Hawk's Hill* by Allan W. Eckert, Little; *The Planet of Junior Brown* by Virginia Hamilton, Macmillan; *The Tombs of Atuan* by Ursula K. Le Guin, Atheneum; *Annie and the Old One* by Miska Miles, Atlantic/Little; *The Headless Cupid* by Zilpha Keatley Snyder, Atheneum

1973 *Julie of the Wolves* by Jean George, Harper

Honor Books: *Frog and Toad Together* by Arnold Lobel, Harper; *The Upstairs Room* by Johanna Reiss, Crowell; *The Witches of Worm* by Zilpha Keatley Snyder, Atheneum

1974 *The Slave Dancer* by Paula Fox, Bradbury

Honor Book: *The Dark is Rising* by Susan Cooper, Atheneum/McElderry

1975 *M. C. Higgins, the Great* by Virginia Hamilton, Macmillan

Honor Books: *Figgs & Phantoms* by Ellen Raskin, Dutton; *My Brother Sam Is Dead* by James

Lincoln Collier & Christopher Collier, Four Winds; *The Perilous Gard* by Elizabeth Marie Pope, Houghton; *Philip Hall Likes Me. I Reckon Maybe* by Bette Greene, Dial

1976 *The Grey King* by Susan Cooper, Atheneum/McElderry

Honor Books: *The Hundred Penny Box* by Sharon Bell Mathis, Viking; *Dragonwings* by Lawrence Yep, Harper

1977 *Roll of Thunder, Hear My Cry* by Mildred D. Taylor, Dial

Honor Books: *Abel's Island* by William Steig, Farrar; *A String in the Harp* by Nancy Bond, McElderry/Atheneum

THE CALDECOTT MEDAL

The Caldecott Medal has been awarded annually since 1938. It is named in honor of Randolph Caldecott, a nineteenth-century English illustrator of books for children. The award is given to the illustrator of the most distinguished American picture book for children. To be eligible an author must be either a United States citizen or a permanent resident of the United States. The award was donated by the Frederic G. Melcher family; the winner is selected by a committee of the Association for Library Services for Children (formerly the Children's Services Division of the American Library Association. The following list includes both the winners of the award and the runners-up, or Honor Books.

If only one name is given, the book was written and illustrated by that person.

1938 *Animals of the Bible* by Helen Dean Fish, ill. by Dorothy P. Lathrop, Lippincott

Honor Books: *Seven Simeons* by Boris Artzybasheff, Viking; *Four and Twenty Blackbirds* by Helen Dean Fish, ill. by Robert Lawson, Stokes

1939 *Mei Li* by Thomas Handforth, Doubleday

Honor Books: *The Forest Pool* by Laura Adams Armer, Longmans; *Wee Gillis* by Munro Leaf, Ill. by Robert Lawson, Viking; *Snow White and the Seven Dwarfs* by Wanda Gág, Coward; *Barkis* by Clare Newberry, Harper; *Andy and the Lion* by James Daugherty, Viking

1940 *Abraham Lincoln* by Ingri and Edgar Parin D'Aulaire, Doubleday

Honor Books: *Cock-A-Doodle Doo . . .* by Berta and Elmer Hader, Macmillan; *Madeline* by Ludwig Bemelmans, Viking; *The Ageless Story,* ill. by Lauren Ford, Dodd.

1941 *They Were Strong and Good* by Robert Lawson, Viking

Honor Book: *April's Kittens* by Clare Newberry, Harper

1942 *Make Way for Ducklings* by Robert McCloskey, Viking

Honor Books: *An American ABC* by Maud and Miska Petersham, Macmillan; *In My Mother's House* by Ann Nolan Clark, Ill. by Velino Herrera, Viking; *Paddle-to-the-Sea* by Holling C. Holling, Houghton; *Nothing at All* by Wanda Gág, Coward

1943 *The Little House* by Virginia Lee Burton, Houghton

Honor Books: *Dash and Dart* by Mary and Conrad Buff, Viking; *Marshmallow* by Clare Newberry, Harper

1944 *Many Moons* by James Thurber, ill. by Louis Slobodkin, Harcourt

Honor Books: *Small Rain: Verses from the Bible* selected by Jessie Orton Jones, ill. by Elizabeth Orton Jones, Viking; *Pierre Pigeon* by Lee Kingman, ill. by Arnold E. Bare, Houghton; *The Mighty Hunter* by Berta and Elmer Hadar, Macmillan; *A Child's Good Night Book* by Margaret Wise Brown, ill. by Jean Charlot, W. R. Scott; *Good Luck Horse* by Chih-Yi Chan, ill. by Plao Chan, Whittlesey

1945 *Prayer for a Child* by Rachael Field, ill. by Elizabeth Orton Jones, Macmillan

Honor Books: *Mother Goose* ill. by Tasha Tudor, Walck; *In the Forest* by Marie Hall Ets, Viking; *Yonie Wondernose* by Marguerite de Angeli, Doubleday; *The Christmas Anna Angel* by Ruth Sawyer, ill. by Kate Seredy, Viking

1946 *The Rooster Crows . . .* (traditional Mother Goose) ill. by Maud and Miska Petersham, Macmillan

Honor Books: *Little Lost Lamb* by Golden MacDonald, ill. by Leonard Weisgard, Doubleday; *Sing Mother Goose* by Opal Wheeler, ill. by Marjorie Torrey, Dutton; *My Mother Is the Most Beautiful Woman in the World* by Becky Reyher, ill. by Ruth Gannett, Lothrop; *You Can Write Chinese* by Kurt Wiese, Viking

1947 *The Little Island* by Golden MacDonald, ill. by Leonard Weisgard, Doubleday

Honor Books: *Rain Drop Splash* by Alvin Tresselt, ill. by Leonard Weisgard, Lothrop; *Boats on the River* by Marjorie Flack, ill. by Jay Hyde

Barnum, Viking; *Timothy Turtle* by Al Graham, ill. by Tony Palazzo, Viking; *Pedro, the Angel of Olvera Street* by Leo Politi, Scribner's; *Sing in Praise: A Collection of the Best Loved Hymns* by Opal Wheeler, ill. by Marjorie Torrey, Dutton.

1948 *White Snow, Bright Snow* by Alvin Tresselt, ill. by Roger Duvoisin, Lothrop

Honor Books: *Stone Soup* by Marcia Brown, Scribner's; *McElligot's Pool* by Dr. Seuss, Random; *Bambino the Clown* by George Schreiber, Viking; *Roger and the Fox* by Lavinia Davis, ill. by Hildegard Woodward, Doubleday; *Song of Robin Hood* ed. by Anne Malcolmson, ill. by Virginia Lee Burton, Houghton

1949 *The Big Snow* by Berta and Elmer Hader, Macmillan

Honor Books: *Blueberries for Sal* by Robert McCloskey, Viking; *All Around the Town* by Phyllis McGinley, ill. by Helen Stone, Lippincott; *Juanita* by Leo Politi, Scribner's; *Fish in the Air* by Kurt Wiese, Viking

1950 *Song of the Swallows* by Leo Politi, Scribner's

Honor Books: *America's Ethan Allen* by Stewart Holbrook, ill. by Lynd Ward, Houghton; *The Wild Birthday Cake* by Lavinia Davis, ill. by Hildegard Woodward, Doubleday; *The Happy Day* by Ruth Krauss, ill. by Marc Simont, Harper; *Bartholomew and the Oobleck* by Dr. Seuss, Random; *Henry Fisherman* by Marcia Brown, Scribner's

1951 *The Egg Tree* by Katherine Milhous, Scribner's

Honor Books: *Dick Whittington and His Cat* by Marcia Brown, Scribner's; *The Two Reds* by Will, ill. by Nicolas Harcourt; *If I Ran the Zoo* by Dr. Seuss, Random; *The Most Wonderful Doll in the World* by Phyllis McGinley, ill. by Helen Stone, Lippincott; *T-Bone, the Baby Sitter* by Clare Newberry, Harper

1952 *Finders Keepers* by Will, ill. by Nicolas, Harcourt

Honor Books: *Mr. T. W. Anthony Woo* by Marie Hall Ets, Viking; *Skipper John's Cook* by Marcia Brown, Scribner's; *All Falling Down* by Gene Zion, ill. by Margaret Bloy Graham, Harper; *Bear Party* by William Pène du Bois, Viking; *Feather Mountain* by Elizabeth Olds, Houghton

1953 *The Biggest Bear* by Lynd Ward, Houghton
Honor Books: *Puss in Boots* by Charles Per-

rault, ill. and tr. by Marcia Brown, Scribner's; *One Morning in Maine* by Robert McCloskey, Viking; *Ape in a Cape* by Fritz Eichenberg, Harcourt; *The Storm Book* by Charlotte Zolotow, ill. by Margaret Bloy Graham, Harper; *Five Little Monkeys* by Juliet Kepes, Houghton

1954 *Madeline's Rescue* by Ludwig Bemelmans, Viking

Honor Books: *Journey Cake, HO!* by Ruth Sawyer, Ill. by Robert McCloskey, Viking; *When Will the World Be Mine?* by Miriam Schlein, ill. by Jean Charlot, W. R. Scott; *The Steadfast Tin Soldier* by Hans Christian Andersen, ill. by Marcia Brown, Scribner's; *A Very Special House* by Ruth Krauss, ill. by Maurice Sendak, Harper; *Green Eyes* by A. Birnbaum, Capitol

1955 *Cinderella, or the Little Glass Slipper* by Charles Perrault, tr. and ill. by Marcia Brown, Scribner's

Honor Books: *Book of Nursery and Mother Goose Rhymes*, ill. by Marguerite de Angeli, Doubleday; *Wheel on the Chimney* by Margaret Wise Brown, ill. by Tibor Gergely, Lippincott; *The Thanksgiving Story* by Alice Dalgliesh, ill. by Helen Sewell, Scribner's

1956 *Frog Went A-Courtin'* ed. by John Langstaff, ill. by Feodor Rojankovsky, Harcourt

Honor Books: *Play with Me* by Marie Hall Ets, Viking; *Crow Boy* by Taro Yashima, Viking

1957 *A Tree is Nice* by Janice May Udry, ill. by Marc Simont, Harper

Honor Books: *Mr. Penny's Race Horse* by Marie Hall Ets, Viking; *1 Is One* by Tasha Tudor, Walck; *Anatole* by Eve Titus, ill. by Paul Galdone, McGraw; *Gillespie and the Guards* by Benjamin Elkin, ill. by James Daugherty, Viking; *Lion* by William Pène du Bois, Viking

1958 *Time of Wonder* by Robert McCloskey, Viking

Honor Books: *Fly High, Fly Low* by Don Freeman, Viking; *Anatole and the Cat* by Eve Titus, ill. by Paul Galdone, McGraw

1959 *Chanticleer and the Fox* adapted from Chaucer and ill. by Barbara Cooney, T. Crowell

Honor Books: *The House That Jack Built* by Antonio Frasconi, Harcourt; *What Do You Say, Dear?* by Sesyle Joslin, ill. by Maurice Sendak, W. R. Scott; *Umbrella* by Taro Yashima, Viking

1960 *Nine Days to Christmas* by Marie Hall Ets

and Aurora Labastida, ill. by Marie Hall Ets, Viking

Honor Books: *Houses from the Sea* by Alice E. Goudey, ill. by Adrienne Adams, Scribner's; *The Moon Jumpers* by Janice May Udry, ill. by Maurice Sendak, Harper

1961 *Baboushka and the Three Kings* by Ruth Robbins, ill. by Nicolas Sidjakov, Parnassus

Honor Book; *Inch by Inch* by Leo Lionni, Obolensky

1962 *Once a Mouse . . .* by Marcia Brown, Scribner's

Honor Books: *The Fox Went Out on a Chilly Night* by Peter Spier, Doubleday; *Little Bear's Visit* by Else Holmelund Minarik, ill. by Maurice Sendak, Harper; *The Day We Saw the Sun Come Up* by Alice E. Goudey, ill. by Adrienne Adams, Scribner's

1963 *The Snowy Day* by Ezra Jack Keats, Viking

Honor Books: *The Sun Is a Golden Earring* by Natalia M. Belting, ill. by Bernarda Bryson, Holt; *Mr. Rabbit and the Lovely Present* by Charlotte Zolotow, ill. by Maurice Sendak, Harper

1964 *Where the Wild Things Are* by Maurice Sendak, Harper

Honor Books: *Swimmy* by Leo Lionni, Pantheon; *All in the Morning Early* by Sorche Nic Leodhas, ill. by Evaline Ness, Holt; *Mother Goose and Nursery Rhymes* ill. by Philip Reed, Atheneum

1965 *May I Bring a Friend?* by Beatrice Schenk de Regniers, ill. by Beni Montresor, Atheneum

Honor Books: *Rain Makes Applesauce* by Julian Scheer, ill. by Marvin Bileck, Holiday; *The Wave* by Margaret Hodges, ill. by Blair Lent, Houghton; *A Pocketful of Cricket* by Rebecca Caudill, ill. by Evaline Ness, Holt

1966 *Always Room for One More* by Sorche Nic Leodhas, ill. by Nonny Hogrogian, Holt

Honor Books: *Hide and Seek Fog* by Alvin Tresselt, ill. by Roger Duvoisin, Lothrop; *Just Me* by Marie Hall Ets. Viking; *Tom Tit Tot* by Evaline Ness, Scribner's

1967 *Sam, Bangs & Moonshine* by Evaline Ness, Holt

Honor Book: *One Wide River to Cross* by Barbara Emberley, ill. by Ed Emberley, Prentice

1968 *Drummer Hoff* by Barbara Emberley, ill. by Ed Emberley, Prentice

Honor Books: *Frederick* by Leo Lionni, Pantheon; *Seashore Story* by Taro Yashima, Viking; *The Emperor and the Kite* by Jane Yolen, ill. by Ed Young, World

1969 *The Fool of the World and the flying Ship* by Arthur Ransome, ill. by Uri Shulevitz, Farrar

Honor Book: *Why the Sun and the Moon Live in the Sky* by Elphinstone Dayrell, ill. by Blair Lent, Houghton

1970 *Sylvester and the Magic Pebble* by William Steig, Windmill

Honor Books: *Goggles!* by Ezra Jack Keats, Macmillan; *Alexander and the Wind-Up Mouse* by Leo Lionni, Pantheon; *Pop Corn & Ma Goodness* by Edna Mitchell Preston, ill. by Robert Andrew Parker, Viking; *Thy Friend, Obadiah* by Brinton Turkle, Viking; *The Judge* by Harve Zemach, ill. by Margot Zemach, Farrar

1971 *A Story–A Story* by Gail E. Haley, Atheneum

Honor Books: *The Angry Moon* by William Sleator, ill. by Blair Lent, Atlantic/Little; *Frog and Toad Are Friends* by Arnold Lobel, Harper; *In the Night Kitchen* by Maurice Sendak, Harper

1972 *One Fine Day* by Nonny Hogrogian, Macmillan

Honor Books: *If All the Seas Were One Sea*, by Janina Domanska, Macmillan; *Moja Means One: Swahili Counting Book* by Muriel Feelings, ill. by Tom Feelings, Dial; *Hildilid's Night* by Cheli Duran Ryan, ill. by Arnold Lobel, Macmillan

1973 *The Funny Little Woman* retold by Arlene Mosel, ill. by Blair Lent, Dutton

Honor Books: *Anansi the Spider* adapted and ill. by Gerald McDermott, Holt; *Hosie's Alphabet* by Hosea, Tobias and Lisa Baskin, ill. by Leonard Baskin, Viking; *Snow White and the Seven Dwarfs* translated by Randall Jarrell, ill. by Nancy Ekholm Burkert, Farrar; *When Clay Sings* by Byrd Baylor, ill. by Tom Bahti, Scribner's

1974 *Duffy and the Devil* by Harve Zemach, ill. by Margot Zemach, Farrar

Honor Books: *Three Jovial Huntsmen* by Susan Jeffers, Bradbury; *Cathedral: The Story of Its Construction* by David Macaulay, Houghton

1975 *Arrow to the Sun* adapted and ill. by Gerald McDermott, Viking

Honor Book: *Jambo Means Hello* by Muriel Feelings, ill. by Tom Feelings, Dial

1976 *Why Mosquitoes Buzz in People's Ears* retold by Verna Aardema, ill. by Leo and Diane Dillon, Dial

Honor Books: *The Desert Is Theirs* by Byrd Baylor, ill. by Peter Parnall, Scribner's *Strega Nona* retold and ill. by Tomie de Paola, Prentice

1977 *Ashanti to Zulu: African Traditions* by Margaret Musgrove, ill. by Leo and Dianne Dillon, Dial

Honor Books: *The Amazing Bone* by William Steig, Farrar; *The Contest* retold & ill. by Nonny Hogrogian, Greenwillow; *Fish for Supper* by M.B. Goffstein, Dial; *The Golem* by Beverly Brodsky McDermott, Lippincott; *Hawk, I'm Your Brother* by Byrd Baylor, ill. by Peter Parnall, Scribner

THE NATIONAL BOOK AWARD

The National Book Awards have included a category for children's books since 1969. The $1,000 prize is contributed by the Children's Book Council and administered by the American Academy and Institute of Arts and Letters. (Prior to 1975 it was administered by the National Book Committee.) A panel of judges selects the juvenile book which it considers the most distinguished by an American citizen published in the United States during the preceding year.

1969 *Journey from Peppermint Street* by Meindert DeJong, Harper

Other finalists: *Constance* by Patricia Clapp, Lothrop; *The Endless Steppe* by Esther Hautzig T. Crowell; *The High King* by Lloyd Alexander, Holt; *Langston Hughes* by Milton Meltzer, T. Crowell

1970 *A Day of Pleasure: Stories of a Boy Growing Up in Warsaw* by Isaac Bashevis Singer, Farrar

Other finalists: *Pop Corn & Ma Goodness* by Edna Mitchell Preston, Viking; *Sylvester and the Magic Pebble* by William Steig, Windmill; *Where the Lilies Bloom* by Vera and Bill Cleaver, Lippincott; *The Young United States* by Edwin Tunis, World

1971 *The Marvelous Misadventures of Sebastian* by Lloyd Alexander, Dutton

Other Finalists: *Blowfish Live in the Sea* by Paula Fox, Bradbury; *Frog and Toad Are Friends* by Arnold Lobel, Harper; *Grover* by Vera and Bill Cleaver, Lippincott; *Trumpet of the Swan* by E.B. White, Harper

1972 *The Slightly Irregular Fire Engine* by Donald Barthelme, Farrar

Other finalists: *Amos & Boris* by William Steig, Farrar; *The Art Industry of Sandcastles* by Jan Adkins, Walker; *The Bears' House* by Marilyn Sachs, Doubleday; *Father Fox's Pennyrhymes* by Clyde Watson, T. Crowell; *Hildilid's Night* by Cheli Duran Ryan, Macmillan; *His Own Where* by June Jordan, T. Crowell; *Mrs. Frisby and the Rats of NIMH* by Robert C. O'Brien, Atheneum; *The Tombs of Atuan* by Ursula K. Le Guin, Atheneum, *Wild in the World* by John Donovan, Harper

1973 *The Farthest Shore* by Ursula K. Le Guin, Atheneum

Other finalists: *Children of Vietnam* by Betty Jean Lifton and Thomas C. Fox, Atheneum; *Dominic* by William Steig, Farrar; *The House of Wings* by Betsy Byars, Viking; *The Impossible People* by Georgess McHargue, Holt; *Julie of the Wolves* by Jean Craighead George, Harper; *Long Journey Home* by Julius Lester, Dial; *Trolls* by Ingri and Edgar Parin d'Aulaire, Doubleday; *The Witches of Worm* by Zilpha Keatley Snyder, Atheneum

1974 *The Court of the Stone Children* by Eleanor Cameron, Dutton

Other finalists: *Duffy and the Devil* by Harve Zemach, Farrar; *A Figure of Speech* by Norma Mazer, Delacorte; *Guests in the Promised Land* by Kristin Hunter, Scribner's; *A Hero Ain't Nothin' But a Sandwich* by Alice Childress, Coward; *Poor Richard in France* by F.N. Monjo, Holt; *A Proud Taste for Scarlet and Miniver* by E.L. Konigsburg, Atheneum; *Summer of My German Soldier* by Bette Green, Dial; *The Treasure Is the Rose* by Julia Cunningham, Pantheon; *The Whys and Wherefores of Littabelle Lee* by Vera and Bill Cleaver, Atheneum

1975 *M.C. Higgins, the Great* by Virginia Hamilton, Macmillan

Other finalists: *The Devil's Storybook* by Natalie Babbitt. Farrar; *Doctor in the Zoo* by Bruce Buchenholz, Studio/Viking; *The Edge of Next Year* by Mary Stolz, Harper; *The Girl Who Cried Flowers* by Jane Yolen, T. Crowell; *I Tell a Lie Every So Often* by Bruce Clements, Farrar; *Jo! Bangla!* by Jason Laure with Ettagale Laure,

Farrar; *My Brother Sam Is Dead* by James Lincoln Collier and Christopher Collier, Four Winds; *Remember the Days* by Milton Meltzer, Zenith/Doubleday; *Wings* by Adrienne Richard, Atlantic/Little; *World of Our Fathers* by Milton Meltzer, Farrar

1976 *Bert Breen's Barn* by Walter D. Edmonds, Little

Other finalists: *As I Was Crossing Boston Common* by Norma Farber, Dutton; *Of Love and Death and Other Journeys* by Isabelle Holland, Lippincott; *The Star in the Pail* by David McCord, Little; *El Bronx Remembered; A Novella and Stories* by Nicholasa Mohr, Harper; *Ludell* by Brenda Wilkinson, Harper

1977 *The Master Puppeteer* by Katherine Paterson, Crowell

Other finalists: *Never to Forget:, The Jews of the Holocaust* by Milton Meltzer, Harper; *Ox under Pressure* by John Ney, Lippincott; *Roll of Thunder, Hear My Cry* by Mildred Taylor, Dial; *Tunes for a Small Harmonica* by Barbara Wersba, Harper

THE LAURA INGALLS WILDER AWARD

The Laura Ingalls Wilder Award is given every five years to an author or illustrator whose books, published in the United States, have made a "substantial and lasting contribution to literature for children." It is administered by the Association for Library Services for Children of the American Library Association, and was first awarded in 1954 to Laura Ingalls Wilder for her "Little House" books.

1954 Laura Ingalls Wilder
1960 Clara Ingram Judson
1965 Ruth Sawyer
1970 E.B. White
1975 Beverly Cleary

THE NATIONAL COUNCIL OF TEACHERS OF ENGLISH AWARD FOR EXCELLENCE IN POETRY FOR CHILDREN

This award was first presented in 1977. It is to be given annually to a living American poet in recognition of his or her entire body of work.

1977 David McCord

THE HANS CHRISTIAN ANDERSEN AWARD

The Hans Christian Andersen Award is given biennially by the International Board on Books for Young People to one living author and, since 1965, one illustrator for his or her entire body of work. The winner is selected by a committee of five, each from a different country.

1956 Eleanor Farjeon (Great Britain)
1958 Astrid Lindgren (Sweden)
1960 Erich Kästner (Germany)
1962 Meindert DeJong (U.S.A.)
1964 René Guillot (France)
1966 Author: Tove Jansson (Finland)
　　　Illustrator: Alois Carigiet (Switzerland)
1968 Authors: James Krüss (Germany)
　　　　　Jose Maria Sanchez-Silva (Spain)
　　　Illustrator: Jiri Trnka (Czechoslovakia)
1970 Author: Gianni Rodari (Italy)
　　　Illustrator: Maurice Sendak(U.S.A.)
1972 Author: Scott O'Dell (U.S.A.)
　　　Illustrator: Ib Spang Olsen (Denmark)
1974 Author: Maria Gripe (Sweden)
　　　Illustrator: Farshid Mesghali (Iran)
1976 Author: Cecil Bodker (Denmark)
　　　Illustrator: Tatjana Mawrina (U.S.S.R.)

1978 Children's Book Awards

THE NEWBERY MEDAL

Bridge to Terabithia by Katherine Paterson, Crowell Honor Books; *Ramona and Her Father* by Beverly Cleary, Morrow; *Anpao: An American Indian Odyssey* by Jamake Highwater, Lippincott

THE CALDECOTT MEDAL

Noah's Ark by Peter Spier, Doubleday Honor Books; *Castle* by David Macaulay, Houghton; *It Could Always Be Worse* by Margot Zemach, Farrar

THE NATIONAL BOOK AWARD

The View from the Oak by Judith and Herbert Kohl, Sierra Club/Scribner's

Other finalists: *Hew against the Grain* by Betty Sue Cummings, Atheneum; *Mischling, Second Degree* by Ilse Koehn, Morrow; *One at a Time* by David McCord, Little; *Caleb and Kate* by William Steig, Farrar.

THE NATIONAL COUNCIL OF TEACHERS OF ENGLISH AWARD FOR EXCELLENCE IN POETRY FOR CHILDREN
Aileen Fisher

THE HANS CHRISTIAN ANDERSEN AWARD
Author: Paula Fox (U.S.A.)
Illustrator: Svend Otto (Denmark)

Given below are the names of the publishers, their addresses, areas of specialization, and average number of titles published per year.

ABINGDON PRESS. 201 Eighth Ave. S., Nashville, TN 37202 Large cross-section of children's books, some religious, for preschool to young adult readers; 15 titles per year.

HARRY N. ABRAMS. 110 East 59th St. New York NY 10022. Art books, some which children might enjoy.

ADDISON-WESLEY, INC. Reading, MA 01867. Picture books, fiction, nonfiction, and science fiction for ages 5 to 12; 18 to 20 titles per year.

ALLYN & BACON. 470 Atlantic Ave., Boston, MA 02201 Breakthrough Series, 25 paperbacks for slow readers, junior high level; 6 short story books, high school level.

AMERICAN ASSOCIATION FOR THE ADVANCEMENT OF SCIENCE. 1515 Massachusetts Ave. N.W., Washington, DC 20005. Science books and reviews of children's books.

ASSOCIATION FOR CHILDHOOD EDUCATION INTERNATIONAL. 3615 Wisconsin Ave. N.W., Washington, DC 20016. ACEI Umbrella Books, 7 stories and verses.

ASTOR HONOR. 48 E. 43d St., New York, NY 10017. Classics for kindergarten to young adult readers.

ATHENEUM. 122 E. 42d St., New York, NY 10017. Wide variety of books, including science fiction, fantasy, and poetry, for nursery school to young adult readers; 70 to 80 titles per year.

ARIEL (Farrar). 19 Union Square, New York, NY 10003. Wide variety of books for preschool to young adult readers; 18 to 24 titles per year.

ATLANTIC MONTHLY. 8 Arlington St., Boston, MA 02116. Wide variety of books, including picture books, novels, and some nonfiction, for readers 3 to 18 years of age; 16 titles per year.

AVON. 959 Eighth Ave., New York, NY 10019. Paperback reprints, mainly fiction, some nonfiction, for readers 5 to 14 years of age; 20 to 30 titles per year.

BANTAM. 666 Fifth Ave., New York NY 10019. "Skylark Books" for readers 8 to 12 years of age; 12 titles per year.

BOBBS-MERRILL. 4300 W. 62d St., Indianapolis, IN 46206. Wide variety of books for readers age 6 to young adult; 12 titles per year.

BRADBURY. 2 Overhill Rd., Scarsdale, NY 10583. Children's books exclusively, preschool to young adult; 15 to 20 titles per year.

CANADIAN WOMAN'S EDUCATIONAL PRESS. 280 Bloor St. W., Toronto, Ont. M5S 1W1, Canada. Children's books about women and social issues; 5 titles per year.

CAXTON PRINTERS. Box 700, Caldwell, ID 83605. Nonfiction and westerns for teens, and an occasional juvenile title.

CHARTER HOUSE. 2121 Belcourt Ave., Nashville, TN 37212. Variety of books for preschool to young adult readers; 10 titles per year.

DEVIN-ADAIR. 143 Sound Beach Ave., Old Greenwich, CT 06870. Very few children's books, one per year.

CHILDREN'S PRESS. 1224 W. Van Buren St., Chicago, IL 60607. Fiction and educational books for preschool to tenth-grade readers; 150 titles per year.

COWARD, MCCANN & GEOGHEGAN. 200 Madison Ave., New York, NY 10016. Wide variety of children's books for preschool to young adult readers; 30 titles per year.

CREATIVE EDUCATIONAL. 123 S. Broad St., Mankato, MN 56001. Children's books for age 3 to young adult; 50 to 75 titles per year.

CROWN CHILDREN'S BOOKS. 1 Park Ave., New York, NY 10016. Variety of children's books for preschool to young adult readers; 16 to 18 titles per year.

THOMAS Y. CROWELL. 10 E. 53d St., New York, NY 10022. Variety of books for kindergarten to young adult.

DELL. 1 Dag Hammarskjold Plaza, New York, NY 10017. *Delacorte Press:* Hardcover general fiction and nonfiction, original works for age 4 to high school; 18 titles per year. *Dell Laurel Leaf Books*: Quality fiction and nonfiction in paperback for junior and senior high school students; 50 titles per year. *Dell Yearling Books*: quality fiction and nonfiction in paperback for kindergarten to sixth grade; 35 titles per year. *Dial Press*: Wide variety of books for nursery school to young adult readers; 24 titles per year.

DODD, MEAD. 79 Madison Ave., New York, NY 10016. General nonfiction, many nature books, but also fiction and picture books for preschool to young adult readers; 50 titles per year.

DOUBLEDAY. 245 Park Ave., New York, NY 10017. Wide variety of children's books for readers of all ages; 100 to 110 titles per year.

DOVER. 180 Varick St., New York, NY 10014. Coloring books, Lang books, Beatrice Potter books, and others for kindergarten to young adult readers; 15 titles per year.

DUFOUR EDITIONS. Chester Springs, PA 19425. Social studies, history, music, drama, literature, and reference books suitable for secondary school use, not written as texts, but suited for class adaptation; 4 titles per year.

E. P. DUTTON. 2 Park Ave., New York, NY 10016. Wide variety of books for preschool to young adult readers; 50 to 60 titles per year.

WM. B. EERDMANS. 255 Jefferson Ave. S.E., Grand Rapids, MI 49503. Two or three children's titles per year.

M. EVANS. 216 E. 49th St., New York, NY 10017. Five titles per year for sixth grade to high school.

FAWCETT. 600 Third Ave., New York, NY 10016. Series books for children, including Peanuts, Dennis the Menace, Family Circus, B.C., Best-Worst books, and science fiction; 180 titles per year.

FEMINIST PRESS. Box 334, Old Westbury, NY 11568. One or two nonsexist children's books per year.

FOLLETT. Children's Book Division, 420 Lexington Ave., New York, NY 10017. Wide variety of children's books from nursery school to age 14.

FOUR WINDS PRESS (Scholastic). 50 W. 44th St., New York, NY 10036. Trade juveniles, fiction and nonfiction for kindergarten through twelfth grade; 48 titles per year.

GARRARD. 1607 N. Market St., Champaign, IL 61820. Juvenile and supplementary elementary

books for kindergarten through sixth grade; 29 titles per year.

GOLDEN GATE JUNIOR BOOKS. 1247½ N. Vista St., Los Angeles, Ca 90046. Every kind of juvenile book; 8 titles per year.

GOLDEN PRESS (Western Publishing). 1220 Mound Ave., Racine, WI 53404. Juvenile picture and story books, teen fiction and classics, activity and coloring books; 5 titles per year.

GREENWILLOW BOOKS. 105 Madison Ave., New York, NY 10016. Wide variety of children's books, including picture books and beginning-to-read books, for preschool to ninth grade; 50 to 60 new titles per year.

GROSSET & DUNLAP. 51 Madison Ave., New York, NY 10010. Mixed juvenile books, leaning toward a specialty in picture books; 100 titles per year.

HARCOURT BRACE JOVANOVICH. 757 Third Ave., New York, NY 10017. Wide variety of books for preschool to young adult readers; 40 new titles per year.

HARPER & ROW. 10 E. 53d St., New York, NY 10022. Wide variety of books for preschool to young adult readers; 75 titles per year.

HARVEY HOUSE. 20 Waterside Plaza, New York, NY 10010. Wide variety of juvenile books, including the Breakthrough Series of high-interest/low-reading-level novels for teens; 30 titles per year.

HASTINGS HOUSE. 10 E. 40th St., New York, NY 10016. Mixed children's books; 7 titles per year.

HILL & WANG. 19 Union Square W., New York, NY 10003. Mixed children's books; 3 titles per year.

HOLIDAY HOUSE. 18 E. 53d St., New York, NY 10022. Wide variety of books for preschool to young adult readers; 30 titles per year.

HOLT, RINEHART & WINSTON. 383 Madison Ave., New York, NY 10017. Mixed children's books for ages 5 to 15; 20 titles per year.

HOUGHTON MIFFLIN. 1 Beacon St., Boston, MA 02107. Wide variety of children's books for preschool to young adult readers; 40 titles per year.

INDIANA UNIVERSITY PRESS. Tenth and Morton Sts., Bloomington, IN 47401. Has published a total of 3 children's books.

ALFRED A. KNOPF. 201 E. 50th St., New York, NY 10022. Wide variety of books for preschool to young adult readers; 20 titles per year.

LERNER PUBLICATIONS. 241 First Ave. N., Minneapolis, MN 55401. Wide variety of children's books, more nonfiction (about 80 percent) than fiction (about 20 percent), for kindergarten through twelfth grade; 60 to 80 titles per year.

LION BOOKS (Sayre Publishing, Inc.). 111 E. 39th St., New York, NY 10016. Variety of books, mostly nonfiction, for elementary school to young adult readers; 16 titles per year.

J. B. LIPPINCOTT. E. Washington Square, Philadelphia, PA 19105. Wide variety of children's books, including Spanish-language books and young adult "easy readers."

LITTLE, BROWN. 34 Beacon St., Boston, MA 02106. Wide variety of juvenile books, mostly fiction; 30 titles per year.

LOTHROP, LEE & SHEPARD (William Morrow). 105 Madison Ave., New York, NY 10016. Wide variety of juvenile books, including storybooks, career books, and handicrafts books; 50 to 60 titles per year.

McGRAW-HILL. 1221 Ave. of the Americas, New York, NY 10020. Wide variety of books for ages 3 to 14; 30 titles per year.

DAVID McKAY. 750 Third Ave., New York, NY 10017. Variety of books for kindergarten to young adult readers; 50 titles per year.

MACMILLAN. 866 Third Ave., New York, NY 10022. Variety of books for nursery school to sixth grade; 30 titles per year.

JULIAN MESSNER (Simon & Schuster). 1230 Ave. of the Americas, New York, NY 10020. Wide variety of books for third to twelfth grade, mostly nonfiction; 50 titles per year.

METHUEN. 572 Fifth Ave., New York, NY 10036. Variety of children's books for prereading to grade 12; 6 to 8 titles per year.

WILLIAM MORROW. 105 Madison Ave., New York, NY 10016. Wide variety of children's books, including novels for the middle reader, science books, and nature books; 40 new titles per year.

THOMAS NELSON. 405 Seventh Ave., S., Nashville, TN 37203. Variety of books for age 9 to young adult readers; 20 to 25 titles per year.

NEW AMERICAN LIBRARY. 1301 Ave. of the Americas, New York, NY 10019. Wide variety of books for young adults, including classics, fiction, and poetry and drama anthologies; 115 titles per year.

OXFORD UNIVERSITY PRESS. 200 Madison Ave., New York, NY 10016. Children's trade book division in England publishes about 30 titles per year; New York Office to resume publishing children's books in the fall of 1978.

PANTHEON. 201 E. 50th St., New York, NY 10022. Variety of books for preschool through twelfth grade; 20 to 25 titles per year.

PARENTS MAGAZINE PRESS. 52 Vanderbilt Ave., New York, NY 10017. Variety of books for preschool to seventh grade; 24 titles per year.

PARNASSUS PRESS. 4080 Halleck St., Emeryville, CA 94608. Two to three juvenile titles per year.

S. G. PHILLIPS. 305 W. 86th St., New York, NY 10024. Juvenile books for age 8 and up; 10 titles per year.

PLATT & MUNK. 1055 Bronx River Ave., Bronx, NY 10472. Variety of books for ages 1 to 16; 30 titles per year.

PLAYS, INC. 8 Arlington St., Boston, MA 02116. Anthologies of plays for young people; books on puppetry, costume, the theater, creative drama, educational dance, and body movement and gymnastics; 10 titles per year.

POCKET BOOKS. 1230 Ave. of the Americas, New York, NY 10020. Archway Paperbacks for ages 8 to 14; 36 titles per year.

PUFFINS (Viking Press). 625 Madison Ave., New York, NY 10022. Wide variety of books for preschool to young adult readers; 30 to 40 titles per year.

PRENTICE-HALL. Englewood Cliffs, NJ 07632. Wide range of books for preschoolers to young adolescents; 40 titles per year.

G. P. PUTNAM'S SONS. 200 Madison Ave., New York, NY 10016. Wide range of books for ages 4 to 16; 60 titles per year.

HARLIN QUIST BOOKS. 192 E. 75 St., New York, NY 10021. Children's books and posters; 8 titles per year.

RAND McNALLY. 8255 Central Park Ave., Skokie, IL 60076. Books for preschool to age 12; 8 titles per year.

RANDOM HOUSE. 201 E. 50th St., New York, NY 10022. Wide variety of books for preschool to young adult readers; 75 to 80 titles per year.

SCHOLASTIC BOOK SERVICES. 50 W. 44th St., New York, NY 10036. Wide variety of children's books for kindergarten through twelfth grade.

CHARLES SCRIBNER'S. 597 Fifth Ave., New York, NY 10017. General titles for preschool to young adult readers, 38 to 40 per year; 6 activity books and projects per year; 8 books for young readers copublished with Sierra Club.

SEABURY PRESS. 815 Second Ave., New York, NY 10017. General books for preschool to young adult readers; 20 titles per year.

SHEED ANDREWS & MCMEEL. 6700 Squibb Rd., Mission, KS 66202. Six cartoon bible stories, five other titles per year for ages 6 to 12.

SIERRA CLUB BOOKS. 530 Bush St., San Francisco, CA 94108. Natural history and environmental conservation; 8 titles per year copublished with Scribner's.

STANDARD PUBLISHING. 8121 Hamilton Ave., Cincinnati, OH 45231. Religious books for preschool to age 12; 50 titles per year.

STERLING PUBLISHING. 2 Park Ave., New York, NY 10016. Nonfiction, including reference and informational books, science, nature, arts and crafts, social sciences, sports, physical education, drama, music and dance, pets, hobby books, and supplementary textbooks; 54 titles per year.

SWALLOW PRESS. 811 Junior Terrace, Chicago, IL 60613. Publishes a very small number of children's books.

TUNDRA BOOKS OF NORTHERN NEW YORK. 18 Cornelia St., Box 1030, Plattsburgh, NY 12901. Juvenile fiction and nonfiction.

CHARLES E. TUTTLE. 28 S. Main St., Rutland, Vt 05701. Juvenile books about the East; 30 titles per year.

TWAYNE PUBLISHERS. 70 Lincoln St., Boston, MA 02111. Ten large-print titles.

VANGUARD PRESS. 424 Madison Ave., New York, NY 10017. General books for preschool to young adult readers; 4 to 5 titles per year.

VIKING. 625 Madison Ave., New York, NY 10022. Forty general hardcover titles per year for preschool to young adult readers. (For paperbacks, see PUFFINS.)

HENRY Z. WALCK. (See DAVID MCKAY.)

WALKER. 720 Fifth Ave., New York, NY 10019. General children's books (60 percent), science-related (40), for kindergarten through twelfth grade; 20 titles per year.

WANDERER (Simon & Schuster). 1230 Ave. of the Americas, New York, NY 10020. General books for ages 12 to 16; 15 titles per year.

FREDERICK WARNE. 101 Fifth Ave., New York, NY 10003. General juvenile nonfiction; 110 titles per year.

FRANKLIN WATTS. 730 Fifth Ave., New York, NY 10019. General juvenile books; 110 titles per year.

WESTERN PUBLISHING. 1220 Mound Ave., Racine, WI 53404. Many picture books, some nonfiction, including novels for ages 9 to 12; 100 titles per year.

WESTMINISTER PRESS. Witherspoon Bldg., Philadelphia, PA 19107. Wide variety of children's books, including high-interest low-reading-level fiction, career books, mystery, adventure, sports, science, books of ethnic interest, for ages 8 and up; 18 to 20 titles per year.

DAVID WHITE. 14 Vanderventer Ave., Port Washington, NY 11050. Variety of books for ages 4 to 8; 16 titles per year.

ALBERT WHITMAN. 560 W. Lake St., Chicago, IL 60090. Variety of children's books including picture books and easy-to-read mysteries and sports stories; 20 titles per year.

WINDMILL. 2 Park Ave., New York, NY 10016. Juvenile picture books and storybooks; 20 titles per year.

WILLIAM COLLINS AND WORLD. 2080 West 117th St., Cleveland, OH 44111. General juvenile fiction and nonfiction for preschool to young adult readers; 40 titles per year.

ACKNOWLEDGMENTS

Excerpt, page 181. From *Four Fur Feet*, by Margaret Wise Brown. Copyright © 1961, Margaret Wise Brown. Used by permission of Addison-Wesley Publishing Company, Inc.

"Bam, Bam, Bam." From *Catch a Little Rhyme*, by Eve Merriam. Copyright © 1966, Eve Merriam. Used by permission of Atheneum Publishers.

"Toaster Time." From *There Is No Rhyme for Silver*, by Eve Merriam. Copyright © 1962, Eve Merriam. Used by permission of Atheneum Publishers.

"Our Washing Machine." From *The Apple Vendor's Fair*, by Patricia Hubbell. Copyright © 1963, Patricia Hubbell. Used by permission of Atheneum Publishers.

"Rain Rivers." From *I Feel the Same Way*, by Lilian Moore. Copyright © 1967, Lilian Moore. Used by permission of Atheneum Publishers.

Excerpt, page 83. From *Alexander and the Terrible, Horrible, No Good, Very Bad Day*, by Judith Viorst. Copyright © 1972, Judith Viorst. Used by permission of Atheneum Publishers.

"Cheers." From *It Doesn't Always Have to Rhyme*, by Eve Merriam. Copyright © 1964, Eve Merriam. Used by permission of Atheneum Publishers.

"Zebra" and "Pretending to Sleep." From *Flashlight and Other Poems*, by Judith Thurman. Copyright © 1976, Judith Thurman. Used by permission of Atheneum Publishers.

Excerpt, page 258. From *The Flat Heeled Muse*, by Lloyd Alexander. Copyright © 1965, Lloyd Alexander. Reprinted by permission of Brandt & Brandt Literary Agency, Inc.

Quote, page 548. From *Hurrah for Alexander*, by Jeri Marsh. Copyright © 1977, Carolrhoda Books Inc., Minneapolis, MN 55401. Used by permission of the publisher.

Excerpt (refrain), page 90. From *Millions of Cats*, by Wanda Gag. Copyright © 1928, Coward-McCann, Inc; renewed 1956. Reprinted by permission of Coward, McCann and Geoghegan, Inc.

Excerpts, pages 657–658, 671, 684. From *An Imaginary Correspondence*, by Rumer Godden. Copyright © 1963, Rumer Godden. Reprinted by permission of Curtis Brown, Ltd.

Excerpt, page 93–94. From *Wildfire*, by E. G. Valens. Copyright © 1963, Evans G. Valens, Jr. Reprinted by permission of Curtis Brown, Ltd.

Excerpts, pages 8–9. From *Emily and The Klunky Baby and the Next-Door Dog*, by Joan Lexau. Copyright © 1972, Joan M. Lexau. Reprinted by permission of The Dial Press.

"What is Brown?" From *Hailstones and Halibut Bones*, by Mary O'Neill. Copyright © 1961, Mary LeDuc O'Neill. Used by permission of Doubleday & Company, Inc.

Excerpts, pages 27, 30, 32. From *The Door in the Wall*, by Marguerite de Angeli. Copyright 1949, Marguerite de Angeli. Used by permission of Doubleday & Company, Inc.

Excerpt, page 232. From *Demeter and Persephone, Homeric Hymn Number Two*, by Penelope Proddow. Copyright (translation) © 1972, Mary Parkinson Proddow. Used by permission of Doubleday & Company, Inc.

Excerpt, page 79. From *Tell Me a Trudy*, by Lore Segal. Text copyright © 1977, Lore Segal. Reprinted with the permission of Farrar, Straus & Giroux, Inc.

"The Ballad of the Burglar of Babylon" (excerpt, pages 156–157). From *Questions of Travel*, by Elizabeth Bishop. Copyright © 1964, 1965, Elizabeth Bishop. This material appeared originally in *The New Yorker*. Reprinted with the permission of Farrar, Straus & Giroux, Inc.

709

INDEX

AUTHOR/ILLUSTRATOR/TITLE INDEX

728

INDEX

SUBJECT INDEX